The Human Side of the War and
Its Aftermath, as shown through
the columns of The Jerusalem Post

YOM KIPPUR PLUS 100 DAYS

The Human Side of the War and Its Aftermath, as shown through the columns of The Jerusalem Post

HART PUBLISHING COMPANY, INC. NEW YORK CITY

*To my dear wife, Beatrice, whose fine editorial judgment
and constant assistance were major aids
in the preparation of this volume.*

YOM KIPPUR PLUS 100 DAYS

The Human Side of the War and
Its Aftermath, as shown through
the columns of The Jerusalem Post

CONTENTS

CONTENTS

The special pathos of Jewish history lies in the immense place occupied by the problem of being Jewish and yet staying alive.

ABBA EBAN

FOREWORD

THIS IS A BOOK about the Yom Kippur War and its aftermath. But it is not a book about the military strategy of the War, nor about the political issues. These pages deal with the emotional experiences of the people of Israel during and right after the War, when they were assailed by unexpected and terrible forces.

Here is the story of a very, very small country rallying to its own defense when it was suddenly attacked on two sides by armies which outnumbered its own forces by about three to one.

In addition, Israel's enemies were supported by one of the great superpowers of the earth, which was supplying the attacking armies unstintingly with the most sophisticated weapons of war, and with an endless stream of military advisers.

At this juncture, the Israelis found themselves bereft of just about all diplomatic support throughout the world. Country after country, in Europe, in Africa, and in the Far East, following its own self-interest and its need for oil, abandoned Israel. Only the voice of Holland was heard condemning the Arab aggression and courageously defending the moral right of the Israeli state to exist. Great Britain announced an embargo on shipments of all parts and munitions to Israel. The only power that came to Israel's aid was the United States.

To the utter chagrin of the United States, members of the NATO group, its own allies, refused landing space for the U.S. cargoes bound for Israel. Spain, in fear of Arab reprisal, denied American planes fueling accommodations in its airports. The same was true of Greece. The only country that acceded to America's request was Portugal.

The entire configuration of events was stunning beyond belief. It seemed as if the entire world had conspired to crush out this little dot of a country. The times recalled the voice of Jeremiah, who in the second verse of Lamentations, cried out:[1]

> *All her friends have betrayed her:*
> *they have become her enemies.*

How did the Israeli public react to this onslaught? For an American to find the answer, the most obvious source would be to consult the newspapers of Israel, especially an English-language newspaper which mirrored the immediate and complete spectrum of reactions. That newspaper was The Jerusalem Post.

The material adjunct to the text of this book has been selected from among the news items, news analyses, editorials, letters to the editor, and advertisements from the columns of The Jerusalem Post for a period of 100 days after the commencement of the Yom Kippur War. These articles reveal the heart and mind of the embattled Israeli.

There are tremendously important news items in these pages which never reached the media of the United States, or the media of any other country. The reader will encounter in these pages a fair sample of representative ads taken by various pressure groups, by political parties, by business groups, and by private citizens, which reflect the multiplicity of feelings and opinions that abound in this democracy.

You will find here, too, a selection of letters which flowed into the newspaper from every corner of the world—letters of sympathy, letters of protest, letters of exhortation.

Here, too, you will find some extremely illuminating articles by Israeli professors, philosophers, and social critics, as well as by famous thinkers from other parts of the civilized world who contributed articles to the prestigious Jerusalem Post.

1. Lamentations I:2.

YOM KIPPUR
October 6, 1973

IN THE 23rd CHAPTER of the Book of Leviticus, it is written:[1]

> *And the lord spoke unto Moses, saying:*
> *Also on the tenth day of this*
> *seventh month there shall be a day of*
> *atonement; it shall be a holy convocation*
> *unto you; and you shall afflict*
> *your souls, and offer an offering made*
> *by fire unto the Lord.*
>
> *And you shall do no work on that same*
> *day: for it is a day of atonement for you*
> *before the Lord your God.*
>
> *For whatever soul shall not be afflicted in*
> *that same day, he shall be cut off from among*
> *his people.*

This Day of Atonement, Yom Kippur, has come to be for Jews the holiest of their holy days. Through rabbinic exegesis, Yom Kippur, over the past 2,500 years, has been a solemn day of fasting.

In Israel, in the early afternoon of Yom Kippur Eve, somewhere around 2 o'clock, everything comes to a halt. Jews close down their shops, their factories, their offices. Schools have been closed since noon. Everyone hurries home to ready himself and herself, physically and spiritually, for the serious day ahead.

During a stretch of some twenty-five hours—from a little before sundown of the eve of Yom Kippur until sundown of the following day—no Jew may partake of food of any kind, nor drink a single drop of water; nor may a congregant anoint himself with an ointment nor with a perfume, nor may one bathe for sensual delight, nor may one indulge in any erotic pleasures of the flesh. Even the wearing of shoes is enjoined.

On this holiest of days, the orthodox dons a white overgarment called a *kitel* for the entire day, the cerement in which he will be buried upon his decease. This garment, utterly plain and entirely white, is intended to blot out all frippery, and to symbolically prepare him as if he were standing before the Throne of God for final judgment.

The focus, then, of this holiday, or rather holy day, is for every Jew to turn aside completely from all sensual pursuits and to assess his behavior. It is a day of reckoning, a day of awe, a day on which the deeds of every man, woman, and child come up before God to be weighed and considered. It is *Yom ha-Din,* the Day of Judgment.

If the prophets of the Bible were intoxicated with the ideal of justice, and if they insisted that ethical behavior was of far more importance than ritual, then surely the fountainhead of this ethos was rooted in the very concept of Yom Kippur, a day dedicated to self-examination. Here, unique in the annals of man, is a day, given over since the beginning of recorded history—not to an affirmation of faith but to searching self-appraisal.

Only a Yom Kippur could have given birth to an Isaiah who derided the hypocrisies of meaningless worship, and exclaimed:[2]

> *Is this the fast that I have chosen,*
> *the day for a man to afflict his soul?*
> *Is it to bow down his head like a bulrush,*
> *and to grovel in sackcloth and ashes?*
> *Will you call such a day a fast,*
> *a day acceptable to the Lord?*

No! chides the prophet. Yom Kippur must be more than a day of supplication and a day of ritual. It must, above all, be a day of rectification!

> *Is not this the fast that I have chosen*
> *to loosen the fetters of wickedness,*
> *To unfasten the bands of the yoke,*
> *and to let the oppressed go free,*
> *and to smash every yoke!*
> *Is it not to share your bread with the*
> *hungry,*
> *And to bring the vagrant poor into*
> *your home;*
> *And when you see the naked that*
> *you cover him,*
> *And that you hide not yourself from*
> *your own flesh.*

Yom Kippur was being transformed from a holy rite into a search for righteousness. It is this pre-eminence of the worth of decent behavior over

1. Verse 26 ff.

2. Isaiah 58:3.

eservist rushing to his unit on hearing
e news of the attack.

13

religious piety and over declarations of faith which constitutes the essence of the Jewish religion.

A Talmudic dictum holds that:

> *Yom Kippur may erase transgressions between man and God (i.e., failure to perform ritual duties); but Yom Kippur can never exculpate or wipe out transgressions between man and his fellow man.*

On this holiest of holy days, a solemn quietude pervades each Jewish household, and the streets of Israel seem to be stilled in sanctification. Most citizens go to their synagogues to engage in worship. The others—the nonbelievers—remain quietly at home. Unlike the social pattern of other holidays, on the Day of Atonement there are no excursions to the beaches, no picnics, no strolling on the boulevards. There is no public transportation, and all radio broadcasting is off the air. *It is Yom Kippur.* If it isn't for some a day of supplication, the least it will be is a day of rest or quiet reflection.

On October 6, 1973, at approximately 2:00 p.m. the quiet of Israel was suddenly shattered by the piercing wails of air raid sirens. The alarm was unmistakable. Everyone shuddered, for everyone knew that anything so starkly interruptive of Yom Kippur had to be grave.

Shortly thereafter, every wave length of Israel's broadcasting system was on the air, and every quarter-hour a newscaster intoned the same portentous statement: "At ten minutes before two, the armies of Syria and Egypt launched an attack on our forces at the borders." Snatches of music filled in the gaps between these announcements, and male voices interspersed code words that called reserve units to their collection points: *Charming Woman, Cucumber, Pocket Screwdriver, Two Pieces of Wool Thread*—these seemingly -meaningless phrases summoned the men of Israel to defense.

The services in the synagogues continued; but here and there, men were called off, some by messengers, some by soldiers in uniform, some directly through an announcement by the rabbi, some so abruptly that they left the *shul*[1] still wearing their *talitim*[2].

In the ultra-orthodox section of Mea Shearim in Jerusalem—where anyone driving a car through the streets on the Sabbath generally risked being stoned by zealots—in the Mea Shearim quarter on October 6, 1973, ultra-pious Hassidic Jews could be seen helping load army gear into buses and into private cars, and sending their sons off to the front—*on Yom Kippur!*

It was precisely because the Arabs misconceived the nature of Yom Kippur that the inevitable loss of Jewish lives was reduced. Mobilization for defense had been effected—*because* of Yom Kippur—so very, very quickly. Had the attack occurred on any other day of the year, it would have been almost impossible to reach the many civilians who constituted this people's army. On any other holiday, many might have been romping over the country, lolling on the mountainsides, and disporting themselves in the Mediterranean, visiting relatives, playing tennis or soccer, or driving hither and yon. The Arabs believed that a strike on Yom Kippur would catch everyone by surprise. It did. But it was the one day of the year when everyone—no matter who—could be readily located.

That evening, at a little after 6:00, just minutes after the close of Yom Kippur, the Prime Minister, Golda Meir, appeared on television and spoke to an anxious nation: "Because the news was so grave," she said, "I was obliged to convene a cabinet meeting on Yom Kippur."

Within a few hours, the entire nation had been galvanized.

Everyone knew that this Yom Kippur attack—by the very day on which it had been planned to take place—was the first blow against Israel's very being. Nasser had brutally declared that "the mere existence of Israel was an aggression against the Arab world." Gadaffi openly lusted for Jewish blood. And other Arab leaders from one end of the Middle East to the other had publicly and repeatedly vowed to destroy Israel.

Perhaps the diplomats of the United Nations saw fit to disregard these constant declarations of intended genocide. Perhaps the editorial writers of the Western world wrote off those diatribes as so much Arab bluster, but the Jews believed the Arab threats. Their enemies were, so to speak, just across the street.

Now the implacable Syrian was hammering away in the North, ably fortified by all the technological sophistication that Moscow could devise.

Egypt, fortified by an awesome array of Russian SAM anti-aircraft missile sites, had thrown bridgeheads over the Suez and was advancing through the thinly held Bar-Lev Line. And Jordan stood poised to throw its army against Jerusalem.

The Islamic world had embarked on a *jihad,* a holy war, a war dedicated to the complete

---

1. Synagogue.
2. Prayer shawls.

extermination of this people.

Six years earlier, the Arab heads of state had assembled in Khartoum, and in one voice had announced: No peace! No accommodation! No talks! No nothing! Only implacable enmity!

Now that Israel was in a two-front war and threatened with a three-front war, was there any reason to believe that the Arabs didn't mean what they had been saying so fervently and for so long?

Survival! That's what every Israeli knew he was fighting for—not for needless acres of sandy wastes, nor for empty phrases buried in windy documents, nor for verbal guarantees that could so easily be violated. Nor was any Israeli fighting for a greater Israel to fulfill some grandiose expansionist dream, as some callous cynics had accused. No, not for any of these, but only for sheer survival.

For many of these Israelis were the sons and grandsons of those who had perished in Hitler's holocaust. These Israelis knew that some

35 years earlier, the world had stood by and watched their people being exterminated. They knew that Israel could not depend on the community of nations to prevent a similar outrage. They knew that an attack by the Arabs was not an attack to retrieve territory. That excuse was mere euphemistic propaganda—The Big Lie. Territory could have been retrieved long before, had the Arabs been willing to offer any indication that they would eventually accept the existence of the Israeli state.

But the Arabs wouldn't even sit down at a peace table to talk. No, the Arabs didn't seek to fashion a smaller Israel—what they wanted was *no* Israel.

As the blast of the *shofar*[1] sounded through the synagogue late that Yom Kippur afternoon, every Jew in Israel knew that he was fighting for his very life.

1. Ram's horn.

Soldiers in the Sinai holding Yom Kippur service.

THE FIRST NEWS reports of the war were dire. The Israeli public learned that the Bar-Lev Line along the Suez Canal had been overrun, that hundreds of Israeli soldiers had been swallowed up in the surprise attack.

The news from the North was equally discomforting. The Syrians had swept through the Upper Golan, inundating the sparse Israeli defense lines.

The broadcasts were grim indeed. The best that could be hoped was that when Zahal—the acronym ZHL standing for *Zava Hagana I'Yisroel,* the Army for the Defense of Israel—was fully mobilized, the tide of battle would turn.

In the meantime, there was hardly a family not plunged into the deepest anxiety. Everyone in the country was touched; everyone had a son, or a

WAR ON YOM KIPPUR

YOM Kippur, 5734. Approximately at the hour that the Jews of Israel were in their synagogues reciting the Mussaf prayer *piyut* describing the high Yom Kippur service in the Temple in ancient days, the Syrians and Egyptians yesterday launched their latest attempt to destroy us.

By their accustomed fairytale logic, the Arabs imagined they would find us too feeble to respond after our long vigil of prayer and fasting. And so riding high on another of their murderous dreams, the Arabs launched what the Prime Minister aptly described yesterday as their "act of madness" and the Defence Minister described last night as "a very, very dangerous adventure."

But as the Arabs will have learned again before the passage of too many hours, the Jews have long since learned the lesson of seven-day-a-week vigilance — a lesson which in recent decades we have again had the opportunity to apply freely. So yesterday we again "violated one Sabbath in order to be able to observe many more Sabbaths."

It is reported that the Syrians and Egyptians did what they did not in any real hope of "reconquering the lost territories" — despite Syrian announcements of intentions to recapture the entire Golan — and "avenging the shame of Palestine." They intended, apparently, to try and gain a foothold on our side of the cease-fire lines — on the east bank of the Suez, in the case of the Egyptians — which, they dreamt, the United Nations would immediately freeze by imposing a cease-fire. Thereby their regimes hoped to regain some of their long-lost prestige in their own countries and in the Arab world generally.

We, on the other hand, aware of their plans and their moves to implement them, took the calculated risk of not striking a pre-emptive blow and allowing them to be seen as the aggressors not only in intent and word but also in act. Another vital reason for this, the Defence Minister said last night, was that the Israel nation wishes — as our history clearly shows — to go on living a life of normal peaceful pursuits, which we could not possibly do if we constantly kept huge fighting forces all along our borders with the enemy.

The United Nations observers have reported to their chiefs how the war began yesterday. One wonders whether this time the so-called "family of nations" will be impressed. One wonders whether they will see any parallel between what happened yesterday and what happened in 1967, in 1956, in 1947-48, and — in other dimensions — many times before that. One wonders whether, as a result, the "international community" will once and for all see the moral, political and tactical bankruptcy of their policy of so-called evenhandedness with respect to a struggle involving aggressors who have no respect for their own let alone others' lives (the Arabs have many times announced how victory will ultimately be theirs because, after all, they can afford to sacrifice tens of millions of lives, if necessary) and the victims or intended victims of the aggression.

Fortunately, we in Israel know by now not to expect anything from the bankrupt morality of the international community. We will fight as we have fought in the past. And the 5734 Yom Kippur season will indeed end and the Succot season begin with the traditional words quoted last night by the Defence Minister: *Gmar hatima tova.*

During the early days of the war, people stopped wherever there wa radio to listen to the news. Anyone the street carrying a transistor rad would immediately attract a crow passersby.

Egyptian-Syria

Tanks battle as Syrians pen
cross Canal, Israel plane

De
ag
pre-e
at

Syrian shells explode in a kibbutz in northern Galilee.

(AP photo)

THE JERUSALEM POST

SECOND EDITION

Price: 65 Ag.

SUNDAY, OCTOBER 7, 1973 • TISHRE 11, 5734 • RAMADHAN 11, 1393 • VOL. XLIII, No. 13911*

Arabs claim success

By ANAN SAFADI
Jerusalem Post Arab Affairs Reporter

The Egyptians last night said
they had no

STRONGER ARAB FORCES THAN '67
Russians flee scapegoat role

By ZEEV SCHUL
Jerusalem Post Reporter

TEL AVIV. — The total deployment of the Syrian and Egyptian
armies — including mobilization of
all of their reserve units — into
the so-called

Finally a continued Soviet presence might also compel the Russians to intervene in the fighting
at a certain stage in order to rescue their citizens.

Both the Syrian and

Jerusal
The joint
began just be
timed delibe
pur. Israel
the attack
The Cabine
extraordinary
Minister Gol
Ambassador
the assault
The Cabin
empt the
authoritative
cision was
military rea
who was r
the war. T
taken delibe
tary disadva
confidence t
rael's border
security nee
ing the init
The attac
and Damas
was design
fort." Th
is believed
of Sinai,
area, Sharr
deis, while
set their w
of the Gol
The Egy
huge tank
two thous
all of thei
about 500
yesterday
heads wes
and bolst
darkness.
Israel s
tians may
Israel citi
The tro
the Syria
were note
was first

n attacks held
rate Golan line, Egyptians
maintain air supremacy

By **HIRSH GOODMAN**, Jerusalem Post Military Correspondent

Israel forces yesterday contained invading Egyptian and Syrian units which crossed into Sinai and the Golan Heights under heavy artillery and air cover. The attack began shortly before 2 o'clock.

Two positions, one on the northern tip of the Canal and the other on Mount Hermon, which were taken by Arab forces in the late afternoon, were recaptured yesterday evening. No casualty figures were available last night, but Syrian and Egyptian losses were reported to be "heavy."

Israel will be fighting an estimated 350,000 troops on both fronts—250,000 of them along the Egyptian front alone. According to Defence Minister Moshe Dayan, the Egyptians have 2,000 tanks, 1,500 artillery pieces and 700 planes readied for the battle, while the Syrians have mobilized 800 tanks and 800 long-range and medium-range guns along the front.

Only limited Egyptian and Syrian forces managed to cross over the cease-fire lines as Israel maintained supremacy in the skies. The Egyptians crossed the Suez Canal at several points, attacking sparsely defended Israeli forward positions, while the Syrians brought troops by helicopter to positions on the Hermon and along the Golan Heights. The attacks were coordinated with massive artillery bombardments aimed at Israeli forces.

Throughout last night, Egyptian forces were attempting to build bridgeheads across the Canal, in an attempt to bolster commando and infantry units, which had taken positions on the Israeli side during the afternoon.

According to the army spokesman, an attempt by the Egyptians to transport troops by helicopter into Abu Rodeis in southern Sinai at 6 p.m. was fought off when Israeli Air Force planes destroyed eight (unconfirmed reports claim 10) of the helicopters in flight. Each helicopter carries an average of 30 men and their equipment.

Air raid sirens sounded off three times in Tel Aviv. According to Defence Minister Dayan, the sirens were in response to enemy planes flying in the direction of the city from the sea. Mr. Dayan said in reply to a question that the planes were equipped with missiles, but he would not elaborate.

Throughout the afternoon there was heavy aerial fighting both in the north and in Sinai. No losses for either Israeli or Arab pl___ were given. M___

Dayan reported, life was normal. Mr. Dayan strongly advised the Jordanians not to enter the battle.

Israeli towns and settlements suffered in no significant way according to Mr. Dayan, who reported that there had been one fatality in the northern town of Kiryat Shmona.

No Israeli settlements had been evacuated, apart from the civilian oil town of Abu Rodeis in southern Sinai, where families were flown north yesterday morning before actual hostilities commenced.

There was no gauging last night how long the war was likely to last, or what it's scope would be. Israel is thought to have lost a certain advantage, observers point out, by not staging a pre-emptive attack. Defence Minister Dayan would not commit himself to a time limit last night, but stated the war would take neither months nor weeks.

The Syrians' air attack was directed in part against the Golan's Druse — several men and women were killed by strafing and 15 injured in the villages of ___ 'as'

---

5 Syrian ships sunk

Jerusalem Post Military Correspondent

Four Syrian missile boats and one torpedo boat were sunk in a naval battle between Israel and Syrian vessels near the Syrian port of Latakia yesterday evening. The Israeli naval unit suffered no losses.

The Syrian vessels, of the Soviet-built Comar and Ossa classes, were sunk with Israel-made Gabriel sea surface-to-surface missiles used in combat for the first time.

U.S. seeks cease-fire

NEW YORK. — Secretary of State Henry Kissinger, on instructions from President Nixon, yesterday sought an immediate cease-fire in the Middle East, the State Department spokesman said in New York.

The spokesman, Mr. Robert McCloskey, said that U.S. attempts to prevent the outbreak of war had failed, but Dr. Kissinger was under orders from the President to "make every effort to see that it is brought to a stop."

Kissinger flew back to Washington from New York — where he had been attending the U.N. session — after a series of urgent telephone consultations with the President.

Dr. Kissinger was to meet with a special task force set up within the State Department as soon as fighting broke out, McCloskey told newsmen.

One White House official said the President was "very, very concerned" and was giving direct ___ ___ ___

---

on st ptive k

Reporter
-Syrian attack _.m. yesterday, or Yom Kip- earlier that take place. called into n, and Prime informed U.S. Keating that ninent.

led not to pre- Arab assault, s said. The de- or political not make it clear le for starting eli decision was despite the mili- involved, out of situation of Is- led the additional nake up for leav- the enemy.

planned by Cairo some time, and a "maximum ef- ptian aim, it o regain parts ally the Mitla kh and Abu Ro- yrians apparently as to retake all ghts.

have amassed a said to number hicles and have anes estimated at e air. Their aim establish beach- ez before nightfall under cover of

believe the Egyp- seeking to attack the air. ncentrations along Egyptian fronts week. However, it ed that the A-ab ved in

brother, or a father, or a sweetheart, or knew of some loved one who had been engulfed in the attack. At every moment, someone dear was known to stand in mortal danger. The casualty lists were awaited with dread.

From the very start, it was clear that this war was not going to be a six-day jaunt. The Arabs had prepared long, and had prepared well. The Israelis, evidently, had been caught off guard.

Though the radio did not announce the precise numbers of the slain, the broadcasts left little doubt that the Israeli losses were heavy. On this second day of the war, the enemy was unquestionably in command; the Israelis were fighting a defensive action, trying desperately not to yield too much ground.

It became quite clear early in the battle that the Israeli Air Force was finding its power sharply curtailed by the sophisticated weaponry conferred

by the Soviet Union on the Arab Armies, who were impervious to Israeli air power under an umbrella of anti-aircraft missiles.

Oddly enough, it was this factor—the Arab dependence on Soviet weaponry and strategy—that eventually proved a boon to Israel. The Eqyptian armed forces hastily crossed the Suez to easily overcome the slight defenses of the Bar-Lev Line. So facile was their progress, that they were quite unprepared for such military success. Had the enemy forces, with their new found strength, utilized their initial advantage to the fullest, they most probably could have pushed all the way to the Mitla Pass or beyond. With little organized opposition in their path, and with the main body of the Israeli Army as yet unmobilized, the Egyptian generals were restrained only by battle orders rigidly imposed on them by their Russian military advisers, who had severely

AIR RAID SIRENS SHATTER STILLNESS OF YOM KIPPUR

By GEORGE LEONOFF, Jerusalem Post Reporter

Air raid sirens shattered the nation-wide stillness at 2 p.m. yesterday on Israel's holiest holiday warning the country of the outbreak of fighting. Within minutes, Israel Radio broke its traditional Yom Kippur silence to announce that Egyptian and Syrian forces had opened offensive operations across the Suez Canal and the Golan Heights cease-fire line respectively.

The radio broadcast orders for Haga, the Civil Defence, to go on full alert.

Although the first "silent call-up" of military personnel on holiday leave and reservists began Friday afternoon, and the sound of jet fighters early Saturday morning provided an incongruous accompaniment to prayers on the Day of Atonement, the 2 o'clock sirens were for thousands of Israelis the first indication of a crisis. The alarms disrupted Yom Kippur services in packed synagogues thoughout the country.

Not all Israelis immediately descended into air raid shelters, but wherever they were, within minutes most of the population almost instinctively gathered around radios, in line with long-standing Israeli practice in times of crisis. As expected, several minutes later Israel Radio came on with the first announcement of the Egyptian and Syrian attacks, and with the warning that the air raid alarms were the real thing. Thereafter news bulletins followed on the quarter-hour, often interrupted for the transmission of code names calling up various units. In between the radio played classical music.

Private vehicles, parked since dusk Friday with the advent of Yom Kippur, appeared on the streets shortly after the initial air raid alarm, followed

shortly by buses — mobilized to take the units which were called up to their various dispositions. Thousands of civilian trucks and light vehicles were requisitioned.

Thousands of tourists in Israel for the holidays were herded into hotel bomb shelters as air raid alarms sounded periodically.

Hospitals immediately set emergency plans in motion, clearing the wards of all but serious cases. Ambulances and private vehicles evacuated hundreds of non-critical cases to their homes to make the maximum hospital space available for war casualties. Doctors were ordered to emergency posts in hospitals and clinics.

The Civil Defence Command ordered all those remaining at home to go to shelters immediately on hearing the air raid alarms, to tape their windows and to observe a strict blackout throughout the night.

In the central part of the country, the first all-clear came 45 minutes after the initial alarm at 2 p.m. Elsewhere, the civilian population was confined to the shelters for several hours, and in Beersheba, capital of the Negev, the first all-clear came only at 7.15 p.m.

Lod Airport, where flights were suspended over Yom Kippur and due to resume only at 8 last night, remained closed until further notice. El Al's entire fleet of 13 aircraft had come home to Lod on Yom Kippur Eve.

Petrol filling stations, closed for the holiday, reopened in urban centres and along highways soon after the first news of the fighting. The several Arab-operated filling stations in East Jerusalem which remained open as usual Saturdays began to do brisk business shortly after 2.30 p.m.

Prayer shawls cover the khaki as Jerusalemites go to war

By ABRAHAM RABINOVICH
Jerusalem Post Reporter

In the crowded Sephardi Synagogue in Jerusalem's Ramat Eshkol, a young man rose from his seat when his name was shouted from the doorway by an army courier. But his father, who was sitting next to him, held him in an embrace and refused to let him go. The synagogue's rabbi told the weeping father that his son could not stay. "His place is not here today,' said the rabbi. The father released his son and the rabbi placed his hand on the young man's head to bless him.

Throughout Jerusalem, men wearing prayer shawls and skullcaps could be seen driving cars or thumbing lifts to mobilization points sometimes with knapsacks over their shoulders. Some had time to stop by their homes to break their fast which began at sundown Friday. In a synagogue in Bayit Vegan, a rabbi interrupted services in the afternoon to tell all men in the congregation that it was permissible to break their fast if they were called up and to use motor vehicles to reach their gathering points. In Beit Hakerem, a synagogue sexton called for silence in order to read out a list of names handed him by a courier. One of the names was that of his own son.

"A war has begun," said a rabbi in Katamon. "Let us pray for our soldiers, may God give them courage and protect them."

The first hint of unusual activity came before 7 a.m. when many Jerusalemites were awakened by the sound of planes overhead. Worshippers who had gone to the Western Wall at dawn were startled by a Phantom flying low overhead.

The streets of Jerusalem, normally deserted of vehicles on Yom Kippur, began to see traffic build up through the morning. With growing frequency, military vehicles braked to a halt in residential neighbourhoods and couriers stepped out to scan house numbers. In many instances, they were directed by neighbours to the local synagogue. Many of those called up drove their wives and children to relatives before heading for their units.

The reaction to the mobilization was a mixture of anxiety and puzzlement. The general public had had no hint of war but the fact the mobilization was being carried out on Yom Kippur indicated that something serious was afoot. "The Arabs must have started shooting," said a man on Six Day War Street, "We never would start anything on Yom Kippur."

Since Israel Radio does not broadcast on Yom Kippur, the country was in a total news blackout without the population knowing whether war was imminent or had actually started.

The growing uncertainty was punctuated shortly after 2 p.m. with the wail of a siren which suddenly made the situation real and, for many people, frightening.

The siren caused many people to turn on their radios, even in religious neighbourhoods. They found that Israel Radio had indeed begun broadcasting almost simultaneously with the siren blast.

At the Western Wall, the sound of sirens sent hundreds of worshippers in search of shelter. Many crowded into the hall beneath ancient Wilson's Arch. Others found shelter in the Jewish Quarter. By sunset, several hundred had returned to the Wall, including the students from the Yeshivat Hakotel, who danced their way down from the Jewish Quarter arm in arm. The approaches to the Wall were guarded by heavy security forces. As the shofar blasts signalling the end of the holiday died away, the yeshiva students and other worshippers broke into a hora. A police loudspeaker boomed across the plaza, halting the dancers in their tracks. "Please disperse immediately to your homes," an officer said, "Happy New Year and good health to you and your families."

SYRIA ASKS U.N. TO EXPEL ISRAEL

UNITED NATIONS (UPI).— Syrian Foreign Minister Abrul Halim Khaddam urged the General Assembly on Friday to approve a resolution expelling Israel, ordering a boycott of the Jewish State and demanding its immediate and unconditional withdrawal from all Arab territory occupied in the 1967 Six Day War.

Khaddam said Israel and "American imperialism" had become isolated in the present-day world.

U.N. legal experts pointed out that Khaddam's expulsion proposal could not be carried out by the Assembly, which he suggested should act because of the likelihood of a U.S. veto blocking anti-Israel action in the Security Council.

The U.N. charter provides that a member may be expelled by a vote of the General Assembly but only upon recommendation of such action by the Security Council.

Khaddam, who also is Syria's Deputy Prime Minister, said in a policy speech to the Assembly that there are two basic conditions for Middle East peace:

Recognition of the rights of the Palestinians to their homeland and to self-determination.

Immediate, complete and unconditional Israeli withdrawal from all occupied Arab territory.

Khaddam charged that Israeli leaders had elevated terror to the level of state policy and arrogated the right to infringe on other nations' sovereignty.

He suggested that Security Council action against Israel would be impossible because of the likelihood of a U.S. veto. Therefore, he said, the General Assembly should adopt a resolution "strong enough to induce Tel Aviv to end its aggressive acts."

cautioned them not to proceed beyond the range of their SAM anti-aircraft coverage. And so the Egyptian Army waited, losing precious hours, until their SAMs could be moved up.

The same thing happened in the Golan. There, too, the Syrians caught the Israelis by surprise. According to military authorities, the Syrians might have advanced their initial thrust right down to Tiberius. Capturing that city would have opened up the entire Valley of Jezreel beyond. But the Syrians, too, dallied to conform to previously laid out battle plans, fearing to advance beyond the cover of their SAM umbrella.

Moreover, it is conceded that had the Jordanians, at the same point in time, attacked on the western front, they might have reached the very walls of Jerusalem. It was, indeed, a most perilous hour.

About two weeks later, the situation, in retrospect, gave rise to some gallows humor, as epitomized in the gag current in Tel Aviv: "If the Syrians advanced through the northern agricultural settlements and captured Tiberius, who would have stopped them from conquering Tel Aviv?" The dour reply was: "The Egyptians!"

Yes, on the day after the Arab attack, the inner cabinet of Israel was badly frightened. The population at large did not know the true extent of the debacle, but Premier Golda Meir and her Defense Minister, Moshe Dayan, and the inner cabinet were all too aware of the extent of the disaster.

Belatedly, every sinew of the nation was tautened to repel the invaders. All combat troops were called up for immediate duty. Every force was brought into action. Every vehicle, public and private, was mustered by the State to carry soldiers to the front. Every man, woman, and child who could do any kind of effective work was put to work.

Those not conscripted, clamored to volunteer their services. The streets of the cities miraculously emptied. Most shops were closed. Non–essential businesses shut down. Postal services were manned by old men and boys. Buses were run by women. A retired general of the Israeli Defense Forces volunteered to drive a garbarge truck. Queues formed in every public sector, next to every hospital, to give blood to save the wounded, to serve in some active way.

One of the more remarkable aspects was the outpouring of support proffered by the Arabs living in Israel. Donations were pleged; services were pledged; Arabs stood in line to offer blood to their Israeli countrymen. Arab women prepared sandwiches and refreshments for Israeli soldiers going off to war.

Likewise, many members of the Christian community in Israel offered help. The Greek Orthodox Archbishop Raya declared he was willing to do anything he could to further the Israeli war effort. If necessary, he was prepared to sweep the streets.

The Rabbinate of Israel regarded the situation with the greatest gravity. As vigilant as they had been in guarding their religious strictures, now they immediately relaxed their prohibition against work on the Sabbath or on religious holidays for anyone engaged in soldiery or in labor which directly aided defense. The doctrine of *pekuach nefesh*—personal succor—was invoked, a Halachic rule which holds that in a case where life is clearly in danger, ritual is of no moment and religious observance may be bypassed.

Early in the morning on Sunday, October 7, the Lod Airport was flooded with foreign visitors attempting to leave a country beset by war. Two thousand had departed from Israel on overnight flights, and now others were at the gates. Still, there were also a great many tourists who clamored to stay, offering to help in any way possible. At the same time, thousands of Israelis were besieging airlines in every country in the world to fly them back to their homeland, and thousands of foreign nationals were appearing at Israeli embassies all over the world volunteering to offer their services.

The Ministry of Education announced that all schools and kindergartens would be closed until further notice. Pressure upon the Ministry to reverse this decision was intense. Many mothers complained that if they had to stay home to watch their children, they could not help in the War effort. Their men were going to the front, they said, and they were needed to take their husbands' places in jobs that they could perform, in some measure.

The Civil Defense was on the radio all day long, announcing to civilians: "Fill all available containers with water. Remove all flammable materials from your homes and from air raid shelters. Tape up your windows. If possible, prepare a first-aid kit. Get together as much fire-fighting equipment for immediate use as you can manage. Store mirrors. Store nonessential items made of glass." The implication was unmistakable: prepare for enemy bombing of major cities and major settlements.

The announcements went on: "Avoid using cars. Avoid using telephones unless such use is

absolutely necessary. Learn the meaning of air-raid signals. Learn to distinguish, and train your children to distinguish, between the rising-falling tones which command residents to go to shelters, and the continuous monotone which signals the all-clear. The all-clear signal will last at least one minute."

By 7·45 on the evening of October 7, 1,000 holy scrolls of the Torah had been transferred to the front line units of the Israel Defense Forces. To the orthodox, these were talismanic artifacts which would protect against doom. The rank and file of the soldiery welcomed the arrival of the holy scrolls more or less as they would welcome old friends. As remote from the War as anything could possibly be, the scrolls were a reminder of peaceful days at home. The parchment might be unable to protect against steel shells, but the presence of the Sefer Torahs proffered comfort. The remnants of mysticism that lurk in even the most rational of us were stirred by the blessed scrolls.

On this day, the first day after the commencement of the War, a writer for the Hebrew daily, Maariv, the most prestigious of Israel's newspapers, penned the following apostrophe:

> *Those who stood back and watched their men go off to war—the fathers and mothers, the wives and the young children —earnestly hoped the prayers they had uttered would be answered.*
>
> *The ancient words of the prayers— the Machsor[1]—acquired new, credible, and majestic significance. Life and death, judgment and mercy—all the old phrases became very direct, very real, very personal.*
>
> *The timeless words continued to resound in their hearts. Neither roaring motors nor the rumble of wheels could drown out the sacred melodies. The roads—leading to the vast expanses of Sinai and the mountains of Golan—were transformed into houses of prayer. Silent entreaties rose from buses and trucks, through the blue skies above, to pierce the very gates of the heavens, up to the seat of the Almighty.*

1. Holiday prayerbook (Hebrew).

BY MONDAY NIGHT, October 8, practically all of Israel's people's army had been mobilized to repel the invaders. Now the cities of Tel Aviv, Jerusalem, and Haifa were transformed. Transportation, except for vehicles engaged in the war effort, was virtually at a halt. The cafés and night life of Dizengoff Boulevard were stilled, for who could be their patrons? The postman was off to war, and the carpenter, the schoolmaster, and the radio repairman, the furniture salesman, and the farmer—all had gone off to fight. Most tourists had left or were leaving, and new tourists were refused passage to the war-stricken country. And those who were too young to fight were trying to fill the shoes of their brothers and fathers.

Of the 300,000 men now mobilized for defense, only 75,000 were regulars, and 20,000 were inductees serving their first regular tour of duty. The other 200,000—two-thirds of the total armed forces—were civilians drafted from all the ordinary walks of life. Among these were the rich and the poor, the educated and the uneducated, the bachelors and the heads of families. No one was spared.

Unique among the armies of the world, Israel's Army is truly a people's army. When Israel goes to war, the economy absolutely grinds to a halt. When this people's army is mobilized, the private sector is immobilized. Every last man is called upon; exemptions are few: even fathers with four children are not exempt, the law specifically stating that only a man who has sired five living children may be excused from combat duty.

Women, too, are part of this army. Between the ages of 18 and 38, they are subject to conscription and are inducted for a period of 20 months of service. Only two reasons warrant exemption: pregnancy, of course, provides an unimpeachable release; and immunity may also be granted to females who come from extremely orthodox homes in which proximity to other unmarried males does not accord with that sect's notions of propriety.

Volunteers from the very orthodox community of Bnai Brak giving blood.

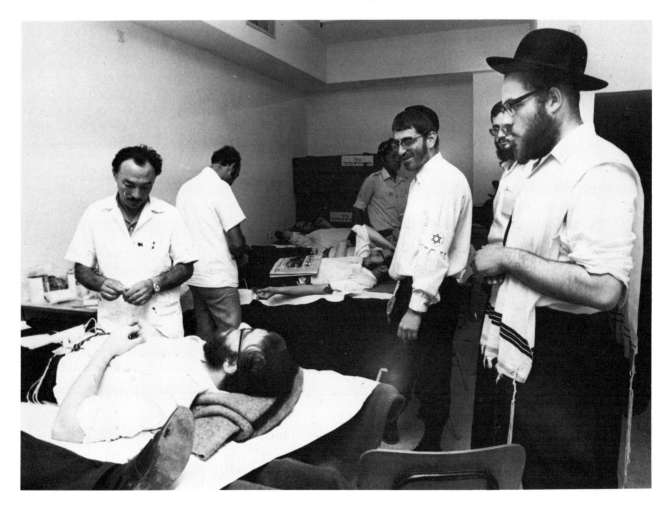

How to paint headlights

Call to observe blackout

Jerusalem Post Reporter

TEL AVIV. — The public is asked to follow Haga (Civil Defence) blackout and other instructions. The Haga spokesman here laid special emphasis on a total blackout at homes and businesses. Drivers are asked to paint over their car lights. (They can leave a small white square in the center of the headlights.)

The Haga spokesman also asked persons who have no shelter at home, or too small a shelter, to dig slit trenches. The trench should be deep enough so that a person can stand up inside without being seen.

There has been only a partial call-up of Haga men, the Haga commander, Tat-Aluf Uri Rom, said yesterday. He explained that this was done in order not to disrupt civilian life in the country. T/A Rom hoped there would be no need for the additional Haga personnel. Among those conscripted are auxiliary Magen David Adom and Fire Brigade men.

Ernie Meyer reports:

In some Jerusalem streets groups of children joined the war effort yesterday by stopping cars and slapping gooey black paint on their headlights. The youngsters were in high spirits but lacked proper directions. on how to do the job, and also endangered themselves.

One Haga officer (a school principal in civilian life) said that he had seen a boy actually pushed aside by a car that refused to stop. He was not aware of any instructions from the Haga command to the youngsters.

In many cases the youngsters did a sloppy job. They painted the entire headlight — plus the enclosing metal rim and other areas — and then used a cloth to wipe open a lightslit. Often the slit was too short and narrow, leaving the driver less than the minimum light needed for safe driving on unlit streets.

Police say headlights must be covered with a thick coat of dark paint or other opaque matter. A horizontal slit 10 by 80 millimetres in the centre is to be covered with light paint only, to allow a minimum of light to emerge. Right rearlights are to be blacked out completely: on the left rearlight, an eight-millimetre light-slit is to remain.

A police spokesman stressed that police officers or Haga men may stop drivers whose cars are not blacked out. Police have issued no instructions to children to help with the blacking-out.

Blood donors queue up

Jerusalem Post Reporter

TEL AVIV. — Long queues of blood donors formed outside Magen David Adom stations, according to Dr. "Abrasha" Atzmon, head of Kupat Holim's "National Emergency Services."

The response of the public has been overwhelming, he said yesterday, adding that "quite a few of them were tourists visiting Israel."

The blood is shipped immediately to the country's various hospitals.

Outstanding work in helping to maintain the stations was being carried out by volunteers, especially members of Gadna, he said

Magen David Adom is selling, for IL10, a family first-aid kit. Dr. Atzmon advised families without a kit of this kind to acquire one.

Kupat Holim yesterday announced that all its services were functioning normally, except the Sprinzak Rest Home in Nazareth, which had been turned over to the army.

Mail getting through

Yitzhak Zemel, deputy director of postal services at the Communications Ministry, told *The Post* last night that "The mails are going through despite the fact that many letter carriers have been called up for military duty. This is because Gadna- boys and girls have been pressed into service."

"I know of no post office that has had to close because of the emergency," he added.

The Ministry yesterday asked the public not to mail parcels weighing more than three kilos. This is to keep parcel post moving smoothly to both civilians and soldiers.

The Examiner of Banks said yesterday that until further notice all banks in the country will be open only until 12.30 p.m., because of the manpower shortage. However, all banking institutions will receive regular deliveries of currency, as needed.

War caught press by surprise

Jerusalem Post Reporter

TEL AVIV. — The war broke out so suddenly that no foreign correspondent could come in the first twenty-four hours to cover it. This was because they had no way of getting here, David Landor, head of the Government Press Office, told *The Post* yesterday. The foreign press and news agencies are regularly represented here by over a hundred professional correspondents, about a third of whom are foreigners and the rest local stringers.

Most girls and women serve their tour of duty working in supply units, or as teachers, or as accountants, and in any other capacity except combat duty.

After their regular tour of duty is completed, all men and women automatically become part of the Reserves, and serve a shorter tour of duty each year. Men, until age 39, must spend 31 days every year in the Army. Between the ages of 39 and 55, this requirement is cut to 14 days per year. Only when he reaches 55 is a man's Army service terminated.

Reserve officers serve a term of 38 days a year. The annual service requirements for a woman in the reserve forces is the same as a man's, but her Army career ends at age 34.

These requirements may seem austere, but in the state of danger in which Israel has always existed there has been no choice. Even the biblical exemptions listed in Deuteronomy[1] have not been honored.

> *And the officers shall speak unto the people, saying: What man has built a new house and has not dedicated it? Let him go and return to his house, lest he die in battle and another man enjoy it.*
>
> *And what man has planted a vineyard and has not yet eaten its fruit? Let him return to home, lest he die in battle and another man enjoy his vineyard.*
>
> *And what man has bethrothed a wife and has not yet taken her to live with him? Let him return to his house, lest he die in battle and another man take her.*
>
> *And what man is fearful and fainthearted? Let him return to his house, lest his brethren's hearts also grow faint, as well as his.*

In present-day Israel, the rabbis have declared these biblical injunctions inoperative in

1. Deuteronomy 20:5.

accordance with Talmudic interpretation of these passages. These laws, the ancient sages said, were never meant to apply to defensive wars. Modern Israel certainly could never afford such permissive rules.

A unique aura pervades this people's army. If anyone believes that military and democratic institutions are necessarily antithetic, he has but to study the Israeli Army. Officers, as likely as not, are addressed by their first names by even the lowliest *turai* (Private). Salutes between the ranks, and other formal considerations of respect, are not a mandatory part of the makeup of these forces. While discipline prevails, morale is deemed to be of higher importance. And morale is high. All men understand their responsibilities, and realize that the lives of their families depend on their actions under fire. Generally, in Israel's wars, the first to have fallen have been the officers, who have deemed it their duty to physically lead their troops into battle.

An army, outnumbered in regular strength as this one was in this last war by roughly three to one, cannot afford to send soldiers into the mouths of

Arabs volunteer in Haifa

By YA'ACOV FRIEDLER
Jerusalem Post Reporter

HAIFA. — Haifa residents were already behaving like veterans yesterday on the second day of the war, and only widespread hoarding marred the home front atmosphere.

Dozens of youths, Arab residents and pensioners volunteered their services to the police.

Boys and girls helped in hospitals, in grocery shops whose owners had been called up, and in putting black paint on headlights.

Police reported a windfall: Crime was virtually suspended in the city, either because the underworld decided to do their bit by making a gesture or because of the call-up. The police spokesman said there had also been a virtual stop to the usual neighbours' quarrels.

The local army recruiting office was overwhelmed by young and not-so-young men demanding to join the forces. A group of Russian immigrants arrived together and insisted they would not stay home while Israel was being attacked. "This is our fight," one of them said; they left only after getting a firm promise they would be phoned when needed.

One 21-year-old Haifa boy recently discharged from the army as physically unfit was practically in tears as he rushed from office to office trying to join up again. "I'm

ready to cook or clean or pass the ammunition, anything to do my bit. I made a fatal mistake in getting a discharge," he told your reporter.

Many of the 9,000 Arab workers from the Galilee who work in Haifa arrived late due to transport difficulties, and some did not come at all. The 3,000 workers from the Areas stayed away.

The port worked at almost full capacity during the day, though the shortage of trucks created difficulties. Arrangements were made to do as much as possible during the blackout as well.

The Israeli liner Nili, due to sail for a Succot cruise with Israeli passengers, cancelled her trip. The four foreign passenger liners due yesterday morning, two of them from Beirut, were informed on Saturday night to stay away.

One of these, the s.s. Romantica, with 209 American Baptist pilgrims on board, was intercepted by the Syrian navy, apparently after leaving Beirut, where she had arrived from Iskenderun in Turkey. She was to have stayed here four days.

There were two air-raid alarms yesterday, a half-hour one in the morning and a 90-minute one beginning at 3.10 in the afternoon. But nothing happened, and quite a few of those who had gone to the shelters came out before the all-clear

sounded.

Unlike Saturday night, the blackout was almost total yesterday, with police smashing the few signs which remained lit in order to put them out. The Retailers' Association, with the agreement of the Commerce Ministry, ordered shops to close at dusk; it would in any case have been impossible to serve customers in the dark. The streets, which were fairly empty the whole day, were deserted after darkness fell.

Despite the repeated assurances that there would be no shortage of foodstuffs, and the order forbidding hoarding, many housewives started a panic grocery buying spree, especially in the supermarkets. Several shops had to close their doors and admit their queues little by little. Shoppers conceded that a lot of the food would probably spoil, but bought it nevertheless, "just in case".

At one supermarket in Kiryat Eliezer there was a mad scramble when the milk arrived. But though some women took up to ten bags, there was no shortage when the scramble was over, and some of them abandoned part of their hoards in the aisles before leaving the store. The lack of hard news from the fronts also set rumour mills going.

Rabbis Waived Fasting For Soldiers

By ABRAHAM RABINOVICH

The first wounded back from the fronts described yesterday how they broke their Yom Kippur fast by eating battle rations as they moved forward into combat.

Three young soldiers interviewed at Hadassah Hospital all said they and most of their comrades had fasted at least until the enemy attack began Saturday at 2 p.m. Some front-line soldiers continued to fast until sundown when Yom Kippur was over despite an announcement by the Military Rabbinate that the obligation to fast was waived with the outbreak of fighting.

THE SOLDIERS' WELFARE COMMITTEE IN ISRAEL
REQUEST TO THE PUBLIC

The people of Israel are requested to show their deep feelings for the Israel Defence Forces' soldiers now on the front line. In order to translate these deep feelings into something practical we request the public to supply us with the following items which our soldiers at the front require at present:

★ **Transistor radios**

★ **Light reading in Hebrew (detective stories, suspense stories etc.)**

★ **Games (chess, draughts (chequers), dominoes, sheshbesh).**

The Soldiers' Welfare Committee have set up the following points for collection:

Tel Aviv: Bet Hehayal, 60 Rehov Weizmann
Jerusalem: Bet Hehayal, Sderot Ben-Zvi
Haifa: Branch Office, 5 Rehov Balfour
Beersheba: Beit Hehayal

Likewise, items can be brought to all branches of the Soldiers' Welfare Committee.

The Soldiers' Welfare Committee and all its branches will see to the distribution of these items according to demand for them.

Thank you.

Civilians reading instructions for Civil Defense on posters pasted on walls.

(Top Left) Volunteer girl painting headlights.

(Top Right) Volunteer boys filling sandbags.

(Center) Volunteer boys assisting in hospital kitchen.

(Lower Left) Volunteer youngsters filling in for sanitation employees called off to war.

cannon like so many unthinking robots. The same respect for individual life that prevails in civilian life carries over in time of war. The sagacity of each sergeant is exercised to preciously harbor life. Whether such concern stems from a democratic philosophy, or just from the knowledge that the Israeli armed forces will always be woefully outnumbered, the character of the Israeli officer encourages self-reliance and self-discipline among the troops. In this army, the usual "Eyes right! Left-Right!" approach is simply inapplicable.

Can a war be successfully waged by such an egalitarian, individualistic, unconventional, unprofessional army? United States Intelligence rates the Israeli Army, on a man-to-man basis, as good as any in the world.

After the Six-Day War of 1967, Yitzhak Rabin, commander-in-chief of the Israeli forces, was awarded an honorary doctorate by the Hebrew University of Jerusalem. In his acceptance speech, he made these significant remarks:

> *The Army, which I had the privilege of commanding through these battles, came from the people and returns to the people—to the people which rises in its hours of crisis.*

THE WAR IS NOW having direct social repercussions. The Tel Aviv Rabbinate has postponed all marriages scheduled for the week— practically all of the intended bridegrooms have been mobilized.

Members of Israel's basketball team, just returned from the European championship games in Spain, have been ordered to change straightaway into Army uniforms.

Two hundred veterans of the Six-Day War, all disabled, many of them amputees, report to emergency headquarters demanding jobs. Some clamor to get their old jobs back, insisting they are fit.

In the Galilee, women and children throng the roads in a constant vigil to distribute apples and drinks to soldiers who are moving toward the Golan front.

In the village of Tura, 41 Christian Arabs sign a petition announcing their willingness to help with money, manpower, and blood—"anything needed to support the state of which we are loyal citizens."

At the police headquarters of Hadera, Arab villagers from nearby offer to haul essential goods in their own carts and autos.

From northern Israel, a group of Arab communal leaders send a telegram to Golda Meir:

> *We pray to God for IDF victory. We, the Arab community of Israel, stand beside the country's soldiers, the Government and the whole nation of Israel, with no distinction of race, community or religion. We are all together in the battle.*

Although the radio from Cairo gloats over a great victory yielded by the surprise attack at the Suez Canal, Mohamed Hassan El-Zayat, the Egyptian Minister for Foreign Affairs, stands up in the Council of the United Nations and declares:[1]

> *The attack on 6 October was not an isolated act; it was the pursuit of the same policy of arrogant power recently escalated by Israel against all neighbouring Arab countries. On this day, Israeli air formations attacked the Egyptian forces stationed in the area of El Zaafarana and El Sukhna on the western bank of the Gulf of Suez while Israeli naval units were approaching the western coast of the Gulf. The time and place for that attack were carefully and deliberately selected. The attack was aimed at El Sukhna, where the construction of an oil pipeline carrying oil from the Suez to the Mediterranean was to begin.*
>
> *The day the attack took place was during the Moslem holy month of Ramadan. Israel's latest act of aggression was preceded by a large-scale aerial attack against Syria on 13 September, in preparation for the co-ordinated further aggression against the two countries. After the attack of 6 October, the Arabs responded to the policy of arrogance. They crossed to the Egyptian territory east of the Suez Canal and raised the flag of Egypt on the territory of Egypt.*

An Israeli, wanted for forgery, appears in uniform before a judge in a Tel Aviv courtroom. He has only one request. He wants his trial postponed until the War is over. In the meantime, he wants to join his unit, and go out and fight the enemy.

Request granted.

1. United Nations *Record of the Month* Meeting of 8 October (page 5).

WHAT NEITHER THE leaders of the government nor the Army commanders knew at the outset of the war was that the Israeli Air Force, on which the outcome of previous wars had depended so heavily, would be somewhat ineffective. Appraised by renowned military experts as one of the finest combat forces in the world, the Israeli Air Force undertook the defense of the country with its usual pluck—only to encounter a startling new factor. No one had foreseen how effective the Soviet anti-aircraft arsenal would prove to be. It proved to be deadly.

The U.S. Defense Dept. estimated that in the first three days of the war, 15 Israeli Phantoms and 40 Israeli Skyhawks were shot out of the skies—wiping out 20 percent of the entire Israeli complement of these types of aircraft. Less than one week later, the U.S. Army figures would rise precipitously to estimate a loss of 25 Phantoms (out of 100), and 50 Skyhawks (out of 160)—an overall depletion of almost one-third of the entire offensive power of the Israeli Air Force.

General Yariv, the Israeli military spokesman, admitted to a dismayed nation, in his broadcast on this third day after Yom Kippur, that "quite a number of planes" had been lost to missiles.

The specific figures were not announced in Israel. But the families of the pilots who were shot down were notified, and word got around that things were pretty grim. The nation was appalled.

Wall's tora scrolls sent to front

By DAVID LANDAU
Jerusalem Post Correspondent

The Western Wall was stripped of its tora scrolls yesterday. An army lorry, authorized by the Religions Ministry, removed most of them to take the scrolls to front-line synagogues.

The lorry arrived in the early morning, to the excitement of worshippers and visitors at the Wall — and departed with the scrolls snugly packed under a big prayer shawl.

Meanwhile, at the other side of the Wall plaza, work continued on the huge *succa* which the Religions Ministry puts up annually. Senior Ministry official Dov Perla said he had secured permission from Central Command to transport the palm-branch *sechach* (*succa* covering) that he had ordered from Jericho.

In the ultra-Orthodox Mea Shearim quarter, thousands of young children assembled with their teachers in the courtyard of the Mea Shearim Yeshiva yesterday evening to recite Psalms and pray for a speedy Israeli victory. The spiritual leader of the *Edah Haredit* (the ultra-Orthodox community), Rabbi Yitzhak Weiss, spoke to the children with tears streaming down his face. He explained to them the facts and dangers of war, and told them that their prayers and charity would help the Israeli soldiers to triumph. On the spot, the children raised IL3,000 for Jerusalem's needy before Succot.

Under Rabbi Weiss' orders, two-hourly shifts of Psalm-sayers are praying around the clock in a yeshiva in the quarter. Every shift numbers scores of men and boys.

Maternity hospital taking casualties

Jerusalem Post Reporter

Jerusalem's Misgav Ladach Maternity Hospital reported yesterday it was cutting confinement periods from 48 to 24 hours, to meet increased demand for beds caused by referrals from Hadassah and Shaare Zedek Hospitals. The latter have already begun receiving war casualties.

The directors of Misgav Ladach and Shaare Zedek, Reuven Kashani and Dr. David Maeir, told *The Post* yesterday they had an overwhelming turnout of volunteers — doctors, drivers, students and housewives. The drivers are taking the women and their newborn babies back home as far as Ramle and Beit Shemesh, he said. They are being accompanied by social workers when necessary.

Crooks cool it during war

Jerusalem Post Reporter

TEL AVIV. — The war has cut deeply into Israel's crime output, police said yesterday. They pointed to a nation-wide total of 49 houses robbed on Sunday, as against 121 on a random day three months ago.

The first full day of the war produced one indecent act, compared with eight on the sample day three months ago. Drug arrests showed no change — one on each of the two days. But there were no armed robberies on Sunday, as against one on the comparison day. And Sunday's two assault complaints fell well short of the test day's six.

'Israel's place under the sun'

ATHENS (UPI). — Prime Minister Spyros Markezinis said in his policy statement on taking office yesterday that Greece supports Israel's right to "a place under the sun."

"Many ties connect us with the Arab countries, but nothing divides us from the state of Israel, which has also the right to have a place under the sun," Markezinis said.

Soviets jam phone links to Israel

MOSCOW (AP). — Soviet Jews complained on Sunday of a side effect of the Middle East war: jamming of their telephone link with Israel. Eight Soviet Jews said in a statement to Western newsmen that the authorities have regularly interrupted calls to friends and relatives in Israel since the Middle East fighting broke out on Saturday.

They said the interference also affected calls among themselves in Moscow. They added that pre-arranged calls from the West were not getting through.

Israeli reservists returning to Tel Aviv from London.

British public rushes to help Israel

By DAVID LENNON
Jerusalem Post Correspondent

LONDON. — Hundreds of Jewish and non-Jewish volunteers wishing to go to Israel's aid met last night in London, Manchester and Glasgow. They were told they will not be called to go to Israel until the war has ended, and were informed that they will have to pay their own fares.

Jewish Agency officials also informed them about the types of work they might be reqiured to do, and divided them into groups according to age and skills.

The money men were also busy yesterday evening organizing the collection of donations — which have already been flowing in to the J.P.A. A spokesman for the organization said the mobilization of both funds and canvassers was greater than in 1967.

A steady stream of callers expressing support for Israel continued to reach the Israel Embassy and Rex House, the Zionist Federation headquarters in London. The Federation has called a solidarity rally for this Sunday at Trafalgar Square which many prominent Members of Parliament are expected to address.

A group of Members of Parliament led by former Foreign Secretary Michael Stewart has already called on the Foreign Office and asked them to condemn the Arab aggression.

BAR OF GOLD

PARIS (UPI). — A Frenchman walked into the Israel Embassy yesterday, laid a bar of gold on a table and said, "I want to give this to you." Embassy officials said they have not decided yet what to do with the gold, worth 14,000 francs (about IL14,000).

Urgent messages now can reach soldiers

Civilians may now send urgent messages to members of their families serving in the armed forces — concerning births, weddings, *britot mila* and sickness — by dialling one of the following numbers: Jerusalem: 63111; Tel Aviv: 254122; and Haifa: 660961.

31

A roaring battle of tanks, involving hundreds of instruments of war, stretches out as far as the eye can see, along that sector of the Suez which came to be known as the "Chinese Farm."

33

ON THE FOURTH DAY after the commencement of the War, the first glimmer of good news reached the Israeli public.

The General Staff of the Israeli Army had decided that the first order of business must be to contain the attack which took place on its very borders, and they directed the major part of their strength to the north against the Syrian armies who had been reinforced by Iraqi troops. Concentrated counterattacks launched along the entire length of the Golan front succeeded in smashing the Syrian salient. Israeli military intelligence estimated that the Syrians lost about 800 of their 1,500 tanks. The Syrian Army, while not in disarray, was at least in retreat.

Now the news was announced to a depressed public, that the Israeli forces had not only repelled the invasion, but had pushed ahead into new Syrian territory. Zahal was on the march. From this point on, until the cessation of hostilities some months later, the movement of Israeli forces would be, by and large, forward.

Rwanda breaks ties with Israel

BRUSSELS (UPI). — The Rwanda Government yesterday severed diplomatic relations with Israel, the Rwandese Embassy in Brussels said.

A statement received by the embassy from the Foreign Ministry in Kigali said the decision was taken because Israel refused to withdraw from the occupied territories and because of the war it wages against Egypt, an African brother country.

Moscow Jews Support Israel

A group of Moscow Jews have issued a message of support for Israel and expressed their conviction that the Arab's "tragic military venture" would be repulsed.

The message, a copy of which was made available to Western correspondents in Moscow said: "It can hardly be put into words how shocked we are by the events and how much our sympathies are with the people of Israel."

More Tora scrolls needed at front

The Union of Israel Synagogues yesterday appealed for many more *Sifrei Torah* to send to soldiers at the front. A large number have already been collected by the Union and sent to the front, but still more are needed.

The Union also called on all synagogues to take special measures to observe the blackout during tonight's services. Services should commence somewhat earlier than usual and end before the blackout goes into force.

A TRADITIONAL JEWISH JOKE asserts that if there are two Jews in a community, there will be three *shuls,* each with a different religious bias. Jews most certainly insist that they have a right to disagree with each other.

By and large, Israeli society is fiercely democratic. Every viewpoint, however minute its following, has a right to be heard and win for itself adherents.

Without doubt, the most unpopular group in Israel today is the New Communist Party, a Moscow-oriented political group which draws the major part of its support from radical Arabs. On October 10, this group, known as the Rakah, held three seats in the Knesset, the Israeli parliament. The New Communists, led by Jews, declared with Gromyko and Brezhnev that the Israelis are power-seeking, expansionist aggressors, the pawns of an imperialist United States. The New Communists baldly advocate the liquidation of the Jewish State.

At the very outbreak of the War, when Israelis were hastening to the front to stem the tide of invasion, Rakah presented an advertisement to The Jerusalem Post which counseled the citizenry of Israel to unilaterally return to the Arabs all the buffer territories which stood between Israel and the annihilation of its citizens.

The ad posed a problem, and the executive staff of the Post was called into session. Should the ad be published? A heated debate took place in which a number of editors, utterly outraged by the Rakah pronouncements, urged that the ad be rejected. However, the majority was persuaded by Ted Lurie, the editor-in-chief, to accept and print the patently traitorous pronouncement. Mr. Lurie pointed out that mere publication of an advertisement did not imply espousal of the cause that was advertised. He argued that ever since its founding The Jerusalem Post had been a bulwark of free speech, and that free speech meant nothing unless it meant providing a forum for those with whom one disagrees, even with those with whom one disagrees violently.

His staff was convinced. The ad was accepted and run as you see it in these pages—with no changes.

The Jerusalem Post met with a barrage of objection. The paper pointed out to those who wrote and called that if it were to sit as a censor on every ad submitted by every political party, by every dissident group, it would then be obligated to abdicate its position as a free newspaper.

African states declare support for Arab side

Volunteer troops from Uganda have left there to assist the Arabs in the ongoing Middle East war, President Idi Amin declared yesterday, as several other African states expressed complete solidarity with the Arab cause.

Uganda President Amin said at an independence anniversary parade at Entebbe that a whole mechanized battalion had volunteered to fight and that there were Air Force and Navy volunteers, too — as well as three million civilians. (The population of Uganda is about 10 million, according to the 1973 "Information Please" almanac.)

President Michel Micombero sent Egyptian President Anwar Sadat a message of support yesterday, saying all Burundi's resources were at Egypt's disposal in the war against Israel. At the same time, Niger and Guinea both declared their support for the Arab cause.

President Tito of Yugoslavia expressed his country's "indignation and deep concern over the recent Israeli aggression" in a message to President Sadat.

(Reuter, AP, UPI)

Demonstrations in French Cities

Demonstrations in support of Israel have been taking place in all the major cities of France. In Nice, on the Riviera, 3,000 demonstrators marched along the "Promenade des Anglais" yesterday, joined by large delegations from the Jewish communities of Antibes, Juan les Pins, Cannes, Monte Carlo and Grasse. Other demonstrations and rallies were held in Bordeaux, Marseilles, Montpellier, Toulouse and Lyon.

Retired Aluf driving garbage truck

Jerusalem Post Reporter

TEL AVIV. — Aluf (Res.) Yisrael Barnea yesterday took the wheel of a city garbage truck and thus joined the ranks the hundreds of volunteers without whom there would have been almost no Municipal services in recent days.

Mr. Barnea, who was once Israel's military attache in Moscow, reported for duty in the small hours of yesterday morning. His boss, former Police Commissioner Yosef Nahmias, who now heads the City's Emergency Headquarters, said the ex-General did a good job.

The City's Information Bureaus are meanwhile being swamped by offers of help.

In the last 24 hours alone, the City spokesman says, 519 men and women have volunteered their services. They included doctors, engineers, students, clerks, workers, and 200 drivers with their private vehicles. The volunteers included foreign citizens, tourists and new immigrants.

Meanwhile, the City is reminding businessmen, plant managers and cafe proprietors that the blackout is still in effect. In many businesses neon signs are still being turned on every night, and on the way to Holon used-car lots were last night faily illuminated with strings of multi-coloured lights. Some cafes were open for business last night on Tel Aviv's Rehov Dizengoff, but were well blacked out.

The Rabbinate yesterday called on all synagogues to see that they are blacked out during Succot services. They recommended that tonight's services be held early. The Succot booths must also be blacked out.

Four species teams

Special teams will be sent by the Chief Rabbinate to soldiers on the fronts to distribute the four species to all soldiers who wish to perform religious rites on the first day of Succot.

Who won the basketball game?

Military Pool Correspondent

"Who won the Israel-Turkey basketball match in Barcelona?" This was one of the first questions a crowd of soldiers asked the Armoured Corps' chief education officer as he distributed newspapers at the front during a brief lull in the fighting on Monday.

For the soldier at the front, cut off from the everyday world of comfortable trivia, the arrival of a newspaper is an important event. Apart from his desire to know what has been happening along other parts of the front, he welcomes the chance to catch up on the smaller news items buried in the inner pages — like the result of a basketball match.

Other simple pleasures take on a new perspective in the grim surroundings. The handfulls of sweets distributed to forward gunners, or the chance to send letters to relatives at home, brought responses of gratitude out of all proportion to the simplicity of the act. And the emissaries from home are amply rewarded with stories of the incredible bravery engendered in the brief but vicious period of fighting.

MOSLEM WARFARE DURING RAMADAN

Jihad guarantees heaven

CAIRO (AP). — The top religious leader in Egypt predicted victory over Israel, because Egyptian troops are fighting in the Moslem holy month of Ramadan and thus "are sure of Allah's support."

Moslems call their fighting "Jihad," or "struggle for God." Under Jihad, any person killed is assured of going to heaven.

Sheikh Abdel Halim Mahmoud, Grand Sheikh of Al Azhar Mosque, told a newsman on Monday, "We are fighting for Allah, for Islam and for humanity."

"Fighting in Ramadan gives the battle great significance," Mahmoud added. "We are sure of Allah's support, and with his help, we shall achieve victory over the Israelis."

Mahmoud did not venture to predict exactly when victory in the current war might come. He seemed to take a historic view, pointing out that Islam's greatest victories came in the month of Ramadan.

During Ramadan, faithful Moslems fast from sunrise till sundown. The soul of soldiers who die in battle during Ramadan rise directly to heaven, the Moslem faith decrees.

Egyptian claims of progress over Israeli forces during the third day of the new war reminded many Moslems of their faith's greatest victories in the 7th Century. That was when the Prophet Mohammed's soldiers triumphed against vastly superior forces of idol-worshippers.

When Islam was only two years old, 300 soldiers under Mohammed defeated 1,000 non-believers near the city of Medina in Saudi Arabia.

The Moslem faith has it that 3,000 angels joined Mohammed's men to ensure victory.

Six years later, Mohammed scored the faith's second greatest victory when he led his men into Mecca and chased out the non-believers.

Smashing their stone idols, he then sparked the spread of Islam into the rest of the Arabian Peninsula, throughout the Arab world and beyond.

One Islamic scholar said, "President Anwar Sadat is a good Moslem and a sincere believer ... Allah will undoubtedly help him in his Jihad."

All mosques in Cairo have preached of Jihad since fighting began on Saturday and urged the faithful to join in the battle.

At the end of each of the five daily prayers, the mosque's Immam, or priest, says "Allah promised us heaven if we fight in his name, so let us all rush to the noble battlefield."

Hospital Volunteers

The hospital again yesterday was besieged by volunteers ready to do everything from treating the injured to washing the floors. Police had to help the hospital keep order, because there was simply not enough work for all. Car owners not called up have organized a car pool for the hospital; and Herzliya Hotel owner Sarah Pearl, known as "the soldiers' auntie," has opened a kiosk in the hospital. It supplies everything from sweets to transistor radios, free of charge, to the wounded, practically round the clock.

SUCCOTH — No Publication

Soldiers on Suez front eating lunch
in a Succah set up by the Israeli
Army rabbinate.

SUCCOTH, ORGINALLY known as the Feast of Ingathering—*Hag ha-Asif*—was, in prehistoric days, an agricultural festival which celebrated the harvest of the summer crops. The date of the festival was variable, and took place whenever the harvest happened to be ready.

Later on, this holiday was endowed with historical significance, and was celebrated to memorialize the dwelling of the Israelites in booths during their sojourn in the desert of Sinai, after they had departed from their slavery in Egypt.

Soldier on leave from Sinai carrying lulav, hitchhiking home to celebrate the Succoth holiday with his family.

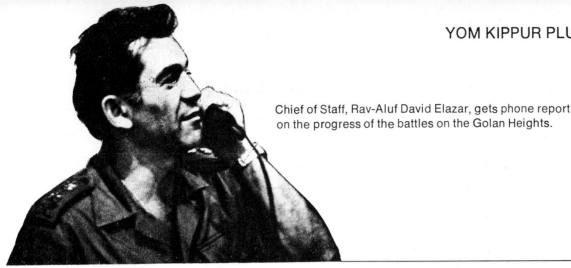

Chief of Staff, Rav-Aluf David Elazar, gets phone report on the progress of the battles on the Golan Heights.

Syrian night fighting and doggedness came as surprise

By RONNIE HOPE
Jerusalem Post Military Correspondent
GOLAN HEIGHTS. — A veteran of all of Israel's wars, Colonel Y., saw combat from a new angle this week. Instead of his accustomed role as a commander in the field, he was in the war room of the Northern Command, watching the battle for the Golan Heights on wall maps, and hearing the reports from the field as they came in on loudspeakers.

It was from this position that he saw how the Israeli forces withstood the initial onslaught in "those terrible two days" until the reserves could be brought up.

The key was the "beautiful co-ordination" between three elements — infantry units in the highly fortified strongpoints strung out along the cease-fire line, the tank force — outnumbered by about 12 to one — and the Air Force which provided the umbrella that made it possible to block the attack.

Col. Y. was speaking to correspondents on Wednesday when the Syrians had already been rolled back, and fighting was in progress on their side of the cease-fire lines. Later, correspondents toured the battlefield, and saw some of the burned-out tanks, evidence of the terrible price paid by both Israel and Syria.

Col. Y. had no doubt that the tremendous investment in the front line strongholds had been justified. Not only had they played a vital part in blocking the invaders, but they had saved the lives of many of the defenders. He told of one bunker, which had been overrun and believed lost.

Two days later, 14 of the defenders mounted on four tanks reached the Israeli line. They told of Syrian attempts to break into the position using tanks, smoke bombs and explosives.

The task of stopping the waves of Syrian tanks that flowed between the strongholds fell to a thinly spread regular tank unit. The biggest of the three Syrian thrusts was south of Kuneitra towards Hushniya, where over a division of tanks poured into a huge bulge, threatening to reach the B'not Ya'acov bridge over the Jordan.

LIKE WATER

Apart from sheer magnitude, there were other elements in the Syrian attack which made it unexpectedly difficult to cope with. For one thing, the invading armour did not confine itself to roads — "they flowed in like water, finding their way through wherever possible," said Col. Y.

He stressed the difficulty of defending terrain like that of the Heights, where the field of vision is always obstructed by hills, rocks, groves, bushes and deserted villages. "You never know what's behind the next turn in the roads. It's not like the desert, where the whole battlefield is visible."

Another unusual element was the fact that the Syrians fought at night. They kept pressing on, firing all the time, ignoring a tank which was hit and immobilized, or ran out of fuel. They would use it as a stationary position, if its gun was still working.

This was the formidable challenge faced, and met, by the defending Israeli armour. The measure of their success was in fact, that while they were outnumbered by about 12 to one, they inflicted losses on the enemy in the reverse ratio.

"Our debt to these men cannot be expressed in words," said Col. Y.

Something of what he meant could be grasped from the sights of the battlefield itself. A short time after reaching the plateau, following the winding climb from the B'not Ya'acov bridge, a line of burnt-out tanks, both Israeli and Syrian, marks the point where the Syrian advance was checked.

As the road goes further into the Golan, there are more tanks, some appearing to be almost intact, others completely demolished. One Israeli Centurion was blown into two — the turret on one side of the road and the body on the other. A blue El Al bag containing one of its crew's personal effects is still wedged into a rack on the side. A charred Uzi submachine gun is on the floor of the wrecked vehicle, and burned scraps of a tankman's uniform are on the side of the road.

Further on, a row of unburied Syrian corpses, frozen into grotesque poses, lies beside what is left of their tank.

On the way back, under arc lights, crews of technicians are seen working into the late hours on the damaged Israeli tanks, preparing them for the battles still ahead.

In Leviticus XXIII: 39, we read:

*In the fifteenth day of the seventh month
when you have gathered in the fruit of
the land, you shall keep a feast unto the
Lord for seven days. On the first day,
you shall observe a Sabbath; and on the
eighth day, you shall observe a Sabbath.*

*And on the first day, you shall take the
fruit of goodly trees, the branches of
palm trees, and the leafy boughs of thick
trees, and the willows of the brook,
and you shall rejoice before the Lord
your God for seven days.*

*And you shall celebrate a holiday
unto the Lord seven days each year;
it shall be for you an everlasting statute
throughout your generations; you shall
celebrate it during the seventh month.*

*In booths shall you dwell for seven
days; every resident in Israel shall dwell
in booths.*

The rabbis have prescribed fulfillment of this commandment by requiring every Jew to eat at least one meal a day during this seven-day festival in a Succah; and whenever possible, also to sleep in the Succah during the holiday.

The Succah is generally a rather simple lean-to, constructed so it can be easily dismantled and its boards stored away for the following year's Succoth celebrations. Most pious Jews regard it incumbent upon them to partake of at least a few meals in a Succah during this season.

In Israel today, Succoth is very widely observed. The nonobservant, as well as the religious, build Succahs for this holiday, perhaps regarding this pleasant occupation more as a part of a folk festival than as a religious rite.

When I was a young lad, my grandfather managed to secure an apartment on the ground floor of a building precisely because he would then be able to build a Succah in the adjoining yard, and pass food and tableware through the kitchen window directly into the Succah.

I remember, too, the time when the voices in the Succah, lifted in prayer and song and thanksgiving, disturbed a neighbor who then brought my grandfather to court to abate the "nuisance." A kindly and understanding Christian judge foiled the curmudgeon: he awarded judgment to the plaintiff, but gave the defendant one week to dismantle the offending structure.

What happy times we kids had pasting up colored paper chains and festooning them across

Volunteer transport, phone services

Jerusalem Post Staff

Israel's home front got its volunteer services into high gear yesterday, with citizens doing everything from funnelling phone messages from soldiers' at the front to organising transport of expectant mothers to hospital.

In Jerusalem, civil servants placed themselves and their vehicles at the disposal of mothers in labour, the seriously ill, the aged, the crippled and others unable to make use of public transport.

The service, which went into operation last night, will be available 24 hours a day until further notice. It is run by the Civil Service Commission and the Transport Ministry in cooperation with the Jerusalem Municipality's Emergency Centre, and will function in five areas.

British join Israelis in volunteering to fight

By **DAVID LENNON**, Jerusalem Post Correspondent

LONDON. — The crews of two British Army Centurion tanks were among the more than one thousand volunteers who attended a meeting at Hillel House in London on Tuesday night.

The Jewish Agency Youth and Hehalutz department which has been responsible for registering volunteers said that it was overwhelmed by the response to its invitation to the briefing meeting.

Yehuda Cohen, the coordinator of the movement, told me that his overworked team simply never had time to count the number who had volunteered. None the less, he was astounded when the meeting had to be held in three large rooms in addition to the hall which had been set aside for it.

All those present were told that Israel has so far said that it doesn't want any volunteers. If a call is issued, they were told, they will be required to pay their own fares, and more important, will be asked to stay for relatively lengthy periods.

Despite being told that they will have to do hard, grey and unexciting work, more than four hundred of the youngsters present said they were ready to go immediately. A group of some fifty doctors and nurses was also standing by, as were older people with special skills which might possibly be of use.

Among the volunteers were many former and even present members of the British Army. The two, non-Jewish, Centurion tank crews said that they were ready to go right away. They explained that they are on leave for a month from duty in Northern Ireland, and felt that their leave could possibly even be extended, if needed, beyond the beginning of December.

Similar meetings were held in Glasgow and Manchester where about sixty volunteers turned up at each hall.

Resuming our correspondence

Ephraim Kishon

DEAR ANWAR,

It's been a long time, eh? I mean, the last time we exchanged letters was about six years ago, though then the address was Gamal, *ahlan wa-sahlan*. We always said you were a cut above him, my dear Anwar, and sure enough, this time you managed not just to outwit us, but to win the coveted title of qualified aggressor for yourself, even if the Russians do deny it — just to spite you of course, as usual. Don't you listen to them, boy, they're simply jealous. To us you're a full-blown aggressor, and we'll say so to anybody who'll listen.

As for your dizzying success — well, that was limited from the start to 48 hours anyway, according to the Bir-Gafgafa Treaty signed between us in '67, remember? It's true our Government is a bit stingy about news from the front just now, but actually we manage pretty well without, using the mixed Supermarket-Security Council system. Our timetable looks something like this:

The U.N.'s taking a nap — it means the Arab troops are advancing.

Her Majesty's Cabinet urges cessation of hostilities — the Arab troops have been halted.

The U.S.S.R. demands a General Assembly meeting — our forces are on the advance ("Israel is playing with fire!" — the advance is swift).

The U.S. convenes the Security Council — the Arab front has collapsed.

The supermarket yardstick is even simpler: when our heroic home front storms the tinned cheese and artichoke barricades, it means the Arabs have the upper hand. When there's no queue at the supermarket then you're lost, Anwar.

What you have a c h i e v e d, is to win a lot of sympathy for the Greater Land of Israel Movement here. It also looks as if you'd put an end to the silly argument about whether we were in danger of our lives in '67 or not. We were.

Actually, we failed to appreciate you this time. Our supermarket supermen snapped their fingers at you. We stood with our backs to you like so many judo teachers saying: Now, chum, go for us with a knife! I guess it's the last time we've used that particular trick: next time we'll forgo the applause from the sidelines.

IT SEEMS as if you, Anwar, had learnt something too. Remember that famous article by your friend Hassanein Heykal in "Al Ahram" before the Six Day War? Stage One: the Zionists have no choice but to attack. Stage Two: the attack is halted. Stage Three: a smashing counter-blow. See, dear, *that's* how it's done

You're lucky we don't trust our own words, Anwar. Then, we told ourselves day in day out that reason didn't play any part in your security calculations, and we refused to believe you'd cross the Canal because it seemed so unreasonable! We begged you to use commonsense, and for that we paid dearly.

So where did you go wrong, Anwar?

In your timing.

If you'd surprised us on a plain weekday, you'd have been faced by worried, fretting, tired Jews with their belly full of steak. On Yom Kippur, everybody's quiet, relaxed, full of pep, positively hungry for some action. You've saved this Yom Kippur for us, Anwar. We'd have expected you to attack us on the day our TV was showing our basketball team playing the Russians. But on Yom Kippur? When there's nothing at all on TV?

What's more, a clever lad like you ought to know better than start a war on us a mere month before the elections. Are you crazy? Have you any idea what a beating you're going to take now so Yehoshua Rabinowitz can stay Mayor of Tel Aviv?

Oh well, we've both learnt something. From now on, we'll put a higher value on your word. *And* on our borders. And we'll discuss the battles when our bank-clerk gets back from his Patton and tells us of a few miracles before he starts collecting petrol-receipts for Sapir again. But that's a thing you'll never understand, Anwar my dear, because sometimes we hardly do ourselves. And with our strikes and our cost-of-living allowances, we'll become a nation of heroes once more.

Translated by Miriam Arad
By arrangement with "Ma'ariv"

"I'm glad I'm here"

Judy Siegel

WHEN THE FIRST strains of the siren shattered the tranquillity of Yom Kippur afternoon, nearly a hundred people in Jerusalem's Kiryat Hayovel quarter promptly headed for the underground shelter in the Beit Giora immigrant hostel. Nervously clutching their children's hands and carrying blankets and shopping baskets hastily packed with food, they hurried downstairs to safety.

Old women, whose memories of past wars were vividly etched into their minds, sat down on mattresses and began to moan. Others listened tensely to transistor radios, while a few closed their eyes and prayed. Although the all-clear signal sounded a short while later, they insisted on remaining in the cramped, concrete room until the following morning.

But upstairs, the immigrant residents, who had arrived with their trunks and suitcases months, weeks or even a few days before, were strangely silent. It was their first Yom Kippur and their first war in Israel, and they did not know what to expect.

Two hours after the *shofar* was sounded most of the lights were extinguished and windows taped and papered over. Pedro Bilsky, a dentist, from Argentina, volunteered to sweep out the debris that littered the shelter and then he stationed himself for four hours near Beit Giora's front entrance, carefully watching all who came and went.

By the second night of the war most of the 110 residents were closeted in their rooms, resting or talking quietly with friends. The realization that Jewish soldiers were fighting and dying to defend them as well as others had finally penetrated.

The feelings of the immigrants about the sudden emergency were not identical, but shaped by their country of origin, personalities, stage of life and previous experiences.

Kato Klein, a photographer who spent a year in Auschwitz and Bergen-Belsen before moving to a small town in Sweden in 1945, first heard the siren from her room on the second floor.

"It was a big shock," she told me grimly. "My first thought was — it's happening again; we are at war." She took a sedative to calm down because "I didn't want to give them another casualty.

"The Jerusalem I saw the next day, with hoarding at some grocery stores and streets emptied of young men, reminded me of my native Hungary during the war," she recalled. "It was a very depressing sight."

Her son, a 22-year-old new immigrant, volunteered to drive a truck during the crisis, and Kato would also like to help. Having been a volunteer soldier in Sweden for 17 years, she knows first aid and how to entertain frightened children. "But I feel helpless," she said, "because no place will accept me. My Hebrew isn't good enough."

Harold and Miriam Hirschfield who emigrated from the United States in May, returned to Beit Giora on Yom Kippur Eve after a month-long business trip abroad.

"A long as it had to happen, I'm glad I'm here in Israel during the war. We didn't take the matter of making our home here lightly," Harold said.

The couple, whose two grown children are back in America, agreed they were not at all concerned for their own safety.

"In the States, no one worries about the country being attacked, but in many of the large urban areas, like Manhattan where we lived, there's a constant fear of being robbed, mugged or murdered. In Israel it's the opposite. Surrounded by hostile Arab nations, there is a sense of precariousness, of war coming every few years, but still complete freedom to walk in the streets."

However, their main reason for "hitching their future to the State of Israel" was not crime on the streets of New York. "We simply wanted to be with our people and to live in a Jewish and not a Christian country," explained Miriam.

Of all the residents, it was, perhaps, the young Americans who found it most difficult to accept the fact of war. Although many of their parents had fought in World War II, for those born after 1945 it was usually just another chapter in their history books. And despite the fact that they had grown up watching scenes of Vietnam bloodshed on television, the shooting seemed distant and unreal, sometimes indistinguishable from battle movies or cowboy thrillers.

Ida Dreyfus, a librarian from Chicago, Matthew Kalisky, a high-school student from Boston, and Jeffery Kowalsky, a musician from suburban Illinois, sat together on that second night to exchange ideas.

Jeffery: I was at services when I heard the alarm, and I thought it was a real air raid. My first reaction was a kind of silent shock.

Ida: I was upset that none of us in Beit Giora knew where the shelter was, or even what the various signals meant. As new immigrants, we're not used to this.

Jeffery: That's true, but everything else was very efficient. I was amazed to see how Israelis tried to create a sense of normalcy, war or no war. The soldiers knew exactly where to report, and even the bakers were mobilized to make enough bread.

Matthew: A few months ago I thought of leaving Israel after finishing school, but I've changed my mind. This emergency made the danger to Israel more real to me, and if they need my help, I'm prepared to serve the country.

One of the Russian immigrants, an articulate doctoral student from Moscow named Alexander said:

"People must live where they feel comfortable, and even during a war I feel I belong here."

He is not optimistic about seeing a lasting peace in the near future.

"I don't see this war as an end to the conflict. Even if Russia were to leave the Middle East, I think Western powers like England, France or the U.S. would sell arms to the Arabs."

THE RESIDENTS of Beit Giora have usually grouped together according to language or country, but the war created a new sense of closeness and concern. People fluent in Hebrew or English translated the latest news for those who did not understand, and contacts were made in a jumble of languages.

"I think that is a good thing," said Felica, a psychologist from Buenos Aires. "Maybe it will even continue after the trouble is over."

This is the second time that Braha Arnon, Beit Giora's director for 11 years, has observed new immigrants in a war situation, and she says she is very proud of the way her current charges have behaved.

"Most of them came to Israel for better or for worse, and they feel this is where they belong. I don't know whether the experience will make them stronger or better citizens, but there's one thing I'm sure of — they will never forget where they spent their first Day of Judgment in Israel."

Syrian saved by wounded Israeli as battle rages

GOLAN HEIGHTS. — A young Israeli tank commander, wounded and left alone after his tank was hit, dragged a **seriously** wounded Syrian soldier for some 10 hours at the peak of the fighting on the Heights before the two were picked up by an Israeli half-track. The episode, which occurred on Monday, was related to Itim reporter Meir Shoshani yesterday.

The lieutenant — who only recently completed his compulsory military service — was left behind after his tank was hit and the rest of his crew rescued by a passing half-track. While evacuating the crew, the half-track came under heavy artillery fire and had to make off before he could climb aboard.

Left alone, the officer took cover until the bombardment ceased, and then tried to make his own way back to rejoin the Israeli forces. On the way, he came across a knocked-out Syrian tank and climbed in to look for water. He found what he wanted, and something else — a severely wounded Syrian soldier, the sole survivor of the tank's crew. He was about to leave, but the imploring look in the man's eyes said more than a thousand words.

So he lifted the man onto his shoulders, despite his own wounded left hand, and started to drag him back to the Israel-occupied part of the Heights. They only stopped to share swigs of water or take cover when shells began to fall. After 10 hours, the two were spotted by an Israeli half-track, which picked them up. Once behind the lines, the Syrian was taken to a hospital. After having his hand dressed, the Israeli rejoined his unit.   *(Itim)*

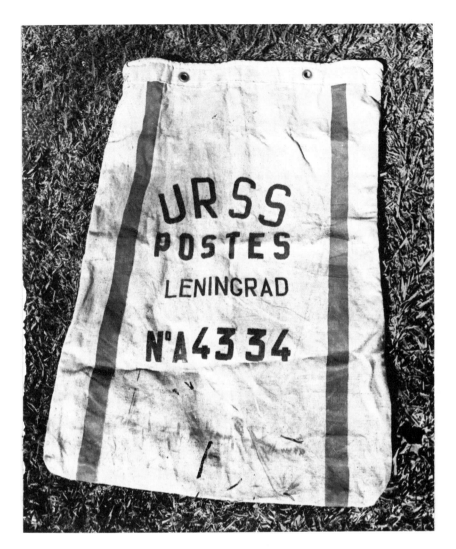

Russian mail bag found on the Syrian front. The Russian contingent, in Syria in force, obviously expected to spend a good deal of time in the country.

---

and under the open-latticed roof. The largest pumpkins, the brightest peppers, the most colorful gourds and squash were hung from the thin rafters, which were strewn with foliage. Tapestries and bright cloths were requisitioned to cover the walls, and even framed pictures were hung to lend charm. A makeshift candelabrum which held lighted candles swung from the ceiling, and candlesticks on the table lent a beatific light. It was a time of bustling about, and busy hands, and beaming faces. We kids were in seventh heaven. Succoth was enormous fun.

I remember, too, how zealously my father once arranged to have his Succah. I was a lad of about eight or nine, and we lived on the third floor of an apartment house in Brooklyn, New York; there was no convenient yard available. But Succoth meant much to my dad, so he built a Succah on the roof, and hauled up the victuals on that now obsolescent contraption, the dumbwaiter.

Since the rabbis had ordained that a properly made booth should be open to the skies, a "kosher" Succah had to be covered with *s'chach,* foliage. Where did one get foliage in Brooklyn? Large

SABBATH—No Publication

Succoth prayers in the bunkers on the Sinai front.

foliage, too! My father solved that one. He personally applied at the offices of the Brooklyn Department of Parks, explained his religious convictions, and asked for the branches that tree surgeons would have cut down during their pruning. His request was granted.

My Succoth experiences were not at all unique. Thousands of Jews throughout the world celebrate the holiday with similar avidity. In Israel, especially, Succoth is a holiday of surpassing joy. To begin with, Succoth is celebrated by closing the schools for a full week. The first day of the festival is a religious holiday observed by and large throughout the land. Most people who live in Israel either build a Succah or join a neighbor in such an endeavor, and most manage to have at least one of their meals in the small lean-to.

During Succoth of 1973, which was exactly five days after the commencement of the Yom Kippur War, despite the fact that the nation was in trauma, the holiday was fully observed. As many men as could be spared from the front were permitted to rejoin their families to celebrate the holiday. For those who couldn't leave, Army Chaplains set up Succahs right behind the front lines, and these Succahs were very well attended by soldiers who enjoyed the convivial spirit and the respite they afforded.

As stated earlier, the holiday started as a prehistoric agricultural celebration. Then, the focal point was the bounteousness of the crop. The Bible dwells on the theme, and mentions the four different types of growth central in the celebration of the festival. The rabbis ordained that four species of botanica should be displayed during the festival so as to make God's munificence evident in the ritual of the celebration.

Rabbinical authorites particularized these species, calling them *arba-a minim.*

"The fruit of the goodly trees" is epitomized by the citron which in Hebrew is called the *etrog.*

For "the leafy boughs of thick trees," myrtle twigs have been nominated. Myrtle twigs in Hebrew are called *hadassim.* The word myrtle in Hebrew is *hadassah,* the name chosen by the league of women who philanthropically support Israel's medical needs. Hadassah, today, has achieved world-wide fame, and I mention with pride that my mother was one of its founders.

The palm branch of the Bible is called the *lulav;* and the willows are known as *aravot.* Thus, in the Succoth of 1973, following this ancient custom, soldiers could be seen on the roads of Israel returning from the Sinai, carrying the precious "four species" for this joyous holiday. Many

Soldier-patients prefer gifts be sent to the front

By **SARAH HONIG**
Jerusalem Post Reporter

TEL AVIV. — Wounded soldiers at Hadassah (Balfour) Hospital here on Friday refused to accept gift packages from Soldiers' Welfare Association volunteers. They said the parcels should be sent to soldiers on the front lines.

The patients said they have families looking after them and that the sweets, cigarettes and books should be sent to Sinai and the Golan.

A compromise was reached under which the wounded accepted the gifts and contributed IL20 each to finance purchase of gifts for the front-line soldiers.

Sizeable donations have been made to the Association. But some of the most touching stories involve the more modest contributors. One oldster turned over his life savings. It amounted to IL1,500 and came in small bills and coins. One woman contributed the IL15,000 she had saved up for a pleasure trip abroad. Children come in daily handing over coins accumulated in their toy banks.

Others have set up stands in the streets, where they also collect gifts for soldiers.

The committee says razor blades are especially useful to front-line soldiers. Persons who contribute games are asked to see that they are well packed. It often happens that pieces fall out of flimsy boxes, so that dominoes appear among pieces of a chess set, and vice versa.

On Friday, more than IL20,000 was raised for the Soldiers Welfare Association in Jerusalem at a concert by the Israel Philharmonic Orchestra, at the Jerusalem Theatre. More funds for the same cause are expected to be raised at today's concert by Issac Stern — also at the Jerusalem Theatre.

Outgoing tourists donate IL4,000

LOD AIRPORT. — Tourists leaving on El Al flights Friday were suddenly overcome with the urge to do something tangible to help the war effort.

A woman from Sao Paulo, Brazil, opened her handbag and gave a DM1,500 travellers cheque to the hostess, to be passed on to the Soldiers Welfare Association. A tourist from the U.S. saw the gesture, and gave all the Israeli money he had on him — some IL1,000—to the hostess. The spirit spread, and the other passengers took out all the Israeli money they had left from their visit and put it in a hat. The total came to some IL4,000—all to go to the Soldiers Welfare Association.   *(Itim)*

hitchhiked back to the north of the country, returning to their homes from the ancient biblical land of Goshen.

But Succoth, 1973, was a low-keyed holiday — a harbinger of many low-keyed weeks ahead, weeks in which the entire population of Israel was cast into the most sober of moods. Many had witnessed the death of their best friends. Throughout Israel, no one had to ask for whom the bell tolled.

THE PUBLIC COMMITTEE FOR THE VOLUNTARY
WAR LOAN

The following have decided to make a personal contribution amounting to one month's salary for the Voluntary War Loan:

Knesset Members; members of the Histadrut Central Committee and of the Managements of Koor, Bank Hapoalim, Solel Boneh and Kupat Holim; and department heads at Beilinson hospital.

The Voluntary War Loan Public Committee urges all directors and senior employees of public and economic institutions to join the effort.

Please notify the Committee of the pledges made at your places of work. The address of the Voluntary War Loan Public Committee is the Finance Ministry, the Kirya, Tel Aviv. Tel.: (03) 256381.

(—) **Yitzhak Rabin** (—) **Zalman Suzayev**
(—) **Asher Yadlin**

Offices open for Israeli Arab volunteers

Jerusalem Post Staff

In view of the numerous requests from Israeli Arabs, offices will open in seven Arab and Druse towns for registering volunteers for essential work and for contributions to the voluntary war loan.

At its own initiative, the Municipality of Nazareth has set up a fund-raising committee for the voluntary war loan, the Government Press Office said yesterday.

In Tel Aviv, religious high school boys filled sand bags and did other volunteer work on the Sabbath and during the holiday. They had the Rabbinates approval.

The Tel Aviv Emergency Authority reports that it continues to be swamped with offers of help. Another retired top-ranking officer has taken to driving a garbage truck. He is Aluf (Res.) Eliyahu Ben-Hur.

Foreign volunteers and Christian clergymen have also offered help.

Youth Aliya has issued a call for volunteers to replace educators and teachers at Youth Aliya boarding schools who have been called up.

Cable from Casals

Prime Minister Golda Meir on Tuesday received the following cable from the internationally renowned cellist, Pablo Casals: "Deeply concerned and want you to know that I am with you and Israel in spirit at this time as always."

A **TRAFFIC** cop on Allenby road, Tel Aviv, caught a young driver going through red lights at corner of Rehov Mazeh. "As it's wartime, I won't give you a ticket but you will have to pay with blood," the cop told the worried driver, and took him to the nearby Magen David Adom station to donate blood.

October 11, 1973

THE PUBLIC COMMITTEE FOR THE VOLUNTARY

WAR LOAN

CITIZENS, FAMILIES

We are in the midst of a difficult struggle, and in order to achieve victory — which we are sure will come — the public must make a special effort.

The rulers of Egypt and Syria have forced us into a war on two fronts at and the same time.

The Israel Defence Forces are at the height of a battle to push back the aggressors.

In order to achieve victory and in order, as far as possible, to reduce losses, the I.D.F. must be strengthened while in the midst of war. The I.D.F. must obtain all it needs without delay — in the way of equipment and weapons. All of us, all Israel, must put these weapons into the hands of our army. Each one of us will imagine that his part in the effort will tip the scale of victory.

The government decided on a compulsory loan to be raised from the public. However, the public in the rear, while standing in the same solid front with our fighting forces, is aware that the needs of war are great and that a compulsory loan by itself will not fulfill its needs. We therefore call upon every citizen and every family to respond to this urgent call:

To voluntarily acquire "War Loans" — either for a small or large sum, according to his means and his conscience.

Those in the rear will not lag behind the dedication of the soldiers on the war front.

The Public Committee uniting all the domestic factors call on all residents of Israel to acquire "War Loans" immediately. This is the time for every one of us to do more than is merely demanded of him.

These loans were available as of Friday at all banks. The bank will give a letter of credit to the buyer until the certificates are issued.

(—) Yitzhak Rabin   (—) Zalman Suzayev   (—) Asher Yadlin

'Keep 'em flying'
El Al mounts its biggest operation

By GEORGE LEONOF
Jerusalem Post Reporter

El Al mounted the biggest operation in its history during the first week of the current war: in the seven days that followed the brutal truncation of Yom Kippur by the Egyptian and Syrian armies, the national air carrier surpassed its heaviest regular schedule in any previous week.

Up to this morning, the national air carrier transported 22,173 passengers to and from Lod Airport, 12,283 of them incoming. The latter were Israelis returning to join their military units, thousands of new immigrants, hundreds of news media personnel, and many tourist groups.

El Al remained the only regular air link with the outside world since Lod Airport was declared closed to civilian air traffic following the outbreak of fighting on October 6. When, the following day, the Civil Aviation Administration permitted special flights subject to clearance for each separate aircraft, only El Al and a single TWA aircraft — which had remained parked at Lod over Yom Kippur — took to the air. Most international airlines operating in Israel remained cautious because formally, the airfield remained closed to regular flights and it was not clear whether Lloyds (with which most international airlines are insured) would permit its policies to cover such "special" flights. Only TWA and Air France each ventured a solitary flight the next day.

On Tuesday Lod was reopened to civilian air traffic. Although the stipulation with regard to clearance for each flight remained, this gave the green light to Alitalia, of the foreign carriers, to resume flight that same day, followed on Wednesday by Air France, KLM and Sabena.

One charter airline, Sterling of London, kept coming most of the week to pick up tourist groups.

New trouble hit the foreign operators in the middle of last week, however, when most national air pilots associations decided that the Middle East remained a danger zone despite the opening of Lod Airport. As a result, the airlines which resumed services became dependent on volunteer crews.

Both Alitalia and Air France told *The Jerusalem Post* on Friday they were making every effort to maintain the service, but only El Al flights remained certain.

El Al spokesman Moshe Eilat said the carrier was flying all its regular routes, although schedules were being shuffled subject to the needs of the hour.

The spokesman, in reply to a question, said El Al would consider chartering aircraft from other companies should the need arise.

A special feature of El Al's service during the first week of war was the urgent delivery to various parts of the world of 150 parcels containing tapes, films, stills and written reports from the host of correspondents and cameramen covering the hostilities.

In a circular to El Al workers Friday, company president Mordechai Ben-Ari lauded the dedication of the airline personnel, which enabled it to maintain regular air communications with the world. He stressed that at this time despite the call-up of all personnel under 40, El Al with a quarter of its normal manpower to "keep 'em flying."

Priority fixed for El Al seats

LOD AIRPORT. — Thousands of Israelis stranded abroad when the war broke out are still besieging El Al offices throughout Europe and the U.S., representatives of the airline said here yesterday.

El Al's 60 offices have been operating around the clock, with their staffs augmented by volunteers. But the airline is finding it impossible to cope with all of those who want to get home. A table of priorities has been worked out with official Israeli bodies abroad to bring some sort of order to the allocation of the limited places on Israel-bound flights.

El Al has increased the number of flights and had five home-bound and four outward bound flights yesterday. Three foreign airlines — Sterling, Alitalia and Air France — also flew into Lod yesterday. In all, 3,205 passengers arrived in the 24 hours ending yesterday evening.

Sakharov on Mid-East

MOSCOW (UPI). — Physicist Andrei D. Sakharov said Friday the West should call on Communist countries to stop interfering in the Arab-Israeli conflict and should take "reciprocal measures" if they refuse.

Sakharov made the remarks in an interview with a man who identified himself as an Arab journalist. Sakharov released the transcript to Western newsmen because he said he was concerned his statements might be distorted.

The interviewer asked what steps the U.S. and other Western countries could take to liquidate the Middle East war. Sakharov replied: "Call upon the Soviet Union and socialist countries to give up a policy of unilateral interference in the Arab-Israeli conflict and take reciprocal measures in case this policy of interference continues," Sakharov said.

He said the West also should work for an immediate cease-fire and direct peace talks.

SUPPORT FROM GERMANY
To the Editor of The Jerusalem Post

Sir, — Israel is at war and men are dying because Arab revanchists want it so. One feels oneself back in the days when Jews had to wear the yellow Star of David on their breasts — only the words are different this time. *"Sieg Heil"* has been replaced by "Free Palestine," and those who attack Israel today have replaced the gas chambers with tanks, bombs and rockets. Those responsible in Moscow and New York suggest resolutions and then go back to the order of the day.

If this ungodly world does not want to remain bogged down in the morass of this wicked war, solutions must be found. Resolutions are of no use to anyone.

We, citizens of this land, feel for Israel in its battle for freedom and peace. And since we believe in justice, we support Israel and her people.

JUERGEN STACH
Aachen (Germany), October 1.

The chicken house of Kibbutz Machanaim was a victim of Syrian artillery.

Soviets did nothing to stop war

Jerusalem Post Staff

The Foreign Ministry spokesman in Jerusalem yesterday accused the Soviet Union of sharing, with Egypt and Syria, responsibility for the war and for the loss of life on both sides.

Reacting to a statement by the Tass news agency about Israeli bombing in Syria and Egypt, the spokesman said: "There is not a shadow of a doubt that the Soviet Government, through its observers who were serving with the armies of Egypt and Syria, had advance knowledge of the aggressive plans of these two governments. Nevertheless, the Soviet Government did nothing to prevent the implementation of these aggressive schemes. In refraining from any measure which might have prevented the Arabs from initiating hostilities — the Soviet Government shares responsibility for the outbreak of the war, and for loss of life in Israel, Egypt and Syria."

The spokesman recalled that Egypt and Syria had begun the war "equipped with enormous quantities of modern Soviet arms," and that this had been reported by the U.N. truce observers.

The spokesman said Israel regretted the loss of Arab and Israeli lives, and regretted too, that Soviet citizens, "caught in the area of hostilities, are among the casualties."

(Soviet nationals were reportedly hurt during air attacks on Damascus, and a Soviet ship was hit during naval operations off the Syrian coast.)

*F*ROM THAT DAY in 1948 when Israel declared its independence, the people of Israel have been obliged to fight four defensive wars. Four times within 26 years have its Arab neighbors sought to destroy this fledgling country. Well might the people of Isreal repeat the words of the psalmist uttered some 2,500 years ago:[1]

> *Much did they afflict me when I was young,*
>   *may Israel now say;*
> *Much did they afflict me when I was young,*
>   *yet did they not prevail against me.*
> *The plowers plowed upon my back,*
>   *they made long furrows.*

In the Yom Kippur War, the furrows were indeed long. The first announcement of casualties made on October 15 revealed that some 600 soldiers had been killed—a horrendous loss of men for such a small country. And when, some five months later, the *Book of the Dead* would be issued, the roster of the slain up to February 12 would include some 2,523 names. Among these would be 581 officers, or more than 20 percent of the total lost, not counting 691 sergeants.

The effect of this news on the citizenry was numbing. Never in any previous war had Israel experienced such losses. Hardly a family was spared; almost everyone had some kin or close friend who had been killed or wounded. By the end of the War, the entire society had been stricken.

I remember talking to my friend, Hadassah Eshel, a woman of about forty. "You know, Harold," she said, "I am a fourth generation sabra. My father was born in this country. My grandfather was born in this country; and his father, too, was born here. When I was a girl, I willingly joined the Army, and I was proud to be a defender of Israel. During the last war, I would have willingly died in battle for this land. But here are my two sons, each more precious to me than my own life. These twin boys, they're eleven now. What am I raising them for? To die in a war? No, I'm not willing to give them up. I was willing to lay down my life, and, yes, even my husband's life, to make this land secure for our children."

She paused to hold back her tears, and then she continued.

"We just can't keep on having wars every five years. We work, we strive, we educate our children, but not just to be killed in battle. I wouldn't mind if I had to go to war, and I were killed. We women of Israel, we all understand that our husbands must fight and might be killed, but I can't bear to think

1. Psalm 129

that my two boys are being raised to be killed in a war."

This is a pervading attitude. Families feel they are living on a crater's edge. They see stretching before them an everlasting expanse of hate. They feel trapped, they see no way out.

If the giving up of territory would placate the Arabs, they would willingly do so. But they fear that this might be the first step toward self-annihilation. The feeling prevails that the Arab demand for the return of conquered territory is but a ruse, and that any appeasement would only whet the appetite of their implacable foes. The more they gave, the more the Arabs would demand. Most Israelis truly believe that the Arabs want nothing less than the total obliteration of the Jewish state.

During these early days of the war, Israel was swept by a mood of dejection. The feeling ran: "We fight because we are attacked; we win because we are fighting for our lives. We are not allowed a decisive victory. The U.N. steps in, the United States and Russia step in, and call a halt

"We are held in check until our enemies get strong enough, or think they are strong enough, to fight another round. Our enemies multiply like rabbits and do not seem to mind the loss of some scores of thousands of men. Their military leaders have said that the depletion of their ranks lessens their problems of overpopulation. For us, the life of each individual is sacred.

"All we want is to live in peace, to till our soil and create a land that is safe for our children, and for any Jew that needs or seeks a haven. Indeed, we must work, slave, live on an austerity level, writhe under most burdensome taxes, expend our all to sustain a crushing military budget; and then, after we've been drained of our substance, we must give the most precious thing we have—our sons."

In the usual course of a lifetime, death within the bosom of one's own family is not experienced until one is well into maturity; and then it is usually in relation to a parent. In Israel, death is a constant companion.

In 1967, Hannah's husband went off to war and never came back. At age 20, Hannah was a widow with a baby. Three years later, she married again. With her second husband, she bore two more children. In 1973, her man was called off to battle. He was killed a few days after the Yom Kippur War started. Hannah is now 26, the twice widowed mother of three.

One hears many stories like this in Israel. Dale, a young American volunteer in Israel, tells me that many of her soldier friends say that they simply don't want to fall in love and get married.

If they are killed in a war, they don't want to leave children and widows behind them.

And the girls, even more so, share the desperate feeling that the future holds incipient tragedy. Perhaps in time, these young people will change their minds; but right now deep pessimism prevails.

This sense of doom has produced its quota of wry humor. A story which went the rounds in Tel Aviv ran somewhat as follows: Sadat, King Faisal, and Golda Meir each spend a night of fitful sleep, and each one dreams of a confrontation with the Master of the Universe. When Sadat in his dream comes before the throne of God, he cries plaintively, "When, O Lord, will I conquer these troublesome Jews?" And God says to Sadat, "Oh, Anwar, not in your lifetime."

King Faisal in his dream appears before the Lord to speak of his troubles. "When," he cries, "Oh, Master of the Universe, will the city of Jerusalem be given over to our Arab brethren?" And the Lord makes answer and says, "Oh, Faisal, I am sorry, but not in your lifetime."

Golda Meir comes before the throne of God, and she, too, asks a question: "Oh, God, tell me, when will there be peace between the Arabs and the Jews?" And then God makes answer and says,

"Oh, Golda, not in my lifetime."

In Israel, when a man is killed in battle, his family is given a sum of money by the Government with which to set up a memorial to his memory. Of even greater significance is the feeling that has spontaneously welled up in the people themselves toward those who have been bereaved in the recent conflict. My friend, Ora Ra-anan—a mother of six—told me that she, along with many other women in Israel, formed neighborhood committees of three, four, or five women and took it upon themselves to visit families who had lost a son in battle to extend to them some comfort and to look after their needs. I was unaccountably moved by one particular story that she told.

She and two of her committee members visited a Yemenite family who had lost an only son. The mother and father were in a state of utter gloom. The ladies attempted to comfort the father and asked the old man what they could do.

"Only one thing," the man answered. "If you could have a Sefer Torah, a holy scroll, written in honor of my son, which I could dedicate to him in my synagogue, the pain of my soul would be eased."

The women were somewhat startled. They had

656 ISRAELIS KILLED IN EIGHT DAYS OF WAR

Jerusalem Post Military Correspondent

TEL AVIV. — The Army spokesman yesterday announced that 656 members of the armed forces had lost their lives since the beginning of the war eight days ago. The families have been informed.

The only name disclosed was that of Aluf Avraham Mendler, commanding officer of the armoured forces in Sinai. No details as to the circumstances of his death were available here yesterday (See biography — page 2).

Announcements were also made to the families of missing men known to have been taken prisoner.

There are also about 2,000 wounded in hospitals.

The IDF Chief Rabbinate has issued directives concerning the mourning for the fallen whereby according to these directions the shiv'a — the ritual week of deep mourning — will begin only after

the Simhat Torah on Thursday.

The delay in publishing the casualty list is believed to have been due to the fact that it took some time for the army's Manpower Division and Adjutant-General's Division to check all details concerning the identities of the dead, the missing presumed dead, and the prisoners-of-war, before the next of kin could be notified.

Since the present struggle began as a defensive war and many front-line positions were overrun, the army could not — unlike in an offensive sweep where the casualties are left within the Israeli lines — obtain immediate details concerning the casualties.

A substantial number of men have managed to trek back through the Egyptian lines.

In a statement over Israel TV last night, Defence Minister Moshe Dayan said the casualties of

the Six Day War were announced after the fighting and the nation could then join in mourning. "Now we are in the midst of war and we cannot give public expression to our profound sorrow. We must fight fearlessly, with the faith and courage of a nation aware that it is fighting for its life.

"The memory and the glory of the fallen we will keep within us, in our hearts. Today all we can say to the bereaved families is how much we are with them in their grief. We are a nation whose destiny is shaped by its fighters and fallen sons. It is through the road which they have helped build that we will attain a secure state recognized by our neighbours, and peace, even though the road is long."

The number of enemy prisoners taken by the IDF at yesterday's count was 414, including 58 officers.

Eager volunteers at Shaare Zedek

By JUDY SIEGEL
Special to The Jerusalem Post

The war has turned housewives into mail carriers, yeshiva boys into kitchen helpers and lawyers into ambulance drivers, as thousands of eager civilians volunteer to fill in for the men and women in uniform.

Jerusalem's Shaare Zedek Hospital, which is now caring almost exclusively for wounded soldiers, has been inundated by offers of help. "Nearly 800 people of all ages and backgrounds — tourists, new immigrants and old residents — have signed up in the last week," says Dr. David Maeir, the hospital's director-general, "and we didn't even ask them to come."

"We've been able to put only 130 of them to work," adds his deputy for administration, Nachum Pessin, "but when the need for more arises, we'll inform the public at once."

The white-coated volunteers, who work in 12-hour shifts along with regular hospital personnel, can be found everywhere, entertaining patients, helping doctors on rounds, filling sandbags, moving beds and distributing laundry.

I found David Estreicher, a bearded yeshiva student from Cleveland, Ohio, in the hospital's bustling kitchen, where many meals are prepared daily. His face smudged yet smiling, he was attacking a greasy oven with a putty knife, steel wool and soapy rags. "I've cleaned ovens before in camp," he grins, "but this big one is a real challenge."

A few steps away, three Israeli high school boys wearing surgical masks prepare to scrub a pile of dirty pots that reach half-way up the wall. An hour later, the tower has been levelled and everything stored neatly away. Commented Haim Nahman, the director of the kitchen: "This place has never been in such great shape!"

Berel Berkovits, a 24-year-old law student who arrived from London six weeks ago, helped build the hospital's *succa*, replenish the warehouse and do other odd jobs. "It may be menial work, but I wanted to contribute in some small way. I feel, more than ever before, that I belong here and that the whole world is against us. I'm no longer British; the break had to come sometime," he says.

Gadna teenagers are also being mobilized as first-line receivers of the wounded. When Shaare Zedek is informed of new admissions, a bell sounds and a dozen of the 16- and 17-year-old volunteers quickly get into formation on the front steps, ready to carry in the stretchers. One chilly night last week, there was a false alarm, and they sat at attention and waited for nearly an hour. Another time, during the day, they raced to open an ambulance door only to find it packed with a shipment of oranges.

Lining the hospital's gate is a queue of private cars belonging to volunteer drivers — tailors, professors, students, factory owners — all of them wanting to be of service. They are prepared to shuttle hospital workers back and forth during the day or in the blacked-out streets at night.

Hospital drivers were given rabbinical permission to work on Shabbat and Succot because of the life and death nature of the emergency. "The hospital rabbi insisted that those who do so are Orthodox and dress in holiday clothes, because it is such a great *mitzva*," explains Zvi Caspi, a former Israeli consul in, New York and now on loan from the Foreign Office to Shaare Zedek. It created the unusual situation of an Orthodox volunteer driving two staff workers — who turned out to be gentiles — to the hospital on the Sabbath.

FATHERS AT WAR

"Twelve *britot* have been performed in the week since Yom Kippur for babies whose fathers were at war," says Yosef Weissberg, the hospital's *mohel*. Volunteers arranged a meal for each family and joined in on the *minyan*. "And during the idle hours of waiting to be called, one of the drivers — a rabbi in normal times — gave a Talmud class for the other volunteers."

Medical specialists have been arriving at the hospitals from abroad for days, without being asked to come. Dr. Arnold Gurevitch, a surgeon at the University Hospital in Birmingham, England, packed a suitcase and fought "the madhouse at Heathrow Airport" to get a seat on an Israel-bound plane. "I asked my wife to tell my boss where I am," he says.

Surrounded by concerned volunteers, doctors and nurses, the wounded soldiers are in fine spirits. A vase filled with pink roses decorates every bed table, and television sets donated by local merchants inform the patients of the latest news.

"Is there any help that you still need?" I ask Tamar Halahmi, the hospital's chief of nurses who has been at work around the clock. "Nothing I can think of," she replies, "except at my house. It's never been so messy."

---

never encountered such a request. They knew that the writing of a Sefer Torah was a prolonged, exacting, and expensive undertaking. The scroll, which consists of the Five Books of Moses, must be painstakingly written on pure, fresh parchment, stitched together with clean special thread by a scribe who devotes himself to nothing else. The writing of a Sefer Torah could never take less than a full year, and probably much more. Such work had to cost a few thousand dollars, and the women were sure the Government could not make such funds available.

They asked the man once again, "Wouldn't anything else do? You know how difficult it is to get a Sefer Torah. You know that we don't have money for this purpose." But the old man adamantly shook his head, "Oh, no, only this one thing will be balm for my soul. My son can live for me only in this one way, only if a holy scroll, a new scroll dedicated in his name, is written especially for him. No, only this, and nothing else will assuage my grief."

The women left. They held counsel. What could they do? Surely the Government wouldn't— couldn't — agree to this request; they would have to raise the funds through private subscription.

Christians scored for keeping silent on war

By DAVID LANDAU
Jerusalem Post Reporter

Professor David Flusser, the eminent Jerusalem Bible scholar, has issued a scathing attack on Christian theologians and intellectuals for not taking a stand against the Arab aggression against Israel. In an interview with *The Jerusalem Post*, Prof. Flusser quoted from Revelations (2,3 15-16) in relation to the Christian intellectual leadership: "I know thy works, that thou art neither cold nor hot: I would thou wert cold or hot. So then because thou art lukewarm, and neither cold nor hot, I will spue thee out of my mouth."

Prof. Flusser, leading authority on comparative religion and early Christianity, said it was the "minimal task of professional men of God" to condemn violent attacks on human beings anywhere. Yet, apart from the Pope's statements deploring the war, there has been nothing in this spirit reported from the Christian leadership.

Not to differentiate betwen attacker and victim is the very antithesis of basic Christian morality, he added.

Prof. Flusser said that, now that Christianity was shaking itself free of medieval trappings, it was obvious to all thinkers that it must seek its roots in Judaism, from which it sprang. The connection between Christianity and the Jews, furthermore, is not one of scholarship and learning alone: it is a vibrant ongoing relationship which must exist between honest Christians and the modern Jewish revival in the State of Israel.

It is perhaps premature, said Prof. Flusser, to speak of a "Christian silence," and there are probably many Christian rank-and-file everywhere who sympathize with Israel. But — unless that sympathy is expressed by Christianity's intellectual leadership — it will be too late, "not for us in Israel, but for Christianity itself."

ARCHBISHOP OFFERS TO SWEEP FLOORS

In Haifa, the head of the Greek Catholic community, Archbishop Joseph Raya, declared he was willing "to work with a broom as a clean-up man, if necessary." The Archbishop, who is recruiting volunteers among his community, has himself offered his services to the Municipality.

"I pray for our soldiers every day," he added.

Meanwhile, the Bir'im Residents Committee, whose cause the Archbishop has championed, has temporarily buried its differences with the Government concerning its claim to return to the village on the Lebanese border. In a telegram to the Premier and the Defence Minister, the Committee offered "to place our people, property and vehicles at our country's disposal, for its security and well-being."

Druse villages, like Bukata, were among the civilian settlements bombed by the Syrians. Treasury officials visited these bombed-out homes to assess damage and arrange compensation.

Londoners queue to give blood

By DAVID LENNON
Jerusalem Post Correspondent

LONDON. — In an unprecedented response to Israel's need, Jews and non-Jews in Britain have been donating thousands of pints of blood and millions of pounds during the past week. This is on top of the thousands of people who have volunteered to go to Israel.

While the early response was somewhat slow in the community, it rapidly accelerated, and after three days donations of money had passed the £15m. donated in the 1967 emergency appeal.

The collection of blood only got under way on Wednesday. But in less than two days more than 3,000 pints were ready for dispatch to Israel. On Saturday afternoon there were still queues of people waiting up to two hours for their turn to give blood at the St. Johns Wood and Marble Arch synagogues here.

The flood of volunteers, too, has continued during the week, following a slowdown after the rush of the first two days. While exact figures are not available, informed estimates put the figure now in the region of 3,000.

A mass demonstration of solidarity is set for today at Trafalgar Square. While at first there was some antipathy to the "uselessness" of such actions, the latest war news has inflamed Jewish emotions here to an unprecedented level. The organizers expect a big turnout.

PRO-ARAB DEMONSTRATION NEARBY

Thousands rally in London to show support for Israel

By DAVID LENNON
Jerusalem Post Correspondent

LONDON. — Politicians, actors, writers and other public figures were among the 10,000 people who gathered at Trafalgar Square this afternoon in a demonstration of solidarity with Israel.

The Arab side was also supported in London, when over 5,000 people marched from Speakers' Corner in Hyde Park to the U.S. and Israeli embassies to protest against "Israeli occupation of Arab lands."

Hundreds of policemen were deployed to cover each demonstration and prevent any clashes between the supporters of the two sides in the Middle East battle.

Speakers at the Israel rally criticized British policy towards Israel, and called on the Government to lift the embargo on arms sales to Israel.

Israel's Ambassador to Britain Michael Comay told the open air rally of 10,000 supporters of Israel: "Let us stop the fighting and move the encounter from the battlefields to the conference table."

He said British Jews should press their Government to work toward this end.

The 5,000 Arab marchers, including contingents of Iranian and Pakistani students, conducted an orderly parade, acompanied by cars with loud-speakers calling "down with Israel."

Traffic was brought to a halt in the Capital's main shopping centre in Oxford Street on the route to the U.S. Embassy, where strong forces of police were on duty.

The Arab marchers delivered a petition to the embassy, protesting against U.S. support for Israel. They continued their march without incident to the heavily-guarded Israeli Embassy about three kms. away.

South African Volunteers in Overabundance

An AP dispatch from Johannesburg said that according to South African Jewish leaders, eager volunteers who want to fight with the Israeli forces don't like taking no for an answer.

"We've had hundreds — it must be thousands by now — of young people phoning up all week wanting to go to Israel to fight in the war," said Julius Weinstein, chairman of the South African Zionist Federation.

"Every day I have phoned Tel Aviv to ask if they want our volunteers, and every day they have answered no... honestly, Israel doesn't want them..."

But Weinstein said some independent volunteers were travelling to Israel via several European cities.

Soldiers' regards to be sent free to France

TEL AVIV. — The Association of Immigrants from France will transmit soldiers' greetings to relatives in France free of charge, it was announced here yesterday. Soldiers are invited to contact 03-53778 or 03-57178 between 8 a.m. and 8 p.m.

Expressions of solidarity pouring in from world over

Jerusalem Post Reporter

The Amsterdam City Council yesterday sent Jerusalem Mayor Teddy Kollek a telegram expressing solidarity with Israel in its struggle. All factions on the Council joined in signing the telegram, the municipal spokesman said.

A similar message was received from the Mayor of Copenhagen last week. West Berlin Mayor B. Schuetz telephoned on Tuesday asking Mayor Kollek's endorsement for a solidarity meeting to be held in the city.

Prime Minister Golda Meir received, among others, a telegram from Hubert Humphrey, expressing his wish that you will be able to repulse the attack on your country and restore peace to the area."

Israel Arabs pitch in to aid war effort

By YA'ACOV FRIEDLER
Jerusalem Post Reporter

HAIFA. — The Prime Minister's adviser on Arab affairs, Shmuel Toledano, yesterday took practical measures to enable the Arab citizens of Israel to volunteer their services and their money to the war effort. Starting off with a meeting of Arab and Druse representatives in Haifa, he later opened seven offices in Arab and Druse towns where volunteers and war loan contributions can be registered. The offices will be run in cooperation with the Histadrut's Arab Department.

Mr. Toledano told *The Post* that the offices have four aims: to persuade Arab workers who have stayed away from their jobs in the Jewish areas to return to work; to recruit several thousand skilled workers for essential plants; to organize contributions to the war loan; and to recruit men for Civil Defence work in mixed towns and in minority villages.

Mr. Toledano said he was gratified by the behaviour of the Arab population since the outbreak of the war and stressed that there had been much more volunteering than during the Six Day War.

"The Arab citizens have demanded to be allowed to share in the war effort, and that's why we decided to open the offices." He stressed that there had been no demonstration of hostility whatsoever, "even in those villages which were 'unfavourable' during the Six Day War." However, he said, during the first days of the war there had been a tendency among the Arabs to stay home because they were not sure how the Jewish population would receive them. "But despite the tension there has been no animosity from the Jewish citizens. The Arabs now feel that everything's as usual and are resuming their normal work," he said.

Before the meeting started a number of young men — Druse, Arabs and Beduin — arrived to volunteer their services "for any work that needs doing."

Yesterday afternoon, Haifa Police Commander Mordechai Kom addressed a meeting of some 200 Arab representatives at the Arab-Jewish Centre here on civilian be-

haviour during the war. He stressed the need to carry on normal life and to go to work as usual, and the need for volunteers for auxiliary services. Archbishop Joseph Raya and leaders of the Moslem community were among the participants.

Several speakers asked for details on how to volunteer. One speaker noted that many Haifa Arabs had already donated blood and money for the war effort but had not publicized their actions because "we consider them our duty."

The meeting adopted a resolution calling on all Arab workers in Haifa to return to their jobs immediately. They expressed their confidence in Israel's victory and called on the Arab citizens to contribute all they can to the war loan. The meeting also denounced the Egyptian-Syrian aggression and called for a peaceful solution to the conflict.

In Nazareth, Arab and Jewish women set up a free food kiosk for soldiers passing through, and many residents brought gifts of Arab delicacies.

Arab women in Nazareth set up a refreshment stand for Israeli soldiers.

ON TUESDAY, OCTOBER 16, 1973, 3,000 soldiers from Jordan left for Syria. While Hussein announced he would not open up a third front, the little King could not refrain from delivering some bluster: "We will teach Israel what war is," he told his troops.

That afternoon, Prime Minister Golda Meir addressed the Knesset. She told of the great losses that Israel had suffered: "They are the sons of all of us. The pain is that of all of us."

She disclosed the disparity in troops between Israel and her enemies: Against Israel's 300,000 mobilized troops, there stood 650,000 Egyptian soldiers, 150,000 Syrian soldiers, an armored division from Iraq, an armored brigade from Jordan, a motorized brigade of 1,500 troops from Morocco. With all Israeli reserves mobilized, the disparity in fighting men was now three to one, and this did not take into account Arab reserves, which were huge.

"There is no need for a fertile imagination to realize what the situation of the State of Israel would have been, had we been on the 1967 lines," Mrs. Meir pointed out.

Her speech displayed the bitterness that every Israeli felt toward the Russians:

The Soviet Union aspires to profit from the war against Israel. The Soviet Union did not prepare the Arab armies for defense, knowing they were in no danger of being attacked, but built up, trained, equipped and deployed these armies for the planned purpose of aggressive action. Above everything else, the Soviet Union's all-out support...has been manifested in the airlift reaching our enemies' airfields, and the ships calling at their ports.

After clamping embargo on Mid-East

Britain announces it is training Egyptians for helicopter crews

By DAVID LENNON
Jerusalem Post Correspondent

LONDON. — Following Britain's announcement of an embargo on all arms sales to Middle East combatants — which was accompanied by her refusal to send Israel spare parts ordered and paid for before the war even as it was shipping five Saracen light tanks to the Persian Gulf oil state of Dubai — another furore has broken out over the Government's confirmation yesterday that Egyptian pilots are being trained on helicopters in this country.

A joint statement by the Foreign Office, the Defence Ministry and Westland, the helicopter manufacturers, admitted that 12 Egyptian pilots and 30 technicians are to be trained by Westland to fly and maintain the company's Sea Cat helicopter. The Egyptians arrived about a week ago and are due to start their three-month training course — which includes visits to R.A.F. bases — today.

The Sea Cat helicopter has a strike power and can be used as an anti-submarine weapon.

In a second statement, the Foreign Office spokesman said the Government would not intervene and the training would proceed as arranged. In the British view, he said, this would not make a difference to the Egyptian war effort; "on the contrary, it ties down Egyptian pilots here."

A Westland spokesman said: "We're under contract only with the British Government, not with the Egyptians. We provide a service."

The matter was first revealed earlier yesterday by several Members of Parliament of both major parties. A debate on Britain's embargo and stance on the war is scheduled to take place in the House of Commons today.

Conservative M.P. Hugh Fraser, former Aviation Minister, accused his Government of cheating Israel.

It is totally unfair, he said, to sell arms to Israel (notably, Centurion tanks) and then refuse to supply spare parts and ammunition when they are needed. "This is **Danegeld;** we are giving in to the Arab oil blackmail," he declared. "We are acting like a dud insurance company refusing to pay the insurance."

Former Labour Foreign Secretary Michael Stewart denounced the embargo as a breach of contract and said that a mere general decision not to supply arms is not impartiality when the embargo is likely to harm one side — Israel — more than the other.

He accused the Arabs of greater intransigence than Israel since 1967, and demanded that they sit down and negotiate with Israel. This sounds like a major shift in the Labour Party's public stance.

Labour M.P. Greville Janner called the programme for training Egyptian pilots "a disgrace" which "ought to be stopped at once."

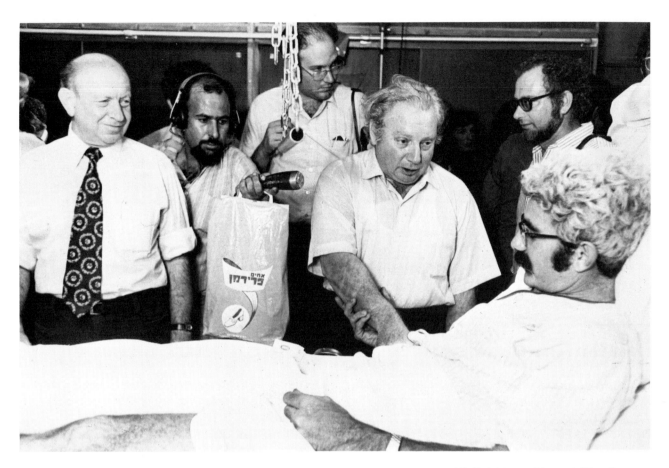

Violinist Isaac Stern visiting the wounded in a hospital.

EGYPTIAN P-o-W's STORY:

'You're not devils like they told us'

By MOSHE SHALEV
Army Pool Correspondent

"I saw your soldiers were surrounding us. The officer beside me had been discovered and was being asked whether he was alone. I rose and raised my hands."

This is the way Sgt. Major Mohammed El Abbady described his capture in Sinai.

"I'm 22." He said, "From the town of Gizeh. I studied weaving and joined the army upon completion of my studies. I was sent to a reconnaissance training course where I have been since 1970. Several days ago, we were told that the Israelis had attacked Egypt. I was one of 21 soldiers flown by helicopter to a hill in the southern sector."

"Did they tell you how you would be evacuated?"

"They told us the Egyptian army would advance and would then collect us. At first, we saw no sign of Israeli soldiers. But later, I don't know exactly at what point, an Israeli force arrived. It was then that we surrendered."

Offering water to several other prisoners (sailors whose boat had been sunk), Mohammed continued: "The Egyptians didn't come to look for us. We suffered terribly from hunger and thirst. We were on the shore for six days until our surrender.

"I have learnt one thing," he said, "You are not the devils we were told about in Egypt. I am being treated well. But if you ask me about peace, well then if the Russians and the Americans cannot bring us peace, who am I to say anything on this subject?"

Nevertheless, Mohammed hopes to be home in another two or three weeks, when the war is over.

CHRISTIANS SHOCKED

To the Editor of The Jerusalem Post

We, members of the Christian community of Israel, and sharing in its destiny, express our profound shock and concern at the new attack by Arab States which has re-opened the war in the Middle East. The fact that this attack was carried out on the Day of Atonement, the most sacred day of the Jewish year, outrages all human and religious feelings. This, and the continued rejection of negotiations, highlights the refusal of the Arab States to recognize the basic right of the Jewish People, which has been affirmed by the U.N., to sovereign and independent existence in peace among the other nations in the Middle East.

We declare that only after this refusal has been truly reversed will Christians have the moral right to require the Government of Israel to meet the legitimate claims of the Palestinian Arabs. We urge all Christians in the world who, like ourselves, feel concerned about the rights of the Palestinian Arabs, to recognize unequivocally this basic right of the Jewish People.

We mourn all those who have died and who are dying in this war. We pray that the hearts of all parties may be opened towards a true acceptance of each other in their own identity, as the beginning of a process leading to a just and lasting peace.

Father Alfred Delmee
  Chaplain of the Catholic Community of Jaffa
Brother Dr. Marcel Dubois OP
  Superior, St. Isaiah House, Senior Lecturer, Hebrew University; former chairman of the Ecumenical Theological Research Fraternity in Israel
Rina Geftman
  Mamre Centre, Jerusalem
Father Michel de Goedt OCD
  Chaplain of the Catholic Community of Jerusalem
Brother Gabriel Grossmann OP
  St. Isaiah House; member of the Ecumenical Fraternity
Brother Bruno Hussar OP
  St. Isaiah House; member of the Ecumenical Fraternity
Father Isaac Jacob OSB
  member of the Ecumenical Fraternity
Hanna Kleinberger
  Catholic community of Jerusalem
Revd. Roy Kreider
  Chairman of the United Christian Council in Israel
Rev. Dr. Michael Krupp
  German Pastor in Jerusalem; Director, Aktion Sühnezeichen; member of the Ecumenical Fraternity
Father Pierre Lenhardt NDS
  Convent of Ratisbonne, Jerusalem
Clotilde Mathys
  Interreligious group, Tel Aviv
Johan Pilon MD
  Nes Ammim
Cecile Pilverdjer
  Catholic community of Jerusalem
Father Virgil Pixner
  Dormition Abbey; member of the Ecumenical Fraternity
Father Jean Roger AA
  Chaplain of the Catholic Community of Beersheba
Father Daniel Rufeisen OCD
  Catholic priest, Mt. Carmel, Haifa
Revd. Coos Schoneveld
  Executive Secretary, Ecumenical Fraternity
Joyce Wilson
  Office Secretary, Ecumenical Fraternity
Rev. Dr. G. Douglas Young
  Director, American Institute for Holy Land Studies
Jerusalem, October 13, 1973

Members of the Christian community of Israel are invited to express their adhesion to this statement by contacting the office of the Ecumenical Theological Research Fraternity in Israel, either by phone (02-66308) or in writing (P.O.B. 249, Jerusalem).

FOR MANY YEARS, I've been a subscriber to the overseas edition of The Jerusalem Post. About two weeks after the Yom Kippur War started, I ran across the letter which appears enlarged on the opposite page. It was this letter that triggered this book.

For me, the contents of this letter were so important that I determined that the letter should have a wider audience.

As you see, the letter was written and signed by leaders of the Christian Community of Israel— by twenty Catholic prelates, chaplains, community leaders, and university scholars who reside in Jerusalem, and who, presumably, are quite familiar with the history of Palestine and with the presumptive rights of its two claimants.

The writers of the letter begin by asserting that they share the destiny of Israel. They deplore the attack "carried out on the Day of Atonement, the most sacred day of the Jewish year," and state in bold terms that the commencement of the war "highlights the refusal of the Arab states to recognize the basic right of the Jewish people which has been affirmed by the U.N. to sovereign and independent existence in peace."

The letter then makes its telling point:

> *We declare that only after this refusal has been truly reversed will Christians have the moral right to require the government of Israel to meet the legitimate claims of the Palestinian Arabs.*

Here, at last, is a Christian voice loudly declaring that the rights of the Palestinian Arabs cannot obliterate the right of the Jews to survive in their own land.

In other words, this group of Catholic dignitaries, close to the scene and familiar with the facts, state from a moral standpoint the rights of the Palestinian Arabs, however legitimate they may be, can be fulfilled only after the Arab world first acknowledges the right of the Israeli Jews to live in peace in a state of their own.

In the face of the Arabs' repeated insistence on their sole right to Palestine, in the face of their insistent denial of the right of the Jews to statehood, how heartening is the following statement:

> *We urge all Christians in the world who, like ourselves, feel concerned about the rights of the Palestinian Arabs, to recognize unequivocally this basic right of the Jewish People.*

It seemed lamentable to me that this letter was not reproduced in any of the news media in this country, or in any other country outside Israel. You could not have read this letter in *Time,* nor in *Newsweek,* nor in The New York Times, nor in the London Times. You may well have read in these publications a great many voices clamoring for the rights of the "dispossessed" Palestinians. But the voices of this handful of thoughtful, long-time residents of Jerusalem—men outside the Jewish faith—were not heard abroad when they publicly asserted that the Jewish claim, if conflicting claims there be, was paramount—historically, legally, and *morally!*

The fact is that there has been much misrepresentation of the truth about the so-called rights of the Palestinians, and of the factors which have led to the shame of the refugee camps. There are hardly any Jews, inside Israel or out, Zionist or no, who do not deplore the horrible situation which has led to the dehumanization of life in the camps where homeless Palestinian Arabs have been obliged to take refuge.

However, the canard that this situation has been due to the heartless dispossession of the Arabs by the Jews as a result of Jewish aggression should be dispelled. Time and again, *Newsweek* and *Time* speak editorially of displaced Arabs implying, by the phraseology of their reports, that it is the Jews who bear the responsibility for this displacement. This lie, carefully nurtured by Arab propaganda, has been kept alive, and has been constantly embellished, until many, if not most, thinking Americans—including many who are deeply sympathetic to Israel—sincerely believe that the Israelis are indeed responsible for the Arabs having been "pushed out" of Palestine. This simply isn't true.

The facts are readily available to those who are willing to read, and willing to learn the truth.

The Arab refugee problem was the result of a war of aggression launched by five Arab states against Israel in 1948. Had there been no war against Israel, there would be no problem of Arab refugees today.

During the years of the British mandate, many commissions had been appointed to determine how the land of Palestine should be apportioned among the rival claimants. No solution seemed to be acceptable to the Arabs. Realizing that the Gordian knot had to be cut, on the 29th day of November, 1947, after prolonged debate, the United Nations passed a resolution to partition Palestine and give part to the Jews and part to the Arabs.

On the very next day, the Arabs began an assault on the Jews of Palestine. From that day on, until

Jews jailed for Moscow protest

MOSCOW (Reuter).—Three young Jews who demonstrated outside the Communist Party headquarters here on Saturday were each sentenced to 15 days imprisonment on Monday, Jewish sources said.

The sources said two of them, Iona Kolchinsky and Alexander Slepak, had been "severely beaten" by Soviet police after their arrest.

The three, one of them a girl, Eygenia Kerzhner, faced charges of "disobeying the militia's orders," the sources added.

During the demonstration, they displayed a poster saying they considered themselves Israeli prisoners-of-war in Russia.

Belgian solidarity

BRUSSELS (INA). — A Belgian "Committee of solidarity with Israel" has been set up here under the presidency of former premier Gaston Eyskens. Several former ministers are among the many political figures who have joined the group.

Sombre Simhat Tora starts this evening

By SARAH HONIG and YITZHAK OKED
Jerusalem Post Reporters

TEL AVIV. — Simhat Tora, which is to be ushered in tonight by special prayers and traditional *hakafot* — festive dances by congregants bearing Tora scrolls — will be quieter and more sombre this year; the mass outdoor celebrations which characterize the holiday will be absent. This year's festivities will be modest and resetricted to the synagogue interiors.

The chairman of the local Religious Council, Pinhas Sheinman, told *The Jerusalem Post* there are a number of reasons for the decision to limit celebrations and to cancel the public, outdoor *hakafot*. "First," he said, "no one is in a mood for such mass celebrations while the war is still on. Second, the gathering of thousands of people in one spot is unsafe in time of war. And there are blackout considerations, as the mass *hakafot* usually take place after sundown."

Mr. Sheinman added that in most synagogues services will be held earlier than usual and the indoor *hakafot* will be scheduled so as to be concluded before the sun sets, both today and tomorrow night. This will spare the synagogue executives the problem of blacking out their buildings. But services in those synagogues which are blacked out need not be held early, he said.

The city's Chief Rabbis, Yedidya Frenkel and David Halevi, have instructed all rabbis to devote their sermons to the war effort. Those congregants who have not yet contributed to the voluntary war loan or who have not yet pledged to purchase bonds will be asked to do so.

The city's rabbis will also be going to the homes of families of the fallen to console them and extend help.

Hundreds of Tora scrolls from synagogues and private homes have been distributed to IDF units on all fronts. Simhat Tora *hakafot* have been organized by the Chief Chaplaincy who hope to reach all units on all fronts. Former Chief Rabbi Yitzhak Nissim has contributed a scroll which was brought out of an Arab country.

The IDF Chaplaincy has printed new editions, running into tens of thousands, of the IDF prayer books and calendar, compiled by Aluf Mishne Gad 'Navon. This book includes Jewish religious laws (*Dinim*) and special prayers for soldiers.

In theory, Israeli soldiers captured by the Egyptians will be able to hold Simhat Tora hakafot: The soldiers on the East bank of the Canal, opposite Port Ibrahim, who were taken prisoner on Saturday, took a Tora scroll along with them.

---

the expiration of the British mandate in May of 1948, Arab leaders plunged the land into turmoil. There were riots, insurrection, looting of Jewish stores, attack, and murder.

Starting in late 1947, thousands of wealthy Arabs began, of their own accord, to leave Palestine.

In May, 1948, the British, unable to enforce the partition resolution of the United Nations, gave up their mandate and summarily left the scene.

On May 14, 1948, Ben-Gurion, the Israeli leader, declared Israel an independent state, in accordance with the resolution of the United Nations. Immediately following Ben Gurion's announcement, the armed forces of Egypt, Syria, Jordan, Lebanon, and Iraq, supported by contingents from Saudi Arabia and Yemen, crossed Israel's frontiers

and marched against Israel's people. Before they reached Israel's borders, they had announced, through the Secretary General of the Arab League:

This will be a war of extermination.
It will be a momentous massacre to be
spoken of like the Mongolian massacres
and the Crusades.

Before the war and during the war—without being driven out by the Israelis—thousands of Arabs left their homes in a mass exodus. On January 30, 1948, the Jaffa newspaper, As Sha-ab, had written:

The first group of our fifth column
consists of those who abandon their

*houses and businesses and go to live
elsewhere. At the first sign of trouble,
they take to their heels and escape
sharing the burdens of struggle.*

On March 30, 1948, the weekly, As-Sarih, accused the inhabitants of Sheikh Munis and other villages in the neighborhood of Tel Aviv of "bringing down disgrace on us all by abandoning their villages."

On May 5, 1948, the Jerusalem correspondent of The London Times wrote:

*The Arab streets are curiously deserted,
evidently following the poor example of
the more moneyed class. There has been
an exodus from Jerusalem too, though
not to the same extent as in Jaffa
and Haifa.*

On October 2, 1948, the prestigious London weekly, The Economist, reported:

*Of the 62,000 Arabs who formerly lived
in Haifa, not more than 5,000 or 6,000
remained. Various factors influenced
their decision to seek safety in flight.
There is but little doubt that the most
potent of the factors were the
announcements made over the air by the
Higher Arab Executive, urging the Arabs
to quit. It was clearly intimated that
these Arabs who remained in Haifa and
accepted Jewish protection would be
regarded as renegades.*

In 1955, in his book published in London, entitled *The Arabs*[1], Edward Atiyah, then secretary of the Arab League Office in London, wrote:

*This wholesale exodus was due partly
to the belief of the Arabs, encouraged by
the boasting of an unrealistic Arab
press and the irresponsible utterances of
some of the Arab leaders, that it could
be only a matter of some weeks before
the Jews would be defeated by the
armies of the Arab states, and the
Palestinian Arabs enabled to re-enter
and retake possession of their country.*

In 1950, writing in a book entitled *New Star in the Near-East*[2], Kenneth Bilby, one of the American correspondents who covered Palestine for several years before and during the war of 1948, observed the following:

*The Arab exodus, initially at least,
was encouraged by many Arab leaders,
such as Haj Amin el-Husseini, the exiled
pro-Nazi Mufti of Jerusalem, and by the
Arab Higher Committee for Palestine.
They viewed the first wave of Arab
set-backs as merely transitory. Let the
Palestine Arabs flee into neighboring
countries. It would serve to arouse
the other Arab peoples to greater effort,
and when the Arab invasion struck, the
Palestinians could return to their homes
and be compensated with the property
of Jews driven into the sea.*

On June 8, 1951, Habib Issa, Secretary General of the Arab League, wrote in the New York Lebanese daily newspaper, Al Hoda, the following:

*The Secretary General of the Arab
League, Azzam Pasha, assured the Arab
peoples that the occupation of Palestine,
and of Tel Aviv, would be as simple
as a military promenade. He pointed out
that they were already on the frontiers,
and that all the millions the Jews had
spent on land, economic development,
would be easy booty, for it would be a
simple matter to throw the Jews into
the Mediterranean. Brotherly advice was
given the Arabs of Palestine to leave
their land, homes, and property, and to
stay temporarily in neighboring fraternal
states, lest the guns of the invading
Arab armies mow them down.*

For a purely local source, I refer to the Jordanian daily, Difoa. On September 6, 1954, reviewing the debacle that occurred six years earlier, this newspaper disingenuously stated:

*The Arab governments told us, "Get out,
so that we can get in." So we got out, but
they did not get in.*

As a matter of fact, the Jews themselves urged the Arabs to stay, to become reconciled to a Jewish state as proclaimed by the United Nations.

The Jews assured the Arabs that they would be safe in life and limb, and that they would be accorded full civil rights in the new state. One of

1. Page 183.
2. Page 30.

the British authorities, the British Chief of Police in Haifa — who, in view of Britain's difficulties in the region and in view of the known British anti-Jewish feeling, could hardly be accused of harboring pro-Israeli bias — reported on April 26, 1948:

> *The situation in Haifa remains unchanged. Every effort is being made by the Jews to persuade the Arab population to stay and carry on with their normal lives, to get their shops and businesses open, and to be assured that their lives and interests will be safe.*

Mr. A. J. Bridmead, who wrote the above, continued in a supplementary report, stating:

> *An appeal has been made to the Arabs by the Jews to reopen their shops and businesses in order to relieve the difficulties of feeding the Arab population. Evacuation was still going on yesterday, and several trips were made by Z craft to Acre. Roads, too, were crowded. Arab leaders reiterated their determination to evacuate the entire Arab population, and they have been given the loan of ten three-ton military trucks as from this morning to assist the evacuation.*

On April 23, 1948 Jamal Husseini, acting chairman of the Palestine Arab Higher Committee, had stated in the United Nations Security Council:[1]

> *The Arabs did not want to submit to a truce. They rather preferred to abandon their homes, their belongings, and everything they possessed in the world, and leave the town. This is in fact what they did.*

And the crowning confirmation of these facts — if further confirmation there need be — can be found in a statement made before an international committee on September 15, 1948, by Mr. Emile Ghoury — the Secretary of the Arab Higher Committee at the time of the Arab invasion of Israel. He declared:

> *I do not want to impugn anyone but only to help the refugees. The fact that there are these refugees is the direct consequence of the action of the Arab States in opposing partition and the Jewish State. The Arab States agreed upon this policy unanimously and they must share in the solution of the problem.*

No less compelling than these avowals by Arab leaders are the judgments of United Nations organs. In April, 1948, when the flight of the refugees was in full swing, the United Nations Palestine Commission inscribed its verdict on the tablets of history:

> *Arab opposition to the plan of the Assembly of 29 November 1947 has taken the form of organized efforts by strong Arab elements, both inside and outside Palestine, to prevent its implementation and to thwart its objectives by threats and acts of violence, including repeated armed incursions into Palestine territory. The Commission has had to report to the Security Council that powerful Arab interests, both inside and outside Palestine, are defying the resolution of the General Assembly and are engaged in a deliberate effort to alter by force the settlement envisaged therein.*

On August 16, 1948, Msgr. George Hakim, the Greek Catholic Archbishop of Galilee, stated:

> *The refugees had been confident that their absence from Palestine would not last long; that they would return within a few days — within a week or two; their leaders had promised them that the Arab armies would crush the 'Zionist gangs' very quickly and that there would be no need for panic or fear of a long exile.*

A survey by an international body[2] in 1957 described these violent events:

> *As early as the first months of 1948, the Arab League issued orders exhorting the people to seek a temporary refuge in neighboring countries, later to return to their abodes in the wake of the victorious Arab armies and obtain their share of abandoned Jewish property."*

---

1. U.N. Security Council, Official Records, Third Year, N. 62. April 23, 1948, page 14.

2. Research Group for European Migration Problems Bulletin, Vol. V—No. 1, 1957, p. 10.

Confidence prevails in East, West Jerusalem

By ABRAHAM RABINOVICH
Jerusalem Post Reporter

As the Egyptian and Israeli armies locked yesterday in bitter battle, Jews and Arabs in Jerusalem mixed peacefully at Mayor Teddy Kollek's annual Succot reception.

Mr. Kollek decided to hold his reception despite the war. The only concession to the times was to conclude the event before dusk so that people could get home before the blackout. The early conclusion meant that most Moslem notables could not attend since they were at home breaking the Ramadan fast. Nevertheless, at least two Moslem mukhtars did come, as well as a number of Arab Christians.

The Russians were also represented, at least the Moscow-based Russian Orthodox Church, whose representative was among the many church dignitaries attending. The diplomatic corps turned out in force, although the British and French Consulates sent only their deputy consuls. The British reportedly explained that their consul could not come because of the change in the scheduled time of the reception. The French offered no explanations, according to a Municipality source.

The mood in both parts of Jerusalem seemed strangely confident yesterday — the Arabs apparently confident that the Egyptian and Syrian armies would prevail this time, while the Jews were confident that they would be smashed. Jewish shoppers could be seen at food stalls in the Old City, and the Arab population seemed to be in good spirits. Security details were posted at the Old City gates, but no incidents were reported.

In East Jerusaem, Egyptian President Sadat's speech could be heard from shop radios and hand-held transistors in the early afternoon as one walked down the street. Two hours later, Premier Golda Meir's speech in the Knesset could be heard in the streets of West Jerusalem. Their expressions of confidence in the outcome of the war seemed to be reflected in the respective attitudes of Jews and Arabs in the city.

Following the release of the Israeli casualty figures Sunday, sizeable security forces were posted at the approaches to East Jerusalem to forestall any possible attempt by elements of the Jewish population to take out their anger on the Arab population. There was, however, no such attempt. A Civil Defence officer who walked through the city after the release of the figures said he sensed a relaxation in the Jewish population.

France trained Egyptian pilots in Libyan guise

Egyptian pilots have been training in France under false Libyan identities, an Egyptian pilot taken prisoner has revealed.

The prisoner, Lt.-Col. Sa'ad Ahmed Zahran, fell into Israeli hands on October 14 in Sinai.

He related that he was in a group of two other Egyptian pilots and a number of Egyptian aircraft technicians which was flown to Libya in August, 1970. After being furnished with false Libyan identities, the group flew on to Marignan, France.

There the men underwent a month's training on Alouette helicopters and subsequently returned to Libya to participate in the Revolution Day parade.

At the end of 1970, Zahran, still carrying his Libyan documents, left for France where he attended a Super Frelon helicopter pilots' course. Zahran said he knows Egyptian pilots who trained on Mirage planes at Dijon, France, under Libyan cover. He gave the names of Farouk Azzawi, Ali Alzin and Mustapha Darwish.

Gush Halav backs the war effort

Jerusalem Post Reporter

SASAD. — The Israeli Arab village of Gush Halav (Jish) on the Lebanese border yesterday sent a message of support to the Government and the Histadrut. The 1,800 villagers, 300 of whom are Moslems, have also sent fruit to the soldiers on the Golan, offered 20 pick-up trucks for civilian needs, and have set up a committee to hasten subscription to the Voluntary War Loan.

Mayor Teddy Kollek confers with neighboring village Mukhtars outside the walls of Jerusalem.

Business as usual in Gaza, despite war

By HERBERT BEN-ADI
Jerusalem Post Reporter

GAZA. — Despite Radio Cairo's repeated description of a Gaza Strip surrounded by Israeli tanks, with a soldier on every rooftop, the only Israeli troops in sight here are two men patrolling the street — just as in more normal times.

Traffic was normal when I drove through yesterday, the streets were crowded, and the shops were full to bursting with goods. Both Jews and Arabs were passing in and out of the Strip without even a pause for checking, and there was no ring of troops or armour.

For days Cairo has been bombarding its listeners in Arabic with stories of troops, severe shortages and heavy terrorist activity in the Strip. Yesterday morning I toured the Strip to see for myself in a car with Israeli plates and a civilian driver. As we passed through Gaza and the Shati, El Burej and Jebalya camps — with no one paying any attention to us — we saw life going on as always, with the children at school and here and there a local policeman directing traffic. The

only sign of the war was the blackout preparations.

In the stores, flour was more than plentiful. So was fuel, after the Military Government in the last three days brought in 650,000 litres. Medical services were operating normally.

The area's industrial centre, which employs local labour, was working at about 80 per cent capacity yesterday, and workers in the port were unloading cement as usual. Gazans employed in Israel are staying home, but are expected to begin returning to their jobs in the next few days.

In nearby El-Arish the local workers employed in Israel went to their jobs as usual, and the Israeli-owned factories were working at full capacity.

One effect of the war on the Strip is that registration for the pilgrimage to Mecca has been suspended. In addition, 700 young Gazans scheduled to study in Egypt are unable to go.

The only complaint Gazans made to me was that hooligans in Yavne — who they stressed were not religious youths — were shooting stones from slightshots at passing Arab cars.

'Satellites aid Arabs'

NEW YORK (Reuter). — The magazine "Aviation Week," reported here that Russian reconnaissance satellites over Middle East battle areas are helping the Soviet Union advise Egyptian and Syrian military commanders on tactics against Israel.

The magazine said one of these satellites was taken out of orbit on October 10, ahead of schedule and replaced by a second whose orbit provides good coverage of the combat zone.

In a separate article,, "Aviation Week" said the Soviet Union had launched a succession of Cosmos satellites over the area since early October and these have given an "unprecedented window" over the whole strategic region.

The magazine predicted that the U.S., "caught without an effective big bird up at the time the war erupted," would hastily launch a satellite.

The Defence Department refused to comment on the report.

DETAILED INSTRUCTIONS and patterns for knitting "Balaclava helmets" for soldiers are available from 8 Rehov Ha'arba'a, Tel Aviv, Tel. 262291. The hats should be knitted in dark colours, such as green, brown or black, and will be received by any office of the Soldiers Welfare Association.

Premier Golda Meir visits a hospital to see the wounded.

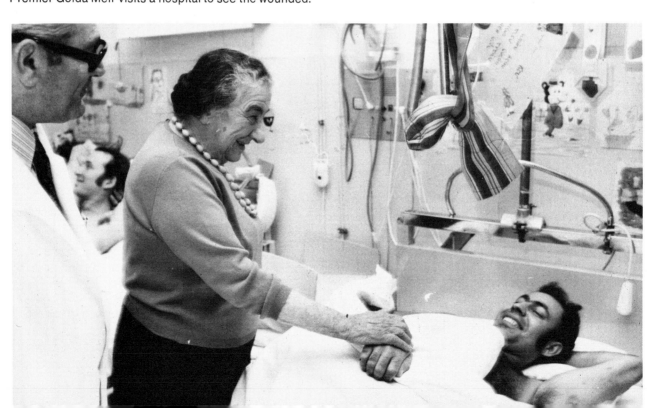

During the War of Independence in 1948, and during its aftermath, some 400,000 Arab residents of the area left their homes. But it is futile and inaccurate to say that they lost their homes because they were driven out of them by the Jews.

I have presented a rather long, and perhaps tedious record, precisely because the lie persists, and is proclaimed by the Arab nations over and over again in the halls of the United Nations. There, not a single voice of protest is raised in rebuttal except by Israel's representative.

Over and over again, journals of opinion have blithely accepted these unfounded assignations of Israeli responsibility. Only in one sense are the Israelis responsible. They disappointed Arab fantasies by refusing to be sacrificed.

Where did the Arab refugees go? They went to camps in Jordan, to camps in Lebanon and Syria. Some trekked across the Arabian peninsula, and eventually found jobs in far off Kuwait. But most of them became the recipients of United Nations relief charity, the major part of these funds being subscribed by the United States.

During the long years of degradation that ensued, what help did these refugees get to restore the self-respect and dignity that comes with being self-supporting?

Very little, indeed, from their Arab brothers. The kingdoms of Saudi Arabia and Libya, wallowing in oily gold, offered scant succor. In no Arab country was a concerted effort made to take in a sizable number of refugees and settle them in homes and jobs. Instead, to their everlasting shame, the Arab countries let their brothers rot in do-nothing refugee camps, keeping their misery alive, fueling the hatred of the self-dispossessed and preserving the camps as a political trump card against Israel.

Israel had created the refugee camps because Israel had refused to commit hara kiri. It was all Israel's fault.

Let us examine the testimony of impartial observers. The Research Group for European Migration reached the following grave conclusion:

> The official attitude of the [Arab] host countries is well known. It is one of seeking to prevent any sort of adaptation and integration because the refugees are seen as a political means of pressure to get Israel wiped off the map, or to get the greatest possible number of concessions.

Throughout the last 26 years, whenever the Jews of Israel have attempted peace overtures to the Arabs, the rejoinder has always been "not until the legitimate rights of the Palestinians have been restored," meaning not until Palestine is returned to the Arabs.

There can be little doubt that if free movement had been granted to the refugees there would have been a spontaneous flow of thousands of them into the expanded Arab economies. It is precisely this that the Arab governments have obstructed.

In a highly significant passage of his report to the Eighth session of the General Assembly, the Director of UNRWA describes Arab policies on free movement:

> The full benefit of the spread of this large capital investment [in Arab countries] will be felt only if restrictions on the movement of refugees are withdrawn. Such freedom of movement would enable refugees to take full advantage of the opportunities for work arising in countries such as Iraq, Saudi Arabia, and the Persian Gulf Sheikhdoms where economic development has already taken place.

There has, of course, been some movement of refugees seeking out the new labor opportunities of the region. The force of economic attraction has sometimes prevailed. But these potentialities could be fully realized only if political resistance were overcome.

There are and have been broad opportunities in the Arab world for refugees to build new lives; but the governments of the Arab kin countries have been singularly—one might say deliberately—uncooperative.

In a survey published by the Carnegie Endowment, the obstructive record of Arab governments is set out in graphic words:

> The history of UNRWA has been a clinical study in frustration. No Agency has been better led or more devoutly served, but the organized intransigence of the refugees and the calculated indifference of the Arab States concerned have brought all its plans to nought. By chicanery, it is feeding the dead; by political pressure, it is feeding non-refugees; its relief supplies have been

subjected in some instances to import duty; its personnel policies are grossly interfered with; and its "constructive measures," necessarily requiring the concurrence of government, have been pigeon-holed. The net result is that relief is being provided in 1957 to refugees who could have been rehabilitated in 1951 with home and jobs, without prejudice to their just claims.

In a survey entitled "Social Forces in the Middle East 1956," Dr. Channing B. Richardson of Hamilton College writes:

Towards UNRWA, the attitudes of the Arab Governments vary between suspicion and obstruction. It cannot be denied that the outside observer gains the impression that the Arab governments have no great desire to solve the refugee problem.

In June, 1957, the Chairman of the Near Eastern Sub-Committee of the United States Senate Foreign Relations Committee reported at the end of an illuminating survey:

The fact is that the Arab States have for ten years used the Palestine refugees as political hostages in their struggle with Israel. While Arab delegates in the United Nations have condemned the plight of their brothers in the refugee camps, nothing has been done to assist them in a practical way, lest political leverage against Israel be lost.

The refusal of the Arab governments to achieve a permanent economic integration of the refugees into their lands must be contrasted with the achievements of other countries when confronted with the challenge of absorbing their own homeless kinsmen.

Israel, with her small territory and her hardpressed finances, has managed to provide homes, work, education, and citizenship for a multitude of newcomers arriving in destitution no less acute than that of the Arab refugees. These Jewish refugees from Arab lands were compelled to leave their property behind. They have had to undergo a process of adaptation to a social, linguistic, and national ethos far removed from

anything they had known before. Integration has been far more arduous than it could possibly be for Arab refugees in Arab lands, where no such differences exist between the immigrants and the host culture. If Israel could and did assimilate half a million Jewish refugees from Arab lands, how much more easy it would be for the vast Arab world—if the same impulse of kinship asserted itself —to absorb a similar number of Arab refugees.

This precise point is made in the aforementioned report published by the Carnegie Endowment:

There is another aspect of the Middle East refugee problem that is also frequently ignored. It is necessary to remember that concurrently with the perpetuation of the Arab refugee problem more than 400,000 Jews have been forced to leave their homes in Iraq, the Yemen, and North Africa. They have not been counted as refugees, because they were readily and immediately received as new immigrants into Israel.

Nevertheless, they were forced to leave their traditional homes against their will, and to abandon, in the process, all that they possessed. The latest addition to their number are the 20,000 Jews for whom life has become impossible in Egypt. Fifteen thousand of them have sought asylum in Israel, while the remainder are in Europe seeking other solutions to their problems.

The same point is made in the report of a Special Study Commission to the Near East and Africa dispatched by the Committee on Foreign Affairs of the United States House of Representatives,[1] the source of a great proportion of U.N. relief funds:

Unlike refugees in other parts of the world, the Palestine refugees are no different in language and social organization from the other Arabs. Resettlement, therefore, would be in a familiar environment. If the local governments are unwilling to tackle the problem except on their own terms, there is little incentive for outside governments to continue financial support. Original humanitarian impulse which led to the creation and perpetuation of UNRWA is gradually being perverted into a political weapon.

1. May 19, 1958.

Abundance of volunteers
4,000 teenagers get work in Tel Aviv

Jerusalem Post Staff

Work has been found in Tel Aviv for some 4,000 teenage volunteers, the Municipal Emergency Headquarters reported yesterday.

Of these, 600 are in city hospitals, in Magen David Adom first aid stations, and in Shekem. Another 200 became wartime bakers and loaders of farm produce, helping assure a steady supply of provisions to the city's groceries and supermarkets.

About 900 youngsters spent the past few days digging trenches in parks and boulevards and putting up sandbags for air-raid shelters. Another 1,300 were engaged in filling sandbags and loading them on vehicles.

The Post Office has 100 volunteer teenage helpers, and Israel Television employed another 300 to conduct an opinion poll among viewers. Many girls do babysitting for mothers who operate businesses while their husbands are away at the front.

Volunteers are also engaged in sanitation work and garbage collection. The City reports that the amount of domestic refuse has dropped by 50 per cent since the outbreak of fighting.

Yesterday, the Emergency Headquarters found it had overlooked one vital area: There is a shortage of *shohatim* — ritual slaughterers. There is plenty of fowl, but not enough people to slaughter them.

DENTAL CARE

The Haifa Dental Surgeons Association yesterday announced the opening today of an emergency service for residents whose regular dentists have been called up. The service will operate daily, including holidays and sabbaths, at the clinic in Rehov Hagefen 26, from 8 to 10 a.m. and from 3 to 5 p.m. The nominal charge will be contributed to the Soldiers Welfare Association.

In Jerusalem, volunteers are being turned away.

"Half of the 4,000 volunteers who came to offer their services since the war began have been turned away because of a lack of suitable jobs," said Avraham Hornig, chief of volunteer services at the Jerusalem Municipality.

"But everyone who wants to do temporary unskilled work should still register with us; those with more qualifications should apply to the Labour Exchange," he added. He had high praise for "the overwhelming volunteer spirit of the people of Jerusalem," and urged them to be patient. "This will make it easier to find places for them."

Mr. Hornig said the long queues of volunteers largely comprised tourists, students "and others with inadequate skills and little knowledge of Hebrew." There are plenty of paying jobs for skilled workers — drivers of heavy vehicles, mechanics, plumbers.

"This is the fifth time I've been here," said Steven Goldberg, a tourist from Vermont, in the queue. "I was lucky to get work loading sugar and helping out at a bakery for a while... It seems you need *proteksia* these days to get a volunteer job."

Protective sandbags—the work of volunteer youngsters— line the entrance to a pedestrian underpass near Tel Aviv's Carmel Market.

No scheme for relief has won Arab acceptance. Many proposals have been rejected precisely because their implementation would help solve the refugee problem and thus remove a source of irritation between Arab and Jew.

A spectacular instance is to be found in the long negotiations conducted between 1953 and 1956 on a project for the coordinated use of the Jordan and Yarmuk Rivers. Israel was prepared to cooperate in this plan. U.S. Ambassador Eric Johnston summed up his experience in the following words:

> *Between 1953 and 1956, at the request of President Eisenhower, I undertook to negotiate with these States a comprehensive Jordan Valley development plan that would have provided for the irrigation of some 225,000 acres....After two years of discussion, technical experts of Israel, Jordan, Lebanon and Syria agreed upon every important detail of a unified Jordan plan. But in October 1956, it was rejected for political reasons at a meeting of the Arab League....Three years have passed and no agreement has yet been reached on developing the Jordan. Every year, a billion cubic meters of precious water still roll down the ancient stream, wasted, to the Dead Sea.*

It cannot be doubted that Arab Governments have determined that the refugees shall remain refugees; and that the aim of wrecking any alternative to repatriation has been pursued by these governments, as Abba Eban has so aptly put it, "with an ingenuity worthy of a better cause."

Make no mistake about it—the phrase "The legitimate rights of the Palestinians" is merely a euphemistic cloak for the utter destruction of the state of Israel, and as a by-product, the liquidation of the Israelis. If you should doubt this, listen to the pronouncements of the Palestinian guerilla leaders.

For years, the Jewish State resisted the notion of re-absorption of the Palestinian refugees on the grounds that a half-million Arabs nurtured on hate would constitute a formidable fifth column in a body of three million Jews.

Events have confirmed the validity of this objection. Hardly a week passes that some bomb outrage does not occur. Terrorism has become the political arm of the Palestinians; their avowed purpose is not the relocation of the refugees, but the destruction of Israel and the "recapture" of Palestine. You have but to listen to them. Their words are clear, and their actions are clearer. They kill athletes at Munich, children at Maalot, and Catholic tourists in the Tel Aviv airport— indiscriminately.

One has only to read the statement made by the Jordanian Finance Minister, Wahab Majli. At the close of the 1967 War, when Israel permitted those displaced by the war to return to their homes in captured territory on the West Bank of the Jordan, that grateful Minister publicly urged refugees to return to the West Bank "to help your brothers continue their political action and remain a thorn in the flesh of the aggressor until the crisis has been solved."

What sane Israeli statesman would have dared to import into the midst of his country a huge group of such "thorns"?

When the world press deplores the plight of the Palestinian refugees, it is quite understandable. But when that same press, regards the Jew as the usurper, it is most irksome.

In an address made on October 9, 1962, the then Israeli Foreign Minister, Golda Meir, said to the General Assembly of the United Nations:

> *What is the basic problem? It is the denial by the Arab states of Israel's right to exist. If this attitude were to change, and if the Arab States and Israel were to discuss their differences at the conference table in a frank and open manner, I am positive that solutions could be found on all the specific issues.*
>
> *Year after year, Israel has come to this rostrum with one demand—peace between it and its Arab neighbors. The Arab denial of Israel's right of existence has a direct bearing on the distressing refugee problem. We are willing, and always have been willing, to discuss with the Arab governments what can best be done to secure the future of the refugees in the light of the political and economic realities in the region. But a natural solution to the problem is frustrated by the Arab dream of destroying Israel, and the openly proclaimed Arab intention of using the refugees for this purpose.*
>
> *This design has been openly propagated even from the rostrum of this Assembly. This small spot of land, in which the Jewish people have revived their*

ancient home and nationhood, must again
be wrested from them, and they again be
scattered to the four corners of the earth.
Our neighbors have tried to achieve this
by various means, open or guerilla
warfare, economic boycott, propaganda,
and threats.

Negotiations and conciliation are
proclaimed from this rostrum as the
method to solve all other problems in
the world except this one, which must,
according to these spokesmen, be
resolved by force. For every other nation,
they claim co-existence, practiced in
peace. For Israel, non-existence, to be
achieved by war.

I recall a conversation with Yehoshafat
Harkabi, the author of *Arab Attitudes Toward
Israel.* Mr. Harkabi speaks and reads Arabic
fluently, and has been monitoring Arab
broadcasts for years. He has also been reading
their newspapers, their books, and the speeches
made by their religious leaders.

I asked him whether he believed that there was
any chance in the foreseeable future that the Arabs
might arrange a peace with Israel.

He thought for a moment, and then said: "Well
even if they did, they would find some excuse to
break it the very next day or so. In their present
state of mind, they just couldn't live at peace with
Israel."

I asked him why, and he answered: "It's really
very simple. Today, the Arab can blame any
failure within his country on the damnable Jew.
He can say 'Well, if it weren't for the Israelis, if it
weren't for the fact that we have to spend all our
money building up armaments, we could
accomplish miracles.' This is their pat excuse for
non-action.

"But comes a peace, and the Arab has no one to
pin his failures on. Then he is confronted with
the stark fact that a great many of his people are
close to starvation, that most of his peasants
are living in poverty, and that the majority of his
population is illiterate, and that he is failing to keep
up with the march of civilization. By comparison
with the Jewish State, he is deemed backward.

"The comparison is a stench in his nostrils.
The only way he can overcome this odious
comparison is to go to war and fight the Israelis
over and over again. Now he can once again
rationally excuse his economic and social failures
by attributing them to the need to make
expenditures of money and effort to retrieve his
honor.

"The jealousy of the Arab is boundless.
It is his undoing."

I T IS WEDNESDAY, October 17th.

Since the outbreak of fighting, U. S. Jews have
collected 675 million dollars in emergency funds
for Israel.

So far, 50,000 volunteers from the United States
are registered to go to Israel to help, however
needed.

Tourists departing for home from Lod Airport
make last minute donations from among their
possessions—giving whatever money they have left,
and even their jewels, to Israel's defense. Some
even leave their wedding rings.

A spokesman for the U.S. Defense Department
reveals that North Korean pilots are flying Migs on
the Egyptian front.

Teddy Kollek, the mayor of Jerusalem, awards a
prize to Abraham Abramovitz for having erected
the city's best decorated Succah.

The Commissioner of Internal Revenue
announces that war costs are running roughly to
10 million dollars each *hour*.

Twenty thousand senior civic employees of Israel
have offered to support the War Loan by each
donating one full month's salary.

Because of blackout regulations, egg production
has dropped severely.

Yeshiva students thread through the wards of the
Hadassah Hospital in Jerusalem, bringing the
Succoth holiday spirit to the wounded who are too
ill to attend services in the hospital synagogue.

SIMHAT TORA—No Publication

Chabad Hassidim bring cheer to the soldiers on the Suez front.

SIMHAT TORA, the Feast of the Rejoicing in the Law, is, after Purim, the most riotous holiday in the Jewish religious calendar. On Simhat Tora, the annual reading of the scrolls of the law is completed; and on that very same day, the reading of those scrolls is immediately begun again, from the first sentence.

On this day, in every Jewish community throughout the world, all Tora scrolls but one are remove from the Holy Ark. Selected worshippers carry the Scrolls of the Law, which have been bedecked with silver ornaments, and circle the pulpit seven times. All men present are called upon to read a portion of the Tora. The reading is repeated as many times as may be necessary, so that every congregant is accorded the honor.

In the Diaspora, for reasons which date far back in history and which are beyond the scope of this book, two days of religious celebration wind up the Succoth festival. In Israel, Simhat Tora was always confined to one day. But the evening of that second day is observed as a holiday, even in Israel. On that last evening, the scrolls of the law are taken out from their places of repose in the Holy Arks of the synagogues, and are carried in

SIMHAT TORA 5734

War Loan collections, 'Yizkor' prayers dominate

By SARAH HONIG
Jerusalem Post Reporter

TEL AVIV. — The Simhat Tora holiday atmosphere was scarcely evident in the city streets yesterday, but the war was felt inside the synagogues.

The traditional *hakafot* — street dancing by celebrants bearing Tora scrolls in their arms — were cancelled this year due to the blackout, and the festivities were thus limited to synagogues. In the few synagogues that were properly blacked out they were held after sundown. But most services and *hakafot* were held earlier to beat the blackout.

A few hundred Bukharan and Salonikan Jews defied the blackout, however, and danced through the darkened streets, bearing Tora scrolls.

Inside the synagogues the atmosphere was far more sombre than usual, as morning *Yizkor* services were held for the IDF's fallen. Speedy recovery wishes went out to the wounded, and prayers were said for prisoners of war. Most rabbis delivered sermons on the war.

The children were there as usual, with their gaily decorated paper flags topped by apples and candles. There was dancing and reading from the Tora, but the conversations revolved exclusively around the war, as congregants analysed the tank battle strategy.

SIZABLE SUMS

Rabbis and congregation leaders took the opportunity to urge the public to make contributions to the Voluntary War Loan, and sizable sums were donated in many synagogues. It is usually a tradition for someone invited to read from the Tora on this holiday to make a donation to some charity. This time there was only one cause to which people were willing to contribute — the War Loan drive.

Even in the most ultra-orthodox (and of the anti-Zionist) centres of Bnei Brak, generous contributions to the war effort were reported.

Residents of the Florentine Quarter here, where especially colourful mass *hakafot* take place every year, told *The Jerusalem Post* they were disappointed that the situation this Simhat Tora did not allow them to hold their public street celebrations. But they promised that "very soon, when we have won, we will hold an extraordinary second Simhat Tora, the links of which this city has never seen. The Arabs will not deprive us of our celebrations."

In Safad, old rabbis and young *yeshiva* students, headed by Safad's Sephardi Chief Rabbi David Dayan, walked seven times around the graves of Rabbi Shimon Bar Yohai and his son Eliezer at Meron, on Wednesday, chanting centuries-old prayers and quotations from the Zohar, the ancient book of Kabbalist mysticism. The incantations, against the dangers and afflictions threatening the People of Israel and for its success in battle, were ordained by the 16th century Rabbi Yosef Karo, author of the "Shulhan Aruch," for times of trial and crisis.

Second *hakafot* to mark the end of the Simhat Tora holiday were held at Jerusalem's Shaare Zedek and Hadassah Hospitals last night, with Gadna youngsters, volunteers and *yeshiva* students giving the wounded an eagerly accepted lift with their singing and dancing.

The synagogue at Shaare Zedek was thronged last night with dancers carrying Tora scrolls some of them injured soldiers with one arm in a sling. Loud music — rarely heard in a hospital — was provided by a combo for four young U.S. volunteers. Doctors, administrative workers and a burly military policeman joined in the *hakafot*, while nurses and Bnei Akiva girls joined the singing from behind the *mehitza* (separting wall) of the women's section.

DANCING IN WARDS

On Wednesday evening, the beginning of Simhat Tora, the young visitors had also gone upstairs into the wards, singing and carrying Tora scrolls (instrumental music is not allowed on Sabbaths and holidays).

The faces of the injured lit up as they kissed the Tora scrolls carried past the beds by the dancers, Dr. Morris Weinberg said. "None of the doctors or nurses could hold back tears," he added.

Second *hakafot* were also held at Beit Hanassi last night, with President Efraim Katzir joining in the dancing. The dancers, *yeshiva* students and members of the Mount Zion Committee had earlier circled the walls of the Old City dancing, in compliance with a Biblical verse.

Oil trouble the cause, not result of war

by Moshe Ater
POST Economic Editor

Israel was taken unawares by the war largely because we underrated the Arab military machine and the resources prepared to attack us. "But the biggest surprise of all," writes the London "Economist," "is the fact that Egypt and Syria should have chosen to go to war just when they were thought to believe that the pressure the Arab oil-producers could bring to bear on the United States, and therefore on Israel, would give them what they wanted within a few years without a war. Why did they do it?"

The answer is close at hand if only one gets rid of the popular notion that American Presidents support this country in order to please the Jewish electors or the money-bags, ready to risk an armed clash with the Soviets in order to defend Israel. It should be self-evident that American policies of such far-reaching extent, of such global implications, can only be dictated by genuine longterm American interests, which may —or may not—parallel our interests. Once one realizes that from the American point of view, the borders — and even the existence — of Israel are subordinate to other considerations, the pieces of the puzzle fall in their places.

Why does the U.S. not show any sign of yielding to the threat of an Arab oil embargo? Obviously because everybody knows that nothing can be gained by yielding to it, because the world energy situation will not be changed by the outcome of the Israel-Arab conflict, and whatever happens here the oil sheikhs will still be in a position to exert pressure on their customers — as long as the latter are not united—to exact stiffer terms, commercial, financial or political, for their deliveries, to a point

where these terms may become intolerable. It stands to reason that a victory over Israel would strengthen their prestige. It would spell the withdrawal of the West from the Middle ast, which would then fall totally under Soviet influence. Nato would be outflanked from the south, with the Mediterranean ruled by the Soviet fleet. In this global strategic issue Israel is a crucial factor.

The explanation proffered by the "Economist" reverses this grim situation by presenting the conflict between the two super-powers as a consequence of Arab hostility and Israeli stubbornness, and the threatening oil crisis as a consequence, and not the cause, of the present war. The simple fact, clear of diplomatic formulas, is that the present war is being fought over Middle East oil and strategic strongholds, that it has been waged with Russian connivance and in accordance with a Soviet-prepared plan, in which the Arabs play the role of cat's-paw, with Israel assigned the role of victim and prize.

Though Dr. Kissinger still hesitates to accept the fact, the Day of Atonement marked the collapse of his laboriously constructed policy of detente and disarmament. Scarcely has the U.S. succeeded in extracting itself from Vietnam before it has become involved in another bloody conflict of even graver consequences. If it is not already the Third World War, it is the prelude to it.

The timing of the Arab attack

can also be understood if it is seen in perspective, in which not Sadat's ruses but considerations concerning the Soviet drive to the Persion Gulf, the Indian Ocean, and Africa, are the major determinants. This drive must have been accorded higher priority in view of the rapid progress made by Iran, which could before long become a major military factor obstructing Russia's advance. The growing Finlandisation of Europe, visible in Chancellor Brandt's "Ostpolitik" and in the weakening of Nato, has untied Russia's hands for another military adventure. The Watergate affair, the internal tieup in the U.S., and the growing isolationist mood both there and in other Western countries, must have been evaluated by the Soviet leaders as a golden opportunity for a strike. Once the decision was taken to make use of it, the resultant tactical moves followed in due course — from the hardened Soviet stance in the Second Salt talks to open support of Palestinian terrorists to the premeditated attack on the Day of Attonement.

This attack is no Pearl Harbour, it is more akin to the Munich appeasement, when Western leaders washed their hands of Czechoslovakia in a vain attempt to avoid "war in our lifetime." This escapist attitude, which now prevails in particular in Western Europe, makes Israel appear as the warmonger, or at least an unfortunate cause of the conflict, while in fact, Israel's borders and the future of the Palestinians are only a pretext for the conflagration. Israel did not submit to aggressors, did not surrender to its fate, like the Czechs. But the outcome of its struggle depends not only on its valour but also on a change in the world political scene.

---

processions through the streets, accompanied by dancing and singing.

Also, in many cities, communities, and army bases in Israel, special celebrations are held. Eminent military and political personnel are accorded the honor of carrying the Tora scrolls at the head of the processions.

In general, in Israel, Simhat Tora is celebrated as a day of fun. The kids are home from school—in fact, this is the last day of their vacation. It is a time for parties, a time for merrymaking. Families go out on

picnics, on jaunts, go a-visiting. A light-heartedness prevails.

In stark contrast to other years, the Simhat Tora of 1973 was tremendously subdued—almost sad— and markedly devoid of the usual levity. The nation, as a whole, was plunged in gloom. By and large, the people were mourning for friends and relatives killed or maimed in war. Everyone was saddened; everyone seemed to have been touched by the hand of death.

Ethiopia sends wishes for peace

Jerusalem Post Diplomatic Correspondent

Emperor Haile Selassie of Ethiopia has conveyed to Israel's government and people his "sincere wishes and hopes for an end to the human suffering and for an agreed solution to the Middle East conflict which will bring lasting peace for the good of all the peoples in the region."

The message was delivered during a 45-minute audience with Israel's Ambassador in Addis Ababa, Hanan Eynor, on Tuesday.

Officials in Jerusalem appeared pleased with the Emperor's sentiments — especially since they were conveyed at this time, when many African states have aligned themselves behind Egypt in the current war.

THE MILLION-MEMBER Mexican Federation of Farmers has sent greetings to Israel, wishing it "victory in your people's war to preserve your independence." The message, received by the Israel Farmers' Federation here, was signed by Carlos Ramos, president of the Mexican organization.

BBC reporters protest biased coverage by their home office

By MACABEE DEAN
Jerusalem Post Reporter

TEL AVIV. — Members of the British Broadcasting Corporation (BBC) "32" news teams and of "Panorama," now in Israel to cover the war, yesterday cabled the head office in England to protest the BBC's "biased reporting of the war."

It is understood that they claimed the BBC's good name for accurate and impartial reporting was in jeopardy.

It was said that the BBC was broadcasting "Arab claims as the truth," even though past experience has shown that "Israeli reports in the main have been accurate," while those from the "Arab countries have often been exaggerated or even untruthful."

In one case, it was pointed out, the BBC preferred to accept a report from the Syrian army spokesman as the truth, even though the BBC's own man was at the spot on the Syrian front and filed an entirely different version of what was happening.

Volunteer M.D.'s From all over the World Head to Israel

Jerusalem's Hadassah Hospital yesterday reported that more than 20 volunteer doctors had arrived from abroad since the beginning of the war. The hospital, which serves as national clearing house for the volunteers, says they include a father-and-son surgical team from Argentina, six doctors from France, and eight from the U.S., including orthopaedic and plastic surgeons. In one husband-and-wife team from the U.S., both spouses are radiologists, in another the husband is a surgeon and the wife a nurse.

Many Hadassah department heads and specialists have cut short their sabbatical years abroad and returned home. The dean of the Hebrew University-Hadassah Medical School, Prof. Aharon Beller, has just come back from a congress of neuro-surgeons in Tokyo.

One of the most spontaneous volunteer movements since the present struggle began has come from the inmates of Israel prisons. Prisons Commissioner Arye Nir told *The Post* yesterday that the prisoners were among the first to donate blood, giving more than 700 blood portions in the war's first few days. Some prisoners wanted to give more than one portion, he added.

A number of prisoners who are heavy equipment mechanics have asked to be allowed to work in army repair workshops. Since the start of hostilities the inmates of Tel Mond's youth wing have been digging trenches and other activities under Gadna supervision.

Prison Commissioner Nir added that all Israeli prisons are quiet. There had been no incidents between Jewish and Arab prisoners, and "some Arab prisoners were even among those who donated blood."

JERUSALEM   MUNICIPALITY

Emergency Branch

The Jerusalem Municipality Emergency Branch requests all inhabitants who built succot to leave the **thatching (schach)** in the yards of their homes until further notice, as at the present time there are no facilities for collecting it, owing to the call-up.

In the Simhat Tora of 1973, a blackout prevailed. As soon as the sun went down, the worshippers in the synagogues were obliged to pull down the blinds so that no light would shine through the windows.

The synagogues, for the most part, were filled with women, with young children, and with old men. The flower of the country was at the front. But, as if to defy fate, the old men grabbed the little children and swung them to their shoulders and danced around the Holy Ark, raising the children aloft as Tora Scrolls. It was a gesture of defiance against fate. It was the will to live incarnate.

The few soldiers in the synagogue who had come home on leave, the women, everyone else, couldn't contain their tears. Perhaps the youth and the grown men had gone off to war, but the old men were now lifting the very new generation. This was their banner. This was the future.

ISRAEL OBSERVERS:

Sadat's aim: dismemberment of Israel

Jerusalem Post Diplomatic Correspondent

President Sadat's speech of yesterday was seen in Jerusalem as clearly revealing his ultimate aim: the dismemberment of the Jewish State. He spoke of two stages in Egyptian policy. First, to force a cease-fire with Israel undertaking to withdraw to the pre-'67 lines; and then to summon an international peace conference to discuss "restoring the rights of the Palestinians"

— which is a euphemism for taking apart the State of Israel.

If the peace conference failed to materialize, observers in Jerusalem pointed out, Egypt could then launch an attack similar to the Yom Kippur attack — but this time from the pre-'67 lines — with imaginable results.

A top Israeli diplomat currently in New York referred to the Sadat speech as "the speech of a man who

wants neither ceasefire nor peace."

Strengthening t h i s assessment was the tone of the Egyptian leader's address. He simply did not relate to Israel as a possible partner in dialogue or negotiation. The tone was "one of dictation, not of negotiation," an observer said. There was "a boastfulness and arrogance born of an initial military advantage which is going to be meagre and transient," the Israeli observer said.

ON THE TOP of this page, there is a news item to the effect that Sadat's aim is the dismemberment of Israel. Many Americans may believe, along with Kissinger, that the Israelis are paranoid, that they credit at face value every bogeyman who talks big and loud and hopes to bluster himself into courage.

Yet in a recent poll, as the columns of the Post will disclose, 85 percent of all Israelis fully believe that Sadat aims to carve up Israel and annihilate its inhabitants.

The people of Israel believe that had they not been strong enough to resist the repeated Arab attacks, there would have been an Islamic holocaust. Along with the psalmist, they repeat:

> Had it not been for the Lord who
>   protected us, may Israel now say;
> Had it not been the Lord, who protected
>   us, when men rose up against us;
> Then had they swallowed us up alive,
>   when their wrath was kindled
>   against us,
> Then had the waters overwhelmed us,
>   the streams would have entirely
>   encompassed us;
> Then had the proud waters rolled over us.
> Blessed is the Lord who hath not given us
>   as a prey to their teeth.[1]

Putting this in other terms, the common Israeli is of the opinion that today's Arab hatred of the Jew does not depend on substantive grievances, and is therefore beyond appeasement.

Moreover, most Israeli leaders hold to this opinion. And most scholars who have studied the situation tend to agree.

In a study entitled *Arab Attitudes Toward Israel,*[2] Yehoshofat Harkabi, a former Israeli Chief of Intelligence and a top Arabist, reached the melancholy conclusion that there was simply nothing the Israelis could do to mollify the Arabs short of committing suicide. A look at some of the statements made by Arab leaders in the past 15 years must convince the reader of the truth of this conclusion.

Writing an introduction to a book entitled *The End of Israel,* Ahmed Said, the director of Cairo Radio, stated:

> The collapse of Israel, this is the hope in
> which we live. The time has come for us
> to consider it, to discuss and map out
> the road to this collapse.

On Cairo Radio on April 20, 1962, the commentator declared:

> Israel is the cancer, the malignant wound,
> in the body of Arabism, for which there
> is no cure but eradication....There is no
> need to emphasize that the liquidation of
> Israel and the restoration of the
> plundered Palestine Arab land are at
> the head of our national objectives.

On February 22, 1965, Nasser, speaking at the Festival of Unity, declared:

> Arab unity means the liquidation of Israel
> and the expansionist dreams of Zionism.

1. Psalm 124.

2. Keter Publishing, Jerusalem, 1971.

On October 6, 1960, the *Middle East Record* reports a statement by Hashim Jawad, in which he said:

> *Israel, being an alien body in the Arab homeland, has no right whatsoever to continue to exist in the territories of the Arab East.*

Arab statesmen have always said that all they want is a restoration to the 1948 borders. Is this true, or is this just poppycock?

Let's look at the record.

On May 18, 1962, Nasser declared to the newspaper Al-Ahram:

> *It is not the intention to restore half of our honour or half the homeland, but the whole of our honour and the whole of our homeland.*

On May 14, 1961, Nasir al-Din al-Nashashibi explained in Al-Jumhuriyya:

> *We do not want to return with the flag of Israel flying on a single square metre of our country, and if indeed we wish to return, this is an honoured and honourable return and not a degrading return, not a return that will make us citizens in the State of Israel.*

The literature abounds with statements and declarations which have spewed forth from every Arab capital. "Israel *delenda est.*"[1] The situation was reviewed and summed up in 1964 in a book written by Professor Bernard Lewis, head of the Department of History at the School of Oriental and African studies of the University of London. Professor Lewis wrote:

> *They [the Arabs] are agreed that Israel must be destroyed, though not on how this should be accomplished. The official Arab demand is no longer for immediate destruction of Israel, but for its reduction to the frontiers laid down in the 1947 partition proposals—obviously as a first step towards its disappearance.*

Yet, say some apologists, "Ah, this was in the long ago, some ten years back. Things have changed now. All the Arabs want is to get a home

for their refugees, and to retrieve their tarnished honor. Give them back the territories they have lost, resettle their refugees, and all will be well."

Let's put on the witness stand Mr. Heikal, for many years the editor of Al-Ahram, the most prestigious newspaper in Egypt, a journal known to reflect government opinion. In one of his articles, Heikal describes what King Hussein had to say to him on November 27, 1963:

> *I have information in my possession that the United States intends to bring all possible pressure to bear in order to get a solution of the refugee problem, imagining that that is all that is left of the problem of Palestine.*

In other words, says Hussein, the world might think that the refugee problem is the big problem for we Arabs, but the settlement of the refugee problem would nevertheless not solve the problem between Arab and Jew. Not by a long shot!

Perhaps the most revealing statement on the matter of appeasing the Arabs was made by Professor Walid al-Khalidi of the American University in Beirut, whose particular field of research is the Arab-Israeli conflict. In an article called "Reappraisal: An Examination of Certain Western Attitudes to the Palestine Problem," the professor wrote:

> *It is sometimes suggested that the way to solve the Palestine problem is to approach it in a piecemeal fashion. You must nibble at the problem until you end up by swallowing it. Settle the refugees and the biggest obstacle to the solution will be removed. But the Palestine problem will remain as acute as ever with every Palestine refugee settled. The refugees may be outward evidence of the crime which must be tidied out of sight but nothing will remove the scar of Palestine from Arab hearts.*
> *The solution of the Palestine problem cannot be found in the settlement of the refugees nor even in the return to the 1947 partition decision.*

The professor makes it clear beyond any peradventure that what the Arabs are seeking is far more than what they talk about in polite conversation. The professor didn't tell any secrets to the Israeli public. They have known about Arab

1. Israel must be destroyed.

intentions for years and years and years. It is only the American public who have been hoodwinked.

Mr. Harkabi's conclusions are most dismal. In his study, he writes that every fiber of Arab life is infected with hatred for the Jew, and that nothing indicates the imminence of an about-face. Until there is a basic change of attitude, Harkabi believes, any hints of accommodation that Arab leaders give to visiting firemen, feature writers for *Newsweek,* senators from Alabama, or members of governing bodies from European countries or from the United States, have no bearing on the basic situation. At this point, the hate is so ingrained that it will take a dedicated movement from within to eradicate it.

If one wants to know whether Arab protestations of their desire for peace are at all sincere, one simply has to ask whether at any time—I repeat, at any time at all—any Arab statesman has said to his people, "I think it is time that we concentrated on improving the lot of our masses at home. I think it is time for us to abandon the fight with Israel, to take all the money that we've been pouring into armaments, and put such money instead into productive public works. I think it is time that we stretched out a hand of peace to our neighbor who has been trying so hard to live in peace with us."

Yes, there was one Arab who once hinted at something along these lines, and a few weeks later he found himself a dead man. His name was Abdullah—father of Hussein—and he was King of Jordan until that fateful day in 1951. As far as the Arabs were concerned, the mere statement that peace with Israel might be considered, was treasonable.

The question then arises, "What is the basic reason why the Arabs hate the Jews with such fierceness?" To answer this question, one must turn the pages of history.

For a period of nearly 400 years before the First World War, the lands of the Near East were under the dominion of the Ottoman Turks. The countries we know as Palestine, Syria, Yemen, Iraq, Saudi Arabia, Kuwait, and Jordan were ruled from Constantinople. They were mere satrapies of a vast empire that ruled unfeelingly, and whose only objective was revenue.

But not for 440-odd years *before* the coming of the Ottoman Turks—not since the dominion of the Arab Caliphates ended in 1071 A.D.—had these lands been independent Arab states. In the course of nearly 850 years, a once flourishing Arab culture had decayed, and Arab nationalism had all but reached the vanishing point.

In 1918, when British armies under Lord Allenby liberated these vast territories from the Turks, feudal overlordship was exercised by local sheikhs.

In 1916, Hussein ibn Ali, the Sherif of Mecca, proclaimed himself King of Hedjaz, a region which is now part of Saudi Arabia. In that same year, T. E. Lawrence, attached to Emir Feisal as liaison officer of the British, was instrumental in arming and financing the Arab rebellion against the Turks.

In 1917, the combined troops of Feisal and Lawrence captured Akaba. In 1918, the troops of Feisal and Lawrence entered Damascus.

During the Versailles Peace Conference, held at the close of World War I in 1919, the Allies decided to ratify Hussein's rule of Hedjaz, and to arrange mandates of other Turkish holdings; these were divided into kingdoms and dominions which subsequently assumed the designations Yemen, Iraq, Kuwait, Saudi Arabia, Syria, etc. The greater part of the land wrested from Turkey was thus formed into Arab polities. Syria was mandated to the French; and Palestine was mandated to the British.

The Jews living in these Turkish-dominated lands had taken part in the war against the Turks and had contributed to the Allied forces a brigade of soldiers who fought with the avowed objective of driving the Turks out of Palestine and putting the land under the control of the Western powers.

During this period, the Aaronsohn family, along with Absalom Feinberg were the leaders of a tiny band of Palestinian Jews known as the Nili spies. Their feats became legendary.[1] "I would set fire to the Turks as one lights a candle if it would achieve our aim," wrote Feinberg. The aim was to release Palestine from the grip of the Turkish Empire. As Yosef Lishansky was hanged in Damascus, he shouted from the gallows: "Long live the English redeemers!"

The Allied leaders deemed it fitting to reward the efforts of the Jews by promising part of the British mandate in Palestine to the Jewish people as a haven and refuge for those who wished to settle there.

Accordingly, on the 2nd day of November, 1917, Lord Arthur James Balfour, then British Foreign Secretary, sent a letter to Lord Rothschild, a respected Jewish leader, as follows:

I have much pleasure in conveying to you, on behalf of His Majesty's Government, the following declaration of sympathy with Jewish Zionist aspirations which has been

---

1. See *The First Million Sabras,* Herbert Russcol and Margalit Banai, page 70, Hart Publishing Co., Inc., 1970.

submitted to, and approved by, the Cabinet.

His Majesty's Government view with favour the establishment in Palestine of a national home for the Jewish people, and will use their best endeavours to facilitate the achievement of this object, it being clearly understood that nothing shall be done which may prejudice the civil and religious rights of existing non-Jewish communities in Palestine, or the rights and political status enjoyed by Jews in any other country.

I should be grateful if you would bring this declaration to the knowledge of the Zionist Federation.

At this point in history, there were no popular Arab nationalist movements, and no one opposed this concession to the Jews. Nor was the promise made to the Jews under the Balfour Declaration regarded by anyone as a violation of any promise made to the Arabs.

Through the intervention of Lawrence, a meeting was arranged at the Peace Conference in Versailles between the Emir Feisal—the son of Hussein ibn Ali, the King of Hedjaz—and Dr. Chaim Weizmann, the Zionist leader. Lawrence acted as interpreter and adviser to the Arabian Emir.

On January 3, 1919, both of the conferees became signatories to the following document:

His Royal Highness the Emir Feisal, representing and acting on behalf of the Arab Kingdom of Hedjaz, and Dr. Chaim Weizmann, representing and acting on behalf of the Zionist Organisation, mindful of the racial kinship and ancient bonds existing between the Arabs and the Jewish people, and realising that the surest means of working out the consummation of their national aspirations is through the closest possible collaboration in the development of the Arab State and Palestine, and being desirous further of confirming the good understanding which exists between them, have agreed upon the following Articles:

ARTICLE I

The Arab State and Palestine in all their relations and undertakings shall be controlled by the most cordial goodwill and understanding, and to this end Arab and Jewish duly accredited agents shall be established and maintained in the respective territories.

ARTICLE II

Immediately following the completion of the deliberations of the Peace Conference, the definite boundaries between the Arab State and Palestine shall be determined by a Commission to be agreed upon by the parties hereto.

ARTICLE III

In the establishment of the Constitution and Administration of Palestine all such measures shall be adopted as will afford the fullest guarantees for carrying into effect the British Government's Declaration of the 2d of November, 1917.

ARTICLE IV

All necessary measures shall be taken to encourage and stimulate immigration of Jews into Palestine on a large scale, and as quickly as possible to settle Jewish immigrants upon the land through closer settlement and intensive cultivation of the soil. In taking such measures the Arab peasant and tenant farmers shall be protected in their rights, and shall be assisted in forwarding their economic development.

ARTICLE V

No regulation nor law shall be made prohibiting or interfering in any way with the free exercise of religion; and further the free exercise and enjoyment of religious profession and worship without discrimination or reference shall forever be allowed. No religious test shall ever be required for the exercise of civil or political rights.

ARTICLE VI

The Mohammedan Holy Places shall be under Mohammedan control.

ARTICLE VII

The Zionist Organisation proposes to send to Palestine a Commission of experts to make a survey of the economic possibilities of the country, and to report upon the best means for its development. The Zionist Organisation will place the aforementioned Commission at the disposal of the Arab State for the purpose of a survey of the economic possibilities of the Arab State and to report upon the best means for its development. The Zionist Organisation will use its best

On the home front Helga Dudman

SUNDAY WAS the day uniforms appeared in city streets with soldiers in baggy, dusty fatigues and khaki work outfits stamped "Zahal" in yellow paint, turning up on brief leaves. Their presence made a world of difference — as did their messages to other families whose sons and husbands had not yet had time off.

The day before, many families set off, bearing cakes and underwear, for border areas to look for their men. One such patrol from the home front did not find their soldier, but instead came home with a long list of messages from other boys, to telephone to *their* families. After accomplishing this mission, the mother was rewarded by an incoming phone call reporting on her son:

"Avi saw your car on the road, but couldn't get off to join you. So he asked me to call you, since I was going on leave."

ANOTHER SIGHT on our city streets, observable ever since this war began, is the large number of young, able-bodied, v e r y healthy young men still going to their usual jobs and still wearing flowered shirts. Our friends abroad, who tend to be far more nervous than we are (just as we at home here tend to be more nervous than the front-line soldiers), would probably be surprised and heartened by the view here. Perhaps just one television shot for the overseas front, covering this aspect of our manpower supply, would help morale abroad.

THE BEIT Sokolow front is a good place to stay away from. In the early days of the war, when nobody knew anything and nobody in the centre of town really had very much to do, the communication commandos and public relations patrols sat around talking hard, frequently wearing odd bits of uniform from previous wars, over paunches and flared trousers. Rumours were manufactured and packaged for export: if only they could just be cracked and used to make omelettes.

Since then, there have been casualties among correspondents. On the front, their bravery and devotion to duty is as great as any. Individually they can be quite all right; but not when the herd instinct has been aroused, and when every seat around every table at the journalists' cafeteria has been taken, as though this were one of the world's finest restaurants (Menu suggestion: *"Schwitz du jour"*).

Perhaps they trudge bravely toward enemy lines, but correspondents refuse to walk a block or two from a legal parking space toward Destination Beit Sokolow where press-carded cars are double-parked and lawn-parked.

"I WANT my mother," came a very young voice, from far away over the telephone, late one night.

"Who is this?" asked the surprised Jerusalem housewife.

"This is Yossi, and I want my mother."

Yossi turned out to be a soldier trying to call home from the front, and had rung the wrong number. So goes our supermen's inner life.

SO YOU thought that Menahem Begin and Yitzhak Ben-Aharon had buried all their arguments for the duration? Not entirely. At an office where government leaders meet, not far from an office where girl soldiers work, Mr. Begin was waiting for a colleague when an unusually attractive — and, incidentally, unusually efficient — Navy girl walked past. Mr. Begin struck up a conversation.

The following day, he was sitting there with Mr. Ben-Aharon when the same girl came by.

"What a darling soldier we have here," the Histadrut Secretary-General accurately observed.

"Oh, I've known since yesterday," said the Herut leader with airy one-upmanship.

"ALL ARRANGEMENTS for the 'Tiyul to Sinai,' which will take place from November 11 till November 14, have now been finalized." So begins a notice from the Hitahdut Olei Britannia dated October 1 and received in Tel Aviv mailboxes on October 15. This could be taken by Arab intelligence as further proof of Israeli plans for aggression; especially as it closes on this ominous note: "Interested persons are advised to book early, as we already have a long waiting list."

Or else, one can take the attitude reflected in the following communication, shouted from one Tel Aviv balcony to the next:

"Yes, Shalom called last night. You know, we were going on a trip to Sinai next week. And imagine — he said he thought it still might be possible!"

ONE OF MANY, a small sad *brit mila* took place in a slum quarter near Tel Aviv last Sunday. The *mohel* was in uniform (one guest wondered what his military function might be); the father was absent and, at one point, the young mother burst into tears. Later, she consoled herself with the silver lining in the cloud: this way, she was spared the expensive celebration which the older generation of the family expected, but which she herself considered a terrible waste of money.

efforts to assist the Arab State in providing the means for developing the natural resources and economic possibilities thereof.

ARTICLE VIII
The parties hereto agree to act in

complete accord and harmony on all matters embraced herein before the Peace Congress.

ARTICLE IX
Any matters of dispute which may arise between the contracting parties shall be

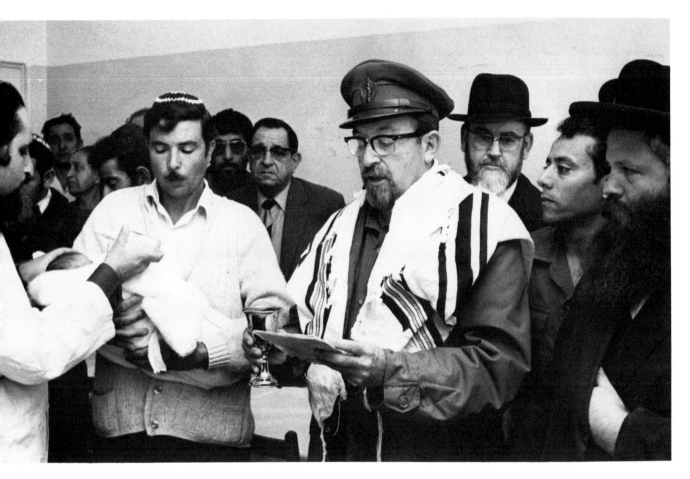

Army Chaplain Aluf Mordechai Piron conducts a Brit Milah ceremony for an infant whose father fell just before his birth.

referred to the British Government for arbitration.

Given under our hand at London, England, the third day of January, one thousand nine hundred and nineteen.
Chaim Weizmann.
Feisal ibn-Hussein.

RESERVATION BY THE EMIR FEISAL

If the Arabs are established as I have asked in my manifesto of January 4th addressed to the British Secretary of State for Foreign Affairs, I will carry out what is written in this agreement. If changes are made, I cannot be answerable for failing to carry out this agreement.
Feisal ibn-Hussein.

Note that in 1919 Emir Feisal, unlike his Saudi Arabian namesake of today, openly agreed to and

encouraged the "immigration of Jews into Palestine on a large scale."

Two months later to the day, Feisal wrote a letter to Felix Frankfurter, who represented the Zionist organization at Versailles. His letter, and Frankfurter's reply follow:

DELEGATION HEDJAZIENNE, *Paris, March 3, 1919.*

Dear Mr. Frankfurter: I want to take this opportunity of my first contact with American Zionists to tell you what I have often been able to say to Dr. Weizmann in Arabia and Europe.

We feel that the Arabs and Jews are cousins in race, having suffered similar oppressions at the hands of powers stronger than themselves, and by a happy

TENDING THE WOUNDED

The army spokesman announced on Sunday that 2,000 wounded Israeli soldiers were being given attention in Israeli hospitals. PHILIP GILLON reports on how Israel's medical profession is meeting the challenge of the Yom Kippur War.

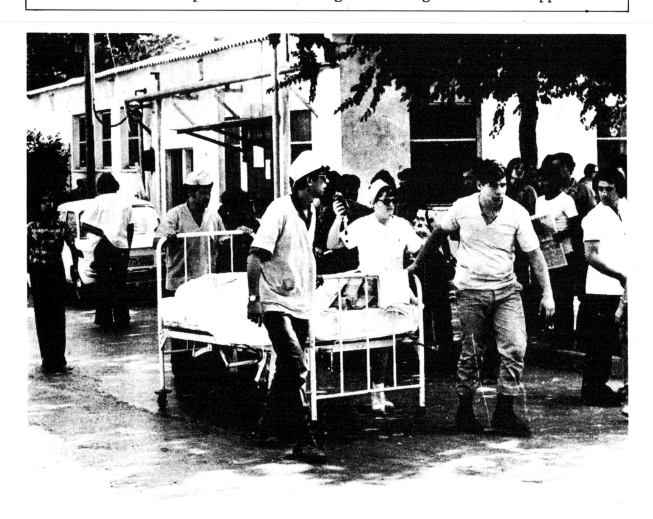

A WOUNDED MAN'S chances of survival depend on the speed with which he is given medical attention; shock, gangrene, or loss of blood can cost his life or cause him permanent incapacity if he is not given attention in time. Minutes a r e precious.

During the Six Day War, the Israel Army Medical Corps perfected a system whereby doctors were attached to fighting units, where they gave the wounded emergency treatment even before they were evacuated. Evacuation was effected, whenever possible, by helicopter — flying ambulances in which further attention was given while the w o u n d e d were being flown

straight to the Hadassah Hospital in Jerusalem, which had at its disposal all the sophisticated equipment needed. The system worked remarkably well, except that Hadassah had to handle over 1,000 casualties in three days, some doctors working **72** hours without sleep. This time, it was decided to spread t h e burden equally among all t h e country's hospitals.

There was another complication—the long lines of communication through the Sinai Desert. These imposed too much strain on transport for it to be possible to evacuate wounded straight to the major base hospitals. Hence a fully equipped field hospital, with two operating theatres, was

set up somewhere in the south, staffed by some of the best young surgeons in Israel.

The system has worked so smoothly that the balance between life and death, between permanent injury or complete recovery, has been tilted in favour of the wounded. Within an incredibly short time of being hit, they are already receiving saline drips against shock, whatever other fluids they may need, treatment to prevent gangrene. Their bleeding is stopped, their wounds are cleaned, broken bones a r e splinted, oxygen is administered.

Many moving stories are being told about the heroism and devotion of the doctors attached to the units or in the helicopters and Nord transports that are serving as flying ambulances. Urgent surgical operations have been performed in the air.

One man suddenly stopped breathing: the doctor operated on his windpipe and applied artificial respiration. The soldier survived. A n o t h e r seriously wounded tank man was suffering from severe shock and such heavy loss of blood from wounds that a needle could not be inserted in the upper part of the body. A tube was inserted into a vein in his leg, so that the necessary fluids could be administered to him. He lived.

AIDED BY this rapid treatment and the resilience of youth, the wounded soldiers do very much better than civilians injured in automobile accidents. Morale among the soldiers in hospital is astonishingly high. Within a day of admission, most of them are doing their best to keep up the spirits of their mothers or wives. They joke with each other about the war, recall their experiences w i t h o u t bitterness. Around them cluster relatives, Chen girls, Ya'al volunteers, any

friends who can get through the guards at the door.

Transistor r a d i o s, games, books, sweets and cigarettes are pouring into the hospital — even television sets. Volunteers by the thousands are offering their services, and are placed somehow in posts as cooks, clerks, telephonists, messenger girls, drivers by the score.

Among the surgeons, the greatest pressure is on the orthopaedists — some cases have bone injuries as well as other wounds. General surgeons, ophthalmologists and neuro-surgeons all face the complicated cases that are flown up north from t h e field hospital. But since the spread of cases throughout the hospitals in the country has been so efficient, and since all non-urgent civilian operations have been postponed for the duration, the surgeons are not overwhelmed by the emergency.

SHOULD THEY have any difficulty, there are literally thousands of doctors — some of them non-Jews — begging for a chance to come to Israel. During the war of attrition, over 20 orthopaedic surgeons came as volunteers from the United States for periods of

one month or more. Seven of them arrived back here within a few days of the outbreak of hostilities.

Dr. Herbert Hechtman, of Boston University, a general surgeon, brought a complete team, consisting, besides himself, of a chest surgeon and three radiologists. Many other surgeons, general and specialist, have come w i t h o u t waiting to be asked to do so.

Particularly moving, perhaps, is the arrival of a team of French doctors — a cardiologist, two plastic surgeons, two anaesthetists a general practitioner and a fifth year student — who turned up without prior notice. From Argentina came a father and son, both surgeons. There should certainly be no shortage of doctors.

Offers of medical equipment are also pouring in from all parts of the world. One night, word came that a consignment of human serum albumen, packed in dry ice, had arrived in Lod Airport, sent by a hospital in San Francisco. It was picked up at 2 a.m. and rushed into cold storage. A woman in England, who owns her own private plane, offered to fill it with medical supplies and to fly it to Israel at her own expense.

---

coincidence have been able to take the first step towards the attainment of their national ideals together.

We Arabs, especially the educated among us, look with the deepest sympathy on the Zionist movement. Our deputation here in Paris is fully acquainted with the proposals submitted yesterday by the Zionist Organization to the Peace Conference, and we regard them as moderate and proper. We will do our best, in so far as we are concerned, to help them through: we will wish the Jews a most hearty welcome home.

With the chiefs of your movement, especially with Dr. Weizmann, we have had and continue to have the closest relations. He has been a great helper of our cause, and I hope the Arabs may soon be in a position to make the Jews some return for their kindness. We are working together for a reformed and revived Near East, and our two movements complete one another. The Jewish movement is national and not imperialist.

Our movement is national and not imperialist, and there is room in Syria for us both. Indeed I think that neither can be a real success without the other.

People less informed and less responsible than our leaders and yours, ignoring the need for cooperation of the Arabs and Zionists have been trying to exploit the local difficulties that must necessarily arise in Palestine in the early stages of our movements. Some of them have, I am afraid, misrepresented your aims to the Arab peasantry, and our aims to the Jewish peasantry, with the result that interested parties have been able to make capital out of what they call our differences.

I wish to give you my firm conviction that these differences are not on questions of principle, but on matters of detail such as must inevitably occur in every contact of neighbouring peoples, and as are easily adjusted by mutual goodwill. Indeed nearly all of them will disappear with fuller knowledge.

ON THE GOLAN WAR-TRAIL

Abraham Rabinovich

THE STORY EXISTS at the moment only in the memories of a few hundred men still engaged in battle or recuperating from wounds. It will take shape eventually as one of the most dramatic tales in Israel's wars — the blunting of the Syrian attack on the Golan Heights. The enormous Syrian tank army thrown across the cease-fire lines at three points on Yom Kippur was met and slowed down by a breathtakingly small number of men in front-line strongpoints and tank units.

Bits of the story emerge in random conversations as one travels through the North.

A middle-aged reservist hitch-hiking to visit his wounded son told how the 19-year-old, a lieutenant, had been in command of four tanks when the Syrians struck. He was a tank instructor and his crewmen were the young recruits he had been teaching. A few hours before the Syrian attack, they were moved up to a position just behind the front-lines.

The small unit went to the aid of a front-line position being attacked by a force of Syrian tanks, and had almost destroyed it when enemy tanks in huge numbers appeared on the flanks. "As soon as they hit one Syrian tank, four more appeared."

For a day and a half, the young lieutenant fought a run-ning action, falling back and fighting. When his tank was finally disabled, he made his way down from the Heights to get a new one. He joined in the powerful counter-attack by reserve units that drove the Syrians back behind the cease-fire line; in the final stages of that fight, he was wounded.

"I used to be in Armour myself," said the reservist, a Galilee farmer, "and I asked my son if the Syrians had improved so much. He said it wasn't that they were so good, but that there were so many of them."

WHEN THE GOLAN Heights was a battlefield last week, reporters were free to roam it almost at will once they had got through — or around — the military checkposts on the main roads leading up from the valley. This week, however, there were military policemen at virtually every intersection, checking credentials. The M.P.s also checked all vehicles leaving the Heights for "souvenirs" — particularly shells and other explosives which might prove dangerous.

MEMBERS OF Kibbutz Yiftah, on the Lebanese border, reported this week that just after the war broke out, they went into the shelters when Syrian planes were reported approaching. They could hear bombs exploding but, when they emerged to look, they saw that the Syrian planes were pounding the Lebanese village of Blida, across the border, in the apparent belief that it was an Israeli kibbutz.

Lisa is a Polish-born girl whose husband, Shaul, from Baghdad, was sent north following last week's mobilization. When she discovered from a friend after a few days that Shaul was still with a rear unit, Lisa started hitch-hiking north from Jerusalem with their 10-month-old daughter, Galit. She fed the baby before they left home and when they reached Haifa, bought her some soup in a restaurant. Mother and baby were picked up as soon as they set foot on a roadside and they were soon at Shaul's camp.

The camp commander, after first telling Lisa that relatives were not permitted to visit, ended up taking her and the baby around the camp in his own vehicle to search for her husband. At her request, Shaul was given a day's leave to drive her and the baby home in the car which he had brought to camp with him.

Lisa reports that the baby did not cry once during the entire outing.

SABBATH──No Publication

I look forward, and my people with me look forward, to a future in which we will help you and you will help us, so that the countries in which we are mutually interested may once again take their places in the community of civilised peoples of the world.
Believe me,
Yours sincerely,
(Sgd.) Feisal.

Royal Highness:
Allow me, on behalf of the Zionist Organisation, to acknowledge your recent letter with deep appreciation.
Those of us who come from the United States have already been gratified by the friendly relations and the active cooperation maintained between you and the Zionist leaders, particularly Dr. Weizmann. We knew it could not be

Shacharit services (morning devotions) in Goshen.

THE BRIDGES ON THE CANAL

THERE are now some first indications that the Israel force sent across the Canal is having an effect despite the continued presence of large Egyptian forces still on this side. This must first of all be to cause the Egyptian command to ask itself just what is happening when Israeli guns can shell the Egyptian invading force from the Egyptian side.

The position of the invading force is much less strong than it was. The tank forays in the direction of the Mitla pass and the general direction of Israel did not prove successful. Around 700 Egyptian tanks are estimated to have been destroyed during the fighting of the past two weeks. Reinforcements have been sent from Egypt, but the units have been broken up too much to have much prospect of continuing the planned invasion.

At the same time the ranks of Israel armour which they might have hoped to destroy have slipped past them and into Egypt. There are reports of some Egyptian forces now seeking to return across the Canal to strengthen the forces on the other side, which were not geared to take up a front-line role in the war. Yet an orderly massive withdrawal is one of the most difficult of all military manoeuvres to carry out successfully, and especially if the withdrawing force is to be kept in fighting condition, with problems of morale and logistics almost equally knotty. A full withdrawal from the Canal is unlikely, and a commander who had the courage to give the order for it might not find his action appreciated at headquarters.

This has enabled the Israel force that crossed the Canal — American sources report 12,000 men and 200 tanks — to begin on its work of destroying the anti-aircraft missiles that protected the waterway, putting the close-packed artillery out of action by moving in on it at close range, and attacking other targets essential to the smooth working of the Egyptian war machine.

It was an extraordinarily hazardous operation whose success was by no means certain at the outset, but if it succeeded infinitely less costly in casualties and equipment than any attempt to smash head-on into the 70,000 men and 1,200 tanks that Egypt at one point had drawn up along the east bank of the Canal. That would make it one totally unexpected piece of military strategy for which the Israeli command has become celebrated.

Defence Minister Dayan said in a television interview yesterday that Israel would not reject a cease-fire as long as the conditions were not unreasonable — such as requiring Israel forces to withdraw from Syria, while permitting Egyptian troops to remain east of the Canal. With Israel forces now firmly established west of the Canal, and some degree of two-way traffic across the water by both sides, the lines of a new cease-fire become a subject for speculation.

Perhaps we shall in time see "open bridges" across the Suez Canal as well as the Jordan?

Markets packed, hotels empty in Cairo

CAIRO (UPI). — "Alfred Hitchcock" and "Ironside" have become casualties of the war in the Middle East.

Canned American television films have been banned from this city at war.

In such small ways, Cairo has begun to count the cost of the war raging 160 kms. to the east.

The long lines at food stores, empty bazaars and hotels and occasional mournful wails of air raid sirens are constant reminders of the conflict.

Cairo — virtually isolated from the outside world for 15 days — has become an oppressive place to live and work. It promises to get worse.

The only civilian lifeline to Cairo is a 24-hour road trip along the northern coast of Africa from the Libyan airport of Benghazi.

———————

DRUSE WOMEN workers at one plant in Isfiya have contributed one month's wages — together over IL5,000 — to the war effort. They said most of them had brothers, husbands or relatives serving in the army.

otherwise; we knew that the aspirations of the Arab and the Jewish peoples were parallel, that each aspired to reestablish its nationality in its own homeland, each making its own distinctive contribution to civilisation, each seeking its own peaceful mode of life.

The Zionist leaders and the Jewish people for whom they speak have watched with satisfaction the spiritual vigour of the Arab movement. Themselves seeking justice, they are anxious that the just national aims of the Arab people be confirmed and safeguarded by the Peace Conference.

We knew from your acts and your past utterances that the Zionist movement—in other words the national aims of the Jewish people—had your support and the support of the Arab people for whom you speak. These aims are now before the Peace Conference as definite proposals by the Zionist Organisation. We are happy indeed that you consider these proposals "moderate and proper," and that we have in you a staunch supporter for their realisation. For both the Arab and the Jewish peoples there are difficulties ahead—difficulties that challenge the united statesmanship of

Command post in Zelig's shelter

By EPHRAIM KISHON

IT looks as if the time has come to reveal some security details, conveyed by our military commentator, concerning the day-to-day activity of the war-room, or as it's called in military slang, the "Pit," which is where the fate of the battles is decided. We don't of course mean that place somewhere-in-Israel where a few senior staff officers sit racking their brains in the absence of any solid information. What we're talking about is the sessions in our Pit, which meet every evening in the Zelig's air-raid shelter with the participation of our whole block — women, children, and Haga (Res.). Our Pit is equipped in plain military style: a couple of mattresses, a transistor, a map of the U.S., a bag of peanuts, and, of course, the red phone — a direct line to Yoske.

The daily Pit session opens as a rule with a bulletin by our chairwoman, who has a brother-in-law planted in the Southern Command. He is a driver there, the brother-in-law, with the rank of corporal (Res.), but he knows a lot.

"Ladies and Gentleman," she announces, "Here's the rumours, and first the headlines."

The material tends to be rich and varied. The O.C. Southern Command urged tonight that we accept Kurt Waldheim's call for a cease-fire. Golda's against. Arik is about to be appointed Interior Minister, after Burg's request to be attached to the Central Command for "special duties" was granted. Dado's in Benghazi.

This last piece of intelligence was relayed to us by Yoske on the hot line. Don't get the idea, though, that anyone can get in touch with Pit Supreme Headquarters (Pitsh for short), just like that. There are strict security checks: if you haven't at least a Tat-Aluf in your pocket you can do an about-face and go home to your transistor. What we want isn't a public, but reliable sources of information. Like Glick the engineer, for example, who's got an uncanny instinct for codes. One morning last week, you'll remember, the radio kept repeating: "Mashed Potatoes, Mashed Potatoes."

"That's a sign," said Glick without a moment's hesitation, "that we've smashed Damascus, smashed Damascus."

"Excuse me," Felix Zelig's 80-year-old aunt who gets on everybody's nerves interrupted at this point, "With how many soldiers?"

"With a force of regimental strength, madam."

"How much's that?"

She does get on our nerves, that woman. A regiment's a regiment, why make such a fuss over it? Yesterday too, after the session was over, she wanted to know whether Hussein was ground-to-air or what. How's one expected to lead a war under such conditions? The rumours come in at a steady flow, but if anyone at Pitsh gets too upset by them, he can always go over to the Recovery Station. That is, in the next room there's a small tape-recorder that plays Haim-Herzog-non-stop, 24 hours a day. Experience has shown that never mind what he says, it's the tone of voice that does it.

We ought to add that our military decisions are extremely responsible. We never cross the Canal without first consulting Danny, our Gadna expert whose best friend's father plays rummy with the chief door-keeper at Beilinson Hospital. Danny is very knowledgeable and can rattle off strategical place-names like Ras-el-Mimsy on the southern axis of the Jebel-Maises and Nebi-Latkeh. What he likes best of all, though, is to bend bend bend bananas with Arik Einstein, which is quite nice as Hebrew pop-songs go, though we've already heard it 12 times on the radio, and the war *still* goes on.

The Pit is on guard and does its duty. If the reader wishes to join our ranks he must supply himself with at least one Aluf (Res.) for rumorous information, and apply in writing enclosing his photograph, the Aluf's. Our sessions begin at 9.02 p.m., after Mabat. If you don't want to be late it's advisable to drive round through the back-streets to avoid the headlight-hunters. Our own headlights, for instance, already wear eight layers of blue paint, and we must grope our way by touch in front of the bumper. War is war. It's true that the Egyptians are still keeping the Canal closed, but on the other hand we are keeping the options open, as the man said, and that's what counts.

Translated by Miriam Arad
(By arrangement with "Ma'ariv")

Abhorrent advertisement

To the Editor of The Jerusalem Post

Sir, — It was with the utmost disgust that we saw Rakah's advertisement in your issue of October 10 and although we know that this is not necessarily your view, we feel that this is not the time to be printing this sort of advertisement.

We assume that the revenue you obtained from this abhorrent organization for this advert will not go into the coffers of *The Jerusalem Post* but will in some way go towards easing the pain of the men injured in the war, and we hope to see a printed notice to that effect in your paper.

FAMILY HERSH, Netanya
FAMILY EMANUEL, Ramat Aviv
ALAN GILL, Holon
EHARIM, Jaffa
SUSI HAND, Bat Yam
MIKY BARAN, Nahlat Yitzhak
ALISA BAER, Ramat Gan
GILLIAN BENATAK, Kiron
L. BLUMBERG, Ramat Aviv
BERTHA SAVDIE, Ramat Gan
TAMI TAVIEFF, Tel Aviv

October 14.
The Jerusalem Post thanks the above readers for their suggestion, which it is taking up. — Ed. J.P.

★ ★ ★

Sir, — If any of us needed insight into the mentality of the followers of Rakah, we surely got it with their advertisement in your issue of October 10.

If this isn't the epitome of bad taste and ruthlessness, I am at a loss to know what is. To choose a time such as this — four days into the worst of hostilities, when the last thought in the minds of Jews is politics — is to show them for what they are.

They are obviously only politicians interested in furthering their own ambitions, without any Jewish "heart" to help them.

Israelis, take heed! If these are their tactics during a crisis, what would they do in normal times to further their own ambitions? Furthermore, why arent these same idiots where they belong — helping to fight for our very survival, instead of having nothing else to do with their time and money than devote them to compiling such a stinking piece of paid advertising.

Theirs is the typical Russian doctrine. Can we afford to have sickness such as this in our midst? Don't we have enough problems? We, and we alone, can put them out of business.

ANITA FEDERMAN
Ramat Hasharon, October 10.

Volunteer women supplying refreshments to soldiers on the way to the front.

Elizabeth Taylor raises funds

ROME (AP). — Actress Elizabeth Taylor, a Jewish convert, gave a private party in a luxurious Rome hotel Friday night to raise funds for Israel.

The Israeli ambassador and his wife were among the first to greet Miss Taylor as she swept into her own party in the reception room of a Rome hotel in which the actress is currently staying.

Actor Lionel Stander and Soraya, former empress of Iran, were among the guests.

Several girls sat at a table, ready to collect donations. A woman who personally greeted the guests said that cheques would also be accepted.

Poll shows French favour Israel

PARIS (UPI). — Frenchmen sympathize more with Isreel than with the Arabs in the present Middle East war, but most want France to stay neutral, according to an opinion poll published in "Le Figaro" newspaper on Wednesday.

Forty-five per cent of those polled said they preferred Israel compared to 16 per cent for the Arab states. But in another question, 60 per cent said they wanted France to remain neutral.

Archbishop Joseph Raya, Head of the Greek Catholic community, told *The Post* that the priests of his diocese would donate blood for wounded soldiers. He has sent letters to the 41 Greek Catholic Churches in Galilee, asking them to contribute what they can from their church funds to the War Loan, and asking the priests and teachers to "contribute all they can from their salaries". He called on the young men of the community to place themselves at the service of the authorities, wherever they may be needed.

Belgians support Israel, but government quiet

By LILI BAT AHARON
Jerusalem Post Correspondent

BRUSSELS. — Despite the exceedingly cautious attitude of the Belgian Government, which to this moment has still failed to identify the aggressor in the current Middle East war, public sentiment in Belgium is running strongly in favour of Israel.

A political Action-for-Israel group was due to begin functioning on Wednesday. The Association of Belgians for Israel is being headed by former Prime Minister Gaston Eyskens and consists of parliamentarians of all political parties.

The streets of Antwerp were the scene on Sunday of a mass organized fund-raising action. Throughout the city, which boasts some half a million inhabitants, loudspeaker-appeals were made for contributions to buy an ambulance for Israel.

At the urging of 500 youngsters, the "man-in-the-street" of Antwerp contributed more than 300,000 Belgian francs (about IL35,000) within a few hours.

Similar action is being scheduled for the cities of Mechelen and Gent, both of them tourist cities with small Jewish populations.

In Brussels, at least three communes — Schaerbeek, Etterbeek and Ixelles — are initiating drives for purchase of ambulances for Israel.

The Mayor of Ixelles made a personal contribution. So did the Socialist Party of the Brussels commune of Anderlecht.

Both in Antwerp and in Brussels, individuals and womens' groups have been forming committees to provide medical aid for Israel.

Belgian and Israeli musicians are offering their talents, and concerts are being organized in private homes and public halls with proceeds going to Israel.

An Israeli artist, a wounded war veteran who was due to give a one-man show, has offered his paintings for sale for the benefit of Israel.

Blood colectilon centres have been established in the cities of Brussels, Antwerp and Mechelen. Hours before the blood collections began long lines of patient donors stood waiting, identifying personally with Israel's struggle.

U.S. public backs Israel

PRINCETON, New Jersey (AP). — A Gallup poll on the Middle East conflict indicates that 47 per cent of all Americans support Israel and 6 per cent back neither side, while 25 per cent expressed no opinion.

A spokesman said it was unusual to have such a large number of persons with no opinion, and he expressed the belief that the figure may reflect a reluctance on the part of many Americans to see the U.S. become embroiled in another war.

The survey was begun on October 6, the day the war broke out, and was based on interviews with 1,500 adults in more than 300 sampling locations.

Those interviewed were asked: "In this trouble, are your sympathies more with Israel or more with the Arab states?"

Arab and Jewish leaders. For it is no easy task to rebuild two great civilisations that have been suffering oppression and misrule for centuries. We each have our difficulties we shall work out as friends, friends who are animated by similar purposes, seeking a free and full development for the two neighbouring peoples. The Arabs and Jews are neighbours in territory; we cannot but live side by side as friends.

Very respectfully,
(Sgd.) Felix Frankfurter.

There was no enmity at this time between Arab and Jew, and Feisal saw no conflict of interest between Jew and Arab. He, in fact, welcomed the Jews as brothers, and fully believed that they could live in peace with one another.

Since the granting of lands to the Arabs by the League of Nations was vast, and the amount promised to the Jews was extremely small, neither Feisal nor any other Arabs of the day were jealous of the Jews, nor had they any feeling that they had been dispossessed or cheated by history.

In 1921, Lawrence served as adviser to Colonial Secretary Winston Churchill. Churchill, along with Sir Herbert Samuel, who was then Commissioner for mandated Palestine, participated with Lawrence in a conference in Cairo. This became known as the Cairo Conference, which confirmed the Balfour Declaration.

The Cairo Conference recommended that Feisal, who had been expelled by the French from Damascus, be made King of Iraq. The Conference also appointed Feisal's brother, Abdullah, to be ruler of Trans-Jordan. It was this Abdullah who later made a declaration in favor of Jewish settlement in Palestine. Shortly after making this declaration, King Abdullah was assassinated.

Lawrence, it appears, was never an anti-Zionist. He regarded Zionism and Arab nationalism as complementary forces in the Middle East.

The seven Arab states in existence in 1947: Egypt, Iraq, Syria, Lebanon, Saudi Arabia, Yemen, and Trans-Jordan — the states whose leaders decided to throttle Israel at its birth — contained an area between them which was 230 times larger than the area of the projected Jewish State.

Turning point seen in Israeli Arab attitude

By YA'ACOV FRIEDLER
Jerusalem Post Reporter

HAIFA. — The Yom Kippur War appears to be marking a turning point in the attitudes of the Arab population of Israel. Judging from a survey made by this reporter in the Northern area on Friday, the war has cemented the loyalty and identification of Arab citizens to the State.

"Even among the more extreme nationalist elements, the feeling now is that war will solve no problems, and that the aggression by Egypt and Syria had not demonstrated those countries' self-confidence," an informed Nazareth source told *The Post*. "Nazareth residents are treating war communiques from Cairo and Damascus, with contempt. There has not been one case of hostile action by Arab citizens," the source said. He noted that the committee established by Mayor Seif edin Zu'abi and other notables, to mobilise funds for the War Loan, has found its work easy. Almost everybody they approached had already subscribed to the loan of his own volition.

"We have no sons in the Army, food supplies are normal, life has not been disrupted, and the least we can do is to show our identification with the war effort", *The Post* was told by one Nazareth Arab. "Older and younger Arabs alike are doing all they can," he said.

In Haifa, an emergency volunteer committee has been established at the Arab-Jewish community centre. Headed by the Arab lawyer, Jamil Shalhoub, the committee operates from eight in the morning to five in the afternoon, finding work for volunteers and especially soliciting contributions to the Voluntary War Loan. "We have set ourselves a target of IL1m. from the Arabs of Haifa and we want to meet it", Mr. Shalhoub said. He noted that 30 young Arab adults are serving as voluntary special constables with the Police, some 20 car owners are helping to transport essential supplies, and many boys and girls are helping in hospitals and at the Post Office. Many Arab citizens have already given blood, and have donated money to the Soldiers' Welfare Committee.

Pilgrims prefer Israel to Arab lands

Two groups of Christian pilgrims from the U.S. have cancelled their plans to visit several Arab states and have come to Israel instead. The Tourism Ministry spokesman, Micha Gidron, said yesterday that the groups, who total over 100 persons, arrived in Israel Saturday night on an El Al flight.

Mr. Gidron said that despite the war Christian pilgrims are evincing considerable interest in visiting Israel. "A relatively surprising number of pilgrims have been coming, not only from the U.S., but also from Germany, Holland, Switzerland and the Scandinavian countries," he told *The Jerusalem Post*.

Mr. Gidron gave one example, of a group of 400 West German pilgrims who were in Athens *en route* to the Middle East when the war broke out on October 6. "The group was divided," he said. "Some wanted to cancel the whole trip and return to Germany. Others wanted to continue. They finally took a vote and over two-thirds decided they wanted to continue to Israel — and Israel only."

They came and toured the country for seven days, despite the war.

Rav Goren at prayer with soldiers on the West Bank of the Suez.

The population of these seven countries was 60 times that of the Jewish inhabitants of Israel, who in 1947 numbered a little more than half a million.

Nevertheless, despite the early rosy beginnings, an enmity did develop. How did this come about?

When I first set foot in Palestine some fifty years ago, back in 1925, I remember sitting astride a horse on the topmost hills of Jerusalem and casting my eyes in every direction. I could find no expanse of so much as an acre that was green. Outside of the indomitable dwarfed olive trees, there wasn't a single tree to be seen as far as the horizon. The land was utterly bare and desolate. The hills were stony; the soil seemed untillable. There were some attempts at small garden cultivation here and there, but the dominant color of the country was brown.

The inhabitants of the land were, for the most part, nomadic Bedouins, not tillers of the soil. The others lived in pitifully unsanitary villages, ridden with trachoma, with little or no sewage systems.

At that time, the city of Jerusalem enjoyed little commerce or industry save for the making of trinkets for the pilgrims who came to the sites holy to three religions. Most traffic consisted of riders on the backs of mules and camels. Life was primitive. There were limited means of disseminating information, education, culture. There were few schools, no libraries, and perhaps two or three daily newspapers for a population that was 98 percent illiterate.

Outside the capital, in other parts of Palestine, the view was even more dismal. The Valley of Jezreel was a swampland, infested by mosquitoes. Malaria was rife. Agriculture, except for little enclaves of orange groves which had been established by Jews who had come to Palestine in the 1880's, was utterly pitiful. Where one might have expected to find the biblical land of milk and honey, one met only with arid desolation.

Forty years later, the situation had been transformed. Mile upon mile of roads had been built, swamps had been drained, farms had risen, nurseries planted. In the 1960's, one could find, for the first time, huge tracts of green land as far as the

No recruitment for Israel, foreign envoys assure Cairo

CAIRO. — The West German, Dutch and Belgian ambassadors assured Egypt's acting foreign minister Saturday that recruitment for the Israeli or any other foreign army is illegal in their countries.

The three ambassadors said the assurances were made to Acting Foreign Minister Ismail Fahmy in separate messages at his request.

Fahmy summoned them after conferring with the French, British and Swiss ambassadors, informing all six diplomats of an Egyptian decision to treat as mercenaries non-Israeli prisoners captured while fighting for Israel in the Middle East war.

The Cairo Government said the decision deprives these prisoners of treatment according to the relevant Geneva Convention on combatant personnel in war.

All the ambassadors said laws in their countries forbid recruitment for foreign armies, but the Belgian, Pierre Anciaux de Faveaux, pointed out, "The Brussels Government cannot prevent individuals taking risks by enlisting in foreign armies if the authorities do not know about it."

U.S. AIRLIFT

Hans Georg Steltzer of Bonn said that among other topics he discussed with Fahmy was the Bonn government's reported confirmation that some U.S.-supplied weapons to Israel are being airlifted via American bases in West Germany.

Meanwhile, a hint that even France is not secure from Arab wrath came over the weekend when the Union of Egyptian Students here criticized French Foreign Minister Mitchel Jobert's statement in the National Assembly last week saying that "France would not oppose minor rectifications of the (Arab-Israel) borders of June 4, 1967."

SHALOM TO GOLDA

Brian Arthur adds from Bonn:

Herbert Wehner, powerful head of Bonn's ruling Social Democrats in Parliament, delivered an unexpected greeting to Prime Minister Golda Meir at a party meeting in Duisburg yesterday.

"Shalom Golda Meir, and all those who want a just peace," he said

suddenly at the end of a speech on labour relations. The 300 delegates to the conference, surprised into silence for a moment, then roared applause. Though Mr. Wehner seemed to have spoken on impulse, observers said his words may have been meant to counter any suggestion his party was lukewarm in its sympathy for Israel.

There is no question among Bundestag parties that Israel's existence and security must be guaranteed. But last week a dispute flared among Socialist and opposition deputies in the "German-Israel Parliamentary Group" over whether to explicitly condemn Russia for its role in the Mideast war.

Christian Democrats in the 100-man group called for "clear language" condemning Soviet arms aid. The Socialist-Liberal wing, which seeks continuing rapprochement with Moscow, preferred less harsh wording.

A final compromise resolution warned Moscow it could not seek detente and "play with the fire of war" in the Mideast, and condemned arms deliveries to the Arabs without mentioning Russia by name.

(AP, Reuter)

89

eye could see. It was a miracle. It was the kind of miracle that the Mormons wrought in Utah. It was the miracle of taking unyielding soil and nurturing it to open up and bloom like a rose. How did this come about?

The first time I went to Palestine, I was impelled by an inner drive. I had to see this land, the land that had a mystic attraction for me as it has had for thousands of Jews throughout the centuries. I was young, brimming with energy, and filled with the careless courage of youth. So I put a pack on my back and went trekking through the barren expanse of the Jezreel Valley.

And there I saw other young men who had come from every part of the civilized world, bending over in back-breaking toil, hour after hour, in the broiling sun, stripped to the waist, pickaxe and shovel in hand, hacking away at the niggardly soil, removing small rocks and huge boulders. And side by side with them were young women who assisted in the clearing of the land. Most worked at least twelve hours a day, and every one of them for mere subsistence.

These young men and young women were working their land, the land of their dreams. The land had been bought by the Jews of the world through the Jewish National Fund, and had been paid for at twice, and thrice, and most often at ten times its value.

As it was—swampy, malarial, unfertilized, roadless, unelectrified—this land was uninhabitable. Neglected for centuries, it was a formidable foe. But these Jews knew this land had to be redeemed, that it *would* be redeemed.

Beginning at the turn of the century, waves of pioneers—*chalutzim,* they were called—had emigrated to Palestine. These young men and women, imbued with the twin ideals of Zionism and socialism, built up a whole string of *kibbutzim,* communal communities in which all property belonged to the commune, and all individuals shared in it alike. Work in these kibbutzim was enormously rigorous: the hours were long; the toil, arduous; the fare, of the simplest. But by dint of dedication, these pioneers turned a wasteland into a habitation and a home.

In a few years, they had visibly achieved that which the Arabs had not achieved in centuries. And although this achievement was an enormous psychological affront to the Arabs, the agricultural miracle did not in itself generate nor trigger the enmity that eventually evolved. In fact, for the Arab peasant, the progress made on the land by the

Jews would seem to have offered promise.

There is a song in *South Pacific* entitled "You Have to be Taught to Hate." That particular ditty is more truthful than entertaining. It reveals what transpired with the *felaheen,* the impoverished peasant of Palestine who generally rented a small plot of land from an absentee landlord. The wealthy effendi, as a rule, resided in luxury outside of Palestine. It was the upper class, especially the absentee landlords who, with the coming of the Jew, saw the handwriting on the wall.

The few affluent Arabs who lived off the poverty of their very many countrymen correctly judged that they could not keep their vassals in an ignorant, subjugated, exploited state. These felaheen were now going to live side by side with the newly arrived Jews, and witness their democratic communities, their building, and their visible achievements in living standards.

In 1925, the Jewish city worker in Palestine was receiving a minimum wage of $1.00 a day, by fiat of the Histadrut—the Jewish Labor Federation. During the same period, an Arab working for a Jewish employer received a minimum wage of 25¢ a day.[1] The same Arab worker had been receiving from his Arab boss no more than 5¢ a day.[2] Obviously, this situation was fraught with danger for the Arab boss. Furthermore, a short time later, the Histadrut raised the level of Arab wages precipitously.

A demon had been unloosed in Arab society. Someone unbidden had come to the lands to show Arab workers that they were entitled to much more than they had been receiving.

It was then that the leaders of the Arabs began to regard the Jews as a dire threat to their way of life, as an alien people who were going to unhinge the Arab's feudal moorings.

How could one cope with this mortal danger?

The Arab leaders conceived a nefarious scheme which enlisted the support of the very peasants they were conniving to exploit. They appealed to the Arab sense of possession and tradition, as if Arab ways were in jeopardy. The Jews were usurpers, they announced. They had come to take over the land; eventually, they would drive the felaheen off the soil. The Arab landowners scornfully pointed to the Jewish women who walked around in shorts, shamelessly exposing their knees. If this were allowed to prevail, the sanctity of the Arab home would be destroyed.

1. Five piastres.
2. One piastre.

No doubt there was a real fear that the supremacy of the male in Arab society would be diminished. In those days, all the Arab women of Palestine wore veils. The social rights of women, from a Western point of view, were minimal.

The leaders cunningly stirred up xenophobic fears; it was so easy to fear and hate someone you did not know. Arab leaders exploited the Arab's loyal observance of his religion, reminding the faithful that the Jews were infidels — a people who did not accept Mohammed, and were therefore to be regarded as enemy intruders.

The campaign to recruit the unsuspecting Arab to the banner of Jewish ouster was an overwhelming success. The irony was that the Arab leader — for whom the Jew and his ways constituted a real threat — could win the battle against the newcomer only by enlisting the poor Arab whom the Jewish presence benefited.

I remember when I was in Palestine in 1927, during the Islamic feast of Nebi Musa[1], I heard carousing Arabs, reveling through the streets of Jerusalem, chanting:

Falastina bladna,
W'Yahud klabna!

Which meant "Palestine is our land, and the Jews are our dogs." This was the rallying cry learnt in the mosques under the tutelage of Haj Amin el Husseini, then Grand Mufti of Jerusalem, the highest Moslem prelate of the region, the man who was to become the friend of Hitler. Thus it was that the Arab leaders incensed an illiterate public against a people who had merely raised the standards of living of the region and the income of the Arab peasant class.

Charles E. Bohlen reports in his book *Witness to History*[2] that President Roosevelt, in a meeting with Ibn Saud, then King of Saudi Arabia, expressed the hope that the 10,000 troubled Jewish refugees from Russia and Germany would find a haven in Palestine. Ibn Saud objected to the immigration, and pointed out that the Jews were "technically and culturally on a higher level than the Arabs." Because of this, the King pointed out, the Arabs had great difficulty in "surviving economically."

The plain fact is that the Jews were bringing wealth into the country, opening up new jobs and new vistas. Despite his words, King Saud could not really complain that the Jews were causing the Arabs to be impoverished. He was just pulling the wool over Roosevelt's eyes. What he really feared was a diminution of unearned increment for the Arab ruling class. "Arabs would choose to die rather than yield their land to Jews," he said.

Moreover, what nettled the King was the introduction of an entirely new way of life into the backroads and byways of Arab life. The eyes of the underprivileged were being opened.

I have no doubt that Ibn Saud was sincere in his fear. He had a right to be. The Arab people had wallowed for centuries in a miasma of ignorance, from which even at this date they have hardly emerged. The literacy rate, even today, in the Arab countries of this region has reached no higher than 50 percent. As Karl Marx said, "Knowledge is power"; an illiterate populace is one without power.

So successful has been the campaign to turn Arab against Jew, that the common Arab is now prepared to accept the perpetration of any outrage against the Jew. Although the wanton slayings by the terrorist guerillas are the actions of a very small group, they are unopposed by the entire Arab world. So massive is the hatred that normal codes of morality are easily suspended when the Jew is the victim. There is no outcry when eleven innocent athletes are mowed down at Munich. There is no responsible organ of opinion which decries the slaughter of 28 children at Maalot. Nor does any public figure, throughout the length and breadth of the Arab world, lament the slaying in cold blood of 39 non-Jewish tourists at the Tel Aviv airport — people who had nothing at all to do with the conflict between Arab and Israeli. These murders simply do not touch the people in whom blind hatred has been deliberately cultivated.

An editorial which appeared in The New York Times on Wednesday, June 25, 1974, was addressed to the subject of Arab justice. Some terrorist gunmen had entered the Saudi embassy in Khartoum, and there had captured, tortured, and then killed a Belgian diplomat and two American diplomats. At the time of the incident, the Sudanese Government condemned the outrage and promised to bring the criminals to justice for what the Sudanese Foreign Minister had termed "brutal killings." Yet the Sudanese Government subsequently failed to punish the self-confessed murderers. The New York Times commented:

Making a mockery of justice as well as of the victims' memory, General Nimeiry engaged in the charade of first commuting the sentences to seven years

---

1. Feast of the Prophet Moses.
2. Charles E. Bohlen, *Witness to History*, W.W. Norton, 1973.

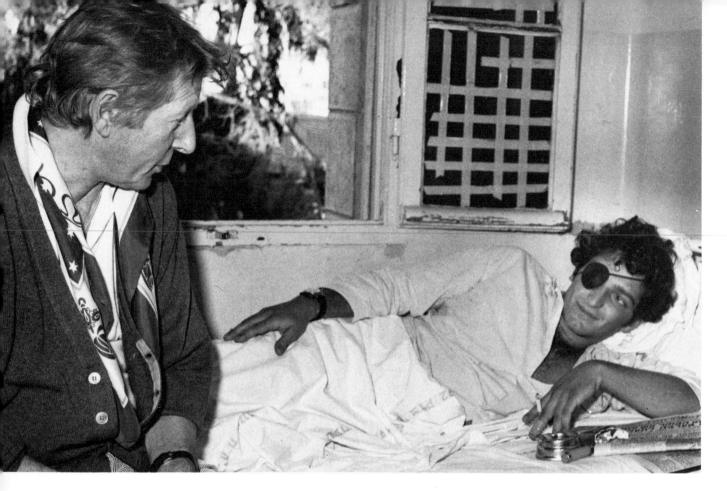

Danny Kaye visits the wounded in a hospital.

Three top entertainers performing for troops

Jerusalem Post Staff

Three world-famous Jewish entertainers — poet Leonard Cohen, comedian Danny Kaye and singer Enrico Macias — are now entertaining Israeli troops. All three came here following the outbreak of war.

Cohen, who arrived unannounced several days ago asking to work at a kibbutz as a volunteer, has already given several concerts at the front. Kaye and Macias arrived yesterday afternoon.

Cohen, the poet-songwriter, accused Israelis of being "militaristic" when he left the country earlier this year, after a stormy concert tour. Interviewed at an airbase yesterday by pool correspondent Yossi Ma'ayani, he still appeared to be suffering from the shock of the war, and to be looking for new answers to questions which had been bothering him for some time.

"I felt like a bird sitting on barbed wire" was how he described his feelings on hearing of the Egyptian-Syrian attack on Yom Kippur. "I just knew one thing — I had to be here with you."

At his first appearance at the base, Cohen was so seized with emotion that he used the interval between one performance and the next to write a new song, singing it immediately afterwards.

HOLY SOIL

The text tells of his seeking his brothers in the desert, who are shedding their blood in the battle against evil being fought on holy soil. Cohen half-sang, half-declaimed this song before an audience of thousands who joined enthusiastically in the chorus: "My love, my love, come back to me."

After the appearance Cohen talked with a group of soldiers who had just returned from a mission behind enemy lines. With evident emotion he said, "At first I was afraid my quiet and melancholy songs weren't the sort of thing to cheer up front-line fighters. But I've learned that these wonderful kids don't need rousing battle hymns. I came to encourage them and they ended up encouraging me. I don't think I've ever known such deep and wonderful contact with an audience."

As for the war, he said he prayed "this nightmare will soon be over." He will remain in Israel as long as the war continues, he added. Cohen is appearing with Ilana Rovina, Oshik Levy, Matti Caspi and Pupik Arnon.

Danny Kaye was grabbed by members of the Air Force as soon as he stepped off his El Al plane at Lod yesterday. The comedian arrived in white shoes, red socks, a two-coloured suit and his familiar hat.

When he reached the V.I.P. lounge he refused to give his passport to El Al's Michael Pinhasi so that the latter could stamp it as required by law — apparently to keep Mr. Pinhasi from seeing his true age. The two men then ran a race to the Border Control counter, where Mr. Kaye stamped the passport himself. On the way he stopped to give onlookers his autograph.

Singer Enrico Macias brought three of his instrumentalists with him, plus all the cigarettes and whisky on his flight, which he bought to give to wounded soldiers. The group went straight from the airport to visit hospitals.

*in prison, and then assigning supervision
of the sentence to the Palestinians—an
act equivalent to releasing a gangland
killer to the custody of his own Mafioso
family.*

As a matter of fact, most of the Palestinian terrorists who committed outright murder were never punished for the crimes. Some who were jailed regained their liberty under reprisal threats.

After the attack on the Olympic Village in Munich in September, 1972, in which 11 Israelis were killed, the three surviving attackers were freed several weeks later when terrorists hijacked a Lufthansa airliner. The hijackers have never been tried.

Five terrorists of the Black September group who killed 31 people at the Rome airport in December, 1973, commandeered an airliner, then added another victim in Athens, and then flew on to Kuwait. That country never brought these murderers before the bar of justice.

A civilization which tolerates the existence of a small minority of exploiters and an overwhelming mass of the oppressed breeds very little moral fiber. In such a society, killers can be applauded, and heads of government can callously send the murderers off to their freedom.

In a country like the Palestine of the 1920's, brutalized and brutish, it was easy to turn the heads of a large mass of ignorant peasants by exaggerated tales of great woe to come, by fantasies of what harm the Jews would do. What was served were the interests of the few at the expense of the overwhelming many. This is the secret of undying Arab enmity.

This enmity has gone to such wild extremes that in Iraq, Zionism is listed as a capital crime. Under the Iraqian criminal code, a person is liable to hanging if two Moslems swear that they know him to be sympathetic to Zionism. For years, any attempt by a Jew to leave Iraq for Israel was treated as a capital offense. Confiscation of property was imposed on a large number of Jews caught trying to leave. Even Jews who had previously left for Israel were tried in absentia and sentenced.

Today, Iraqi law permits a Jew to leave the country provided he renounces Iraqi citizenship, but he is only allowed to take along a small amount of cash. Whatever property he leaves behind remains legally his, but actually is confiscated by the State.

In contrast, no land was ever taken from the Arabs. Every inch of the soil of Israel was paid for.

And paid for at unbelievably inflated prices. A study has been made comparing the prices paid for prime Iowa farmland in 1920—land composed of fine black topsoil—with the prices demanded by Arab landowners for barren wasteland in the hills of Judea. The prices in Palestine were ten times as high per acre as that of prime Iowa farmland.

Up to 1947, the Jewish National Fund bought 234,000 acres in Palestine, slightly more than half of the total Jewish holdings at that time; the rest was purchased by private funds. From 1920 to 1948, the Jewish National Fund raised in the United States some 26 million dollars, most of which found its way into the coffers of wealthy Arab landowners.

In the Arab world, misrepresentations about Jews are diligently propagandized and perpetuated. From the cradle, Arab children are taught to hate and mistrust Jews by being fed lies.

In 1962, the Egyptian government disseminated in the schools a text entitled "Talmudic Human Sacrifices." This new edition contains an up-to-date foreword by Abdel Qati Jalal which states:

> *The Talmud believes that the Jews are
> made of different material from the rest
> of mankind. Those who do not share
> the beliefs of the Jews, being animals
> devoid of sense for they are servants and
> chattels of the Jews. Their wise men
> laid it down that there is no law but their
> own desire, and no doctrine but their
> own lust. They commanded their people
> to bring harm to the other peoples, to
> kill their children, and suck their blood,
> and take away their wealth.*

This material is given to Arab teenagers and taught as a factual work, as proof of a Jewish admission of its conspiracy to dominate the world. Generation after generation of Arabs are being brought up to hate all Jews. They are taught to believe that it is vital to destroy Israel. Under such circumstances, what kind of a peace can one expect with the Arab world?

Peace in the Middle East can come about only if the Arab world becomes convinced that it is to their own interest to stop sowing seeds of hate in the minds of their young. Until this is brought about, the war between the Arabs and the Jews will, like the Biblical war with Gog and Magog, run to the end of time.

After the 1967 Six-Day War, Israel insisted on the

removal of such school texts in the Arab areas it occupied. Israel launched a program of education and rehabilitation for its Arab inhabitants.

Vocational training centers were established to raise Arab youth out of the rut of unskilled labor. Many Arabs took advantage of these opportunities for self-improvement. By 1972, 40,000 workers from Arab towns and villages found employment on Israeli building sites and in Israeli factories.

The status of Arabs in Israel since its founding has steadily improved both socially and economically. Arabs are not subject to hatred. They are treated as citizens with equal rights and opportunities.

Today, at least 600 Arabs attend Israel's universities. Today, five Arabs are members of Israel's governing body, the Knesset. And today, many Arabs operate in the country's administrative structure. And perhaps that is why, during the Yom Kippur War, as evidenced by so many articles in these pages, the Arabs who are resident of Israel came to the support of the country. After living in the State of Israel for many years, they came to learn that the stories they had heard of Jewish deviltry and exploitation were so much poppycock. The reality exorcised the propaganda.

Israel permits the Arabs on the western bank of the Jordan, and the Arabs residing in Jordan proper, to send their products for sale across the border into Israel. The result has been the elimination of unemployment among the refugees still living in camps in these areas.

Even though the Arabs maintained a state of belligerency with Israel after the '67 War, allowing no accommodation, no talks, no peace, Israel kept open the bridges across the Jordan, permitting Arabs to visit their relatives in Israel. Israel has also permitted Arab students residing in Israel to go abroad to study in Cairo, and in other Arab universities.

Moreover, every year during the summer holiday season, thousands of people from Arab states, from as far away as Kuwait, come to visit relatives in Israel. Even while many voices in these countries —both official and unofficial—were threatening the annihilation of Israel, large numbers of well-to-do Arabs were making jaunts to Israel for summer holidays on Israel's beaches. A Druse journalist by the name of Mansour, a staff member of the daily Ha'aretz, referring in the issue of July 30, 1971, to this usual summer influx, declared in ironic

hyperbole that the Arabs had descended on Tel Aviv "to take a vacation in the Zionist hell."

As mentioned at the outset of this section, this "Zionist hell" was the object of Sadat's aim of dismemberment. Nearly all Israelis were aware that Sadat's lethal sentiments were also exactly those of his Arab allies. Yet when Sadat's armies moved against Israel on October 6, Gaddafi of Libya immediately disassociated himself from the War. Egypt had announced that it wished to get the stalemate off center. Sadat had said that all he wanted to do was to retrieve lands which he had lost during the 1967 War. As far as Gaddafi was concerned, these demands were much, much too moderate. The Lybian made no bones about it— what he wanted was nothing less than the complete disappearance of Israel—at one stroke!

Most students of Near East affairs believe that Gaddafi's big talk and Sadat's aims actually coincided.

What separated the two leaders was the matter of means. Sadat did not believe that his Army and the armies of his Syrian allies, plus Jordanian forces, enlarged by contingents from Algiers, Morocco, Saudi Arabia, and other Islamic lands, were strong enough to overrun and conquer Israel. What he did believe was that he could achieve sufficient thrust so that he could force Israel to concede strategic areas.

The Arabs are using the refugee argument simply as a weapon, a strategic weapon, to pry the Israelis out of the country. It is very important to view the euphemistic words used by the Arabs with clear eyes, and to hear the intent behind the words in their full meaning and force. The Arabs are saying, "We want the Palestinians to return to their former homes." Translated, this means, "We want to dispossess the Israelis, to liquidate the State of Israel. If the Israelis won't deliberately commit suicide, then we will kill them off."

This is the meaning behind the Arab intransigence of the last 26 years. *Why sit down and bargain with someone you intend to butcher?* Any kind of face-to-face negotiation, discussing matters of principle, would only disclose what the Arabs really have in their hearts.

They do not seek monetary compensation, they do not want any kind of territorial accommodation; they do not want any kind of compromise. They simply want body and soul.

Workers all over the World Support Israel

Messages of sympathy and support for Israel and the Histadrut have been received from all over the world by Y. Ben-Aharon, General-Secretary of the Histadrut.

DAN GALLIN, Secretary General of International Union of Food and Allied Workers, informed the Histadrut of a message sent by him to Presidents Sadat and Assad, stressing that the interests of the Arab peoples cannot be solved by military conflict — calling for an immediate cease-fire and direct negotiations for a durable peace in the Middle East.

The Executive Committee of the Belgian Transport Workers convey to the Israeli workers their fullest feelings of fraternity and sympathy at this moment when all their efforts to build a modern democratic and free nation on a basis of peace have been endangered.

From Holland comes a message signed by the Presidents of the three trade union Federations, W. KOK for N.V.V., SPIT for N.K.V. and F. LANSER for C.N.V., expressing their sympathy with the inhabitants of Israel and the victims of the War, and wishing the Histadrut all strength during this ordeal. They too hope for an end to hostilities and a lasting peace.

"Deeply shocked by the acts of aggression against Israel. We express our sincere sympathy with your people" . . . cabled A. BUELENS, General-Secretary of the Universal Alliance of Diamond Workers.

The Norwegian Trade Unions and the Secretary of the Norwegian Labour Party have urged their government to support Israel in its struggle.

Messages of support were telephoned by the Assistant to the German Minister of Labour and trade union leaders in several states of the Federal Republic of Germany.

The Post, Telephone and Telegraph Workers' International at its European Conference held in Belgium, supports Israel's right to exist, condemns the violation of the cease-fire by Egypt and Syria and conveys its fullest sympathy and solidarity to the people of Israel. This message was sent by S. NEDZYNSGI, the General-Secretary of P.T.T.I.

U.S. TRADE UNIONS SUPPORT ISRAEL

GEORGE MEANY, President of AFL-CIO sent the following cable to Y. Meshel, Deputy General-Secretary of the Histadrut.

"The AFL-CIO condemns the unprovoked aggression against Yom Kippur, the holiest day of the Jewish Religion. This treacherous attack, in flagrant violation of the agreed cease-fire, is another expression of Egyptian and Syrian leaders' determination to destroy Israel's independence and sovereignty. We support Israel's fight against aggression. As the Israelis well know, the only effective answer to aggression is defeat of the agressors.

"We express our deep sorrow for the loss of lives in the war and reiterate our firm belief that the only way of achieving a settlement of the conflict and secure any defensible borders, is through direct negotiations.

"In this grave hour of the Israeli nation, we again express our solidarity with and full support of the State of Israel, the Histadrut and Israeli workers in their struggle for a free society based on democracy and social justice."

Fraternally
George Meany

LEONARD WOODCOCK, President of U.A.W., the Automobile Workers' Trade Union, issued a statement unreservedly condemning the unprovoked Egyptian-Syrian military attack. He expressed deep sorrow for the loss of lives and his Union's solidarity with and support of Israel, the Histadrut and all Israeli workers.

In their message, S. STETIN, General President and W. DU-CHESSI, General Secretary-Treasurer, of the Textile Workers' Union of America, pledge their full support to Israel in its battle for freedom.

JERRY WURF, President of American State, County and Municipal Employees condemns the brutal aggression of Egypt and Syria and reiterates his support of Israel's right to exist in peace and security.

The United Federation of Teachers in its message, signed by A. SHANKER, Union President, condemned Arab aggression and called upon the U.S. Government to provide Israel with the materials necessary to secure its existence.

(Advertisement)

Shooting continues at Canal despite Israel-Egypt cease-fire

THE JERUSALEM POST

SECOND EDITION

Price: 65 Ag.

TUESDAY, OCTOBER 23, 1973 ● TISHRE 27, 5734 ● RAMADHAN 27, 1393 ● VOL. XLIII, No. 13922S*

Kosygin expected in Damascus to push cease-fire

By ANAN SAFADI
Jerusalem Post Arab Affairs Reporter

Soviet Premier Alexei Kosygin was expected to arrive in Damascus last night, apparently to persuade Syria to accept the the cease-fire. Earlier Mr Kosygin was reported to be in Egypt, which announced its acceptance of the cease-fire in time for the Security Council deadline.

Jordan, which kept a low profile throughout the war, last night declared it would abide by the cease-fire. But it said its troops on the Syrian front were subject to instructions and decisions from Damascus.

Lebanon, the fourth Arab state neighbouring Israel, said it was withholding comment on the decision pending Syria's decision. Lebanon, which was not a party in the latest war, had to deal with the Palestinian terrorist movement which is based in Beirut and which last night pledged to defy the cease-fire and continue the armed struggle until the liberation of all Palestine.

Egypt's acceptance of the cease-fire was condemned by a number of Arab countries. Most outspoken were Iraq and Libya, which called for the continuation of the war. Saudi Arabia, Morocco, Algeria, Kuwait and Sudan, all of which had troops on either the Egyptian or the Syrian fronts, maintained silence and seemed to be waiting to hear Syria's attitude.

The Soviet Union appeared to be concentrating its efforts on Syria, the only country which is military relevant and which had not yet accepted the cease-fire.

The Syrians last night said they were still studying the cease-fire resolution. Their dilemma was that in accepting the resolution, they would also have to accept Security Council Resolution 242, to which they have never agreed before. In addition, a large Iraqi force, whose government has already rejected the cease-fire, is located inside Syria.

The Syrians ignored the cease-fire call most of the day yesterday. Damascus Radio reported it only late in the evening, along with Egypt's acceptance of it.

Egypt announced in a broadcast statement at 2.30 p.m. in a acceptance statement attributed to the president's office. The statement said that President Anwar Sadat had instructed his army command to observe the new cease-fire at the time set by the Security Council. Later Cairo Radio repeatedly broadcast a terse announcement stating Egypt has decided to observe a cease-fire at 6.52 p.m. last night.

The statement said the decision was
(Continued on page 2, col. 7)

Likud will oppose cease-fire agreement

Nixon 'confident he can't be impeached'

WASHINGTON — President Nixon is 'quite confident there are no grounds to impeach him, a White House spokesman said yesterday. Mr. Nixon, it was stated, was at his desk at 8.45 in the morning and during the day consulted by cable with Secretary of State Kissinger and also worked on a statement to the nation on why he fired Watergate prosecutor Archibald Cox.
● Pressure for impeachment, page 3

Mig 25s over Canal

TEL AVIV — Two Mig 25s ('Foxbat' in the Nato code), flew over the Suez Canal area at a high altitude yesterday, apparently photographing the area. It is understood that the Egyptians do not fly the Mig 25 and it is assumed here that the pilots were Russians.

Henry Kissinger waves to onlookers as he arrived yesterday at Lod Airport, where he was welcomed by Foreign Minister Abba Eban. Behind them are (centre) Assistant Secretary of State Joseph Sisco and, extreme left, his deputy Alfred Atherton.
(Werner Braun)

Kissinger-Meir meet 3½ hours

No statement issued after talks

By DAVID LANDAU
Jerusalem Post Diplomatic Correspondent

TEL AVIV — Premier Golda Meir and her senior Ministers met for over three hours yesterday with U.S. Secretary of State Henry Kissinger to discuss the cease-fire resolution, that he and Soviet leader Leonid Brezhnev had only the day before succeeded in bringing about.

... in the morning the Israel ... contacts between him and the Soviets which had led to the cease-fire. The radio quoted Israeli sources as saying they were naturally ... with the talks.

Dr. Kissinger was greeted by applause and cheers from newsmen and other workers who ... US Air Force boeing touched down just before one a.m. He emerged waving and smiling to the crowd, and exchanged friendly welcomes with Foreign Minister Abba Eban, US ...

The UN's cease-fire resolution

UNITED NATIONS (AP) — Following is the text of the U.S.-Soviet resolution approved by the Security Council at 6.50 a.m. Israel time yesterday (12.50 a.m. New York time)

Union of Soviet Socialist Republics and United States of America Resolution

The Security Council

● Calls upon all parties to the present fighting to cease all firing and terminate all military activity immediately, no later than 12 hours after the moment ...

A cease-fire was accepted by Israel and Egypt yesterday on the 17th day of the war as of 6.50 p.m., but shooting continued at the Suez Canal front.

Syria by late last night had still ignored the cease-fire which was initiated by the U.S. and Soviet Union.

In another sudden move, U.S. Secretary of State Dr. Henry Kissinger flew into Israel from Moscow at noon yesterday for talks with Prime Minister Golda Meir. Soviet Premier Kosygin flew to Cairo and Damascus. (See separate stories this page).

The lightning developments came on the heels of an American-Soviet agreement in Moscow in talks between Dr. Kissinger and Soviet leaders.

The cease-fire was promulgated in a Security Council resolution, that also called for immediate peace negotiations between the sides, and for implementation of the 1967 Security Council Resolution 242 "in all its parts."

Jordan also yesterday accepted the cease-fire, but said its expeditionary force in Syria would meanwhile remain under Syrian command. Iraq, which sent larger forces to Syria, rejected the cease-fire call.

MILITARY POSITION FAVOURABLE IN BOTH SECTORS

By SRAYA SHAPIRO, Jerusalem Post Reporter

TEL AVIV. — All Israeli troops in the Suez Canal area were ordered to cease-fire at 6.50 p.m. yesterday, in conformity with the government decision to abide by the Security Council resolution of yesterday morning. But during the next hour, the Egyptians staged a massive artillery barrage on three targets — Israeli positions in the north, our Canal sector, the bridgehead north of the Bitter Lake and on units near the town of Ismailya. The Army spokesman said later the Egyptians were continuing to fire on Israeli positions "in many places."

The cease-fire found the Israeli forces in a favourable position west of the Canal about a mile from the Ismailya-Cairo road in the north and straddling the two roads and the railway leading to Cairo from Suez in the south.

Israeli units also broke through to a front of four kilometres at the Canal, south of the Little Bitter Lake. Three airfields in the area are also in Israeli hands, the Army spokesman said.

The area controlled by Israel west of the Canal is roughly 1,200 square kilometres and its western-most perimeter is about 75 kilometres ...

HE cease-fire is a calculated gamble: it may do no more than freeze the situation for the time being, and save lives and limbs until such time as fighting breaks out again. As things stand now, the Egyptians may have retained sufficient military strength to regroup and make a further attempt to "regain by force what we lost by force." Ample supplies of military hardware are assured to them during a cease-fire.

There are reports of a super-power agreement on limitation of arms supplies to either side in the conflict that refused the cease-fire. Even if that is so, the Russians might not have been too scrupulous about observing it, or have outflanked the arms ban somehow. A period of cease-fire might thus serve them to rebuild their strength and prepare for the next round.

However, that is not all the cease-fire proposal says. It is in fact a grab-bag of proposals from all sides. No doubt both super-powers were suddenly anxious to see an end to a conflict that both viewed with equanimity at the outset. The Russians saw prospects that their advanced arms would at last prove themselves in the field, and the Americans may not have been reluctant to see Soviet arms destroyed by their own weapons once again, or to have growing Soviet dominance in the area cut down.

Two short weeks have proved the present conflict far more furiously destructive of men and arms than any of the preceding clashes. Without a jungle to conceal personnel and armour, the weapons now in use, drawn up in great numbers in an open area, a modern version of a Napoleonic battlefield, the wastage has been unexpectedly great.

We may now assume that Mr. Kosygin used his four days in Cairo to impress on the Egyptian President that he could not afford to continue fighting, but that they would write into the terms of the cease-fire the 242 U.N. Resolution, which is open to varying interpretations from total Israel withdrawal to the 1967 lines down to minor changes. The Resolution was then balanced by a further paragraph requiring "prompt negotiation between the parties," the essential provision of the original armistice agreements between Israel and the Arab states which has been most persistently and deliberately ignored.

If we accept the cease-fire it is because our ultimate target is peace, not the destruction of Egypt. The cease-fire will be well worthwhile if there is a prompt move towards negotiations, and we can then afford the loss of whatever consolidation our forces would no doubt have still achieved on the west bank of the Suez Canal.

If negotiations are unduly delayed, our present position on the road to Cairo should still prove a major obstacle to further Egyptian aggression.

Losing the fruits of victory

Yediot Aharonot (non-party), commenting on the surprise element in the agreement reached at the Brezhnev-Kissinger talks, finds it "far from conducive to lightheartedness." Kosygin must have brought back from Egypt her agreement, if not her pleas, for the acceptance of the programme presented to Kissinger. Further evidence of this is Cairo's appeal to the Chinese representative at the U.N. not to hinder the adoption of such an agreement. Furthermore, the Russo-Egyptian consensus must have been arrived at with the knowledge and acquiescence of the U.S. The details of this agreement represent an attempt to deprive Israel of the fruits of her victory, and are even less advantageous to us than the Rogers Plan. The Moscow agreement was made behind our backs, and the haste with which it was put together was dictated by a desire to save the Arabs from defeat. There may, indeed, also be additional secret clauses — and it would be advisable that both the Government and the IDF should not use a stopwatch in observing the cease-fire, but rather re-double their efforts on the field of battle.

Ma'ariv (non-party) points out that the Israel Government's acceptance of the American-Soviet cease-fire proposal is conditional upon bilaterality and an exchange of prisoners. The paper reviews the current military situation and points out that, despite Egypt's territorial gains on the eastern bank of the Suez Canal, Israel will have won considerable territorial advantage from this war at a comparatively low cost in lives. We shall not forget the lessons learnt from previous cease-fires, which have shown that the Arabs, far from honouring their undertakings, utilize the lull in the fighting in order to prepare for the next round. This time we require substantive guarantees and a working supervision of the truce, so that it should not be used for the emplacement of new missile bases and troop concentrations.

The paper goes on to declare that the U.S.-Soviet proposal "represents an attempt to obscure Israel's military victory and save both Egypt and Moscow from their military and political defeat by attempting to leave territorial gains in Egyptian hands... A cease-fire under the proposed conditions signifies that Sadat may be permitted to claim political advantages, thanks to the war he initiated, despite his military defeat... Israel is in favour of a cease-fire, but not one arrived at in haste, and not one that makes negotiations with a view to peace conditional upon Security Council Resolution 242."

5,000 Englishmen want to help

By DAVID LENNON
Jerusalem Post Correspondent

LONDON. — Five thousand people have volunteered here to go to work in Israel, and by the end of this week over 400 will actually have arrived in Israel.

Working according to well-laid contingency plans, the Youth and Hehalutz Department of the Jewish Agency here carefully screened all the applicants and has already found that 1,100 of those who came forward are suitable.

All of the volunteers are paying their own way and have undertaken to stay at least five months. A number of them asked if it were not possible to stay longer.

Having learnt from the experience of 1967, the Agency is now only sending people in response to specific requests from Israel. Most of those who have already left have gone to kibbutzim, and now some are going in response to requests from industry.

EDITORIALLY, THE JERUSALEM POST on this day greeted the news of the cease-fire with this line: "The cease-fire is a calculated gamble."

By and large, this was the attitude throughout Israel. Most people had little faith that the cease-fire would last; most people felt that war was likely to break out again. Few entertained illusions that the Egyptians really wanted to live in peace with Israel.

But the Israeli hunger for a surcease from war was so great that the cease-fire was greeted with a sigh of relief. Husbands would return; sons would return. Dear ones, on the Egyptian front, would no longer stand in mortal peril. That, in itself, to a war-weary country was enough to make the cease-fire palatable.

I say war weary, even though the War had lasted only 17 days. But the War had been fought with such unbelievable intensity, and the anxiety had been so all-pervasive, that it seemed as if the country had been at war for months, rather than for days.

Of course, there were many who decried the cease-fire, feeling that at the last minute they had been robbed of a victory. The most vocal of these dissidents was General Arik Sharon, the man who had been responsible for the daring thrust to the West Bank of the Suez. He was enraged, along with members of the Likud Party, who felt that they had been let down by a spineless government. It was their contention that Israel couldn't afford inconclusive wars. The price, both in lives and in material costs, of mobilizing the entire nation only to achieve another stalemate, was just too heavy. It was their feeling that the Egyptians, who had initiated this War, should be made to pay for their folly, and that the only way payment could be exacted and future deterrence insured would be for the Egyptian armies to suffer a most grievous defeat. There were many among Israel's citizens who supported this point of view.

But the public did not know what the

Ethiopia breaks ties

ADDIS ABABA (Reuter). — Ethiopia yesterday broke off diplomatic relations with Israel, one of its oldest associates.

Emperor Haile Selassie said in a declaration that diplomatic relations between his country and Israel would remain severed until Israel withdrew from Arab territories occupied in the 1967 war.

Ethiopia and Israel have long been linked with close cultural ties, and the Ethiopian Constitution specifically mentions that the Emperor is directly descended from the union of King Solomon and the Queen of Sheba.

There are many Israelis at present in Ethiopia administering the aid Israel has been giving to Ethiopia.

The Emperor closed his statement saying: "We express the hope that all nations will make their maximum contribution towards bringing permanent peace in the Middle East."

Not one anti-State action by local Arabs

Since the beginning of the current war there has not been a single action, direct or indirect, by Israeli Arabs against the security of the State. This was announced yesterday by the Prime Minister's Adviser on Arab Affairs, Shmuel Toledano, to a meeting in Tel Aviv of Arabs supporting the voluntary War Loan.

Mr. Toledano noted a wave of identification with the State, including volunteering both of manpower and money, which has swept all communities and groups in Israel.

ISRAEL'S COMMITMENT TO FREEDOM

To the Editor of The Jerusalem Post

Sir, — I wish to refer to the two letters published on October 21 regarding the Rakah advertisement. While a staunch opponent of Rakah myself I must register my admiration for *The Jerusalem Post* for having printed the advertisement.

Israel is not only at war for its existence, but also to protect our way of life and our ethical and moral codes, of which one of the most basic is freedom of expression.

What makes us a great nation is not only our military prowess, but also our strict protection of those things we hold sacrosanct. Israel's might lies as much in its social, cultural and human freedom as it does in its military capabilities. The maintenance of these freedoms even in time of war is gratifying evidence of Israel's unshakable commitment to peace, truth and freedom.

ADAM B. KAHAN
Jerusalem, October 21.

Nahariya youngsters collect souvenirs of a Syrian plane that disintegrated over the town on October 20th.

Not one anti-State action by local Arabs

Since the beginning of the current war there has not been a single action, direct or indirect, by Israeli Arabs against the security of the State. This was announced yesterday by the Prime Minister's Adviser on Arab Affairs, Shmuel Toledano, to a meeting in Tel Aviv of Arabs supporting the voluntary War Loan.

Mr. Toledano noted a wave of identification with the State, including volunteering both of manpower and money, which has swept all communities and groups in Israel.

Sir, — I had hoped that the French Government and all western governments would condemn the Arab aggression, but was bitterly disappointed. I am ashamed to be French, to be European. The same cowardly governments rule Europe today as before World War Two. The French and European policy is only guided by the interests of the oil companies. What is Israel's blood compared to the wealth of Arab oil?

I am not a Jew, but I understand that your fight is ours — that you are fighting for freedom and our civilization against totalitarianism and fanaticism. In the past, France was considered the second fatherland of all free men, but today it is Israel. Every free man would be proud to fight side by side with your army.

CLAUDE PAYRE
Perpignan, France, October 10.

Sir, — As a Dutchman, I can tell you that our people always felt close to Israel and the Jews as shown in World War Two. When we heard of this horrible war started by your Arab neighbours in such a cruel manner, my family felt we must let you know our feelings of support in these awful days.

B.D. CREMER
Stadskanaal, The Netherlands,
October 7.

APPEAL FOR PEACE
To the Editor of The Jerusalem Post

Sir, — As the entire region of the Middle East has again exploded into bitter conflict, tragic suffering and loss of life, we as representatives of the United Christian Council in Israel express profound shock and dismay that frustrated hopes and dreams of peace have resulted in resumption of fighting. That this outbreak of hostilities occurred on the most sacred and solemn Day of Atonement offends all religious feelings and human sensibilities.

We earnestly call upon all Middle Eastern states, in accordance with the highest aspirations of their religious ideals, to abandon once and for all this easy recourse to bloodshed instead of responsible and fair negotiations, and with equal energy and dedication to begin to devise a strategy of peace, that all who live in this region who have known the full measure of suffering may now be privileged to know the fruits of peace.

We mourn all who have sacrificed life, and grieve for all who suffer. We pray that the one God whom we all fear may mercifully grant that neighbour will yet come to love and accept neighbour, and that a new spirit of tolerance will prevail, and that out from the fires of this conflict will be forged a desperate will for peace and a new path to fruitful coexistence.

*THE UNITED CHRISTIAN
COUNCIL IN ISRAEL
Executive Committee*
Ramat Hasharon, October 19.

THE TALL ISRAELIS
To the Editor of The Jerusalem Post

Sir, — I am a Roman Catholic sister from the U.S. visiting here in Jerusalem. Back home, I have just completed my term of office as Executive Director of the National Catholic Conference for Interracial Justice, a church-related agency which I have served for ten years.

In the countless pages of the sacred history of Israel, there is no leaf telling a more epic story than the past 25 years of struggle and success. The current battle in Sinai and on the Golan Heights will only tell us once more how tall are Israelis, tall enough to match the mountains.

The sacred history of Israel is more than carving names onto a rock. It is fashioning a nation — people who are walking through time with the ensign of their Maker upon their lives. By what she is, Israel tells the world that persons, not machines, truth, not power, balance the scales of justice in our universe.

*SISTER MARGARET ELLEN
TRAXLER,
School Sister of Notre Dame*
Jerusalem, October 8.

Blind veteran, Druse father, 30,000 others buy bonds

Jerusalem Post Economic Reporter

A veteran blinded in the War of Independence has given all his savings (several tens of thousands of pounds) to the War Loan, according to the Haifa Branch of the War Invalids' Association.

A Druse father of six from the village of Rama, in Galilee, who was wounded in the 1967 conflict, undertook to buy IL2,000 in war bonds — the money to be deducted from his pension in 10 monthly instalments.

When the association tried to dissuade him, pointing out that this leaves him with only IL300 a month to support his family, he said: "I owe this to the State, even if my children and I have to eat bread and olives."

Some 30,000 individuals have purchased war bonds through the banks so far, to the sum of IL40m., it was announced yesterday.

behind-the-scenes pressures actually were. In supporting Israel's defense against the Arab armies, the United States had been pushed to the very brink of ultimate confrontation with Russia.

Shunning further brinkmanship, which was endangering a hard-earned but fragile detente, Kissinger now pressured Israel into a cease-fire. Unless they followed American advice, Israeli leaders were given to understand, they could not depend on receiving further military supplies from America. Without these supplies, Israel couldn't

possibly prosecute a war.

Mrs. Meir, bone weary from tension and not yet recovered from the shock of the closeness of Israel's brush with disaster, was now being faced by the stark threat of abandonment by her major ally. She saw no other course other than acceptance of the American proposal.

When the cease-fire was announced, there was no rejoicing in Israel. Many were relieved, but nobody was happy.

Lights on

Jerusalem Post Staff

The lights went on again all over Israel last night, after 18 nights of darkness.

hTe end of the blackout was officially announced over radio and television at about 5.30 p.m. by the National Haga Commander, Tat-Aluf Uri Rom. Promptly, blacked-out windows all over the country were flung open, and the home-lights — enhanced by the beaming faces of the apartment occupants — shattered the darkness.

In Jerusalem, the Old City walls and the Citadel glowed again by the light of the artistically installed Municipal floodlights, and the Hanukka candelabrum atop City Hall blazed its announcement of last night's Feast of Lights.

In Tel Aviv, many who had not heard the announcement started arguing with people who had turned on their lights along the city's "Great White Way," Dizengoff Street. Car owners went down to wipe the paint off their car lights. And the traffic lights were a confusing mess for several hours till the Municipal technicians got them all working properly again.

Moscow Jews try to send blood

Eighty-eight Moscow Jews yesterday asked the Red Cross in Geneva to let them send blood to Israel. In their cable they claimed the Soviet authorities are only prepared to send blood to the Arabs.

A similar telegram, signed by 100 Moscow Jews, was sent on Monday asking the Red Cross to send a representative to Moscow to organize the dispatch of blood to Israel.

FIRM SUPPORT

To the Editor of The Jerusalem Post

Sir, — My wife and I have come to Israel in order to declare publicly our full and firm solidarity with the State of Israel in the name of "Midnight Call" and "Beth Shalom," representing over 200,000 Christian friends of Israel in Europe and the Americas. Israel's war is our own war. And we are thoroughly convinced that all enemies of Israel who threaten its land and its people, shall be routed. This conviction of ours is based upon the message of the Prophets. As to the numerical superiority of the enemies, we remember what Moses said:

"And five of you shall chase an hundred, and an hundred of you shall put ten thousand to flight." (Lev 26:8).

WIM MALGO President
Beth Shalom

Jerusalem, October 20.

The Israel Philharmonic, with conductor Zubin Mehta and violinist Isaac Stern, gave a concert on Tuesday for combat airmen and ground crews at an airbase somewhere in Israel. The programme consisted of works by Beethoven, Dvorak, Verdi, Bizet and Mendelssohn.

Christian group supports Israel

By JUDY SIEGEL
Special to The Jerusalem Post

The president of an organization representing 200,000 Christians in Europe and the Americas has announced their "unconditional solidarity with the State of Israel in its struggle against the Arabs."

William Malgo, an Evangelical minister from Holland, declared yesterday on behalf of the 18-year-old Beth Shalom Society for Bible Studies that "Israel's war is our war, and we are sure that all the enemies of the Land and People of Israel will be defeated."

"There is no European government that stands firmly for Israel, because they have all abandoned the principles of Christian belief," he said.

The organization's leaders, who plan to meet here in March, hope to raise substantial funds for the State of Israel.

8 ACRE ARAB FISHERMEN have collected IL4,500 to give to the army. They told Acre Mayor Yisrael Doron, to whom they gave the money, that they were also buying IL4,500 in Voluntary War Loan bonds.

OIL ARCHITECTURE

LONDON IN THE DARK

Script for a revenge story

YOM Kippur. Armoured battles. Sam missiles. Uncle Sam. Uncle Herzog, Profesor Shamir, Gotteniu.
CUT

Oilfields somewhere-in-a-principality. Prime Minister Edward Heath. Embargo.
CUT

An Israeli Centurion crippled in Sinai. Demonstrations in Trafalgar Square and British Parliament. Tanks. Tankers. A smiling sheikh: "With Allah's help we can paralyse England. We can plunge London into darkness."

Sir Alec Douglas Home: "I say. We're neutral." Chamberlain's umbrella. Bevin's ghost. A camel's yawn. Reoilpolitik.
CUT

A colossal explosion. Map of the area goes flying. Israeli flag aloft. Cease-fire doves in the air. U.N. building in N.Y., Golda addressing the Assembly:

"...And finally, now that the battles are over, permit me to unveil one of the most secret and wondrous chapters in the saga of our victory. I feel the nations of the world should know that, behind the smoke-screen of its embargo declarations, Britain provided us with powerful military supplies in the most critical hours of our war..."

The Libyan delegate rises and squints. The eyes of the British delegate turn glassy. The Saudi, Baroodi, kicks Tekoah.

Golda: "... We extend our profound and eternal gratitude to the noble British People and its courageous Government, who stood by a small beleaguered nation in its time of need."

The Kuwaiti delegate departs cursing in Russian. Shot of the glassy eyes. Abandoned fuel station. Lone cat.
CUT

Heath: "We did not stand by any small beleaguered nation, we never have and we never shall! Nohow!"
CUT

From the Israeli Press: Three-column picture spread of British shell. Title: The weapon that turned the tide. Subtitle: A friend in need is a friend indeed.
CUT

Sir Alec: "Perfidious slander! We observed the embargo to the letter, honour bright! We can prove it! We'll appeal! HELP!"
CUT

Ramat-Gan high school students in demonstration of sympathy before British Embassy

by EPHRAIM KISHON

King Faisal in profile.
CUT

Sir Alec: "We might discuss substantial economic assistance to Israel in exchange for an immediate stoppage of the gratitude campaign."

Abba Eban: "We shall forever be indebted to Britain for its staunch and indomitable resistance to Arab blackmail...."

Close-up: Sheikh turning off tap somewhere-in-the-desert.
CUT

In London the lights go out. Traffic stops. A thin layer of ice covers a random stove.
CUT

Golda, winking: "That's all, folks!"

Translated by Miriam Arad
By arrangement with "Ma'ariv"

BREAK WITH AFRICA

THE government cannot at this time give official expression to its feelings as one after another Israel's erstwhile friends in Africa break their diplomatic ties with us. Sharp condemnation would heap obstacles on the path of possible reconciliation, and possibly prompt other states to break their ties with Israel too.

But public opinion in this country is angry. If it were not occupied with the more pressing concerns of the war, it would doubtless have been much more embittered, and more volubly embittered.

More than half the countries in Africa with which we had ties at the start of this year have now severed them — and only 14 states in Africa are left now.

And the situation with regard to some of those is so delicate that official spokesmen in Jerusalem cannot even permit themselves to praise those African leaders who are withstanding the pressures and maintaining their links with Israel. A word of praise might be the kiss of death.

Yet the fact is that the pressures upon these leaders are intense, and their courage and political integrity is correspondingly high.

The pressures did not begin on Yom Kippur. The time bomb was set a long time before that — at the Organization of African Unity conference in Addis Ababa in May, and at the Non-aligned summit in Algiers in September. In fact, the anti-Israel resolutions p a s s e d at those conferences must themselves be seen in the context of the process of radicalization that has been eroding Africa's fledgling political stability during recent years.

Some states in black Africa draw their inspiration from Peking. Others find affinity with Moscow. Many more take aid and technological assistance from everyone who offers while managing to steer clear of political ties. But even these are prey to the wave of fierce and growing antipathy towards the ex-colonialist West, and even more so towards the U.S.

Israel, merely because of its identification with the U.S. and the West, would have suffered from this process even without the added unpopularity of the Six Day War aftermath. But the continued occupation of the areas won in that war has been represented to these newly radical African states as the embodiment of modern-day imperialism. Territorial acquisition by force of arms is a genuine threat to the African states which themselves are artificial creations, whose borders follow no geographical or even ethnic logic. Israel's concern for defensible borders that do not invite aggression were never comprehensible to them; perhaps they did not want to understand.

Coupled with the internal radicalization was external pressure — from the newly activist Arab oil states. It is hard to remember today that only recently have Libya and Saudi Arabia emerged as states determined to use their wealth to acquire power and influence.

Israel saw the storm build up — but found that it was unable to prevent it. There could be no question of competing dollar for dollar with Libyan or Saudi financial inducements. I s r a e l tried in some cases to adopt a low profile — even agreeing in one instance to reduce the status of its representation — in the expectation that the storm would blow over. In other cases it tried the opposite course, stepping up technological and development aid. Both courses failed.

There is no denying the political damage that Israel has suffered as a result of its growing isolation in Africa. The repercussions carried across to Western Europe and accounted to some extent for the cool attitude to Israel's plight in the war exhibited by some European states compared with their wholehearted sympathy in 1967.

If the cease-fire opens the path to a political settlement in the Middle East, no doubt many of the African states will seek to renew their links with Israel — and Israel will certainly be glad of it. But those links will never be the same again. The taste of betrayal at a time of crisis will remain.

IN EUROPE, THERE WAS a great disparity between the feelings of the people and the acts of their governments. Generally, throughout the Continent, public opinion favored Israel. The polls showed that 45 to 50 percent of the population of Great Britain favored the Jewish cause. The same was true in France. In West Germany, 57 percent of the country supported Israel.

On the other hand, the Arabs, applauded by only six percent in Great Britain, found their greatest support in France, where 16 percent of the people favored an Egyptian and Syrian victory. This was probably due to the fact that France has a strong segment of Communist voters, and also because of the large Algerian population.

The British Government refused to permit spare parts for British-made Centurion tanks to go to Israel. The Government was roundly criticized by both Tory and Labor members in Parliament, and Sir Alec Douglas Home, the Foreign Secretary, had a difficult time defending his position in the House of Commons. In a radio interview, Harold Wilson baldly admitted the Foreign Office was traditionally pro-Arab.

In Africa, Israel fared very badly, indeed. During 1971, 1972, and 1973, Uganda, Chad, Mali, Nigeria, Congo-Brazzaville, Burundi, and Togo had broken off diplomatic relations with Jerusalem. A few days before the beginning of the Yom Kippur War, Zaire and Rwanda recalled their diplomatic representatives, and during the War, diplomatic links were cut by Tanzania, the Malagasy Republic,

Ask your father and he will tell you...

By MEYER LEVIN

On the morning of the maybe-cease-fire-day, a municipal official telephones. "We have a notification of death to make to the next-of-kin."

The notification committee is gathered in his office. An army reserve officer. A local doctor who knows the family. Two middle-aged women and a quiet-looking man.

The volunteer car is driven by a recent American immigrant, Philip Groob, who came to Israel largely because his two daughters and sons-in-law decided to settle here, the younger having left the day after her marriage. The woman next to me says that last night at the very hour of the cease-fire she had to go to a family in the immigrant housing area, people from Morocco, five children. "I asked a boy, about eight, where were his older sisters or brothers and he said he was the eldest." Their father had fallen.

The family we seek has just moved to a new section of terrace-houses, each with two flats. The car is parked a block away while the doctor and the officer — in civilian clothes — walk over to the house. By the time the rest of us approach, we can already hear the sobbing. Grotesquely, as we open the door, there comes the odour of baking cookies. Truce day. The mother had hoped one of her boys might get immediate leave.

She sits on the sofa between the two women, silent, stunned. Her fingers move over a number of postcards from the front, on the low table before her. Each one says he's fine, everything is fine, not to worry, and is signed with love, These are the soldiers' postcards printed by Carmel wines; we carried a pocketful of them back from Sinai a few days ago, so they would arrive sooner. One of these cards does not bear the army stamp so it might have been brought back and mailed in Tel Aviv by someone like ourselves.

The car is sent to bring the father, from his small household wares shop in Tel Aviv. The family came from Poland in 1956; the elder son, 22, is in the Air Force, and our army man goes next door where there is a telephone, to send for him. had been studying in America and had come rushing back when the war broke out.

The neighbour who has the telephone is sobbing wildly. "Such good people. In some families there is something bad, but this family, all so good, all so good, why did it have to happen to them? Only a few days ago had a chance to phone Ima. He asked to speak to his mother and I ran at once to fetch her."

His mother is now wandering from one room to another. There are only two bedrooms in the immaculate flat. In the boys' room two ironed shirts are hanging ready, there is a shelf of schoolbooks with a shortwave set half taken apart, class pictures on the walls from the Technical School A poster of a tiger.

In the livingroom, there are romantic pictures, cupids in a wood, two pictures of young men serenading girls in white. On a shelf, a Bar Mitzvah picture, the boy in *talit* and *tefilin*. Another picture of the two boys in white jackets and black bow-ties, almost like twins. They were very close.

The mother wanders into the kitchen and one of the women follows her. Sometimes, the woman tells me quietly, they suddenly seize a knife. The doctor has prepared a sedative. But the mother only leans her head against the wall.

A large man with a strong face enters hurriedly, the father. He clutches his head in both hands, rushes into the boys' room and falls on the bed. His wife runs to him, kneels over him. Now there are racked, primeval sobs.

On the bookshelf I pick up a Passover Haggadah. On the cover is a picture of sages around a table. Underneath the picture is printed: "Ask your father and he will tell you. Ask of your elders and they will explain."

Meyer Levin, author of "The Settlers," "In Search," "Compulsion" and "Yehuda," lives in Herzliya.

Dahomey, Upper Volta, Cameroon, Guinea, Senegal, Ethiopia, and Nigeria.

Israeli relations had been close—very close—with many of these countries. Thousands of Africans had received their professional and military training in Israel. Many Africans had been attending, and had graduated from, Israeli institutions of higher learning. Amin, the President of Uganda, and Mobutu, the leader of the Congo—both of whom had been enthusiastic supporters of the Jewish State but a few years earlier—had now become vociferously and fanatically anti-Israel.

I recall traveling through Africa during 1967.

Whenever I heard Hebrew spoken in the streets of Addis Ababa in Ethiopia, in the streets of Abidjan of the Ivory Coast, and in the streets of Dakar in Senegal, I would accost the persons whose language I recognized and strike up a conversation. Delighted to meet an American Jew, my new friends would generally invite myself and my wife to their home. Here, I learned at first hand what these young Israelis were doing in Africa—or rather what Israel was doing in Africa.

The people I met were all dedicated young men and women who had been sent by their home government to assist these underprivileged

Belgians send 'love letters' to the Knesset

Jerusalem Post Knesset Reporter

"Israel — je t'aime."

Hundreds of red-and-white postcards bearing this legend reached the Knesset yesterday, mailed by Belgian Jews under the auspices of the Jewish Community Centre of Brussels.

The postcards are addressed to "The people of Israel, Knesset, Jerusalem, Israel," and are dedicated to the IDF's soldiers. Each postcard is signed by a contributor to the Israel Solidarity Fund, which sold many thousands of them in its fund-raising drive.

In response to the deluge of postcards, Knesset Speaker Yisrael Yeshayahu yesterday cabled the chairman of the Community Centre, David Susskinds, to thank him for the heartening gesture.

CHRISTIAN VOICES RAISED

To the Editor of The Jerusalem Post

Sir, — As Christian scholars who have in common with our Jewish colleagues historic roots in the Land of the Bible and commitment to Biblical faith, who now have gone through the crisis of war alongside Israelis, we share, in so far as we can, the present trial of the people of Israel. Our Christian conscience and our common humanity demand that we make our voices heard.

1. The initiation of the Yom Kippur War through the deliberate breaking of the cease-fire by the Egyptian and Syrian governments is an act of aggression which we deplore.

2. In the face of this renewed threat to destroy the State of Israel, we reaffirm the right of this State to sovereign existence and to secure borders, as provided by the United Nations.

3. We regret not only the tragic loss of life and waste of resources in this war, but also the inevitable hardening of lines which will follow. We believe that the hope of a military solution is a cruel illusion, and we seek to strengthen the hand of those who strive to build a peaceful community of peoples based on mutual respect and brotherhood.

4. Believing that open, direct negotiations between the parties in the Middle East offers the best hope for a peace settlement, we support Resolution 242 as a possible basis for peace talks.

5. We hope for a new and more urgent initiative for peace, one which will transcend the bitterness of the post-war situation. We call upon all parties to implement the cease-fire, to release all prisoners of war, and to turn their attention instead to the root causes of the hostilities in the Middle East. Specifically, we urge the recognition of the State of Israel by the Arab states, a renewed search for a just response to Palestinian claims, and the compensation or re-settlement of all refugees.

*PROF. THOMAS E. AMBROGI,
D.Sc.R.,*
University of the Pacific
Stockton, California, U.S.A.
DONNA MYERS AMBROGI,
Stockton, California, U.S.A.
*BROTHER DR. MARCEL DUBOIS
OP.*
Superior, St. Isaiah House, Jerusalem
SISTER MARIA EDWARD,
Madison, Conn., U.S.A.
*SISTER DR. MARIE GOLDSTEIN,
RSHM,*
Ecumenical Theological Research
Fraternity in Israel
*REV. PROF. NORMAN K.
GOTTWALD, Ph.D.*
Graduate Theological Union,
Berkeley, California, U.S.A.
*BROTHER GABRIEL GROSSMAN
OP.*
St. Isaiah House, Jerusalem
BROTHER BRUNO HUSSAR OP,
St. Isaiah House, Jerusalem
REV. PROF. W. KLASSEN,
University of Manitoba, Canada
BENGT KNUTSSON,
Director of the Swedish Theological
Institute, Jerusalem
*REV. PROF. ARTHUR L.
MERRILL, Ph.D.,*
United Theological Seminary,
New Brighton, Minnesota, U.S.A.
*REV. PROF. DALE MOODY, Th.D.,
D. PHIL. (OXON),*
Southern Baptist Theological Seminary,
Louisville, Kentucky, U.S.A.
SISTER MICHIKO OTA,
Oecumenical Commission for the
Translation of the Bible, Tokyo, Japan
DR. JOE SEGER,
Archaeological Director,
Hebrew Union College, Jerusalem
*REV. DR. WILLIAM R. WATTERS
JR.*
University of Iowa, Iowa City,
Iowa, U.S.A.

Jerusalem, October 22, 1973.

---

countries in the fields of education, agriculture, and electrical and engineering technologies. They received no special pay bonuses, nor did the Israeli Government receive any compensation for these gestures of friendship. The aim of the Israeli Foreign Office had been merely to build up a reservoir of good will among the African nations.

But the work of 20 years had now collapsed. Gone were the thanks, forgotten were the protestations of everlasting gratitude. The efforts of the Israelis had all gone for naught.

It should be borne in mind that most African countries contain sizable Muslim minorities. The governments of these countries conceded to the feelings of their Mohammedan countrymen who followed the call of a holy war against Israel.

Besides, many of these African countries courted Arab political support in the United Nations and elsewhere. They were, therefore, ready to dump Israel in favor of the more powerful support— numerically speaking—of the Arab countries. Moreover, the African nations had been swayed by propaganda identifying Israel with Western capitalism, and they were eager to affirm their membership in the Third World.

But above all, the most persuasive argument was

oil money—oil money paid to African leaders. Jomo Kenyatta, who observed the phenomenon of the stampede away from Israel into the Arab camp, remarked: "We do not want to become prostitutes."[1] Nonetheless, two weeks later, his own Kenya broke off relations with Israel.

Gadaffi was not too far wrong when he boasted that he, singlehanded, had defeated Israel on the diplomatic front in Africa. There is no doubt that Libyan money was the greatest single force in changing the diplomatic picture on the African continent. Perhaps Gadaffi's boast was not altogether fair to the Saudi Arabians and to the Kuwaitis who had also made substantial contributions towards Israel's discomfiture.

The African leaders had been paid—paid in cold cash—for breaking relations with Israel. They had simply succumbed to filthy lucre. Yet all in all, what great moral difference was there really between the baksheesh accepted by the Africans and the turnabout of the European countries? Save for Holland, every European country regarded its need for oil as much more compelling than the cries of three million Jews to be allowed to live.

The Bible said it all some three thousand years ago:

> *For bribery blinds the eyes of the clear-sighted.*[2]

In today's world, each man is still for himself, and each country follows self-interest. It is a world that knows no moral order. And perhaps the Israelis and their supporters were naive to have expected or hoped for anything else. Yet Holland defied the Arab threat of an oil embargo.

> *How far that little candle throws his beams!*
> *So shines a good deed in a naughty world.*[3]

While Israel was absorbing the rebuffs of its sister nations in all parts of the world, its representative in the United Nations was fighting a losing battle in trying to rebut the outrageous statements made by the supposedly responsible ministers of major countries.

The Chinese Foreign Minister, Chu Peng-Fei, condemned "the large-scale military attack by the Jews." The Yom Kippur attack had been planned by the Israelis, in every detail, he declared. The Israeli aggressors had undertaken a surprise attack, much to the indignation of the Chinese people. American imperialism had made this attack possible by providing massive arms to Israel. But Soviet social imperialism was at least equally responsible, for the Russians had permitted many Jews from their country to emigrate to Israel, and the Russians had even considered the renewal of diplomatic relations with Israel.

It was true, continued Peng-Fei, that the Soviets had provided arms to the Arabs, but that minor gesture only operated to prevent Israel from achieving all its aims.

The Chinese Foreign Minister went on to say that the Soviet Union was tying the hands of the Arabs. It was the secret understanding between Moscow and Washington, he insisted, that made it impossible to find a lasting solution in the Middle East.

The halls of the United Nations had resounded during its history with many assertions, but on that day, the Chinese representative scaled the topmost summit of absurdity.

But China was not the only Arab supporter in the Far East. Japan, thirsty for oil, jumped on the Arab bandwagon. Nippon now saw the light. The Arab position was unassailable, and the Israelis, said Tokyo, had better knuckle under. That about completed the picture, but not quite.

Mrs. Indira Gandhi, attempting to achieve an all-time high in double-talk, declared that Indian support for the Arab countries in no way affected the neutral stand of India.

Mr. Rahman of Bangladesh offered Sadat 50,000 guerrillas willing to leave, as he put it, "at a few minutes' notice." After a few days, Rahman modified his offer. Instead, he sent 50,000 pounds of Bengalese tea.

In Islamabad, President Bhutto of Pakistan contented himself by asking his compatriots to pray for an Arab victory.

Save for the United States and Holland, Israel now stood diplomatically isolated.

1. Neue Zurcher Zeitung, October 24, 1973, reporting the Nairobi radio broadcast of October 20, 1973.
2. Exodus XXIII:8; also, Deuteronomy XVI:19.
3. *The Merchant of Venice*, Act V, Scene I.

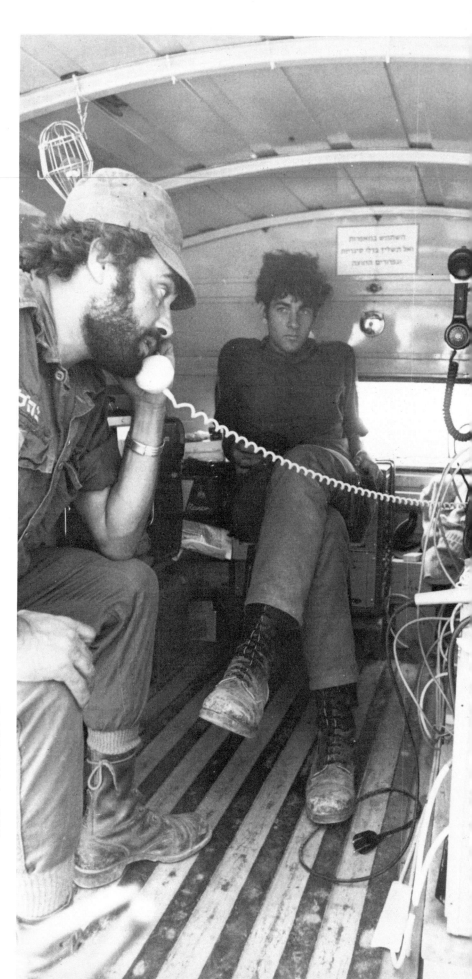

Direct dialling now from Egypt

Soldiers west of the Suez Canal have been dialling home direct, thanks to a mobile telephone unit brought over by Communications Ministry engineers. The unit, which permits a large number of calls at a time, is also being used to relay reports by Israel Broadcasting correspondents.

A similar unit is operating in Syria, which among other things served the soldiers who retook Mount Hermon. All calls are free.

Throughout the fighting, Ministry engineers worked to keep communications open, often under fire. Some even found themselves behind enemy lines at the beginning of the war, the Government Press Office said yesterday.

THE DAY THE CEASE-FIRE CAME

'Nothing between us and Cairo'

By BILL MARMON
''Time'' magazine

WITH ISRAELI FORCES IN EGYPT. — "We could be in Cairo for late lunch," said an Israeli soldier in west central Suez. As he stood on top of his armoured personnel carrier and scanned the road ahead with field glasses. "There is nothing to stop us . . ."

At that point we were on one of the two main access roads from Cairo to Suez and the most direct line from Cairo to the Egyptian forces on the east side of the Canal in the southern

region. We were 50 kms. west of the Canal on that road, the deepest penetration the Israeli forces made into Egypt, only 60 kms. from Cairo.

The Israeli operations in our area were mopping and blocking. And the Israelis were, as the U.S. Marines say, "kicking ass." They stormed a whole series of Egyptian missile bases which had been largely evacuated. One Egyptian unwisely fired at our personnel carrier with small arms fire and was promptly disposed of by the Israeli machinegunner.

When the news came over the radio that a cease-fire was likely to go into effect at 7.00 that

evening (this was the first cease-fire on Monday, October 22) we abandoned our forward position in the west and sped south and east to cut off a vital junction. On the way we encountered four Egyptian tanks moving east to west. The commander cut them off and caught them in a cross-fire from the north and west. At least three of the tanks were destroyed. Standing up on top of the carrier, the commander cheered at the hits.

Most soldiers we spoke to seemed cautious about the cease-fire. Said one officer: "They can't go starting wars whenever they choose and then stop them when they want to."

Women petition Gov't on prisoner exchange

Several hundred Jerusalem women, including mothers and wives of captured Israeli soldiers, petitioned the Government to secure an exchange of prisoners "within 24 hours." The women asked the Government to insist on the exchange as a pre-condition for any cease-fire. "If the enemy fails to comply, it is up to the Government of Israel to take the most far-reaching action to ensure that our demand for the return of prisoners is met," the petition concluded.   *(Itim)*

Id El Fitr

Jerusalem Post Arab Affairs Reporter

Several Arab countries last night ordered the cancellation of traditional festivities marking the three-day Moslem feast of Id El Fitr, which begins today. The feast ended the month-long fast of Ramadan.

Festivities in Arab capitals were called off amid a mood of depression, stemming from the outcome of the war.

The holiday will be marked by about a million local Moslems in Israel and the administered areas. Schools and other institutions in the Arab populated areas were closed for the holiday.

Israel agrees to supply plasma to Third Army

Jerusalem Post Military Correspondent
TEL AVIV. — Israel has agreed to supply plasma to the Egyptian Third Army at the southern end of the Suez Canal.

Arrangements for the transfer of the plasma are being made through the International Red Cross, which asked Israel for the processed blood for transfusions. Egypt had notified the IRC that it was urgently in need of the plasma but had not been able to get it across the lines.

Israel was acting out of humanitarian motives and would transfer the plasma as soon as possible, said a senior army officer who announced the agreement yesterday.

Asked if this meant that Israel would also allow food and water to be transferred to the stranded Egyptians, he said that as a human being he hoped so, but he could not comment as a military man.

He said that the fact that the Egyptians had run out of plasma did not mean they were short of other supplies. Plasma was perishable, but it could be assumed that the Egyptians had transferred enough water and food to last them for some time.

British arms to Arab states

Despite the British embargo on arms to the Middle East, a "veritable airlift of arms" is going to the Persian Gulf emirates from Britain, according to a detailed report on France Inter Radio by Edouard Sablier yesterday.

Sablier began by analysing the hostile attitudes to Israel of the U.S.S.R. and France.

It is believed that the arms sent to the Persian Gulf go from there to Syria and Egypt.

Holiday in France for needy children

TEL AVIV. — One hundred and two needy children whose families suffered severely from the war will spend a month's vacation in France at the expense of a group of Jews living in Paris. A 51-man group, representing the sponsors of the project, left Israel yesterday after a four-day tour during which they visited the Suez Canal and distributed woolen wear to soldiers.

The spokesman for the group, who asked to remain anonymous, said the group was formed spontaneously from among immigrants from North Africa. "We wanted to express our solidarity with Israel," he said.

A phone call to the family from Africa.

One of the most striking features of the war on the home front during the past three weeks has been the firm identification of minority communities, some 400,000 strong, with Israel's cause.

ARABS VOLUNTEER FOR EMERGENCY

IN NAZARETH, beyond the tall green road sign indicating the Haifa-Nazareth-Afula crossroads, a poster in Hebrew reads: "Soldiers! the women of Nazareth and Upper Nazareth welcome you to their free buffet"! On the opposite side of the road, a row of folding tables, put up in the shade of the "Nazareth Hotel," are laden with cold drinks, fruit, sandwiches and cigarettes. Miss Fuma Tawail, an employee of the local post office, relates how Arab and Jewish women in the capital of Galilee organized the first-ever operation of this kind.

"Our buffet is open 12 hours a day and each woman volunteers for a 4-hour shift. There are about 12 of us Arab women here and the bulk of the food, drinks and cigarettes are donations from local merchants and Arab families. The rest is provided by the Nazareth Municipality. In addition to the buffet, we provide the soldiers who stop for a snack and a rest with a free telephone message service to their families at home."

Her shift partner is Mrs. Georgette Amuri, a Nazareth housewife, who says that between 350 and 400 soldiers stop at the buffet every day. When they realize that Arab women are serving them, they often remark, "All honour to the women of Nazareth."

Mrs. Amuri is very sad about this new war.

"As a woman and a mother I feel with every woman and mother, Arab or Jewish, who has lost her son. What we are doing here is the least one can expect us to do to help our country, Israel, through these critical days and ease the suffering of its soldiers..."

At the town hall, Nadim Batish, secretary of the emergency committee, tells me that a special delegation headed by Deputy Mayor Mussa K'teili has just started visiting 200 well-to-do citizens to urge them to subscribe to the voluntary war loan.

"Within the first three hours, they collected over IL20,000," says Mr. Batish.

At the local branch of the Discount Bank, the manager, Jamal Sa'ad, reports that his 13 employees have contributed IL15,000 to the loan. Bank activities are normal, both on the deposit and the withdrawal side. Waiting for Mr. Sa'ad's attention is a local building technician, Mr. Yousef Danial, who wants to make a contribution of IL1,500 to the loan.

"You see" he tells me, "for us Israel is our State, we don't want any other. I pity the youth from both sides. We must do everything we can to help and perhaps our contributions will bring peace sooner."

ANOTHER DONOR is Mr. B'shara Sa'id, a tyre repair man from nearby Yafia village. He has come to pay a first instalment of IL500, but promises to be back soon with a second payment.

"You know," he says, "we independent craftsmen are not capitalists and have no reserves. I bought war loans in 1967; today I feel it my duty to contribute again. I enjoy full rights in Israel, so I must also fulfil my obligations."

At the volunteer registration centre, some 50 qualified workers and craftsmen have already registered, according to Sa'id Khalil, director of the local labour exchange.

Riadh Sakhnini, a concrete blockmaker, is next in the line.

"My boss in Natanya has been called up" he says.

"I am ready to do any job, go to work in the fields of a kibbutz, anything. *El Hamdu li'llah*, I don't need the money, I'll give my pay to the war effort."

Behind him is an electric welder, Jamil Ihbeis, who used to work in the settlements on the Golan Heights. "I felt I just couldn't stay behind. Israel needs support, so just let us give her this."

Doesn't he feel a contradiction between this step and being an Arab?

"A contradiction?" he replies with surprise, "No, why? Israeli soldiers defend me as well. The Syrian rocket which hit Yafiah village and caused destruction last week didn't distinguish between Arabs and Jews, did it?"

AILABUN on the road to Safad is a village of some 1,600 inhabitants. Shortly after the outbreak of the war, the villagers set up their own emergency committee. First task: opening a first aid post. Second task, says Suleiman Rizik, a member of the committee:

"We are urging our workers to resume their normal jobs from which they stayed away at the beginning of the war for three reasons: the closing down of many enterprises; the lack of transport; and the fear that Jewish work colleagues or passers-by in the streets would seek revenge on Israeli Arabs for what the Syrians and Egyptians did."

As a result of the committee's efforts, 60 per cent of the workers have gone back; the fear of maltreatment from Jews had proved to be unfounded, and with the aid of the Nazareth labour exchange, transport has been secured.

At Fadl Matar's greengrocer's shop, I hear him telling two of his customers:

"We here lack nothing, all our needs are supplied amply. It is therefore our duty to the State to make sacrifices in order to help in the defence of our country."

THE LARGEST of Israel's 18 Druze villages is Daliyat al-Carmel. In the first 48 hours of the war, these singular people paid their blood tax once again with several of their sons who lost their lives in the front lines. Yousef Fakhr e-Din, manager of the local Bank Hapo'alim branch, tells the story of

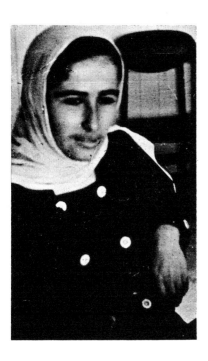

Amunah Nasser e-Din

a peasant woman who came to his counter in tears. She' had just seen a TV scene showing Israeli casualties. Her husband is a simple day labourer. She brought all her savings, IL200, to contribute to the war effort.

At the Gibor factory, which makes women's underwear, Miss Amunah Nasser e-Din, a member of the local workers' committee, representing the more than 70 Druse girls employed here, says:

"Last week we collected IL1,600 to buy presents for the soldiers at the front. Now we are trying to meet another IL1,500 for the war loan."

MY LAST STOP is Tayiba, the biggest of the Moslem villages in the southern part of the "Little Triangle." After three days of absenteeism, concentrated efforts by the local Histadrut branch yielded results: the first of Tayiba's 2,000-strong labour force, the village women, returned to work. Lutfi J'barah, the Histadrut secretary, says that 300 women and girls returned to the agricultural sector and 150 to industry.

"A number of Israeli factories, such as Dubek, could only resume production thanks to our girls returning to their jobs," Lutfi tells me.

Hassan Kamel Ubeid, secretary of the local emergency committee, relates how that body is watching shopkeepers, looking after the enforcement of the blackout and doing everything it can to get life back to normal as quickly as possible.

"Scores of Tayiba's fleet of tenders and trucks have been mobilized for the war effort, some with, others without their owner-drivers." says Hassan.

At the labour exchange I meet Sharif e-Tibi, a self-employed electrician, who has come to register for voluntary work.

"If we don't volunteer to help, who will? Who will replace our soldiers at the front?" he asks me.

He is ready to do any job, even if he earns less than in his own field. Speaking with emotion, Sharif reminds me:

"After all, don't forget that in 1967, Tayiba itself was hit in the Arab attack against Israel. Any attack against Israel is an attack against every single Israeli Arab. Bombs and rockets don't make any distinction. Our duty is to give our State everything it requires to defend its citizens, Jews and Arabs alike."

Hassan Ubeid.

GIDEON WEIGERT

SABBATH
No Publication

IT IS MONDAY, October 22, just a little over two weeks since the War began.

In Haifa, the University's psychology department has begun to focus on helping war-bereaved families, offering special guidance for the now fatherless children.

U. S. Ambassador Kenneth Keating receives a letter signed by over 1,000 Tel Aviv school children thanking America for its aid, and adding: "We hope that your help will speed the coming of true peace, and will prevent death and destruction."

West Germany's Federation of Labor Unions issues a statement condemning aggression, and supporting Israel's right to secure borders.

The Post Office handles more than 100,000 letters for soldiers each day, and treats them as if they were telegrams.

In Tel Mond prison, 200 convicts donate blood, and ask to serve in the Israel Defense Forces.

Finance Minister Sapir states that "Israel's secret weapon is the mobilization of the Jewish people."

Soviet Red Cross refuses blood plasma for Israel

LONDON (INA). — Eighty Soviet Jews from Moscow, Novosibirsk, Vilna and Tallin have protested to the International Committee of the Red Cross that the Soviet authorities did not accept from them offers of blood plasma for Israel, while plasma for Arab combatants was being accepted from donors and dispatched.

Jewish sources said Arkady Lurie, who telephoned the Red Cross headquarters in Geneva, was told that if the blood plasma reached Geneva they would dispatch it to Israel. But when Mr. Lurie, Valery Krikhak and Leonid Tsipin went to the headquarters of the Soviet Red Cross, an official told them their request must be referred to a higher authority. They had no further reply.

Twenty-five Riga Jews, meanwhile, have protested to Tass against biased reporting of Mid-East war news. They pointed out that they did not approve of the anti-Israel policy of the Soviet government either, but they expected at least factual and unbiased reporting from the fronts by the Soviet media.

'West Europe would let Israel go under'

By DAVID LENNON, Jerusalem Post Correspondent

LONDON. — "There wasn't one country in Western Europe that, if pushed to the wall, wouldn't have let Israel go under," the "Daily Telegraph" yesterday quoted a Pentagon official as saying in Washington.

There is a strong feeling in the Pentagon that America's Western allies were less than helpful during the war, and one official said that Britain seemed more interested in arms sales to the Persian Gulf than in Israel's fate.

Pentagon officials were particularly disappointed at the attitudes of Greece and Turkey in declining to permit bases in their territory to be used in the arms airlift, said the "Daily Telegraph." This feeling was accentuated by the fact that Spain and Italy also publicly forbade American planes from staging through their territory.

"The West Geman attitude, including a sharp rebuke over ship-loading at Hamburg late in the week, was also a shock to the Americans. They didn't bother to ask France to cooperate as it is already in the Arab camp. Nor did they ask British cooperation, as the Foreign Secretary was quick to state that if asked Britain would refuse."

Another source of irritation to American officials, the newspaper said, was the way in which Italy, Belgium, Holland, Austria, Sweden, Spain and Luxembourg imposed controls and special conditions of the re-export of refined petroleum products to America.

The negative attitude of Western Europe during the Middle East war had added pressure to the demand for a cutback in U.S. troop commitment in Europe, the "Daily Telegraph" said.

Dilemma of over-aged men

To the Editor of The Jerusalem Post

Sir, — I read with interest Doris Lankin's article, "Dilemma of over-aged men trying to serve" in your issue of October 19. Two days later, you published a report about gas deliveries in Tel Aviv, to the effect that the city emergency headquarters had announced that when gas companies were not able to make home deliveries, the consumers could collect the gas balloons themselves.

Most women are without their menfolk. We may be able to hire a taxi to transport the balloon, but how can we carry it to our apartments? Can a woman carry a gas balloon alone, when the gas companies always have two men delivering? I would suggest that this is definitely a job for over-aged men to do in pairs.

SARA MILLER

Bnei Brak, October 21.

...rning prayers in the desert.

18 Russian Jews arrested

MOSCOW (UPI). — Soviet secret police on Thursday arrested 18 Jews planning to deliver a petition to the Presidium of the Supreme Soviet (Parliament) on behalf of an imprisoned woman, a Jewish source said.

The 18 were picked up separately as they made their way to the Presidium headquarters, the source said. An officer at the militia (police) headquarters at the Ministry of Internal Affairs confirmed the arrests to relatives.

The Jews were attempting to deliver a petition signed by 85 Jews calling for the release of Silva Zalmanson, whose birthday was on Thursday.

Miss Zalmanson received a 10-year prison sentence in 1970 for her part in an alleged plot to hijack an airliner to Sweden.

The appeal said Miss Zalmanson's poor state of health would not allow her to survive the sentence, according to a text made available to Western correspondents.

It also asked for the release of 29 other Jews it said were jailed for seeking to go to Israel.

Israel hoopsters barred from Europe matches

By PAUL KOHN
Jerusalem Post Sports Reporter

TEL AVIV. — The International Basketball Federation (FIBA) has ruled out the participation of six Israel basketball teams in various European championship matches "because of the situation in the Middle East," Mr. William Jones, FIBA secretary, told the chairman of the Israel Basketball Association, Mr. Assael Ben David, on Friday.

FIBA claims it is too dangerous for the foreign teams to play in Israel, and rejected a suggestion by the Israel Basketball Association that all matches be played abroad, on the grounds that visiting Israel teams pose security problems.

The basketball squads of Ramat Gan Maccabi, Jerusalem Betar and Jerusalem Hapoel were due to play on November 6 against Bamberg, Germany, Ankara University and Aek of Athens respectively. Return games were to be played in Israel. The Israel teams' scheduled opponents will receive byes into the next round.

Israel champions Tel Aviv Maccabi, which received a bye in the first round, was to play its second-round match in Amsterdam on November 29, and the girls' teams of Tel Aviv Maccabi and Tel Aviv Hapoel also had matches scheduled for November 29.

Mr. Jones told Mr. Ben David that if all were peaceful in the Middle East by mid-November, FIBA "might reconsider," but officials here were not hopeful.

Danny Kaye conducts IPO for soldiers

Jerusalem Post Reporter

TEL AVIV. — Nurses from local hospitals gave injections and distributed pills at the Mann Auditorium Friday night — to wounded soldiers who had been brought there to hear a special IPO concert.

Some 200 soldiers — in blue pyjamas, plaster casts and bandages — occupied the front rows as Shalom Ronly-Riklis and then comedian Danny Kaye conducted the orchestra.

It was Mr. Kaye's debut as a guest conductor. But he only gave photographers 50 seconds to take his picture — then he ordered them out so the boys could have a clearview of the stage.

After breaking his baton in little pieces and dancing a little jig, Mr. Kaye conducted a Strauss polka, part of the "Nutcracker Suite" and several other pieces, to the applause of the audience of 4,000. He conducted "The Flight of the Bumblebee" with a fly swatter.

He wound up his appearance saying: "I was on the Golan Monday, in Jerusalem Tuesday, in Africa Wednesday.. Tomorrow I'm off to Istanbul for a few days with Unicef, and then I'll be back. I'm going to visit every single hospital with wounded soldiers in the country, I'm going to see every one of those who gave their heart, soul and blood for Israel... That's why we too should all give everything we can."

Proceeds from the benefit concert went to the Soldiers Welfare Association.

Sombre festival in Cairo

CAIRO (AP). — Id el-Fitr, the festival ending the Ramadan fast, is not the same this year. Usually at this time, the streets are like a carnival, gardens crowded with frolicking children. At night, strings of coloured lights festoon the shops.

This year there is no festive atmosphere. The government has closed the public gardens. At night, Cairo is blacked out and police and civil defence guards patrol the streets, checking the passes of the few pedestrians who venture forth on business. Cars with blinking, blue-painted headlights feel their way in the darkness.

For many Egyptians, pride over initial Arab victories has been tempered by the realization that Egypt is paying a heavy toll in battle casualties.

Leaning against his car, a taxi driver remarked: "These people baking *kahk* and *ghorayeba* at this time should be jailed. It's a shame. They should wait until the boys come back from the front." He watched a girl walk past with a tray of freshly baked cookies rich with butter, date paste, almonds and peanuts. "Eat it. I hope you get sick," the cabbie yelled at her.

Danish anti-Nazi leaders arrive

LOD AIRPORT. — Nine members of the Danish World War II underground arrived here yesterday as guests of the Friends of Denmark Association in Israel.

While in Israel, the delegation hopes to visit the battlefronts in Sinai and the Golan Heights, will visit Yad Vashem, the Denmark High School in Jerusalem, and other sights in Israel.

THE HANDWRITING ON THE WALL

To the Editor of The Jerusalem Post

Sir, — Israel is encircled by neighbours who are getting continually more bellicose and making war more frequently. Signs of tightening the noose around the Jews of Israel today remind one all too clearly of Europe in the 1930's, when Hitler was building up to the liquidation of Europe's Jews. Other nations then made compromises at the expense of the Jews; so it is happening again today. Who can forget former Prime Minister Chamberlain of England and his umbrella trip to see Hitler and the resultant compromise? As then, so today too many morally minded organizations and individuals are not speaking out about the threat to Israel's very existence. As a clergyman and educator, I especially deplore this near total silence abroad. Sad to say, even here in Israel, where they enjoy many benefits under Israel's leadership, many important church leaders and organizations are silent. It is not that Israel may not survive the present emergency. Far from it. After this emergency is over, anti-Jewish and anti-Israel pressures in the world will still be present and must be dealt with.

The handwriting on the wall is clear. Why are men silent?

The Rev. Dr. G. DOUGLAS YOUNG
President,
American Institute of Holy Land
Studies

Jerusalem, October 17.

ADMIRATION FROM SPAIN

To the Editor of The Jerusalem Post

Sir, — May I, as a non-Jewish admirer of the State of Israel, express my deep satisfaction at the behaviour of the Spanish public towards the Israeli basket-ball team playing in the Catalan towns of Barcelona and Badalona for the European Championship.

According to the Barcelona leading sports paper, "El Mundo Deportivo," the Israeli team had "the most fervent and passionate hinchada (mass of unconditional supporters)" in all matches for their group. "La Vanguardia," a newspaper of European stature, along with Madrid's "ABC," Spain's leading daily, never failed to reflect at every match the Spanish public's ardent support for the Israeli sportsmen.

On this occasion, it may be worthwhile mentioning the Spanish public's deep admiration for the State of Israel. Everything Israeli is taken here as an example to be followed of strenuous effort, unfailing perseverance, efficiency and intelligence.

We feel that the State of Israel can offer a positive contribution to the world, which is thereby all the richer.   *MIGUEL ROVIRA*

Barcelona, October 6.

President Ephraim Katzir in discussion with a wounded soldier.

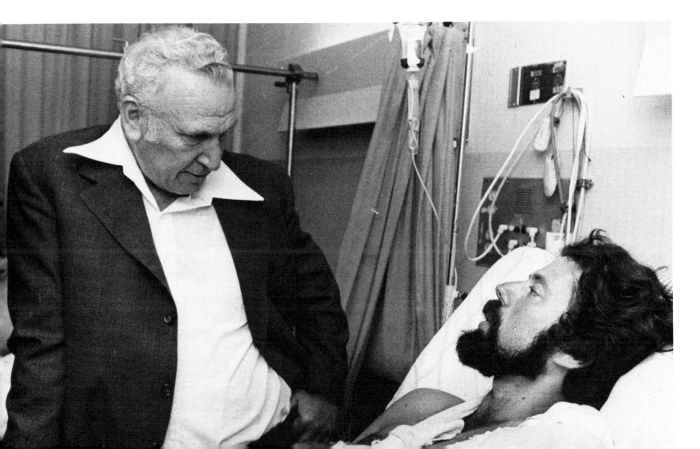

MAN IN THE STREET:
AID TO THIRD ARMY 'INCOMPREHENSIBLE'

By SARAH HONIG
Jerusalem Post Reporter

TEL AVIV. — News that the Government had agreed to allow food supplies through to the beleaguered Egyptian troops in Sinai aroused anger, gloom and frustration in the Israeli street yesterday. The most common reply to *The Jerusalem Post's* random opinion sample was that the "decision is incomprehensible. There is no reason for us to be so humanitarian. We can't go on playing the role of the merciful Jew while cruel losses are being inflicted on us."

Perhaps the bitterest comment of all came from a medic who was demobilized on Friday. "The men to whom we are sending plasma and food are not a bunch of innocent civilians accidentally caught up in the hostilities. These men are aggressors and this is a war," he argued.

"They attacked us and mercilessly machinegunned our boys in the Bar-Lev line outposts," he said. "I saw pictures of these same Arab soldiers gloating in foreign publications and I also saw the results of the awful blood-letting of this war. It turns my stomach to think of what they would do had they succeeded in surrounding our troops. If they want to eat they can surrender. No other army would do what we are doing," he said.

An elderly Yemenite woman had a special reason of her own for opposing the Government's decision. "I lived in Jerusalem when the War of Independence broke out. I remember how hard it was to feed my five children because the Arabs wouldn't let provisions through. My children were not soldiers on tanks.

"All we want is that these Egyptian soldiers give up and go home to their families," she said. "We shouldn't feed them so that they can use their weapons against our boys," she said and added: "My five boys are all in the front now."

All of the some 120 people I spoke to agreed that given the Arabs' record of atrocities we should not have yielded to humanitarian considerations. After several hours of approaching people in Tel Aviv's main streets, I could not find a single person who agreed with the Government's decision.

What troubled most people was the fact that although Israel made yet another concession, "no concessions were forthcoming from the other side."

A middle-aged woman shopping in the Carmel Market said that not only have the Arabs made no concessions "but they have not even done what they are obliged to do under the Geneva Convention of War. They have not turned over the list of the prisoners of war to us or let the Red Cross visit the wounded.

"Our PoW's are being neglected," she said. "God only knows what tortures these men are going through. I don't know if they are given food, water and plasma, and as long as I don't know what their condition is, I don't want my Government to be humanitarian."

KNESSET INCIDENT

To the Editor of The Jerusalem Post

Sir, — A Member of the Knesset was attacked today, his notes were destroyed, he was hustled forcibly away from the rostrum and was refused the right to finish his speech.

This sort of thing will grow overnight into an uncontrollable monster if the three M.K.s responsible are not punished. They ought to be banished from the Knesset for at least three days.

I hate what Willner stands for, but if he can be muzzled by force, anyone else can — and will be.
ROBERT GREENGARD
Holon, October 23.

SOUTH AFRICA'S SUPPORT

To the Editor of The Jerusalem Post

Sir, — With reference to your editorial of October 26 concerning Africa's break with Israel, it seems to me that it would have been opportune to mention the extremely friendly stand taken towards Israel by at least one country on the African continent, namely the Republic of South Africa.

Whatever reserves and criticism one may, rightly or wrongly, have about the internal policy of that country, it seems to me that it should be frankly admitted and recognized that there is apparently one state in Africa on whose friendship Israel can rely, and that is the Republic of South Africa.
Y. YANNAY
Jerusalem, October 26.

WHEN THE ENTIRE VILLAGE CAME TO SYNAGOGUE

New Moon day of mourning

By David Gross

IN normal times our village synagogue has a bare quorum for Sabbath services. Most of us are non-observant and prefer to spend the one weekly day of leisure on outings with the family or fixing up the chicken run, pottering in the garden or simply idling.

But last Shabbat our synagogue was full. Taking into account the fact that almost all our young and not-so-young men were away on active duty, the congregation was as large as on Yom Kippur. On the morning of Yom Kippur that is, before they began drifting away when the sirens alerted us to the radio.

The (reserve) colonel's son, a pleasant young man with a neat, arty beard, had been at that Yom Kippur morning service with his father. They were both among the absentees for the afternoon service; the young man, a newly commissioned officer, was already on his way to the front.

This Shabbat, the entire village came to synagogue to console the father and to pray for the lad's soul, and for the souls of all who had fallen in defence of the Land and People of Israel.

It was the New Moon, semi-holiday, when the Hallel thanksgiving psalms are recited. It was an occasion for a special service of Thanksgiving. The guns silenced, the enemy driven back, his tank corps mauled, his front line missiles obliterated, his air force crippled and his navy cowering in its harbours. The boys will soon be back. Thanks be to God.

Bereaved village

But our New Moon was turned to a day of mourning. The colonel's son had been killed in action. The while village felt bereaved. Instead of fixing up the chicken run, or pottering in the garden, they came to synagogue, all of them, even the professor, who had not come even on Yom Kippur. Also among us were those slim 16-year-olds who, since the war began, have been heaving sacks of chicken feed, crates of poultry and stacks of eggs to keep the village going in the absence of the hired labourers.

The colonel was called to the reading of the Law and to recite the Kaddish at its conclusion. The portion of the week was the story of Noah, "a righteous man in his generation."

I don't know how many in Israel who heard the story of Noah this Sabbath would lay claim to saintliness. Modesty was the hallmark of the first of the prophets and we were taught by another to walk humbly with our God. We do not claim perfection; why, indeed, the confession on Yom Kippur? We have our faults: we lust for material gains, our national wealth and culture is not spread evenly or fairly; some of our youth takes drugs; we maim one another by reckless driving; we maintain an educational system four decades behind the times; we talk too much and sing too little.

But false modesty is also a fault. What are our failings compared with others of our generation? While our enemies deliberately conceal the identities of the prisoners they hold, piling anguish on anguish on the heads of mothers and wives of the missing, we submit lists of all those in our hands who have been categorised. When we occupy Syrian villages we feed and comfort the inhabitants instead of committing rape and rapine as other occupiers do. While those Jews who have failed to flee Syria and Iraq choke in the solitary confinement of their ghettoes, the Arabs who chose to remain in Israel in 1948-9 are free citizens, who volunteered their services for the war effort. And those who came under Israel rule in 1967 are free to come and go as they please and even in these days of war, no iron heel is to be seen in the administered areas.

Open-handed aid

But let us not talk of those with whom we are at war. We extended open-handed aid to the poor and economically retarded in Africa, to have this hand bitten when we could have used a little sympathy if not active help. And what of the Western world, whose nominal religion and whose culture emerged largely from our own, and whose political and social system is to be found in the Middle East only in our country? Germany forbids the use of its port for the transfer of materiél to us.

Germany is now neutral between the admirers of Hitler, and the remnant of his victims. This is what Chancellor Brandt must have meant when he said on his recent visit to this country that relations between Bonn and Jerusalem would no longer be special. Germany can now treat us as unfairly as France and Britain do.

At our synagogue on Shabbat the "El Male Rahamim" prayer for the souls of the colonel's son and his comrades in arms was recited by one who had been imprisoned in Hungary with Hannah Senesh and who saw her executed by the Germans. In those days, too, there were very few who cared a damn for the writhings of European Jewry in its death agony. I suppose it is an improvement that Germany is neutral this time. The western half, that is. The "Democratic People's Republic" that the Soviets created in the eastern half sides, of course, with the (national) socialist republic of feudal Egypt and party-caucus gripped Syria. The free countries of Europe are neutral between free Israel and the Soviet-ensnared Arab bloc; the non-Aligned states of Africa bend away from the only nation in the world that is not part of any alliance.

Jewish solidarity

But we are in ourselves an alliance. Our isolation has strengthened the *alliance israelite*, the brotherhood that is Israel. And not only that part of Israel which dwells in the Land of Israel. As the men in the battle line know they are joined to the people in the rear, so are the Jews of Israel heartened by the expressions of solidarity from the Jews of the world, those in the free world who give of their resources and influence and those who brave the communist tyranny to express their oneness with us.

This generation of ours fears more for the possible loss of its petrol than for the spilling of the blood of our young. Evil and apathy to evil survived the flood. As long as we resist evil and mourn its victims; as long as an entire village feels bereaved when one of its sons dies in defending his people and their land, we are indeed walking in the footsteps of Noah and are righteous in our generation.

J-P Sartre:

Hits Arab aggression, Israeli inflexibility

Jean-Paul Sartre, the leftist French writer and philosopher, said last week that the true war aim of the Egyptians and Syrians was the destruction of Israel.

In an interview published in last Friday's "Al Hamishmar," Sartre said his initial reaction to the news of the Egyptian and Syrian attack was that this was "despicably hopeless war." He added that the Arab aggression was "obvious, well-prepared and backed by great military force."

Sartre spoke with contempt of the French press which, he said, predicted "with satisfaction" the defeat of three million Israelis by one hundred million Arabs.

Asked if he was convinced the Arabs were the aggressors, Sartre replied: "According to their statements it appeared that their official war aim was to retrieve the territories they lost in 1967, and that Israel itself was not in great danger. But I am against the Arabs for their brutal and massive initiative in starting this war, although, as you know, I take no sides in the global dispute.

"I was very concerned," the writer went on to say, "at what emerged behind the official excuses for this war: the destruction of Israel..."

Nevertheless, Sartre said he felt the Israeli government could have exercised "greater initiative and flexibility" after the 1967 war, despite the stubborn refusal of the Arabs to recognize Israel. He said he still believed the occupied areas were one of the causes of the conflict and that Israel's insistence on holding on to them diminished the chances for peace.

OPINION POLL:
Arabs' loyalty to State rose during war

HAIFA. — Forty per cent of the population believe that the loyalty of the Arab minority in the country and their identification with the state increased during the war. Only 13 per cent believe that it declined. This emerges from a survey conducted by the Applied Social Research Institute in Jerusalem. In a similar survey conducted in March 1971, 23 per cent affirmed their identification, and 34 per cent did not.

Last month, Arabs made over hundreds of thousands of pounds to the war effort. Negev Beduin alone subscribed close to IL200,000 in War Loan bonds. They also put at the disposal of the armed services 80 trucks.

In Haifa, several Arabs hitherto regarded as nationalists contributed to the voluntary War Loan

The Prime Minister's Adviser on Arab Affairs, Shmuel Toledano, believes that the basic attitude of fanatical nationalists had not been changed by the Yom Kippur war.

WIZO THANKS HOLLAND

TEL AVIV. — The president of World Wizo, Raya Jaglom, yesterday sent a cable to Queen Juliana of Holland thanking her and the Dutch people for refusing "to yield to Arab pressure and . . . standing by the Jewish People and the State of Israel." The cable was sent in the name of 50 Wizo federations throughout the world.

Jerusalem artist Ya'acov Pins yesterday donated one of his woodcuts, "Moon Over Jerusalem," to the Dutch Embassy in Jerusalem in appreciation of the Dutch people's support of Israel and their refusal to bow to Arab oil blackmail. *(Itim)*

CHRISTIAN COLLABORATION

To the Editor of The Jerusalem Post

Sir, — The Christian world was very largely silent and complicitous before the Nazi genocide of the Jews. Its silence and "neutralism," and even pro-Arabism, amid the attempted second Holocaust of 1967, are well known. With the Yom Kippur War of 1973, Christians and the churches are given the opportunity to collaborate yet a third time in the unceasing effort to annihilate the Jewish People. The available devices are familiar ones: "evenhandedness" and "calls for peace."

The answer will be given almost immediately. And to the extent that Christian collaborationism is once again forthcoming, a new fact will afflict our conscience: consent to the wicked blasphemy of utilizing the holiest day of the Jewish year to the end of destroying the Jews.

REV. A. ROY ECKARDT
Coopersburg, Pa., October 6.

Rev. Eckardt, Professor of Religion at Lehigh University, is, together with his wife, Alice, and a small number of other American Christian theologians and professionals, one of the moving spirits of a group known as Christians Concerned for Israel. Rev. and Mrs. Eckardt have separately and jointly written several books and numerous articles on the subject of Christian-Jewish relations and on the Jewish origins of Christianity. *Ed. J.P.*

TEXACO PROPAGANDA

To the Editor of The Jerusalem Post

Sir, — I recently received a booklet which was sent to me by Texaco Inc. With all that has been said about the oil corporations and their strong anti-Israel involvement, I think that there is still room for denouncement of Texaco's propaganda "Balancing Regulation and Energy." This booklet was published before the Yom Kippur War, but reflects the attitude that what is good for the Arabs is good for the oil companies and therefore good for the world. This propaganda which was sent to thousands of American university professors, lecturers and instructors, should be publicly denounced.

CHAIM KROPACH
Eilat, December 26.

OPEN LETTER

TO THE PRIME MINISTER, Mrs. GOLDA MEIR

Dear Mrs. Meir,

In view of the failure of the Egyptian Government to supply lists of Israeli prisoners of war now in their hands to the International Red Cross,

We, the friends and relatives of those missing on the Suez Front, demand that the humanitarian action of the Israeli Government in permitting the passage of supplies to the encircled Egyptian Third Army be accompanied without delay by the exchange of prisoners of war between Egypt and Israel.

We have today, October 28, 1973, collected in excess of 2,000 signatures supporting this position. These signatures will be delivered to you shortly.

We hope that this grass roots support on the part of private Israeli citizens will strengthen you in your efforts towards this end.

Sincerely,

COMMITTEE FOR THE IMMEDIATE RELEASE OF ISRAELI PRISONERS OF WAR

Copies of the petition can be obtained in English and Hebrew at 21 Rehov Sheshet Hayamim, Jerusalem, or by calling Tel. 02-286144.

Chief Rabbis appeal to Pope on P-o-Ws

Chief Rabbis Shlomo Goren and Ovadia Yosef yesterday appealed to Pope Paul VI and other world religious leaders to help persuade Egypt and Syria to hand over the names of Israeli prisoners of war and to grant them their rights under the Geneva Convention.

Rabbi Goren said the refusal of the Egyptian and Syrian governments to do so was in violation of the Convention, human morality and the rights of man, while Rabbi Yosef pointed out that most prisoners were captured "during prayer and fasting on the day holiest to Judaism."

A similar appeal was made by Religious Affairs Minister Zerah Warhaftig.

Amnesty International in Israel has set up an actions committee to arouse world public opinion on the P-o-W issue. The committee will counsel families of P-o-Ws and men listed as missing on how to solicit the help of international organizations.

Those wishing to can apply in writing to the Actions Committee to save the P-o-Ws, P.O.B. 3260, Tel Aviv, or phone 03-227730 or 03-229483.

The Israel Union of University Students yesterday appealed to unions in 30 countries to protest against the refusal of the Egyptian and Syrian governments to publish lists of Israeli war prisoners. They also asked their fellow students to exert pressure on their governments and the International Red Cross in this matter.

Unions appealed to incluse those in Austria, Czechoslovakia, India, Japan, Uganda and Tanzania, a spokesman said. University students are among Israeli soldiers listed as missing, he added.   *(Itim)*

The mood at Gevat: 'It's not so bad'

By YA'ACOV FRIEDLER
Jerusalem Post Reporter

GEVAT. — "It's not so bad, we've still got one of our walls standing," an eight-year-old girl from this kibbutz wrote to another kibbutz child recently about her children's home. Her letter reflects the attitude at this kibbutz, badly hit by a Russian-made Frog missile from Syria three weeks ago. "Compared to the lives lost in this war, the damage to Gevat, bad as it is, is after all only a secondary problem", kibbutz secretary Malka Meran told me yesterday.

She said that damage is now estimated at some IL3m. and despite war-damage payments, "we'll have to bear very heavy expenses too. We have already shelved all our regular building plans for the coming year, and will concentrate on rebuilding and repairing the damaged houses."

Seven of the dozen children's homes have been razed for rebuilding, which will take at least eight months. The reconstruction has been complicated by the lack of manpower.

The 150 or so children made homeless by the attack have been temporarily moved into the rooms of the men away on active service. They include all the infants. The older children have moved in with their parents. The Housing Ministry has sent 18 prefabricated rooms with showers and toilets attached, and the foundations, water and electricity mains for them should be completed in a month.

Work at the kibbutz is continuing, though the settlement is very shorthanded due to the call-up of most of its younger men. Worst hit is the plastics plant, "our major source of income."

The harvesting of the grapefruit in the 450-dunam grove is being carried out with the help of 40 young Jewish volunteers from Britain, who arrived at Gevat last week. The grapefruit must be picked and exported before Christmas, when they fetch the highest prices in Europe. The primary cotton harvest was accomplished mainly by the older children, standing in for their fathers. "We were pleasantly surprised at how the teenagers handled the complicated and very expensive machinery," one member commented.

Mordehai Zur, a veteran kibbutznik, told me with a wry smile, "For the time being we have suspended kibbutz democracy. We held our first assembly since the war last night. It was an 'old' assembly, with all the young men away. We made it short and decided to let a building committee decide everything concerning the rebuilding. It will determine the character of the kibbutz for years to come, but this is not the time to be fastidious."

I talked to three of the 40 volunteers, 18 to 25 years old, most of them university graduates or students, who have pledged to stay six months in Gevat. Colin Chadwick, 25, a London systems analyst said, "I felt that what I could do in England, donate blood and money, was not enough. I wanted to help while my Jewish brothers in Israel are giving their lives." His non-Jewish employers understood his eagerness to go, "and have promised to keep my job open for me. But now I'm here, I think I may stay if I can find a job in the computer field," he said.

Wendy Roseman, 23, of Brighton, where she worked as a supervisor for a soft drink firm, stands to lose her job. At the kibbutz she is quite happy washing dishes. She has been in Israel before "and I couldn't sit at home while Israel's fighting for its life," she said.

Hospitality needed

Among the fighting men are scores of new immigrants from English-speaking countries. Some of them arrive in Jerusalem for a few hours' leave but have no homes of their own in the capital. They would like a hot shower, perhaps a meal, a few friendly words in their own language and sometimes a bed for the night.

Jerusalemites willing to give such hospitality to boys, who might otherwise have to spend their few leisure hours stretched out on benches in the parks, are asked to telephone the following numbers: 65538 or 66872 or the office of the Association of Americans and Canadians (36932 and 69598) and give their names and addresses.

Follow the Dutch example

To the Editor of The Jerusalem Post

Sir, — We suggest that, in view of the courageous and self-depriving position taken by the people of Holland, we should also limit our pleasure driving.

Let us at least follow their moral leadership by not driving our cars on Shabbat. This is the time when most people here use their cars for pleasure.

We are also of the opinion that the fuel saved by this measure should be exported to Holland.

DOROTHY ROBBINS
KAROLA DESSAUER
Kiryat Ata, November 3.

Kenyan paper bewails African 'ingratitude'

Jerusalem Post Diplomatic Correspondent

A leading newspaper in Kenya yesterday wrote a strong editorial against the African breaks with Israel, terming them "national ingratitude and diplomatic ineffectiveness".

The "Sunday Nation" said that Israeli aid programmes "have been more succesful than those of most of the major and richer nations", and continued: "It is national ingratitude that only one of the African countries thanked the Israelis for anything, choosing rather to dwell on the anti-Arab evils of the 2.5-million-people nation. Evil or not — and every nation has its share — the Israelis have put a great deal in this continent," it said.

At a public meeting a week ago, President Kenyatta declared his intention of maintaining diplomatic ties with both sides to the Middle East conflict.

In Tel Aviv, the Ethiopia-Israel Friendship Association yesterday sent a cable to Emperor Haile Selassie expressing "shock and sorrow" at his country's decision to sever diplomatic ties with Israel.

The cable, signed by Avraham Ne'eman, president of the association, went on to stress the long-standing historic ties between the Ethiopian and Jewish peoples, and to regret that Ethiopia has now disqualified itself from playing an active part in laying the grounds for peace talks between Israel and the Arabs. *(Itim)*

Soldier writing letter home from the Sinai.

Parents of Israeli P-o-Ws demand action

TEL AVIV. — Parents of missing soldiers yesterday called on Israel to cut off all contact with the enemy, the U.N. observers and the Red Cross until the Egyptians and Syrians furnish lists of prisoners they hold.

The parents made the demand in a leaflet calling on Prime Minister Meir to "do more" towards freeing the prisoners. The leaflet was distributed at Beit Sokolow, headquarters of the Israel Journalists Federation.

They called on Mrs. Meir to declare that the cease-fire will not be binding on Israel until the enemy submits the lists and commits itself to exchange of prisoners.

The group said that every additional minute without the prisoner lists puts the lives of the captive Israelis in danger. They were particularly disturbed by Israel's agreement to allow supplies to cut-off enemy troops.   *(Itim)*

The Action Committee for the Release of the Prisoners

Under the auspices of Amnesty International, Israel

P.O.B. 3260, Tel Aviv. Tel. 227730

In view of the grave situation of Israeli prisoners, denied the status of prisoners-of-war, with all the elementary rights ensuing from the Geneva Convention and international law,

We hereby appeal to the governments of the world and international public opinion and demand:

1. The governments of Egypt and Syria must immediately publish a full and detailed list of all the Israeli prisoners in their hands.

2. The Arab governments must permit the immediate release of the wounded as ruled by the Geneva Convention.

3. The Arab governments must ensure the early exchange of prisoners — as promised with the declaration of the cease-fire.

The Government of Israel and the Knesset are obligated to ensure and insist on the principle of mutuality when extending aid to the encircled Egyptian forces, midst preservation of the legitimate rights of the Israeli prisoners anchored in international law, the Geneva Conventions and international law commitments.

The Founding Committee:

SHMUEL ABUTBUL
MORDECHAI BEN-ARI
SHAUL BEN-SIMHON
MOSHE BARNEA
MICHAEL CASPI
ARYE DISSENCHIK

NOAH MOSES
MARK MOSEVICS
HENRI OCHANA
Dr. MOSHE BERNARD
REZNIKOFF
DAN RECANATI

A demonstration outside the Red Cross Building in Tel Aviv.

Criminals in Egypt are 'patriotic'

CAIRO (AP). — Crime in Egypt reportedly has dropped to almost zero since the Middle East war began, and a top official is quoted as saying it may be because thieves are being patriotic.

"It seems the criminals feel it is shameful to commit crimes when their country is at war to liberate their occupied lands," said Gen. Mustafa el Sheikh, chief of the national police.

"They know that our sons are giving their blood and lives at the front to bring us victory, honour and respect."

Sheikh, in an interview with a Cairo newspaper, was quoted as saying that even the nationwide blackout did not encourage such crimes as breaking and entering.

Many known criminals, as well as men recently released from prison, had reported to police stations to volunteer for the national cause. Some asked to be sent to the front lines, he said. The government put some in rear area jobs such as hospital laundries while others were assigned to civil defence units, he said.

Sheikh said that blood feuds between families — a fact of life in Egypt for centuries — also appear to have been suspended by the war.

"Astonishingly enough, the families who were supposed to be taking part in revenge killings have become reconciled," he said.

"Free my father!" this sign reads. The girl is taking part in a demonstration held in protest against the retention of prisoners of war by Egypt and Syria.

OUTRAGED CHRISTIAN

To the Editor of The Jerusalem Post

Sir, — As an American, I was deeply disturbed by the inaccurate, damaging and incomplete article by Dr. William Watters entitled, "Christianity can't be trusted in time of need" (October 28).

I have heard and watched one big American cargo plane after another coming in to Lod with help for Israel's defence. America stood up beside the Jews. We don't ask for too much thanks because we love Israel. But don't say Christians can't be trusted in times of need. President Nixon is openly a Christian. Harry Truman was a Christian. Senator Jackson is a Christian. I am a Christian. I flew to Israel as fast as El Al would bring me when the War of Atonement came. Within the past 12 days, I have lectured in support of Israel in Braunschweig, Germany, Belfast, Ireland, and London.

Many Christian missionaries here now are not only praying for and loving Israel, but working for her too. We believe in fighting for God's People, the Jews, as well as praying. You gave Christianity its very foundation. We love you all. When will you get that straight? Don't class all Christians together just because they call themselves that. All real Bible-loving Christians are one with Israel.

GEORGE OTIS

Tel Aviv (Northridge, Calif.), October 28.

IN SUPPORT OF ISRAEL'S RIGHT TO SECURITY AND PEACE

Immediately after the outbreak of the war of the Day of Atonement, 21 faculty members of the Hebrew University of Jerusalem, some of whom had in the past been critical of their government's policies, declared their full support for Israel's self-defense effort, as well as for Israel's basic approach to the issue of reaching peace with its neighbors.

They appealed to their academic colleagues, to students, to people of good will all over the world, to "use their influence to the utmost to bring home to the Arab countries the demand of the world that the language of hate and vilification, and the dialogue of war, must be replaced by the dialogue of peaceful co-existence."

This is a message of response to that plea for understanding and support.

We believe in the justice of the Israeli cause and are convinced that the people and government of Israel seek nothing more in this war, which was thrust upon them, than enduring peace in the Middle East. We know that this war follows upon and is a consequence of 25 years of Arab refusal to recognize the sovereignty and independence of Israel and to deal openly with its leaders.

We have not forgotten the holocausts of the past. The 3 million people of Israel, many of them survivors of the Nazi terror, cannot be allowed to fall victim to the concerted attack of more than 60 million Arabs backed by the tremendous power and resources of the Soviet war machine. Nor can the world accept this Soviet effort to exclude Israel from the security of international *detente.*

It is our hope that the people of Israel may build their nation without periodic threats of annihilation and without wars that waste their substance and take their young.

As citizens of the United States and members of the international community of learning, we send this expression of solidarity and assure the Israeli people that we shall do all we can, and seek to persuade our government to do all that it can, to sustain them in their struggle for the right to live in peace within secure boundaries.

Abel, *Dean, School of Journalism Columbia University*

stian B. Anfinsen, *Nobel Laureate, National Institute of Health*

eth Arrow, *Nobel Laureate, Professor of Economics, Harvard University*

t F. Bales, *Professor of Social Relations, Harvard University*

el Baskin, *President, Union for experimenting Colleges and niversities*

e Beadle, *Noble Laureate, Professor meritus, University of Chicago* ellow

d Bernstein, *Charles Ev...*

John R. Everett, *President, New School for Social Research*

Harold A. Feiveson, *Lecturer, International Affairs, Woodrow Wilson School, Princeton*

John H. Fischer, *President, Teachers College, Columbia University*

Edward W. Fox, *Professor of History, Cornell University*

Milton Friedman, *Distinguished Service Professor of Economics, University of Chicago*

Harry D. Gideonse, *Chancellor, New School for Social Research*

Eli Ginzberg, *Hepburn Pr...*

Arthur Link, *Edwards Professor of American History, Princeton University*

Seymour Martin Lipset, *Professor of Government and Sociology, Harvard University*

Louis Loss, *William Nelson Cromwell Professor of Law, Harvard University*

Brendan A. Maher, *Professor of the Psychology of Personality, Harvard University*

Frank Manuel, *Kenan Professor of History, New York U...*

Herbert Scarf, *Professor of Economics, Yale University*

John Schrecker, *Associate Professor of History, Brandeis University*

Harvey B. Scribner, *Former Chancellor, New York City School System*

Edward Shils, *Professor of Sociology, University of Chicago*

John R. Silber, *President, Boston University*

John A. Simpson, *Professor of Physics, University of Chicago*

'Israel will remain independent'

The demands that war and its aftermath have forced on Israel and the questions raised by the cease-fire are discussed here by Transport and Communications Minister SHIMON PERES in an interview with Jerusalem Post Political Reporter MARK SEGAL

Shimon Peres

The complicated question whether the cease-fire was a mistake and whether, to judge from Arab talk, it contains the seeds of an even fiercer war, was broken down into simple reasoning by Transport and Communications Minister Shimon Peres.

"The war broke out because we were attacked. The reason for the cease-fire was because it was offered us. We did not want war, so there was no reason to oppose the cease-fire.

"In the Middle East, there is the atmosphere created by the countries involved in the conflict and there is the stratosphere created by the Big Powers. If the Russians had not built a war machine for the Arabs, they would not have gone to war. After all, we have seen how the Russians built war machines model 1, model 2 and model 3, which caused war on three occasions."

Now the Soviets have to show moderation, for if they build another Arab war machine the temptation to make war will be too great for the Arabs. The chances for peace also depend on whether peace negotiations are held with all the Arab states together, or each country by itself. If the former, then prospects for peace are much lower. For if Sadat, Assad and Gaddafi all sit together at the table, then Gaddafi's fanaticism will set the tone. But if talks are held with each Arab state separately, then the prospects seem much better."

Our interview took place in Mr. Peres' office in Tel Aviv. The Minister looked utterly exhausted. His secretary Aviva tells of her boss putting in 20-hour days in tending to his ministerial duties, apart from the daily Cabinet sessions. On a purely personal level, Mr. Peres has just had news that both his son and son-in-law emerged unharmed from the war on the Suez front.

Mr. Peres refused to comment on reported American pressure on Israel to acquiesce in saving Sadat's position and prestige by rescuing the Third Army and whether this might be a foretaste of talks on the border.

However, the Minister was more amenable to the question of what kind of margin is left to little Israel to maneouvre with the Super Powers and whether Israel's independence would henceforth be limited by its overweening dependence on the U.S.

"Israel should and indeed can remain as a firm rock, irrespective of the severity of the threat. In this I profoundly believe and it is not just a matter of fatalism. When it comes to the real crunch, we have no alternative and this becomes the focus of our policies ... The need to receive aid from the U.S. was a function of the massive help extended by the Russians to the Arabs.

"Believe me, Israel will continue to be the most independent country in the world. My old friend Guy Mollet, who of late has been attacking Israel, continues to call for the retention of American troops in Europe. So who is more sovereign? True, Israel has American military equipment, but they have the equipment and American soldiers. Who is more independent, Israel or Hungary, Poland and Czechoslovakia? They sent tanks and other weapons of death to the Arabs and any child may ask why these countries need to send such arms against Israel? Only because they are subject to Soviet dictate. African countries that suddenly in 1973 remembered that Israel had not evacuated the territories, are they more sovereign than Israel?

"If we compare Israel to these other lands, then we are one of the decision makers. We are not 'hawks,' but we are in a 'hawkish' situation.

Mr. Peres said that although this war like the previous ones evokes questions, the real question is not if there were any mistakes, but how we emerged victoriously. "After all, the true lesson to be learned from this war is the defeat of the enemy. When one sees the disproportionate odds against us, the combined forces and resources of the entire Arab world with massive Communist aid, and despite this, that Israel is now west of the Suez Canal and north of the Hermon range, then the war comes into true focus. Historians will draw their conclusions from the results of this war much more than from its problems."

We then turned to his reported proposals for putting the economy on a war footing.

He stressed that the question facing a developed economy like that of Israel was not how to exist but of the standard of living. "We have to grasp that the nation

that won the war by hard fighting in wartime must become a hard-working nation to win the peace." He called for the declaration of an emergency period of economic recovery when "we will have to work harder, and have a longer working day." In practical terms this meant extending the present collective labour agreement unchanged (i.e. no wage rises) for at least six months.

No profiteering

He wanted measures taken to ensure that no one profits from this programme. "Everyone will be ready to make the right kind of effort if they know that there will be no dodging by a minority." (He has already raised the outline of his views before the Ministerial Economic Committee.) He did not envisage compulsory, but rather voluntary, measures with full coordination and cooperation by the Government, the Histadrut and the employers in a national planning board.

What conclusions should be drawn from the boycott during the war by foreign airlines and shipping companies? The Minister declared that "I can only express my strongest possible displeasure at this unnecessary interruption of Israel's links with the outside world.

"The fact that 50 per cent of air freight and passenger traffic was handled by El Al and 50 per cent of sea transport by Israeli flag ships indicated in which direction Israeli policy must cleave in the future. He said he had also learned from coping with land transport problems in the recent emergency that Israel must develop its railway system to an even greater extent and thereby solve its transportation problems thoroughly. "In war we run out of trucks and in peace fear that if things go on as they are, we will run out of roads."

ONE OF THE REMARKABLE THINGS about Israeli life is that the population is, by and large, completely at home with the full spectrum of the ancient Scriptures. Boys and girls study the Bible in public school, where it is taught not as a religious document, but as the prime literary heritage of their past. On their school holidays, children often take hikes and excursions to visit the sites of the Bible, which are, so to speak, just around the corner. Here is Mount Gilboa, where King Saul and his son Jonathan fell at the hands of the Philistines—just about an hour's drive from Tel Aviv. And here are the Stables of Solomon, a mere 20-minute stroll from the throbbing business center of Israel's capital city. Have you ever heard of the Witch of Endor? Well, they say she lived right around here....

Thus, most school children from the age of nine and up are quite familiar with the narratives recounted in the Bible, having read them in the original tongue.

From the age of eleven, boys and girls are introduced to the prophetic literature. As a matter of course, they study Isaiah, Jeremiah, Ezekiel, Joel, Zephaniah, Jonah, Job, Ecclesiastes, and Esther, as well as other more unfamiliar works of the Old Testament; and as they grow older, they

study the Talmud and the poetry of the great Jewish medieval sages. It is, therefore, not uncommon in Israel to come upon ordinary posters or signs quoting what in other countries would be deemed esoteric passages of Scripture, known only to Biblical scholars. These quotations are used in full confidence that the man in the street will understand the reference.

Speakers, too, in their public addresses are likely to use Biblical phrases with little fear that they may be talking above the heads of their audience, or that they may be flaunting their learning.

For centuries, the Jews have thought of

themselves as *Am ha-Sefer,* "The People of the Book."

Today, statistics bear this out. In this nation of 3,200,000 people, there is publication of as many as 518 newspapers and magazines of general interest, plus 393 periodicals of special interest. Every day, 23 newspapers are printed in 10 different languages: 13 in Hebrew, two in Arabic, and one each in English, French, German, Yiddish, Hungarian, Polish, Bulgarian, and Rumanian.

I remember visiting a rudimentary kibbutz in 1925, and although the housing was nothing more than four walls of bare lumber with scarcely space

One of the signs reads "There can be no peace conference without a solution to the problem of the missing." Another sign reads "Golda, where are our dear ones?" A third proclaims "The government is responsible for the fate of our sons." The one on the left quotes Yehuda Halevi's well-known verse, "O, Zion! Wilt thou not be concerned for the welfare of thy captives!"

127

The unwavering loyalty

IN a world of nations where loyalty wavers with shifting interest, Israel is truly blessed with the unwavering loyalty of the Jewish communities in every part of the world.

Jews in the Soviet Union in expressing solidarity with us during the past weeks displayed an extraordinary brand of courage, of a kind we generally associate with the battlefield.

In the Western world where vocal support may be given freely, the Jewish response has an important material dimension as well. And when at the outset of the war Finance Minister Pinhas Sapir left on his mission to rally monetary support from Jewish communities abroad he had reason to expect that his appeal would evoke appropriate response. But even he was unprepared for the massive outpouring of financial help especially among the Jewish communities of the U.S. and Canada.

The United Jewish Appeal collected more than $100 million in the first week of the war and has set a goal of $750 million. The UJA has undertaken to bear the burden of immigrant absorption and social welfare.

The Israel Bond Organization has undertaken to shoulder Israel's entire development budget, and forged a programme to sell $642 million in bonds during the current year. Since the war began bond sales have totalled $250 million, surpassing the $210 million sold during the entire year of 1967.

This tremendous outpouring of funds expresses the fundamental truth which is now engraven on the Jewish consciousness — namely the awareness of the unity of Jewish existence and Jewish fate.

And while Israel, endangered but resolute, stirs the emotion and sense of loyalty of the entire Jewish world, Jews abroad should also always know that their sense of solidarity is also an inspiration to us.

1,000 volunteers already here from abroad

Jerusalem Post Reporter

More than 1,000 volunteers from abroad have arrived in Israel since the war broke out, and are now helping out on those kibbutzim most severely hit by the call-up of their members. This was reported by Mordechai Bar-On, head of the Jewish Agency's Youth and Hehalutz Department, at a meeting of the Zionist Executive on Sunday.

Mr. Bar-On told the Executive that another 1,000 volunteers are expected to arrive shortly. Half are from the U.S. and the rest from England and other countries in Europe and Latin America.

The volunteer programme is being run by the Youth and Hehalutz Department, but all volunteers are expected to pay their own fares and undertake to remain in Israel for at least six months. Mr. Bar-On said Jewish Agency offices abroad had been flooded with requests from some 50,000 young people wanting to come to Israel to help. But a careful screening process had eliminated all but those for whom work would be readily available.

Not a single volunteer from abroad had found himself without work when he arrived, Mr. Bar-On said.

Difference of standards

Israel's decision to allow supplies to reach the Egyptian Third Army and its "moderate response" to the Arab refusal to observe the Geneva Convention on P-o-Ws moved the London **Daily Telegraph** yesterday to call on the Arabs to meet the same standard of conduct. In an editorial the paper said:

"Israel's enemies say she dare not rout the Egyptian Third Army now because America would not allow it. But there may not be much that America could do to stop it. Instead, Israel has agreed to let a supply column through to her stranded enemies.

"Here in essence is the difference between the standards of conduct of the two societies confronting each other in the Middle East. For, on the same day Egypt was refusing to grant Red Cross access to captured Israelis, Israel responded by stopping evacuation of captured Arabs — which, considering she could have denied the means of survival to 20,000 men, was a moderate response indeed. Let the Arabs now show similar standards."

The **Guardian**, Liberal, discussed the U.N. peace force:

"As for Dr. Waldheim's peacekeeping force of 7,000 men, it is not much use, but better than nothing. It is no more than an expanded group of observers, it offers no security to either side and by the time it has been stretched out along two fronts, it will only be a thin blue line.

"At least once in position it can report what is happening and can clear up minor incidents. That is the limit of its capability. Again the urgency of proper peace negotiations is evident. Moscow and Washington will have to get their clients to the conference table."

Phone van in Egypt handles 2,000 calls a day

Jerusalem Post Reporter

The Communications Ministry's mobile phone van in Egypt is handling about 2,000 calls a day, the Ministry announced Sunday. The van, offering direct dialling, is connected into the Tel Aviv "03" central.

On the home front, phone installation priorities are being set aside temporarily, and engineers are installing phones first in buildings where there are none. The move is designed to ensure communications between soldiers and their families. In a related move, another 600 public telephones will be installed in remote areas of the country within the next week or 10 days, according to the Ministry.

Meanwhile, telephone repairmen are continuing to work around the clock, to make sure soldiers calling home get through.

U.S. ethnic leaders support Israel

NEW YORK. — Leaders of various ethnic groups in the United States, including the Polish, Italian, Greek, Japanese and other communities, have expressed their support of Israel's right to exist with defensible borders and have condemned the Egyptian and Syrian assault on Israel.

"Defending its freedom, independence and safety in the current Middle East War, Israel has earned the sympathy and good will of countless Americans who adhere to the principle of self-determination for all nations," declared Aloysius A. Mazewski, President of the Polish American Congress.

Ross M. Harano, of the Japanese American Citizens League, declared that "the deliberate shattering of the 1967 cease-fire agreement by the Egyptians and the Syrians and the general unwillingness to negotiate a lasting peace is especially disturbing to those of us who are striving for understanding and cooperation among all peoples."

Similarly, Andrew T. Kopan, President of the Hellenic Council on Education, said that "a solution must be found for the vexing problem confronting Arabs and Jews. But the solution must be premised upon the right of Israel to survival with defensible boundaries."

Another important leader in ethnic concerns, Rev. Andrew M. Greeley, Director of the Centre for Studies of American Pluralism of the National Opinion Research Centre, declared that "the only solution to the Middle East problem will come from negotiations between the parties involved... It would be madness for Israel to withdraw from the cease-fire lines until her neighbours are willing to guarantee her right to exist."

Seven Catholic religious leaders concerned with ethnic and urban affairs, have expressed their recognition of "the right of Israel to exist with defensible boundaries and to peacefully fulfil its destiny as expressed by the democratic ideals of that nation state." Signatories to the statement were: Rev. Msgr. John Egan, Notre Dame University; Rev. Msgr. Geno C. Beroni, President of the National Centre of Urban Ethnic Affairs; Rev. Paul J. Asciolla, Editor of Fra Noi Italian American News; Rev. Silvano Tomasi, Director, Centre for Migration Studies; Rev. Edward Flahavan, of the St. Paul Archdiocese Urban Affairs Commission; Rev. Les Schmidt, of the Catholic Commission of Appalachia; and Rev. Thomas Millea, of Chicago. *(A.J.C.)*

Chess contest for soldiers

By ELIAHU SHAHAF
Jerusalem Post Reporter

TEL AVIV. — The Israel Chess Federation has launched a special contest designed for soldiers at the front as well as civilians. The contest consists of two problems and one study (endgame). Some 50 prizes will be awarded, among them chess sets, clocks and books, as well as free tickets to the forthcoming Israel chess championship, scheduled to be held at the end of this year.

Thousands of leaflets about the contest have been sent to registered chess players, clubs, recreation camps, youth centres and soldiers (through the Chief Army Education Officer).

Peres sees Danish resistance fighters

Jerusalem Post Reporter

TEL AVIV.—"The war may not yet be over, although the battles probably are," Minister of Communications Shimon Peres told a group of Danish resistance fighters of the Second World War yesterday. They were here for a ceremony marking the issue of a special Israeli stamp commemorating the 30th anniversary of the rescue of Danish Jews.

"We have paid a very high price to ward off the threat of annihilation from an army of a million soldiers armed to the teeth," Mr. Peres added.

The Danish delegation of eight is headed by Morgens Ryefelt, who said the Danes did for their Jews "what we would have done for any other Dane."

The stamp, designed by Assaf Berg of Jerusalem, depicts a boat, enveloped in the Danish colours, carrying the figure of a refugee.

---

enough in which to turn around, the community had set up a reading room with books, magazines, and newspapers from all over the world.

Israel boasts of 77 publishing houses, and 124 bookstores. There are approximately 700 libraries in the country, a towering figure for a country of this size. There is hardly an Israeli community—

no matter how tiny—that does not have a library.

Literally speaking, Israel is undoubtedly a people of the book, but the phrase *Am ha-Sefer* has always meant, specifically, the people of *the* book par excellence—the book being, of course, the paramount book of all time, the Bible.

IONESCO ON MID-EAST WAR:

'A persecuted people should have a country of its own'

By JACK MAURICE
Jerusalem Post Correspondent

PARIS. — The Arabs' "determination to destroy Israel is something that I fail utterly to understand," the French playwright and essayist, Eugene Ionesco, wrote in "Le Figaro" yesterday.

Ionesco, who was awarded the Jerusalem Prize at the Sixth Jerusalem International Book Fair last April, wrote that the Arabs claim "all they wish is to reconquer their territories; but in 1967 it was not a matter of reconquering territories but of exterminating a people."

He added: "It is just that a persecuted people should have a strip of land to cultivate where it can live in peace. That is why the Jews wanted a country of their own. But they were threatened with finding a cemetery there."

OTHER WINNERS

The 1967 Jerusalem Prize-winner, André Schwarz-Bart, ("The Last of the Just") arrived in Jerusalem just after the war began, to lecture French-speaking school-children and radio audiences and to "help out in any way I can," he said on arrival. No word has been heard in Jerusalem from any of the other prize winners: Swiss novelist and playwright Max Frisch (1965); Italian novelist Ignazio Silone (1969), and Argentine short-story writer and fabulist Jorge Luis Borges (1971). The first laureate, in 1963, was the late Lord Bertrand Russell.

The present war was launched by the Arab bourgeoisie for their own profit, the French Nobel Literature Prize winner, Jean-Paul Sartre, wrote in the extreme Left-wing French daily he edits, "Liberation," yesterday. Thus, he said, this war, "instead of advancing, is bound to set back the Middle East's progress towards socialism."

He wrote: "Their admirable effort since the beginning of this century, when the Israeli nation did not yet exist, is enough to justify the presence of the Jews on this land which nobody had ever made fruitful before. The destruction by violence of the Israeli nation is, therefore, inadmissible."

However, "Israel will be a viable country only when it succeeds in reconciling its own rights with those of the exiled Palestinians. There can be lasting peace only if (Israel and the Arabs) solve the problem of the frontiers and occupation themselves, without allowing the big powers to impose a solution."

BRITISH JEWS ASHAMED

To the Editor of The Jerusalem Post

Sir, — I write this to you as a Jewish wife, mother, and grandmother. I have no family or friends in Israel, so send this as an open letter to all.

I am a third generation British Jew, and up until now have thought of Israel as my second country. I have never even visited Israel, but the ties a Jew feels for Israel I too have felt. I cheered during your Six Day victory in 1967, but still the spirit for Zionism was not in me. Now things are different and my thoughts are with you day and night.

My family and I feel such shame and disgust at this country's embargo of the spare parts you need, that I hope, please God, when we visit Israel, which I trust will be soon, you will not turn your backs on us as British Jews, and call us cowards. We, in our hearts, feel this shame, and it will remain with us always.

DELLA WHITCOMBE
London, October 16.

Arab women knit for the soldiers

TEL AVIV. — Members of the Arab Women's Clubs of Moetzet Hapoalot are volunteering to make life more comfortable for Israeli soldiers in the field.

The Arab girls and women in more than 30 Moetzet Hapoalot clubs throughout the country have responded to the national call for "balaclava" knitted helmets to keep the men warm in the cold nights of the desert and Syrian fronts.

The project, launched earlier this week, will cover approximately 2,000 members of Arab Women's Clubs sponsored by the Moetzet Hapoalot. The girls have volunteered not only to knit the helmets for their countrymen, it was noted, but are also buying the wool themselves.

Mrs. Violet Batat, director of the Arab women's programme of the Moetzet Hapoalot, reported that the project was suggested by the girls themselves.

This statement has been cabled to the Secretary General of the U.N., to the President of the International Committee of the Red Cross, and to International Women's Organizations.

We, the Council of Women's Organizations in Israel, are profoundly distressed at the refusal of the governments of Egypt and Syria to submit the names of Israel prisoners-of-war to the International Committee of the Red Cross, to permit that organization to visit these prisoners, and to repatriate wounded prisoners. Their refusal is a manifest breach of the obligations laid down in the 3rd Geneva Convention Relating to Prisoners-of-War to which the governments concerned are signatories. As has been confirmed by the International Committee of the Red Cross, Israel, for its part, has provided and continues to provide full information to the Red Cross on Arab prisoners-of-war in its hands, and is permitting Red Cross delegates to visit these prisoners in accordance with the Geneva Convention.

As mothers and wives, we are profoundly anxious over the welfare of our husbands and sons held captive by the Egyptian and Syrian governments.

Human decency requires that the international voice of women be heard in protest against this behaviour. We therefore appeal to you to speak out and use every influence to bring pressure on the governments of Egypt and Syria to fulfil the minimal humanitarian requirements that the Geneva Convention demands of them with respect to Israeli prisoners-of-war in their hands.

(Mrs.) Pnina Herzog
President
Council of Women's Organizations in Israel

Jerusalem, October 30, 1973

CONCERNED HUMAN BEINGS

Please phone or cable your friends and relatives in the United States immediately to relay the following message through all effective channels:

We urge the President and Congress of the United States to bring all possible influence to bear on the Governments of Syria and Egypt to implement an immediate and full exchange of prisoners of war. We further urge the Government of the United States to insist that the Soviet Union keep its promise on the prisoner of war exchange issue.

CITIZENS' COMMITTEE FOR THE IMMEDIATE RELEASE OF ISRAELI PRISONERS OF WAR.

For information and/or offers of help, please call 02-286144 or 02-528525.

A QUESTION THAT MUST BE ASKED
To the Editor of The Jerusalem Post

Sir, — Lea Ben Dor's article ("What Happened? What Went Wrong? — October 19) offers a spate of possible explanations as to Israel's lack of preparedness for this latest and, very likely, costliest of our wars with the Arabs.

Her proposition that in the event the Arab forces massed at our borders were only military manoeuvres, the bringing up of Israeli tanks and men could have sparked a conflict, is questionable. Such reasoning could argue against all military preparedness.

Mrs. Ben Dor caps off her article claiming that "the whole of Israel was party to the error, hawks, doves and all; we would not let the army believe otherwise." Such strained logic could serve as an explanation for just about anything. It explains everything and nothing. The fact is that we have military experts; we have our intelligence service; and we have political leaders entrusted with the responsibility of deciding and implementing national and military decisions. The very need for military secrecy and the complex nature of modern warfare plus the fact that the public is neither privy to such classified information nor in a position to affect such policy directly would preclude otherwise.

Few would dispute the Government's decision not to strike first. This is not the question. The question that must be asked and ultimately answered is why almost nothing was done to prepare for and to counter the known Arab build-up on our northern and southern frontiers until it was already too late.

ALFRED MILLER
Ramat Hasharon, October 22.

MOTHERS AND WIVES!

We call on all women to join in protesting against the barbaric disregard by the Syrian government of the Geneva Convention in respect to Israeli prisoners of war. Join the demonstration today, Wednesday, October 31, at 3.30 p.m., outside the offices of the International Red Cross, 32 Rehov Ben Yehuda, Tel Aviv.

THE ORGANIZING COMMITTEE:
YONAT SENED—Revivim
SHULAMIT ALONI—Kfar Shmaryahu
Dr. CELA SCHECHTER—Beersheba
TEHIA BAT OREN—Jerusalem
MARCIA FREEDMAN—Haifa
ESTHER HANIN—Haifa

Outside Knesset

Protesters demand action on P-o-Ws

Jerusalem Post Staff

Some 300 parents and wives of soldiers listed as missing or taken prisoner demonstrated outside the Knesset yesterday to urge the Government to take immediate action for the exchange of the men.

They carried placards in Hebrew and English which read: "Geneva Convention For All," "Exchange of Prisoners First — Then Help to the Enemy," "Where is my Father?," "Nixon — Keep your Promise," and "Nixon — You Gave us a Cease-fire — Now Give us Our Boys Back."

The demonstration spilled down into the roadway, forcing Knesset members to drive in and out of the Knesset building in one lane. There was no shouting, and there were no incidents.

Demonstrators who talked to reporters said they felt the authorities could have taken firm action to ensure reciprocity on humanitarian issues several days ago, as soon as the problem of the encircled Third Army cropped up.

A number of the P-o-Ws' families entered the Knesset earlier to talk to ministers and Knesset members.

Another demonstration is scheduled for 3.30 p.m. today outside the Israel office of the International Red Cross, at 32 Rehov Ben Yehuda, in Tel Aviv.

The Israel Medical Association and the deans of the country's law schools yesterday cabled the International Red Cross, the World Health Organization and the International Medical Association, asking them to use their good offices to persuade the Egyptians and Syrians to honour the Geneva Convention governing war prisoners.

In a similar move, heads of Israel's institutions of higher learning yesterday cabled some 200 colleagues all over the world with an appeal that they use their influence to have the Syrian and Egyptian governments comply with the Geneva Convention.

A similar cable was sent to U.N. Secretary-General Kurt Waldheim, United States Secretary of State Henry Kissinger, Eric Martens, President of the International Committee of the Red Cross; UNESCO, and Gen. Ensio Siilasvuo, Chief of Staff, United Nations Truce Supervisory Organization.

It was learned that the Israel Student Union will ask for a High Court injunction against the Government's decision to feed the beleaguered Egyptian troops if the Arabs continue violating the Geneva Convention.

IN ISRAEL, the catch phrase used to describe the War and its immediate aftermath was *ha-Maapacha,* "The Earthquake." For the cataclysm of those few days turned over and upset many strongly held opinions.

For one thing, no one in Israel could conceive that the country's leadership would ever be caught by surprise. Everyone had unbounded faith in the strength of Israeli Intelligence. It was unthinkable that Israel's enemies could be preparing any kind of major assault without Army Intelligence being well aware of what was going on. True, it was later asserted that Intelligence reports were in fact delivered to the Premier and to the Defense Minister, but that these reports were improperly interpreted. If so, this was no more heartening.

The quickness with which the Bar Lev Line collapsed was depressing. True, everyone knew that it was only slightly manned, but for years the ingenuity of its construction had been esteemed, and to have it fold up like a pack of cards was indeed a shock. But probably what was most appalling was that the Israeli Air Force had proved not to be invincible after all. Under the relentless blows of Russia's SAM missiles, the losses were horrendous.

Truly an earthquake had struck Israel. Inevitably, a reaction set in. Questions of political, military and moral responsibility were painfully explored. Who was responsible for pulling the rug from underneath our feet?

For nigh onto three months, the country addressed itself obsessively to these questions. The general tenor of unrest reflected itself not alone in the debates held in the Knesset, which at times grew extremely acerbic, but also in the parlor debates held in every private gathering in every living room throughout the land. What to do? How would a troubled nation restore its equilibrium?

The austerity program that lay in the wake of the War didn't help the mood very much. The Israeli became the highest taxed person on the face of the earth. Proportionately, Israel carries the heaviest

Lesson on P-o-Ws

To the Editor of The Jerusalem Post

Sir, — I now serve as chairman of the Long Island, New York, POW (prisoners of war) Organization, as well as a National Board Member of the National League of Families of P.o.W.s and MIAs in Southeast Asia. Both of these groups represent the families and concerned leaders in the United States who are trying to ameliorate the tragic plight of the P.o.W.s and MIAs in the Vietnam War. I have had a great deal of exposure in the ongoing discussions with the White House and Dr. Henry Kissinger in the plans to get the P.o.W.s home from Vietnam after the truce and the difficulties in getting the honest facts about the MIAs.

I must make this plea to the Israeli officials dealing with the P.o.W. problem: do not enter into any negotiations until all Israeli prisoners-of-war have been released and all the missing-in-action have been properly accounted for.

I know whereof I speak. The United States had about 1,900 P.o.W.s and MIA men listed at the time of the cease-fire in Vietnam. After much threatening and contention, about 585 men were released. It is nearly ten months after the fact and we still have had no word about the other 1,300. In spite of the fact that North Vietnam and its allies in Laos, Cambodia and others have given many indications that other men are alive and are held in jungle cave camps, not one word has come out about the 1,300 MIAs.

We have made repeated demands of the President and his Secretary of State; all we get is sanctimonious answers of sympathy and promises that have proved empty. Even though the United States Government has installed a special unit to seek accounting for the 1,300, they have not been able to get the required permission to make the on-the-spot inspections and investigations. The unfortunate and unabashed truth is that they have been scrupulously kept away from each and every opportunity to find out the truth about the 1,300.

I am certain that Israel now, as the United States then, honestly and carefully fulfil the entire Geneva Code in their treatment of prisoners of war. We have a right to expect that the other side should perform in like fashion, and until we are certain that they do, I implore Israel again to heed my plea:

RABBI RUBIN R. DOBIN
Tel Aviv (Lawrence, N.Y.), Oct. 29.

Feelings run high at rally of P-o-Ws' families

Jerusalem Post Reporter

TEL AVIV. — Hundreds of anxious relatives of Israeli prisoners held in Egypt and Syria tried to storm the American Embassy and Red Cross offices here yesterday. They were held back by prompt police intervention.

Feelings were running very high, and the demonstrators — many of them women — worked themselves into a frenzy, shouting threats against the Arab leaders and also, in some cases, against the Government.

Shulamit Aloni, M.K., who addressed the crowd outside the Red Cross offices in Rehov Ben Yehuda, tried to explain that the demonstration was not meant to be a criticism of the International Red Cross. It was, she said, "an expression of the anxiety of the prisoners' relatives." Red Cross officials promised to do their best.

Psychological help for the civilians

By JUDY SIEGEL
Special to The Jerusalem Post

While the Yom Kippur War brought little physical danger to the populated areas of Israel, many civilians were subjected to considerable emotional stress.

Women, anxious about their husbands in uniform, were suddenly faced with sole responsibility for their homes and children. Young men physically unfit for military service felt useless or guilty as they watched their friends go off to the front. And in the minds of their elders, memories of past wars and of the Holocaust were stirred by yet another siren blast.

In an effort to provide practical help to normal people overburdened by the pressures of war, a number of professionals in the mental health field in Jerusalem set up an *ad hoc* voluntary organization called Moked.

They use the Jerusalem Mental Health Clinic in Bethlehem Road as a base of operations and share the telephone number of Aran the 24-hour hotline for emotional problems run by the Municipality and the Ministry of Health since 1970 (the number is 69911).

"A free service of this kind never existed here before," says Judy Heller, a volunteer social worker at Moked. "We had to feel our way around and look for the gaps in regular social and mental health services during the emergency."

They found the atmosphere tense and uneasy in the cramped corridors of the Town Major's office in Jerusalem, where families who had not heard from soldiers came to get information. A team of psychologists and social workers were sent to help make the waiting easier.

"Most of them sit quietly and keep their troubles to themselves," said Naomi Sheffer, a volunteer from the Paul Baerwald School of Social Work at the Hebrew University. "But if one woman is overwhelmed by the unknown and starts to scream hysterically, everyone sitting here is liable to explode.

"I can't solve their problems, but I do try to discover where their strength lies and encourage them to use it," she continues. "It's amazing to discover the great reserves of personal toughness that come to the surface in a time of crisis."

Many Moked workers have been sent on home visits to distressed families who have been referred to them by relatives, neighbours, Magen David Adom or the Town Major.

The problem may be easily solved — a woman who wants to visit her wounded husband in hospital and needs a babysitter for her children, or one whose husband left on Yom Kippur without leaving her any money for household expenses.

But some families need detailed and deliberate advice. How does a wife go about her usual tasks at home and those normally done by her husband, while keeping in good spirits and explaining their father's absence to her children?

The Moked psychologists advise her that household routine be kept as normal as possible. She should sit down with her children — even those she thinks are too young to understand — and try to dispel any fears of danger and abandonment. If they are irritable or aggressive, have little appetite or sleep poorly, the children should not be punished, but given a lot of love.

Moked volunteers have found that, if handled properly and in time, the emotional wounds of the war usually heal completely.

defense burden in the world; and after the War started, almost 50 percent of the gross national product went into defense. Compare this with the figures in the United States where the citizenry pays some six percent of its gross national product for defense. The Israeli was being told that he would have to pull his belt in even tighter; luxury items were completely out.

"The earthquake" had rocked Israel. One month after Yom Kippur, the tremors were still strong. November was anything but a happy time in Eretz Israel.

Israeli Army personnel getting rid of the desert dust.

CHRISTENDOM'S OFFICIAL SILENCE

To the Editor of The Jerusalem Post

Sir, — If Israel, in order to prevent what happened on Yom Kippur, had opened fire first, the Christian press would have been full of sarcastic comments about this shocking lack of respect for such a holy day. If Israel, in order to protect her very existence, had once opened fire, on a Moslem holy day, this same press would have exploded with shocked comments and protests. I am not exaggerating: Let us only remember June 1967, when one or two shells hit the St. Anne Catholic Church in the Old City, near the Lions' Gate. A wave of protest rose from the Catholic world. And as far as the Protestants are concerned, one need only remember the shocking reaction of the Lutheran Federation, demanding the immediate departure of the "occupying Israeli forces" from Lutheran ground on Mount Scopus. Yet the Lutheran Federation never protested when the Jordanian King's occupying forces started to transform the Augusta Victoria Hospital into an army base weeks before the June war.

But when the Jewish people is murderously attacked on Yom Kippur and, moreover, in the very month of Ramadan, Church leaders (who like to be called Holy Father, Beatitude, Grace and Monsignore, when Jesus came as Servant!) remain silent. They pray, of course, for the cease-fire, thus putting the murderer and the victim in the same category. There are many Christians like me who are fed up with pious prayers which are not followed by declarations or action.

The Christian hierarchy and Christian theologians have not accepted the deep prophetical meaning of Israel's resurrection on her land — they refuse to see the evident messianic implications of this unique adventure.

There are, I believe, some 40 patriarchs, beatitudes, graces and monsignori in the Old City of Jerusalem alone. They have all kept quiet since Kippur, although this nation is still in grave danger. Some Christians did publish a protest ("Christians shocked," October 16), and it is certainly a good move. But unfortunately the signatories represent only themselves. They do not speak in the name of their churches. Will one — only one — of the leaders of official Christendom speak up and save the honour of Christendom?

THE REVEREND
CLAUDE DUVERNOY
Jerusalem, October 17.

THE LETTER PRINTED and enlarged on the opposite page represents a protest written by an individual, a clergyman who is resident in Jerusalem. He expresses his deep chagrin and disappointment that the church hierarchy — both Catholic and Protestant — have remained silent in the face of what he deems to be outrageous behavior towards the Israelis. He wonders why official Christendom has not protested the desecration of Yom Kippur, has not lifted its voice against the harassment of the Jewish State, and why the churches "have not accepted the deep prophetical meaning of Israel's resurrection on her land."

Throughout the pages of this book, the reader will encounter many letters of support from all over the world written by sympathetic Christians. The Reverend Claude Duvernoy does not stand alone in his protest. Nuns, leaders of religious orders, and ordinary laymen have been aghast at the immorality displayed by the policy of most nations toward the Jewish State. These words of support have been extremely heartwarming to the Israelis.

I recall meeting a Swiss doctor in the home of my friend, Mordecai Raanon, an Israeli publisher. I did not know as I talked to the doctor and his wife for an hour or so that they were not Jewish. Their interest in the country was so intense, their sympathy so profound that I took it for granted that they were bound to the land by blood ties. Ora Raanon, Mordecai's wife, told me that immediately after the outbreak of hostilities, the doctor's wife had phoned her from Switzerland to ask her how they were, and that she had followed up her first phone call with a couple of others to find out how things were going. "You would think,"

Syrian inhumanity

THE cease-fire may have silenced the guns and stopped the tanks in their tracks, but the looking-glass war continues, with the defeated claiming victory, and every statement by the enemy apparently made in mirror-writing. Thus the Egyptian Third Army is said to be encircling the Israelis on the western bank of the Suez Canal and the Syrians, according to an English correspondent's report, do not consider that they have been beaten even though their troops have been driven back beyond the former cease-fire line.

We may have to wait until reason disperses this desert mirage, and past history has shown that Syria has always been the last of our neighbours to accept realities. But we cannot tolerate any further delay on the issue of our prisoners-of-war. It is not only that every Israeli personally feels the anguish of the wives and parents involved. We are not prepared to accept Syria's flagrant disregard of the Geneva Convention, nor its latest extraordinary exhibition in laying down "conditions" before it even provides the International Red Cross with the lists of prisoners in its hands.

Any nation claiming to belong to the civilized world accepts humanitarian concepts as regards treatment of prisoners of war, as does Israel meticulously. If the world is still capable of being shocked, then the photographs in the press and on television of manacled, even shackled Israeli prisoners of war must indeed shock. Egypt, at least, has promised to provide the Red Cross with the requisite lists, but this, too, at a snail's pace. Past experience has shown that Egypt takes more care of its image than Syria does. Indeed, Syria has a long history of uncivilized behaviour.

No wonder, then, that there are demonstrations at the Knesset and in Israeli cities demanding action for the immediate return of the prisoners. No wonder that thousands flock to sign petitions for their release to be sent to President Nixon, to the International Red Cross, to every body of decent public opinion everywhere.

Perhaps the most damning testimony to the attitude of the Syrian leadership to human beings has come from a Syrian pilot who baled out when his plane was shot down in a dog-fight. He was left to fend for himself, without food or water, for 12 days. Before he died, he scrawled on his parachute: "Next time you send your citizens to fight, give them some thought." World opinion cannot allow such a government to drag its heels on the P-o-W issue.

Security suspects contribute to soldiers' welfare

NETANYA. — Detainees awaiting trial in the Kfar Yona jail here for alleged security offences have contributed more than IL3,200 to the Soldiers Welfare Association. The contributions range from IL10 to IL1,000 (the latter given by a Druse prisoner from Majdal Shams, on the Golan Heights).

One prisoner from Ramallah, who said he had no money, took two rings off his fingers as his contribution.

Jailers had explained the purposes of the Association and said contributions were strictly voluntary.

The Histadrut has meanwhile announced that Negev Beduin have subscribed IL190,000 towards the national war loan. The subscriptions are made through the secretary of the Histadrut branch in Beersheba.

It said the committee of Arab taxi drivers' cooperatives resolved that soldiers on their way home on Fridays and holiday eves would be taken without charge. The committee of the Arab producers' cooperatives has announced that its members will subscribe IL1,000 to 1L7,000 apiece to the war loan.

'Rehearsal for Worl

Axel Springer, head of the powerful German publishing empire and a sturdy friend of this country, says the Russians gained an important political victory when Bonn refused to allow transhipment of American arms to Israel. He says the behaviour of Nato countries during the Middle East crisis is "the shame of Europe."

Springer arrived three days ago in his private plane "because I felt I had to be with my Israeli friends at this time." He terms the West German halt of vital arms shipments to Israel "appalling and indefensible," and says it will have serious consequences for the future of Europe.

"Many Germans like myself, who have laboured for three decades to improve relations with the Jewish people, bury our heads in shame.

"Make no mistake. This was not a policy that Foreign Minister Walter Scheel determined on his own. It is the policy of Chancellor Willy Brandt.

"It was quite in character that Mr. Brandt went off on holiday to southern France at the height of the crisis. He doesn't realize what's happening. We are again in Spain in 1936. The Soviet Union is testing its most modern arms and equipment at the price of Israeli blood.

"The bridging equipment used by the Egyptians to successfully cross the Canal is a tiny sample of the Soviet amphibious bridge-carriers massed on the banks of the Elbe, threatening the very heartland of Germany — and this in the midst of European disarmament talks. Despite all the talk of East-West detente we may be facing a great dress rehearsal for World War Three.

"German Defence Minister Georg Leber, who is also a good friend of Israel, realizes the danger of scores of Soviet Russian mobile bridges ready to be put across the Elbe in a matter of minutes. But he has been asked to keep quiet about it so as not to spoil Willy Brandt's 'Ostpolitik.'

"I very much dislike being an 'I told you so' man, but it is a fact that I predicted at an early stage that Brandt's 'Ostpolitik' must bring about the destruction of the West European community.

"The Bonn Government cannot do anything that might upset the Russians in any manner. In the present stage of European apathy, I don't

German publisher AXEL SPRINGER, who is in Jerusalem for a flying visit, says we are "again in Spain in 1936." He calls Nato's behaviour regarding U.S. arms shipments to Israel "the shame of Europe," in an interview with The Post's ARI RATH.

know who would lift a finger, if the Russians decide to move on West Berlin. As a Berliner, I feel even more let down by Bonn's sterile and unforgivable neutrality towards Israel in its hour of most dire need.

"The U.S. is the only guarantee for a free West Europe, and to deal with the Americans over the arms shipments to Israel the way the Brandt Government did is unspeakable, quite apart from the betrayal of Germany's moral commitment towards Israel."

Germans appalled

Mr. Springer says the majority of the German people do not support Brandt's present policy. "Millions of Germans were horrified when Israel was attacked by the Arabs over three weeks ago, and they are appalled at Bonn's attitude both towards the U.S. and Israel. A C.D.U. Government would never have acted that way, and I am saying this as a non-party man. I know Willy Brandt very well, from his years as Mayor of Berlin. I often wondered why people tended to overestimate his character and personality, the same way many Germans underestimated Konrad Adenauer, because of his simplicity.

"Egon Bahr, Brandt's close associate and chief architect of Bonn's 'Ostpolitik,' once told me that a German like Willy Brandt, who in 1945 felt liberated, has no need to feel guilty towards the Jews."

Adenauer's testament

Axel Springer recalls here what

Axel Springer.

Adenauer told him shortly before the former Chancellor's death six years ago. "It was like a spiritual testament. He made three points:

- Don't trust the Russians in their talk.
- Be careful with the unbalanced German people.
- Keep up Germany's friendship with Israel and the Jewish people.

"Unlike Brandt, who often chooses to remain silent in times of crisis and political embarrassment — as he is doing now — Adenauer always had the courage to speak out. He was convinced that his love and support for Israel were also in the best service of Germany.

"The Opposition and my newspapers had warned the Americans that they were supporting the wrong people, just for the sake of promoting an East-West detente. The majority of the German people is definitely pro-American. A recent public opinion poll by the well-known and reliable Allensbach group showed that the U.S. arms air lift to Israel has raised all-out German support for Washington from 57 to 66 per cent. Most Germans are still very much concerned over the Russians and would want to see a united Europe in transatlantic union with the U.S."

Accompanying Mr. Springer on his current visit is Ernst Cramer, one of the top managers of the Springer concern and a former edi-

Var III'

He sent a letter to the conference, expressing his solidarity with Israel and warning that Germans sit at the table of the world powers in "borrowed tailcoats..."

Unbalanced neutrality

"Bonn's so-called balanced Middle East policy and its sterile neutrality are not even balanced any more. The German protest to the Americans over the arms shipments to Israel was first made public by the West German Ambassador in Cairo, Hans-Georg Steltzer, at a meeting with the then Egyptian Deputy Foreign Minister Ismail Fahmy (who is now in Washington). The ambassador acted at the explicit order of State Secretary Paul Frank, head of the Bonn Foreign Ministry, who lost no time in soothing the Arabs.

"I was never so sad in this city," Axel Springer reflects on his current visit to Jerusalem. "The empty King David Hotel reminds me so much of the empty hotels in Berlin during the dark hours of the Russian blockade.

"You have suffered so many losses, among them sons of many of my friends here. And there is this European shame, the immoral attitude of West Europe towards the Jews.

"But I do believe that in the long run, it is the moral issues that determine policy."

tor of "Die Welt." He interjected a few choice quotes from some of the Springer papers.

A recent editorial in the "Berliner Morgenpost" said that Bonn's move against U.S. arms shipments to Israel was a "step from Nato into no-man's-land." "The German Government has lost its view for both world policy and a balanced national interest," the paper said.

Brandt's 'kneel service'

Referring to Brandt's historic gesture, when he knelt at the Warsaw Ghetto memorial, Hans Habe comments in "Die Welt": "Was that anything else but sheer 'kneel-service?' It has been proved that it is easier to bow to yesterday's victims of murder, than to support murder victims of today... Willy Brandt's rejection of Jews in their hour of need has extinguished the glory of his emigration period... The Federal Republic's neutralization, which has so often been denied by Brandt, has become reality in Bremerhaven (where the Israeli ship Palmach was sent away before it could load American arms). In Bre-

merhaven 'desk-culprits' were at work..."

And in an editorial in last Sunday's "Welt am Sonntag," Mr. Cramer himself warns that the "Soviet leaders have proved once more that they are not harmless, peace-seeking people, but remained the same dangerous wolves as before, disguised occasionally in sheep-fell... It was Soviet policy that strengthened the Arabs. It was Soviet weapons — among them the most modern rockets and other arms — which made the attack of October 6 possible... All this does not fit into the picture of a peace-loving Soviet Union, which Brezhnev has tried to create in the West with so much effort... Suddenly the world began to listen, when it learned that the same type of arms that were so successfully used in the attack in the Middle East, together with even deadlier weapons, are amassed in East Europe in unimaginable quantities, manned by excellent soldiers — all directed against the West..."

Axel Springer preferred to come to Israel this week, instead of attending the annual Springer Correspondents' Conference in Berlin.

said Ora, "that she had a child at the front, or that she had some family here, or some property interests," Ora continued. "Her involvement was so strong that I even found it hard to credit her sincerity."

"But," continued Ora, "these people *are* sincere. They are simply in love with Israel, so deeply in love that they just bought a house in Jerusalem and are going to settle here. They have both started to take Hebrew lessons."

This may be an unusual case, but not an isolated case. There are others.

But why, one must ask, has the church itself been so indifferent to the moral issues involved?

Shortly after the beginning of the War, a block party was held on 13th Street in Manhattan. A platform was set up, and from it a rather small crowd was addressed by prelates who headed the various churches in the vicinity. A Catholic priest recited one of the psalms in English. His choice and reading of the piece, and his relating it to the present conflict were unspeakably moving. Each

of the five churchmen who spoke was visibly involved. Each clearly considered that in the violation of the rights of the Jews, his personal rights had been trespassed. Yet these men spoke only as individuals, and during the 100 days that followed in the wake of the Yom Kippur War, throughout the length and breadth of this land, there was a notable dearth of official pronouncements by churches condemning the Arab attack on Israel's Day of Judgment.

Sometime during the month of February, the Pope saw fit to hold personal conference with a man whom the church considered for years to be anti-Christ. In the past 60 years, nothing has been more anathema to the Catholic Church than the Communist regime of the Soviet Union, which has openly avowed that it considers the church its natural enemy. Yet in the aftermath of the Yom Kippur War, the world was permitted the spectacle of His Holiness meeting with a prime representative of the Soviet. Were they meeting to discuss

WHAT THE ISRAELI THINKS TODAY

By general consent, the war has had a profound impact on the thinking of the average Israeli. Or has it? PHILIP GILLON sought the answer by accompanying a young interviewer working for a public opinion survey, and by talking to Professor Louis Guttman, the sociologist who heads the survey.

VERY FEW PEOPLE in this country really know what the average Israeli is thinking about war, peace, the Government, Arabs, the credibility gap or, indeed, about any of the things that affect his daily life. The media occasionally ask questions of men, women and children selected at random in the streets. But this is obviously not enough, and there are fortunately some public opinion polls carried out on a more scientific basis.

The other day, I tagged along with an interviewer for one of these surveys, a volunteer high-school student in his matriculation year. He smiled disarmingly at the first householder to answer his ring at the door, and explained the aim of the exercise. The man looked a bit dubious, but then obviously began to feel rather flattered — probably nobody had ever bothered to ask him his opinion before.

The questions are profound and wide-ranging. They start quite innocuously with problems of supplies and transportation — are you getting all you need? From your usual shop? Do you go to another shop? The interviewee has a choice of four, five or six answers — yes, I get everything; no, one thing is lacking; two or three things are lacking; a lot of things are lacking; everything is lacking. And so on. The interviewer notes the answers to 76 carefully worked out questions in his 12 foolscap interview sheets.

HAVING DISPOSED of the not-so interesting question of supplies, we get down to the real problems. Do you think the Government is strong enough to beat the enemy? Yes, certainly. How is the Government handling the situation? Very well. What is your own mood like? All right.

What do you worry about most? Here he is given a choice of the following answers: a relative or friend in the Army; terrorist activities; Israel's military position; Israel's political position; Israel's economic situation; his own and his family's financial position; his family's health; a combination of these factors; other things entirely; nothing at all.

It seems to me that there is a built-in weakness in this question: it is hard to imagine any Israeli admitting that he is worried about his finances when boys he knows are killed, wounded or missing. The answer in this particular case is the predictable one: the interviewee's major concern is a boy at the front.

Should Israel continue to hold the areas occupied in 1967? Which areas, and how much? Do you hate the Arabs? Emphatically no — but perhaps here, too, the answer is built in; it would require perverse courage for a Jew to admit hatred of a people. Have the Arabs proved that they are better fighters than they used to be? Rather surprisingly: very doubtful. Have they redeemed Arab honour? Very doubtful. What do you think of the Government information services? All right. Do you believe what the Government says? On the whole, yes.

And so on.

The young interviewer is the essence of tact. Later, interviewing a woman, he ends his questioning with the reassurance that all the information she is giving him is absolutely confidential. When she nods her approval, he adds: "What is your age?"

THE SURVEY is being conducted by Professor Louis Guttman, one of the world's leading sociologists, who came here from the United States after World War II and began his surveys of public opinion as a voluntary service way back in Hagana days. He is now Director of the Israel Institute of Applied Social Research and Professor of Social and Psychological Measurement at the Hebrew University. He is doing the present survey together with Professor Elihu Katz, of the University's Department of Communications.

Some 300-500 people are visited by the volunteer team of interviewers each day — and Professor Guttman stresses the importance of doing the survey daily, since the answers to some of the questions may vary from day to day.

"In general," he says, "Israeli attitudes tend to harden when things are going badly, and to soften when the country is on the upswing." He then analyzes for me the conclusions to be drawn from the day-to-day survey. Fortunately, he began a system of surveys during the Six Day War, and has kept it going ever since. Thus, he had his pollsters out within two hours of the start of the Yom Kippur War, and is in a position to review public postures before, during and after hostilities.

MORALE ON THE home front was very high at all times, much higher than it was during the Six Day War. The mood changed from one of euphoria at the beginning of the War to a more sombre one at the end of t h e first week, but there was never any doubt about Israel eventually winning. Before war broke out, 31 per cent had been concerned about the military situation, 16 per cent about their own finances, 14 per cent about their health. During the war, the major anxiety was about people at the front — varying between 46, 55, 54, 43 and 41 per cent from one day to another — and the general military situation — 22, 23, 20, 33, and 21 per cent. Nobody cared a damn about his own finances.

CONFIDENCE in the Government's handling of the situation, somewhat surprisingly, soared as a result of the war. Before Yom Kippur, there had been considerable doubt about the Government's ability to deal with the situation, due to dissatisfaction with the economy — presumably the inflation — and Government steps to deal with it. Eighty per cent were nevertheless satisfied with the military direction.

From the day the war started, general confidence in the Government was entertained by no less than 80 per cent of the public, and the percentage remained at this level throughout the days that followed. There was a slight shift in the degree of satisfaction, with fewer people saying "very good," and more, just "good." Before the war started, the percentages with regard to the handling of the military situation were: very successful, 32; successful, 59. This changed to very successful, 23; successful 63 on October 15; by October 24, they were: very successful, 24; successful, 51; with 19 per cent saying grimly, "not so very successful."

ATTITUDES TO ARABS were rather unexpected. Nobody hates them, which is obviously a good thing, if we are ever to have peace. But very few think that they have improved their image as soldiers, despite all the evidence of how well they planned and fought the war. To the question whether Arab honour has been redeemed on the battlefields, the reply of the majority was only, "somewhat." Few Israelis think that the Arabs have destroyed the image of the Israel Defence Forces as invincible. This view was expressed throughout the war, even during the bad days.

On the question of Israel agreeing to the cease-fire, the answers on October 23 were: 22 per cent, very justified; 51 per cent, justified; 17 per cent, not so justified; ten per cent, not justified at all. It is curious to note, despite this 73 per cent endorsement of acceptance, that 70 per cent of the population didn't believe on October 22 that the Arabs would observe the cease-fire. Thus, correlating these answers, it seems that a majority of Israelis thought that Israel should accept the Soviet-American proposal, even though they were convinced the Arabs would not abide by their undertakings. There was no question

about Israel observing the cease-fire.

There is considerable scepticism as to whether the Arabs are ready to make real peace, but hopes have increased. A year before the war, 77 per cent of Israelis answered "not yet" to this question, and only 21 per cent replied in the affirmative. In the first week of the Yom Kippur War, the percentage of optimists about Arab attitudes to peace rose to 38 per cent, went up to 45 in the second week, soared to 52 when the cease-fire was announced, only to drop to 38 when the fighting was resumed.

ONE OF THE CURIOUS implications of the survey, Professor Guttman points out, is that there is no correlation between the lack of confidence in the Arab desire for a real peace and attitudes about the return of the territories occupied in June, 1967.

In the first week of the war, 42 per cent said that Israel should not give back an inch of the territories; this figure rose to 52 per cent in the second week, dropped to 40 per cent at the beginning of the third week, and went down to 32 per cent on the day after the cease-fire went into effect.

A year ago, 46 per cent wanted to return a good part of Sinai, 17 per cent, a small part, and 37 per cent, nothing. The figures were about the same at the end of the war. Thus the Arabs do not appear to have effected a change in attitudes to the Sinai by this enormous endeavour, and the terrible cost in blood.

About the Golan Heights and Sharm e-Sheikh, Israelis have been almost unanimous before and during the Yom Kippur War: the answer is definitely "no." Percentages on the Golan — 92 noes

before the war, then 87, 94, 93, 93. Sharm e-Sheikh — 96 all the time, against any return. Opponents of return of the Gaza Strip were 66 per cent before the war — then the figures fluctuated to 69, 80, 86, and dropped sharply back to 72.

As to the West Bank (of the Jordan, not the Canal — nomenclature gets very difficult with the march of history), a year before the war there were 58 per cent nay-sayers. The figure went up — 63, 77, 84 — and then dropped again — 74, 70. The downward trend seems likely to continue.

BEFORE THE war, Israelis apparently had a very doubtful opinion of Government spokesmen. Only 13 per cent believed everything they were told, 42 per cent believed most. Surprisingly, despite the suppressions and distortions of the news during the first three days, belief in the Government's credibility went up from the first day — 32 per cent believed everything, and 40 per cent, most, of what they were told about the war. With some fluctuation, the percentages stabilized at 42 and 37 by October 15. Presumably the public believes the Government about the war, but not about Netivei Neft.

Both in peace and war, the figures are much higher for belief in what the radio and television reporters say. This is a distinct feather in the often battered cap of the Israel Broadcasting Authority, a proof that giving it independence is vital for Israeli democracy.

Despite Jordan Television's efforts every now and then to be impartial, virtually nobody believed or believes the Arab TV or radio reports, although 25 per cent of Israelis watched Arab TV throughout the crisis.

---

religious freedom in the Soviet Union? Hardly. The only subject on which they met on common ground was how to dispossess Israel from Jerusalem, a subject of obvious and deep concern to their mutual religious feelings. Perhaps one could not expect Gromyko to have any acquaintanceship with the prophetic literature, but surely the Pope must be familiar with Scripture. Surely the Pope must know the lines in Psalm 125 which read:

*O Jerusalem! the mountains surround
   you!
So may the Lord surround his people
   from now on, and forever more.*

Surely the Pope might sense in these lines, if not a logical connection, the mystical connection which binds the city and the people and God's love into one undying creed.

We've lost the world's sympathy again

THERE'S GREAT anger everywhere against Israel the aggressor. Perhaps only the displeasure with Israel for fighting off its aggressors is greater.

The 1973 Hit Israel Parade is reaching new peaks of popularity these days, both in the number of its participants and in the impressive show of hypocrisy put on by them. It's got to a point where the few friends we still have are gradually coming to be suspected of eccentricity or pure one-upmanship. We're positively uniting the civilized world just by being our provocative selves.

Our efforts to prove to the international community that we had *not* prepared for this round and that it was *not* we *who* started this war were so much good negligence down the drain. At the time of going to press, 18 African states have indignantly severed relations with Israel on account of the Egyptian and Syrian armies' open attack on us and Gaddafi is still going strong. Socialist Bonn protests loudly against its neutral ports serving to deliver arms to those Jews who happened to survive the German slaughter; Paris considers that cease-fire lines don't apply to oil-producing countries; and England sticks to its traditional type-casting whereby every British Government betrays Israel, while the Opposition shakes its head.

The International Movement for the Encouragement of Contemporary Aggression is taking on a quite surrealist dimension; it embraces former victims of aggression like Ethiopia and Czechoslovakia, Holocaust survivors like

Ephraim Kishon

Bruno Kreisky, and non-aligned nations of Cuban proportions. Everybody jumps on the bandwagon.

Sometimes we feel like taking a look at ourselves in the mirror: what the hell is it about us that puts everybody against us? And all we see in the mirror is just bearded kids crossing the Canal, their eyes swollen with lack of sleep, and scared parents rushing about after foreign weeklies for pictures of their P-o-W sons. We see nothing in mankind's distorting mirror except a breathless tribe fighting half the world again and again since birth, and retaining its human image in an ocean of cynicism and deceit — a small, brave, hard-working nation whose fate hangs on nine tapes being bandied about in Washington.

We'd cry if it weren't so funny. We haven't a friend left in this whole wide world except Dr. Kissinger, Holland and Jordan. And Portugal. A rather embarrassing reflection on humanity.

AREN'T THE nations of the world ashamed of themselves? Don't *they* have a mirror?

Many years ago, after the Sinai Campaign, we happened to write a satirical piece which was quoted widely every time Israel had the effrontery to win a war. We called the piece: "How We Lost the World's Sympathy," and explained that in order to gain the world's sympathy, we ought to stick our heads out and let the Arabs kill us all. Then, we said, after the splendid funeral, everybody would love us at last.

Actually, we would now like to apologize to the reader for our bitter mistake. One of the harshest lessons of the Yom Kippur War is that we won't manage to win people's sympathy and understanding even by being beaten. More than that: the worse our situation, the more obviously just our cause, the lonelier we stand — the more ready they are to sell us out.

Why? Because there isn't anything people hate more than somebody who reminds them they're scoundrels.

So there's nothing we can do except live and die without their sympathy. And we'll manage, thank you. Even if the Security Council breaks its latest record and votes in one min., **17** secs. for our withdrawal from the entire globe.

By God, we're beginning to be proud of ourselves!

Translated by Miriam Arad
By arrangement with "Ma'ariv"

CHRISTIAN COMMENT

War and Dialogue

WHAT MAY BE happening to the Jewish-Christian dialogue in Israel and, perhaps, other parts of the world, is reflected in the following statement made by an official of the Israeli Ministry for Religious Affairs·

"The telephone is silent; none of our usual Christian friends have come to call. There w a s only one other time I can remember it so quiet in this office, and that was during the Six Day War."

What effect will this, the Yom Kippur War, have on Jewish-Christian relations?

IT IS TRUE THAT, whereas some, if not most, Christians regard Israel as a political state like any other modern state, there are also Christians who see in Israel the realization of a reality promised in Scripture. They see a close relation between God's chosen people and the land that was once called Palestine. There are those who accept, as history, that God linked his covenant with the Jews with a gift of l a n d but cannot bring themselves to admit that the identity of the contemporary Jewish people is also linked with that land.

When Christians were silent about the Six Day War, Jews were shocked — perhaps as shocked as they were about the silence of the Churches during the Holocaust of the Second World War. They realized that individual Christians came out in support of Israel in 1967 as did many individual Christians come to the aid of some Jews during the '40s. Nevertheless, they were shocked and disappointed. E s p e c i a l l y disheartened were those who had engaged in dialogue with the Churches. They felt let down and betrayed because the Churches to which their Christian friends belonged remained silent. S o m e asked themselves if the silence was not a subtle manifestation of the problem that had been posed by the death camps of Hitler.

In 1967, it became clear to World Jewry to what extent the existence and the survival of the State of Israel was bound up with

Dialogue between a bishop and a Jew, 12th century, Douai, France.

Oikoumenikos

their own existence and survival as Jews. Many began to feel that Israel as a Jewish state is a living, spiritual expression of Jewish aspirations for the fulfilment of Messianic hopes of freedom, justice and peace. Even those whose Jewishness had until then expressed itself, practically, only in religious terms, and who had little to do with Zionist activity, suddenly discovered the ethnic dimension of their Judaism.

WE CHRISTIANS cannot ignore the sense of Jewish disillusionment over "Christian silence" during these past weeks. However, from what is known about what individual Christians have done, especially here in Jerusalem, it appears that this silence was far from complete, and that the charge requires careful qualification.

We may need to inquire into the underlying causes of the silence of Christian officialdom.

In doing so, we cannot fail to acknowledge that there was a failure on the part of the Churches in Israel to communicate to the outside world that there is always very grave Jewish anxiety over the threat of the destruction of the state of Israel, which always carries with it a threat of genocide.

IT CANNOT BE GAINSAID that much Christian thinking on the subject of Israel's right to exist derives from spurious theological presuppositions. As a Catholic writer has stated:

"Fundamentally, the traditional Christian position towards t h e Jews, for a certain category of churchmen, is undeniably t h e theological impossibility to get accustomed to the idea that for the Christian order, the Jewish people can still have a personality of its own and can exist apart; and that in our days, this existence can manifest itself in realizations such as the creation of a Jewish State in Palestine."

Hence the need to subject to a critical examination the legitimacy of anti-Judaic views to the present day situation. Among these anti-Judaistic views are such concepts as the decadence and displacement of the Jewish people a n d the theological necessity for the dispersion of the Jewish people.

Should we not be astonished at the self-assurance and the lack of a sense of mystery displayed by writers who do not hesitate to determine the ways of God in the history of salvation by dismissing out of hand the possibility of God's continued work in the history of the Jewish people? Unless he chooses to ignore Romans 9-11, can a Christian theologian reject the legitimacy of the continued existence of the Jews as a people having a function in the unfolding of God's economy of salvation?

There is a continuous trend in Christian theology and apologetics linking the loss of sovereignty and the dispersion of the Jewish people among the Gentiles with the design of God. But if such a theological evaluation of historic effects is legitimate, then there is no reason to deny a theological significance for t h e return of the Jews to the Land and the achievement of sovereignty.

I WAS BORN in New York City. My mother was born in New York City. My father was born in Poland.

This is a partisan report. No matter how I have tried to state the facts as objectively as I possibly can, I know in my heart of hearts that this is a partisan report. For it is written by someone who regards the question of the survival of Israel as inseparable from his own personal survival.

I start with this bias: If Israel is obliterated, the chance for physical and spiritual survival of any Jew anywhere in the world will be greatly diminished. And even if a few Jews escape extinction, the likelihood that they will live out their days in peace, without molestation can be accounted as very dim.

The great holocaust of the 20th century, the unthinkable disaster in which Hitler exterminated six million Jews, was simply one particularly heinous disaster in a long line of massacres in which Jews were slaughtered in droves for no other reason than that they were born Jews—were born into a stubborn minority that has refused to be obliterated. Their crime was the crime of being different.

And even those who tried to deny their differentness by taking on protective coloration were not spared. Ultimately they, too, were identified and persecuted as Jews. Not even obliteration through assimilation is a right tendered Jews. The story is told, perhaps apocryphal, about Otto Kahn, a Jewish tycoon who was strolling with a business acquaintance who was equally affluent. Kahn's companion was a hunchback.

As they strolled down Fifth Avenue in New York, they passed the magnificent Temple Emanu-El at 65th Street facing the park. Kahn, referring to the fact that he had been converted, pointed to the sumptuous edifice and remarked: "You know, I was once a Jew." His companion then quietly noted: "You know, I was once a hunchback."

History has accorded the Jew limited choices. A thriving Jewish community seems to be regarded as unpalatable. Whenever Jews have managed to settle anywhere long enough to achieve material and intellectual status, a murderous reaction has inevitably set in.

After each tidal wave of blood, those who were sufficiently audacious or lucky enough to survive,

Sapir says Diaspora response 'overwhelming'

LONDON (INA). — Finance Minister Pinhas Sapir said here yesterday "the overall target of the emergency campaign in the U.S. is $750 million."

The overall target for Europe, including the United Kingdom, South Africa, and Australia is $500 million.

Mr. Sapir said the response was overwhelming.

"Sometimes, Leon Dulzin and I had tears in our eyes at the response of Jews in all walks of life. People of limited means, who could only afford small contributions, were those who moved us most. It should also be stressed: This campaign is reaching wider circles than even the campaign of 1967. We have had assimilated Jews whom we had considered completely outside the Jewish orbit, coming forward with substantial contributions."

Mr. Sapir said the campaign was for education and social welfare in Israel. "Because of the burden of the war, we appealed to Diaspora Jewry to make sure that the social welfare structure and the education of the children of Israel can be maintained. And we are sure that this will be the case."

Israel Bonds working around the clock

NEW YORK (INA). — The Israel Bond organization here is working around the clock, seven days a week. National officers and leaders and chairmen of community campaigns have volunteered to take a week off from their jobs or businesses in order to devote all their time to the sale of Israel Bonds.

Sam Rothberg, General Chairman, announced that extraordinary measures were being taken to meet the Israel Bond emergency national goal of $142 million.

Jews and friends of Israel have been asked to accept a self-imposed compulsory loan to Israel of at least one month's income through the purchase of Israel bonds.

Minorities subscribe to war loan

HAIFA. — Some 600 leaders of the minority communities — Moslem and Christian Arabs, Druse and Beduin — yesterday reaffirmed their solidarity with their Jewish fellow citizens in the defence of Israel against aggression.

Yitzhak Rabin, head of the Voluntary War Loan drive, told the gathering that the peaceful cooperation of Jews and Arabs in Israel could serve as an example of what could be achieved in the region as well. He praised the contribution of Israel's minorities in the war effort, pointing out that they had already purchased ILlm. worth of war bonds..

The participants at the meeting included Deputy Communications Minister Sheikh Jaber Mu'addi, Nazareth Mayor Seif e-Din Zuabi, Greek Catholic Archbishop Joseph Raya, the Kadi of Acre, and local council heads from all over the country.   *(Itim)*

MOSLEM LEADERS URGE RELEASE OF PRISONERS

Jerusalem Post Reporter

The Moslem religious leaders in Israel have appealed to the governments of Egypt and Syria to treat prisoners of war, in particular the wounded, in accordance with the Geneva Convention.

In a letter signed by Sheikh Tawfiq Mahmoud Asliya, the Kadi of Jaffa, Sheikh Muhamad Hubeishi, Kadi of Acre and Galilee, Mr. Shuhayl Shukri, the Chairman of the Haifa Moslem Committee, and Advocate Wajdi Tabari, the Honorary Secretary of the Israel Interfaith Committee, the Egyptian and Syrian Governments are called upon to release their prisoners of war as soon as possible in view of the fact that the Israel Government has already declared its readiness to return its prisoners immediately.

"This human step" says the letter, "which will make possible the return of prisoners to their homes and families will certainly hasten the establishment of peace between the two nations. This step will honour you in the eyes of all nations and be proof to the world of your being faithful sons of the Moslem tradition which has always taken care of the weak and the poor."

Kenya breaks Israel ties

NAIROBI (Reuter).—Kenya broke diplomatic relations with Israel yesterday for "as long as Israel continues to occupy Arab lands taken by force of arms."

The decision was announced in a statement issued from the Presidential lodge at Mombasa, where President Jomo Kenyatta is on holiday. Kenya had been regarded as one of Israel's closest friends in Africa.

Kenya is the 24th African country to break diplomatic relations with Israel.

Group of Israeli prisoners held by the Syrians.

SABBATH—No Publication

One of the Israeli bridges over the Suez Canal.

were hounded, degraded, and despoiled wherever they had fled, so that once more their numbers were decimated. The pattern became so familiar that the Jews coined a stock phrase to describe those left after a holocaust. They were called *sh'arith haplaita,* the remnant of the escaped.

So it was after each of the horrible massacres which occurred during the 300 years of the Crusades; so it was after the countless outrages of the Middle Ages in Europe; so it was after the expulsion of the Jews from Spain in 1492.

And so it will be with Jews—no matter where they may be, even here in the United States—who might survive the obliteration of the *Yishuv*[1] in Israel. Jewish survivors, if there are any, cannot rely on succor in a world that has been sufficiently callous to stand by and see the kin of those who perished in the ovens of Auschwitz and Treblinka immolated by their Arab neighbors.

Why is the Jew such an intolerable threat? Is it that the world is not ready to forgive the Jews for having given them a Jesus who saddled them with the yoke of brotherly love?

1. Settlement.

Bar-Lev about War

Jerusalem Post Political Reporter

TEL AVIV. — Commerce and Industry Minister Aluf (Res.) Haim Bar-Lev has stated that he has "no doubts that the Government and the I.D.F. will conduct a thorough enquiry" into the questions surrounding the start of the war.

"Let it hurt whoever it hurts," he told "Ma'ariv" interviewer Dov Goldstein.

Back at his ministerial duties after serving as the Chief of Staff's representative on the Southern Front, Bar-Lev denied reports of friction with O.C. Southern Command, Aluf Shmuel Gonen. "He called me his personal Chief of Staff," said Bar-Lev, who was C.o.S. until two years ago.

Army intelligence had plenty of reliable information on Egyptian and Syrian preparations for war, Bar-Lev said but "the evaluation did not stand the test... I know people think the war caught intelligence by surprise. That is utterly untrue ... but the likelihood of war was not great... only after Saturday morning did the evaluation change."

Stressing that if Sadat carries out his new threat, the I.D.F. will be ready for him, Bar-Lev stated "We are well placed at the soft under belly of Egypt."

NO FAILURE

Bar-Lev said the initial achievements of the Egyptians and Syrians did not come from any failure of the I.D.F. doctrine. "It was a result of surprise and inadequate warning. The army has proven itself, and its operative concept is palpably right. Once the I.D.F. machinery was set in gear things began to move in the right direction... It did not help the Syrians that the Iraqis and Jordanians came to their aid. It did not help Egypt to have such great armed power and huge quantities of missiles... If not for the cease-fire the Egyptian army would have been wiped out."

As to an enquiry, Bar-Lev said: "On the basis of the facts we will draw conclusions against those responsible. One thing I am sure of — the Army will never again be caught by surprise. Henceforth we will not only have reliable information but the conclusions and the evaluatic will be different."

Declaring that the "Bar-Lev line," as such, had never really existed, he noted that the strongholds were built during the war of attrition to facilitate Israel's presence along the Canal, and without them Israel would have been pushed back. But he emphasized that the 20 strongholds were not intended to hold back an all-out attack of five or more Egyptian divisions, and were part of the total deployment.

"Whoever says the strongholds did not succeed in curbing the Egyptian attack is talking rubbish," he said. "The Egyptians intended in their initial attack to reach the passes, some 30 kilometres away, but they were held to 8-10 kilometres. I say that our deployment in Sinai did not collapse. The strongholds fell because they were not intended to be more than advance posts."

Asked whether the Egyptian soldier had changed so radically as is now claimed, the former Chief-of-Staff noted that this time the Egyptians had a stronger motivation, more advanced weapon systems and unlimited quantities of men and equipment. This made the fighting in some areas much tougher than in past wars.

"In battles, where initiative, resourcefulness, inventiveness and speedy reactions are called for, the Egyptians were the same as before, with one outstanding difference — they were more ready to take risks.

MORE RISKS

Bar-Lev said the Egyptians showed readiness to sacrifice themselves but lacked battle sense and professional capability. This was indicated by their commando attacks, for the Egyptian commandos suffered heavy losses and produced only minor damage. The Egyptians sacrificed thousands of infantry soldiers "in keeping with their norm of 'throwaway soldiers.' Before the war they repeated exercises many times over and accompanied this with brainwashing. I have heard that the infantry was supplied with special pep pills."

Israeli soldier holds Soviet-made Sagger anti-tank missile captured in large quantities and incorporated in the Israeli defense arsenal.

From the Anglican Archbishop
THE WAR OF THE TURNING POINT

To the Editor of The Jerusalem Post

Sir, — The cease-fire is being honoured and all can now work together to fulfil Mr. Abba Eban's hope that what started as a month of horror may become the month of the turning point, bringing peace after 25 years of intermittent war.

People in all the countries of the Middle East are weary of war, killing, anxiety and grief. Israelis stress that they did not make a pre-emptive strike in this fourth war; a sign of their desire for peace. Arab nations say that they did not want to destroy Israel, but only to recover the territory lost in 1967; surely another sign of hope.

Four chronic problems have become so acute that they can no longer be ignored:

a. Israel's need of acceptance and security within secure and recognised borders.

It needs to be remembered that the nation of Israel has been in a virtual state of war since it was founded, and that Jews have not felt safe in the world community or with the Christian Church for many centuries.

b. The resentment and frustration of the Arabs in having territories occupied since June 1967.

c. The urgent need of a settlement for the refugees, whether they live in hopeless conditions in the camps or in embittered exile elsewhere.

d. The desire of the Palestinians to have their own identity recognised and to be involved in the planning of their own future.

These four interlocking problems need an interrelated solution.

Many people inside and outside Israel had hoped that Israel would have taken a courageous and generous initiative which might have pre-empted this last war. Now, we must hope that (in Mr. Eban's words) "Israel will devote itself to the cause of peace with the same patience and perseverance it showed in defending itself."

I find among all communities in Jerusalem a growing understanding of the rights and grievances of others. More Arabs and their friends are coming to realise that the State of Israel is necessary for Jews and that its achievement has given new confidence to Jews throughout the world. Jews now have a place to come to, where they will feel safe, find a welcome, and work out the principles of Judaism in national life.

There is a need for Israelis and Arabs to meet, so that the members of each community may discover that there are good, peace-loving people in the other community. Arabs tell me how hurt and critical they feel when Israeli leaders speak of teaching the Arabs a lesson. Israelis say that they feel equally resentful by the Arabs' refusal to meet round the peace table.

In the first days of the war millions of people throughout the world were deeply worried about the fate of Israel. In the last days of the war many of the same people were thankful that there had been no overwhelming defeat for either side, for that might have resulted in further humiliation and the fear of another war in a few years' time.

Israelis and Palestinians have been meeting one another in the West Bank during the last six years and have been finding a new respect for each other. I believe that the Palestinians of the West Bank are a key group in the search for peace, because they have links with both Israel and Palestinians in Arab countries. I believe too that the Arab community in Israel has an important role to play. Can we all engage in an "operation understanding" in which small groups of Jews and Arabs can meet and explain themselves to one another? The stereotypes which each has of the other would soon be seen to be mistaken, and the fact reported to supporters outside.

One of the things I have discovered in recent travels is the renewed pain in Jewish hearts of the Holocaust. We who are not Jews can only feel a fraction of that deep pain. It seems as if that awful tragedy was so great that feelings had to be anaesthetised to some extent to make the pain bearable. Now the numbness is wearing off and the pain is being felt more acutely. Six million Jews were exterminated, hardly a European Jewish family did not mourn a victim of the gas chambers. There is an urgent need that this vast wound shall be healed.

It was not the Arabs who inflicted that wound, but the Western world; un-Christ-like attitudes and theological assumptions in parts of the Christian Church were contributory factors. Jews all over the world need to be assured that nothing like this can happen again.

I have been very moved by the high value that our Jewish friends place on one human life, and their concern for the wounded, the prisoners, the anxious and bereaved of both sides. Equally I am moved by the intense grief in an Arab family when a young man is killed or wounded. We must all let our humanity prevail and seek to bind up the wounds of war and search for the right peace which will make this fourth war the last one.

Yesterday, at my own request, I visited with an Arab colleague wounded Arab prisoners of war. We must have shaken hands with nearly a hundred men, mainly Egyptians, a few Syrians, an Iraqi and a Moroccan. They were getting magnificent medical care and much human kindness. One of the youngest of them said: "To hell with war!" to which all of us present in that small ward — Moslems, Jews and Christians alike — said a hearty "Amen!" Quite a number of the men begged me to do everything I could to hurry up the exchange of wounded prisoners.

I speak with great tension of heart, for I have a pastoral responsibility for Anglicans in all the countries of the Middle East. It was said of the philosopher Hegel of the inner tensions of his own being — "He was not one of the combatants but rather both of the combatants, and also the combat itself!" I know how he felt.

GEORGE APPLETON
Anglican Archbishop
Jerusalem, November 2.

Fast today on 30th day of the war

Jerusalem Post Staff

Today has been declared a day of fasting and prayer by the Chief Rabbinate. All Israelis who feel up to it are asked to fast, and those who cannot are to give charity instead.

Today is the 30th day since the outbreak of the war, but it is also a fast day in the Jewish calendar — one of three obscure fasts after Succot and Pessah which very few people usually observe.

According to Jewish Law the fast is "to atone for any transgressions committed in the course of over-enthusiastic observance" of those festivals.

The fast was to have begun at sunset yesterday and is to end after sunset today.

Special additions to the regular weekday service are the "Avinu

Swiss postal workers show their amity

A Swiss tourism organization which has vowed not to send anyone to an Arab state yesterday became the first tourism group to send an organized party to Israel since the war.

The party, 31 Swiss postal workers led by the head of their union's cultural and tourism section, Mr. Willy Bahler, have come for a 14 day stay. Mr. Bahler said his group had decided to counter the Arab oil embargo with a ban on tourism. "As long as I am president of the Postal Workers culture and tourism organization," he said, "not one group of our workers will travel an Arab country."

Mr. Bahler said the members of his party had decided, "against all logic," to go through with their planned visit here because they knew Israel needs friends, and to help see that Israel does not lose politically what she won on the field of battle.

FORTY-THREE volunteer Arab and Druse taxi and pick-up truck drivers in the North on Friday ferried soldiers on leave from Acre to Kiryat Shmona and to Hadera, in response to an appeal of the Arab Department of the Histadrut.

ON THE 30th DAY after the commencement of the War, on November 6, 1973, the rabbis of Israel declared a national fast day.

Yom Kippur is the only fast day decreed in the Mosaic Code. The religious calendar of the Jews contains five additional fast days, not ordained in the Pentateuch.[1] Four of these fasts, which memorialize historical events, were first mentioned by the prophet Zechariah[2] who described them in the following somewhat cryptic terms:

> *The fast of the fourth month, and the fast of the fifth, and the fast of the seventh, and the fast of the tenth, shall be to the house of Judah joy and gladness and cheerful feasts.*

Since Zechariah lived about 518 B.C., scholars believe that the four fast days he makes reference to were instituted during the Babylonian exile. It is thought that the fast of the tenth month[3] commemorates the commencement of the siege of Jerusalem by the Babylonians; that the fast of the fourth month, which falls on the 17th of Tammuz,[4] commemorates the first breach in the walls of that city; that the fast of the fifth month,

the fast of Tisha b'Av,[5] commemorates the destruction of the temple; and that the fast of the seventh month, which falls on the third day of Tishrai,[6] commorates the assassination of Gedaliah, who had been appointed Governor of Judea by Nebuchadnezzar, the King of Babylonia.

However tenuous these historical ascriptions may be — some scholars doubt their authenticity — pious Jews throughout the centuries have observed these four minor fasts as days of mourning.

The most widely known of these fasts is the fast of Tisha b'Av, which according to tradition marks the day in 586 B.C. on which the first temple was destroyed. This ninth day of Av proved, again and again, to be an ill-omened day of calamity. It was likewise on this same day, some six centuries later in the year 70 of the Christian era, that the second temple was destroyed by the Roman, Titus. In distinction from the other minor fasts, the fast of Tisha b'Av, like that of Yom Kippur, begins on the eve of the day before, and continues for a full twenty-four hours.

1. The Five Books of Moses.
2. Zechariah VIII:19.
3. The Fast of the Tenth Month is known as *Asara B'Tebet* in Hebrew.
4. *Tammuz* is the fourth month of the Hebrew lunar calendar. It generally falls during the month of July.
5. *Av* is the fifth month. It generally falls during August.
6. *Tishrai* is the seventh month.

CIVILIANS' FINEST HOUR
Treating the enemy wounded

By MACABEE DEAN
Jerusalem Post Reporter

BE'ER YA'ACOV. — The "finest hour" of Israeli civilians during the current crisis is seeing that enemy wounded are treated the same as Israelis, according to a staff doctor of the 376-bed Shmuel Harofeh Hospital here. This hospital was emptied of most of its Israeli patients on the first day of the war to make room for wounded enemy soldiers.

So far, some 600 wounded soldiers have received medical treatment. About 350 of the serious cases are still hospitalized. Of these, some 300 are Egyptians, 40 are Syrians, and there are a few Iraqis and Moroccans. (But this situation changes from hour to hour, the doctor said, since patients whose condition improves materially are sent to a prisoner-of-war camp.)

The medical director of Shmuel Harofeh is Dr. Walter Davidson, and his two chief assistants are Dr. Emil Hereczeg and Dr. Ya'acov Adler.

"It takes superhuman effort for a nurse whose son was shot down over Syria to walk up to a wounded Syrian soldier, ask him how he feels, and attend to him. It puts a great strain on her bedside manner. Her smile may be stiff; but it is still a smile," the doctor told me.

"Or take the case of a young girl in the Gadna who has held up an Egyptian soldier and fed him. Her mother was expelled from Egypt. And so it goes. There are few families in Israel who have not suffered loss, either to close members of their families or to distant ones. Yet they never questioned their responsibility to treat enemy as unfortunate human beings," he added.

Outstanding in their help were members of the Gadna (high school paramilitary) from the Lydda-Ramle area, who not only fed the prisoners and washed them, but also hauled them around on stretchers from place to place. Students from the nearby Ort school worked in the laundry and kitchen, which had to supply food not only to the wounded and the hungry volunteers, but also to the military policemen who guard the prisoner-patients.

"Two main things motivate these kids and the other volunteers," the doctor said. "One is their belief that the Arab soldiers are people just like us. The other is the hope that their example will be followed by physicians and civilians in the hospitals in Egypt and Syria."

He added: "I must admit that a lot of the enthusiasm of these volunteers began to evaporate when they saw there was no reciprocity among the Egyptians and Syrians; but, nevertheless, they are continuing to work here with a smile."

Question: How do the wounded Arabs themselves react? Are they at least grateful?

Answer: Only one out of 600 was really hostile — he said we were performing experimental operations on the patients — and another was not thankful. But ninety-nine-point-nine per cent said they were grateful, and they indicated it in various ways.

Question: But will they still say they are grateful when they get back to Egypt?

Answer: It depends how much pressure is put on them to say the opposite.

NO COMPLAINTS

At any rate, on a tour through the wards, none of the wounded Arabs expressed any complaints. The wards were spotlessly clean, and doctors and nurses were in attendance everywhere. Only one of the wounded appeared disturbed. "When will we be repatriated?" he wanted to know.

"One hour after Sadat agrees to repatriate the Israeli wounded and begins to do so," the staff doctor answered.

The wounded Arab shook his head in disbelief.

The regular medical staff of Shmuel Harofeh has also displayed an outstanding capacity to put up with hardships. Although many of its doctors and nurses were mobilized, the hospital continued to function on a three-shift basis with the skeleton staff that remained.

In one day the hospital received 100 wounded prisoners-of-war, between 30 and 40 per cent of them in serious condition. During one 24-hour period some 50 operations were performed in the four operating theatres. Considerable help came from teams of doctors and nurses who arrived as volunteers from the U.K., U.S. and Canada.

"Only three of the wounded died here during the entire period," the staff doctor said. "This in itself is a splendid medical record." But Shmuel Harofeh did get outside help. For example, neurosurgery cases were sent to Beilinson; Ichilov did the jaw-bone operations; and Assaf Harofeh handled eye injuries. Sometimes, however, doctors from these hospitals come to Shmuel Harofeh to operate.

The most misleading medical diagnosis yet was made by an Egyptian doctor, who was also a patient. He had been wounded in the throat, chest, thigh and hand. All the wounds were serious. His diagnosis: he was going to die of his wounds.

But I saw him lying on his back, sleeping peacefully. At his side was a pile of medical literature (in English). "He's trying to keep up with the latest advances in medicine," the staff doctor told me.

Today, doctors and other staff at Shmuel Harofeh are still working round the clock. There is a feeling here that if they do not get outside relief soon the staff will join the wounded prisoners in bed.

Shmuel Harofeh first treated enemy wounded during the Six Day War. Then some 400 wounded Arabs passed through the hospital. One of the visitors to see the wounded Arabs then was U.S. President Richard Nixon.

A recent visitor was Anglican Archbishop George Appleton of Jerusalem, whose jurisdiction encompasses Egypt. "It is hoped he will report to the Egyptians that the Israelis have set an example which they should emulate," the staff doctor said.

In Israel, on the eve of Tisha b'Av, most restaurants, cafés, kiosks, and places of entertainment shut down as a gesture of respect for the pious, who on this anniversary still mourn the destruction of the venerated situs of their ancient religious rites. In commemoration of this doleful event, tens of thousands of the residents of Jerusalem walk to the Wailing Wall to chant dirges and recite the lamentations of Jeremiah.

Zechariah referred to these fast days prophetically. He envisioned a day when Judah would be returned to its homeland, and when these days of mourning would no longer need to be observed.

The fifth fast day, the fast of Queen Esther, commemorates the appearance of this Jewish heroine before her husband, the Persian king, Ahasuerus. After imposing on herself a three-day fast, Esther approached the monarch to beseech him for the life of her people.[1] *Ta'anit Estair,* as it is called in Hebrew, is not regarded as a day of grief, but rather as a fast of thanksgiving for deliverance. The fast of Esther would appear to have been instituted some few hundred years after the other four minor fasts became part of Jewish observance.

But apart from historic memorialization, the fast as an institution has always played a significant role in Jewish life. For ages, the fast has functioned as a talisman against impending disaster.

I remember that my grandfather would, for no apparent reason, refuse all food on some self-chosen day. And when urged by my grandmother to sit down at the table, he would answer simply, "I'm fasting today." If prodded, he would admit that he had had a bad dream the night before in which some awful thing befell him. In order to ward off personal catastrophe, he was fasting to humble himself before his God, and to implore forgiveness for whatever sin he might have committed, to forestall the punishment hanging over him.

On a literal level, my grandfather could be regarded as a simple, superstitious primitive. In reality, he was not. He was a highly moral man who lived by a strict code in which consideration for others, especially for those less fortunate than himself, was primary. His periodic fear of divine punishment was basically an expression of his inner uneasiness that he may have relaxed his normal ethical standards, may have become too complacent, too self-centered.

To the religious Jew, God is a very real presence, who demands the highest level of humane behavior. A visitation of suffering is a reminder that one has not fully observed the Mosaic injunction: And you shall love your neighbor as yourself.[2]

This mode of thinking has deep roots in the Jewish psyche. Going back to roughly 200 B.C., one can find in the earliest books of the Talmud a Mishnaic tractate called *Ta'anit,* which means "Fasts." An entire section of Halachic thought was devoted to this specific subject, testifying that the matter of fasting occupied a central place in the life of the people. It is instructive to examine

1. Esther IV:16.
2. Leviticus XIX:18.

Supplies to the Third Army

To the Editor of The Jerusalem Post

Sir, — I cry with tears of rage and frustration when I hear the demands for humaneness for the soldiers' of the Egyptian Third Army. They are hungry and thirsty and need blood plasma for their wounded, but still have ammunition to fire. Where was humanenss for the beleaguered city of Jerusalem in 1948? Its citizens were also hungry and thirsty — not just for days, but for weeks. They weren't soldiers, but old men, women and children, whose only crime was that they were Jews.

EVELYN HENIG

Halfa, October 29.

To the Editor of The Jerusalem Post

Sir, — I am hurt, grieved and appalled. Why must we always display our humanitarianism at the expense of our own soldiers and people, to an inhumane world which neither appreciates nor cares? Why did we so readily agree to permit the passage of supplies to the encircled Egyptian Third Army without first demanding the exchange of prisoners of war, or at least a detailed list of all Israeli prisoners in their hands, as promised when the cease-fire was declared?

These, and many other questions are being asked by parents, wives and close ones of those who are lost or prisoners.

ROSE BELKIN

Givatayim, October 30.

Liz Taylor art auction raises IL 800,000 for Israeli victims

Actress Liz Taylor in her role as auctioneer at the Amsterdam-Hilton Hotel.

To the Editor of The Jerusalem Post
Sir, — In your leader of October 26, "Break with Africa," there is one sentence I have to take strong exception to.

You state, in your closing paragraph, that "no doubt many of the African states will seek to renew their links with Israel and Israel will certainly be glad of it."

I think that this eventual desire of these states should be met with complete indifference. More than that, we should refuse to renew the development assistance to any state which severed relations.

The heavy burden of our taxation which most of us are willing to bear in order to repair the damages of this war would become intolerable if even a penny were spent to bolster the economy of those who let us down when the pinch came.

DR. M. JACOBSEN
Savyon, October 28.

To the Editor of The Jerusalem Post
Sir, — As an English visitor currently spending my second sabbatical term under wartime conditions (the first was in Nigeria during the Civil War), I should like to comment on your leading article, "Break with Africa" (October 26).

Nigeria severed her links with Israel last Thursday.

She does not draw her inspiration from Moscow or Peking, and has resisted moves to spurn the Western powers.

She shares with Israel the experience of having to go to war for her survival as a nation.

In 1972, General Gowon played an impartial role in the OAU's mediation initiative in the Middle East.

But it must not be forgotten that half of Nigeria's population of 60 millions are Moslems. Undoubtedly, Islamic leaders put out worldwide pleas for solidarity when the war broke out, just as Jewish leaders here appealed to their communities abroad, and political pressure was brought to bear as a result of this.

It seems to me a logical outcome that Nigeria should have felt obliged to act when lives of Moslem civilians were lost and further territory taken. Viewed in this light, her actions do not conform to your analysis as a "betrayal" of Israel.

DAVID M. GOODALL
Visiting lecturer in
Physical Chemistry
Jerusalem, October 28.

AMSTERDAM (UPI). — Elizabeth Taylor appeared at an art auction here yesterday which raised about 500,000 guilders (IL800,000) for widows and orphans of Israelis killed in the war.

"The reason I am doing this kind of Elizabeth Taylor stunt for war victims is that we have to care for those who are bereaved," Miss Taylor told the crowded auction room where hundreds had to be turned away from the door although they were willing to pay the 125 guilder (IL200) admission.

"I am clearly pro-Israel, but even more pro-humanity," the actress said. She had interrupted film work in Germany to take part in the auction.

A middle-aged man raised bids on a dinner set to 3,000 guilders on condition that Miss Taylor would kiss him. She said she would if he would go up another 1,000 guilders. The man got his kiss and the dinner set.

To the Editor of The Jerusalem Post
Sir, — Of late there seems to be a race between the African countries to sever diplomatic relations with the State of Israel. It makes me wonder whether these countries have any independent foreign policy at all. May I ask one simple question of all these countries: In what way has the position changed since they recognized this country?

I happen to be an impartial observer of the drama enacted by the Arab countries invading this country with all their modern weapons borrowed from others, on the very day when every citizen of this country was busy at prayers. I also observed the strong determination of only 3 million people of this small country to defend their land only because they want to exist as a nation. I am fully convinced this country has no territorial ambition at all and the Israelis are really interested in living with their neighbours in peace. I hope common sense will prevail and the Arab leaders will sit around the table in order to come to an agreed solution of outstanding issues.

The African nations will benefit more from diplomatic relations with this country than anything else.

B. K. ROY CHOUDHURY
Tel Aviv (Bombay), October 30.

To the Editor of The Jerusalem Post
Sir, — I am utterly disgusted and heart-broken to read that our Government is helping the Egyptian Third Army with plasma and convoys of food, water and medicine. I know that the pressure from the U.S. Government on our Government is tremendous, but our Government should stand firm. If the U.S. Government tells us what to do and how to handle the Egyptians, then let Israel become the 51st state of the Union and then the American Army can come and fight our war. Why should our men have to die in the front line in the name of survival, freedom and independence, when this is really the war of America and Russia?

If our Government cannot be strong enough to stand up to American pressure, let younger and stronger people take over.

CHARLES FOUKX
Shoresh, October 30.

WHAT'S THE

Ephraim Kishon

GENERALLY speaking, the average Israeli either floats on air with self-confidence or crawls in the mud with dejection — there's no middle-mood. The spoilt Israeli doesn't know how to lose. He positively wallows in self-made gloom these days. The average Israeli does nothing but search for prophets of doom and high-priests of negligence, as if not he himself, like all of us, is to blame that Yoske lost the keys again, this time at the Canal.

We want to get angry at ourselves? Very well, that's quite healthy. But for doldrums of such national dimensions we ought to . demand a more logical explanation of ourselves, especially as the black line of the Jewish Despair Zone starts 70 km. from Cairo and ends on the road to Damascus.

ALL RIGHT, so let's figure the score! And let's go about it as meticulously as our colleague Hassanein Heykal:

The Arabs achieved their objective but didn't realize their expectations. They managed — by drudgery, long-range planning and skill, and above all by avoiding expressions like "Leave it to me!" — to shake our position in the area and the world; they proved that strongholds can be captured and Israeli soldiers taken prisoner; but they failed to fulfil their great dream of defeating us, let alone recover the legitimate-rights-of-the-Palestinian-People, that is, wipe us out.

Another point for them: our care for every soldier, our concern for the loss of young life. That's our moral advantage in war, and our political weakness after. In Syria and Egypt, apparently, there are no mothers.

And now for the greatest military achievement of our friends: their Brother is stronger than ours. One's a Superpower & Co., the other's a Superpower Ltd. And as long as the relationship between them stays as it is, the Arab armies will remain undefeated. It's not as if the U.S.'s might were in any way inferior to that of the Peace Camp's, but that Russia is better at getting angry and that Comrade Brezhnev isn't obliged to hand over his tapes. That's why Russia presses, and the U.S. only resists the pressure. The name of the game is "Balance." And one of the ways it's played is by mumbling "Well, what can you do?" when the Egyptians moved their missile sites, remember, and we shouted Gevalt!

PROFESSOR Kissinger is a clever intercontinental missile and we'd like to hope he's our friend in spite of his Jewish ancestry and that he isn't too mad at us for refusing to provide the Third Army with its requirements in arms as well. At the same time, we're a bit afraid the brilliant professor might be suffering from a slight "Bridge over the River Kwai" case.

The hero of that film is a proud British colonel who withstands all the physical and mental torture of his Japanese captors, but after they've got friendly and he's built a bridge over the river with them, he starts getting anxious for the constructive cooperation between them, till he's ready to shoot the American soldiers who've come to blow up "his" bridge. Only at the last minute does the colonel realize what's happened to him, but then it's already "The End."

Professor Kissinger doesn't see, or doesn't want to see, that behind the warm embraces of the "détente" the U.S.S.R. is cutting the ground from under his feet with frightening efficiency. They've already got Europe under the Arab oil whip, and presently the great North Vietnam offensive'll break out and rock the free world on its foundations. The votes against: Israel. The U.S. itself is still smiling. It's anxious for the bridge. Only China can still save the West.

A FEW words about that wretched bunch for whom the existence of a small nation is a question of central heating. The mass prostration of Western Europe before the oil-wells, the wholesale abandonment of Holland, their Nato and Common Market ally, is nothing but a cynical repeat of the Munich affair. If they'd just put up a united front and told the Arabs firmly ...

Oh well. Why endanger the smooth running of your public transport for the sake of Czechoslovakia?

WE ARE not Czechoslovakia.

And with that basic premise, if the reader permits, let's now finally start counting *our* points:

No blackest nation-wide depression can change the fact that *we* are at the gates of *their* Capitals, *we* are sticking in *their* troats, *we* are feeding *their* encircled army and not vice versa, *we* are forming regiments of *their* tanks in a variety of colours, *we*, the surprised, unprepared, negligent, arrogant three million, have turned

SCORE?

the well-stocked tables of 19 Arab States on them, and if it hadn't been for the panicky intervention of the automaton in New York we'd have put the fear-barrier back where it belongs ...

If that isn't an Arab defeat we should rewrite the dictionary. We admit there used to be a myth that the I.D.F. is unbeatable. And that isn't true: it's not a myth any longer but a fact. You can cause us losses and they hurt, you can give us the black and blues, but you can't wipe us off the map because we aren't Czechoslovakia but quite the opposite.

Besides, Yoske with the keys has learnt something. One may suppose this has been the last time he's been caught without them. Now it's *our* turn.

IT ALSO isn't true that the whole world is against us. The whole world is for us, only their governments aren't. The public flocks to our show, only the reviews are bad. Don't underestimate the public.

And then there's always World Jewry still, which hasn't been mobilized to the full extent of its yelling capacity yet. There are 12m. Jews in the Diaspora, 10m. of them in key positions. They're our oil, with the slight advantage that oil doesn't have the vote in elections.

One look from the Arab viewpoint: is their position really that good? They were a bit surprised too, weren't they, by our behaviour in a crisis, by our astounding striking power, and above all by the absolute and unequivocal support of the U.S. in this war. And not only they but the Russians too, and we ourselves.

If I were an Arab I might wonder rather uneasily: what're those spiteful Jews going to do to us at the next round for having been surprised and humiliated by us on their holiest day? Because we Jews have our honour too, haven't we?

And we still have a few technological-scientific tricks up our sleeve. Let's not forget that in these days of long-range depression.

WE COULD go on and on, but we're ready for the impatient reader to interrupt us at this point: What're you doing "boosting our morale" over half a page? Who wants any more rounds? Who wants any more victories?

Dear reader, this half-a-page was written exactly for that purpose — so there wouldn't be any more wars or victories. If it's peace you want you can learn it by heart.

Because in negotiations over a just and dictated peace every international factor is taken into account except justice. A strong and self-confident, or even over-confident, Israel is going to come to a fair settlement with its neighbours some day. A whining and dispirited Israel is going to be put on the lowest shelf of history by its enemies and friends alike. What you've got to prove in the universal poker-game isn't so much your strength as your authentic anger, the fact that you really and truly intend to commit follies. And that's not a game one can play in the jittery atmosphere that you, dear reader, with all respect, spread round you these days. You want the Old Lady's hands to tremble with the cards? You want a shaken Golda?

Our future'll be decided in that inevitable moment when our Golda turns to "a friendly power" for the first time and says loud and clear:

"No!"

"But Mrs. Meir," her American hosts'll answer politely, "if you won't accept our dictates we'll withdraw our support and throw you to the Russians." And then — then Mrs. Meir will have to answer with her delightful simplicity:

"Very well!"

And look'em straight in the eye and not blink even once, till the House turns white all over. Because that's the only answer that will ensure us American support for a just and feasible peace with the Russians. But for that Golda needs the whole State of Israel behind her, three million Mediterranean madmen who're capable of smashing the world to bits if they're not given a place under the sun. So stop the depression cult for a bit and shut up, for heaven's sake, and remember that the war with the Americans has only just started. Every charge, and certainly every justified charge, on the subject of the war that was — is a trump-card for the Arabs; every sign of weakness, doubt, internal strife, every whimper — take us that much farther from our slight chance for peace. A depressed nation doesn't count in the balance. A people that deserves to be pitied gets only consignments of pity.

Translated by Miriam Arad
By arrangement with "Ma'ariv"

155

the opening passages of the Mishna *Ta'anit*:

> When should one begin to mention "the power of rain"?
>
> One should not pray for rain until shortly before the season of rain.
>
> If the seventeenth of Marheshvan[1] has come and there has been no rainfall distinguished individuals begin to fast. On the nights preceding the fast, they may eat and drink, and on the fast days proper they may engage in work, may bathe, anoint themselves, wear shoes,

> and cohabit with their wives.
>
> If the first day of the month of Kislev[2] has come and no rain has yet fallen, the Court orders three fasts for the community. On the nights preceding the fasts, the people may eat and drink, and on the fast days they may engage in work, bathe, anoint themselves, wear shoes, and cohabit with their wives.
>
> If these fast days are over and the

1. *Marheshvan* is the eighth month.
2. *Kislev* is the ninth month of the Hebrew lunar calendar.

Bishop Raya protests

To the Editor of The Jerusalem Post

Sir, — I can assure Dr. Watters that we, the "Christianity" of this country, have always been trusted, trustworthy and loyal to friends, and even to foes, and we shall remain so forever. We have been trustworthy and loyal to our Government, to Israel and to our Jewish people. We are proud to be that "Christianity" and we shall never allow mud nor malice to mar its beauty. No Jewish brother, be he a Sabra or a returnee, shall ever look at us as "can't be trusted in times of need," or at any time. What we need now in this beautiful country is healing hearts and clasped hands of brothers.

The first complaint against "Christianity," says Dr. Watters, came to him from the "Ministry of Christian Affairs." At the outbreak of the war, a representative of the Ministry said to him: "The telephone of the Ministry is silent; none of our usual Christian friends have come to call." Is that why we can't be trusted? *Et tu, Brute!?* I wish the Ministry of Religious Affairs would let me know why should I call on them? Is it a war against religion, theirs or mine?

I know where my duty lies in time of war. Not with the Ministry of Religious Affairs, but with the Government represented in the person of our Prime Minister. At the very moment the war broke out, we, the "Christianity" of Israel, sent a telegram to Mrs. Golda Meir and said that we were ready to serve in every way we could. My priests gathered around me until very late that night to study means and way for us to be effectively helpful to our country. We immediately donated money and offered our blood. I personally called the Municipality of Haifa where I live, and the Police Force, to offer my services: "Even if you need someone with a broom to sweep the garbage in the streets, I am ready" (sic). I can-

not understand the attitude of the Ministry of Religious Affairs in this respect.

Secondly, Dr. Watters turns his attention to all the suffering the Jews endured in the West at the hands of "Christianity." Why don't we be honest? If there is so much to condemn in the "Christianity" of the West, there is also, I think, some tiny little expressions of love we could sometimes bless. I might be wrong, but I think it is cowardly to always look at the past, especially when the past is so sad, can paralyze and stir hatred or division. We, in this country, Israelis of all stocks and backgrounds, we want to look at our future. Enough blood has been spilled. Hatred and suspicion paralyzed our relations and our enthusiasm for life. The poison of division and opposition spoiled the most beautiful things the people of this country, the pioneers and their sons, have created. It is time for openness, for forgetting sadness and mistrust. It is time for peace and love.

JOSEPH M. RAYA
Archbishop of Galilee

Haifa, October 29.

GREEK CATHOLICS BUY WAR BONDS

A representative of the Greek Catholic community in Israel yesterday handed a cheque for IL23,160 to the Ministry of Religious Affairs — the first instalment of the IL250,000 worth of war bonds the Greek Catholics have pledged to buy.

The representative, Salah Darsi, said that IL5,000 of the sum was a personal contribution by Archbishop Joseph Raya, head of the Greek Catholic community in Israel.

SUPPORT FROM BERLIN

To the Editor of The Jerusalem Post

Sir, — You certainly know how much we are with you in our thoughts. We can only pray that this frightful war will soon be over and end in your victory. You deserve all our admiration. We are highly indignant about the Arabs. Israel must be triumphant and finally be able to live in peace.

MARGARETE GRUEBER

Berlin, October 16.

Margarete Grueber is the wife of Dean Heinrich Grueber, who was incarcerated in Oranienburg and Dachau by the Nazis for rescuing Jews, and was honoured with a tree in the Avenue of Righteous Gentiles at Yad Vashem. Ed. *J.P.*

CHRISTIAN HELP

To the Editor of The Jerusalem Post

Sir, — I hope that Mr. Landau, in his article, "Christians scored for keeping silent on the war" (October 15), excluded many Christians who live here in the Holy City and have been helping with cars and physical work in an effort to keep civilian life running smoothly during this awful war. The Lord Jesus Christ Himself said that anyone who takes up the sword will die by it (St. Matthew — 26,52). This is being evidenced by the tremendous casualties experienced daily by Egypt, Syria and their allies.

Real Christians throughout the entire world bleed in their hearts for the plight of Israel.

MRS. MARIE NANCY BROWN

Jerusalem, October 16.

WHOSE SINAI?

Col. Richard Meinertzhagen, chief of intelligence to Gen. Allenby in World War I and later an adviser on the Middle East to the British Government, became a lifelong supporter of the Zionist cause. Some of his reasons are made clear in the following remarkably prescient letter to Premier Lloyd George in March, 1919, which, over half a century later, is still also an authoritative statement on the legal situation of the Sinai Peninsula.

My Dear Prime Minister,

You asked me yesterday to send you an unofficial letter on the subject of the sovereignty of Sinai. I regard this question as supremely important — not at the moment but in years to come. May I enter more fully into the question than I was able to do yesterday.

We are very wise in allowing the Jews to establish their national home in Palestine; we have also freed the Arabs from the Turkish yoke and we cannot forever remain in Egypt. This Peace Conference has laid two eggs — Jewish nationalism and Arab nationalism; these are going to grow up into troublesome chickens.

In fifty years' time, both Jew and Arab will be obsessed by nationalism, the natural outcome of (President Wilson's) self-determination. Nationalism prefers self-government, however dishonest and inefficient, to government by foreigners, however efficient and beneficial. Nationalism, moreover, involves the freedom of the state but ignores the freedom of the individual. It is a sop to professional politicians and agitators, and may involve gross injustice to the people.

A national home for the Jew must develop sooner or later into sovereignty; I understand that this natural evolution is envisaged by some members of H.M. Government. Arab nationalism will also develop into sovereignty from Mesopotamia to Morocco.

Jewish and Arab sovereignty must clash... The Arab will do his utmost to check the growth and power of a Jewish Palestine. That means bloodshed.

The British position in the Middle East is paramount; the force of nationalism will challenge our position. We cannot befriend both Jew and Arab. My proposal is based on befriending the people who are more likely to be loyal friends — the Jews. They owe us a great deal and gratitude is a marked characteristic of that race. Though we have done much for the Arabs, they do not know the meaning of gratitude; moreover they would be a liability; the Jews would be an asset.

Palestine is the corner-stone of the Middle East; bounded on two sides by desert and one side by the sea, it possesses the best natural harbour in the Eastern Mediterranean; the Jews have, moreover, proved their fighting qualities since the Roman occupation of Jerusaem. The Arab is a poor fighter, though adept at looting, sabotage and murder.

I now come to Palestine's position vis-a-vis Egypt. The Egyptians, even with superior numbers, are no match for an inferior Jewish army. But as modern weapons — tanks and aircraft — develop, offensive power rests more and more on human bravery and endurance. This is why I regard Egypt as Palestine's potential enemy.

Loss of Canal

With Jewish and Arab nationalism developing into sovereignty and with the loss of the Canal in 1966 (only 47 years hence), we stand a good chance of losing our position in the Middle East. My suggestion to you yesterday is a proposal to make our position in the Middle East more secure.

Previous to 1905, the Turkish-Egyptian frontier ran from Rafa in the North to the neighbourhood of Suez. The whole of the eastern and southern Sinai was part of the Hejaz province of the Ottoman Empire. In October 1906, Egypt was granted administrative rights in Sinai up to a line drawn from Rafa to the head of the Gulf of Aqaba, Turkey expressly retaining the right of sovereignty. General Allenby, with British Forces, unaided by the Egyptian army, conquered and occupied Turkish Sinai, which, by right of conquest, is at Britain's disposal. This bare statement can be verified by the Foreign Office.

If Britain annexes Turkish Sinai, the following advantages accrue:

1. It establishes a buffer between Egypt and Palestine.
2. It gives Britain a strong foothold in the Middle East with access to both the Mediterranean and the Red Sea.
3. It gives us room for a strategic base and, with Jewish consent, the best harbour in the Eastern Mediterranean.
4. It not only places us in a position whence we can frustrate any Egyptian move to close the Canal to British shipping, but it enables us to build a dual canal connecting the Mediterranean with the Red Sea.
5. No question of nationalism can arise in Sinai, as its nomad inhabitants are but a few thousand.

(Reprinted from Middle East Diary, 1917-1956 by R.H. Meinertzhagen. The Cresset Press, London, 1959.)

Meinertzhagen in Mesopotamia in 1914.

community's prayer has not been answered, the Court orders three more fasts for the community. On the days preceding these fasts, one may eat and drink until sunset only; and on the fast days proper, work, bathing, anointing oneself, wearing shoes, and cohabitation are forbidden. The bath-houses must be closed.

If these fast days, too, are over and the community has not been answered, the Court orders seven additional fasts for the community, making in all thirteen fasts.

In what respect are these seven fasts more rigorous than the three immediately preceding? In that on these the alarm must be sounded, and the shops must be closed. On the fasts falling on a Monday, the doors of the shops may be slightly opened toward nightfall, while on Thursdays they may be kept open all day for the sake of the approaching Sabbath.

First lines and last

By LEA BEN DOR

U.S. Secretary of State Dr. Kissinger is only rarely short of an answer, but before he left the U.S. on his present swing round the Arab capitals he said it was "hard to be profound in the rain." It won't have been raining in Egypt when he got there, so we may expect him to take a careful look at statements made there, aided by all the clarity of blue skies.

The first point that we would like him to take into consideration concerns borders. A great deal of world-wide sympathy has lately been poured out for the Arab states, who are seen to suffer under the loss of territories in 1967; the Nine in Europe confirmed this last night. No doubt they have suffered, but the suffering is almost entirely a matter of prestige. Many tens of thousands of refugees in Gaza and on the Jordan West Bank have made more progress towards rehabilitation and a return to normal life in the six years since 1967 than in the 19 years preceding.

Egypt and even Syria have shown the political good sense to concentrate their appeals, threats and propaganda on the issue of the territories lost to them in 1967 and a sympathetic reaction has swept the world press. For many commentators it has become the only issue in the Middle East of which they are fully aware.

"This is the first target, the first line at which they are aiming," a senior military commentator observed recently. "This is all they are willing to talk about at the moment. But will Dr. Kissinger please ask them what the *last* line, the final border is to be?

"Will any of them, in fact, commit themselves to the acceptance of the June 4, 1967 borders as peace borders for Israel? They certainly did not accept them prior to 1967: then the popular, the appealing, phrase was that Israel should go back to the U.N. Partition Scheme borders, which sought to create a state consisting of three separate areas linked only by so-called "crossing points."

And we have not forgotten — though most other people have — that it was this unlikely, rickety structure that seven Arab states combined to destroy in 1948 even before it was established.

Perhaps we should be appreciative that most of the terrorist organizations make no secret of the fact that they are not seeking a change in borders or any other arrangement that would involve them in recognizing the existence of the State of Israel, but simply its destruction in its present political form, that is, the ending of Jewish independence in Israel, regardless of borders.

Thus the essential question for Dr. Kissinger to ask is what are the last, the final, borders you envisage for Israel, to which you will commit yourself?

If all these fast days have passed and the community has not been answered, all business transactions, building, planting, betrothals, marriages, and greetings should be limited, as behooves persons excommunicated in the sight of God. Distinguished individuals begin again to fast till the end of Nisan.[1]
If there is no rainfall after the end of Nisan, it is the sign of a curse.

In the view of the early rabbis, all things were controlled by God; natural disasters, too, took place by His direction. Since God was all-beneficent, nothing so evil as a death-dealing drought could occur unless it had been ordained by the Deity as well-deserved retribution. The surest means of deflecting the wrath of God was for man to afflict himself, to humbly acknowledge his guilt. In so doing, he would be deemed to have foresworn his

1. *Nisan* is the first month of the Hebrew year.

evil ways. Then God, in His infinite mercy, might relent and grant the wrongdoer forgiveness, absolution from further punishment.

So began the tradition of self-examination, of introspective soul-searching. If I am being punished, in what way have I sinned? How can I mend my ways? How can I once again find favor with a righteous God who demands of me nothing short of goodness?

And so, in this same time-honored tradition, on Monday, November 5, 1973, on the 30th day after the commencement of the Yom Kippur War, the rabbis of Israel, in the belief that the catastrophic destruction of their sons in battle could only have occurred as a just punishment, sought to humble the hearts of the entire nation. They called upon the national community to engage in a day of fasting, a day of prayer and atonement. The imperiled nation, they inferred from events, must retrieve a mood of sobriety and thoughtfulness befitting the awesome fact that its youth were facing deathly fire at the front.

Graduation exercises for artillery men.

Parents of fallen receive insignia at graduation

Military Pool Correspondent

Flags were lowered to half-mast at an artillery officers graduation ceremony somewhere in Israel yesterday, as the parents of graduates who fell in the war came forward to receive their sons' certificates and insignia.

The officers course was interrupted when the war broke out and the cadets rejoined their units to take part in the war. Chief Artillery Officer Tat-Aluf Natan Sharoni told the graduates that this course "was different from any that preceded it. You have already taken part in the most difficult of all Israel's wars and have shown unlimited devotion and courage."

Turning to the bereaved parents, Tat-Aluf Sharoni said: "The memory of the fallen will accompany us always. They fell for the right to live in this country."

HOW A CURIOUS CONVOY BROUGHT ICE-CREAM TO THE FRONT-LINE

By **SARAH HONIG**
Jerusalem Post Reporter

TEL AVIV. — It was on the eve of Simhat Tora, which even back home this year lacked the traditional rejoicing that typifies this holiday in normal times. At the Sinai frontline, where tank corpsmen were reorganizing after a long day of particularly ferocious fighting, the holiday atmosphere was altogether absent. Until, almost out of nowhere, ice-cream arrived and with it, Simhat Tora.

The friendly ice cream men making their deliveries at each tank, half track and encampment, were several middle-aged businessmen. This war, the army passed them up and they were not mobilized for active service. But Bank Leumi executive Moshe Amit, diamond dealer Yitzhak Dankner and textile marketing executive Boris Sakow could not sit it out at home.

They spent the first few days of the war doing various driving jobs. They then started collecting transistor radios, snacks, games, underwear and toilet supplies for soldiers. "But that just wasn't it. It didn't seem to satisfy our need to do something more concrete to help the war effort. We weren't allowed to fight, so at least we thought that we would personally bring the goods we obtained and the love of everyone left at home directly to those who needed them most at the very first lines," Mr. Sakow explained.

"With a little *protectzia*" the businessmen managed to convince the military authorities to let them have a civilian tender that had been mobilized. A large ice-cream company donated 5,000 ice-creams packed in dry ice. They also took along 4,000 packets of cigarettes, bags of pop corn, toilet items, fresh underwear, socks, and 10,000 post cards for the troops to write regards to their anxious families. They were received by a new immigrant from South Africa, Jack Reisen, who brought his car, and an American tourist, Michael Katz, who contributed towards the operation.

"During the days of fierce battles, we weren't stopped much," I was told. "The officers just took our appearance there as a fact. We didn't know the way either. We more or less got directions as we went. Once we nearly made a wrong turn and an officer later told us that we very narrowly missed distributing our ice-cream to the Egyptians — the Third Army, as it turned out," Mr. Sakow says with a chuckle.

Since the eve of Simhat Tora he and his friends undertook four such trips, each lasting three to four days. But the impression of the first one is still the most powerful. "We just surprised the men there and they absolutely did not know what to make of us. To see real rejoicing, one had to be there. We took out wine and made a *kiddush* there under the open sky, and, suddenly, despite the guns and the grubby uniforms and the situations, there was a real warm holiday atmosphere."

"Before we left we forced each and every soldier to write a post card." Mr. Sakow said. He and his friends also took down many of the soldiers' telephone numbers and when they got home spent hours on the phone passing on fresh regards to worried mothers, wives and children. They organized the speedy delivery of the postcards to the soldiers' homes by volunteer messengers.

The next trip they took two more tenders, plus Mr. Reisman's car. "We bought 10,000 ice cream portions, 8,000 cigarette packs, more toilet supplies, pop corn and many, many home-baked cakes. You have no idea what a hit the cakes were. We also carried a load of pocket flashlights, more transistor radios and batteries," Mr. Sakow recounts.

This time they crossed the Canal into Egypt. At one point, the curious convoy found itself under mortar and katyusha shelling. "Shells were exploding all around us. When I told a soldier that we didn't have to be there, he gave me a startled look and asked if I wasn't crazy and if I was married. When I replied in the affirmative and added that I am the father of two, he suddenly embraced me, gave me a kiss, turned away and disappeared," Boris Sakow recalls.

One dark night, when they were sleeping on the roadside, a column of tanks almost ran over them. "We started waving out flashlights and they came to a halt. That was a very close call," Mr. Sakow says very matter-of-factly.

The fourth trip took place last weekend. This time they decided to adopt a certain unit and establish ties with the unit's wounded in hospitals. "We also thought that this would best be done in the Rotary framework," says Mr. Sakow, who is President of the East Tel Aviv Rotary.

His club, along with the Holon and Bat Yam clubs decided to join in sponsoring the contacts with the "adopted" unit, which turned out to be one of the most remote ones near the port of Abadiya, south of Suez City.

They were joined by Oded Pessensohn, who was injured during naval manoeuvres in 1960 and left a quadriplegic. He surmounted his difficulties, became a lawyer and after a long hard struggle won a driving licence. "All through the war he helped out doing volunteer work, and he came with us despite the fact that it is very difficult for him. He even slept on the ground with us and the rest of the soldiers. The trip was a terrific effort for me. Imagine what it was for Oded," Mr. Sakow says.

The most popular items on this trip were newspapers.

But the best of all "was the little help we gave in maintaining personal contact between home and front. At one point, for instance, we met a soldier who told us that he has heard nothing from home and is worried because he left his wife expecting a baby any day. As soon as we got home, we started inquiries and found out that the wife had just given birth and managed to let him know he was the father of a beautiful baby daughter."

Abba Eban, Minister of Foreign Affairs, delivering an address.

BELIEVING THAT "those who do not remember history are doomed to repeat it," in Israel, the Holocaust has become a subject for deep study. As painful as that study might be, as shocking as the details are, the gruesome facts have not been buried out of sight. The Holocaust is one chapter of history that was altogether too terrible to ever be repeated. The Holocaust must never, never be forgotten.

All over the world there are memorials to the martyred Jews, but the most notable edifice stands atop one of the mountains of Jerusalem. This memorial is known as Yad Vashem. The name derives from a passage in Isaiah.[1]

I will give to them in my house, and within my walls, a hand and a name better than I would give to my sons and my daughters;

an everlasting name will I give them which shall never be cut off.

In Hebrew, *yad vashem* literally means "hand and name," but in the context above where these words appear, they signify "a monument and a memorial."

When Absalom warred against his father David and was slain, the tomb in which he was interred was called *Yad Avshalom,* literally "The Hand of Absalom." Scholars tell us that the figure of a hand is often found on Phoenician and Punic monumental stones. It is therefore likely that in Canaanitish times a hand was a symbol of death, more or less used as it is in the phrase in archaic

1. Chapter 56, Verse 5.

Double standard

To the Editor of The Jerusalem Post

Sir, — The hypocrisy and double standards of the so-called non-aligned nations, which in unison accuse Israel of "aggression" against the Arabs, is best revealed in a recent statement of Mrs. Indira Gandhi, Prime Minister of India, at a press conference in Kerala Province.

Mrs. Gandhi stated that India's support of the Arabs is based on the principle of non-recognition of acts of aggression and on the demand that Israel retreat from the occupied territories.

- However, when she was asked whether her stance against aggression is also applicable to the areas captured by India in Kashmir, her reply was that this is India's position in principle, "but when it applies to us, we have to act in the best interests of our country."

Kashmir, a predominantly Moslem region, has been in dispute between India and Pakistan since 1947, after the end of the British rule. In August 1965, the armed forces of both nations became involved in a spreading war. It is interesting to note that, in September of that year, both sides agreed to accept a U.N. Security Council demand for a ceasefire but did not comply with a call for them to withdraw their forces across the old cease-fire line.

However, in the case of Israel, both India and Pakistan are vehement supporters of the demand that Israel withdraw to the pre-1967 lines. Another case of do as I say, not as I do.

DR. REUBEN EFRON
Jerusalem, November 1.

WEST BANK ARABS

To the Editor of The Jerusalem Post

Sir, — In your issue of October 10, there was a letter from Evelyne R. Engelberg of Pittsburgh, Pennsylvania, enquiring as to the Israelite origin of the West Bank Arabs.

The land of Israel has been the scene of so many invasions and other population movements that its peoples are truly a mixture. The Arabs were relative late-comers to the area (early 7th century C.E.), and were followed by Persians, Crusaders, Mongols, Turks, and many others. The problem of defining an "Arab" has been solved by t h e Arabs themselves, who give that title to anyone whose native language is Arabic, including the inhabitants of North Africa.

A very common but false supposition is that all Jews in the land of Israel disappeared into the Diaspora following the Roman wars of 70 and 135 C.E. This is true only in a religious sense, however. Jews who were willing to change their religion (paganism, of course, being preferred by Rome) were allowed to remain. Even at that, there were always communities of religious Jews, particularly in Galilee.

The first Christians were, of course, Jews. How many Jews became followers of Jesus prior to the Bar Kokhba Revolt one cannot really ascertain, though it was at least in the thousands (Acts 2:41; 4:4). When the Moslems came in 636 C.E., they found an essentially Christian population. Large numbers were converted to Islam, and all eventually adopted the Arabic language, thus becoming "Arabs."

The Arab invaders settled, for the most part in the larger towns, and hence the villages retained more of their original character. Thus it is that we find Christian (and Moslem) Arab towns in the West Bank whose inhabitants may actually be Jewish in origin.

While certain political problems would obviously be solved by official recognition of the West Bank Arabs' right to live in the land of Israel (by virtue of their Israelite heritage), nevertheless other socio-political problems could arise.

JOHN A. TVEDINES
Jerusalem, October 10.

Firm backing from U.S. labour

TEL AVIV. — American Labour's firm backing for Israel was reaffirmed this week by AFL-CIO President George Meany when he met Histadrut Secretary-General Yitzhak Ben-Aharon, now on a speaking tour of the United States.

This report was conveyed by cable to Histadrut head offices here. Mr. Ben-Aharon took the opportunity to convey Israel Labour's gratitude to the American labour movement for its support in Israel's hour of trial. Mr. Meany responded: "There is no need to thank us for things we do so willingly." He said their traditional backing of Israel would be maintained.

English, "Someone has laid a hand on him," meaning "Someone has harmed him," (perhaps killed him.)

The reference in the verse of Isaiah is clear: the monument will be an everlasting resting place where the memory of those whom it honors will never be erased.

The feeling that the names of the martyrs must be commemorated runs deep. In 1945, three years before the State of Israel was established, at the first Zionist Congress that met after World War II, a committee was formed to develop this project.

The task of erecting a fitting memorial was outlined specifically:

To gather in material regarding all those Jewish people who laid down their lives, who fought and rebelled against the Nazi enemy and their collaborators, and to perpetuate their memory and that of the communities, organizations, and institutions, which were destroyed because they were Jewish.

The Yad Vashem Memorial houses a central archive which contains some 25 million documentary pages on the Holocaust. Millions of microfilms, museum objects, films, and records have been amassed. The adjunct library contains

Bereaved parents at the grave of their son in Mishmar Hanegev.

'America had better remember that Israel is a democracy'

Man in the street irate at concessions

By SARAH HONIG
Jerusalem Post Reporter

TEL AVIV. — The announcement that 50 more truckloads of supplies are to be sent to the encircled Egyptian Third Army has incensed the public following the publication of the Yom Kippur war casualty figures.

Most people I spoke to in Tel Aviv yesterday linked the two announcements and felt, as one high school senior told me: "Our grief over the fallen should at least stop us from making more harmful concessions and make us more resolved that Israel's security — for which so many boys gave their lives in the past month — is not compromised. We should make sure the blood spilled has not been sacrificed in vain, whether or not Kissinger or anyone else likes it." I caught the 17-and-a-half-year-old high school pupil as he was leaving the Kiryat Shaul Cemetery, following services for the war dead. One of the soldiers killed was his best friend, only 18 months his senior.

Away from the mourners and back in the city streets I found the same reaction. Waiting to cross the street I struck up a conversation with a girl — a former army lieutenant — who said, "If the Government cannot resist pressures, it had better tell the nation so today, as we commemorate our too-many fallen. Any government which makes concessions in this tragic situation will not survive, and the Americans had better remember that this is a democratic nation in which people have the power of the vote. The Arabs are dreaming of completing Hitler's work, but this time the Jewish people are not helpless. We have a strong army, and there is no reason for us to allow the new Nazis to erode our resistance by agreeing to concessions which the Arabs figure will enable them in the end to throw us into the sea."

"We said that without the return of the PoWs and the lifting of the Bab el-Mandeb blockade there would be no cease-fire. Well, there is a cease-fire just the same. Why should anyone think they must honour commitments made to us?"

The issue of the PoW's was raised by many of the people I spoke to.

A youngish junior high school teacher added: "There is no justification for Israel concessions in a world where black gold is dearer than Jewish blood, and in which Syrians can demand that we abide by the Geneva Convention while they murder bound prisoners. The problem," she went on angrily, "is that the world can't and doesn't want to understand the price we have just paid. Proportional to our population, it is more than three times higher than the American losses in all the years of fighting in Vietnam. If any other nation could even begin to realize the Jewish reverence for each human life, and the magnitude of our loss, they would be at a loss to understand how we can agree to keep an enemy army alive and kicking so it can inflict more casualties on us in a future round," she exclaimed.

A passerby who eavesdropped on our street-corner conversation — and then, along with several others, joined it — felt that "we did not win this war to become puppets. If we don't look out for ourselves, no one will. Our interests right now mean the surrender of the Third Army; and it will not be achieved if we keep it well fed," he contended. An orthodox woman laden with shopping bags shouted: "So many of our boys were killed so that the Egyptians could be encircled. Lifting the siege is an insult to their memory."

Everywhere I went feeling ran high on the issue. "I couldn't understand why the first 135 trucks were allowed through to begin with," a reservist, strolling with his wife and a baby daughter during a short leave, told me. I kept consoling myself that it was a one-time gesture, for Kissinger; but the news that the Egyptians will get 50 more truckloads of food and water has hit me like a ton of bricks, he said.

A cab driver said: "I am a simple man. I am not a clever politician. All I understand is straightforward, plain logic. To my mind, when you give something you should get something in return. We already gave the Third Army food and water once. I figure we should have got something for our generosity. Our PoWs should at least have been home by now. But we didn't even get their names. We were cheated. Anyone can be cheated once, but I can't understand why we should allow ourselves to be made fools of twice," he argued.

An old-timer, listening to heated debates in the outdoor Sderot Rothschild "parliament" here, said the renewed supply transports to the Third Army "are the first sign of concessions Golda made in Washington. We must beware of Kissinger. He did not achieve peace in Vietnam, and we can't afford precarious agreements like that here. At a time when the Arabs are talking of a new round, we should not feed them. If they want us to help their soldiers they cannot make threats against us."

Members of a group calling itself "Citizens Against Surrender" demonstrating outside the Hanashbir Department Store in Jerusalem. The group collected signatures on a petition calling for the replacement of the government by a "Nonpartisan National Emergency Cabinet," and they demanded closure of the supply route to the Egyptian Third Army.

more than 35,000 books and periodicals. Here the researcher can find eyewitness accounts, detailed by survivors from every ghetto and every hamlet that was ravished.

In every generation, history has produced villains who have not scrupled to attack and destroy the weak and the unprotected. In every generation, too, history has provided men of righteousness who have understood that regardless of circumstance and regardless of birth, all men are brothers. The sages of the Talmud talked about these kind people as *Hasidei Ummot ha-Olam,* "the saintly ones of the nations of the world." The rabbis spoke of these great souls with enormous reverence.

At the Yad Vashem Memorial, one can find a most edifying archive entitled "The Department for the

Righteous Gentiles." This was set up to honor individuals who risked their own lives to rescue Jews during the horrors of the Holocaust. Here are inscribed the names of Christians from every European country who came forth in the days of trouble. These saintly ones represented the very best teachings of their faith. Their names, written for all to see for generations to come, are inscribed as a monument to man's faith in Man.

On page 162 of this book, the reader will find a letter written by Margarete Grueber, a resident of Berlin, who sends her support to the Israeli people through the columns of The Jerusalem Post. The editor appends a note stating Margarete Grueber is the wife of Dean Heinrich Grueber who was incarcerated in Oranienburg and Dachau by the Nazis for rescuing Jews. Mr. Grueber is

Memorial services for the 1,854 men killed during the war. Scene is the military cemetery in Tel Aviv.

(Inset.)
Father at the graveside of the two sons he has just buried.

everlastingly honored with a tree planted in his name in the Avenue of Righteous Gentiles at Yad Vashem.

It is quite likely that just as many Ukrainians and Poles were destroyed as Jews. Certainly the number of Hitler's martyrs must amount to over 20 million. But what makes the destruction of the Jews especially poignant is that they were the only people whom Hitler determined to blot out simply because they were born under a religious stigma. In the case of the Poles, or the Ukrainians, or the Belgians, or the French, or in the case of any other peoples whom Hitler destroyed—however wantonly—he attacked these people because he construed them to be enemies of Germany and not because he despised them because of their forbears.

NATION MOURNS ITS 1,854 SONS

Jerusalem Post Staff

A mourning nation paid homage to its 1,854 war dead yesterday with solemn music and prayers on the radio and calls by the brigadiers of the country's three geographical commands for the people of Israel "fighting alone" to stand firm so that the fallen will not have died in vain.

The national flag flew at half-mast over Israel Defence Forces camps as memorial services were under way at provisional military cemeteries following Tuesday's disclosure of the price in blood paid so far in the country's latest war for survival. Services are to be held at the other cemeteries today and Sunday.

The three temporary cemeteries where bereaved families and comrades-in-arms gathered in anguish yesterday are at Kiryat Shaul near Tel Aviv for Central Command; Afula for Northern Command, and Mishmar Hanegev, some 30 kilometres from Beersheba for Southern Command.

Herbert Ben-Adi was at Mishmar Hanegev:

Addressing some 6,000 mourners, Aluf Shmuel Gonen, O.C. Southern Command, said that "we are fighting our fourth war in 25 years. While it is a cruel hard war, we did not start it. Only a thin line of regular soldiers saved us from a catastrophe until the reserves could be called up—"and few realize just how close we were to another holocaust. We are fighting alone and we shall finish this war alone," he said.

More than 300 soldiers from all parts of the country who fell on the southern front have been buried in the temporary cemetery at Mishmar Hanegev. Hundreds of buses and private cars brought mourning families and friends to honour the memory of the fallen. Academic staff from the University of the Negev have been taking care of the families of fallen soldiers in the Beersheba area and they brought them to Mishmar Hanegev in their own cars.

The Chief Chaplain to the Forces, Tat-Aluf Mordechai Piron, eulogized, and the chief army cantor chanted "El malei rahamim." The service closed with three salvoes fired by the guard of honour and the strains of "The Last Post" played by an army bugler.

Sarah Honig reports from Kiryat Shaul cemetery:

"It is thanks to the heroism and boundless devotion of those who gave their lives in this latest of Israel's wars that we can stand here under clear blue skies, with tree branches over our heads and our homes intact," O.C. Central Command Aluf Yona Efrat told the thousands of mourners who filled the temporary burial grounds at Kiryat Shaul.

He termed the Yom Kippur war "the worst attack ever launched on the State of Israel. Our enemies were encouraged and armed by a great power, and their aim was to annihilate this nation and turn this beautiful land into a valley of death and slaughter. With their very bodies, our soldiers stopped this onslaught and turned back the attacking tide," he said.

Aluf Efrat described the whole nation as "one single family, to which we all belong."

Bereaved families started streaming from early yesterday morning to Kiryat Shaul, where 91 are buried, their graves outlined in white stones in three rows.

Wives, mothers, sisters and grandmothers of the dead sat around the sites, some of them wailing, scratching and beating their faces, in oriental tradition. Others stood silently in family groups, fighting back the tears.

A young wife sat near one grave repeating one word: "Why?" A young soldier carried his small orphaned niece, telling her that she must be brave and not cry. At another neat patch of freshly turned ground, a grandmother wept as her bearded husband, his hand on her shoulder, recited Psalm 23 out loud.

A fleet of ambulances was standing by to help persons overcome by grief. First aid men and women circulated among the mourners, offering them drinks and giving medications to those who felt faint. Soldiers bearing stretchers had to be called out several times to take parents who had fainted to the first aid station.

Against this background of lamentations and grief, Aluf Efrat reminded the mourners that the fallen had been "born to live, and they wanted to live as citizens of a free and independent nation. They would have wanted us to be strong. Their voices still call on us to be courageous."

Ya'acov Ardon writes from Afula:

At the temporary cemetery at Afula, which adjoins that of the Six Day War dead, many thousands gathered from eight in the morning for the 11.30 service, and lingered on long after. The throng grew towards 11 and it included many soldiers who had been given special leave to attend the service for their comrades. Some of them mingled with the mourning families and told them of the fallen men's last hour. Flowers were piled high on many of the 241 graves.

The chaplain of the Northern Command, Rav-Seren Israel Ariel, opened the service with a reading from the Psalms and a cantor recited *kaddish*.

BIBLE PORTION

The Deputy Chief Chaplain, Aluf-Mishne Gad Navon, used as his text the verse from this week's Bible portion, Abraham answering "Here am I" when called to sacrifice his son Isaac. "These men answered the call to protect their country and their people, as Abraham did, here am I, with body and soul, so that our people, Israel, may live."

On behalf of Yad Le'Banim, Nathan Shnur, who lost a son in a previous war, told the mourners of his deep conviction that "we raised our sons in the right way."

O.C. Northern Command Aluf Yitzhak Hofi, said that "every man fought as if the fate of the nation was on his shoulders. Though they were heavily outnumbered by the enemy, they battled relentlessly to push him back into his own territory. They fought like lions, in burning tanks, moving through minefields; they repaired tanks under bombing; their devotion knew no bounds. In their death, they enabled us to carry on."

grieving parents at graveside of son just buried. Tomb stone carries the name of the boy, Chayim.

The Nazi hordes crushed whole communities because they stood in the way of Hitler's military advance. But the Germans did not seek them out and go out of their way to uproot these communities just because of their religious origin. Not so with the Jews. It is this which is the very special horror of the Holocaust in human history.

The people of Israel are the sons and the daughters and the relatives of those who were trapped in Hitler's giant death vise; they are everlastingly bound to the memory of that tragedy. In his notable book, *The Israelis: Founders and Sons,*[1] Amos Elon sums up in a few pithy sentences the impact of the Holocaust on the people of Israel.

The holocaust remains a basic trauma of Israeli society... It explains the obsessive suspicions, the towering urge for self-reliance at all cost in a world which permitted the disaster to happen... The lingering memory of the holocaust makes Arab threats of annihilation sound plausible.

For most Israelis today, the Arab threats do not merely sound plausible: they loom as a stark

1. Pages 259 ff. Bantam Books, 1971.

HOUR OF TRUTH

THE "Hour of truth" is what Defence Minister Dayan has called the present significant stage in the aftermath of war: what we hope is the aftermath and not a lull before the resumption of fighting.

Truth could be very important, for it is needed for confidence. We, as well as the Arab countries, will have to do some rethinking and not only, or even mainly, concerning territories. One does not have to read the brief interviews with men-in-the-street in Tel Aviv to know that the great majority of Israelis today have no confidence that a peace agreement will be kept, however much they yearn for peace, more so than ever after this war.

It is, nevertheless, possible that President Sadat is ready for peace. The stupendous effort put into the preparation of the Yom Kippur war has not succeeded in taking more than a hand's breadth of Sinai, has left a large Israel force poised on the western bank of the Canal, and trapped the Egyptian Third Army in a very precarious position that could change at any moment into open disaster.

Thus a bargain has been carefully stitched together by the flying U.S. Secretary of State, Dr. Kissinger. He no doubt knows that the priorities are not the same for the two sides.

For Egypt there are some urgent and immediate goals. Firstly, the desperate need to save the Third Army from collapse because it is encircled and receiving only subsistence supplies; secondly, a prospect that Israel will withdraw from some at least of the territories occupied in 1967, and in particular western Sinai and the Canal — and do this as the result of a war, and not as a voluntary gesture for peace for which the Egyptians would have to be grateful. What lies beyond that in time is of course the question of truth. These aims achieved, will Egypt maintain the peace?

The Israeli priorities run almost in the opposite order. Almost any agreement on small strips of land in Sinai would be worth while if it leads to a negotiated settlement in which our borders are agreed and accepted and the general principle of unlimited war against Israel's existence is abandoned. Any promising step in this direction is worth trying if it does not involve any direct danger to our forces in the area. Secondly, an exchange of prisoners, and particularly wounded prisoners, is of overwhelming immediate importance, and would also justify concessions as long as these did not endanger or prejudice future peace negotiations. The opening of the marine passage at Bab el-Mandeb is important.

The provision for continuing contacts between Israeli and Egyptian officers for the maintenance of the cease-fire may in the end prove to be of great significance. In the long run only joint Israel-Egyptian control of the cease-fire or border lines can be effective, and the foundation for some such body could be laid in the present contacts, if they are successful.

Truth and mutual confidence remain the essence. Confidence could certainly be aided by rapid progress on the exchange of prisoners.

Crime rate on the rise

By YITZHAK OKED
Jerusalem Post Reporter

TEL AVIV. — As far as Israel's criminals are concerned, the war is over. The crime rate, which dropped drastically during the month of October, is beginning to rise again, according to the national police spokesman.

Sgan-Nitzav Nahum Bosmi said the police are continuing 12-hour shifts, partly because they lack manpower and partly because they expect an increase in the rate of misdemeanors after the war. (One popular post-war misdemeanor is illegal possession of weapons—often enemy firearms which are brought home by soldiers as souvenirs but later end up in the hands of the underworld.)

S/N Bosmi said the police would become more visible now. Border Police and policemen who normally do office work will be recruited to patrol the streets of the big cities.

He added that the police were on a 24-hour-a-day alert during the war. Some of their activities included clearing the roads, guarding sensitive installations, enforcing blackout regulations and... repairing broken windows in border villages.

Voluntary war tax

To the Editor of The Jerusalem Post

Sir, — Since the Yom Kippur War has strained the finances of Israel to an almost unbearable extent, I would suggest that people convert the war loan into a voluntary war tax, so that the Treasury will not have to repay the amounts received. I myself have signed up for the equivalent of one month's indemnity which I receive from Germany and declare hereby that I have paid this amount as a voluntary tax.

I hope many people will follow suit.

Dr. BARUCH TOMASCHOFF
Jerusalem, November 1.

APPEAL TO INTERNATIONAL COURT OF JUSTICE

To the Editor of The Jerusalem Post

Sir, — If ever there was a case crying for submission to the International Court of Justice, it is the complaint of the State of Israel against Egypt and Syria for their brutal, arrogant and consistent violations of the Geneva Convention in the matter of Israeli prisoners, especially the wounded, in their hands. Israel should lodge her complaint immediately, with all the vigour at her command.

Of course, it will be pointed out — and with reason — that the chances of accomplishing anything by this complaint are almost zero, in view of the fact that the International Court of Justice is an organ of the United Nations and, therefore, subject to the same baleful influences always operating there against us. True. But, if we are to have left any faith at all in human decency, especially in the free world, we must tell ourselves that there are many people who are not willing to let our case go down the drain by default, and who would wholeheartedly applaud and support the act of bringing the case before the one international body which stands primarily for justice — regardless of the outcome. We must ask the Court to listen, we must demand it.

A. H. SAKIER
Tel Aviv, November 6

'Israel seduces our scientists'

MOSCOW (UPI). — A Soviet Jewish historian accused Israel Wednesday of "seducing" Jewish scientists to leave this country, and said their departure causes serious material damage.

Prof. I. I. Mints, 77, outlined his views in an article in the weekly "Literaturnya Gazeta."

The subject of Jewish emigration is rarely mentioned in the Soviet press, and observers said publication of Prof. Mints' article may reflect official concern over the number of well-educated Jews seeking to leave the country.

"Why should not bourgeois Israel... concentrate its efforts on training its own personnel for the needs of research?" he wrote. "Why should it resort to such unseemly actions in seducing cadres?"

Prof. Mints was dismissed from his posts during the late dictator Josef Stalin's campaign against Jews, but was later restored to favour and is a member of the Academy of Sciences.

He said Israeli leaders were "diligently supporting and propagating the freedom of migration of scientists from the U.S.S.R.... but only to their own country."

Prof. Mints said freedom of migration of scientists "cause a serious material damage to countries losing specialists."

Silent churches

To the Editor of The Jerusalem Post

Sir, — I would like to thank Archbishop Raya for his letter outlining the activities of which his churchmen are a part during this war (November 6). His kind of response was exactly what I hoped to see as a result of my article of October 28. Unfortunately, there were no other responses to equal his.

That *individual* Christians (mainly Western Protestant, Roman Catholic, and Anglican) have helped in the war effort, is not the issue. As in the case of the Holocaust, the Six Day War, and the Yom Kippur War, the real issue is that responsible Christian *denominations* both here and abroad have failed to react to the crisis. Amid the silence of ecclesiastical leaders, the efforts of the individuals become lost.

It was the singular purpose of my article to move church leaders to make clear to Israelis what they have done and how they feel. The loneliness of the Christian Affairs representative of the Ministry of Religious Affairs was not merely an artistic entry into my article, but what I felt (and still feel) to be the gut-level feeling of many Israelis, namely, that while Christian individuals will help, groups will not. When a man is in danger of death, he needs to know who his friends are. He must therefore interpret silent groups and individuals as his enemy.

REVD. DR. WILLIAM R. WATTERS, JR.
Jerusalem, November 6.

The unwavering loyalty

To the Editor of The Jerusalem Post

Sir, — Thank you for your editorial, "The unwavering loyalty" (October 30). This will be particularly encouraging to Jewish communities in countries whose attitude towards Israel leaves much to be desired. In Britain, for example, the Jewish community are completely behind Israel and great efforts continue to be made, collecting money, donating blood, etc. At the same time, many volunteers have come to Israel to help; e.g. it has been my privilege to work alongside my Israeli colleagues for the past three weeks in a Tel Aviv hospital.

Please be sure that no matter what the Government in Britain may say or do, the Jewish community are solidly pro-Israel.

Dr. MERTON SEIGLEMAN
Tel Aviv, October 30.

dear Friends in Israel

Darmstadt-Eberstadt/West Germany
October 19, 1973

All of us who live in the little "Land of Canaan," a religious centre in West Germany, and many friends both here and abroad have a special love for Israel. The bitter, hard-fought battles with their bloodshed have filled us all with deep grief and sympathy for Israel. With our daily prayer and entreaties, we hope to help build a wall around your people as a protection against the outnumbering enemy forces. We live from one news broadcast to the next, sharing Israel's suffering.

The incredible occurred. Roughly 3,300 years after the Covenant was made on Mount Sinai, and Israel really became a nation, she acquired this historical site, after her people had returned from many nations to their own land. It would now have been possible to make Mount Sinai a place of pilgrimage, like Jerusalem with the Western Wall or Hebron with the Tombs of the Patriarchs.

Three and a half years before the momentous occasion when G-d's chosen people gained possession of the Sinai Peninsula, I had the privilege of spending forty days in prayer there, on the Mountain of Moses. It was my deep longing that Mount Sinai would become a holy place for G-d's people, since it is a place of divine revelation. *"Hear, O Israel: The LORD our God is one LORD" (Deuteronomy 6:4).* We are reminded of these words especially here at this site, where G-d made a Covenant with His people and gave them the laws of the Covenant, the Ten Commandments, which later became the ethical basis for many nations, the standard of good and evil. It seemed to me as though the Lord was waiting for His people to keep the Commandments holy, since the nations who received the Law from Israel have taken up the slogan of the times, "The foundations of Mount Sinai have been shaken." They are declaring the Commandments of G-d invalid, rejecting them and thus rejecting G-d. Amorality, criminality, drug addiction, and riots have followed; and the nations are threatened with chaos and disaster.

"For out of Zion shall go forth the Law" (Isaiah 2:3).

What tremendous significance Mount Sinai has today! It is indeed a holy site. As the Scriptures say, *"The LORD our God made a covenant with us in Horeb" (Deuteronomy 5:2).* So remember the Covenant; remember the Commandments!

I beseeched the Lord for Israel — where today when the nations are preparing the way for disaster — that her people might build a powerful dam against the deluge of permissiveness, immorality and the abolition of law and the rejection of the Commandments. I prayed that Israel would not imitate the other nations in discarding the Commandments of G-d, but that she would turn back to G-d in prayer, with tears of repentance for every time the Covenant of the Commandments was broken and the foundations of Mount Sinai shaken. If Israel does this, G-d will remain her partner in the Covenant and fight for Israel and perform miracles, also in time of war.

As Gentiles, we must humble ourselves greatly, for our people have discarded the holy Commandments of G-d. Constantly we beg on our knees, for the nations today disregard G-d's holy Commandments, and we are filled with pain and have to look upon our own immeasurable German guilt towards Israel: We entreat the Lord continually,

"Bless Israel. Let her keep the Covenant and the Commandments holy, so that You can be her shield and helper.

This is our fervent desire and prayer.

Shalom! Shalom!
Yours sincerely,

MOTHER BASILEA

(Communicated)

frightening reality.

In Israel, Holocaust Remembrance Day has been appointed a national holiday. It falls on the 27th day of the month of Nissan, and its chief celebration takes place at the Yad Vashem Monument.

There is still another significant memorial in Israel to the martyrs of the Holocaust. It is a museum which stands in a kibbutz named Yad Mordechai in southern Israel, between Ashkalon and Gaza. This impressive building, designed by Aryeh Eldar Sharon, houses artifacts, posters, photographs, and memorabilia, mostly from the Warsaw ghetto. As one enters these awesome halls, one reads the dire inscription:

> In this place
> Seek and look, for what can be seen no
>   more;
> Hear voices that can be heard no more;
> Understand what is beyond all
>   understanding.

This experience of an hour is unforgettable. It eats like bitter wormwood into one's vitals. One is minded to inquire why this building was erected in this particular spot, and what special significance lies in the name of the kibbutz *Yad Mordechai,* "The Hand of Mordechai."

Yes, this kibbutz is indeed the hand of Mordechai, the hand of Mordechai Anilewicz stretching from his grave, his everlasting memorial. For Mordechai Anilewicz was the Commander of the Warsaw Ghetto Uprising. Until May 8, 1943, he led a brave band of survivors in a last desperate battle against the Nazi foe. He, along with his comrades in arms, was slain in his command bunker at 18 Mila Street. So perished the last remnants of Polish Jews who refused to be marched to extermination or to remain passive in the huge crematorium that was Warsaw.

Mordechai Anilewicz realized his ideal to die as a fighting Jew in armed combat. He had the satisfaction of knowing that he had resisted those who conspired to take his life and the lives of his people. During the last months of his life, he edited an underground newspaper in Hebrew, called *Neged ha-Zerem,* which means "Against the Stream." Mordechai knew that all was lost. No not all — he could still save his pride.

Today, a statue of heroic proportions of Mordechai Anilewicz stands on the grounds of Yad Mordechai. It was sculptured by Natan Rapaport, an Israeli artist.

There is a kibbutz today that was founded and peopled almost entirely by survivors of the Holocaust. It is called *Lohamei Hagetaot.* Translated, the name of the colony means "Fighters of the Ghetto." A military cemetery adjoins this colony. On Monday, November 12th, memorial services were held here supervised by Deputy Chief Chaplain Gad Navon. The *Aluf-Mishne* (Colonel) pointed out the symbolic signficance of burying the fallen soldiers at this particular situs (see page 177).

SABBATH—No Publication

8 Jewish graves found in British cemetery at Fayid

HAIFA. — Eight Jewish graves, including four of Israelis who had been serving in the British Army during World War II, have been discovered at the British military cemetery at Fayid, in the Israel-occupied sector of the Suez Canal's western bank.

Some of the families concerned have requested the Chaplaincy Corps to arrange for reinterment in Israel.

The first grave was discovered about two weeks ago by Ittamar Weinstein, a 39-year-old reservist who is now stationed on the western bank, as was reported in *The Jerusalem Post* at the time. It was that of his father, who was killed in a road accident in 1942 while serving in a British transport unit.

The graves were easily identifiable by the Magen David markers on them. One grave is a woman's, Rose Harvey (née Mizrahi), whose family now lives in Jerusalem. She was married to a British sergeant-major, Harold Harvey.

Mrs. Tova Feiner, of Bnei Brak, told "Itim" that one of the graves was that of her father, David Peretz, of the Royal Engineers, who was killed in an air attack on a British convoy in 1943. She was six years old at the time.

Three of the eight graves are of South African Jews, who were serving in the R.A.F.   (*Itim*)

Soldier finds father's grave in Egypt

TEL AVIV. — A soldier serving on the southern front has discovered the grave of his father, killed 33 years ago while serving in a transport unit of the British Army, on the West bank of the Suez Canal.

Itamar Weinstein, himself serving in an I.D.F. transport unit, said his family had known that his father, Aharon, had been buried somewhere in the area. After locating the grave he asked the Chaplaincy Corps to arrange transfer of the remains to Israel.   (*Itim*)

Moslem rites for Arab fallen

HAIFA. — Israel Defence Force burial teams are transferring the remains of Egyptian and Syrian soldiers killed in the recent fighting to specially designated military cemeteries.

Each soldier is given a proper burial according to Moslem religious rites. Documents and effects found on the body are placed in a special file for eventual return to Egypt and Syria. The Chief Army Chaplain, Tat-Aluf Mordechai Piron, told "Itim" the I.D.F. was doing everything to ensure honourable burial to all the fallen.

A memorial service will take place today at the military cemetery at Kibbutz Lochamei Hagetaot, where 150 Israeli soldiers who fell in the war have been buried.

Writers seek dialogue with Arab colleagues

Jerusalem Post Reporter
TEL AVIV. — The Hebrew Writers' Association has published an open letter to writers in Arab countries, urging a "direct and frank dialogue in an effort to understand each other."

Taking issue with the "mistaken and perilous view that the State of Israel is a foreign body in this region," the Hebrew writers stress that "the Land of Israel is the cradle of the Jewish people, whose physical and spiritual connections with it were never broken."

The Arab writers were asked to pass on to their peoples "the fundamental awareness that the State of Israel is real," and to put an end to the "dangerous illusion that it will ever be possible to wipe Israel off the map by war."

Israel and the Arabs are destined to live together in this region, and, the letter ends, writers, "who have more than once anticipated reality through their vision," are called to begin a dialogue-in-writing "as good neighbours, not as enemies."

ewish cemetery of World War II in Faid, Egypt. When this cemetery was ediscovered by the Israeli Army in 1973, the authorities immediately laced a sign on the fence which read "This place is holy. Entrance is orbidden."

Demonstrators ask tough stand

TEL AVIV. — Several score citizens demonstrated here yesterday in favour of firmness in negotiating any peace settlement with the Arabs.

Carrying placards reading "There is no need to surrender. We are strong, but the Government is weak," "The Israel Defence Forces were victorious on the battlefield — don't let the Government raise the white flag," the demonstrators marched through the city's streets signing up passers-by for a petition calling for a tougher Government stand. They handed the petition in to the Prime Minister's Office in Tel Aviv, where a large contingent of police were stationed to prevent any incidents.

The demonstrators belonged to three organizations — "Citizens against Surrender," "The Movement for a Plebiscite" and "The Movement for Political Courage."   *(Itim)*

Mixed feelings greet cease-fire

By SARAH HONIG
Jerusalem Post Reporter

TEL AVIV. — News that the cease-fire agreement was about to be signed after all was greeted with mixed feelings in the Israel street yesterday. People said that while they very much wanted to hope it would be the first step on the long, hard road to peace, at the same time they found it difficult to free themselves of gnawing doubts.

One passerby in Rehov Allenby summed up best what appeared to be the general feeling when he told *The Jerusalem Post* that he "very much wants to believe that a chance for peace exists. After all, it will be the first time since 1949 that Israeli and Egyptian representatives affix their signatures to the same piece of paper. Still, so many of our fervent hopes were dashed in the past that I keep telling myself not to indulge in any wishful thinking." Another passerby said his "heart was trying its best to be optimistic. It wants so badly to believe. But the brain is as pessimistic and full of suspicion about Arab intentions as ever."

The note of hopefulness and cautious optimism was far more evident on Friday, before any one-sided interpretations of the agreement were published. (At that time there were only press speculations, according to which Israel had managed to achieve most of what it wanted.) "But what we first heard was almost too good to be true," a school nurse said. "Then we were slowly brought down to earth by the distorted Egyptian version of the agreement; by the fact that all was not so rosy and our Government was having second thoughts; and, most of all, by what was happening on the ground —

the clashes, the downing of the Phantom, and the mining of a civilian ship. These do not bode well; they indicate something about the intentions of the other side."

"The more I think of it, the more I think we gave in and were forced to agree to something which leaves too much to be desired. (U.S. Undersecretary of State Joseph) Sisco came here and told us in so many words to sign on the dotted line. If the Arabs do not fulfill their part of the bargain we still will not be able to get out of this agreement," she felt.

A man standing nearby disagreed. He maintained that "Israel will always be able to shut off the supply tap to the beleaguered Egyptian Third Army in case this is yet another Arab trick. We want to trust that it isn't, but we must be wary. We cannot afford to contract a non-peace of the type that U.S. Secretary of State Henry Kissinger imposed on Vietnam."

The nurse, however, was joined in her scepticism by a number of passersby who took part in our conversation. One, a book salesman, felt that the "wording of the agreement is far too ambiguous to afford us any comfort. Vagueness in phrasing may have its usefulness in some parts of the world, but we must remember that we live in the Middle East, realism is a very rare commodity."

Others hoped that, "despite everything, something good will come of it all." But, as one gas delivery man bluntly put it, "I wouldn't want to bet on it."

A Holon grocer voiced similar fears when he asked: "What's to stop Yemen from saying that it is solely responsible for the blockade. The Egyptians will put on their most innocent manner and say they can't control the Yemenis, who are

not bound by their signature. This is just what is happening with the terrorists. We all know who backs them, and yet all Arab states deny responsibiltiy."

He also complained, as did many people, that the agreement did not apply to all PoWs, including the ones in Syrian captivity. "The two fronts must not be separated. Egypt and Syria launched a carefully coordinated attack together. They are a single party in this dispute," he said.

Other people's fears concerned what might happen when peace talks open. "I am afraid of the ideas mooted now, according to which we are to withdraw deep into Sinai with a U.N. force separating the two sides. Our past experience with the UNEF does not lead me to be optimistic," a middle-aged school principal said carefully. "Such an arrangement can lull us into complacency, and then the Egyptians can suddenly move in and disarm the U.N. troops and occupy larger sections of the Sinai than they do now."

A colleague of his voiced the complaint that the Government has yet to interpret clearly for the public just how it regards the agreement. "We have heard every possible reading of the document but our own, and the interpretations we hear are not such as to instill joy in our hearts. We are not told clearly what we gained and where we gave in. I keep suffering from the nightmare that we are about to give up the fruits not only of the costly 1973 victory but also of the 1967 one. I have nothing against concessions made at the negotiating table of our free will. But we are being pressured into a hasty 'solution' that will solve nothing and only whet the Arab appetites," he sighed.

MIXED-UP MEDIA

By
HELGA DUDMAN

Cairo's information planners achieved a cute victory early in the war. It did not cost them a penny. They simply announced that this time, unlike their performance in the '67 war, they would be truthful, non-hysterical, "classic and calm."

And so, what was Cairo Radio broadcasting? On Friday night, one item covered the "touching scene of an Egyptian soldier giving a drink of water to an Israeli prisoner — proof of the Arab policy that once a soldier is taken prisoner, he gets the best of care, in sharp contrast to the barbaric treatment Israelis give ·prisoners."

The announcer — this was the "English Programme of the Hebrew Section of Cairo Radio" — also referred to Israel's "shooting of innocent Arabs in Gaza without trial."

Dov Yinon, Israel Radio's Arab affairs analyst, pounced on Cairo's "new policy," giving examples which show that they are in fact merely doing business at the same old stand. Stories from our reporters at the front showed up, in addition, the gap between changes accepted by correspondents accredited to Arab countries and current reality.

Example: A Reuter's report, printed by *The Jerusalem Post* last Friday, and filed after journalists crossed the Canal from Egypt, claimed "the gap between officers and men, once believed to be wide in the Egyptian army and which was said to have contributed to the 1967 defeat, seemed all but forgotten."

But Israeli soldiers were not reading the papers; they were encountering Egyptians.

"We had specific orders to treat wounded officers ahead of wounded soldiers," said a captured Egyptian doctor.

An Israeli officer reported our troops found it incredible that Arabs landed commando units "with no possible means of escape — helicopters brought them and left," leaving men in the desert for as long as six days with inadequate supplies, until their surrender.

"When we gave them food, they fell upon it ravenously..."

'Bitter Lake' of tears at memorial services

Jerusalem Post Staff

The last two memorial services for soldiers who fell in the recent war took place yesterday —— one at Kibbutz Lohamei Hagetaot, where 146 soldiers who fell on the Golan Heights are buried, and the other in Beersheba, for 204 soldiers who fell on the Sinai front.

Some 6,000 mourners gathered at the temporary military cemetery in Beersheba, where the Chief Chaplain to the Forces, Tat-Aluf Mordechai Piron, eulogized the fallen who "through their incredible bravery, saved the nation from another holocaust."

A senior officer described how his men fought like "pillars of fire," refusing even to leave burning tanks as long as they were still capable of fighting. "But should there really be some hope for genuine peace, then their sacrifice will not have been in vain," he concluded.

A small insight into the personal anguish of the bereaved families was given by the father of one of the fallen who told *The Jerusalem Post:* "Now we have our own Bitter Lake, filled with the tears of mourning families."

Among the mourners in Beersheba was Commerce and Industry Minister Haim Bar-Lev, who lost a nephew in the war.

At the second ceremony, at the military cemetery adjoining Kibbutz Lohamei Hagetaot, more than 5,000 mourners heard the Deputy Chief Chaplain, Aluf-Mishne Gad Navon, point out the symbolic significance of burying the fallen soldiers at a kibbutz established by survivors of the Nazi Holocaust in Europe.

The service closed with the recital of the Kaddish, led by an army cantor who then chanted "El malei rahamim." Among the mourners was the President's wife, Nina Katzir, who visited the graves after the service accompanied by Aluf-Mishne Yitzhak Zeid, Commander of the Haifa District.

KLM refused ground service in Damascus

DAMASCUS (Reuter). — Damascus airport workers last night refused to provide ground services for a KLM Royal Dutch airlines plane because of Holland's alleged pro-Israeli attitude. The airliner which flew in from Beirut, returned to the Lebanese capital 40 minutes after landing.

Air transport workers said in a statement that the boycott was in accordance with resolutions voted by Syria's general workers federation and by a pan-Arab labour federation conference in Libya earlier this month. Under the conference resolutions, all Dutch and U.S. transport and goods were to be boycotted, the statement said.

Civilian air traffic here returned to normal only yesterday when the airport was reopened after being closed for 36 days because of the Middle East war.

Airport workers placed a large placard on the tarmac saying in French and English: "The air transport workers in Syria strongly condemn the imperialist-Zionist aggression against their Arab nation and condemn the American and Dutch aid to Israel."

this space is donated by danish interiors

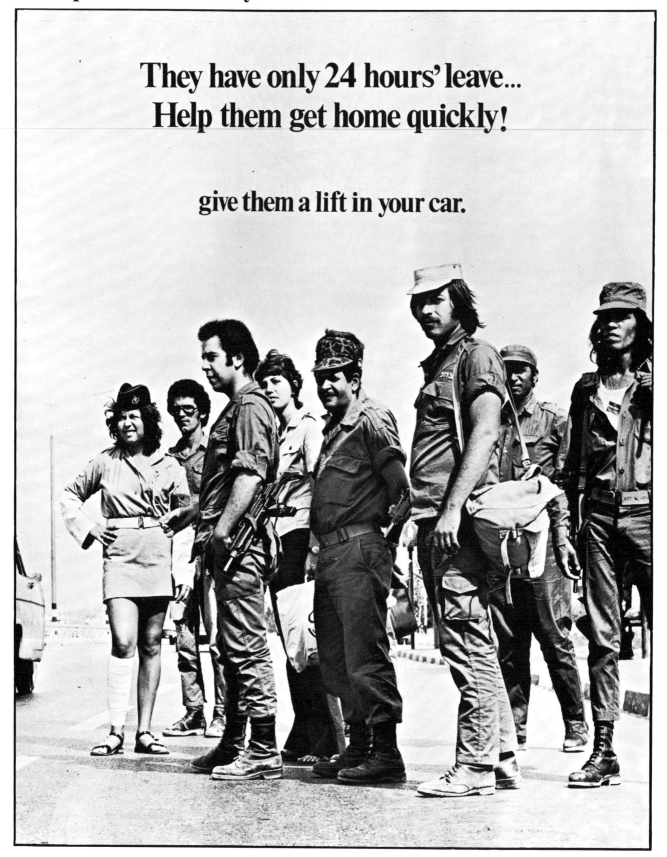

They have only 24 hours' leave...
Help them get home quickly!

give them a lift in your car.

A typical public service ad by a commercial firm.

'Generals' war' could re-politicize IDF

By YA'ACOV FRIEDLER
Jerusalem Post Reporter

HAIFA. — The "Generals' war," which developed in the wake of the Middle East war of October 6, may have grave consequences for the Israel Defence Forces. It is likely to impede the advancement of able officers and reintroduce the political factor in military promotions — a factor which was eliminated in the early days of the State by former Premier and Defence Minister David Ben-Gurion.

This is one of the conclusions of a preliminary study caried out by Dr. Shevah Weiss, senior lecturer in political science at Haifa University, at the urgent request of an unnamed American journal.

Dr. Weiss found that, in the Yom Kippur War, "20 per cent of the senior officers were men active in politics — such as Arik Sharon, Aharon Yariv, Haim Bar-Lev, Yosef Geva, Uzi Narkiss, and Shlomo La-

hat. In addition, former officers active in politics, to a greater or lesser extent," served as military commentators, such as Haim Herzog, Yosef Nevo, Meir Pa'il and Matityahu Peled.

"What happened this time was something unprecedented. Former senior officers who were active in politics were called up, but in fact continued their political work, albeit in uniform. Now they have doffed their uniforms again. As a result political doctrines were integrated with military doctrine, and this found expression while the battles were still being fought," he said. As an example he cited the running fight of Aluf Sharon with the high command.

This, he believes, "has returned us to the days just before and after the establishment of the State, when we had military units under political patronage through the medium of their generals."

SUPPORT FROM HOLLAND

To the Editor of The Jerusalem Post

Sir, — Israel's real friends in Holland are fully aware of the situation in the Middle East. We do hope that Israel will not confuse the attitude of the Dutch Government (which we consider cowardly) and the disgusting statements of the official Churches, with the stand of the Dutch people, in particular, the Christian fundamentalists, who are absolutely pro-Israel.

We consider the oil boycott

against Holland as an honour. It will only strengthen our solidarity with the people of Israel.

For Israel to withdraw from its present borders, even a single inch, would be a disaster. We pray that Israel will not give in to any pressure.

HUIB VERWEY, Editor
"Koers" Magazine
Sliedrecht, Holland, October 30.

LONG HISTORY OF DUTCH SUPPORT

To the Editor of The Jerusalem Post

Sir, — The Government and people of Holland deserve acknowledgement and appreciation for their refusal to be cowed by the Arab oil threat into an abandonment of Israel in its present struggle against the conspiracy of the Arab states, backed by the USSR, to destroy this small bastion of democracy in the Middle East.

The Jewish people have had many occasions in the past to express gratitude to the Dutch people and Government for friendly acts and policies, going back to the 17th century settlement of a number of Jews in Brazil, Dutch Guiana, Curacao and New Amsterdam. In 1954, on the occasion of the Tercentenary of American Jewry, it was my privilege, on behalf of American Jewry, to present the then Prime Minister of Holland, Dr. Willem Drees, a testimonial of appreciation from the Jewish community of the United States. This precedent has had many noble sequels, of which Holland's recent stand, is the latest.

In a critical time for Israel, when many European nations, professing Christianity, are placing economic self-interest above religious professions, the Dutch people and Government are holding high the banner of moral priorities. May their moral strength be reinforced from On High.

DR. ISRAEL GOLDSTEIN
Jerusalem, November 7.

Hearts and flowers

Jerusalem Post Reporter

TEL AVIV. — Volunteers during the war rescued a wounded soldier and his family from economic ruin by saving and selling the tens of thousands of flowers in his Kfar Kadima greenhouse.

The volunteers, organized by Wizo, picked up the flowers, including carnations and asters, from the soldier's greenhouse, transported them, and sold them at large petrol stations, major crossroads and the Wizo centres in Tel Aviv, Hadera and Netanya.

The proceds went directly to the wounded soldier's wife. The Kfar Kadima couple have a four-month-old son.

The Kfar Kadima Wizo branch organized the project when its members heard the couple stood to lose the thousands of pounds they had invested in their business. They had been left with greenhouses full of colourful blooms when the husband was called up. To make matters worse, many orders, both domestic and foreign, had been cancelled.

Since then, flower exports have resumed and the Kfar Kadima blooms are now going out to their original destinations.

'Thanks to Holland' committee set up

Jerusalem Post Staff

TEL AVIV. — A committee headed by Hillel Seidel, of the Histadrut Central Committee, has been set up to seek ways of expressing to the Dutch people Israel's appreciation of their valour in refusing to bow to Arab oil blackmail. One of its first projects has been to sponsor the sending of citrus fruits to Dutch schoolchildren.

Another gesture is a decision taken by the Histadrut's vocational training department to order all electronic equipment for the Amal vocational schools exclusively from Holland. Nathan Almoslino, head of the department, has also suggested inviting Dutch schoolchildren for a holiday in Israel as the guests of the Amal schools.

Meanwhile, the Dutch are continuing to demonstrate unstinted support for Israel. The Jewish Agency spokesman said yesterday that Dutchmen have contributed hundreds of thousands of dollars towards the Israel Appeal, and three former Dutch Prime Ministers and three former ministers have published an appeal to raise funds for Israel.

The Dutch support has not been limited to money, and a group of about 30 Dutch youngsters — all non-Jews — arrived yesterday to work on kibbutzim.

Also here at present is a delegation of Dutch trade unionists, here on a six-day visit as the guests of the Histadrut. The delegation yesterday called on Knesset Speaker Yisrael Yeshayahu, who presented each of its members with a Knesset medallion and a scroll with a poem by Haim Hefer called "Somewhere there is a Land"—translated into Dutch. The poem expresses the respect of the Israelis for Holland, which has once again proved its friendship for the Jewish people.

THROUGHOUT THESE PAGES, the reader will find innumerable news items showing the flood of grateful responses of the Israeli people to the people of Holland who staunchly refused to tolerate the Arab aggression or to be intimidated by Arab blackmail. No threat by the Arabs of an oil embargo would induce Holland to change its moral judgment that the Arabs had wantonly attacked the State of Israel without provocation.

Benjamin Disraeli once told the Duke of Portland, "I come from a race which never forgives an injury nor forgets a benefit." The gratitude of Israel toward Holland is expressed all through the leaves of this book.

We read that the children of Beersheba have dried flowers and pressed them onto postcards to send to other children in Holland. We read that Israeli youth organized a bicycle parade for no other reason than to advertise their thankfulness to the Dutch who calmly and happily took to their bicycles when the Arabs punished them by withholding oil. We read that the Dutch people have been inscribed in the Israeli Golden Book.

In addition to these organized gestures of gratitude, hundreds of letters were mailed by individuals to friends and acquaintances, and even to leaders of government in Holland, in sheer gratefulness that one country in the moral wasteland of Europe had had the courage to stand up against the Arabs and say out loud, "We shall not sell our souls for a barrel of oil."

Actually, Holland's support of Israel in the Yom Kippur War is not its first overt expression of sympathy for the plight of the Jews. There has been a long-standing history of cooperation between the Jewish people and the Dutch people, beginning

Mormon support

To the Editor of The Jerusalem Post

Sir, — As a member of the Church of Jesus Christ of Latter-day Saints (commonly called "Mormons") and as one of the officers in its Jerusalem Branch, I have been somewhat dismayed by certain statements of late regarding the "trustworthiness" of Christians. While not wishing to speak for Christianity (an impossibility, inasmuch as we agree with them only on the question of Jesus, while theologically being closer to Judaism), I would like to make a defence of my own coreligionists.

Mormonism was born in a Zionist spirit, in the 1820s and 30s. It has always regarded the immigration of Jews to the land of Israel as not only their right, but as their *duty*. In 1841, the Mormon Prophet Joseph Smith sent one of the 12 Apostles, Orson Hyde, to Jerusalem to dedicate the land for the return of the Jews. This he did, calling upon God to restore the land to its "rightful heirs," and to inspire the powers of the earth to aid in the establishment of a Jewish "nation."

On Yom Kippur, Mormons from throughout the world were meeting in conference in Salt Lake City. Some of our friends in attendance have reported the concern publicly manifest at that time for Israel in its hour of peril (the conference is broadcast nation-wide and around the world on radio and TV.)

The same day, Mormons of the Jerusalem Branch were gathered in fasting and prayer in Jerusalem. In the midst of our activities, we heard the first air-raid sirens. Upon learning of the war, those of our number who had come down from Galilee rushed home to assist. They included a Mormon family from Kibbutz Shamir, just on the border, and another Mormon woman who works at the Safad Hospital, where she has been caring for the wounded (as she did in Beersheba during the 1967 war).

In our rush to try to assist our Jewish friends, none of us thought it necessary to call on the Ministry of Religious Affairs or to write letters condemning the Arabs. We were content to volunteer our services. One of our members is serving in the I.D.F. and was sent to Sinai before the end of the first week of the war. On the following Shabbat as we again gathered for our weekly services (minus a few who were engaged in more urgent matters!), we concluded our morning by going *en masse* to Magen David Adom to donate blood.

I hesitated to write this letter, fearing that — as is often the case — it might be viewed as bragging or as an attempt to "prove" some false loyalty to the Zionist cause. The thought even occurred to me that some would consider it an attempt at free publicity for Mormon beliefs. But, as I have seen criticism mounting, I have deemed it necessary to state the reasons for which our Jewish brethren may rest assured that we are their friends, in both good and bad weather.

JOHN A. TVEDTNES
Jerusalem, November 7.

Libyan thief is sentenced to have hand chopped off

BEIRUT (UPI). — A Libyan court has ordered a Libyan citizen convicted of stealing to have his right hand chopped off, the Tripoli newspaper "Al Balagh" said yesterday.

The newspaper said the verdict meant that Libyan courts have started implementing Colonel Mu'ammar Gaddafi's instructions for a return to Islamic law.

The scrapping of existing laws and a return to Islamic law formed part of the "cultural revoltuion" Gaddafi launched in April.

"Al Balagh" said the Tripoli criminal court, which handed down the verdict, gave the defendant the right to appeal against it. The newspaper did not give the man's name nor other details of the case.

notably after the expulsion of the Jews from Spain and Portugal at the close of the 15th century, and continuing with demonstrations of support and acts of rescue during the Nazi occupation of the Netherlands.

The Anne Frank House in Amsterdam stands as an everlasting monument to the charity and kindliness of the Hollanders during the horrible days of the Holocaust, when many Dutch burghers risked their own lives to succor Jews who were about to be sent off to Hitler's ovens.

On November 29, 1947, the Netherlands voted in favor of the U.N. plan to partition Palestine allowing for the establishment of a Jewish State. Soon afterwards, the Netherlands officially recognized the new State of Israel. Formal diplomatic relations were established on the ambassadorial level, with Holland being the first country to set up its diplomatic representation in Jerusalem.

The Netherlands has supported Israel in the United Nations on other international issues, for example, supporting the struggle of persecuted Jews in the Soviet Union and in the Arab countries to emigrate.

Holland was also Israel's major ally in its efforts to establish ties with the European Economic Community. From 1953 on, whenever the Soviet Union severed diplomatic relations with Israel, the Netherlands have represented Israel's interest in the U.S.S.R.

Each year, a steady stream of tourists comes from Holland to visit Israel. There are frequent cultural exchanges, such as a major exhibit of Dutch art in Israel, and exhibits in Holland from the Land of the Bible. The Israel Philharmonic Orchestra has often performed in Holland.

In Brussels 'even Arabs gave'
Belgians rally for Israel

Jerusalem Post Reporter

"We wanted to see how the non-Jewish population would react to Israel's crisis. So we organized a drive on street corners in six districts of Brussels, to get money for an ambulance. It was a hurried, last-minute operation and the weather was terrible — rainy and stormy. We thought we might collect enough for one ambulance.

"In less than two days, we had money for four. One of the strangest things was that Arabs were among our contributors. We actually found Syrian money in our collection boxes.

"One Arab explained his action by saying that he had fought in three wars against the Jews, and all the time he was in an Arab army he never had enough to eat. 'Now that I'm in Europe and have plenty of food, I want to give money for the Jews.'

This report was made to *The Jerusalem Post* by a four-man delegation from the Jewish Community Centre of Brussels here this week on a five-day visit to make concrete contacts for Belgian contributions to Israel, including meetings with the Minister of Health and the Defence Ministry's Rehabilitation Division.

"The people of Belgium are not particularly sympathetic to the Arabs," Maurice Elbaum, 31, a chemical engineer and spokesman for the delegation, said. "Our leading newspapers have supported Israel. Our group has many contacts with high government officials who, while officially even-handed, are in fact very friendly to Israel."

His observations again point up the fact that Western European governments today do not reflect public opinion on all issues: "Never before has there been such widespread support for Israel," he emphasized.

TWICE THE NEED

"Priests, police in uniform, and soldiers were among those who lined up for hours to give blood, when we organized a donation campaign. We had to turn down nearly twice as many as we accepted."

The Centre organized a public demonstration in Brussels which drew over 6,000 persons (in all of Belgium, there are fewer than 40,000 Jews.) "The Arabs organized a meeting the following week, and drew only 1,500 — mostly the New Left and some Arab students. You must not forget that we have 100,000 foreign workers from Morocco alone, and the Moroccan Embassy called for attendance at this demonstration."

Yet Belgians are a comfort-loving people, observed a young secretary who came with the delegation, "and we probably have less civic spirit than the Dutch." The moment of truth may come during the damp, cold Belgian winter. Some 80 per cent of Belgium's fuel come from Arab lands, and 60 per cent of this comes through the Dutch port of Rotterdam. "For us, heating will be much more of a problem than transport — and as for riding a bike, why not? We're very concerned about pollution, and some people see the Sunday driving ban as a kind of blessing in disguise."

In addition to Holland, Israel has maintained a particularly warm friendship over many years with Denmark, whose people have been traditionally sympathetic to the Jews.

It is said that during the Nazi occupation, to show his contempt for the German Nuremberg laws, the Danish monarch himself, King Christian, had a yellow star affixed to his garments and publicly appeared wearing this indicia of revilement. The story most likely is apocryphal, but if nothing else, it indicates the great reverence for the Danish King held by the Jewish community — and with good reason. The fact is that the Jews of Denmark fared better during the Nazi terror than their brethren did in any other country that fell under the heel of the swastika. So protective was the steadfast behavior of the Danish authorities and the Danish citizenry vis-a-vis the Jews that the Germans did not deem it prudent to proceed openly against the small Jewish community. The Nazis feared to earn the active hostility of practically the entire Danish population.

Public opinion in Denmark was expressed by a leader of the United Danish Youth Movement, who openly proclaimed that justice and respect for the Danish Jews was inseparably linked with the preservation of Danish freedom and Danish law.

When, despite the strong Danish posture, the Nazis decided to move against the Jewish enclave, a rescue organization spontaneously sprang up. In less than three weeks, some 7,200 Jews were snatched out of the claws of Hitler's henchmen and carried by Danish captains and Danish fishermen in small craft across the sea to Sweden. It was a rescue operation almost without parallel.

Since those perilous days, the Danes have stood staunchly by the Israelis. Today, Israel and Denmark maintain active friendship leagues. In most cities of Israel, there is a street or a square named in honor of a Danish befriender. In Jerusalem, on the 25th anniversary of the rescue of the Danish Jews from the Nazis, a commemorative monument was raised. In the small village of

Eitanim, the local hospital has been named The King Christian X Hospital in honor of that noble monarch. Every year, thousands of Danish youth pay extended visits to Israel's kibbutzim, working on the farms in a gesture of helpful friendship.

On page 365 of this book, Ephraim Kishon, Israel's Art Buchwald, tells about a letter received towards the end of December 1973 from a Danish lawyer. It runs in part:

Dear Sir of the Israeli Press!

I have been a fervent admirer of the Jewish people for a long time, which is the reason why I'm taking the trouble to write these lines sitting in an unheated flat early in the morning when I'd rather have stayed lazily in my warm bed. If I'm writing to you all the same it's because I have a feeling you need me.

Now then, you say you've lost the world's sympathy again, and that everybody's mad at you for having been attacked. With all respect, I don't see how you can offer such a dubious claim. To begin with, you couldn't have lost the sympathy of all those African states because you never had it. That bunch care for nobody but their own selves, and if anyone had illusions otherwise then I'm surprised at him, to say the least.

Britain and France, on the other hand, took exactly the stand you expected of them, so there again you didn't lose anything except the good manners which have gone by the board in Europe long since.

As for my own little country, Denmark, the latest public opinion polls show that 83 per cent of its population sympathize with Israel, 15 per cent haven't the faintest idea what it's all about, and two per cent support the Arabs through thick and thin. I'm convinced the picture's the same in all civilized countries.

Now give me leave to ask whether you figure it would be any practical use

Distraught relative at a demonstration concerned with Israeli prisoners of war held by the Syrians.

The joy of reunion.

60 Dutch trucks, drivers here

By YA'ACOV FRIEDLER
Jerusalem Post Reporter

HAIFA. — A fleet of 60 articulated 25-ton trucks complete with their `drivers arrived via Trieste in the m.s. Nili yesterday, to help overcome the transport shortage resulting from the war. A team of two mechanics and six operating staff accompanied them.

They were brought here by the De Lely trucking company, under contract with the Ministry of Transport, and will work in Israel for a minimum of three months, with an option of renewal.

The company's general manager, Jan De Lely, told *The Jerusalem Post* that they were "happy to be able to help Israel out." His drivers, who will stay in local hotels, are ready to work up to 16 hours a day, wherever needed. He has been informed that they would work mainly to clear goods from the ports in Haifa and Ashdod.

In answer to a question, Mr. De Lely said they were "not at all worried" by possible Arab reactions. "We're not politicians, and we're not doing anything military, just helping to transport cargoes," he said, adding that his company worked in many countries in Europe, as far as Russia.

Arabs walk out as Israeli addresses FAO

ROME. — Arab and Chinese delegates walked out of the plenary session of the U.N. Food and Agriculture Organization (FAO) governing conference here yesterday when the Israel delegates prepared to deliver a speech.

Most of the Arab delegates, who quietly left their seats accompanied by some African colleagues, returned after Israel representative F. D. Maas had read his country's statement on FAO proposals to ward off the danger of future famines.

Mr. Maas supported the proposals for a system of international food stockpiling to tide the world over periods of shortage and widespread crop failures.

Commenting on the walk-out, Mr. Maas told Reuter: 'It doesn't worry me, but it is very dangerous when people stop listening."

'U.S. MUST NOT SELL ITS SOUL FOR OIL'

NEW YORK (INA). — The second highest ranking Episcopal clergyman in the U.S. warned here this week that America must not "under any circumstances sell its soul for a guaranteed flow of oil." The Rev. Dr. David R. Hunter, Deputy General Secretary of the National Council of Churches, made t h i s statement in an address to the conference of the Metropolitan Council of Bnai Brith here.

"We must resist every temptation to let our foreign policy be affected by the gross misuse of force on the part of the oil-rich nations of the world and their allies," Dr. Hunter said. "So long as Israel is threatened by military aggression, we need to affirm clearly and loudly that Israel has the right to exist," he added.

He said he was "pleased that many Christians have spoken o u t meaningfully with both indignation and compassion since the desecration of Yom Kippur by the Syrians and Egyptians," on October 6. "This time we are faced with a moral obligation to settle for nothing less than a peace settlement," Dr. Hunter said.

Soviets okayed crossing into pre-1967 Israel

KUWAIT (AFP). — The Russians told the Arabs soon after the war began last month that they need not stop at Israel's pre-1967 boundaries, a Kuwaiti member of parliament told a gathering of university students here yesterday.

The member of parliament, Ahmed al-Khatib, told the students that the Kremlin leaders had made this clear to Algeria's President Houari Boumedienne when he visited Moscow the day after fighting started in the Middle East. He said that President Boumedienne had told the Russians "to charge Algeria for all Soviet military aid to the Arabs." The Russians replied that it was not the time to make accounts. They said their support for the Arab cause was total — even if this meant going beyond the pre-1967 borders.

*if we here in Copenhagen began all of a
sudden to read your buddy Anwar Sadat
the riot act for his riotous behaviour.
What on earth can Israel benefit from a
friend who weakens himself by political
statements without having any real power
to back them up? Politics is a power
game, my dear sir. A foreign policy without power is, if you'll forgive me, sheer
idiocy. I hardly imagine you aren't aware,
for instance, that France's position in face
of the Arab threats is a great deal weaker
than your own, and that as for Great
Britain — its ruling-the-waves days are
over. The only one who can stand up to
the Arabs is you.*

So don't you tell the Iraelis you've

*lost the world's sympathy because, on the
contrary, we love and admire you, and
we're trying to help you now more than
ever — but quietly, on the sly, because
that's the only way in winter. We make
believe, if you know what I mean. Like
when Colonel Gaddafi demanded that
Denmark provide military training for
Libyan soldiers, and by agreeing to we
did Israel an immense service, seeing
that we've got the shortest and lousiest
military training in the world.*

How much of this letter was written by the
Dane and how much by Kishon is anyone's guess,
but the message is clearly authentic.

INITIAL 26 PoWs, ALL WOUNDED, EXCHANGED FOR 412 EGYPTIANS

By ZE'EV SCHUL, Jerusalem Post Military Reporter

LOD AIRPORT. — Twenty-six Israeli prisoners of war, all wounded during the October war on the Egyptian front, were flown home yesterday. The thin, pale men, in their loudly striped Egyptian pyjamas and their heads shaven, were the first Israelis to be repatriated under the cease-fire agree-ment with Egypt. In exchange, Israel returned 412 Egyptian prisoners, including 162 wounded men, on four Red Cross flights.

The 26 were the only Israelis to be returned yesterday. Sixteen others who were supposed to arrive — including nine who have been in Egyptian captivity for four years (since the War of Attri-tion) — did not show up, for what the Egyptians called "technical reasons." They are expected today.

Two of the returnees had to be carried down from the plane on stretchers, one of them accompanied by a nurse supervising an infusion. The others limped and hobbled, but made their own way. ...rried little bouquets of flowers which had been given to ...diers when their plane landed at 11.30 a.m. ...at One man, both his legs in plaster, was carried down the gang-... by two welcomers,

THE FINE ART OF SURVIVAL

Philip Gillon

AHARON BAR, a fourth-year student of mechanical engineering at the Haifa Technion, was called up on the night of Yom Kippur and rushed down to the central sector of the Southern front. He and the other three members of his tank crew had served together in the reserves, and knew each other well. They took part in all the great tank battles that raged on their sector that first night and for the next ten days.

"On October 15," Aharon recalls, "we got orders to organize for the crossing of the Canal. Our task was to drive north against the Egyptian forces pressing on the Israeli corridor to the Canal. The idea was to keep the corridor open so that the bridgehead could be established. Right through the night we advanced, slowly, slowly, against fierce resistance. In the morning, fog covered the area. As it dispersed, we found that we were facing huge masses of missile-carrying infantry: our small force had fallen into an ambush.

"We got into a hollow, below a crest. From time to time we tried to get out, but the missile fire against us was too heavy, Then we got an order to attack."

Aharon goes on: "We talked about the order to attack on the intercom, and, frankly, we decided that it was suicidal. Despite this, we drove out of the hollow, over the crest, and went forward. After three or four minutes, I felt something I had never felt before in my life. I didn't understand what had happened to me, but I knew it was something very serious. I knew I was badly wounded but didn't know how. The tank was full of gas and I felt I couldn't breathe. I wasn't surprised; I'd been expecting to get hit. I was fully conscious, and I didn't feel any particular pain. But I was 99 per cent certain that this was the end and that, I was going to die. All the same, I shouted into the inter-com, 'I'm hit!' But nobody heard, the connection was broken.

"So I decided that I had to get out. Then I found that I'd had my foot hard down on the accelerator all the time and the tank was advancing into the Egyptian ambush. By a conscious effort, I moved my foot. I opened the driver's hatch and got out: only then did I realize that there was empty space below my left knee. I stood on one foot, holding on to the tank.

"The rest of the crew didn't understand what had happened. The missile had penetrated the tank very low, taking off my leg and filling the tank with gas, but they didn't realize how badly we'd been hit. They looked out and saw me standing down below. The commander shouted to me to get back inside and drive on. Then they got out and saw how bad the position was.

"There was no stretcher in the tank: two or three days before, we had been attacked by MIGs, and somebody had been hurt, so our stretcher had been used to evacuate him. The crew was in a state of shock: they said afterwards that I was the coolest among them. They dragged me along the ground by my overalls: all the time we were under fire from light arms and artillery.

"I saw that my leg was torn off below the knee and that the lower part was still in the overall. Usually I'm very sensitive about blood and wounds, but the sight of my own leg like that didn't disturb me. I said to myself: 'So I've lost a leg. So what? I'm still alive — as long as there's life, what's so terrible about losing a leg?'

"I didn't realize then that one piece of shrapnel had entered the bone under my eyebrow, just above the eye, while another piece had made a hole in my chest. The rest of the crew saw blood flowing from these wounds, but didn't know how serious they were. They were in a state of shock from seeing my condition, as well as from what had happened. The Egyptians were still firing. It was very hot; by then it must have been noon. Yet the crew dragged me along for more than a kilometre. They didn't try to bandage me or anything: afterwards, in the hospital, I was told that nothing would have helped.

"Suddenly, we saw an Israeli armoured car coming towards us. Where it came from, what it was doing there, we were never able to find out. It was under the command of a major. They put me down on the floor. I insisted on my crew coming with me. We started off."

AHARON HAS BEEN TALKING with great animation. His left eye is still bandaged, although his sight, by a miracle, will be unaffected: the piece of shrapnel never got through the bone. There is a scar on his chest. His wife, Osnat, a psychology graduate of Bar Ilan University, and mother of a three-month-old baby, suggests that he rest a while, and take a drink of water. "After all," she says, "Even Abba Eban interrupts himself to drink a little water." But Aharon is too involved in his narrative to rest.

"We were travelling along when a shell burst in the area. The major got some terrible wounds in the face. I never found out what happened to him. We went on, and got to one of the front-line doctors. He gave me some transfusions. All the time I remained fully conscious. I can't remember feeling any pain, only that I was determined to stay alive. That was why I wouldn't allow myself to lose consciousness. When we talk about the war, lying here in the ward, some of the chaps say they lost consciousness, others didn't. It also seemed to me very important that the crew should stay with me.

"I must have got very weak. The crew told me that they took me further back.

"Then I was put in a helicopter — I remember thinking that this was the first time I had been in a helicopter. The trip seemed endless. I got to the field hospital and a wonderful team of doctors took over. It's impossible to describe how marvellous the doctors were — the front line man and the men at the field hospital. Even before I was flown from the field ambulance to Jerusalem, I felt that I was getting back to being a a human being again."

Osnat produces two plastic bags containing pieces of shrapnel about the size of a silver Israeli pound coin. "War souvenirs," she says.

Now that the first stage of euphoria because he is still alive is passing, what does Aharon think about it all? Does he brood about losing a leg?

"As far as I think I understand myself, I'm not crying over spilt milk. I know it doesn't help: what's done is done. I'm determined to do the maximum in the future. I'll go back to the Technion and will carry on with my profession. Luckily, I have no internal injuries."

IN THE WARD, they all follow the news on the radio all the time (unfortunately, they have no television, one of the boys points out). What does Aharon think of the latest developments, the talk about mistakes? Does the war of the generals make him feel bitter? Osnat pulls a face, and urges me to drop politics, but Aharon answers readily:

"Obviously there will have to be a full enquiry into what happened. I'm not the kind who passes judgment before all the facts are investigated and known. But I think that this is not yet the time to start with the wars of the Jews, fighting our internal problems.

"I must say one thing for Arik Sharon. When we heard of the plan to cross the Canal, we thought he was crazy. We were having a hard enough time fighting on the east side: it required great imagination to appreciate that the way to win the war was to get on to the west side. At the time, we were against the idea; now we realize it was quite right."

There are two views about Israel accepting the cease-fire: some people are delighted that the fighting has stopped, others say that Israel was denied the fruits of victory. What does he think?

"These are very difficult questions you're asking. On the one hand, it's very important to prevent anybody being killed or wounded; one unnecessary casualty would be too many. On the other hand, it's clear we would have gained a lot by advancing. There's also the question of the Russians: Arik Sharon says they wouldn't have intervened, but I don't know. Frankly, I don't know what I'd have done -- or what I'd do — if I were king."

Was he surprised by the strength of the Egyptian attack, and the quality of the Arab soldiers?

"Yes. Before the war I never thought the Arabs would attack. The Canal line seemed absolutely safe. I hope they've now got over all their complexes, and can make peace."

Would he give up the areas occupied in 1967 for peace?

"Before the war, I thought we shouldn't give up anything, that doing so would put us in a very weak position. Now there are signs of peace which we never had before. As I said, the Arabs have got back their self-confidence: this may make them more reasonable. If it's clear that giving up most of the areas would help to bring peace, I'd give them up.

"It doesn't depend on us, but on the Arabs — and on the Americans and the Russians. But I'm a natural optimist, a super-optimist. Somehow things seem to be different now: maybe we're in sight of peace at last."

Syria charges Israel with 'body-snatching'

DAM CUS (UPI). — Syri said yesterday that Israeli and Dutch doctors removed corneas and ear drums of wounded and dead Syrian soldiers and transplanted them to wounded Israeli soldiers. The charge was carried on Damascus Radio.

The Syrian claim was raised in a meeting between Foreign Minister Abdel Haam Khaddam and Robert Guyer, visiting aide of U.N. Secretary-General Kurt Waldheim.

Mr. Guyer arrived in the Syrian capital Tuesday night for talks with Government leaders.

12-ambulance convoy to Tel Hashomer

By THOMAS ACKERMAN
Pool Correspondent

TEL HASHOMER. — The 26 wounded PoWs, all wearing green, blue and white striped pajamas and all with close-cropped haircuts, arrived at the emergency ward of Tel Hashomer in a convoy of 12 ambulances. From there, they were transferred to respective wards depending on their injuries.

The 26 include five pilots, all of them shot down during the war. Some of the 26 emerged from the ambulances and walked with some support under their own power. Others were carried on stretchers. Some had head wounds and others had their legs in casts.

Crowds of several hundred bystanders and friends were repeatedly forced back by police from enveloping the ambulances as they rolled up to the emergency ward, their sirens wailing and their red lights flashing. Most of the ambulances bore the Magen David Adom, with the names of their American donors printed on the doors.

Several hundred metres away, the families of all the prisoners were kept waiting at a special reception centre until the soldiers and airmen had been sent to Wards 30 or 35 that had been set aside for them.

WITH NEWS

A woman Air Force major was first with the news of the five pilots who were aboard the first flight. "All of our veteran pilots from before will apparently be on the next flight. So you'll just have to sit patiently a little while longer," she said.

When the name of one of the fliers was called out, his black-haired, petite wife said: "Did you tell him that he has a son?" The major said "Yes." The woman said she had given birth last week.

The wounded, even many of those who were carried into the ward on stretchers, smiled wanly. One with a cast on his right hand waved weakly to the crowd of applauding bystanders. All the ambulances had been staffed with girl soldiers on the 10-minute ride from the airport.

One nurse opened the back door of the ambulance and held the arm of an ambulatory soldier. As he alighted from the vehicle, she handed him a bouquet of pink, yellow and violet chrysanthemums. The soldier, his head swathed in a bandage, grinned in embarrassment, shrugged his shoulders and said. "I haven't got the strength. You'll have to carry them." But then he walked slowly up the octagonal-shaped stones of the path to the ward entrance. He was greeted with more applause.

Above the main entrance to the hospital, the bystanders had put up a banner stretched between two poles that quoted the Bible in blue letters, "Your sons shall return to their own land." (Jeremiah 31, 16).

3 religions in Jerusalem donate blood to PoWs

By GEORGE LEONOF
Jerusalem Post Reporter

A group of 25 Jerusalemites — Moslems, Jews and Christians — donated blood Wednesday morning for transfusion to wounded Israel and Egyptian war prisoners who are to be exchanged under the auspices of the International Red Cross.

The donors were members of the Meditran association for the enhancement of cultural and social relations in Jerusalem. The donations were given at the blood bank off Via Dolorosa in the Old City. The majority of the group were Christians, Lev Schwartz, one of the founders of Meditran, told *The Jerusalem Post* yesterday. "We

have more than 50 donors registered so far. Others will follow."

He said, " our objective, both as an organ and as individuals, for Jew d Arab to live together in a rel onship more enduring than armis es and stronger than treaties."

Meditran was found more than two years ago, establishing its headquarters in Rehov Hanevi'im, near Damascus Gate. The organization, which has no membership drive, today counts about 200 Jewish, Moslem and Christian members.

Its other activities on behalf of soldiers includes visits to wounded and collection of gifts for war prisoners both here and, through the International Red Cross, in Egypt.

The first prisoners released by Egypt arrive at Lod Airport.

Behind the façade of Washington-Moscow detente
'The assault of Soviet imperialism'

In the following open letter to U.S. Secretary of State Henry Kissinger, Land of Israel Movement leader **SHMUEL KATZ** challenges the idea that putting pressure on Israel to make concessions is a desirable step in the direction of achieving peace in the Middle East. He warns the American statesman that it is in America's best interest to check the growing presence of the Soviet Union in the Middle East and Africa—a menace whose only stumbling block is the Jewish State.

Dear Dr. Kissinger,

The statement you made in Washington on October 26 to the effect that the conditions which brought about the Yom Kippur War were "intolerable to the Arabs" and that Israel would have to make substantial concessions both vindicates the Arabs and condones wanton aggression. It shows, moreover, that our Government failed to convince you that the Arabs were in fact the aggressors.

The only "intolerable condition from which the Arabs suffer is the fact of the existence of a Jewish State in the midst of their vast territories and their continued failure to annihilate it. The worst "condition" that Israel's secure and peaceful existence could mean for the Arabs is that of their 100 million people, one per cent would be living as a minority in the Jewish State with full rights.

The immediate practical consequence of the dictate you are trying to impose on Israel is quite clear. Every Israeli step backward will increase the combined Arab and Soviet pressure for more and then more concessions, until the balance of strategic circumstances makes successful resistance by the victim impossible. I do not have to tell you that there is a point beyond which the quality of men and of arms cannot compensate for loss of strategic depth. And surely you do not put your complete trust in Arab or even Soviet signatures on the guarantees in a peace-treaty.

Moreover, it is a serious error to think that by sacrificing Israel's security, Western interests and world peace will be preserved. The scenario of your policy, it seems to me, could have been written by Neville Chamberlain. The punitive cease-fire agreement and later the incredible saving of the Egyptian Third Army are all too reminiscent of the Munich Pact. What is being done seems as incredible to us as Munich seemed to the Czechs.

Let me spell out the truth, however obvious, of the international implications of your apparent policy.

Israel is the last bulwark of the West against the assault of a purposefully pursued policy of Soviet imperialism, the last line of defence against the swamping of the entire Middle East and of the African continent by Soviet influence and expansionism.

If Israel withdraws in Sinai, the whole zone will be overrun at a speed — already being planned in Moscow and Cairo — which will be irresistible.

Middle East oil, which for all its economic importance also symbolizes the gilded and gluttonous decadence into which Europe seems to be sinking, would pass directly into the control of the Soviet Union. Within months, perhaps, the peoples of the Middle East and Africa would become vassals of the Soviet Union. The way of life and, before long, the very survival of the West as a meaningful entity in the world would be at the mercy of the Soviet Union. Its defence system would have become grotesquely devalued.

You, Dr. Kissinger, are behaving towards us as though you believe that by your policy you are preventing a war between the Super-Powers. The Russians are no more anxious for a war than you are.

Perhaps you honestly believe that their threat is real, that the Russians are in fact prepared to take the risk of an armed clash with you *now*, when you have the overall strategic advantage. But what kind of perverse logic suggests to you that their readiness will evaporate precisely when they have turned the strategic balance in their favour, when they will have laid hands, *inter alia*, on a large part of the world's oil?

Can you prevent this? Once the Soviets are astride both banks of the Suez Canal, and freely deploy their naval strength in the Mediterranean how will you prevent their purposefully pursued penetration into the oil-countries of the Middle East? On what local forces will you depend to resist their demands? On King Faisal and his sons and brothers? On the major military powers of Abu Dhabi and Kuwait?

Yet there is still hope that this process can be halted, even in this black hour.

First mistake

We trust that our Government will not persist in its first mistake of giving way to pressure. The time to stand firm is now, while we are still strong. If we stand firm *now*, while still holding the fort against Soviet expansion, the people of the United States will not abandon us. If *you* stand firm, Dr. Kissinger, the Soviet Union will not go to war. There is no reason to believe otherwise.

If, however, we are forced to withdraw from the Suez Canal to vulnerable boundaries, we shall in the end still fight. We shall not be a second Czechoslovakia. We *cannot* be a second Czechoslovakia. The Czech people did not disappear when they lost their independence. But if the Arabs are enabled to deal us the final blow, what will be at stake will be the physical existence of our people. It is idle for us to pretend to be horrified at the thought of civilized America, Britain and the rest "permitting" genocide. How were six million Jews murdered by Hitler if not by the silent resignation or acquiescence of the civilized world? And we have not forgotten Biafra, nor the hundreds of thousands of Nilotic Sudanese whose extermination hardly merited a headline in the Western press, nor the mass killings in Bangladesh. We have no illusions.

If our *State* goes under, it is the end of our people — our *people*, not only the three million living in Israel, sustained and driven by the memory of the millions eliminated by Hitler. The destiny of the three million Jews in the Soviet Union, of all Jewish communities throughout the world, including those of the United States, will be decided by Israel's fate.

We would not go down without a fight. Any pragmatic statesmen, who under the threat of Arab and Soviet barbarism, have toyed with the thought that the interests of Israel's three million — and the three million themselves — may have to be regarded as expendable on the altar of world peace — are making a dangerous miscalculation.

The altar will burn with the sacrifice.

A demonstration parade held in Tel Aviv before the beginning of the Geneva peace negotiations. The signs read, in effect: "There can be no negotiations unless our boys are free."

SABBATH—No Publication

FROM ISRAEL — WITH LOVE

THE CARTOON BY DOSH, showing Israel smiling at a Dutch tulip flowering in the European rubbish heap, inspired Mr. and Mrs. Wim Van Leer of Haifa to obtain the cartoonist's permission to reprint the drawing on 20,000 postcards. These cards were mailed to friends of Israel in Holland as a gesture of appreciation.

The Van Leers also gave several thousand cards to schools and to the Tel Aviv Soldiers' Welfare Association. Proceeds from the sale at 50 agorot[1] per card went to the Soldiers' Welfare Fund.

1. An agora is a coin. There are 100 agorot to the Israeli pound.

'All I did was to come home'

Pilot back at kibbutz after 3½ years in Egypt

By YA'ACOV FRIEDLER
Jerusalem Post Reporter

"All I did was to come home," said Seren Rami Harpaz.

The 34-year-old pilot, released by the Egyptians on Friday after 3½ years' imprisonment, spoke calmly but with emotion as he addressed the members of Kibbutz Hazorea at a party in his honour in the kibbutz dining room. Several times he sought to play down the effects of his imprisonment.

"It is no problem to readjust for men who have a home like I have and who think like me. Then I went, and today I returned. Then I took leave of two children and today I returned to four." (His wife gave birth to twin girls two months after his Phantom was shot down during the War of Attrition.)

"The intermediate period has passed. I remember it, but it was not all that terrible."

The kibbutz turned out as one man to welcome Seren Harpaz home, but they started decorating for his return only after they had received phone confirmation from Lod that he had indeed landed in Israel. "We've been disappointed by too many false alarms," they explained.

At 1.50, Harpaz arrived in a car, and was greeted by fireworks and applause. The pilot, with some white in his short black hair, had tears in his eyes as he made his way from the gate through a big crowd to the club room, shaking hands, kissing, backslapping, joking and accepting little bouquets of flowers from all the kibbutz children, who also threw confetti. He remembered everybody's name, bellowed a hearty "*mazal tov*" to one of the women who told him she had become a grandmother, and there was one poignant scene as he was embraced by one of the women who had lost a son during last month's war. (He himself has lost a brother-in-law and a cousin.)

At the club, Kibbutz Secretary Rafael Tabori welcomed him with a few words, a champagne toast was drunk, and the returning PoW said, "You are much more excited than I am, because all of you had to wait for me, and all I did was to come home."

He stayed only long enough to give instructions for a cat, Sazu, which he had brought back from prison camp, delivered to Dan Avidan, at nearby Kibbutz Ein Hashofet, as a present. Avidan returned three weeks ago, after four years of imprisonment.

Then Harpaz, accompanied by his wife Nurit, went to their room where he met their twin daughters, Dalia and Deganit, for the first time. They were born in August, 1970. His elder children, Nettah, 10 and Amir, 8, had welcomed him at the airport.

The twins were wearing dresses he had knitted them during his imprisonment, and sent home. They had been brought up "as though their father had gone on a journey end would be back soon," members said. Later, Harpaz said that "when Dalia and Deganit sat on my knees and told me about the dog, Shehori, I felt that it was all over and that I was really back."

The party was restrained in deference to the members in mourning and those who had relatives wounded during the war. The dining room was furnished with little round tables, each with a candle and a bottle of champagne. It was packed.

Dan Avidan and three pilots who had been prisoners in Syria and were returned last June also attended the evening get-together and sat with the Harpaz family.

There were songs and recitals of poems written by the children, and a kibbutznik welcomed Harpaz and assured him that "every child knew that Dalia and Deganit had a father too, a pilot who would return one day and take them to the swimming pool and to walks in the woods." He said, "The God of the Hebrews smote the Egyptians with ten plagues; there are miracles no more, and now we must smite them ourselves, and face losses."

Harpaz replied that "people think that being a war prisoner is like going beyond the hills of darkness. But actually there are worse things in the world, and three and a half years is not all that long."

While it was impossible to give an account of those years in a few minutes, he considered the period closed, as abruptly as it had started when he bailed out, he said.

And, looking around at the assembled friends, he said: "This is the moment I thought of again and again."

Pro-Israel stand by 50 Europe MPs

By JACK MAURICE
Jerusalem Post Correspondent

PARIS. — Supporters of Israel from 11 Western European parliaments decided here on Friday to act together in order to back Israel against political pressure from the Arab and Soviet countries and also from Western Europe.

The 50 MPs condemned the nine Common Market nations' pro-Arab statement in Brussels recently as a surrender to oil blackmail by the Arabs.

The MPs came from all the Common Market countries and from Sweden, Switzerland and Austria. They represented both government and opposition parties.

In a statement issued after their talks here, the MPs said they had decided to set up a European parliamentary committee with a permanent secretariat in order to promote friendship with Israel.

The parliamentarians added: "Europe must show its will to see the future of the State of Israel safeguarded. We denounce any form of economic blackmail. Acceptance of such blackmail is bound to lead to new pressures and new threats."

ASTURIAS CABLES HIS SUPPORT

Miguel Angel Asturias, the renowned Guatemalan novelist and 1967 Nobel laureate, yesterday cabled the Central Institute for Israel-Spanish American Cultural Relations in Tel Aviv, expressing his support for the Israel people during this time of crisis.

Soviet Jews in hunger strike

MOSCOW (UPI). — Jews in four cities began a two-day hunger strike Saturday to protest the recent arrest on "hooliganism" charges of a Kiev engineer denied permission to emigrate to Israel, a Jewish source said.

The source said the engineer, Alexander Feldman, 35, was scheduled to go on trial today, but that the proceedings have now been indefinitely delayed. He faces up to five years in prison.

According to the source, Feldman's arrest appeared to be part of a new Soviet secret police campaign against Jews seeking to emigrate to Israel.

The hunger strike was being conducted by at least 17 Jews — two in Moscow, one in Leningrad, five in Tbilisi, and nine in Novosibirsk, the source said.

The Moscow Jews were identified as Alexander Luntz and Alexander Prestin. Luntz was one of six Jewish scientists who conducted a 14-day hunger strike in August to protest Soviet emigration restrictions.

The source said Feldman applied to emigrate to Israel 13 months ago and was denied permission on the grounds he knew classified information. Following his arrest, police confiscated several books on Judaism from his home.

In London yesterday 35 members of the Women's Campaign for Soviet Jewry chained themselves to the entrance of a Soviet art exhibition to mark the beginning of a world-wide "Prisoners' Month."

The girls, each bearing the name and picture of a Jewish prisoner in the Soviet Union were cut free by police.

The demonstrators said they wanted to draw attention to the case of Alexander Feldman.

Mr. Panov's plight and Mr. Wilner's complaint

Valerie Panov with his wife.

Valery Panov's courageous fast has now lasted eighteen days — as long as the Yom Kippur War.

He is not trying to change his country's policies, as Jan Palach did tragically in Czechoslovakia, when he burnt himself to death. Panov is not claiming the right to take any Russian goods, civilian or military, out of the Soviet Union.

All he wants to do is what 100,000 Israelis do per annum — when they board a plane in Lod airport, or a ship in Haifa harbour, without ever telling the Israeli authorities whether they intend to come back or not.

He wants to activate a clause in the Declaration of Human Rights, which entitles him to move his own body freely from one portion of the earth's surface to another. He simply desires to be one of the ticket-carrying multitude who throng the world's international airports every day of the year.

Rakah, the New Communist Party of Israel, has published big advertisements in the press saying that the Soviet Union is a peace-loving state, solicitous for the welfare of mankind. I have heard Meir Wilner declaim in the Knesset (in answer to an interjection from the floor) that Russia cares more for the interests of the Israeli people than does the Israel Government.

Yet Wilner — an anti-Zionist party leader — was allowed by the "reactionary" government of the country he inhabits to enter a travel agency in Tel Aviv last week in perfect freedom, and buy a ticket to Moscow.

Perhaps Rakah would put in an another advertisement, explaining why the Soviet Union lets Valery Panov — an innocent ballet dancer — starve himself almost to death rather than grant him the same small privilege.

Are Panov's sufferings a necessary part of the USSR's peace policies, that serve the interests of the Israeli people more than does the Israel Government?

DAVID KRIVINE

WHAT IS ZIONISM? When did it start?

The root of the word itself goes back some 3,000 years in history, when the word *Zion* was interchangeable with the word *Jerusalem.* Strictly speaking, a Zionist is a person who loves Jerusalem. And Jerusalem, in a generic sense, stands for *Eretz Yisroel.*[1] Zionism represents the oldest love of country in human history.

We find dramatic mention of this all-encompassing love in Psalm 137, presumably written around 586 B.C. The first temple built by the Jews in the holy city of Jerusalem had been destroyed; the population of the city had been carried away, captive, to Babylonia. The psalm recounts the sequel:

1. The Land of Israel.

By the rivers of Babylon, there we sat down; yea, we wept, when we remembered Zion.
There in the midst we hanged our harps upon the willows.
For there, they that carried us away captive required of us a song,
And they that wasted us required of us mirth, saying, sing us one of the songs of Zion.
How shall we sing a song of the Lord on a strange soil?
If I forget thee, O Jerusalem, let my right hand forget her power.
If I do not remember thee, let my tongue cleave to the roof of my mouth.
If I prefer thee not, O Jerusalem, above my chiefest joy.

TO MAKE UP LOST CLASS TIME

Abolish holidays, say some high schools

By SARAH HONIG, Jerusalem Post Reporter

TEL AVIV. — Amal, the Histadrut's vocational system, has called on the Ministry of Education to do away with the Hanukka and Pessah school holidays this year, since studies in some secondary schools have been severely disrupted since the war. The problem is particularly acute in the vocational schools, where many of the pupils have been helping out in essential industries in order to alleviate the manpower shortage.

The Amal system network says holding classes during the holidays would help make up for lost classroom time.

Over 2,500 of Amal's 11th and 12th graders are working full time on a volunteer basis in the Military Industries, the Aircraft Industries, and other defence plants. High school pupils are also employed in metal works around the country.

(Vocational high school juniors and seniors come under the jurisdiction of the Ministry of Labour's Manpower Controller in times of emergency, when many of the employees in essential industries are called up for military service. Pupils who have been learning some of the necessary skills can alleviate the situation by filling vacant posts.)

These pupils still attend classes when they're not working, or are given their lessons to prepare at home. However, they cannot make up for the classes they miss. Their teachers hope that with almost an extra month (which the combined Hanukka and Pessah holidays would give) they might be able to reduce the lost material.

Some educators believe there may be no choice but to shorten the summer vacation — or possibly even to eliminate it altogether — to enable the seniors to complete their curriculum and graduate on time.

Ministry of Education officials are considering the various proposals, but as yet have made no decision. Hanukka is still four weeks off.

Chief of Spanish Red Cross to intercede in Syria

LOD AIRPORT. — The president of the Spanish Red Cross, Francisco Queipo, said yesterday that he intends immediately to ask the Red Crescent in Syria to step up its pressure on the Damascus Government to exchange prisoners with Israel, or at least to submit a list of the names of Israel prisoners in Syrian hands.

Mr. Queipo has been visiting Israel with Manuel Fiol, head of his organization's youth department, at the invitation of Magen David Adom. He told Itim at the airport before he left that he had supported the abortive Israel motion at the recent International Red Cross convention in Teheran, calling on Syria to respect the Geneva Convention. He added that Red Cross headquarters in Geneva are maintaining contact with the Syrian authorities in an attempt to secure the release of the Israelis held there.

197

AN APPEAL OF A CITIZEN!!!

As a plain citizen, I appeal to my co-citizens, to the Government, and to our neighbours, to be more flexible and more compromising in our efforts for peace.

I APPEAL TO:

My Co-citizens:

1. To strive for peace and only for *peace*, not for territories and not for military victories.

2. To show full and complete confidence in and support for our Government and our leaders — who are experienced and want the best for our people. Even the "hawks" have now learned from their mistakes, and are ready to return part of the territories to achieve peace.

3. To be united and to discourage "witch hunting," looking for scapegoats and "wars" between Jews. There is no point in public inquiries into what went wrong. Everyone should make his own inquiry into his own domain. We are all to blame, we are all guilty for what happened. The Six Day War gave us a false sense of security, comfort, tranquility, encouraging unlimited and excessive improvements in standards of living, "cockiness" and even arrogance. Hopefully, the last war has taught us a lesson — but unfortunately the price was too high. We should not want to pay again.

4. To be more tolerant, humble, flexible and understanding — we are not alone in the world — and, whether we like it or not, we have to consider the necessities, the "face-savings" and the internal and external pressures our neighbours have to face. We have to go at least halfway, so that they can also come to us.

Our Government:

1. To be strong in representing our beliefs in Independence, Autonomy, Democracy and the "Value of Human Life," but to be tolerant, flexible and compromising in negotiations, so as to achieve these aims and beliefs.

2. To encourage direct negotiations, but, if these are impossible in some cases, to accept indirect negotiations — as long as there is no major imposition from the major powers. To use the conquered territories and the military victories only as means for achieving peace. Our final aim should in no event be territorialist or expansionist and we should only use these means for achieving our true aim: PEACE.

3. To avoid interference by the Great Powers and their use of our region as a field of experimentation and our soldiers as guinea pigs for their newly developed weapons.

4. To encourage, initiate, promote and force negotiations with our neighbours. To recognize and try to solve the problems of the territories and of the Arab refugees. To avoid the repetitions of past errors made between 1970 and 1973, during which time we "sat pretty," without doing very much towards peace and settlement of the "status quo." Since we are the ones that want true peace, we should be the ones to take the initiative.

World Jewry:

To continue to give us the help, the backing and the assistance — moral and financial — in achieving peace; to stand united with us and to continue to identify yourselves with our homeland Israel, not only in war, but also in peace.

Our Neighbours:

To let us live together in peace, and join us in developing jointly the whole of the region for the good of your and our people.

Let us replace the arms — the cannons, planes, tanks, bombs and missiles — with social, economic and cultural intercourse. Let us jointly develop our resources through our combined means for the good of the people and humanity, and not for the enrichment of the major powers.

If you, co-citizen, believe in peace, make yourself heard; write today to our leaders, backing these thoughts.

H.D. FRENKEL, P.O.B. 1018, Haifa, Israel

A **70-YEAR-OLD** Russian immigrant, Shmuel Pikus, has made 800 hats and gloves for soldiers in the Golan Heights since October 6. The army has asked Mr. Pikus, a retired tailor, to train 20 women in sewing warm clothes for soldiers.

Throughout their exile in Babylonia, the Jews clung to their everlasting hope of returning to Zion. Isaiah, their prophet, sings of this dream in Chapter 61.

The spirit of the Lord God is upon me,
For the Lord has anointed me;
He has sent me to bring good news to the
    lowly,
To bind up the broken-hearted,
To proclaim liberty to the captives,
And release to the prisoners;
To proclaim the year of the Lord's favor,
And the day of our God's vengeance;
To comfort all mourners,
To provide for the mourners of Zion,
To give them a crown instead of ashes,
Oil of joy instead of a garment of
    mourning,
A song of praise instead of a drooping
    spirit,
That they may be called oak trees of
    righteousness,
The planting of the Lord, with which he
    may glorify himself.
Then shall they rebuild the ancient ruins,
They shall raise up the desolations of old;
They shall renew the wasted cities,
The desolations of age after age....

No more shall you be named "Forsaken,"
    nor your land be named "Desolate";
But you shall be called
    "My-delight-is-in-her," and your land
    shall be called "Married";
For the Lord delights in you, and your
    land shall indeed be married.
As a young man marries a maiden,
    so shall your Builder marry you;
And as a bridegroom rejoices over his
    bride, so shall your God rejoice
    over you.

Over your walls, O Jerusalem, I have
    appointed watchmen,
Who never keep silent by day or by night.
You who are the Lord's remembrances,
    take no rest for yourselves,
And give him no rest, until he establish
And make Jerusalem a praise in the earth!
The Lord has sworn by his right hand,
    and by his strong arm:
"No more will I give your grain to be food

for your enemies,
Nor shall aliens drink your vintage
    for which you have labored;
But those who have garnered the grain
    shall eat it, and praise the Lord,
And those who have gathered the vintage
    shall drink it in my holy courts."
Pass through! Pass through the gates!
    Prepare the way of the people!
Grade up! Grade up the highway! Clear it
    of stones! Raise a signal over the
    peoples!
See! The Lord has made proclamation
    to the end of the earth:
"Say to the daughter of Zion, 'See! your
    salvation has come;
See! The reward has come! and the
    recompense is here!
You shall be called, 'The holy people,
    the redeemed of the Lord'."[1]

It was words like these that kept the spirit of the Jewish people alive through all vicissitudes, words so ringing they were transcribed for all time.

During the Babylonian captivity, Nehemiah, one of the Jewish captives, rose to become cup bearer to King Artaxerxes I, a position of great power. The story of Nehemiah is recounted in the beginning of Chapter 2 of the book by the same name:

And it came to pass in the month of
Nissan, in the twentieth year of Artaxerxes
the King, that wine was set before him:
and I took up the wine, and gave it to the
King. Now I had not ever been sad in
his presence.

So the King said unto me, 'Why are you
so sad; yet I see you are not ill. This can
be nothing but sorrow of the heart.' Then
I became afraid.

And I said to the King: 'Let the King live
forever! Why should I not look sad, when
the city, the place of my fathers'
sepulchres, has been laid waste, and the
gates of my city have been consumed
by fire?'

Then the King said to me, 'What are you
requesting?' Then I prayed to the God of
heaven.

1. Isaiah LXI:1-6, LXII:4-12.

EGYPTIANS AGREE TO SEARCH FOR DEAD

By ZE'EV SCHUL
Jerusalem Post Military Correspondent

TEL AVIV. — Agreement has been reached with the Egyptians to begin combing the battlefields east and west of the Suez Canal for the bodies of soldiers — both Israeli and Egyptian — the O.C. Manpower, Aluf Herzl Shafir, told military correspondents here yesterday.

Aluf Shafir said the IDF was willing to deploy a large number of search parties immediately, to operate jointly with the Egyptians.

Some missing Israeli soldiers are believed still in the strong-points of the Bar-Lev Line, and Israel is asking for permission to have at least one man enter these positions.

If this and other proposals prove unacceptable to the Egyptians, Israel is suggesting, as an alternative, that each army comb the areas under its control and hand over the bodies to the other side for proper identification and burial.

Aluf Shafir said he expected the exchange of prisoners with Egypt to be concluded today. Debriefing of the returned Israelis should help clarify the fate of some of the missing and unidentified men.

Concerning the number of men reported missing and believed to have been killed in action, Aluf Shafir explained that the army was caught unawares by the suddenness of the war. Men were rushed down to the fronts as fast as they reported for duty — often not as complete units. Problems were compounded by the character of the fighting, the duration and the heavy losses. Some tank crews exchanged vehicles four or five times — changing the original composition of the crews and often serving in different capacities (doubling for injured tank drivers, gunners or tank commanders).

INITIAL RETREATS

Matters were further complicated by the initial retreats and the necessity of conceding territory to the enemy — a factor not experienced by the army since the War of Liberation (1948/49) — which meant leaving strongpoints in the hands of the enemy. Large segments of the battlefield are still held by the Egyptians, and they are believed to contain the bodies of Israeli men.

Aluf Shafir believed he would be able to give a tentative estimate of the number of men still missing (including the number of prisoners of war held by the Syrians) in a few days.

In the meantime, a missing persons centre has been set up. A file is opened for each case and the files are separated into categories such as "Mt. Hermon battles." As incoming information is sorted, it fills in the blanks in the files. In some cases, information received from a comrade is enough to classify a given man as "dead" or "in Syrian captivity," for instance.

On the other hand many "missing men" later show up. They may have been reported missing during the first few days by distraught parents only because they had not contacted their homes.

A computer has been put at the disposal of the centre to help speed up the sorting of facts. A total of 182 officers are employed by the centre, including 95 investigators.

Aluf Shafir disclosed that a large number of bodies, buried as "unknowns," have been identified during the past few weeks thanks to the systematic investigations continuing on each missing person file. He expected to be able to complete a large number of additional files in the near future, although the refusal of the Syrians to supply PoW lists or cooperate in any other way is complicating the centre's work.

Sir, — Let me assure you that no matter what statements are made at the official level, the 400 million people of this country are with you (I won't say anything about the remaining 150 million.) I have yet to come across a person of my acquaintance who favours the Arabs. If you would allow it, there are thousands who would like to come to Israel and fight against the Arabs. Lest this letter be dubbed a propaganda stunt, I am giving my address so that young Israelis can write to me — a 22-year-old student.
BHUPENDRA DOGRA
c/o Dr. Paul Love
B.U.C. College
Batala (Punjab) India, October 17.

SUPPORT FROM ABROAD

Sir, — The whole world knows that the Arabs have been the aggressors against Israel in all the wars in the Middle East. I am pained at the short-sighted policy of my own country in not using the Gandhian yardstick of equity, justice and truthful assessment in the present West Asian problem.

Many of us wish for Israel's success because we feel the fight of one small Israel against 16 fanatic Arab States is unequal and unjustified. That is the main reason why there are from 70 to 80 Indo-Israel Cultural Friendship Societies flourishing despite many impediments placed in their way.
N.V. IYER, Secretary, India-Israel
Cultural Association
Nagpur, India, October 22.

Sir, — I think your readers should be aware of the fact that you have a true silent majority of praying Christian friends all over the world, and thousands of them in Scandinavia, who do love Israel.
ANDERS WIGHOLM
Field Secretary of the Salvation
Army of Sweden
Stockholm, Heshvan 8.

COMMISSION OF INQUIRY NAMED

Jerusalem Post Staff

The President of the Supreme Court, Judge Shimon Agranat, yesterday named four men — including two former chiefs of staff — to serve with him as the Commission of Inquiry into the recent war. The former chiefs of staff are Hebrew University archaeologist Professor Yigael Yadin and Haim Laskov, who is now the Army ombudsman. Serving with them will be State Comptroller Dr. Yitzhak Nebenzahl and Supreme Court Judge Moshe Landau.

The Government decided on setting up the inquiry committee on Sunday. Judge Agranat has appointed himself chairman.

The Commission was expected to convene at an early date, probably this week. Its members were informed personally of their appointment by Justice Agranat yesterday afternoon.

The composition of the Commission denoted that the Supreme Court President had resolved to choose widely respected public personalities who could enjoy public confidence, particularly since the inquiry is to be held *in camera*.

The Commission will apply itself to these three broad issues:

- Evaluation and assessment of information and intelligence reports before the war (by both military and civilian authorities);
- The IDF's general preparedness for the war;
- The enlistment of the reserves and their deployment.

The Commission of Inquiry to investigate the causes of unpreparedness for the Yom Kippur War sits in session.

'War of the Sons' may be final phase in six-year-long war

"We are vitally interested in negotiations with the Arabs, but they must be direct negotiations at all stages," writes Minister of Transport and of Communications SHIMON PERES. "Israel's security is guaranteed by territories, relations with the Arabs and our defence capability; our security does not lie in guarantees by foreign powers."

THE Yom Kippur War — which might perhaps more correctly be called the War of the Sons — can be regarded as the continuation and possibly the final phase of a six-year war consisting of four battles: the Six Day War, the War of Attrition, the War of Terror, and the War of the Sons.

During the past six years the days of fighting outnumbered the days of quiet. Every battle, of course, had its own particular character The waiting period preceding the Six Day War created the impression of an Israel in mortal peril, while our swift victory in the actual fighting created the opposite impression. The War of Attrition proceeded in a "leisurely" fashion and therefore seemed more of a nuisance than a decisive test. The War of Terror was the first stage, preceding the use of the "oil weapon," in hitting at Israel abroad. Finally, in the War of the Sons, enemy aggression preceded Israeli reaction, and the battle brought days of fateful crisis the like of which we had never known before.

World War Two

In terms of duration, this six-year-war can be compared to the Second World War (1939-1945). The comparison is almost similar in terms of weaponry (at least as far as tanks, planes and missiles are concerned) when we recall that the Germans in their attack on Russia used 1,300 tanks — 100 fewer than the Syrians poured onto the Golan Heightx.

Yet there is no comparison between the series of defeats suffered by the Allies and the fact that during its six years of war Israel chalked up a series of victories, with almost no serious defeats. And Israel throughout the six years fought alone, without allies.

In addition to the purely military aspects of Israel's struggle over the past six years, the period also put to the test theories which are partly political and partly military. Those who say that "the entire theory on which our security was built has collapsed" are expressing a judgment both hasty and premature.

1) There are those who claim that we could have avoided the war by not conquering Arab areas, or by promptly retreating from them. This theory was disproved by our retreat from Sinai and the Gaza Strip after the 1956 campaign. This pull-back in 1957 did not prevent the Six Day War only ten years later.

2) Another theory to be examined is that of secure borders and strategic depth. If war is unavoidable, the Government must ask itself whether the battles should be fought at the gates of Beersheba or in the sands of Sinai; in the Huleh Valley or the rocky hills of the Golan Heights; on the banks of the Jordan or at the gates of Jerusalem; at Shaar Hagai on the Tel Aviv-Jerusalem road or in the Straits of Bab el-Mandeb.

President Sadat says that once Israel has retreated from all the conquered areas, the question of the Palestinians must be "considered." And what is that likely to lead to?

3) The theory of the pre-emptive strike proved itself militarily correct in the case of the Six Day War but it cannot be applied automatically. It has to be carefully re-evaluated politically in each case, lest repeated application brand its practitioner as the perpetual aggressor. If we had resorted to the pre-emptive strike technique this time, the world would have claimed that we had not really been in danger but had acted out of cussedness. Quite possibly American public opinion would have swung against us.

4) We have always done our utmost to avoid a collision with any of the world powers, or to remain without the support of one of them. This policy demands very delicate judgment. When in 1956 the Russians threatened to intervene with missiles, I tended to consider their threat a bluff. But when we were told in this war that the Russian helicopters (perhaps painted white instead of red) would attempt to

ferry supplies to the Third Army, I believed this to be a real possibility and not a bluff.

The attitude of the Americans, on the other hand, from their airlift of weapons to their global alert, was such as to deserve that their every demand on us, even if it is called pressure, receive the greatest consideration in order to demonstrate our willingness to advance toward peace.

5) - The theory of reliance on "ourselves alone" has been fully realized in the field of manpower and is being increasingly implemented in the sphere of arms production. The Israel Navy is perhaps the outstanding example of this self-reliance, with its all-Israeli crews, vessels, missiles and doctrines. In the field of aircraft production, such relative independence is unattainable because of constant technological development and changes.

These efforts at eventual technological self-sufficiency need to be constantly pushed ahead and deserve the best we can put into them.

6) David Ben-Gurion has always stressed that our destiny will be decided by *aliya* and the quality of each individual among us. The chief lesson to be learned from the Yom Kippur War is that, because of the great numerical disproportion between us and our enemies, continued *aliya* must be one of our foremost goals, together with the continuing high level of courage and readiness for self-sacrifice of our people.

7) As far as demography is concerned, the policy of the "Open Bridges" more than proved itself. Perhaps we do not fully appreciate the meaning of the quiet that reigned among the million Arabs living in the West Bank, and the many things that could have happened — but did not. However, from the demographic point of view, we have to realize that border-villages are no longer enough and that we may have to build border-cities. Because of the need to mobilize the reserves rapidly in an emergency, we may have to establish three such cities, in the south, the north and the centre of the country.

★ ★ ★

THE peace we so fervently desire requires three factors that are beyond our control: restraint on the part of the Soviet Union; a readiness for reasonable negotiations on the part of the Arabs; and greater stability in the Arab world.

The dispatch of Soviet armaments constitutes a constant spur to aggression, since they are directed to nations which have no tradition of institutions designed to induce restraint. Most Arab countries have no real parliaments or a free press, no real parties or trade unions capable of making realistic demands. It is doubtful whether the Middle East will ever have peace, so long as the Russians keep up their indiscriminate supply of aggressive weapons to the Arabs.

For negotiations to be reasonable and fruitful, it is essential that each Arab state speak in its own name and on subjects that concern it. Gradualness and compromise must be of the essence for such negotiations.

I do not recommend an Israeli attitude of "all or nothing," of constant war or total peace. Due to the problem of the Palestinians I doubt whether it is even possible to trade "all the territories for absolute peace." The Arabs seem no more inclined to grant us absolute peace than we are able to relinquish all the territories.

Fruitful talks

Perhaps a combination of returning some areas, partial demilitarization of others, disengagement of the various armies, and certain arrangements concerning citizenship and ownership, will lead sooner to fruitful negotiations than a one-way moving about on the geographical map. Dealing with a political map makes it possible to take into consideration factors of time, national honour and of logic. It can satisfy demands for freedom of movement in the air, on water and on land. It can take account of individual needs of citizens and safeguard the aspirations for national identity of various groups.

We are vitally interested in negotiations with the Arabs, however long drawn out they may be, *but they must be direct negotiations at all stages*. The real guarantees of Israel's security are contained in a combination of three factors: territories; relations (with the Arabs); and our defence capability. Our security does not lie in guarantees by foreign powers.

In view of the attitudes of the Arabs, the European countries and the super-powers, it is incumbent on Israel to start negotiations as soon as possible with at least one of the Arab countries. At the same time we must retain areas for defensive strategic depth and to maintain our military preparedness.

Lessons of war

The main lessons of the War of the Sons, however, are directed to Israelis themselves. On the eve of the war our society was characterized, more than at any other time, by an indescribable complacency, an impatient covetousness and a pursuit of material advantage absolutely detrimental to high standards of work morale.

The hard-fought war must be followed by a period of hard work. Our most important natural resource is the industriousness of our citizens. We have the elections just ahead of and we must decide whether the coming four years will be years of reconstruction and progress, or a time characterized by further pampering and illusions.

We can emerge strengthened and victorious if we apply all our energies in three areas: aliya and immigrant absorption; the promotion of science and technology; and the advancement of the underprivileged sections of our population.

And I said to the King, 'If it please the King, and if your servant has found favor in your sight, please send me to Judea,[1] to the city of the sepulchres of my fathers, that I may build that city once again.'

The King was moved, and granted the request of his cup bearer; and Nehemiah went back to Jerusalem, to rebuild under the royal aegis the city for which he longed.

1. Geographical section surrounding Jerusalem.

About 600 years after the Second Temple had been built by Nehemiah, the Romans, in 73 A.D., conquered Jerusalem, destroyed the temple, and carried off the physically able to Rome as slaves. The rest of the Jews were scattered to the four corners of the earth.

The Arch of Titus, still standing in Rome, commemorates this Roman victory. The Jewish subjugation is graven in stone on a bas-relief which portrays Roman soldiers carrying off booty from the temple they had despoiled.

SABBATH—No Publication

Two soldiers, standing some 35 kilometers from Damascus, take time out for an ice cream cup.

Year after year, on the 9th day of Av, the anniversary of the destruction of the Temple, Jews came back to sit in the rubble of their beloved Jerusalem. Since Roman law excluded them from setting foot in the area, they would bribe the Roman guards to allow them to enter, and sit down and mourn.

It was in Talmudical times — probably around 200 A.D. — that the sages composed the prayer which ever since has expressed the core of Jewish hope:

Any may our eyes see the return to Zion in your mercy.

This prayer has taken its prime place in the liturgy, and Jews have recited it three times each day for generations. It remains in every Jewish prayer book until this very day.

In 1086, Judah Ben Samuel Halevi was born in Toledo. Halevi became a noted physician in Castilian Spain, and grew wealthy and influential. But this Jewish doctor's major acclaim was as a prince of medieval poets. His inclination was ever toward Eretz Israel, and the paean he penned about the land of his dreams has become famous in Hebrew literature:

My heart is in the East, and I am in the uttermost ends of the West.
How can I find savor in food, and how can viands be sweet for me?
How shall I render my vows, while Zion lies in the fetters of Edom, and I lie in Arab chains.
It would seem right for me to leave all the good things of Spain, could my eyes but behold the dust of the desolate sanctuary.

Prisoner tells of torture in Egyptian captivity

By YAACOV FRIEDLER
Jerusalem Post Reporter

HAIFA. — Sergeant Kenneth Handler, one of the PoWs released by the Egyptians last week, said here on Friday that the prisoners had been "sadistically beaten" during their first week in captivity.

Handler, 21, had both his legs in bandages, and his nose was broken — the result of Egyptian beatings. He was taken prisoner on October 21, after his tank was hit by a missile.

He said the month in Egyptian hands had been "both physically and mentally difficult."

The jailers beat the prisoners "with the full knowledge of their officer." He could think of no reason for the beatings, "except pure sadism."

During the second week, the torture became more systematic — interrogations had started. His hands had been tied behind his back for days, and "they are still numb," he said.

The PoWs had been held in solitary confinement, in small cells, with nothing to do all day.

"I watched the sun and the shadows moving across the cell, and tried to keep busy counting the insects crawling up my legs, or playing with grains of rice from the meals."

The food was small portions of "bad pitta and beans," pushed into his cell under the door.

One day, his cell door was opened, and gas was pumped in filling the small cell and making him cough.

"I thought it was the end, that they were poisoning me," he said. But the gas turned out to be disinfectant, sprayed without any warning or consideration.

He also believed the shaving of their heads had been intended to humiliate and depress them, rather than serve any sanitary purpose. All his personal possessions, including his watch and spectacles, had been taken away and never returned.

The treatment improved only a couple of days before the release, which came as a complete surprise to Handler.

The prisoners were taken on a tour of Cairo and the pyramids. Handler said the pyramids were "smaller than I expected, but the Sphinx is very interesting." They were accompanied on the tour by a Hebrew-speaking officer.

Despite everything, Handler said, he "had no hard feelings for the Egyptians," believing that they had been incited by their own propaganda.

He was somewhat worried about having been born British — he has been in Israel seven years — in case the Egyptians carried out their threat to exclude "mercenaries" from the Geneva Convention.

Sergeant Handler was reunited with his parents in Haifa on Friday night. They had gone to England for a visit three months ago, and returned on the Nili. They did not know their son had been taken prisoner, because his brother had decided not to tell them. Their first question was, "Why didn't you write?"

History recounts that Halevi, ignoring the entreaties of friends and family, did actually leave his home, his wealth, and his position, and undertook the long, arduous journey over sea and over land to Palestine. He died in Egypt, and like Moses, died without setting foot in the Promised Land.

A legend penned by Heinrich Heine has it that Halevi did reach the land of his dreams, but at the very moment when he bent down to kiss the beloved soil, a Saracen passing by on horseback, whipped out his scimitar, and decapitated Halevi with one blow. What symbolism is conveyed in this story, I leave to the reader to conjecture.

Eretz Israel has, indeed, been watered by the blood of dreamers, even beyond those who are but dreamers in legend. For history tells us that throughout the long years of exile, from 70 A.D. until the first stirrings of political Zionism in the late 1800's, Jews always constituted a substantial segment of the population of Palestine the recent declarations of that profound researcher, King Faisal of Saudi Arabia notwithstanding. Drawn to

---

PAGE FOUR *(ADVERTISEMENT)* **THE JER**

MENAHEM BEG

Between Rosh Hash

Yom Kippur Why D.

Mobilize the Res

On November 13, the Knesset held a debate on a statement by Prime Minister Mrs. Golda Meir on the political situation. The first speaker in the debate was Mr. Menahem Begin, M.K.

The full text of h tion of the Prime entire Cabinet) f

Mr. Speaker, Members of the Knesset,

Lieutenant General David Elazar, the Chief of Staff of our Armed Forces, said two days ago: "If the reserves had been called up 24 or 48 hours earlier, there can be no doubt that the war would have run differently and we would have suffered fewer casualties. The decision not to call the reserves was taken at the highest political-military level, on the basis of the assessment that, in spite of all the signs of mass concentrations of Egyptian and Syrian troops, there

why did you not call up the reserves? Why did you move the equipment up? How do you try to live with lie that the question was whether to start shooting? W do you not say that the question was whether to mobi in time, as we could have done; we have erred, we h done wrong, we have sinned, and because of our decis not to call up the reserves, the Israel Defence Force v in the first 48 hours of the fighting, in a state of quantita and qualitative inferiority at the front.

The entire philosophy of the few against the many,

the land by the power of a million magnets embedded in their psyches, and regardless of which government held domain, an appreciable number of Jews have always chosen Jerusalem as their temporal home, just as many Jews, throughout the long exile, have maintained Jerusalem as their spiritual home.

Jerusalem, the golden! There have always been men, some Jewish, some Christian, with their roots in scripture, who have regarded Jerusalem as their

symbolic capital, the fountainhead of their spiritual strength. So did the visionary poet, William Blake, the apostle of gentleness. So did the prophet who proclaimed:

For from Zion shall go forth the Law,
And the word of the Lord from Jerusalem.[1]

Generations of Jews, living over a stretch of 2,000 years, have regarded Eretz Israel, the Land

1. Isaiah II:3.

POST (ADVERTISEMENT) **SUNDAY, NOVEMBER 25, 1973**

N:

na and

n't You

ves?

ch, in which he called for the resig
r (and therefore automatically of

plicitly that they are bound by no cease-fire, including the
t, stabilized one at Km. 101.

Is there any nation in the world that is being asked to
ive its national security in such a way? Has anyone,
wever strong he may be, the right to demand this of our
ople, with its experience? But then Dr. Kissinger goes
: Admittedly, there will be a very serious problem of
rael's security; Israel will to all intents give up its se-
rity; but we have a remedy: we will give her guarantees.
uarantees! Mr. Kissinger is not only a statesman, but also

with you, but in all our conversations you have let us know
things after the event, with the one and only exception of
the Sadat-Kissinger agreement; and then we made our remarks, but you did not take them into consideration.

Why do I say that you were irresponsible in accepting
that agreement? Really, why did you make all that to-do
about it? Agreed, you have made an agreement. What does
Egypt get from that agreement? The Third Army, which
was encircled, besieged, doomed to surrender, is brought to
life again. What do we get? A promise to release our prisoners in Egypt. Not all our prisoners, and we know that

Katzir: Everyone at fault for mistakes of the war

President Ephraim Katzir said in a radio interview yesterday that many military and political mistakes were made in connection with the war — for which "we all are to blame." He said "we wanted to live in a utopian world which was not exactly identical to the real world in which we live."

The investigation of the mistakes that were made should not be aimed at "punishing one another," but at learning the lessons which might determine the fate of the Jewish people, he said.

Asked if he thought the nation was in a state of shock, the President replied: "I wouldn't describe it as shock. The Jewish people are a wise people. But we felt suddenly the powerful Arab military might and the need for common action — something we were unaccustomed to. In addition there was the pain felt at our losses. As a result we have begun to review our actions soberly, with muted pain and no small sorrow at what has happened to us."

On the chances for peace, he said the talks at Kilometre 101 provided the first opening. "Perhaps the Arabs also understand now that the Jewish people will do everything to defend their state. Maybe the Arabs will now think twice whether it pays for them to once more sacrifice their sons and fathers for the dubious goal of satisfying their hatred."

(Itim)

Africans to tell Pope their views about Jerusalem

KHARTOUM (UPI). — President Jaafar Numeiry and Ethiopian Emperor Haile Selassie will visit the Vatican to inform Pope Paul of the viewpoint of African Moslems and Christians on "the continued armed occupation of Jerusalem by a single religious sect," the government announced on Friday.

An official statement said Numeiry, who visited Addis Ababa on Thursday and later Riyadh, Saudi Arabia, conferred with Emperor Selassie and conveyed his viewpoint on the matter to Saudi King Faisal. Numeiry returned to Khartoum on Thursday night.

It added the three leaders believe that Jerusalem is a Moslem and Christian shrine "as well as a Jewish one."

SUPPORT FROM SWITZERLAND

To the Editor of The Jerusalem Post

Sir, — Having been in this land with a group of Swiss pilgrims — for the twelfth time — it seems providential that we were in Jerusalem on Yom Kippur when war broke out. Our group unanimously decided to stay on as scheduled. We shared with Israel the indignation and grief at the mean aggression of the enemy on that holy day. We admired the sober courage with which the Government, army and people faced the grave situation, and also the calm with which they endured the bitter losses. We wept with those that wept.

And now, as we return home after four weeks, we wish to assure Israel that there are millions of Pentecostal believers all over the world — besides many other Christians — who are with Israel in their claim to the right to live peacefully in the land which, since Abraham's time, has always been and still is their own.

LEONARD STEINER
First Chairman of the
World Pentecostal Conference
Jerusalem (Basel), October 26.

Golda: We can't live like others

By ABRAHAM RABINOVICH
Jerusalem Post Reporter

Premier Golda Meir said last night that Israel had lulled itself into thinking in recent years that because it saw no point to war the Arabs didn't either.

"We were so absolutely certain that war can solve nothing and that we wanted peace that we transferred this feeling to a very large extent to our neighbours. The intelligence reports (about war preparation) came in and the best of our people said 'it can't happen'." Mrs. Meir was speaking at a Knesset dinner for leaders of Anglo-Jewry.

For the first time in any of Israel's wars, Mrs. Meir said, the feeling existed in the first two days of the October war that Israel may lose. On the outcome of the war, she said, depended not only the fate of Israel but of the Jewish people. "I'm convinced as I never was before that the continuity of the Jewish people depends on us."

"The lesson we have to learn and teach our children and grandchildren. — and it is a bitter lesson — is that we just cannot live like all other people in the world. If we turn away for a moment because it's too dark to face this truth, then we're lost. We have to learn how not to give up one iota of our desire for peace and never again to believe that because we want it they will give it to us." Israel must increase its strength every hour and augment its population, she said.

"There is no Jew in Israel who can say he is the same today as he was on Yom Kippur Eve. I don't believe I will ever be the same." The Premier said she was not a pessimist and believed that Israel would one day live with its neighbours as do other countries.

of Israel, as the land that was Biblically promised to them through their fathers; the land to which they are bound by history and tradition; the golden land their mothers sang of as they lay in their cribs; the land they read about as soon as they were old enough to hold a book.

It was too, the land of their mythology, the land through which there flowed the mystical river Sambatyon, the awesomely, turbulent river that, running its fearful course, heaved up stones during six days of the week, and wondrously came to rest on the Sabbath. It was the land in which the giant Leviathan sported off the shores of the Great Sea, as the Mediterranean was called. This was the land, too, that was peopled by the folk heroes of which the Midrash[1] spoke at length. Miracles were piled on miracles, but none too weird nor absurd nor incredible to be rejected by the thirsty minds of the young, who reveled in these stories of mystery and wonderment.

It was a familiar land, too, a land peopled by names as familiar to them as the names of their own sisters and brothers. It was the land of the patriarchs, of Abraham, of Isaac, of Jacob. It was the land of the arch-heroes, Samson, David, and Bar Kochba.[2]

Nor were these characters of fiction. To every Jewish child, these were intimates, people to emulate, characters whose deeds they could recount, and whose words they could quote verbatim. The bonds were as strong as iron. No distance of time or space, and no oppression could blot out the dream of return. For it was this dream

1. A rabbinic anthology of Biblical narrative and exegesis.
2. Hero of the Jewish revolt against Rome circa 138 A.D.

that nourished the Jewish heart, and that fortified the Jew to withstand the persecution of centuries. It was not a dream of dominion, nor a dream of power, nor of possession. It was a dream of peace, and of belonging.

Throughout the long pages of human history, there are no pages so blood-drenched as those which describe in so repetitive a monochrome the massacre of Jews, decade after decade, century after century. That the Jews survived these bloodbaths is a miracle. The Haggadah recites the inevitability of this unending cycle:

> *For in every generation, they are arrayed against us to consume us; but the Holy One, blessed be He, delivers us from their hands.*

The deliverance came, in many cases, somewhat tardily; and in others, was somewhat spotty, so that the roster of the massacred echoes as a mournful dirge through the corridors of time.

But whatever black forces assailed them, and however many the Jews who were immolated, the *sh'earit ha-p'la-tah,* the remainder of the remnant, was always sustained by the hope of a redeemer who would lead them back to the land from whence they had sprung.

Throughout the long centuries of the dispersion, this hope was never relinquished. No matter how great a celebration any individual Jew enjoyed, he had been taught to be always mindful that the temple of his forefathers had been destroyed. Thus, even at a wedding ceremony, at the very height of jubilation, the custom—which survives down to this

Dried flowers sent to Dutch children

Jerusalem Post Reporter

TEL AVIV. — Schoolchildren in Beersheba have been drying flowers and sending them on postcards to Dutch children, Hillel Seidel, head of the "pro-Holland committee," said on Friday. The committee met to devise new ways to show the appreciation of Israel to the Dutch people for their refusal to give in to an Arab oil boycott.

Some of the suggestions raised: naming of streets for Holland (Netanya has already done so); sending citrus fruit; and lectures and a national bicycle tour. The committee also plans to make badges expressing sympathy for Holland for people to wear or to stick on the car windows.

Call for a more coherent team

To the Editor of The Jerusalem Post

Sir, — If any proof was needed, the Yom Kippur War offered it: that you can achieve victory on the field of battle, yet be held to a draw, if not worse, at the negotiating table; that diplomacy and military might are different political tools towards the same end; and that they should be used to the same end by rational governments.

In Egypt and Syria, these two tools are effectively controlled and wielded in clever alternation. At home, we are witnesses to a situation where our Ministers of Defence and of Foreign Affairs disagree on essentials, criticise each other in public and wish to see each other removed from office. Golda must re-strain their zeal as best she can under the pressure of conflict within her own party, and must handle the critical issues herself. In this, she is doing outstanding work against odds like age, overwork, incomprehension of the ways of the Orient and the inevitable limits of her own personality.

But the acute clash of views within her Cabinet cannot but affect her efforts and the vital decisions affecting the nation's fate. Perhaps our next Government will include more adults, as distinct from mere fullness of years, and give us a more coherent team.

YAACOV AZOUR
Haifa, November 12.

---

very day—has been for the bridegroom to smash a glass underfoot, so that all those present may be reminded that the walls of Jerusalem were crushed, and that the Jewish people were driven into exile.

Many a Jew has saved his last pennies to make the long journey back to the land of his forefathers, if only to spend his last years in the land that he had yearned for throughout a lifetime.

From the Roman destruction of the Second Temple until the late 19th century, the Jewish people were scattered in communities throughout the world. During all this long period of time, without let-up, a small trickle of Jews made their way back to Palestine. But it was not until the late 1880s that the trickle became a stream. And some years later, the stream became a river. How did this come about?

Up until the end of the 18th century, most European Jews resided in tight Jewish communities in small towns and villages, *shtetles*,[1] cut off from the mainstream of Christian life and thought. In the shtetle, there was little, if any, secular education. The young were taught by Rabbis; and learning, for the most part, was confined to the Talmud.

During the 1700s, there began a movement of enlightenment called the *Haskalah*,[2] which stressed the importance of secular learning. Jews were now introduced to the study of mathematics, foreign languages, foreign literature, etc. By the late 1800s, on the heels of the Haskalah movement, Zionist societies had sprung up all over Europe. Along with the new secular learning came new horizons, and a new sense of history. Some Jews began to think further than the rigid confines of their large Talmud tomes, and began to speculate and ponder what could be done to get them in closer contact, pragmatically speaking, with the land of their spiritual bonds. These groups became known as the *Hovevei Zion* (the lovers of Zion). By 1880, their membership totaled about 14,000 people.

Modern Zionism was sown by the seeds of disillusion. It started as a reaction against the dramatic and tragic events in 19th century Russia. After Czar Alexander II was assassinated early in 1881, the succeeding government took repressive measures against all elements it deemed radical. This repression had as its inevitable consequence pogroms against the Jews.

Jews were attacked for their alleged exploitation of the Russian peasantry. There was some element of truth in these accusations, but what was ignored was the fact that anti-Jewish restrictions had locked the middle class Jews of Russia into a few miserable trader occupations. The Jews were as much victims as those whom they were allegedly victimizing. Many revolutionaries

1. Yiddish for "small towns."
2. Hebrew for "enlightenment."

privately applauded the outbreaks of violence as catalytic agents which would lead to profound social change.

The radical movement counted some Jews in its vanguard, and these Jewish populists hailed the pogroms as the first necessary revolutionary convolution. But revolutionary reforms failed to materialize. In fact, the hand of repression only grew heavier.

It became apparent that under the existing regime there was no future for the Jew in Russia. About two and one-half million Jews from Russia and its immediate neighboring countries emigrated to America during the years between 1881 and 1914.

Leon Pinsker, one of the leaders of the Hovevei Zion group, drew important conclusions. He did not believe that anti-Semitism was limited to Russia, or that the problem would or could be solved by

emigration to a friendlier country, or by emancipation through legal measures. No codification of law could wipe away the deeply ingrained bias.

Cowering before the pogrom mob, Pinsker saw in a flash of light that even a full-blown anti-czarist revolution might not bring freedom to the Jews. Today, almost 100 years later, we can only marvel at his prophetic insight. The Communist society, while it eliminated every vestige of capitalism, has certainly not brought freedom to the Jew in Russia. Pinsker rightly predicted that even in a newly burnished polity the Jew might still be resented. He concluded that the future of the Jew lay only in a return to Jewish nationhood.

In 1882, Pinsker published a pamphlet which he entitled "Auto Emancipation." The simple proposition of this essay was that anti-semitism,

---

GROWING READINESS FOR CONCESSIONS

Only 1 in 20 sees Arabs really ready for peace

Jerusalem Post Reporter

Only five per cent of the population believe the Arab countries are "definitely" ready to discuss a real peace with Israel. But another 44 per cent said "perhaps" this was the case when interviewed last week by pollers.

Although most Israelis do not believe Arab readiness for peace is a function of Israel territorial concessions, there is a growing readiness since the outbreak of the October war to withdraw from some of the territories, especially parts of Sinai.

These are some of the findings of a poll carried out November 19 and 20 by the Israel Institute of Applied Social Research and the Communications Institute of the Hebrew University. The November 19-20 poll, which encompassed 660 urban residents aged 20 and above, was part of a continuing survey.

Prof. Louis Guttman, director of the Applied Social Research Institute, told *The Jerusalem Post* last night that the continuing survey showed a considerable change in the public's attitude toward giving back occupied areas.

During the second week of the

war, 52 per cent of those polled said they did not believe Israel should give up a single inch of territory. Last week only 11 per cent gave this answer.

In October, 27 per cent thought Israel should agree to relinquish some of the territories; last week this figure had swelled to 48 per cent (a reduction from the previous week's 53 per cent).

Only about 12 per cent of the population support the "Rogers Plan" — namely, that Israel should give up "all" the territories or "almost all, with slight adjustments." This figure is slightly higher than it was earlier.

Among the poll's other findings:
● Some 71 per cent of the population do not believe the upcoming peace conference will result in a real peace in the coming months.
● More than 50 per cent now believe the present cease-fire will end in renewed fighting (seven per cent fewer thought so a week earlier).
● Only 16 per cent believe the more territory Israel gives back, the greater will be the Arabs' readiness for peace.

Druse farmer buys IL10,000 in war bonds

Jerusalem Post Reporter

HAIFA. — A Druse farmer from Issfiyeh, Amin Minhal Mansour, yesterday bought IL10,000 worth of war bonds, the largest sum subscribed by a non-Jewish citizen.

A Christian resident of Shfar-Am who applied for a IL300 loan at a downtown bank branch here, turned out to be unemployed. Asked what he wanted the money for, he explained he wanted to buy war bonds. The loan was approved.

Disunity in the ranks: The War of Words

THE late unpleasantness apparently failed to produce a "Tipperary" or a "Jerusalem of Gold," let alone an agreed-upon name for the war. It seemed at one time that it would be known as "The Yom Kippur War" though this was challenged by "The War of the Day of Judgement." Now, Mr. Shimon Peres has taken to referring to it as "The War of the Sons" while the enemy seems to fancy "The October War."

Judging by what has been happening in the rear echelons, an apter definition would be "The War of Words." Never before in the field of human conflict can there have been a greater outpouring of rumours, accusations, counter-accusations, breastbeating and parading of opinions on the conduct of the war (and the peace) in such a short space of time.

Now things are not always what they seem and I've managed to derive some comfort from the words of that lovely fella, Edmund Burke, written nearly two centuries ago: "Because half a dozen grasshoppers under a fern make the field ring with their importunate chink, whilst thousands of great cattle... chew the cud and are silent, pray do not imagine that those who make the noise are the only inhabitants of the field; that, of course, they are many in number; or that, after all, they are other than the little shrivelled, meagre, hopping, though loud and troublesome *insects* of the hour."

Unfortunately Mr. Burke did not venture an opinion on the damage these creepy-crawlies may cause, but I think it's fairly plain that they can persuade the enemy that we are a divided people and tempt him to take advantage of this apparent weakness. In fact, one of the main themes of "The Causes of War," a book published recently by the Professor of Economic History at Melbourne, Geoffrey Blainey, is that a mistaken perception of disunity in the enemy's ranks may propel a nation into war. His thesis is that a false notion of the relative strengths of rival powers brings about war and that a reappraisal ends them. In terms of President Sadat's calculations at the beginning and end of October, it would seem that Professor Blainey has something there.

It would be a pity if the Egyptians were to be misled by the strident cries of the politicians and the press, calling for inquiries into the conduct of the war, demanding and opposing elections or supporting and opposing changes in the law whereby serving officers may not stand for the Knesset.

What we need, more than all these issues combined, is some sort of moratorium on washing our dirty linen in public. Now, more than ever before, we have to close ranks and present a united front — even at the cost of what is mistakenly called democracy.

Precious freedom

That true democracy existed in England during World War II is, I think, beyond question, yet during the Emergency, as it was officially termed, the people were eager to surrender some of their precious freedom in return for positive leadership waging a vigorous war.

Following the passing of the Emergency Powers (Defence) Act all known Nazi or Fascist sympathisers were rounded up under Regulation 18b and imprisoned without trial for the duration of the war. Hardly a voice was raised in protest, and the general feeling was that Voltaire could go and get stuffed. Here, on the other hand, Communist Members of the Knesset took the rostrum to publish their poisonous views and while I was patrolling the blacked-out streets I was interested to see a number of eligible young men belonging to Matzpen huddled around a candle in "their" cafe, night after night, presumably plotting the overthrow of the Government.

In 1940, the British made it an offence, punishable by a £50 fine (approximately five months average income), to pass on any rumour likely to cause alarm and despondency. If such a law had been enforced here Mr. Sapir wouldn't have found it necessary to slap on more taxes.

Following Chamberlain's dismissal, Churchill formed a National Government and the General Elections scheduled for 1940 simply never took place until the enemy had been defeated. I don't believe for a moment that the election circus is necessary or desirable except for a handful of professional politicians who, anyway, should have been taken into some form of coalition weeks ago. Who can afford all these distractions when the goal is clear? We went into the war blinkered by all sorts of side-issues including the pressing problem of staff appointments at Israel Aircraft Industries and we're still dithering about.

Make no bones about it, this sort of nonsense is damaging to morale — an incalculable factor in waging war. The steadying factors have been few, almost drowned out by the shrill cries of little men. A place of honour must be reserved for Aluf (Res.) Haim Herzog who, in my opinion, is worth a division as a morale-builder. I can only compare his broadcasts to those "Postscripts" by J.B. Priestley which rallied Britain in the dark days of 1940.

Munich architect

Despite the re-emergence of Lord Dunglass (briefly metamorphosed as the Earl of Home), one of the architects of Munich, into the corridors of power as Foreign Secretary Sir Alec Douglas-Home, we should not be misled about Britain. We can learn a lot from their conduct of the war against the Nazi evil.

One of their slogans, in those dark days, was "Britain Can Take It," generally expressed by the ordinary man in dog-Latin as: "Nil Illegitimum Carborundum" which, in translation, means "Don't let the bastards grind you down." Their common-sense, determination and humour, in the face of appalling casualties and, for a long time, complete isolation, should serve as an example to us all.

Football season started late this year.

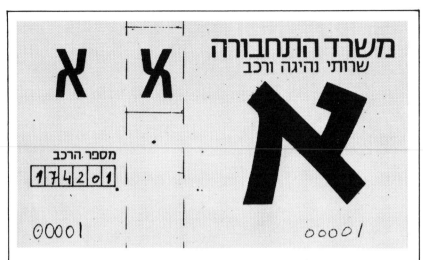

CARLESS DAY TAG: This is what your tag will look like if you choose Sunday as your carless day. The next six letters in the Hebrew alphabet will indicate the rest of the days of the week. Cars of handicapped drivers will bear tags with a "Peh," standing for patur (exempt.) The tags are to be affixed to the right-hand side of the front windshield. The left-hand tear-off section goes into the vehicle licence.

Carless days from Dec. 16

Jerusalem Post Reporter

The once-a-week carless day programme goes into effect on December 16, with each motorist choosing his own day.

A "day" for the purposes of the regulations, is the 24-hour period beginning at two a.m. and ending at two a.m. the following day. Drivers who choose Saturday will receive a bonus: they may get on the road 30 minutes after sundown rather than wait until two a.m. Sunday.

The carless day remains fixed from week to week, and if a motorist wishes to change days he must apply to the local licensing office — not earlier than six months from

his earlier choice of day.

Windshield identification tags showing the day on which the car may not be lawfully used will be distributed at post offices on presentation of the vehicle licence, between December 9 and 14. The licence will be marked with the chosen day. Persons on active duty who cannot apply to a post office personally or by proxy, will be able to get their tags at their regional licensing office whenever they can come for it.

Penalties for violation of the carless day regulations have been set at IL3,000 fine and/or suspension of licence for three months. A car caught violating the rules will be

driven to the nearest police station, and kept there until 8 a.m. the following day.

"Cars" include commercial vehicles under 2,500 kg.

The Transport Ministry's information office in Jerusalem (Tel. number 02-233305) will answer all queries concerning the carless day.

The following vehicles are exempt from the regulations: military vehicles, police cars and vans, emergency vehicles such as ambulances and fire trucks, tow cars, cars belonging to handicapped persons.

The Sabbath will be the carless day for all Netanya municipal vehicles, the city council decided yesterday.

which he called *Judophobia,* was a fixed psycho-pathological phenomenon, not just a social factor. The Jews were a ghost nation—everywhere a minority, nowhere a national majority. Everywhere "guests," nowhere "hosts."

Anti-semitism was xenophobia, hatred of the stranger, thrice multiplied. Anti-semitism was the longest lasting and the most pervasive form of this malaise.

The pogroms disabused Pinsker of the notion emerging from the Haskalah movement that if Jews

made an effort to change themselves over into the image of their Gentile neighbors, they would gain acceptance into the society of the majority culture. The Jews, declared Pinsker, were irretrievably and forever alien, not because the Jews could not assimilate, or would not assimilate, but because the majority would not let them assimilate.

It followed that the only way to solve the Jewish problem was to remove the Jews from the places where they were surrounded by hatred to a territory

TALENT EVERYWHERE BUT IN THE GOVERNMENT

The public wants answers

by EPHRAIM KISHON

WITH Arab pressure for direct negotiations increasing in view of Jerusalem's triple negative — no surrender, no full withdrawal, not before the elections — it looks as though the Israeli public has a few questions which the leadership is hard put to answer, both for want of answers and for want of a leadership.

The powers that be have apparently not yet grasped the fact that the Israeli public feels frustrated because they didn't prepare it for this war but for the one before. The public can't conceive why, after such enormous errors of judgment and such effective mismanagement, only three American Intelligence employees and Justice Minister Shapira have handed in their resignations — the first because they took our "nothing to worry about" on trust, and the Minister of Justice because they committed all the blunders without him. No one else made any mistakes, apparently.

If we can read the signs, the Judicial Inquiry Commission will sit behind closed doors for about a year, and by the time it's finished the job we'll probably have forgotten whether it was a matter of blunders or something about a Third Man or what.

The Israeli public feels lost and bewildered, though in fact it shows the sound judgment of a computer which stops working when it hasn't got the facts. The public is proud of our military achievements, all the more now it knows the odds, but refuses to accept that the aims of this war have been accomplished with the exchange of Israeli prisoners against an entire Egyptian division. The public is afraid we may give up the borders that saved our life for a "rely on me" of foreign make. The Israeli is afraid of his own self, afraid he'll opt willy-nilly for a dictated settlement.

The Israeli public is made up of three million wonderful people who've proved over and over that they can stand up to the stiffest fight and make immense sacrifices if they must. This public can bear the most painful blows. It cannot bear the thought that they were unnecessary.

It can't grasp why, when right is so obviously on its side, the whole world is against it.

It can't understand how its leaders go on as if nothing had happened.

And its leaders aren't aware of any of it.

IN times of war, prices go up and you pay more for everything. Just now we're paying in a big way for the fact that our closed party set-up, fossilized election system and outworn taxation have prevented our best brains from choosing politics as a vocation. A man who wants to soar isn't going to climb ladders. The Establishment has turned into an exclusive club. The rule of rotation was only applied where we still did have talent in our Army. Everywhere else, admission was on a strictly third-rate basis.

So now we're paying.

The thing's particulary obvious in a field where the Administration and the Army occasionally put their heads together, namely, in Information. We get the feeling sometimes that this department just doesn't exist.

Because how else explain the fact that the world doesn't know who the aggressor in our region is? Was there ever a war in which one side went so far out of its way to prove it hadn't started it? Then why the hell don't we make the point? We're licking our wounds because we sat and waited, and the whole world screams that Israeli aggression must be abolished.

To this day, the nations of the world don't know that that small paragraph about "a just settlement of the Palestinian problem" means, according to the official Palestinian standpoint, a just wiping out of the Jewish State. It's a military secret apparently.

We also take pains to save world public opinion the shock of looking at what the Syrians did to our PoWs. We've got the documents but we hide them. They're strictly for domestic consumption.

These things are handled by mediocre people.

★ ★ ★

HAVE our mentors ever considered that the Arab oil embargo ought to have ended up making the world detest the Arabs and not us? It's our best weapon, informationwise! Public opinion is bound to revolt against this moral rottenness *some* day, if only somebody ups and asks: "Look, do you really have to freeze just because a hundred million Arabs have lost every war they waged against a handful of Jews?"

There are some among us who argue that we ought to demand an end to the oil embargo before we agree to a peace conference. It's the last thing we should do. The oil's working in our favour, however crazy that may sound. Another cut in oil production in January, another trip by our Gaddafi, and the nations' fury will be laid at the proper doors till even governments won't be able to ignore their people's disgust.

We may end up yet with Saudia doing our information job for us.

This kind of reasoning, only half meant in fun, naturally demands that our leaders won't keep shouting from the rooftops about how awfully scared we are of Russian intervention, because that exactly is the big threat our persuaders beyond the ocean keep holding over our heads. It's not the only declaration made by our leaders, over and under the Knesset table, that we could very well do without.

We don't, for instance, see the point of telling the world that it isn't humanitarian motives that make us feed the Third Army. Even if it's true, why say so? And just what was the profound security calculation lying behind the announcement that we had run out of shells on the eighth day of the war?

★ ★ ★

TO judge by his performance, Professor Kissinger has more brains than all of us put together. Even so, he never moves without a few dozen brilliant, non-partisan minds in his entourage to advise him what not to do. I doubt whether he himself really belongs to any party, because he was a university don before they took him away to manage U.S. affairs. American Presidents surround themselves with the best talents available in the country without going into political account-keeping.

And with us?

With us, every decision is made by three party members in charge of the political hush-hush. No one is consulted who has not climbed *their* ladder. No professor, no genius, will be allowed into the closed circle. Just watch the frightened objections of both Establishment and Opposition to a reopening of the candidates' lists: God forbid someone from outside might get in...

This country is positively bursting with talent. You can find it everywhere except in government.

Translated by Miriam Arad
By arrangement with "Ma'ariv"

215

IN WAKE OF WAR
CRASH PROGRAMME TO TEACH ZIONISM

By SARAH HONIG
Jerusalem Post Reporter

TEL AVIV. — The Ministry of Education has embarked on a crash Zionist education and current events programme in high schools. The step was decided on after questions raised by the war and its aftermath had teachers stumped.

The Minister of Education's special assistant, Dr. Dan Ronen, told *The Jerusalem Post* that an education to Zionist values programme has been in the works for the past three years, but it is still not ready — despite the fact that it has for long been apparent that many children are getting far too little information about recent Jewish history, about the state's *raison d'etre* and about the Zionist revolution. This educational vacuum was especially noticeable during the war, when bewildered youngsters started confronting their teachers with such questions as "till when will we have to fight?" "is there something wrong with us that the world is always against us?" "why is there no peace here?" and "what are we fighting for and is it worth dying for?".

We put it to Dr. Ronen that something must be very much amiss in our educational system if there were no ready answers to such very basic questions. He agreed that very often the teachers themselves had only a scant superficial knowledge of Zionism, its philosophy, values and history, and could hardly pass on to their pupils what they themselves did not possess. This, he admitted, makes the pupils easy prey for extremists, particularly from the left, including such groups as Matzpen and Siah.

"There is obviously a great danger in the possibility that the school will not be providing children with answers and with the ability to judge issues, to form opinions intelligently and to resist demagogic propaganda. If we don't give them answers, some one else will and they may be completely vulnerable without any means of their own to evaluate what they hear," Dr. Ronen says.

Why were things allowed to deteriorate on this front while Ministry experts were busy putting together sophisticated courses of study? we asked.

Dr. Ronen replied that the Ministry was hampered by the general atmosphere in the country. There was a tendency to put quotation marks around the word "Zionism." We felt that the Zionist aim had been achieved with the founding of the State. We must now remove the ironic quotation marks and stress that the Zionist revolution is by no means completed, that it is an ongoing process and that not all of the Jewish people's problems have been solved.

"We must strengthen understanding of the ties between the pupils and the world's Jews as well as enrich their awareness and appreciation of the Jewish heritage," he said. "We will try to give the teacher a far more active role. He will now be less neutral and try to have the children identify with Jewish and Zionist values. But," he admitted, "these are rather long range goals."

The Ministry's pedagogic secretariat is now working on them. As he has it, it will still take some time before it puts the finishing touches on the teaching material it is putting together. Its staff is currently working on monographs about the history of Jewish settlement, about pre-state organizations, about pre-State leaders and about their philosophies.

For the very immediate future the Ministry's crash programme is mainly geared to providing factual information. Thus, there will be classroom explanations about the energy crisis, about the situation at the front, about the worldwide solidarity of the Jewish people, about the aims of the Jewish state, about the Geneva peace conference, about how to interpret the news and even about what a rumour is. This will, according to Ministry of Education policy makers, provide the pupils with the basic tools with which to form opinions of their own.

The second stage will be to hold discussions on topical issues, as well as try to reply to questions about Zionism and Israel's history. Dr. Ronen, who promised that the Ministry will see to it that the embarrassing incident of the pamphlet advising teachers to prepare their pupils for the emotional shock of returning the territories will not be repeated, also promised that in these discussions the teachers will not force the views of any political party on the youngsters.

But he also admitted that as most of the children's knowledge is scant, the technique of classroom discussion and of group dynamics cannot be overdone. "It must not be exaggerated. This is what has caused much of the crisis with American youth during the 1960s," he said.

"We have to be very careful not to give a child the feeling that he is omniscient. Otherwise the result will be a discussion not based on values, knowledge and experience, but an all-round sharing of ignorance. This must be avoided at all cost," he said.

INQUIRY COMMISSION—YOM KIPPUR

PURSUANT TO THE INQUIRY COMMISSIONS LAW, 1968

ANNOUNCEMENT BY THE COMMISSION

In accordance with a decision of the Government made November 18, 1973, the Commission has been charged with investigating the following subjects —

1. The information available during the days preceding the Yom Kippur War regarding the activities of the enemy and the enemy's intentions to start a war, and also the assessments of this information made by the authorized military and civilian authorities, and their consequent decisions.

2. The general state of preparedness of the Israel Defence Forces, the preparedness of the I.D.F. during the days preceding the Yom Kippur War, and the I.D.F.'s operations up to the time the enemy was halted.

Anyone wishing to give evidence or to submit to the Commission any document or other exhibit, relevant to the subjects of the inquiry, should provide the Commission with a written summary of his evidence, a statement of the content of the document, or a description of the exhibit he wishes to submit.

I.D.F. soldiers of all ranks may apply to the Commission, without going through a superior officer.

The summary of the evidence, the statement of the content of the document, or the description of the exhibit should be sent to the Commission, P.O.B. 1251, Jerusalem.

The Commission will consider all summaries of evidence, statements of the content of documents, and descriptions of exhibits, and will decide whether to regard such written material as sufficient, or to invite the person applying to give oral evidence.

Judge D. Bartov
Secretary to the Commission

Protestant church groups in Geneva support Israel

Two Protestant church groups in Geneva, with a total membership of about 200,000, have issued a statement supporting Israel's right to secure borders. This was reported yesterday by the Rev. Claude Duvernoy of Jerusalem, following his return from a two-week visit to Geneva.

The groups are The Free Evangelical Church and the Assembly of the Revival Churches, which also has parishes in France.

They have decided to launch a fund to aid Israeli children whose fathers fell in the war.

In their statement, the two churches urged the Arab countries to absorb the Palestinian refugees and protested against the refusal of the International Red Cross to recognize Israel's Star of David emblem although it recognizes the Red Crescent of the Arab states.

APPEAL FOR ALIYA

To the Editor of The Jerusalem Post

Sir, — Following the publication of messages of solidarity and intended continuation of support by the various missions at present visiting Israel, may I add my own welcome and deliver my own appeal to the leaders of these missions.

They are indeed welcome to be with us to witness the results of their unstinting efforts and study our further needs. I am positive that a realistic study of the situation can only lead to one conclusion. That is, whatever moneys are raised can only be a blood transfusion, a medication that keeps the patient alive, but does not and will not cure the ailment.

The ailment is lack of population. Nothing, not blood, not money, not sympathy, will ever replace our heroic and beloved fallen. We need people to take their place and more. I suggest that the Yom Kippur War is final and conclusive proof, if proof was needed, that now is the time of decision.

Leaders of the missions which visited Israel must not allow history to shake its head in bewilderment at the dereliction of the Jewish People, who witnessed the miracle of the rebirth and building up of our State and did not make more than a feeble effort to take part physically in the consolidation of this miracle. If a further miracle is possible, it is only they who can help to achieve it through aliya.

NORMAN COHEN
Netanya, November 23.

217

Distraught mother being pushed back by policeman, and being restrained by her daughter.

A demonstration during one of Kissinger's visits. One of the signs reads: "For the sake of peace, return our boys." Another asks: "Kissinger! What of your promise?" Still another declares: "Kissinger! Our sons are not to be discounted!"

'No one cares or understands'
RELATIVES OF MISSING STORM KNESSET GATES

By ASHER WALLFISH
Jerusalem Post Knesset Reporter

Several dozen relatives of missing soldiers forced their way past Knesset guards yesterday morning, through the Palombo Gates, and up to the entrance of the building, to protest that the Government was neglecting their plight.

They threatened to burst into the building itself and wreck the place, demanding that Premier Golda Meir or Defence Minister Moshe Dayan appear to hear their pleas and answer them. They also demanded that food supplies to the encircled Egyptian Third Army be halted till Egypt and Syria free all the Israeli prisoners.

A few of the more overwrought among the demonstrators said they were giving the Premier and the Defence Minister "a one-hour ultimatum," to appear or to act. They broke several windows in the office by the Palombo Gates and a plate-glass door at the Knesset members' entrance. Many were shouting and sobbing.

The Knesset guards and ushers who sensed the plight of the relatives of the missing abstained from use of force, and seemed torn between their sympathies and their duties. Policemen and women were called in, and stood by a considerable distance away.

One young man was taken to the Magen David Adom clinic with cuts caused by broken glass. An ambulance waited in the Knesset parking area. It was not needed.

A delegation of the relatives went inside the building at noon, when a crowd of 80 or 100 was still outside the Palombo Gates. They spoke to six M.K.s of various factions. Their main complaint was that, from the very first day, when they feared their relatives were missing, they encountered deaf ears and "harshly inconsiderate" replies in their contacts with the town majors. They endured one run-around after another, they complained. It seemed as though nobody cared, nobody understood, and nobody was in charge, the delegation said.

After the crowd surged through the Palombo Gates to the building entrance itself, a second delegation went inside to talk to Speaker Yisrael Yeshayahu — whereupon the rest calmed down somewhat.

The Speaker came out and said he had tried in vain to arrange meetings between the relatives and Premier Meir and Mr. Dayan for the same day. But he promised he would arrange for delegations to meet both of them within 36 hours, and he would convey all the complaints to the appropriate military authorities. He would urge that every family get a chance, as soon as possible, to talk their problems out face to face with the army officers who could give them an answer.

Interior Minister Yosef Burg, who happened to be in the building and had sat in on the talk between the Speaker and the delegation, also tried his best to calm the crowd.

Both the Speaker and the Minister were constantly interrupted by bitter shouts and reproaches, in a confrontation unprecedented for its unrestrained emotions on Knesset premises. Finally the crowd agreed to select delegations to meet with the Premier and the Defence Minister whenever this could be arranged, and meanwhile to draft questions to put to them.

PROTEST CANCELLED

The demonstration originally planned to take place outside the Knesset yesterday had been cancelled when the Knesset session on the plight of prisoners of war and missing soldiers was postponed.

A few of yesterday's crowd had not heard of the cancellation, and a handful turned up despite the cancellation.

The scene became violent when a group of several dozen Beit Shemesh residents joined the crowd. They had never intended to demonstrate. They had gone to the Mount Herzl Military Cemetery in the morning, with a printed invitation from the military authorities, to mourn two soldiers from their town.

At Mount Herzl they did not find a grave with the name of one of the soldiers and, on asking an IDF officer, were told his name was not on the list. The officer then took away their invitation. The mourning family, accompanied by its friends and neighbours, crazed with grief and feeling itself spurned and belittled, at once rushed to the Knesset, still carrying the flowers they had brought for the non-existent grave.

Throughout the six or seven hours the crowd was at the Knesset, more complaints were voiced over the matter of the missing soldiers — whose fate had been unknown or concealed till recently — than over the case of the prisoners of war. Some demanded intensive efforts to search for the bodies of the dead.

---

of their own where they would become an independent nation. Pinsker favored a refuge that would be readily available for settlement, and expressed preferment for the American continent, in which, at the time, there were huge unoccupied areas of land.

Other leaders of Hovevei Zion, in deep agreement with Pinsker's theoretical formulations, nevertheless responded more strongly to their emotional ties to Palestine.

In the early 1880s, their fervor set in motion the first emigration.

Since Jerusalem is situated on a hill, every Biblical reference advises pilgrims to "Go up to Jerusalem." In time, the literal reference to physical ascent took on a spiritual connotation. "Going up (to Jerusalem)" came to signify a dedication to a higher cause. The emigration to Israel thus became known as "the first going up," in Hebrew, "The First *Aliyah*." This first emigration was

The Long Trail Home

Uri Ehrenfeld, one of the P.o.W.s captured by the Egyptians when the pocket of Israelis who held out on the Port Tewfik pier surrendered, is back in Israel.

ALL THE TIME he worried about what was happening to his country and his friends.

"I knew that the Northern front was all right, that Israel was close to Damascus, but I thought that Israel was being defeated on the Canal. I knew that we were the last to hold out on the Line. There was a fog over everything. I told myself that Zahal would somehow win in the end; I clung to my faith in Zahal and in God. On the other hand, the Egyptians kept telling me during the interrogations that the whole of Sinai was in their hands, that Israel had suffered 17,000 dead."

Uri fainted many times from lack of food and water, and from the beatings. He could not tell how long he was kept tied and blindfolded. He does not remember anything clearly except for the last fortnight; the rest is a blur of pain and privation. Even now, he cannot work out how many days he spent under these horrendous conditions of captivity.

At one stage he talked over Radio Cairo.

"I don't remember what I said. They kept me without water for hours, told me they'd give me all the water I wanted if I talked over the radio. They gave me a prepared document to read — anti-Israel, anti-Dayan. Afterwards, they gave me a small glass of water."

One of the people who picked up the broadcast was a Druse in Galilee, who at once phoned and also wrote to Uri's parents.

DURING the last two weeks, conditions improved considerably. He was given more food and water — the same kind of food as the Egyptians themselves got, mainly *pitta* and rice, but in smaller quantities than the Egyptians received. Blankets and a cigarette-thin mattress were issued to him. His clothes were changed for the first time, and he was allowed his first shower. All the time he was in captivity, he was allowed only two showers. Although still kept in isolation, the blindfolds and bonds were removed, and he met his comrades sometimes in the

toilets. Through a small peephole in his door, Uri was able to see something of what was going on outside his narrow cell. But the first time he saw a cigarette was when he was visited by the Red Cross — the only such visit — on the day before he was sent home. There was nothing to read. No letters or parcels were handed to him.

"I prayed a lot," recalls Uri. "It helped me a great deal — a very great deal — that I am religious and had something in which to believe. I don't think that I would have got through those 35 days without my belief. When I felt a little better, I did a few exercises."

THE SMALL GROUP of Nahal paratroopers who held the Port Tewfik pier for a week, until they were ordered by Zahal to abandon

PHILIP GILLON

the hopeless fight and surrender, consisted at first of 42 men. Five of them were killed; most of the others were wounded. They still had adequate supplies of food and water, but ammunition was running very low, and, says Private Uri Ehrenfeld, they could not have carried on for long even if they had not been told to surrender.

Most of the 42 were Orthodox, as is Uri himself. They came from different units, and had been concentrated at Port Tewfik because of the high holidays.

Uri, the son of Professor Nahum Ehrenfeld, head of the Clinical Endocrinology Department at the Hadassah University Hospital, will turn 20 in a few weeks' time. He is now in Hadassah undergoing tests for internal injuries sustained in innumerable beatings. At one time it seemed he might require an operation, but his father hopes that this can be avoided.

On the day of the surrender by the Israelis to the Red Cross, the behaviour of the Egyptians started off being as impeccable as any gentleman in Geneva could desire. Of course, at that stage the "Newsweek" representative and other reporters were present to witness the Israeli ignominy. After the Israelis had been taken across the Canal, the Egyptians had another idea, and the Israeli commander was instructed to pick two men to go back with him across the water to salute the Egyptian flag as it was raised on the last redoubt of the foremost section of the Bar-Lev Line. One of the two he took with him was Uri.

Immediately the flag-saluting ceremony was over, and the Red Cross and newsmen had departed, the Egyptians' copy of the Geneva Convention was thrown into the Canal. Uri was blindfolded and bound, his boots and socks were taken away, and everything portable was stolen from him, including even his skull-cap. Taken to a port somewhere in Egypt, still bound and blindfolded, he was kept isolated in a cell six feet by six in area. He was given very little food or water, and he had no blankets. He was beaten incessantly, apparently at whim, with no specific reason given to him why he was being savaged.

The attitude of some of the warders changed considerably as time passed. The more compassionate among them gave Uri a little extra food, and talked to him. They swopped dirty jokes, discussed Judaism, the possibility of peace ever breaking out between Jew and Arab. The day before the PoWs left Egypt, two Saturdays ago, his clothes were changed for the second time.

URI HOLDS NONE of the views he voiced over Radio Cairo.

"I don't blame Dayan or anyone else for what happened to us — war is like that. One side always catches the other by surprise — this happens in every war. People get killed, wounded, taken prisoner. There isn't a new type of Egyptian soldier. They are still 20 years behind us; the only thing is that the Russians have given them better arms. If they had been better soldiers, we couldn't have held out as long as we did."

He hopes, like everyone in Israel, that peace will result from the present negotiations, although he doesn't see how the trick will be worked.

"It's hard to believe that the Arabs will ever make real peace with us. Still, I'm a great optimist by nature, I keep hoping. As to the areas, I think we should be prepared to give up part of Sinai — even most of it — in order to get a settlement with the Egyptians. But Jerusalem? Hebron? Certainly not. And the Golan — also not."

Somewhat surprisingly, he has never thought deeply about the problem of the Palestinian Arabs.

"They asked me about the Palestinians while I was in Egypt. I can't say that I know the answer. Certainly not to give them back East Jerusalem or Hebron. It's a very difficult problem."

Uri's *garin* is linked to kibbutz Kfar Etzion, but he had already decided not to join the kibbutz at the end of his army service. Before the war, he had planned to go to the Hebrew University to study geography and English.

"But now I don't think I'll go on with it — somehow it seems rather pointless, studying English and geography. And I don't want to be a doctor, like my father. And yet I don't see myself going to a yeshiva or a kibbutz. Really, I don't know what I'll do. I've been in the army two-and-a-half years: we still don't know what Zahal will want from us. When I finish, I'll try to decide what to do with my life."

Uri Ehrenfeld, an Israeli paratrooper captured by Egypt and returned in the POW exchange.

The Great Silence...

Friedrich Duerrenmatt

THERE IS silence among the writers. The great name-signers don't sign their names any more.

It was easy to sign protests against the war in Vietnam, against the occupation of Czechoslovakia and against the overthrow of Allende; of course you would stand up for Solzhenitsyn and Sakharov. Being involved with the left, you would want to have an at least halfway decent left. But you better not protest against the new Arab-Israeli war; in the end you might be confused with Hans Habe or Axel Springer. The result is silence.

For years it has been fashionable to dismiss the Israelis as fascists and to regard the Palestinian terrorists as heroes moved by sheer despair to do what they are doing (as if there were no pleasure in terrorism). The good-and-evil system of coordinates set up by the intellectual left has prevailed in all but the rightest of rightist publications and has become the moral currency of the world.

Still, even the densest ideologists — unless they have to be ideologists as they do in the East — realized that it was impossible to fit the new Arab-Israeli war into the Procrustean bed of ideologies.

The reasons for their embarrassment are clear. Israel's policies before the war were in many ways wrong (that is an opinion I still hold). And I also believe that pitted against each other in this tragic conflict were two just causes. But the wrong policies of Israel have paradoxically been justified by the Arab attack on the Jewish Day of Atonement, a conclusion which makes a thinking person shudder.

"Appeal to reason" is a phrase that enjoys currency where there is no reason. The winner did not know how to win and the loser did not know how to lose. The winner put justice on the side of the loser, and now, afterward, the loser returns justice to the winner's side.

The Arabs should not try to fool us. In 1967 they wanted to attack Israel but couldn't because Israel anticipated them. They have been wanting to attack Israel ever since. The difference is that now, having become better soldiers, they were able to attack.

But just because we need their oil, we don't have to buy their lies. Had Israel accepted the United Nations resolution, there still would have been war, only Israel's military position would have been that much more desperate. And knowing that — besides enormous amounts of blood — a little more ink had flowed for her sake, would have been wretched consolation.

This supposition will look monstrous only to those who haven't yet been able to understand that we live in a monstrous world, a world in which there is nothing more cynical than peace.

Only those can afford peace who no longer can afford war — the great industrial powers and the superpowers. The superpowers engage in subsidiary wars — as they do currently, if reluctantly, in their Mideast war — while the small countries must manage with peace.

That Israel, as a small country, always has to afford war — that is her tragedy. But the Arabs, with their oil, can afford any war. Soon we shall finance even this one for them.

For the Arabs nothing was more inopportune than a detente, even a detente between two corrupt superpowers. No sooner did Brezhnev put his arms around Nixon than the Arabs struck — had to strike — a successful blow.

The Russians supply the Arabs with arms, and the United States, perforce, supplies the Israelis. The Arabs blackmail both sides at once — and if this should lead to a world war, it was Allah's will all along.

Not only the Israelis but we, too, have underestimated the Arabs: A people steeped in an old culture cleverly managed to play a political trick on all of us.

No protest rallies, no speeches, as there still were during the Six Day War. Amid the embarrassed silence of the West and the howling applause of the East, the Arab lambs tried to devour the Jewish wolf.

With these words I want to put myself behind Israel, for the sake of Israel and for the sake of all of us. For Israel as a matter of decency. For all of us so we won't soon all be silent.

This article by the famous Swiss playwright orginally appeared in the "Neue Züriche Zeitung."

composed entirely of European Jews who derived mainly from Rumania, Russia, Poland, and the Austro-Hungarian Empire.

In July of 1882, Zalman Levontin, one of the leaders of the Havevei Zion movement, left Kharkov, Russia, with a small group, to establish a settlement in Palestine. They purchased a tract of 835 acres of land from the Arabs. Here they began an agricultural settlement, which they called *Rishon le Zion,* First in Zion.

Shortly thereafter, another agricultural settlement was established in the very north of Palestine by settlers from Rumania. It was called *Rosh Pinah* (Cornerstone). Also at the same time, the settlement of *Petah Tikvah* (The Gates of Hope) was founded by a group of Jews who had been living in Jerusalem.

However, their meager funds, their inability to adapt to the rigorous climatic conditions, their unfamiliarity with local agricultural requirements, and the harassment of the marauding Bedouin, proved too much to cope with. The settlers needed help.

Their sponsoring societies in Russia and in Rumania could provide no assistance.

An appeal was sent to France to Baron de Rothschild, an extremely affluent French nobleman and philanthropist, who was Jewish.

And so most of the early Jewish settlements in Palestine came under the aegis of Rothschild. Under his sponsorship, the colonies persevered, and ultimately flourished.

Historians have entertained, if inconclusively, the argument of whether an individual makes history,

Jews have always been a lone

To the Editor of The Jerusalem Post

Sir, — We in Britain see and hear Israelis describe their feelings at the events of recent weeks and the attitude of almost every government in the world towards Israel. Let me tell Israeli Jews that the Jews in Britain feel exactly the same as they do. You have an advantage of being physically involved; we are frustrated. On the other hand we can, and do, constantly let our M.P.s and our craven political leaders know what we, as Jews and as British citizens, think of their immoral conduct. Although we may live 2,000 miles away, our thoughts, minds and feelings are as one with you — we are one people. Your losses are our losses, your worries are our worries.

We say to you: Fight again if you believe it better to risk more lives now than 3 million in a few years' time. Do not concern yourselves with foreign opinion or "isolation." Since when have Jews ever been anything but alone? Whatever you decide, fight or stand fast or negotiate, do it from strength, secure in the knowledge that your decisions will be ours. We are and will be 100 per cent behind you and, should you say the word, we shall be alongside you as quickly as it takes to travel to the Jewish Homeland. **L. MARX**
Cockfosters, Herts., November 10.

We the undersigned* call upon the citizens of Israel to join us and sign the following petition:

PEACE INITIATIVE NOW!

- The Yom Kippur War exposed the illusion and errors of the politics of stalemate and creeping annexation which did not lead to peace and did not prevent war.
- In the wake of the cease-fire, a historical opportunity for peace has arisen.
- In the absence of peace, further wars are to be expected, possibly even more difficult and cruel than the Yom Kippur War.
- Israel should take the initiative in immediately formulating a realistic peace plan.
- Israel's security will not be achieved by annexation and/or occupation of territories but through peace agreements, creation of demilitarized zones and increasing the strength and vigilance of Israel's Defence Forces.
- Peace is more important to us than territories.
- Israel should recognize the existence of the Arab Palestine people and help promote their participation in the peace efforts.
- The new situation requires a leadership, capable of exploring without misgivings all avenues leading to peace.

The initiators of the petition are: Simcha BAHIRI (Netanya), Chanan EIT (Beersheba), Gordon LANGHOLZ (Ramat Gan), Dov SITON (Beersheba Yoram ROSENBERG (Tel Aviv).

Yakov AGMON
Gila ALMAGOR
Prof. Daniel AMIT
Yossi AMITAI
Prof. Aharon ANTONOVSKY
Dr. Yakov ARNON
Prof. David ASHRI
Emmanuel BAR-KADMA
Dan BITAN
Prof. Chaim BLANK
Dr. Pinhas BLUMENTAL
Heda BOSHES
Ori BERNSTEIN
Dr. Menahem BRINKER
Prof. Michael BRUNO
Baruch CHEFETS
Nahum COHEN
Yitzhak DAGAN
Zvi DEKEL
Nina DINUR
Latif DORI
Eliyahu DRUKMAN
Michael DRUKS

Prof. Moshe HILL
Prof. Zeev HIRSCH
Dr. Yehoach HIRSCHBERG
Ella HOFFMANN
Theodore HOLDHEIM
Dr. Tikva HONIG-FRANS
Yair HOROWITS
Dr. Dov IZRAELI
Dr. Yossi IZRAELI
Yoram KANIUK
Dr. Kurt KANOVITS
Dr. Olga KAPELIUK
Dani KARAVAN
Zvi KESSE
Dr. Naomi KIS
Ran KISLEV
Hellen KOPILEVITCH
Oded KOTLER
Dr. Zvi LAM
Nina LANIR
Dr. Israel LEF
Dan LEON
David LEVIN
Uri LIFSCHITS

Prof. Chanan OPPENHEIMER
Mordechai OREN
General (Mil.) Matityahu PELE
Lr. Yochanan PERES
Menachem PERRY
Prof. Nahum POZNER
Prof. Erwin RABAU
Prof. Amos RICHMOND
Dr. Yossef SADAN
Shmuel SEGAL
Moshe SFADI
Dr. Uri SHAFRIR
David SHAHAM
Dr. Tsilla SHECHTER
Yoel SHECHTER
Prof. Akiva E. SIMON
Dr. Nahum SNEH
Dr. Sasson SOMECH
Prof. Gavriel STEIN
Yitzhak TAUB
Raoul TITELBAUM
Dan TSALKA
Ygal TUMARKIN
Prof. Amos TVERSKI

*Call for review of security doctrine;
various methods for assuring safety; not only territorial changes*

THE WINDOWS SHOULD BE OPENED

Abba Eban

IT IS hard to believe that less than two months have passed since Yom Kippur. The world in which we lived before that day, recedes further and further into a distant haze of recollection. The war has shaken Israelis out of the images and ways of thought in which they had lived for over six years. Nothing now seems more discordant than the slogans and vocabulary that seemed adequate at the beginning of last month. Since all these became suddenly obsolete in a single week — the intellectual and emotional shock is hard to sustain. We are summoned almost overnight to a far-reaching reconstruction of our conceptual world.

The paradox is that the agonized national debate goes forward within the objective reality of triumph. There has been no decline in the typical Israeli virtues — tenacity, courage, responsibility, self-sacrifice, pragmatic resourcefulness and above all — an immense power of recuperation.

If these qualities had failed, we would have been overwhelmed. Because they existed o u r forces were able to embark on a brilliant thrust which pushed the tide of aggression away from our gates. Without these successes in the field there would have been no cease-fire, and the Arab Governments would not have agreed to negotiate at a Peace Conference. My experience tells me this: whenever I hear a cease-fire being seriously discussed at the United Nations I know that Israeli forces are doing very well. When Israel was hard-pressed and in peril, the idea of a cease-fire was regarded by most delegates at East River as an eccentric joke.

The sombre and reflective mood of our nation today is a tribute to its realism and emotional integrity. But it should not be carried to an apocalyptic degree. We have not been defeated or conquered; our non-combatant population was spared the worst rigours of war; and the Arab attacks did not achieve their military aims. Indeed, it is hard to imagine how combined assault forces of 5,000 tanks and 1,300 aircraft with vast missile support and the advantage of surprise could ever achieve a more meagre or negative result than the result reflected in the difference between the October 5 cease-fire lines and lines of today

YET WHEN all is said and remembered this is a victory without celebration. In other arenas of combat little counts except the final result: and if the final result is victory — who cares how the score stood at half-time? But war is not like any other form of rivalry or competition or conflict. Here the hazard is nothing less than human lives. So Israel looks sadly on its own victory. We understand that the perils of the first week are just as much a political reality as the triumph of the subsequent days. It has in some degree modified the standards by which the world appraises Israelis and Arabs — and by which they appraise each other. It appears that the uniquely crushing extent of our 1967 triumph — a hundred per cent Israeli victory and a hundred per cent Arab defeat — was not an authentic or permanent reflection of the real military balance.

Arabs and Israelis should not have constructed their images of what they and we are in accordance with that particular encounter. I still hold that our nation retains a remarkable preponderance in those elements of strength which counterbalance the quantitative superiority of those arrayed against us. But if the gap is wide, we should not believe that it is unlimited or infinite.

The danger, of course, is lest we allow the pendulum to swing too far — from excessive buoyancy to an excessive pessimism, which would be sterile in its results and unfounded in objective fact.

The sudden need to achieve a new proportion in our relationship to our environment is chastening enough. But it is not our only, or even our primary ordeal. When we speak of a sense of irreplaceable loss we mean the thousands of lives lost and crippled. Let this be clear: nothing else is irreplaceable, and therefore nothing else can be put on the same level of discussion as this. The tanks and aircraft and guns can be replaced — and by the grace of our partnership with the United States, *they have been and are being replaced*. The money can be replenished, the lost production can be made up, and with the transition from war to a more stable order of relations, many political positions can be regained or fortified. Families in Israel are not coming together to mourn a tank or a plane or an African embassy or a depleted exchequer. We have many categories of adversity to overcome: but we should be false to our humanistic values if we evaded the uniqueness and centrality of the specific anguish arising

from the loss of the only thing that can never be replaced. It may be comforting for some and convenient for others to consider this human tragedy in the context of other disappointments from which no loss of life has ensued. But our Jewish instinct commands us to see the spectacle of death as an experience of unique scope. It involves responsibilities and moral predicaments that cannot be emulated or shared in any other context whatever.

The October war brought us face to face with the crisis of our human vulnerability. Anyone who reads or writes about Jewish history comes up against this preoccupation again and again. The special pathos of Jewish history lies in the immense place occupied by the problem of being Jewish and yet staying alive. The Israelis who have given their lives in this war compound a previous toll — of those who were lost in 1967 and 1956 and 1948, and in the attrition and violence in between. And these memories are enacted against the dark and unforgotten background of the Holocaust with its six million martyrs. There is no other national experience even remotely similar to this.

Perhaps this is one of the factors that makes Israel's security "obsessions" so hard for others to grasp. And even when the right of individual Jewish survival has been secured in some places and some generations, we have stood before the other Jewish predicament: how to survive in our collective identity, in our own image, our own frame of values, our own particularity, our own faith and tongue — in short in our own nationhood. How rarely have the twin rights of individual and collective survival been a matter of course for Jews for any length of time!

In a country with these memories and these conditions, it is not surprising that the national security doctrine should be the decisive element in the nation's life and policy. Since 1967 our security doctrine was clear. We had sufficient preponderance to deter any likely assault; or if an assault took place to defeat it with such speed and, therefore, with such little cost as to strengthen our power of deterrence still further. In that event there would be no time or occasion for the conflict to get caught up in the Great Power rivalries, so that Israel's autonomy of political movement would remain intact. With no hope of changing the established situation by force, our neighbours would find negotiation to be their only option.

So long as this appraisal of the military balance was valid, all the other aspects of Israel's official policy were at least intellectually coherent whether anyone accepted them or not. Israel's policy, diplomacy, posture, as well as her social and domestic priorities all fell into place. Once the first link in the sequence of assumptions fails to stand firm, nothing else is solid, and the whole chain comes under the need of review.

The review cannot afford to stare into the future and turn its back on the past. "He who does not remember the past is doomed to repeat it." The truth is that even our pre-war policies were sometimes undermined by being taken out of their own balance and proportion. A doctrine based on absolute confidence caused the national style and rhetoric to become overly strident. Domestic rivalries led to the proliferation of maximalist statements. Israel's rights and claims, legitimate in themselves, were often proclaimed in a vacuum, without a due attempt to bring them into harmony with the rights and claims of others. It was properly recognized — as it still must be — that previous borders must be changed or adapted in such manner as to give Israel a strong chance of withstanding the first momentum of an assault. The October experience, if anything, reinforces this principle. But this does not mean that it was right for many Israelis to present the position of boundaries as the sole condition of security, rather than as one of its conditions.

AN INTEGRAL SECURITY doctrine would include, along with the territorial component, such elements as the balance of forces, the vigilance and spirit of defenders, precision in organization, the technical productivity of the economy, the moral quality of the public sector as a whole, the ability to draw strength from external connections. It was not everywhere realised that without these our security would be undermined no matter what boundaries we had. Those who listened to what was said from many platforms might have attributed to us — quite wrongly — the fallacious belief that a list of the places which we would never abandon constituted in itself a total and adequate statement of our national policy.

The style of the national rhetoric became an immensely important element in the formation of policy and in determining Israel's policy abroad, including in places where vital security interests could be affected by decisions outside our sovereign control. It was not always taken into account that policy should be directed not only to making the enemy unable to fight us again, but also to the hope of making him unwilling to fight us again. The logic of war is power, and power has no inherent limit. The logic of peace is proportion, and proportion implies limitation. Deterrence and persuasion are not incompatible. But their combination implies a certain restraint.

Meanwhile on the fringes of our political spectrum some illusions were sprouting fast. (Alas! They did not always remain on the fringes. They sometimes invaded the centre.) These were not at all inherent in our official policy, but they often threatened to swamp and silence the official voices. I mean the illusion that the cease-fire could exist indefinitely in a diplomatic vacuum, with no constancy of political activity. I mean the illusion that a million Arabs would be kept under Israeli control forever provided that their economic and social welfare was impressively advanced; the illusion that Zionism forbade a sharing of national sovereignty between two nations in the former Palestine Mandate area; the illusion that Israel's historic legacy was exclusively a matter of geography and not also, and principally, a heritage of prophetic values of which the central value was peace. The fallacy that to see anything temporary in some of Israel's positions west of the Jordan was tantamount to alienation from the Biblical culture. The fallacy that a nation could not be strong unless it demonstrated its toughness in every contingency.

WE SHOULD NOT underestimate the provocations from outside which made all these things understandable. The task before us today is to rebuild our concepts and our style in the sequel of the terrible drama that we have lived. This does not mean that we should jettison everything from our past attitudes, whether valid or not. I see a real peril both in extreme tangential departures — and in continuing inertia. But it does mean that the windows should be opened, for I believe that there is a new air to breathe. We should not abandon the idea of strategic depth to protect our populated centres. But there is a versatile range of methods by which this can be achieved — sometimes but not always by territorial change. The problem can be aggravated if we think of erecting vast population centres deep in Sinai — and then look for additional strategic depth to defend them — and so on to infinity — or absurdity.

These and other problems will arise in the new context of the Peace Conference. There is no reason to be rhapsodic about this prospect — for the intrinsic difficulties are immense, and dialogue does not make peace inevitable. It does, however, make it less improbable. Our national Jewish experience makes it inevitable that in most situations we should be more aware of risks than of opportunities. But the duty of leadership must sometime transcend the national experience and not be committed to it to the point of inertia. Our task is to bridge the gap between our nation's experience and its vision, between our tradition and our future. The peace conference

must be approached as an opportunity and not only as a danger. The readiness of Arab States to break a long inhibition and to enter a civilized negotiating context could of course turn out to be illusory. But it could also be significant and even revolutionary. Only a positivist approach can put the issue to a valid test. We should construct a model of a Middle East without enemies, a community of sovreign states united in a regional devotion. The prospect may be far, but the architect makes a picture of the finished structure before he begins arduously to build.

THESE QUESTIONS are destined to be resolved in our Israeli society in the coming months with our characteristic intensity. I could wish that they might be discussed with some calmness and coolness, even with some tenderness and mutual compassion, for grief has struck in every camp and every party. There is an excessive personalization of the public debate. This also belongs to the particular heritage of the past decade. For the future let us recognize that virulent gossip is no substitute for candid analysis. Leadership has the duty of creating an atmosphere conducive to the expression of diverse and sometimes disconcerting ideas.

Text of address to the Conference of Presidents of the major Jewish organizations in the U.S. and Canada delivered in Jerusalem on Tuesday before the Labour Party formulated its new election platform on security and peace.

---

or whether the times bring forth the man. Answer this, if you can, in the case of Theodore Herzl, the founder of political Zionism.

Herzl was born in 1860 in Budapest. When he was 10 years old, he announced his intention to build a canal across Panama to link the Atlantic and the Pacific Oceans. At age 14, he founded a students' literary club.

When he was 18, his sister died, and his family moved to Vienna, where Herzl enrolled at the University in the Faculty of Law. Three years later, Herzl joined *Albia,* a German student fraternal society. After two years, he left the society in protest against the anti-semitism he had encountered there. His protest had nothing of the casual about it.

When Karl Lueger was appointed Mayor of Vienna on an anti-semitic platform, after Kaiser

Franz Josef had three times previously vetoed Lueger's election, Herzl was shocked. That such a party could prevail in cosmopolitan Vienna! From that point on, the Jewish problem occupied his deepest attention.

Herzl, it may be noted, also wrote plays, some of which had successful runs on Austrian and German stages. Some of his plays were humorous, others serious; all dealt with timely social questions. A man of superior imagination, Herzl even fantasied about the possibility of leading all the Jews to the Great Cathedral of Saint Steven in Vienna where their baptism would make an end, once and for all, to anti-semitism. But he knew it wouldn't work. Anti-semites hate Jews even after Jews have been totally assimilated.

From 1891 to 1895, Herzl served as the Paris

SABBATH—No Publication

Yigal Allon, then Deputy Prime Minister, facing a barrage of demonstrators outside of the Prime Minister's residence.

correspondent of the Vienna Neue Freie Presse, the influential liberal newspaper of the day.

It was the Dreyfus case that led Herzl irrevocably to his life's work. He witnessed that cause célèbre as the correspondent for his newspaper, and observed the riotous behavior of the Parisian mob when the falsely accused Jewish officer was publicly humiliated in a ceremony stripping him of his military rank. This impressive rite occurred on January 5, 1895, accompanied by shouts of "Death to the Jews."

It was then that Herzl became convinced that the only solution to the Jewish problem lay in the mass exodus of the Jews from their countries of residence, countries infested by ineradicable anti-semitism, to a territory of their own. He decided to apply himself to the realization of his idea.

As though driven by a superior force, his every thought was devoted to this aim, "Am I working it out?" he asks in his diary. "No, it is working itself out through me. It would be an obsession if it were not so rational from beginning to end. This is what used to be called inspiration." These notes became the first draft of his seminal work *Der Judenstaat,* a book which Herzl completed in 1895.

When Herzl read the draft of his proposal for the founding of a Jewish homeland to his friend Friedrich Shiff, a medical man and a journalist, the doctor feared that Herzl had suffered a nervous breakdown. He counseled rest; he even hinted Herzl had gone insane.

At this time, Herzl went to see the Rothschilds to recruit them to his cause. He suggested that their wealth, which roused the envy of the Gentile

---

RESPONSE TO ARAB OIL MINISTERS

Dutch reject call for anti-Israel gesture

BRUSSELS (UPI). — Holland yesterday turned down Arab demands that it make a special anti-Israeli "gesture" to end the embargo on its oil supplies.

"We are not prepared to give the wrong impression to others and to buy some oil out of this," Dutch Economics Minister Ruud Lubbers told newsmen. "We are not going to buy oil on a Saturday morning after making a declaration that could be misunderstood by others."

Mr. Lubbers met for 75 minutes with Sheikh Ahmed Zaki Yamani, the Saudi Arabian Oil Minister, and Algerian Energy Minister Abdesselam.

Afterwards he said Yamani carried out his earlier promise to demand from the Dutch "a very clear-cut position which condemns the Israeli occupation, asks for a complete withdrawal from all occupied territories and shows a gesture to repair the damage."

It was this statement which Lubbers refused. His aides said the Arabs did not specify what gesture" they had in mind, but

said the issue of a possible break in Dutch-Israeli diplomatic relations did not come up.

Lubbers also said there would be negotiations this month between the Netherlands and the U.S. on the possibility of American oil shipments to Rotterdam. State Department officials indicated on Friday that there is, at least in principle, an agreement between the U.S. and Holland on how America can aid the Dutch.

Former U.S. Under-Secretary of State George Ball, writing in the "New York Times" on Friday from London, suggested that the U.S., Europe and Japan pool oil supplies so that "none suffers greater hardship than the others — and that includes the Netherlands which has been quite unfairly singled out for special punishment."

The Arab oil ministers Yamani and Abdesselam are to fly to the U.S. tomorrow for talks with U.S. officials. Yamani said yesterday he would urge the U.S. to pressure Israel to give up conquered Arab territories.   *(UPI, AP, INA)*

ISRAEL — Never an Arab Land

One of the myths related to the Arab-Israel conflict is that Israel and the whole of Mandatory Palestine before it was stolen from the Arabs as a result of imperialist machinations and settled by alien Jews.

The fact is that until the defeat of the Turkish Ottoman Empire during World War I, there was no geopolitical entity called Palestine, no Arab nation lived on this soil and no national claim was ever made to the territory by any group other than the Jews.

Between the expulsion of the Jews by Rome in 70 to 132 C.E. and the defeat of the Ottoman Empire in 1918, Palestine was occupied by fourteen conquerers over thirteen centuries. The following table shows the approximate historical periods of the various rulers of Palestine:

1. Israel Rule (Biblical period)	1350 B.C. to	586 B.C.
2. Babylonian Conquest	587 B.C. to	538 B.C.
3. Israel Autonomy (under Persian and Greco-Assyrian suzerainty)	538 B.C. to	168 B.C.
4. Revolt of the Maccabeans	168 B.C. to	143 B.C.
5. Rule of the Hasmoneans and their successors	143 B.C. to	70 A.D.
6. Jewish Autonomy (under Roman and Byzantine suzerainty)	70 A.D. to	637 A.D.
7. Rulers of Arab Caliphates	637 A.D. to	1072 A.D.
Mecca	637 A.D. to	661 A.D.
Umayyides	661 A.D. to	750 A.D.
Abbaside	750 A.D. to	870 A.D.
Fatimides	969 A.D. to	1071 A.D.
8. Selijukes Rule	1072 A.D. to	1096 A.D.
9. Crusaders	1099 A.D. to	1291 A.D.
Ayyubids	1175 A.D. to	1291 A.D.
10. Mameluke Rule	1291 A.D. to	1516 A.D.
11. Ottoman (Turks)	1516 A.D. to	1918 A.D.
12. British Mandate	1918 A.D. to	1948 A.D.

Thus, during the whole period of recorded history, Palestine was never ruled by the Arabs of Palestine. The rule of the various Arab Caliphates, which was a foreign Moslem rule, extended for a period of 432 years — Jewish rule of Palestine extended over a period of 2,000 years.

The inhabitants of the region consisted of the conquering soldiers and their slaves and only during the Arab conquest of the area were these diverse ethnic inhabitants compelled to accept Islam and the Arab tongue or be put to the sword. The Jews in fact are the sole survivors of the ancient inhabitants of Palestine who have maintained an uninterrupted link with the land since the dawn of recorded history.

FACTS AND FIGURES ON THE MIDDLE EAST

Refugees, How many Refugees?
590 thousand Arabs left Israel during the period of the 1948 war.
— 20 per cent of them soon found permanent homes in the Arab world (U.N. figures).
— 160 thousand remained in Israel. These are United Nations figures.
— 450 thousand Arabs are now citizens of Israel.
600 thousand Jews left Arab countries following the 1948 war.
— 100 per cent of them were helped to find permanent homes in Israel.
— 5 thousand still reside in Arab countries.

Who owned the land in Israel in May 1948?
8.6% — owned by Jews
3.3% — owned by Israeli Arabs
16.9% — owned by Arabs who had left
71.2% — public land owned by England, reverting to the State of Israel as its legal heir by U.N. action.

Am. Ed. League for a Secure Israel
SOL. A. DANN, Chairman

TO ALL CITIZENS OF ISRAEL OF WHATEVER OPINION OR PARTY

IN THE ELECTIONS for the Eighth Knesset, we ask you to authorize Likud to form a Government of National Unity called for by our political and security situation.

THE GOVERNMENT of the day, whose overlong rule has resulted in a deep social, moral and economic crisis, has also failed to guard and to maintain the peace and security of the nation.

OUR ENEMIES prepared for a war of aggression. From the eve of New Year until Yom Kippur, the Government received information of these preparations — of massive concentrations of troops in the South and North. But the Government failed to call up our reserves, in time, and to move adequate forces, which were at our disposal, to the front lines. These failures of the Government have led to most serious military and political consequences. Only the heroic stand of our soldiers saved the country from the threat to its existence.

OUR WARNINGS against the unwise policies of the Government have proved justified.

THIS GOVERNMENT deserves no confidence. It cannot be trusted to run the country.

THE DECLARED POLICY of the Alignment Government, which seeks to re-partition the Land of Israel, spells future peril, peril to the existence of the State. The Alignment's policy may well bring the centres of our civilian population within artillery and rocket range of the enemy, and thus expose us to continuous warfare and bloodshed.

Likud offers an alternative policy, calling for:

- Direct negotiation of peace treaties at a peace conference with the Arab States.

- Rejection of withdrawals which would endanger the peace and security of the nation.

- Upholding our right to the Land of Israel, national security, and true peace.

- Enlisting the support of the Jewish people and all friends of Israel throughout the world, particularly in the United States of America, in order to prevent and overcome pressures.

LIKUD

Gahal, The State List, The Free Centre, The Labour Movement for a Whole Land of Israel

גח"ל, הרשימה הממלכתית, המרכז החפשי, תנועת העבודה למען ארץ ישראל השלמה

SUPPORT AND SYMPATHY

From Denmark

Sir, — As a non-Jewish Dane, 1 wish to express my heartfelt sympathy for your country. It is with indignation and shame that we have recently witnessed one country after another make anti-Israeli declarations regarding the Yom Kippur War. Free European nations have never behaved more unworthily in peacetime.

As a Dane, I was delighted to hear our own premier state his honest opinion to Israel's advantage, even if it must cost us some inconvenience on the oil front. I can assure Israel that, even if our Government has now fallen, it was not due to this question, quite the contrary, and a possible liberal government will certainly follow the former government on this question.

Your readers may be interested to know that a recent public opinion poll in Denmark has shown that 62 per cent of the people support Israel, 30 per cent are neutral (and I really mean neutral), 6 per cent do not know and only 2 per cent support the Arabs.

Finally, I believe that, with t h e oil boycott and rising oil prices, the Arabs have got things moving in the western world and, within a few years, it will be independent of Middle East oil. Then the Arabs will have a new Suez Canal problem in the form of what to do with their oil.

ASBJORN KLOPPENBORG-SKRUMSAGER

Egaa, Denmark, November 18.

From Holland

Sir, — As a small group of non-Jewish believers in the God of Israel, we want to express our strong disagreement with the official announcement of the Dutch churches saying they do not want to support Israel. We believe there is no future left for the churches as they abandon their roots by opposing Israel. We cannot identify ourselves with a treacherous policy like that and wish to turn our backs on them. They do not hear. They do not listen. We would like to say that we feel very close to your people and your country. The struggle you are in is our struggle.

ANNETTE VAN DER SCHAAF and ten other signatures

The Hague, October 21.

Peace by accord is the only hope

To the Editor of The Jerusalem Post

Sir, — Professor William Freedman's letter (November 16) was like a breath of fresh air with its bold assertion that peace through agreement seems Israel's only hope.

The smog closed in again with Gordon Austin's letter and Shmuel Katz' "open letter" to the American Secretary of State of the same date. Both are heavy with popular myth and fallacy.

Mr. Austin says: "The gratitude we owe to the U.S. is immense, but surely not so great that we must put aside our own need for self-determination and a possible chance of victory. The decision to stop fighting was America's, not ours..."

What the U.S. did, it did in its *own* interest. So much for gratitude. Much more important is the myth of Mr. Austin's "possible chance of victory." It didn't and doesn't exist. Russia is not going to allow Israel to win a decisive victory, nor is the U.S. going to risk war in order to secure such a victory for Israel.

Equally fallacious is the thesis, so often heard, that the cease-fire was imposed on Israel in contravention of Israeli interests. The decision to stop fighting obviously was Israel's, and obviously it was made in her own interest after a weighing of all factors — including, presumably, the probability or certainty that the U.S. would not support a continuation of the war.

Mr. Austin and Mr. Katz seem to have a comfortable scenario for a Middle East solution: the U.S. supplies and supports Israel, keeping the U.S.S.R. at bay (but not interfering with Israel's "self-determination"), while Israel knocks the daylights out of Egypt and Syria and lives happily ever after.

This isn't going to happen. U.S. policy and action are going to be governed by a cold-blooded U.S. determination of U.S. interests at any given point in time. Israel's security is a U.S. interest, and so is a peaceful settlement in the area. An Israeli "victory" is not.

This is not 1948, 1957, or 1967. Circumstances have changed, weapons have changed, leaders have changed, people have changed. It has to be time for new thinking and new approaches. Who can guarantee that this is not actually happening in Egypt? Only negotiations will tell.

Negotiating does not mean giving up. It simply means talking, trying, exploring, learning, understanding as much as possible — and then deciding.

I for one am hoping and praying that the process Dr. Kissinger initiated will continue and prosper — as Mr. Katz says, "for all our sakes."

(MRS) MARY SHUKRI

Haifa, November 17

From Britain

Sir, — I would like to put on record that, whereas the average Israeli now thinks poorly of his British counterpart, he should know of the indisputable fact that the English man-in-the-street has every sympathy with the cause of Israel and every admiration for the achievements of Israel in times of peace and of war. There has been a tremendous response from non-Jews in providing material and money without direct appeal from agencies, which might help bear out what I write.

British politics are as devious as any other country's, but I think that the average Englishman would be perfectly willing to go short of his petrol or suffer any other embargo if he was convinced that this was the right and proper thing, and I do earnestly hope that in good time, relations between Israel and England will once again be good and fruitful.

PETER KATZ

Brighton, November 3.

To the Editor of The Jerusalem Post

Sir, — I think your readers may be interested to know that at least one leading New York department store has demonstrated its sympathy for Israel in a very original way.

A relative of mine has written to tell me that the exclusive and expensive store, Bergdorf Goodman, had planned a display of French perfumes to be held during October. When the Yom Kippur War broke out, Bergdorf Goodman cancelled this plan as a protest against the French attitude to Israel. To make the point even stronger, they substituted a promotional display of the Israeli perfume "Chutzpah."

MIRIAM FELDMAN

Tel Aviv, November 25.

world, should be sanctified to this superior goal. The Rothschilds were left cold.

These discouraging reactions had a profoundly depressive effect. Shaken to his roots, Herzl wrote "I have given the matter up for the present. There is no helping the Jews."

Later on, Herzl described the crisis of that period using the figure of speech of a white-hot body thrown into cold water: "If that body happens to be made of iron, it turns into steel." Herzl emerged from his crisis with greater strength.

Thereafter, Herzl arranged meetings with many prominent Jewish leaders, but couldn't seem to stir any of them. The only exception was Max Nordau, a noted Hungarian doctor and writer and the only one willing to put his reputation and ability at the disposal of Herzl.

Herzl concluded that his only recourse was to put his case before the public. He revised both the style and the content of his writings, and broadened the scope of his approach.

Der Judenstaat was now published in Vienna. It was the year 1896. Translations appeared almost immediately in Hebrew, English, French, Russian,

and Rumanian in that selfsame year. Eventually, Herzl's masterwork was published in 80 separate editions, and in 18 different languages.

Herzl's thesis was that the Jewish problem could not be solved by assimilation, because of the existence of anti-semitism on the one hand, and the Jewish will to survive on the other. The only possible solution would have to be a political solution—the establishment of an independent Jewish state. This could only be accomplished with the consent of the great powers.

Herzl's idea was received with mixed reactions. For the most part, eminent Jews in Western Europe challenged Herzl's assumptions, and rejected his plan. Even some who were ardent Zionists regarded Herzl's notions as too extreme.

It appears that Herzl had independently duplicated—not plagiarized—Pinsker's thoughts. The opening passages of Der Judenstaat follow:

The Jewish question still exists. It would be foolish to deny it. It is a remnant of the Middle Ages which civilized

All PoWs in Egypt were tortured

By ZE'EV SCHUL
Jerusalem Post Military Correspondent

TEL AVIV. — The defence establishment — both Army and Ministry — are collecting evidence concerning the maltreatment and torture of Israel prisoners of war held by Egypt and will submit it at an early date to the U.N. as well as to the International Red Cross Committee.

Although no formal response is expected from either of these bodies — dominated as they are by large majorities openly siding with the Arab states — the exposure will, it is hoped, shock world public opinion. The facts built up to a picture of cruelty unmatched since the Nazi era, perhaps the Bangladesh concentration camps.

(Evidence has been collected from the prisoners who have been returned. This is why no factual case can be made against Syria —apart from the 28 known murders which have already been brought to the attention of the U.N.).

All Israel prisoners of war regardless of rank were tortured. Fur-

thermore, Israel will accuse the Egyptian authorities of having participated in or permitted the murder of prisoners of war, especially of pilots who ejected safely from their damaged aircraft.

Some prisoners are believed to have died while under interrogation.

One of the reasons for the Government's insistence on the speedy repatriation of the PoWs was the knowledge that they were experiencing a terrible time in Egyptian jails.

A typical story is that of David Senesh, nephew of Hanna Senesh (who parachuted into Nazi-occupied Europe during the final phase of the Second World War, was captured and executed by the Germans in Budapest.)

The story, as told to "Ma'ariv" reporter Aharon Dolay, by the 19-year-old bearded and bespectacled soldier, began on the second day of the war, Sunday, October 7, when his strongpoint on the Canal front was overrun. In the final phase, smoke grenades were thrown into their bunkers and the 37 survivors — one of the men was killed — trooped out into the

strongpoint compound.

"The Egyptians pounced on us, plucking off our identification discs, taking our watches and other valuables, personal papers, steel helmets. Then they told us to remove our boots and socks. It looked as if they had rehearsed this many times. Then they brought a reel of telephone wire and tied our wrists with it, as tightly as they could, wrist crossed over wrist. Most of us soon lost all sense of feeling in our hands."

The prisoners were laid on the floor of a troop carrier. Their guards stood on top of them, continuously kicking them or spitting at them. "Every time I tried to lift my head I was knocked down again by a blow from a fist; but not before they all had a chance to spit at me. The spittle dribbled down my face."

During the various transit stages to the first interrogation point, mobs of Egyptian soldiers attacked the prisoners time and again. David was knocked unconscious by a rifle butt blow, and came to to find blood streaming down his face. The others fared no better.

nations do not even yet seem able to shake off, try as they will. The Jewish question exists wherever Jews live in perceptible numbers. Where the Jewish question does not exist, it is carried by Jews in the course of their migrations. We naturally move to those places where we are not persecuted, and there our presence produces persecution.

This is the case in every country, and will remain so, even in those highly civilized—for instance, France—until the Jewish question finds a solution on a political basis. The unfortunate Jews are now carrying the seeds of anti-semitism into England; they have already introduced anti-semitism in America.

I believe that I understand anti-semitism, a really highly complex movement. I consider it from a Jewish standpoint, yet without fear or hatred. I believe that I can see what elements there are in it of vulgar sport, of common trade jealousy, of inherited prejudice, of religious intolerance, and also of pretended self-defense. I think the Jewish question is no more a social problem than a religious one, notwithstanding that anti-semitism sometimes takes these and other guises. It is a national question, which can only be solved by making it a political world question to be discussed and settled by the civilized nations of the world in council.

We are a people—one people. We have honestly endeavored everywhere to merge ourselves into the social life of surrounding communities, and to preserve the faith of our fathers. We are not permitted to do so. In vain are we loyal patriots, our loyalty in some places running to extremes. In vain do we make the same sacrifices of life and property as our fellow-citizens. In vain do we strive to increase the fame of our native land in science and art, or her wealth by trade and commerce. In countries where we have lived for centuries, we are still cried down as strangers.

In the world as it now is, and as it will probably for an indefinite period remain, might precedes right. It is useless, therefore, for us to be loyal patriots, as were the Huguenots who were forced to emigrate. If we could only be left in peace.

But I think we shall not be left in peace.

Oppression and persecution cannot exterminate us. No nation on earth has survived such struggles and sufferings as we have gone through. Jew-baiting has merely stripped off our weaklings; the strong among us were invariably true to their race when persecution broke out against them.

This attitude was most clearly apparent in the period immediately following the emancipation of the Jews. Those Jews who were advanced intellectually and materially entirely lost the feeling of belonging to their race. Wherever our political well-being has lasted for any length of time, we have assimilated with our surroundings. I do not deem this is discreditable. (Hence, the statesman who would wish to see a Jewish strain in his nation would have to provide for the duration of Jewish stay guaranteed political well-being. Even a Bismarck could not do that.)

For old prejudices against us still lie deep in the hearts of the people. He who would have proof of this need only listen to the people where they speak with frankness and simplicity; proverb and fairy-tale are both anti-semitic. A nation is everywhere a great child, which can certainly be educated; but its education would, even in most favorable circumstances, occupy such a vast amount of time that we had best remove our own difficulties by other means long before this process were accomplished.

Assimilation, by which I understand not only external conformity in dress, habits, customs, and language, but also identity of feeling and manner— assimilation of Jews can be effected only by intermarriage. But the need for mixed marriages would have to be felt by the majority; their mere recognition by law would certainly not suffice.

No one can deny the gravity of the situation of the Jews. Wherever they live in perceptible numbers, they are more or less persecuted. Their equality before the law, granted by statute, has become practically a dead letter. They are

Members of a pro-Israeli, non-sectarian Japanese Christian organization parade through downtown Tokyo to demonstrate against what it called the Japanese government's "Anti-Israel" mideast policy. One of Japanese placards reads "Save the Great Israeli Race."

debarred from filling even moderately high positions, either in the army, or in any public or private capacity. And attempts are made to thrust them out of business by "Don't buy from Jews!"

Attacks in Parliaments, in assemblies, in the press, in the pulpit, in the street, on journeys—for example, their exclusion from certain hotels—even in places of recreation, become daily more numerous. The forms of persecutions varying according to the countries and social circles in which they occur. In Russia, imposts are levied on Jewish villages; in Rumania, a few persons are put to death; in Germany, Jews occasionally get a good beating; in Austria, anti-semites exercise terrorism over all public life; in Algeria, there are travelling agitators; in Paris, the Jews are shut out of the so-called best social circles and excluded from clubs. Shades of anti-Jewish feeling are innumerable. But this is not an attempt to make out a doleful category of Jewish hardships.

I do not intend to arouse sympathetic emotions on our behalf. That would be a foolish, a futile, and an undignified proceeding. I shall content myself with putting the following questions to the Jews:

Is it not true that, in countries where we live in perceptible numbers, the position of Jewish lawyers, doctors, technicians,

RISING TO THE

TO THE INDUSTRIALISTS AN

Zahal is drawn up and ready to do its duty, an
Aviv road. The integrity and strength of the people
and behaviour, in the light of Zahal's victories in
home must emulate Zahal's stamina, strength, res
maintain a stand against sustained pressure. It is
as long as such support is required — until a jus

We appeal to every plant manager to run his pla
the workers' committee and the workers themselv
and its trust in the strength and stamina of the Sta

WE APPEAL TO YOU —

★ **Non-use of vehicles, one day a week**

Don't wait till the stickers are ready. Kee
one day a week all your plant's vehicles an
the plant helps to maintain. Put a homema
the right-hand corner of the windscreen, t
day the vehicle is not to be used.

★ **Encourage awareness of the need for eco**

Encourage awareness of the need for ec
fuel, electricity, materials, manpower and

This advertisement occupied a full page in The Jerusalem Post of Monday, December 3rd. It is too large to reproduce here on one page, and therefore has been broken up into two sections.

HALLENGE

NDUSTRIAL WORKERS OF ISRAEL

lks with the Egyptians are being held on the Cairo-Suez road, not on the Ashdod-Tel
el have again been put to the test. We on the home front must examine our actions
vy battles which were forced on us, and make sure we are doing our part. We at
lness and capability. We are able and must dispel the idea that Israel is unable to
to show our enemies and friends that we can provide firm support for our army, for
sting peace is achieved.

way becoming a people at war. Every plant management team, in cooperation with
st become a force on the home front which will increase the people's self-confidence,

e road
ehicles
ker in
ate the

★ Cut down commercial lighting

Have all shop-window lights and illuminated advertising
signs put off at 9.30 p.m.

Your neighbours will follow your example.

★ Economize on heating in offices and work locations

ing on
ort.

Give instructions for the use of heating stoves to be
reduced throughout the plant.

★ ## Take and make deliveries outside working hours and on nonworking days

If you have been allocated a lorry for times outside normal working hours, take and make deliveries at whatever times, and on whatever days are necessary; ensure that a proper team is available to handle the goods. In this way, we can double and triple the utilization of the transport available.

★ ## Introduce a nine-hour working day

In cooperation with the workers' committee, introduce a nine-hour working day in your plant. Pay the full cost of this ninth hour into a special fund, under the control of the management and the workers' committee, for the assistance of the families of your employees who have been called up.

I appeal to workers to work longer hours — whatever is asked of them — in order to raise production and support the war effort.

★ ## Mutual aid between plants

Contact neighbouring plants, and together find ways of rendering mutual aid in the fields of transport, equipment, maintenance personnel, etc. Help your neighbour, and he will help you.

★ ## Adopt a neighbouring plant whose owners have been called up

Offer help to the wives of plant owners who have been called up, in the day-to-day running of their plants. Give advice and guidance. Devote some of your time to supervising workers with no manager to guide them.

...aeli products — buy "kahol lavan"

...an example for others. Insist on the purchase of ...eli products; give them preference over all others. ...lain to your suppliers, clients, employees, and every- ...you come in touch with that it is always important ...ıy Israeli products, but today it is vital.

...s

...an example to all your employees — pick up workers ...others going your way. Make sure all your ...loyees with cars do the same. Suggest to your ...ds and relatives whose time is at their own disposal ...they give lifts along busy routes.

...e plant a "home address" for the ...of those called up

...ent the links with the families of those called up. ...help in all possible ways (small repairs, welfare ...lems, etc.) to the families of your workers who have ...called up. Encourage employees who have not been ...d up to help the families of those who have. Arrange ...visits to the families of those in the army. Keep in ...h with them by post.

...weekends for work on the land

...our days off, give help on the farms of those serving ...e army, and organize your employees to do the same. ...tact farms near your plant and offer your help, and ...of your workers who volunteer, in picking and ...lar work.

MARK MOSEVICS, President
Israel Manufacturers' Association

teachers, and employees of all descriptions becomes daily more intolerable? Is it not true, that the Jewish middle classes are seriously threatened? Is it not true, that the passions of the mob are incited against our wealthy people? Is it not true, that our poor endure greater sufferings than any other proletariat?

I believe this external pressure makes itself felt everywhere. In our economically upper classes, it causes discomfort; in our middle classes, continual and grave anxieties; in our lower classes, absolute despair.

Everything tends, in fact, to one and the same conclusion, clearly enunciated in that classic Berlin phrase: "Juden Raus!"[1]

1. Out with the Jews!

My plan is in its essence perfectly simple, as it must necessarily be, if it is to come within the comprehension of all.

Let sovereignty be granted us over a portion of the globe large enough to satisfy the rightful requirements of a nation; the rest we shall manage for ourselves.

The creation of a new state is neither ridiculous nor impossible. We have in our day witnessed the process in connection with nations which were not largely members of the middle class; but poorer, less educated, and consequently weaker than ourselves. The governments of all countries, scourged by anti-semitism, will be keenly interested in assisting us to obtain the sovereignty we need.

The plan, simple in design, but complicated in execution, will be carried

FULBRIGHT AND M.E. REALITIES

To the Editor of The Jerusalem Post

Sir, — U.S. Senator Fulbright of the powerful Senate Foreign Relations Committee coupled the idea of an American-Isreli security treaty with an Israel pullback to the pre-1967 borders. He stated that because of the possibility of pullback, he feels the prospects for the cease-fire and a peace settlement are hopeful.

A pullback to even the 1967 lines (never mind the pre-1967 lines) would be suicide for Israel and genocide for more Jews. It is unfortunate that Mr. Fulbright is so detached from the realities here, especially commitments of any kind made by our neighbours, that he cannot see that, under conditions of modern warfare, Israel could not survive with enemies on those borders again. He should remember that cease-fire treaties signed by them before were broken by them at will. What certainty is there that this will not be repeated?

Let us not forget that the attacks of 1948, 1956, 1967 and 1973 were initiated by our neighbours who were refusing to come to peace terms, or even to talk to Israel, and all the while Israel was saying that she was willing to meet to discuss conditions. How much can anyone depend on the "talk" of belligerents?

REV. G. DOUGLAS YOUNG
President, American Institute of
Holy Land Studies
Jerusalem, November 27.

MINISTRY OF DEFENCE / Rehabilitation Dept.

NOTICE TO FAMILIES OF THE DEAD AND MISSING

Under the auspices of the Israel Bar Association, a service providing advice and the handling of the legal affairs (inheritance, administration of wills, debts, etc.) of the dead and missing is being provided free by lawyers who are volunteering their services.

Free legal services will be provided, under the supervision of the Judge Advocate General, in accordance with the professional ethics of the Bar Association.

Families interested in receiving information should apply to the Judge Advocate General's Branch, Army Post 2329, Zahal — Sgan-Aluf Aviva Dor.

The Branch can be contacted by telephone: 03-262367/693177 between 10 a.m. and 12 noon, and 2-3 p.m.

Detailed notices will be sent to families through the post.

out by two agencies: The Society of Jews and the Jewish Company.

The Society of Jews will do the preparatory work in the domains of science and politics. The Jewish Company will continue with the practical application.

The Jewish Company will be the liquidating agent of the business interests of departing Jews, and will organize commerce and trade in the new country.

We must not imagine that the *departure of the Jews will be a sudden one. It will be gradual, continuous, and will cover many decades. The poorest will go first to cultivate the soil. In accordance with a preconceived plan, they will construct roads, bridges, railways, and telegraph installations; they will regulate rivers; and they will build their own dwellings. Their labor will create trade; trade will create markets, and markets will attract new settlers. For every man will go voluntarily, at his*

An appeal to good sense

IT is a sign of changed times, of the enhanced sense of civic duty, that a passionate appeal to "the industrialists and industrial workers in Israel" has been made by the President of the Manufacturers' Association concerning matters which have little to do with business activity.

The page-long advertisements published in yesterday's newspapers reflect Mr. Mosevics' concern about the very basis of our economy, the nation's stamina, morale, and resolve to maintain a stand against sustained enemy pressure.

Mr. Mosevics does not indulge in fine phrases. He makes a dozen practical suggestions directed to his fellow-industrialists and their employees, which range from giving free lifts and economizing on fuel and commercial lighting, to helping plants left without managers now in the army, use of weekends for volunteer farm work, a nine-hour workday, with the additional earnings used to assist the families of those called up.

By pointing out that we can rise to the challenge of this grave hour only by changing our way of life, by disregarding convenience for the sake of productivity, saving, and mutual aid, he is of course voicing evident truths. And it is to be hoped that his appeal will be widely heeded, that citizens will stop relying in every respect on state assistance and administrative controls, and will begin to help themselves and their fellow creatures as best they can.

It is however also symptomatic of the current confused state of our public affairs that such an appeal has come from a relative outsider instead of from the accredited leadership, that one looks in vain for public initiatives to make the practical adjustments needed in our changed circumstances. Despite all the talk about emergency, state and municipal departments are still being conducted on a business-as-usual basis, and it is that they tend to be imitated by private concerns.

Nor have we seen public figures giving a personal example by volunteering or reducing their living standards. Despite the labour shortage there has been no attempt to organize self-help in neighbourhoods for such practical jobs as, say, street cleaning. Nor has anything been done to stagger business hours in order to reduce traffic peaks and make better use of the buses available or to adjust shopping hours to the needs of working housewives.

Even such a trifle as the introduction of daylight saving time is not yet in sight, and it is by now clear that in most cases the one-day ban on private driving will be carried out at the expense of business, not of pleasure.

It is little wonder that changes involving more inconvenience are not proceeding at all, and as a result a gap is developing between the men at the frontlines and those of us at home, generating grievances and undermining national morale.

Mr. Mosevics' appeal is therefore a timely, indeed an urgent, reminder that something ought to be done, and quickly.

10,000 petition for recognition of Palestinians

TEL AVIV. — Over 10,000 signatures were appended last week to a petition calling on the Government to draw up an immediate plan for peace and to "recognize existence of the Palestinian nation." This was claimed at a press conference here yesterday by the sponsors of the petition, a group calling itself the "Committee for a Peace Initiative—Now."

The group says it has supporters in many political parties, including Labour, Mapam, the National Religious Party, Independent Liberals, Moked, Meri and Siah.

Dr. Dov Siton of the Negev University said the group represented the broadest common denominator among "all those who believe there is an alternative to the policy that preceded the Yom Kippur war — a policy of stagnation and creeping annexation that precluded any chance for peace." *(Itim)*

Jews take time off to work for Israel

More than 30,000 Jews in the United States and other countries left their regular work during the Yom Kippur War to devote their time to collecting money for Israel and to engage in information work, according to Jewish Agency Director-General Moshe Rivlin.

Mr. Rivlin said yesterday that the identity of Diaspora Jewry with Israel during the war surpassed that during the Six Day War. He noted that since Yom Kippur at least one planeload of immigrants has arrived in the country every day.

own expense, and his own risk.

The labor expended on the land will enhance its value, and the Jews will soon perceive that a new and permanent sphere of operation is opening here for that spirit of enterprise which has heretofore met only with hatred and obloquy.

We could offer the present possessors of the land enormous advantages, assume part of their public debt, build new roads for traffic, which our presence in the country would render necessary, and do many other things. The creation of our state would be beneficial to adjacent countries, because the cultivation of a strip of land always increases the value of the surrounding districts in innumerable ways.

Let all who are willing to join us, fall in behind our banner and fight for our cause with voice and pen and deed.

Students embraced Herzl's notions with enthusiasm, and called upon him to assume the leadership of the Zionist movement. Almost automatically, Herzl became the leader of the Hovevei Zion societies.

Considering the political climate of the day, Herzl's ideal appeared somewhat quixotic if not altogether mad. Who except a madman would conceive of approaching the Turkish sultan to negotiate for a piece of Palestine for the Jews? But Herzl shrugged off the practical difficulties, saying, "If you but will it, it need not be a legend." It was this slogan that became the rallying cry of the Zionists.

There was something about Herzl's appearance that suggested the ancient prophet. His august stature and noble demeanor commanded respect, and the resonance of his voice charmed his audiences. He was a particularly moving figure to the masses of Jews in Eastern Europe—perhaps because he was a sophisticated, urbane Westerner who had come back to his people.

In perspective, one might judge that Herzl's

Israeli actress Daliah Lavi with soldiers in Hadassah Hospital.

242

tactics of practical politics were his most important contribution to Zionism.

Moreover, into the teeth of the anti-semites who had made the word Jew an insult, Herzl flung the word *Judenstaat,* which means not only "The Jewish State", but literally "The Jew State."

Herzl perceived the Jewish question as an *international* political question. Therefore, in 1897, he organized the Zionist movement at an international Zionist Congress in Basle, Switzerland, in a manner that bestowed upon it the aura of a parliament in session. He conducted his presidency of the Congress with a mien that commanded the respect accorded to the head of a state.

Here, at the Zionist Congress, Herzl launched the program of paying a shekel as an act of allegiance to the international Zionist movement. When the Congress was over, Herzl wrote in his diary "I have created here the Jewish State."

Herzl sought to get "a land without a people for a people without a land." He therefore made his first and major effort by proposing to the Sublime Porte the granting of a charter to Jews to settle in Palestine, or in the immediate vicinity of Palestine. When the Sultan of Turkey turned him down, Herzl was willing to consider other geographical localities.

In 1903, the British Government proposed that a Jewish settlement be established in Uganda in East Africa. This proposal was championed by the noted Jewish writer Israel Zangwill. Herzl found himself opposed by Zionists who objected to this proposal. Up until this point, Herzl's commitment to Zionism had been stirred by his recognition of the plight of the Jews; his was not a cultural nor a historical commitment to Zion. It was only when Herzl learned through the Uganda episode that Jews were inextricably bound up with their heritage and their ancient land that he changed his orientation. From that point on, Herzl became convinced that the Jewish future lay in Palestine.

In the few years that were given him to lead the Zionist cause, he consistently proclaimed that only the attainment of a political document granting Jews sovereign rights to settle in a specific territory could lead to viable statehood. He, therefore, opposed the movement toward piecemeal settlement in Palestine. Whatever aid he reluctantly gave to settlements during his lifetime, he did as a practical concession to his opponents.

In his last will, Herzl asked to be buried beside his father's grave in Vienna until such time as the Jewish people would acquire Eretz Israel. In good time, in the Biblical tradition of Joseph, the Jews would transfer his remains to the land he yearned for. In August of 1949, shortly after the State of Israel was established, the remains of Theodore Herzl were re-interred on Mount Herzl in Jerusalem. Nearby, a grateful people have built the Herzl Museum, which houses his original study in Vienna. Each year, the anniversary of his death, the 20th day of the month of Tammuz, is celebrated in Israel as a national memorial day.

After Herzl died, the Zionist movement continued to slowly and steadily gather strength.

In 1914, the German Reich made war against England, France, and Russia. On the side of the Kaiser were arraigned the Hapsburg Austro-Hungarian Empire and Turkey.

During the war, Jews from all over the world, but especially those in Palestine, were fired with the idea of helping to wrest Eretz Israel from Turkish dominion. Some of the early Zionists, especially Joseph Trumpeldor, Vladimir Jabotinsky, and such young labor pioneers as David Ben Gurion and Izhak Ben-Zvi, believed that helping to defeat the Ottoman Empire would be one way of insuring that Jews would be taken seriously at the peace table after the war. The Zion Mule Corps was formed in Palestine and fought at Gallipoli in 1915. Thereafter, a Jewish legion, recruiting most of its contingent from Palestine and a large part among English Jews, was formed under the leadership of Ze'ev Jabotinsky. About 2,700 volunteers came from the United States to join the cause of the Allies. This force operated under the English commander, General Allenby, and later played a role in the capture of Palestine.

As military formations, these Jewish corps were of some importance; but their main significance was in the creation of a modern Jewish military tradition as a conscious national act. In the preparation for nationhood, something more than a symbolic army had been responsible for the victory.

Even earlier, with the very beginnings of Zionist settlement, Jewish armed guards called Shomrim (The Watchers) had protected settlements against armed robbery. Later, when difficulties developed between Jews and Arabs, a Jewish self-defense organization was formed called the Haganah, which had at its core, the men of the Jewish Brigade, the Zion Mule Corps, and the Shomrim.

In 1917, the British Government, acting through its Foreign Secretary, Lord Balfour, issued the historic Balfour Declaration in the form of a letter written by Arthur James Balfour to Lord Rothschild, a leader of the Zionist movement. *(See page 76.)* While the Balfour Declaration did not have the force of law, it was a document of

243

MINISTRY OF TRANSPORT

CARLESS DAY — CHOSEN BY DRIVER

The regulations covering the non-use of vehicles one day a week come into effect on December 16, 1973.

VEHICLES AFFECTED

1. Private cars, motorcycles, motor tricycles, and commercial vehicles of gross weight not exceeding 2,500 kg.
2. Vehicles to which the regulations do not apply:
   a. Israel Defence Forces vehicles, bearing I.D.F. identification marks;
   b. Vehicles of the Israel Police, bearing red police registration numbers;
   c. Touring vehicles;
   d. Ambulances fitted with a siren, fire-fighting vehicles, etc.;
   e. Breakdown lorries;
   f. Vehicles of disabled persons —
      (1) who require a vehicle because of leg disablement
      (2) whose degree of disablement is 60% or more, and whose health is liable to be adversely affected by street traffic.

The vehicle types coming under the regulations are also subject to the regulations in the occupied territories.

CARLESS DAY

The carless day will be Saturday, but if the vehicle owner so wishes, he may choose any other day of the week. Those who choose Saturday as the carless day will be able to use their vehicles Saturday evening *(Motz'ai Shabbat)*. For the other days of the week, the carless day will last 24 hours — from 2 a.m. to 2 a.m.

THE MINISTRY OF TRANSPORT APPEALS TO THE PUBLIC TO CHOOSE SATURDAY AS THE CARLESS DAY.

The carless day for any given vehicle will be the same day every week. The carless day may be changed by application to licencing offices throughout the country. Such applications may be made six months after the carless day has been established, and only once in six months.

CARLESS DAY STICKERS

Carless day stickers will be given out at all post offices throughout the country, December 9 — 14, 1973. These stickers will indicate the day the vehicle owner has chosen as his carless day. The sticker is to be affixed to the right-hand side of the windscreen; owners of vehicles which have no windscreen should stick them to the front mudguard.

Take your vehicles licence when applying for the sticker. A slip identifying the carless day, stamped with the post office stamp, will be attached to the licence. Vehicle owners now serving in the army who are unable to go personally or ask someone else to collect their stickers may apply to their local licencing office at a later date for a sticker.

Disabled vehicle owners who are exempt from observing a carless day will receive through the post a sticker bearing the Hebrew letter "Pei" on a grey background. They need not apply to a post office for this sticker.

Doctors will also observe a carless day. However, the Medical Association will send them a movement permit, enabling them to make journeys on their carless day for the purpose of providing medical attention.

PENALTIES

Vehicle owners using their cars on the carless day are liable to a fine of IL3,000 and/or the withdrawal of their driving licence for a period of three months. Vehicles found to be in use on the carless day will be taken straight to a police station, where they will remain until 8 a.m. the next day. Vehicle owners must remove their impounded vehicles at this time.

These regulations are intended as a means of saving fuel. Observance of the permitted road speeds will also yield a significant saving in fuel. Accordingly, police vigilance in this respect will be intensified.

Any questions regarding these regulations may be addressed to the Liaison Section of the Ministry of Transport, Jerusalem, Tel. 02-233305.

Likud M.K.s apologize for House scuffle

Jerusalem Post Knesset Reporter

The Knesset House Committee yesterday expressed regret over the scuffle in the Knesset on November 23, when three Likud M.K.s assaulted New Communist Avraham Levenbraun, punched him at the rostrum, grabbed his notes and prevented him from speaking.

The House Committee also expressed its regrets over remarks by Mr. Levenbraun's colleague, Meir Wilner, earlier in the debate on the Government's political statement of that day.

Benzion Keshet (a Gahal deputy speaker), his Gahal colleague Matityahu Drobless, and Yigal Horowitz (State List) made a statement to the House Committee in which they said they were sorry and explained they had been carried away by the provocation of the New Communists.

The three M.K.s said the incident was caused by "intolerable and unprecedently slanderous hate-statements by Mr. Wilner, which exceeded all bounds."

They quoted, as examples of this, Mr. Wilner's remarks in the debate: "You conquered another strip of land...the Hermon position...for prestige reasons, and brought about bloodshed...It was because of you Herut and Gahal people that our boys shed their blood...You are the foe..."

Movies desperate, 50 cinemas face closure

By MACABEE DEAN
Jerusalem Post Reporter

TEL AVIV. — If the authorities do not extend immediate financial help to the country's cinemas, they are in danger of closing down for good. This was stated yesterday by Gavriel Mograbi, chairman of the Cinemas Association.

The Association has 245 member cinemas throughout the country. Mr. Mograbi said 50 are in immediate danger of closing.

He did not specify what financial aid was demanded, but he did say it was "up to the Government to decide if the cinemas are a vital part of the country's entertainment and culture. If it rules they are as outdated as an icebox, let it say so plainly, and we will close down and look for other sources of income."

He noted that the number of movie-goers since the war broke out was down 50 per cent or more from last year. For example, attendance in October of this year was only 1,220,000, as compared to 2,951,000 in October last year. Figures for November were not yet in, but they were believed to hover around the 50 per cent mark.

Attendance was down, he said, for a simple reason. Most movie-goers were young people. Most of them were mobilized today.

Most of the 50 cinemas facing closure, he said, are in towns and villages where they constituted the "focal point of social gatherings." However, three are in greater Tel Aviv, two in Jerusalem and two in Haifa. The 50 employ some 500 persons of the 2,000 employed in the entire industry.

He said that "with the introduction of television five years ago, the cinemas suffered a severe heart attack. We managed to recover and struggle along at a much slower pace. If the Government wants to save the cinemas from closing, it must consider giving us a financial heart-transplant."

Wounded commando describes one of Sharon's missions

KAETZELE'S PRIVATE WAR

By ZE'EV SCHUL,
Jerusalem Post Military Reporter

BEILINSON HOSPITAL. — "My name is Ya'acov Katz, but everybody calls me Kaetzele," the youngster said. His bed had been moved next to the window of a plastic surgery ward, overlooking the lawns and tall green trees below. This is as close as he is going to get to the outdoors for many months.

"I intend to get well," Kaetzele says. "Not only that — I'm going to save this game leg of mine so they'll take me back into my old unit. I owe it to my friends who didn't make it. I made a pledge."

The pledge means a lot to 22-year-old Ya'acov. More than to most.

Ya'acov, a Yeshiva student from Bnei Brak, was on his pre-discharge leave when the October 6 war broke out. Before that he had been a deputy company commander with the rank of lieutenant in one of the elite reconnaissance units attached to the Southern Command.

"I was getting ready to drive to Jerusalem that Friday, the eve of Yom Kippur. I wanted to spend the holiday praying in Yeshivat Harav Kook, where my brother is studying. Only a few hours before my departure I received a phone call, ordering me back to my unit.

"I had already signed out of my unit, turned in all my equipment. I had planned to study at the Yeshiva. No, I don't think I'm cut out to be a Rabbi. But I wanted to gather some values before making up my mind. Maybe I'll teach delinquent youth, or join a moshav. Do something worthwhile, you know."

He continued, "When I showed up at the camp they still had my equipment. It was all there, waiting for me. My Kalachnikov rifle and all the rest of my stuff.

"We still didn't know what was going on. But I had a feeling this was going to be a war of *mitzva* (religious duty) and that it would release me, partially, from many of the holy day's restrictions. I prayed in the vehicle that carried us southwards the following day, the Day of Atonement. We rejoined our battalion. I fasted, although I learned later that I shouldn't have, under the circumstances.

"We were hoping that the fighting would be a local thing and that we'd soon be returning home.

"But about two o'clock that day — Saturday — all hell broke loose. The skies were filled with Egyptian planes, swooping down at us from all directions. A camp behind us became one blazing inferno. We could hear the sound of artillery fire from across the Canal, although we were beyond its reach, and we prepared to defend our installations in the area. Each time the Egyptian planes came over I would jump into a half-track and open fire at them with a swivel-mounted machine-gun. I didn't hit any of their planes. But at least I fired back.

"I don't know what prevented them (the Egyptians) from over-running our lines at that stage. There were pitifully few Israeli tanks, but they fought back, contesting every inch of ground. But the Egyptians could have advanced."

"Sunday Arik Sharon (a divisional commander) came down to join us. There were a number of us, myself included, who didn't have any clearly defined tasks. There weren't enough troops for us all to command, so I rounded up a small number of officers — nine of them, including two lieutenant colonels, former battalion commanders. We also 'borrowed' a half-track and a couple of jeeps and organized ourselves into a special task force.

"We spent the first few days roaming around near the Egyptian lines, picking up their artillery spotters and Egyptian pilots who had bailed out and were trying to regain their positions. We captured four of them — some high-ranking officers, including one full colonel and a major. The other two were captains.

"It was all sand dunes. From time to time we found ourselves sandwiched in between the two armies, and we were often under artillery fire. But we were an agile unit and always managed to evade them in good time. We filed reports on Egyptian spearheads. We reported directly to Arik.

"Six of us were in the half-track," Ya'acov continued. "Three more were piled in the jeep.

"Most of our encounters were minor — rounding up Egyptian commando units and stuff like that. But my last battle was more serious.

"It occurred on Sunday, the following week. We were alerted about four o'clock in the morning. They said a sizable unit of Egyptian commandos had landed somewhere behind the Israeli lines. The nine of us went out to find them.

"They were supposed to have landed somewhere near the line where the tanks of the two armies were slugging it out. Well, we found them all right. About 6 a.m. 60 or 70 of them, well dug in. We called in a couple of tanks to support us with their guns. Then we charged — the nine of us, in two jeeps and my half-track. But they scored with a bazooka. A bull's eye, killing the driver and another man.

"Me — I was lucky. They say it doesn't pay to stick one's neck out, but in my case I suppose it did. I was standing up, exposed, firing my machinegun. If I hadn't been, that missile would have gone right through me. As it was, it hit me in the thigh.

"Are you squeamish? See? They can't even put a bandage on it yet, and the bone is still broken. It isn't even all there. But they'll put in a piece of metal or something..."

(I looked under the open-ended canopy that covered Kaetzele's lower body. Where his left hip should have been there was a deep pit.)

"It's ever so much better now," he assured me. "They are already doing skin grafts.

"Well, I knew I'd had it. But I still had enough strength to pull myself up towards the edge of the half-track and roll off it. I groped for my personal bandage, but it was gone, along with most of my hip. I knew I had to stop the blood, so I put my fist right inside the wound. I could feel the smashed bones with my fingers.

"The boys couldn't help me. There were only six of them left. The driver, a second lieutenant, got it in the head. He was gone, instantly. The other guy, behind me, was also dead. And I was out of action. So the remaining six had to keep on doing what they were doing. I don't think many of those Egyptians got away. My unit mopped them up. But two more were wounded. There were only four of them left.

"They came over to me. Later they told me that after taking one look at my leg they decided I wouldn't live more than five minutes. Since the area was still under fire, they couldn't call in a helicopter. So they bound me to a tank and got me back to an evacuation point.

MEDICAL FREAK

"Yeah — they think I'm a medical freak around here. I kept on losing more blood than they could pump into me. It took over 20 pints of blood to bring me round. The professor says I was dead for all intents and purposes by the time I got here. It wasn't a question of whether or not they should amputate my leg — but of whether I would last a few more minutes.

"Thank God I am recovering. What annoys me is that they lowered my health profile to 24 — from 97. But I'll show them, I don't want a duty-free car. I don't intend to become an invalid. I've seen officers fight with artificial legs. Praise God, I've kept my two legs and I in-

tend to use them again — in the army."

Kaetzele explains that he is now the only survivor of a group of three friends who volunteered for the reconnaissance unit. "We all went to the same school (Kfar Haroeh) and graduated together. One of them had intended to go to a yeshiva after completing his army service. But he changed his mind during the war. He told me just before he died that since so many officers had been killed, it was up to him to contribute his personal bit to plug the gap. Since he was killed I intend, if I can, to fill in for him."

Yaacov Katz—a handsome youngster with deep-set, dark blue eyes — is the unchallenged favourite of the ward. He has been lying immobile for weeks now on his back. He has no complaints, and only one wish — could I bring him a cassette recording of "My Fair Lady?"

I said I would.

"But be sure you don't bring it on Saturday — I wouldn't want you to violate the Sabbath."

I promised I wouldn't, that I would bring it on Sunday.

My Fair Lady for Kaetzele on Sunday.

Ya'Acov Katz in the hospital.

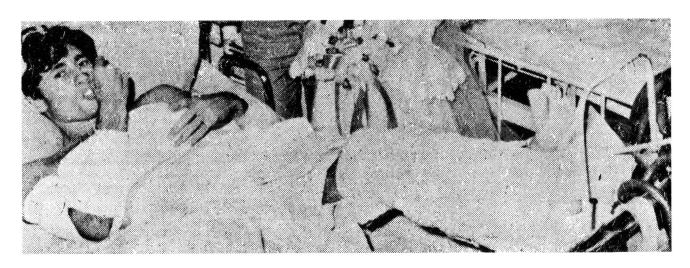

great significance, since it pledged Great Britain's support, after consultation with France and with the United States, toward the realization of the Zionist dream of creating in Palestine a homeland for the Jews.

At the Versailles Conference at the end of World War I, the mandate over Palestine was awarded to Great Britain. All the Allied nations who had participated as major parties in World War I had subscribed to the Balfour Declaration, and their intention clearly was that England would administer Palestine as a trustee for the Jewish people, and help in the establishment of a Jewish State in that territory. As a matter of fact, the Zionists had sent a commission to Palestine even before World War I was over to provide food and medical supplies for the local population and to aid the British officials in planning the administration of the territory.

The promulgation of the Balfour Declaration in 1917 was the powerful impetus that led to a new

wave of immigration, which became known as the Second Aliyah. These immigrants of the Second Aliyah gave a tremendous lift to the kibbutz movement.

But the British Foreign Office which succeeded Balfour had other ideas. It believed that the Arab countries, although disorganized and not politically minded, could be welded into a force Britain could control. The Foreign Office was of the opinion that the Arab potentates sat on huge natural resources. Perhaps, at that time, the British did not envisage the enormous oil wealth of the Arabian peninsula; but they surmised that there was more benefit to be derived from favoring and controlling the Arabs than from developing a friendship with the Jews.

Difficulties started almost immediately. One of the problems emanated from the fact that the English, in trying to persuade some of the Arab sheikhs to join in the fight against Turkey, had promised them grants of territory. But the British

---

Rejects Israel complaint to ICRC
Syria accuses Israel of serious war crimes

GENEVA. — Syria yesterday denied that its soldiers had killed Israel prisoners of war and said such allegations by Israel were part of a "campaign of hatred" aimed at covering Israel's "own war crimes."

In a statement sent to the headquarters of the International Red Cross Committee (ICRC) here, Syria called on the committee to undertake an immediate inquiry into alleged Israel violations of the 1949 Geneva Conventions protecting war victims.

Syria was replying to a request made by the Red Cross on November 13 that it should observe the Geneva Conventions, give lists of Israel prisoners captured during the October war, and allow Red Cross delegates to visit them.

The Syrian statement said Israel accusations that its PoWs had been tortured and killed after capture by the Syrians could have no validity because they came from Israel itself and were not based on impartial or neutral testimony.

On the other hand, the statement cited a report in the French newspaper "Le Monde" of October 27 which, it said, quoted an Israel military officer as saying Syrian PoWs had been used to cross minefields in front of Israel troops in the region of Jabal al-Sheikh. It also said a Dutch surgeon had been quoted on October 25 in two Belgian newspapers as saying that the Israelis had used Egyptian and Syrian PoWs as material for transplants on injured Israel soldiers.

The statement alleged that Israel had executed about 30 civilians in the Syrian village of Beit Jann on the Golan Heights after the cease-fire in front of other villagers to terrorize them and force them to flee their homes. It added that Israel forces had used anti-personnel weapons and bombs disguised as toys to kill civilians and innocent children.

(The I.D.F. spokesman last night categorically denied these four allegations.)

The story we must tell the world

By EPHRAIM KISHON

SOME subjects are hard to write about. Some are *impossible* to write about, but one must. I'm talking of our PoWs.

The Government's handling of this dark side of the War has been wretched from the first. Instead of telling our boys' parents the sad truth, instead of explaining to them that every outcry at home would only increase the difficulties and add to the price of freeing their sons, our leaders fell over each other to make the general anxiety public, effectively turning the desperate relatives into pressure groups. Needlessly so. Anyone who saw the tears in Golda's eyes when she welcomed our returning prisoners would know she doesn't require prompting by microphones and slogans.

*

ON the other hand, let it be said that the Egyptians' treatment of their Jewish captives not only shows the moral abyss between our two peoples, but also serves as a harsh warning to those who are trying to explain the Arabs' attitude toward us on rational grounds. Their attitude is, regrettably, one of fanatical hate. They don't beat our soldiers to wring any military information out of them, they torture shackled and blindfolded boys just for the sadistic pleasure of it. And their officers look on and do not interfere. It would be enough to turn the stomach of any sane person in the world.

If he knew.

Because what does the world know about this vile barbarity? Nothing. Our Egyptian friends, who can lick us any day in planning and political acumen, invited all the Press and every TV station in the world to the PoW release ceremony. They showed them how their War Minister and Chief of Staff took leave of our prisoners the way only a great power can afford to show chivalrous magnanimity towards its defeated enemy.

We returned an entire army of Egyptians quietly and unobtrusively so as not to hurt their sensibilities. Their honour. The Arab honour.

Then some of our boys came home and were permitted to tell their hair-raising tales. Tales that would have been enough to put the entire civilized world on its feet. But that mustn't happen, apparently. That's cut by the censor.

The Dutch TV filmed the sickening evidence of the Syrians' bestial treatment of our prisoners on the Golan. Did anyone trouble to ask them for copies of their documentary in order to distribute it the world over?

Our U.N. delegate, Mr. Tekoah, hands Secretary Waldheim a formal complaint against the Syrians and informs him that "he won't attach photographs in view of their shocking nature." The mind boggles.

*

NOTHING will save our prisoners in future, nothing will protect our boys in Syrian captivity as much as a wild yell of pain and protest to fill the whole world, as much as photographed proof, a stream of reportage and broadcasts through every communications media on earth, *now*, this minute, so long as they're still listening, so long as Km. 101 and PoWs are still fashionable.

This is political impotence in an advanced degree.

All the speeches of our Foreign Minister won't come up to one single picture of the Syrian Vale of Tears, all our arguments about the need for defensible borders will carry less weight than David Senesh's harrowing account of his Egyptian Via Dolorosa.

Our handling of the PoW affair is unbelievable: *at home*, where silence on the subject is a matter of vital national interest, we shout and smash windows; *abroad*, where we must wake up sleepy humanity, we go in for discipline and restraint.

Translated by Miriam Arad
by arrangement with "Ma'ariv"

---

promises had been vague. Most historians are of the opinion that these promises, for the most part, embraced the territories now known as Yemen and Saudi Arabia, but that there may have been an overlap of promises made to Arabs and Jews regarding Palestine itself. One thing is certain, there was no clear line of demarcation.

As is apparent from the documents set forth on page 77 between Feisal, the Arab emir to whom England had promised rule over Trans-Jordania, and Dr. Weizmann, the leader of the Zionist cause, it was agreed that Palestine was to be the homeland of the Jews. But there were Arab forces in Palestine that were not quite so acquiescent.

The landowners, the *effendi,* were of two minds. On the one hand, they viewed the advent of the Zionists as a golden opportunity to sell large tracts of unproductive land at huge prices. On the other hand, they viewed with alarm the coming of the Europeans who would have a revolutionary impact on the poor, ignorant, rightless fellaheen, the Arab peasants. Although not bound to the land in a strictly feudal sense, the condition of these peasants was tantamount to economic serfdom.

What made the situation so enormously difficult was that the British administrators did not act with clear-cut purpose to implement the Balfour Declaration. The British had no interest in Palestine, except as a colony of England from which the adjoining Suez Canal could be guarded. The British deplored the prospect of Jews coming in masses to Palestine because it would complicate their dealings with the Arabs. Unresponsive to the Jewish dream of a national renaissance, the British bureaucracy had no feelings of cordiality toward

Swiss Jewry makes up for size with quantity

By MARK SEGAL
Jerusalem Post Reporter

TEL AVIV. — The small but influential Swiss Jewish community is fully mobilized on Israel's behalf, and has set itself a target of $27m. for the emergency Israel appeal. This is nearly three times the $10m. collected after the Six Day War, according to Jean Nordmann, the acting chairman of the Swiss Federation of Jewish Communities. He is now ending one of his innumerable visits here together with his entire family.

Swiss Jewry makes nearly the highest per capita contribution to Israel of any community in the Diaspora.

The sign in Hebrew reads "All honor to the Dutch people." The sign on the right is written in Dutch.

Youngsters ride bikes in solidarity with Dutch

TEL AVIV. — Hundreds of youngsters rode their bikes down Ibn Gvirol Street yesterday in a demonstration of solidarity with the Dutch nation. The bicycles symbolize the mode of transportation adopted in Holland on its car-less Sundays.

Taking part in the demonstration were local high school pupils and kibbutz youngsters from out of town. Their bikes were decked out with the Israeli and Dutch national colours and they carried placards reading "Holland — We Love You," "Israel Thanks the Dutch People" and "The Netherlands is Super."

Some posters were in Dutch.

The head of the public committee of solidarity with Holland, Hillel Sei-

del, told the demonstrators that the Dutch are not only under strong Arab pressure to turn their back on Israel, but that no less pressure is being exerted on them by the French and British. Nevertheless, they have refused to sell Israel out for a mess of oil, and the Dutch Foreign Minister has announced that his government has not changed its policy.

The Dutch Consul in Tel Aviv, Joop Voet, addressed the demonstrators in Hebrew saying that he is happy to see the bike riders who prove the sympathy of the Israelis for the Dutch and promised to pass on to the people of the Netherlands the deep friendship of the Israeli people.

(Itim)

Bomb explodes on bus

NETANYA. — One passenger was seriously wounded and 14 others slightly hurt in an explosion yesterday morning aboard a Tel Aviv-Netanya bus.

The seriously injured man, identified as a 20-year-old Arab from Tulkarm, was in Kfar Saba's Meir Hospital last night. All the other injured — who had been taken to Meir and Hillel Yoffe hospital in Hadera — were released after treatment, mostly for scratches.

The packed Egged bus had been passing Ilanot on its way north along the old coastal road at about 10 o'clock when the explosion rocked the rear section. It uprooted the seat on which the Tulkarm man was sitting, injuring both his legs and blowing off an arm. Driver Shabtai Yakar called for help and the injured were taken to the two nearby hospitals.

Police last night refused to go into details of the case, but said they had made no arrests yet. Unofficial reports put the size of the explosive charge at 200 grammes, and said it appeared to have gone off earlier than intended.

World Jewry's donations up 2 1/2 times 1967

Jerusalem Post Reporter

TEL AVIV. — World Jewry outside the U.S. contributed $410m. to Israel within the seven weeks since the beginning of the war, Ezra Shapiro, chairman of Keren Hayesod-United Israel Appeal, told the press here yesterday. The sum is 2½ times greater than the $165m. raised in this framework after the Six Day War.

(The figure for the U.S. was over $500m., including pledges.)

Perhaps the most impressive instance of fund-raising Mr. Shapiro witnessed was in Rome, where the community contributed 100 kilos of gold. "It was on the 30th anniversary of the day when the Jews of Rome were ordered to hand in 50 kilos of gold to the Nazi authorities to ransom the life of 1,000 Jews Of course, the Nazis rounded up the 1,000 men all the same."

the Jewish people. They were playing politics all the way down the line, tacitly supporting the Arabs, and taking no measures to stamp out the fomenting of disturbances by Arab leaders.

Consequently, during 1920 and 1921, riots broke out in Jerusalem, and erupted in Jaffa on an even larger scale. As a carry-over, some of the outlying Jewish settlements were also attacked. Many Jews were wounded, and some were slain.

In 1920, the village of Tel Hai in the north of Galilee was attacked. Its small group of defenders fought off the Arabs. In this attack, Captain Joseph Trumpeldor, an early leader of the Zionist cause in Europe, was killed. His death under dramatic circumstances, while holding off a large enemy force, became a national legend. A monument at Tel Hai marks the incident. Trumpeldor has been revered ever since as a hero and a symbol of fearless defense of country. Today, he stands as the counterpart of America's Nathan Hale. His last words were: "How good it is to die for one's country."

Many English bureaucrats resented the Jews because they could not treat them like backward colonials. Some of the Jewish leaders spoke forthrightly to the administrative officials, and rebuked them for their evasiveness. This kind of straightforward talk didn't sit well with the English, who found the sycophantic style of the Arabs much more to their liking.

The British administrators and constabulary simply turned a deaf ear to complaints by Jewish leaders that Arab instigators, both Moslem and Christian, were spreading propaganda among the peasants to the effect that Jews were going to deprive them of their holy places, and intended to destroy the Mohammedan religion.

In the summer of 1920, Sir Herbert Samuel, an Englishman of the Jewish faith, and a man of lofty ideals and experience in government, was appointed to be the High Commissioner of Palestine. It was believed that under his jurisdiction, conditions would quiet down.

But wishing to appear evenhanded—even generous—Sir Herbert distributed government lands to certain Arab notables. The Jews raised a great outcry, but the High Commissioner was determined to pursue his own course toward greater tranquility. Sir Herbert Samuel also set about to establish a civil government in which the Arabs would have an equal share. The effects of these policies turned out to be the very opposite of what Sir Samuel had hoped for. The Arab upper classes, finding their methods quite successful, accepted the lands that had been proffered, then later sold these very same lands to the Jews at unbelievably inflated prices. They also insisted that the government be entirely placed in their hands. And now, they accelerated their objections to Jewish settlement, demanding that the Jewish homeland, as a concept, be entirely abandoned, and that the Balfour Declaration be declared a nullity.

Why is it that whenever a Jew assumes high office he feels compelled to demonstrate his impartiality by giving the advantage to the opponents of the Jews?

The situation of unrest continued, under the regimes of Herbert Samuel's successors. During the years before 1948, different commissions had been appointed by various countries, by the League of Nations, and by several organizations to examine the local situation in Palestine. Any report that acceded to the Jews the previously confirmed right to the establishment of a National State, was rejected by the Arabs.

In the late 1930s, local warfare continuously broke out between the Jewish and Arab communities. The British not only did not intercede, they actually encouraged the Arabs. At the same time, the British restriction on immigration closed off every avenue of escape for those Jews who had managed to flee Hitler's Europe.

In 1939, with millions of Jews facing destruction by Hitler's S.S., the British issued a white paper which restricted Jewish immigration into Palestine for the next five years—to 75,000 Jews! A quota of 15,000 a year was being imposed on the escapees from Europe.

Hitler's intentions had been made clear; he was going to wipe out every Jew he could lay his

Oi, Oi, What's Going to Happen?

Ephraim Kishon

IN THESE DAYS of war and peace and almost-war and maybe peace, the population of this country is turning into a socialist dream: we think alike, talk alike, and twiddle our thumbs alike. We all walk around with split personalities, and the only difference between us is the number of eggs we manage to wangle under the counter. On the one hand, that is, we feel an irresistible impulse to shout at the top of our lungs about the great botch-up and demand the botchers' heads, but on the other, we know quite well that every shout of ours is music to the ears next door. Consequently we either keep our mouth shut and get stomach ulcers, or shout and get a bad conscience.

"What's going to happen?" people ask in their leisure moments — i.e. between one news-broadcast and the next — "What's the solution?"

The solution is the truth.

Because in truth lies strength. The strength to face the fact that the Egyptians achieved precisely what they wished to achieve: putting up bridgeheads on the eastern bank of the Canal and holding on to them till the Great Powers could intervene. We'd been hearing about this plan for the past six years and in the end it caught us by surprise. It's probably the most surprising surprise in military history, the first Pearl Harbour in the middle of a war.

YET IT isn't true that it's the fault of the Israeli public, that we lived, ate, drove too well. Where does it say that a man who's got a car and a nice flat fights less well than one who lives in a shack and goes to work on a bicycle?

Nor is it true that we were too security-minded and that that's why. It's rather as if a precious treasure had been guarded by an intricate and expensive alarm-system, complete with cops, dogs, electronic devices and all, and had then been stolen after all because somebody forgot to set the switch.

But the treasure's gone — that is the truth.

Still, whatever is going to happen depends on us, on you personally, dear reader. We're in the middle of an Olympic fight, but we've got a champion representing us so we'd better back her up. We are going to come in for pressure, threats, sanctions and booming guns, and we won't be able to stick it out if we go on with our jittery muttery "Oi, oi what's going to happen?" — which is unfounded anyway.

We're sorry to have to remind the reader again and again that he doesn't just have a Government, he has a marvellous country too.

The reader wants to get mad at his leaders? Fine! But what does he want from his country?

True, schizophrenic that he is, he can look at it two ways: from close up or from a distance. From close up, our country is a grain of sand with a handful of miserable creatures crawling over it,

sweating and trying to push each other off. At a distance it's a beacon of light in this dark age, a nation the size of an American suburb which has built a democracy in the middle of nowhere, and developed it between wars at a dizzy, statistics-defying pace.

In much the same way you can judge the war that was in two ways, depending on your mood. At close range it's a comparative failure. At a distance — say from a perspective of just six years — it's a mighty victory which started at the municipal boundaries of Ashkelon and ended within shouting distance of Cairo and Damascus: an incredible military and political achievement which has finally convinced our neighbours to talk to us.

The Arabs want to wipe us out? Sure they do! There's a lot of other things they want besides. We played with the idea of a greater Land of Israel ourselves, and then found out that the Arabs didn't like it. As far as our future and our security are concerned, what matters is our self-confidence and our staying-power, however elementary that may sound. The people of Israel are beginning to look the truth in the face, and they've already told their Government what they think, and felt the better for it. Now the people of Israel must overcome its uncertainty and start exploiting its atomic power of fury for peaceful ends.

Translated by Miriam Arad —
By arrangement with "Ma'ariv"

SURPRISE ATTACK AT THE HEIGHT OF A PICNIC!...

Such a thing could definitely happen . . . if the Arab leaders decided to launch a surprise attack at, say, Rosh Hashana. They would then find us far less organized; they would find a quarter of a million people at mass picnics in the forests of Galilee, even on the Golan Heights.

Yes, this could well happen, and who knows what the price in human lives would be. This could happen as a **DIRECT RESULT** of the secular culture the State has adopted, and of the "fashion" of desecrating the Sabbath — our **HOLY SHABBAT**, and, from pride, of setting no value on our **FESTIVALS** and **RELIGIOUS HOLIDAYS**.

in recent years, responsible (or, more correctly, irresponsible) bodies in our secular government have been only too quick to encourage mass picnics during holy days and Sabbaths, as we saw during last Rosh Hashana.

This grave danger was averted, as a result of the fact that, on Yom Kippur — and only on Yom Kippur — and only on Yom Kippur — almost the whole House of Israel joins, together in prayer and soul searching, and consequently all citizens were in the right place. Hasn't the time come for us all again to keep the Sabbath and festivals holy, and to return to our religious values!

In the series of shortcomings of the secular government, the most serious is the fact that the people have strayed from its religious values, and that despite the failures the government lacks the courage to make changes.

Join us, strengthen the movement demanding a return to tradition!
A return to our holy Tora and its commandments!
A return to tradition — the only strength for us in the future!

PUT YOUR TRUST IN THE PEOPLE WITH FAITH

ישראל בטח בה' !

VOTE
TORA RELIGIOUS FRONT
Agudat Yisrael — Poalei Agudat Yisrael

חזית דתית תורתית

אגודת ישראל פועלי אגודת ישראל

ודתיים בלתי מפלגתיים

hands on. Rejected by the world, the Jews had no place to run, except to Palestine. The United States was operating under a strict quota system which effectively limited the influx of Jews into this country. The same was true of all other European countries.

In 1938, a conference on refugee problems was held at Evian-les-Bains on the French shore of Lake Geneva. President Roosevelt of the United States had invited European, American, and Australian delegates.

The outcome of the deliberations was sorely disappointing to the world Jewish community. Australia agreed to accept 15,000 refugees during the ensuing three years. A few South American countries undertook to accept an unappreciable number of settlers. Only the tiny Dominican Republic announced its willingness to accept a sizable quota of immigrants.

In November 1938, the British government proposed placing a large tract of land in British Guiana at the disposal of refugees. No European country, nor the United States, agreed to take in any refugees.

But public pressure in the United States and in the British Commonwealth urgently persisted in demanding that the victims of the Nazi regime be rescued.

On January 20, 1943, the British Foreign Office, proposed a joint consultation between Britain and the U.S.A. to once again examine the problem and the possible solutions. After an exchange of diplomatic notes, an Anglo-American Conference on Refugees was held in Bermuda from April 19th to 30th. While the western powers were dragging their heels, millions of Jews were being marched into the ovens. On April 30, 1946, the Anglo-American commission recommended that 100,000 displaced European Jews should enter Palestine.

The British then agreed to admit 2,000 Jews *a month!*

World Jewry, and especially the Jewish community in Palestine, were enraged. The shores of Palestine were being set with barbed wire by British Tommies to repel brothers and sisters who stood on the beaches of Palestine with arms outstretched to receive their own flesh and blood.

Defense Minister Moshe Dayan holding a press conference with a group of Arab notables.

NO JUSTICE FOR ISRAEL

To the Editor of The Jerusalem Post

Sir, — On November 29, Egypt suspended negotiations with Israel at Km. 101. Egypt didn't have to give any reasons, for the whole world stands ready to accuse Israel of intransigence. If it had been the other way around and Israel had been the party to break off the talks, the world would have likewise concluded that Israel was the guilty party. Because Israel has only 3m. people as opposed to 100m. Arabs, because Israel has no oil riches on which the world depends while the Arabs are literally swimming in black gold, because anti-Semitism is an endemic disease in the world at large — for all these reasons, Israel cannot possibly be right in a conflict of interests with the Arabs. There is about as much justice in the world as there is sanity.

ARNOLD RUBENSTEIN
Bnei Brak, December 2.

JOSEPHINE BAKER, the well-known Franco-American entertainer, yesterday ordered a wreath for Ben-Gurion's grave through a Beersheba florist.

TRUE FACTS ABOUT 'OCCUPIED "ARAB" LANDS'

To the Editor of The Jerusalem Post

Sir, — I find it appalling that so few Israelis know that:
1. The so-called "occupied 'Arab' lands" which Egypt daily calls on Israel to surrender, are not Arab lands at all. These lands, including the Gaza strip, were seized by Egypt as late as 1948 in its illegal war of aggression against the infant State of Israel and in defiance of the U.N. decision.
2. The so-called "occupied 'Arab' lands" which Jordan claims, including East Jerusalem and the West Bank, came into Jordan's hands illegally in the same war of Arab aggression against Israel only as late as 1948.
3. In 1967, in a war of self-defence brought on by the closing of the Tiran Straits (a recognized act of war), threats and a massing of forces on her border, Israel took these territories and therefore has a superior right to them.
4. The lands in the Golan Heights were taken by Israel in 1967 and in 1973 in wars of self-defence.

Every day, one hears the master imperialist aggressor of our time, Russia, proclaim that Israel must cease her "aggression" and return these lands, and this is repeated by a chorus of one Arab country after another *ad infinitum.*

A tremendous job of information remains to be done in Israel and in every country in the world.

ROSE S. BERENSON
Jerusalem, November 26.

ISRAEL IS BEING SOLD DOWN THE SUEZ CANAL

To the Editor of The Jerusalem Post

Sir, I think your readers may be interested in some of the comments on the Middle East crisis broadcast by Robert Holiday in Canada, where the Russian and Arab versions of the conflict are widespread.

Mr. Holiday said *inter alia:* "Looking at a series of reports from the region, it is apparent the Israelis have been sold down the Suez Canal. They were forced to re-furbish the Egyptian Third Army, they are being forced to accept the U.N. peace-keeping force and, keeping in mind the activities of the U.N. in the Congo, I refuse to put very much trust in the U.N. It is not a very objective organization.

"For Henry Kissinger, Israel has become a major liability in his misguided campaign of detente. He is riding a tiger and he knows it. But, because he is an internationalist, more committed to world government than to justice, Israel can and is being sacrificed. Looking at U.S. foreign policy over the past 20 years, I find it curious that, in every country where U.S. presence was depended upon for moral, financial and military support and where U.S. presence was subsequently withdrawn after a so-called peace agreement, that country has either fallen directly to communism or has fallen under the influence of the Kremlin. And much as I empathize with the people of Israel, I fear that nation is caught in the pincers of detente with the future obscured by a peace agreement dangerous to its very survival."

J.A. BLUSTEIN

Netanya (Willowdale, Ontario), November 26.

It was in response to the hard face of the British that the Irgun came into being. The British had been sending all the illegal immigrants they captured to the Mediteranean island of Cyprus. British soldiers waylaid ships and searched houses. Anyone in Palestine who could not produce a proper identity card was subject to deportation.

In 1937, a group of young Israelis, some of whom were recruited from the ranks of the Secret Defense Forces, the *Haganah,* formed the *Irgun,* an organization whose purpose it was to thwart the British. The Irgun was impatient with the slow gains achieved by the Haganah. The Irgun, believing that a desperate situation required a desperate remedy, became involved in daring schemes and artifices to outwit the British constabulary, and to land as many immigrants as it could on Palestinian soil.

In June of 1938, the Irgun contracted for a Greek ship, and renamed it the *Af-Al-Pi,* which translated into Hebrew means the "Nevertheless." This was the Irgun's way of announcing that despite the British blockade, it was going to land escapees and refugees into Palestine. The ship became the flagship of a rag-tag, nondescript convoy which though not especially seaworthy still succeeded in transporting many Jews, who otherwise would have been doomed, into Palestine.

In 1940, after still more repressive measures by the British, including flogging and hanging, the

THE ALIGNMENT FAILED IN DEED THE LIKUD IS IDEA-BANKRUPT NOW WHAT?

The Independent Liberals consider that the political and military outcome of the Yom Kippur War make it essential to re-appraise the totality of political and military conceptions.

The idea that the **status quo** is the most desired situation, and that it could continue for many years, has toppled.

The proposition that the occupied territories exclude the possibility of war, and constitute a kind of substitute for peace has been shown incorrect.

The mode of action of the Government and its method of reaching decisions have been shown to be basically defective.

The shortcomings in the fighting and in the state of preparedness are being investigated by a committee appointed for the purpose. Conclusions affecting policies and persons will have to be drawn.

However, before that can be done, the people will be called to go to the polls — not only to pass judgement on the shortcomings of the past, but — and this is the main thing — to plot the paths into the future.

In these elections, the public will have to indicate clearly the direction in which the State is to go, without the election lists being opened, and without the points of disagreement being expressed clearly in the party setup.

The right-wing Likud demands rigidity, the consequences of which would be war, a renewed and continuing war.

The Alignment continues to maintain a confused medley of ideas, the aspect of which given most importance is the image created. Dove and hawk groups girate about each other — no-one forgets anything, but no-one learns anything.

The newer parties on the sidelines are mostly concerned about peace, but their chances of representation in the Knesset are small, and their prospects of attaining a position of influence are negligible. A vote for such a party is no more than a vote of protest.

Against this background, we offer the voter who yearns for peace, and who wishes to promote this point of view in the government of the country, one safe road:

Vote for the Independent Liberals.

The Independent Liberals have always been, and are today supporters of a **policy of peace initiative,** open to territorial compromise in a framework of defensible borders. The Independent Liberals have exerted and continue to exert all their strength, in endeavours to realize every real peace option, provided such option also ensures security.

At the same time, the Independent Liberals will continue to fight for the maintenance of citizens' rights, the establishment of correct, democratic procedures for government decision making, the separation of the political process and Zahal, the control of inflationary processes in the economy, the just fair application of the tax burden, and the promotion of solutions to the the country's pressing social problems, within the limits of practical possibilities, and with the application of a yardstick which is not arbitrary, and which ensures social jutice.

After the elections, there will be a possibility of a situation in which the power of the Independent Liberals could tip the balance in favour of a policy of peace.

The voter who desires this will weigh the matter carefully, and decide.

INDEPENDENT LIBERALS

256

Israel needs to launch propaganda offensive

By FOREST A. BROMAN

THE current Middle East peace initiatives are presenting alternatives to Israel which are more threatening than the reversals suffered in the war's first few days. Abroad, both friend and foe now anticipate Israel's ultimate withdrawal not only from Sinai, but from most of the Golan Heights as well. And the notion that a new Palestinian state should exist, headed by Mr. Arafat's or other terrorist organizations, is gaining credence throughout the world. The only question which seems to be an "open" one is the type of guarantee or treaty arrangement Israel will be given.

One need recall only the outline of Israel's brief history with her Arab neighbors to appreciate how dangerous this situation is. Nor does one need a crystal ball to see that tension in Israel's relations with the U.S. will increase, and that soon the depth, as well as the breadth of U.S. public support for Israel will be tested.

Preoccupied with assessing October's defensive failures, the Israeli government seems to lack either the commitment or the capacity to contend with the erosion of support now occurring in the western world. While Israel looks on helplessly, the Arabs are persuading many that peace with Israel is their ultimate goal; and that it is contingent only upon Israel's withdrawal from Arab territory conquered in 1967.

Israel seems to lack an offensive propaganda capacity for delivering to the people of the world some telling and little understood truths about Israel, its neighbors, and the Middle East conflict. This is a major foreign policy failing, one result of which is that Americans and citizens of western countries, who have personally supported Israel in the past, remain woefully ignorant of critical information which will determine their reactions to the paths their governments pursue in this area.

This includes information relevant to (1) What justice requires for the Palestinian Arabs; (2) what is nec-

essary to preserve the security of Israel; and (3) which parties in the conflict are real obstacles to peace in the area.

Mass communication

So little information relevant to these questions has been communicated to the American people, in a format conducive to mass consumption, that Israel can contemplate a serious erosion of non-Jewish popular support in the United States and elsewhere. But an intelligent and aggressive information policy could reverse this trend.

One instance of Israel's long-standing inaction is its continuing failure to communicate the facts about Israeli Arabs. Few people outside of Israel are aware of the mode of existence enjoyed by most of Israel's large Arab population. Nor is information reaching them of the considerable and surprising expressions during the recent war of Israeli Arab support for Israel, which was well-covered by the Israeli press and T.V. These events are a telling commentary on Israel's efforts to include its Arabs in its general prosperity. They also reflect the changing attitudes of many Israeli Arabs over 25 years, from outright hostility to both real and symbolic expressions of support for the country's efforts to defend itself.

The story of the Druse people and their continuous loyalty to Israel is even less known or publicized outside of Israel; and the same must be said of Israel's efforts since 1967 to elevate the level of Arab existence in Gaza, the West Bank and the Golan Heights. The obvious point that successful Arab-Jewish co-existence exists in both Israeli and Israeli-held areas, and surpasses that which any Arab country has permitted within its own borders, must be conveyed and continuously reinforced. In their ignorance of these facts, most citizens of America and Western Europe still have the impression that Arabs in Israel or in Israeli-held territories live in squalid U.N. refugee camps of the type frequently pictured in Gaza during the 1950s.

Israel's capacity to take advantage of short range propaganda opportunities is equally inadequate. For example, the government's handling of Syrian war crimes committed since October 6 has been astoundingly inept. After announcing that photographic and other

proof of Syrian murders of Israeli captives exists, Israel has done nothing of any effect to press these facts upon the attention of the world. Why has the proof not been distributed to the world for publication? Why have Jewish organizations throughout the world not been enlisted to press home to their countrymen the barbarity of the state to which Israel is now expected to return the Golan Heights? And what about the condition in which former Israeli prisoners from previous conflicts with Syria have ultimately been returned?

Prisoner exchanges

There may have been some argument for underplaying these facts while negotiations for prisoner exchanges with Egypt were underway. But the continuing failure to exploit this information internationally can only raise serious doubts about the veracity of Israel's charges. At the same time the Syrians are learning that they can behave this way with relative impunity so far as reactions around the world are concerned.

Israel now seems willing to pursue the same low-key course in pressing evidence of Egyptian torture of Israeli captives only on the U.N. and the International Red Cross. Clearly, in this fateful period, even consideration for those most bereaved by the deaths of those prisoners must give way to the need for publicizing these atrocities as widely and as dramatically as possible.

Battered as she may feel by the current actions and attitudes of many western governments, there are clear signs that even outside of Holland and the U.S., Israel has not lost her place in the hearts of free peoples. Yet the time is rapidly approaching when the personal commitment of many, left unnurtured by some critical facts about Israel and its belligerent neighbors, will be sorely tested. Unless Israel undertakes immediately the kind of aggressive information campaign which seems thus far to have eluded its grasp or its capacity, her isolation will increase. By any standard, Israel is being routed in the propaganda battle with the Arabs.

(Mr. Broman is a former Deputy Commissioner of New York City, currently spending a year as a Fellow in the National Programme or Educational Leadership in Kfar hmaryahu.)

Information services aren't doing enough

SABBATH—No Publication

Two soldiers on duty on Mount Hermon make the best of a job in freezing weather.

'DON'T SWAP LAND FOR PROMISES'

TEL AVIV. — U.S. foreign policy expert Professor Hans Morgenthau on Friday cautioned Israel against trading territory for guarantees, which he said were worth no more than the paper they were written on. It was better to stay on the present lines than to go back to the 1967 ones with such paper guarantees, he added, as the present lines at least left Israel some hope of staying alive if attacked again.

The New York City College-University of Chicago professor was speaking in New York to Israel Television's Haim Yavin, who also interviewed two other American academics who have served as policy advisers to the U.S. Government. These — Columbia Professor Zbigniew Brzezinski and Yale Professor Eugene Rostow — called for Israel to settle on America's terms.

Prof. Morgenthau, who served as consultant to both the State and Defence departments in the sixties, said that under the present circumstances peace would be at Israel's expense alone. Since the outbreak of the recent war the Middle East situation had changed in four ways: Israel's military supremacy had been called into question; the Russians had shown that they would not allow another Arab defeat; the Arab states had scored a considerable success with the oil weapon; and U.S. foreign policy had undergone a meaningful change.

The pro-Arab undercurrent, which he said had always been strong in the State Department, was gaining. Americans were no longer interested in unreservedly supporting Israel, as they were competing with the Russians for decisive influence with the Arabs.

Prof. Morgenthau said he thought the U.S. would press Israel to make a settlement on the Arabs' terms, not one according to its own wishes. He strongly cautioned Israel against withdrawing from territories in return for guarantees. The worthlessness of these had been proved in the past, he said, reminding his listeners that free passage through the Strait of Tiran had been guaranteed in 1957 by the U.S. and other powers, who then stood by when Egypt closed the strait in May 1967.

He noted that the 1967 boundaries were impossible to defend, and indicated that withdrawing to them in return for guarantees would mean the destruction of Israel in a future war. Referring to the idea of a U.S. guarantee in exchange for a massive withdrawal, he said that if Israel had to rely on that, "it would already be too late by the time the U.S. help arrived."

He did, however, support the idea of a withdrawal from Sinai if the area could be demilitarized. But not that of giving it to the Egyptians for another attack on Israel.

Speaking on the same programme, Columbia University's Zbigniew Brzezinski maintained that both America and Israel had lost a historic opportunity for peace right after the Six Day War. There was a great need now for peace, but it would cost Israel dearly, far more than it would have after the 1967 war.

Prof. Brzezinski, who was a foreign-policy adviser to President Kennedy, urged Israel to go to the peace conference with a definite plan. This should involve only minimal annexations, since it was necessary to remove some of the sources of Arab hatred, and one of these was Israel's holding of Arab land. The Soviet penetration of the Middle East had been made possible by the Arab frustration which the long-drawn dispute had produced, and it was therefore necessary to reach a settlement as soon as possible.

Yale law professor Eugene Rostow, who served as an Undersecretary of State under President Johnson, saw the very convening of a Geneva peace conference as a giant step forward. This was what both Israel and the U.S. had been hoping for for the last 25 years, he said, explaining: "When I was dealing with these problems, it was forbidden to even mention Geneva or Lausanne — places where peace is made."

(Itim)

Druse officials buy war bonds

HAIFA. — The three members of the Druse Spiritual Authority and the two kadis of the Druse religious court here yesterday contributed a month's salary each to the Voluntary War Loan.

They asked the Religious Affairs Ministry to have their contributions deducted in one lump sum — not in six monthly payments, as is usual for civil servants.

One of the two kadis, Sheikh Nur e-Din Halabi, added a personal contribution of IL2,500 in cash. He has been making over his pay cheques to the defence establishment since he was appointed to the court three years ago.

Time for renewal — not pessimism

By Yitzhak Shapira

IN the wake of the Six Day War, Israel was swept by a wave of optimism and exaggerated self-confidence, which had a harmful effect on our lives in the following years. Today, after the Yom Kippur War, the prevailing mood in the country is one veering strongly to pessimism and self-castigation.

It is of the utmost importance that we succeed in checking this mood, which unfortunately has affected even some of our thinkers and men of action, and which finds expression, partly in mutual recriminations and demands for punitive dismissals among our leaders. If we fail to do this, we shall not only be aiding our enemies and endangering generations of Zionist achievement, but we shall also be likely to do lasting damage to the spirit of our Israeli youth.

In order to check these dangerous developments in our national life, it is essential to present to the public a more sober and balanced attitude to the recent events, and to see not only the dark side but also the more positive aspects of this War. Such a sober attitude is demanded of us above all in our evaluation of both the shortcomings and the achievements of the first phase of the War, which we fervently hope will also be the last.

There is every reason to assume that the judicial investigation being carried out by the authorized national bodies will reveal that serious, perhaps even fateful, errors were committed just before and immediately after the outbreak of the War, and it is both a national need and duty that the appropriate conclusions should be drawn from these blunders. However, fateful mistakes have been made by other great nations in wartime, and only those lacking in real backbone have allowed such mistakes to throw them off their balance. It should be recalled that a nation like the British went on from grave blunders to achieve "its finest hour."

It is essential, moreover, to emphasize that apart from the blunders, the War revealed magnificent displays of resourcefulness, planning, and above all of infinite courage and self-sacrifice. Indeed, the Yom Kippur War has given the strongest possible proof that our young people today, even those with the long hair and the blunt, biting manner of speech, are no less patriotic and no less ready for heroic self-sacrifice than the most glorious of their brothers in previous generations.

As one whose lot it has been to visit the families and comrades of the fallen, I can unhesitatingly say that the spirit of those who have gone through the grimmest ordeal remains as strong as ever, and that they are not the ones who are looking for scapegoats.

There are those who maintain, with a great degree of justice, that the War shattered "illusions": illusions about the omnipotence of our Army, about our non-dependence on outside forces, illusions about the weakness of our enemies, and the like. But surely it is just as well that the War shattered these illusions, since they were the cause of the various negative tendencies and phenomena which bedevilled our national life in recent years, and which, we must hope, will never again recur.

A strong demand is now being voiced in various quarters for a thorough national stocktaking in the wake of our "failures" in the War. This demand was also at the centre of the exchange of views at a gathering of educators, scholars, and writers recently called by the Director-General of the Ministry of Education. Undoubtedly there is need for such a stocktaking in many areas of our national life, but this need was no less real and pressing even before the War and has not arisen out of "our failures" in the War.

On the other hand, since the War has given rise to special conditions which facilitate the process of self-examination, we should take advantage of the incentive provided by the War and use it as a lever rather than a reason for national stocktaking. There is no justification for presenting the Yom Kippur War as a national failure or as a wholly negative event in our national history. We were not responsible for the War, and we did not want it; it was forced on us by our enemies. It may have laid bare many weak points in our national life, but at the same time it has also given us, and the whole world, a demonstration of our national strength, resourcefulness and powers of resistance in the most difficult situation, and above all of the priceless treasure that we possess in the spirit of our intrepid youth.

If, therefore, we make use of this War as a means and incentive to a transformation of certain national attitudes, and in particular, if we realize, and make our young people realize, that our strength as a nation without friends and surrounded by enemies lies primarily not in the superlativeness of our Army but in the superlativeness of our national values and spiritual inheritance, as a "chosen people" in the full sense of that term — if we do all this, then perhaps the Yom Kippur War will go down in Jewish history not only as a bitter and bloody conflict, but also as an event that contained the seeds of the consolidation and completion of our national revival.

Mr. Shapira is the principal of the Reali School in Haifa.

Persecution of Jews 'threatens detente'

NEW YORK (INA). — Professor Hans J. Morgenthau told the Soviet Ambassador to the U.S. on Friday that reports of renewed persecution of Soviet Jews "pose anew the question of the stability of detente."

Morgenthau, chairman of the 10,000-member Academic Committee on Soviet Jewry, in a letter to Ambassador Anatoly Dobrynin, cited the recent renewal in the USSR of judicial proceedings against Jews who have applied for visas to leave for Israel.

The new pattern of trials "is as disturbing as the purpose is clear: intimidation aimed at limiting the number of exit visa applications by Jews desirous of being reunited with their families in Israel," Morgenthau declared.

Irgun was hard pressed.

At this juncture, a new splinter group was formed under the leadership of Abraham Stern. Stern was then in a British jail, having been arrested in 1939 by the English for subversive activities. Getting word from his comrades on the outside that the British repression had become still more heavy-handed, Stern formed the *Lohamei Herut Israel*—"Fighters for the Freedom of Israel"—which became known as *Lehi* through a contraction of its initials. Lehi was pejoratively called the "Stern Gang" by its detractors, who sought to brand this activist group as thugs and gangsters.

Stern was the furthest thing in the world from a hoodlum. He was an intellectual who had arrived from Poland at the age of eighteen, and soon became a student at the Hebrew University in Jerusalem. His indignation at the acts of the British led him to write inspirational poetry for the underground. But Stern was above all an activist; and simultaneously, he compiled a manual in Hebrew on the use of the revolver. The group he headed was instrumental in causing the British to desist from open acts of cruelty towards Jewish prisoners. When two Jewish boys were flogged by the British soldiery after protests had failed, Stern

seized two British soldiers and treated them in like fashion. It was then that the British took notice. If conscience couldn't dissuade from brutality, then Stern's measure for measure could—and did. But Abraham Stern lasted but a short while. In 1942, the British tracked him down, forced entry into his home in Tel Aviv, and shot him dead on sight.

I must digress here to recount a personal experience. One night in 1945, I was walking on upper Broadway in Manhattan when I heard some young people speaking Hebrew. I greeted the group, and asked them from what city they had come, and what news they might have. After a few minutes' conversation, I invited them to my home. In the conversation that ensued, I learned much about these young people. One of them, Saul Eshel, has become a lifelong friend.

Saul was then seventeen. He was studying engineering at Pratt Institute in Brooklyn. He had been sent away from Palestine by his parents, who had managed somehow to spirit him out of the Jaffa jail where he had been incarcerated for his anti-British activity. His two older brothers had been caught by the British, and had been deported to Kenya.

Some years later, when I was in Israel I met these two dreaded members of the Stern Gang. I was

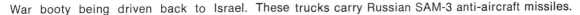

War booty being driven back to Israel. These trucks carry Russian SAM-3 anti-aircraft missiles.

shown the notebooks that they had kept while in detention along with the other villainous characters and Jewish blackguards held in the British prison camps of Kenya. To make constructive use of their time, these Sternists had formed an educational group. Each one had volunteered to teach everyone else in the group what he knew about any subject. The notebooks contained lessons in mathematics, in geography, in sociology, in economics—a hodgepodge of knowledge not too different from a secondary school curriculum.

I can only record that the two boys I met were gentle souls. Today, they are heads of families and respected citizens of Israel.

I write in some detail here only to counterbalance the propaganda that has surrounded this dedicated group. I am convinced in retrospect that nothing except the eye-for-an-eye approach would have been sufficient retaliation to swerve the British. Nothing but the kind of harassment administered by the Sternists would have caused the British to call it quits. For, in 1946, the British had not only increased their commitment to the Arabs, but had increased their military strength in Palestine to 100,000 men. They had in fact all but repudiated the Balfour Declaration. However extreme some of the tactics of the Irgun may have appeared to

Scene in an Israeli enclave on the West Bank of the Suez.

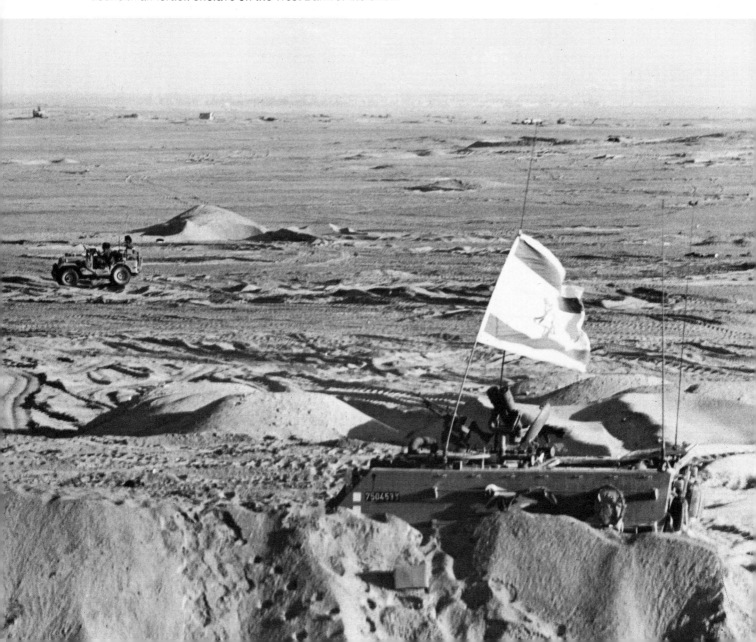

outsiders, to those who knew at first hand the relentlessness with which the British were flouting their commitment to the Jews, and the cruel mockery the British were making of their international obligation, the measures taken by this small band of resisters can be understood. The desperate actions of those days were dictated by overwhelmingly crushing events. Could any other measures have succeeded? I doubt it. I know that there are many Israelis, and perhaps some historians who share my view.

In February of 1942, a ship named the Struma left the shores of Rumania carrying 770 refugees from Nazi oppression. While the boat was still in Mediterranean waters, the British made it clear that they would not allow the Struma to land in Palestine. They had spotted the vessel, and had lined up British men-of-war in readiness to fire at the craft with its pitiful human cargo.

The Struma then headed for Turkey; but the Turkish Government, too, refused to allow the boat to land its passengers. The ship had no other recourse than to head back to Rumania from whence it had come. For whatever reason, on its way back, the Struma foundered in the Black Sea, and all aboard were lost.

When the news of this tragic event reached Palestine, the Jewish community was outraged. To have survived the Nazi holocaust, and then to not be allowed entry to a land where willing people were waiting to receive them was deemed monstrous. Outcries issued from Jewish

Even in peace Saudia won't recognize Israel

WASHINGTON (INA). — Saudi Arabia will not recognize Israel even if it concludes a peace settlement with its neighbours and withdraws to the pre-June, 1967, borders, Sheikh Ahmed Yamani, the Saudi Minister of Petroleum, said on the CBS' "Face the Nation" television program yesterday.

Yamani, replying to reporters' questions, drew a distinction between Israel's immediate neighbours and other Arab countries. He said that if Israel withdrew from all of the Arab territories, including East Jerusalem, under the terms of Resolution 242, 1967, "what matters is that the countries that surround Israel" recognize it and its borders. For those far away, it was not important. It was "not important or significant for all Arab countries to recognize and live in peace" with Israel.

UNIVERSITIES REOPEN

SOME soldiers home on brief leaves from the front complain that they cannot stand the long faces they find at the rear. Some senior officers, on the other hand, have complained that life should not go on in its normal fashion while some men are having to spend long months in the reserves. There is enough unavoidable hardship, they claim, in the fact that some units of the army are more urgently needed than others, and that an army medic may be released while a mechanic continues to serve.

This has worried some soldiers. "People won't want to give jobs in future to men with a 'fighting' classification because they are the first to be called up and the last to come home," one has said. Their periods of duty will have to be equalized in some fashion in due course.

Yesterday, the universities announced that they would reopen later this month, but set a second date in March for students not released now, and that these would be able to complete their year during the summer. Teachers not on military service will donate their summer months to continue courses for the late-comers. This second date should go a long way towards calming the anxiety of students afraid they were going to miss the year if the universities begin work now. If the reserves cannot be released by March, then some form of rotation will have to be devised by the army to balance out the present admitted inequalities, for students as well as for others needed by the army.

A student who misses a year out of the middle of his studies is liable to give up and abandon the course. The planned summer semester obviously will not give the army students all the time they should have had, but they have already been promised all possible consideration in the matter of timetables and examination dates — though not achievement levels. There is enough hardship in continued service without the added fear that their whole civilian future will be imperilled.

Life in the rear could reasonably become more modest while the threat of war has not yet receded and so many men remain in uniform, but it would be self-defeating to close the universities for the rest of the year, and that is what is now at stake. There are approximately another 30,000 students waiting for courses to start, either women, men released from the reserves, or those not in the reserves at all. It is not an injustice to allow them to get on with their work as long as proper provision is made for the others to get an equal chance in another three months.

Diana Rigg of TV's 'Avengers' here to do 'whatever I can'

By YA'ACOV FRIEDLER
Jerusalem Post Reporter

HAIFA. — "It is awkward for an Englishwoman to be in Israel today because of the British policy towards Israel," English actress Diana Rigg said last night. "But I felt the need to be here and do whatever I can, which is unfortunately very little."

Miss Rigg, best known in Israel as Mrs. Peel of the TV "Avengers" series, is here for a week's visit with her Israeli husband, the painter Menahem Gefen, to entertain the wounded and the troops and visit his family.

Interviewed in the Dan Carmel Hotel here, she said that they had been in the U.S. when the war started, and her husband, who was himself wounded in the Palmach, wanted to come back. "We came as soon as we could," she said.

Her appearances before the wounded in the Rambam Hospital and before Navy personnel on board one of the ships on Saturday marked the first time she had attempted such entertainment, she said. "I'm an actress and work with texts. I can't speak Hebrew, except for a few words, but nevertheless I feel I did well. Maybe the pleasure lies in the sense of communication with another world my visit gave them, after their weeks in hospital. I gave them a different kind of contact."

In addition, she was photographed with each of the men, and the photos would no doubt also give them pleasure and hopefully help them a little over the suffering still facing them, the actress said. She noted that in the Navy "they were so proud to show me their ship, and despite my bad voice they got me to sing for them."

Diana Rigg with some of the crew of an Israeli Navy missile boat which she visited.

For the rest of their stay she will visit more wounded soldiers and troops, and though the "Avengers" did not have a long run on Israel TV ("I can understand that it was too English") she seemed thrilled that she is widely recognised wherever she goes.

Asked whether she was considering converting to Judaism, Miss Rigg said she would not do so until she felt a need. So far she did not know enough about the Jewish faith and she would certainly not convert for the sake of convenience. But she was learning Hebrew, and would "certainly" consider coming to live here, if the right job were available. "I love acting, and that's a problem for me here as an English actress. But we'll come as often as possible."

communities all over the world. The British were universally denounced. But they kept fast to their policy. And public support for the Irgun increased mightily.

On April 13, 1947, the refugee ship, *Theodor Herzl,* arrived at the port of Haifa. Along its sides, it carried a huge banner emblazoned in English which read: "The Germans destroyed our families —Don't you destroy our hopes." The *Herzl* was one of a large flotilla of ships, large and small, which peppered the Palestinian coast, struggling to sneak in as many refugees as it could salvage from the human wreckage of Europe. Some were saved;

but many of the boats were captured by the British and the human cargo disgorged at Cyprus. Here the refugees were placed behind barbed wire like so many criminals. They had survived one detention camp run by the Nazis only to end up in another run by the British. And they had been incarcerated in both for no other crime than the crime of having been born Jewish.

Finally, the dormant conscience of the world was stirred. Concern to provide a homeland for the remnant of European Jewry inspired the General Assembly of the United Nations to call a session

German-Israel group from Bundestag due here today

By BRIAN ARTHUR
Jerusalem Post Correspondent

BONN. — A five-man delegation from the Bonn parliament's "German-Israel Group" arrives in Israel today for a four-day visit and talks with Government and Knesset leaders.

Mr. Metzger, 40, is also a deputy chairman of the ruling Socialist wing in the Bundestag and a staunch friend of Israel. When the October war broke out he issued one of the strongest pro-Israel statements to be heard here.

While the Socialist-Liberal government of Chancellor Willy Brandt tries to pursue a "balanced" line towards Arabs and Israelis, the German-Israel Group has never made

any bones about its pro-Israel sympathies. It takes up about 20 per cent of the 496-member Bundestag.

After the war ended Metzger said he did not believe Israel should give up all the territories and rely on international guarantees alone for its security. "The decisive factor has to be the safety of Israel," he explained

While the coalition and opposition wings believe the parliamentary group should clearly state its support for Israel, they tend to split over whether the Bonn government should also take a pro-Israel stand. Coalition members tend to feel the government can help Israel more by remaining officially neutral. The Christian Democrats lean towards a more open pro-Israel policy.

Argentine Jewish help

Jerusalem Post Reporter

TEL AVIV. — Argentinian Jewry threw its entire weight behind Israel during the Yom Kippur War — and is doing so today — not only with word and money but also with deeds, Jose Moskovits, president of the Association of Survivors of Nazi Persecution in Argentina, said here yesterday. He reported that with the war's outbreak all the Jewish organizations banded together to form a "general emergency committee" which directed affairs.

Not only did this committee "collect three times as much money" as in the Six Day War, but it also asked President Peron to use his good offices among non-aligned countries to support Israel.

Other acts included public pro-Israel demonstrations, and anti-Soviet demonstrations (which led to 21 members of Bnei Akiva being arrested); publishing large ads in the daily papers in support of Israel; publishing Sadat's letter to Hitler in which Sadat supported Hitler; and taking steps to reveal a forgery of the Arab organization in Argentina, which circulated a pamphlet saying that the Peronists supported the Arabs (which they did not); and collecting packages for the Soldiers Welfare Committee.

in April, 1947. A United Nations Special Committee on Palestine was established. This committee was immediately boycotted by the Arabs. In August, the UNSCOP (as this Committee came to be known) proposed a plan to divide Palestine into three parts: a Jewish State, an Arab State, and a small internationally administered zone which would include Jerusalem.

On November 29, 1947, the General Assembly of the United Nations, led by the United States and Russia, approved the UNSCOP proposal. In the vote that followed, Great Britain abstained. The Arab states, in one great huff, left the meeting, and announced their intention to oppose implementation of the Partition plan. They weren't going to listen, no matter what, to the United Nations.

Many Zionist leaders, and a great portion of the Jewish people, were dismayed by the amount of

land that had been whittled away from the original promise. The land now granted to them by the vote of the U.N. was now less than half of that promised by Balfour. But the Jewish people, as a whole, were content to accept the plan, for at last a legal home had been found for their refugees.

Not so with the Arabs. It didn't make any difference how small, how miniscule, how minute the land grant was.

On May 14, 1948, when the British High Commissioner left Palestine, a Declaration of Independence was proclaimed by the Israeli leader Ben Gurion. Simultaneously, five countries of the Arab League—Lebanon, Syria, Jordan, Egypt, Iraq—began war against Israel.

Again, in 1956, and once again in 1967, Israel was forced to defend itself. The Yom Kippur War is the fourth war the Jews have been compelled to fight within a period of twenty-six years.

TREATMENT OF POW'S

To the Editor of The Jerusalem Post

Sir, — I refer to your report, "All prisoners in Egypt were tortured" (December 3). It is agony even to read of the tortures and suffering to which your men were subjected during their captivity in Egypt and right-minded citizens of all nations must join in condemning and preventing the recurrence of such brutality.

At the same time, I feel duty-bound to bring to your notice one of the exceptions: Our eldest son was wounded and taken prisoner by the Egyptians, but he fortunately fell into the hands of decent people, was given immediate and adequate medical treatment both in the field and later the prison, and he recalls with gratitude the fair behaviour of his doctors and the kindness of some of the jailers who washed and looked after him when he was too weak to take care of himself.

We owe it to all those still in captivity to do everything in our power to protect them from abuse and to secure their speedy release, but we also owe it to ourselves and all fair-minded people wherever they may be to record such acts of humanity; for it is deeds of compassion like these, performed by ordinary people, regardless of borders and creed, that will eventually help us towards mutual understanding and peace.

R.E.

(Name and address supplied.)
Ra'anana, December 4.

BRITONS ADMIRE GOLDA MOST

LONDON (AP). — Israeli Premier Golda Meir is the woman most admired by the British public, according to a Gallup poll published in the "Sunday Telegraph."

The poll showed President Nixon as the third most-admired man close behind Prime Minister Edward Heath and Prince Philip, husband of Queen Elizabeth.

During the previous two years the Queen gained first place.

'Take a hitch-hiker' campaign is launched

By MACABEE DEAN
Jerusalem Post Reporter

TEL AVIV. — The Ministry of Transport yesterday launched a "give a lift to the hitch-hiker" campaign among the country's 200,000 private car owners. Gad Ya'acobi, Deputy Minister of Transport, said that many volunteer bodies, as well as the Histadrut and other organizations, were cooperating fully, and many were organizing car pools among their employees.

Each private car owner would be approached by a member of Gadna — generally at a petrol station — and asked to stick a "volunteer driver" tab on his car. Anybody needing a lift would be asked to carry a large placard printed with his destination.

Mr. Ya'acobi pointed out that public transport is only functioning at about half its normal capacity. "Public morale would be raised by creating a bond of solidarity between civilians and civilians and between civilians and soldiers, and the carless day would impose an added burden on public transport," he said.

'We'll go a long way' to meet the Arabs

By JESSE ZEL LURIE
Special to The Jerusalem Post

NEW YORK. — A slight figure in a black dinner jacket, black tie, and black eyepatch, standing in the spotlight at one end of the cavernous Hotel Hilton ballroom on Saturday night brought over 300 U.J.A. leaders to a high pitch of enthusiastic applause with his ringing declaration "we have never been so strong as we are now."

Minister of Defence Moshe Dayan may be under attack at home, but he has lost none of the great admiration in which he is held by those who have raised fantastic sums for the U.J.A. since the disastrous Yom Kippur attack just eight weeks ago. His charisma is undiminished here and in need of no assistance, but he had the aid of his blonde, beautiful new wife, making her first appearance at his side before an American audience.

Israel forces will remain mobilized "until we can negotiate an agreement in Geneva, even though it may take months," Dayan declared. "We are going to negotiate not only peace but the final permanent boundaries of Israel," he said.

Once again he stated that Israel "will pay a lot" for a settlement with the Arabs. "We are ready to pull back from a part of Sinai and other places," he promised, but he warned that Israel "needs political wisdom to insist only on what is really essential."

This is Israel's first chance for a peace conference, he said. "We waited a long time for it." Israel must try to understand the Arab viewpoint and "we will go a long way to meet them."

More appreciation for Dutch backing of Israel

Jerusalem Post Reporter

HAIFA. — Honorary membershp in the Israel Seamen's Union was conferred yesterday on the honorary consul of Holland, Avraham Uriel.

It was granted as a sign of recognition and apprecation of the courageous stand of the Dutch people and government against the Arab oil blackmail, and their present support of Israel in its greatest hour of need and of the Jews during the Nazi terror, union spokesman Moshe Gutter said.

Union secretary Shlomo Avitan presented Mr. Uriel with a membership scroll and a union lapel badge.

Hillel Seidel of the Histadrut Executive, who is chairman of the Israel Committee for Holland, announced at the ceremony in the union offices that the Citrus Marketing Board had decided to present 1,000 cases of oranges to the children of Holland. The Board would hand over the gift from one of its shipments to Rotterdam shortly.

Mr. Seidel said he had asked the Communications Ministry to issue a special stamp next February 21 to commemorate the general strike of the Amsterdam transport workers on February 26, 1941, against the deportation of Dutch Jews during the German occupation of the Netherlands. Some of the strikers were executed by the Germans.

He said that thousands of letters of appreciation — many of them with pressed flowers — had been sent to the children of Holland by Israeli schoolchildren, and he had asked the Education Ministry to arrange for a "Holland Day" to be marked in schools soon. Mr. Seidel said that the Israel Ambassador in The Hague had informed him that the Israeli reaction to the Dutch stand had met with widespread public appreciation.

Egyptians murdered 28 PoWs

Jerusalem Post Diplomatic Correspondent

Israel yesterday submitted to the International Red Cross a preliminary report on Egypt's torture and murder of Israel prisoners-of-war, referring to at least 28 attested cases of murder of PoWs. A copy of the report was sent to U.N. Secretary-General Dr. Kurt Waldheim.

On Saturday the Government complained to the Red Cross that on the Syrian front, 42 soldiers were murdered after their capture. In a letter sent on Saturday night to Dr. Waldheim, enclosing a copy of this complaint, Israel said that atrocities, including murder and maiming, were carried out by Moroccan and Iraqi troops serving with the Syrians.

Yesterday's report attesting to 28 PoW murders at the hands of Egyptians also refers to attested cases of torture and humiliation at the time of capture, during transport to the prison camps, and in the prison camps themselves.

Officials in Jerusalem said last night that there would certainly be more reports as evidence is collated from PoWs returned from Egypt. All the cases of torture and murder reported to the Red Cross yesterday were based on evidence of returning PoWs.

The officials said that the 28 cases of murder were by no means a comprehensive list. At one strongpoint that surrendered, for instance, the Egyptians bayonetted the dead and wounded Israelis lying on the ground and it was impossible to know how many wounded men had been killed in that episode. Their deaths had not been included in that first report. What is already clear beyond doubt is that a great many more than 28 men are known to have fallen into Egyptian hands alive — and have not returned.

An initial complaint on Syrian atrocities last month listed 28 murders, but the latest document submitted on Saturday said new cases had come to light, indicating that "no fewer than 42 separate cases of murder have been committed."

Giving details of violations of the Geneva Conventions, Israel said five soldiers captured at a Mount Hermon strongpoint had been maltreated and killed in the games room of the military post. Their grave was pointed out by a Syrian prisoner-of-war present at the time.

In another case, a downed Israel pilot was stabbed to death at the military airfield at Dumeir by Iraqi troops.

Other information indicated that six Israeli pilots who parachuted into Syrian territory at different times were killed by bursts of small arms fire.

The complaint to the Red Cross also said the Government had "reliable information" that a Moroccan soldier serving with the Syrian forces had a sack filled with parts of bodies of Israeli soldiers (palms and tongues) which he intended to send home as souvenirs.

Most of the slain soldiers had been stripped of their uniforms as an act of humiliation and dishonour.

Even before the outbreak of the war, the complaint to the Red Cross charged, instructions were given to Syrian troops to remove identity discs from the bodies of dead Israelis to make their subsequent identification more difficult

This history of Zionism as set forth in these pages, sketchy as it is, has been related in order to convey the historical commitment of the Jew to his homeland. For without this awareness, one must fail to understand how it is that a small group of people is willing to stand up and fight against foes that outnumber it by something like 200 to 1. The Arab world is huge, and the Moslem world even greater, extending far into the Asian continent, and deep into the recesses of Africa. Moslems constitute most of Indonesia, and there is even a substantial Moslem community in the Philippines.

Against such formidable opposition, and against the boundless wealth created by Arab oil, how then can the Jews hope to prevail? Is not the struggle hopeless? Why do the Jews carry on?

The answer is *ain brera* — possibly the most popular catch-phrase in Israel — "There is no alternative." If the choice is *accepting annihilation without a fight* versus *fighting against all odds*, there is no choice.

Yet this new Israeli generation enjoys one advantage: It has grown from the loins of fighters. It is the generation that was reared on the story of Masada. These are the sons and daughters of parent who have *fought*.

It has been estimated that 80 percent of the Jews now residing in Israel have spent approximately 60 percent of their lives in war, in serious conflict, or in some kind of vital crisis.

Eight deported for subversion

Jerusalem Post Arab Affairs Reporter

The authorities yesterday deported to Jordan a prominent East Jerusalem lawyer and seven West Bank political activists including the mayor of El-Bireh, the twin town of Ramallah. All were accused of "undermining security, law and order and of inciting the population to cooperation with the terrorist movement."

All eight deportees were sent across the border somewhere in the Arava at about 8 o'clock yesterday morning.

The expulsions came a day after the Cabinet discussed the recent outburst of pro-terrorist activity in the West Bank, coupled with three major sabotage attacks in the Old City of Jerusalem, Hebron and Nablus, and distribution of leaflets calling for civil disobedience. The Cabinet was believed to have considered reprisals, reflected in the arrest of subversive elements, the blowing up of a number of houses and the banishment of leading activists.

Yesterday's deportations were the first in some four years when subversive political activity came to a virtual end. Amman radio yesterday gave the total number of those banished since 1967 as 1,508.

Heading yesterday's list was Abdul-Mohsin Abu Maizer, 45, who is a member of the Old City Moslem Supreme Council. The charge against the Jerusalem lawyer indicates that he was behind the political statement of the Moslem Council last week, supporting the recent Arab summit conference's decision to regard the Palestine Liberation Organization as the sole representative of the Palestinian people. The authorities accused Abu Maizer of having incited the population to cooperation with the terrorist organizations and to rebellion and disobedience against the authorities. The charge recalled that, in 1967 Abu Maizer was banished for a number of months for "incitement to rebellion."

Abu Maizer's expulsion was personally ordered by Defence Minister Moshe Dayan, while the banishment of the seven residents of the Administered Areas was issued by the Commander of Judea and Samaria, T/A Rafael Vardi.

The seven were headed by the mayor of El-Bireh, Abdul-Jawad Saleh, 45, who was said to have been "active in the town and region in mustering support for terrorist organizations and opposition to the authorities." Another El-Bireh resident, Jeries Awwad Kawwas, 35, a teacher, was deported for having been "active in an underground organization which preached support for the terrorists." He was also said to have attempted to undermine normal life in the region, while "inciting to oppose Arab work in Israel, set up roadblocks and distribute leaflets."

Similar charges were laid against a 40-year-old Ramallah resident, Jamil Hassan Odeh, who was also among the deportees.

The other four deportees were all from Nablus. They were a physician, Dr. Walid Kamhawi, 50; a lawyer, Hussein Mohammed Jabour, 40; a teacher, Shaker Abu Hajaleh, 40; and a political activist, Arabi Moussa Awwad, 40, who was described as a "ranking member of an underground subversive organization."

T/A Vardi yesterday called the members of the Nablus City Council to his offices and warned them it is their responsibility to see that the atmosphere in the town is not conducive to acts of sabotage such as the attack on the military governor.

The publisher and editor of the Jerusalem Arab weekly "Al-Fajr" yesterday obtained an order *nisi* from the High Court, calling on the Ministers of Defence and Police to show cause why they should not refrain from deporting them.

Editor and publisher Joseph Nasri and his assistant editor Jamil Hamad claimed that the eight political activists were expelled yesterday because they had publicly supported the decisions of the Algiers summit which called for recognition of the Palestine Liberation Organization as the sole representative of the Arab-Palestinian people.

Since they too shared these views, the applicants feared they would also be expelled. They said their expulsion to Jordan would constitute extradition to "a hostile country" since they opposed the Hashemite regime.

QUIET ON EGYPTIAN FRONT DESPITE DAILY INCIDENTS

By CHARLES WEISS
Jerusalem Post Reporter

The situation on the Egyptian front is threatening, at the least. The U.N. reports as many as 30 truce violations a day along the cease-fire lines, most of them shooting incidents. The Egyptian Minister of War, Ahmed Ismail Ali, claims the Israelis on the west bank of the Canal are completely surrounded and have trouble getting supplies. A senior Israeli officer last week spoke of a high state of alert on both sides.

None of this eve-of-war tension came across in the course of a 1,000-kilometre tour of the lines Sunday. The front seemed peaceful, almost bucolic, and no shooting was heard.

Now that the talks at Kilometre 101 have broken down, the famous tent has been converted into an officers' mess for the U.N. personnel stationed there. The Finns have set up a field sauna that everyone uses together — U.N., Egyptians and Israelis.

The area commanders seem to hit it off much better than the generals, who couldn't come to agreement on most things. The Israeli, Segen "Pinny," holds daily meetings with his Egyptian opposite number, Colonel Youssef Maki, to arrange for the relief convoys to the town of Suez and the encircled Egyptian Third Army. They decide what supplies will be let through the Israeli lines on how many trucks.

Segen "Pinny" says they also exchange Hebrew and Arabic lessons for one hour a day.

There are two Russians serving with the U.N. Truce Supervision Organization assigned to this sec-

tor. One of them, Captain Alex, came over to talk to us.

In awkward-but-fluent English, he apologized for his obvious hangover. There had been a birthday party the previous night for one of the Swedish officers, and everyone had attended. He proudly recited the to-your-health toasts in Hebrew, Arabic, Swedish, Finnish and Russian.

The Russians go out on patrol separately, accompanied by a Swedish officer. They are not allowed to enter Israel-held territory.

While we were talking, a long line of trucks carrying the day's relief supplies began to form up on the Egyptian side of the 101 compound. Finnish U.N. drivers took over and drove them past the Israeli sentries on to Suez, 33 kilometres away.

(Incidentally, Kilometre 101 is a misnomer. The kilometre marker closest to the tent reads 100, and the next one is 99.)

SUPPLIES CHECKED

In Suez, porters recruited from the town's civilian population form up in work gangs to unload the trucks and lay the cartons of canned goods or sacks of rice or flour out on the ground for inspection. An Israeli sapper went over them carefully, shaking the cans and running a mine detector over the sacks.

The empty trucks turned around and set off back to Cairo. Other empties came out of Suez, fuelled up with petrol brought by the convoy, and loaded the supplies for the town.

Thirty-three trucks make the trip every day, carrying less than 200 tons. The operation takes half a day from start to finish. The U.N. does not interfere.

In another relief operation, north

of Suez, supplies are ferried across the Canal to the Egyptian Third Army. Till now the daily quota, seven days a week, was 25 trucks— about 150 tons. It has now been raised to 30 trucks so that the Finnish drivers can have Sunday off to attend church services.

The Israelis allow 100 Egyptian soldiers to come over to the west bank and unload the trucks onto amphibious armoured personnel carriers or launch-driven lighters. No more than 10 can be in the water at one time, but the Israelis say there are now fewer than 10 as even the Egyptians are trying to conserve fuel. Once a week the Israelis fill the gas tanks, allowing as much as they can consume in a week's trips back and forth.

The picture is much the same as at Suez. The trucks are unloaded first onto the ground and the goods checked to see there is no military contraband.

The Israeli officer in charge said there have been no attempts to smuggle weapons or ammunition, but the Egyptians have tried to get fuel across. He told of one case last week when jerricans containing 500 litres of medicinal alcohol were stopped. An army doctor was consulted who said it was far more than could possibly be needed. Only 45 litres were permitted.

Pure alcohol can be used as a fuel or even converted into an explosive.

In the course of the day-long trip we heard no shooting, and no one seemed to be anticipating any. There were none of the feverish logistical or armour movements associated with an imminent war.

Nevertheless, towards evening the Army Spokesman reported the usual quota of daily incidents.

The new generation has been brought up in pride, and recognizes its strength. It is not likely to give up very easily. Like the sabra, the native prickly pear after which they are named, these boys and girls, however sweet, carry thorns.

Many Israelis are taken to Masada by their parents when they are thirteen, at the time of their Bar Mitzvah. They are taken to Masada to be shown

the last stronghold of the zealots who held out against the Romans in 73 A.D. Rather than have the Romans dislodge them from this mountain fortress, each man slew himself, his wife, and his children. The Romans took no captives.

The young see Masada and they understand. They know that they might have to die for their country.

'War pinpointed industry's failings'

Arafat 'won't allow' peace with Israel

HAIFA. — "Israel's industry is too small in scope and has accepted low standards of quality. A great investment of effort and resources to remedy the situation is called for," Technion President Amos Horev said yesterday. "This is one of the lessons of the Yom Kippur War," he said at a press conference.

Mr. Horev, who was for many years the defence establishment's chief scientist, stressed the importance of a developed industry for the strength and security of the country. It was his opinion that "there is no objective reason for industry's relative weakness."

During the war, he said, it had shown itself incapable of quick solutions to problems that cropped up, "and our dependence (on overseas supplies) proved to be much greater than we had thought. Our industrial capacity is not up to long-term challenges. A small country like Israel cannot be entirely independent, but it can be much more independent than we are, and defence strength is directly related to industrial strength."

Mr. Horev, who is himself an engineer, said the war had proved that far from having a surplus of technological manpower, Israel needs many more trained people in many fields — electronics, mechanical and aeronautical engineering, metallurgy and chemistry.

BEIRUT (UPI). — Terrorist leader Yasser Arafat said on Sunday that the "Palestinians" will "not allow" any Arab to recognize or sign peace with Israel, the Iraq News Agency reported yesterday.

Arafat was speaking at a rally of the Palestinian Engineers Union in Baghdad.

He said, "We will not allow any Palestinian or Arab to compromise our historical rights (in the liberation of Palestine), recognize or sign peace with Israel." The "Palestinian revolution," he said, "will continue until it realizes all of its goals."

Syrian area yields rich ancient finds

ROSH PINA. — Well preserved buildings dating to the second and third centuries C.E. (the Roman period) were found during a three-week survey of the Syrian area captured during the October war.

The study was carried out last month by the Archaeological Survey Society with the aid of the Government Antiquities Department. It covered an area of about 20 by 25 kms.

Altars and temples found among the dozens of villages and ruins in the area indicate that it was inhabited during the Roman period by a Semitic pagan population. The name by which they called themselves is not known, but a number of Greek inscriptions were found and await deciphering.

Many of the buildings continued in use by present-day villagers who used them as stables, storage sheds and even residences. The finds are to be published for the benefit of the general public and scholars.

This structure, which dates to the second century C.E., was found at Nasei village by an Israeli archaeological team which last month surveyed the Syrian territory captured in the October War. The building owes its fine state of preservation to the strong basalt stones and excellent building techniques which went into its construction.

271

EGYPT GENERAL DESCRIBES HOW HE 'TRICKED ISRAEL'

CAIRO (Reuter). — Egyptian forces used 65 different ploys to distract Israel's attention from Cairo's build-up for the October war, the Assistant War Minister, Major-General Saad Maamoun, has revealed.

The general, whose remarks were published by "Al Ahram" yesterday, said these included having Egyptian soldiers swim in the Suez Canal as usual every day and ensuring that soldiers left their helmets off until the very moment of battle.

The general said he warned his men that anyone putting his helmet on one moment before attack would be forced to enter battle without it.

Giving details of tactics and battle losses, General Maamoun said the officer corps sustained negligible casualties despite the fact they were always at the head of their men. He said officer losses were only one-tenth of original estimates.

General Maamoun was the commander of the Second Army for the first eight days of the war, before suffering a heart attack. He became Assistant War Minister after his recovery.

He said soldiers who used to swim in the Canal at the same time every afternoon were ordered to continue the practice on October 6, the day the war erupted. They were in the water when the first shots were fired, he said.

He said the infantrymen who first crossed the Canal were armed only with short-range anti-tank guns and "a very limited number of long-range anti-tank rockets."

To enable them to withstand Israeli counter-attacks pending Egyptian establishment of pontoon bridges, "we resorted to a very primitive method, providing the troops with handcarts carrying more ammunition."

He said some 80,000 men crossed the Canal on the first day and 15 Israeli strongpoints were captured, the first one — south of Port Said — falling 83 minutes after the war's start. The second position, in the el-Shatt area, was taken seven minutes later.

It took up to six days to capture other points, he said. "All counter-attacks were repelled," he said.

On Israel's gains on the western bank of the Suez Canal in the Deversoir area, General Maamoun said that a 30-hour armoured battle, one of the biggest in military history, took place.

This was followed by seven days of bitter fighting before the Israelis were able to establish a bridgehead, he added.

Major-General Gamal Mohammed Alywn, the commander of the engineering unit, said the Egyptians managed to reduce the time of establishing a pontoon bridge from 24 to five hours. The Egyptian missile base system was an example that was followed later by the Warsaw Pact countries, he said.

Air Vice Marshal Mohammed al Fahmy later said the Egyptian Air defence missile system was the strongest in the Middle East.

Marshal Fahmy said that although Western sources had estimated Israel's aircraft losses at 200 planes and Eastern sources put them at 285, the real number was much higher.

Three South American soldiers,
part of the U.N. corps,
on a sightseeing stroll in Tel Aviv.

WHO ARE THE PALESTINIANS?

To the Editor of The Jerusalem Post

Sir, — In one of our regular get togethers of former British officers of the Palestine Police, some of them wondered who and what are the so-called Palestinians and how long they had lived in the country up to 1948, and where they had come from. They also wondered why these so-called Palestinians were refugees.

My former colleagues, all of whom were British officers in the Palestine Police, tell me they have documentary proof that the "Palestinians" are not and never were "Palestinians." They were and are illegal migrants into the Land of Israel from all the surrounding Arab countries, and they came searching for work and food from the Jewish settlers, because in their own Arab countries, they were homeless, jobless and on the verge of starvation.

BILL WILLIAMS
Kiryat Ono, November 30.

Church paper: Jewish link to J'lem is tenuous

Jerusalem Post Reporter

HAIFA. — The Jewish claim to Jerusalem is tenuous and of recent origin, according to the latest issue of "Er-Rabita," the monthly publication of the Greek Catholic Church here. In what is presented as an objective historical study by one George Takhoury, the magazine ignores 1,000 years of Jewish history and states that the Jewish link to Jerusalem "begins in 70 A.D." — when the temple and much of the city was destroyed by Rome.

Between 135 and the middle of the 19th century, the publication says, there were hardly any Jews at all in Jerusalem. It was only after 1838 that Jews began "infiltrating" Jerusalem and building synagogues.

After the Balfour Declaration of 1917 opened Palestine to large-scale Jewish immigration, the magazine continues, the newcomers built what is today new Jerusalem. Because of the tenuous claim of the Jewish Johnny-come-latelys — and because of the many Christian holy places in Jerusalem — the article concludes that the solution for the city is "internationalization."

Volunteers attack fleas at the front

By ABRAHAM RABINOVICH
Jerusalem Post Reporter

A squad of volunteer Jerusalem sanitation men last week crossed the Suez Canal to provide covering fire for servicemen who have been engaged for weeks in a bloody battle with hordes of Egyptian insects.

The sanitation men spent three days spraying disinfectant into billets and front line bunkers as close as 100 metres from Egyptian lines. The Egyptian soldiers have been less of a concern for the reservists in the area than the fleas, flies and other insects which have been attacking on all fronts since their arrival. The round the clock battle has left many of the Israeli troops covered from toe to head with insect bites.

The idea of dispatching the sanitation men came from Jerusalem City Manager Ronnie Feinstein, while serving with a reserve unit. Although the army has its own sanitation teams, there are not enough to cope with the legions of insects infesting the whole west bank area, particularly abandoned houses and Egyptian army bunkers now being used to billet Israeli troops.

The soldiers now rank these insects with the Sam-6 and Sagger anti-tank missiles as surprise Egyptian weapons.

An initial reconnaissance across the Canal was carried out two weeks ago by Yehuda Reider, deputy manager of the sanitation department. After spending two days being briefed by army sanitation experts and doctors, he returned to Jerusalem — covered with bites — and organized two pick-up trucks with insecticides for the trip back to Africa.

They came from the ample stocks maintained by the Municipality in the event that cholera or other plagues ever strike the capital. Accompanying Reider on his return trip were six men from his department, ranging in age up to 55.

The team used more than 100 litres of insecticide, mixing it with 20 times that amount of water pumped out of the Suez Canal. The material was sprayed from canisters carried by each man on his back.

"The work was difficult," says Reider. "We worked the whole day long and the canisters were heavy. But the soldiers were very appreciative."

It will take more than one spraying to stay ahead of the Egyptian fleas, however. Reider estimates that they will be back in their old lodgings within a week, and new spraying teams may be sent down within a few days on a blocking mission.

SOVIETS GAVE BEST WEAPONS TO ARABS FOR OCTOBER WAR

By Edward Luttwak

AMONG the weapons left behind on the Golan Heights by t h retreating Syrian army are dozen of BTR-60s — long, low eight-whee armoured troop carriers. Some are in standard Syrian camouflage colours; others are still in the deep green of the Russian army — these last no doubt brought over by the Russian airlift and t h r o w n into battle too hastily to be repainted.

Amidst the profusion of tanks, guns and carriers that litter t h e Golan Heights, the BTR-60s may not attract particular attention. But they should. For in a precise technical sense they demonstrate t h e extent of Russian recklessness in their arms supplies to the Syrians.

Most BTR-60s in Russian service (the standard carrier of the mechanized divisions) are the basic model, with no turret, no roof and a rudimentary machinegun pintle; first-line Russian divisions have an improved model — the PK, which does have a closed top. But the BTR-60s supplied to the Syrians were the latest and best model — the PB, which has a 14.5 mm gun turret, good radio equipment and many expensive refinements. Few Russian divisions have yet received the PBs, while the Syrians were given these vehicles in substantial numbers.

If in 1967 the Arab armies fought with a mixture of standard and obsolescent Russian equipment, in 1973 they were amply provided with the very best in each class of weapons, and in very large numbers.

The anti-tank missiles which blunted the cutting edge of Israel armour in the first days of war in the Canal sector included a large number of the PUR-64 Saggers, the latest weapon of its class, while the standard weapon in Russian service is still the older PUR-61 Snapper. Nor did the Russians refrain from exposing their most modern operational tank, the T-62 with its 115 mm smooth-bore gun of novel design, to possible capture.

Until now, all that was known in the West about these weapons was what could be learned from the examination of fuzzy parade photographs; n o w the Israelis have quite a few for conversion and use, as well as for detailed examination. According to press reports, s o m e captured T-62s (found intact) have been made available to the United States as a token of Israeli gratitude.

FROGS AGAINST CIVILIANS

Of much more obvious political significance, although not of a n y great tactical utility, are the Frog bombardment rockets, which the Soviet Union supplied to Syria and which the Syrians fired into Galilee. Though unguided, these weapons (Free Rocket Over Ground) are by no means unsophisticated. In t h e Russian army they are the standard battlefield nuclear weapon.

Much too costly to warrant use with non-nuclear warheads, these three-ton bombardment rockets — carried one apiece on heavy truck-launchers — are of an entirely different class from the Katyusha rockets which have been supplied to the Arabs for many years.

It has been said that the United States had refused to sell the high-accuracy Lance missile to Israel on the ground that it was "provocative," although the Israelis wanted it for a precise tactical purpose — to destroy high-value targets such as SAM batteries. As against this perhaps excessive American restraint, t h e Russians supplied at least 40 Frogs to the Syrians in the full knowledge that their only possible use would be the indiscriminate bombardment of civilian settlements. (They are too inaccurate for realistic use against military targets.)

ENTER THE SCUD

Of course — in comparison with the Soviet introduction of Scud missiles into Egypt — the entire Frog business is reduced to insignificance. Alongside the Scud, even heavy nuclear-capable bombardment rockets are little more than lethal toys. In fact, it is an ominous sign of the degeneration of the West that t h e entire world seems to have absorbed the news without any visible reaction.

In 1967, the Soviet Union did not attempt to resupply its Arab clients until the fighting was over and the cease-fires had come in force; in 1973 the Soviet Union mounted the biggest military airlift in history in a clear bid to reinforce an apparent Arab victory.

This did not suffice to prevent the Syrian defeat nor to keep the Israelis from crossing the Canal. But t h e airlift did negate the Israel air strategy of the first days of war whose goal was to exhaust the stocks of Arab anti-aircraft missiles: SAM-6s and SAM-7s were fired by the volley until the fighting came to a stop. The Israelis were consciously depleting their airpower in order to destroy and absorb the Arab missile systems. They must have thought that the rules of the game would be those of 1967, when neither side resupplied until the fighting was over.

But the real meaning of detente was made clear when the Russian airlift began and when the Israelis had to face the bitter realization that they lost pilots and aircraft to no purpose, since their small stock of fighters was being countered by an unending flow of missiles.

LIMITED STOCKS

Issued only to the first-line AA battalions of the lead Russian divisions, the SAM-6 is not cheap; even the Soviet Union has a limited stock of these complex missiles. But the Russians did not hesitate to strip their own AA units in order to keep the Arabs supplied with SAM-6s and the Arabs were using them as if they were 10-cent shotgun shells.

First of all, the Scud is a full-fledged nuclear delivery weapon. Fired from Egypt with its standard warhead, it could do at least as much damage to Tel Aviv as Hiroshima suffered in 1945.

As reported in the press, U.S. Intelligence sources now believe that the weapons are indeed in Egypt (30 is the figure given) and that they *are* fitted with nuclear warheads. But once the presence of these sophisticated missiles (Scud-B/MAS-543 carrier) was confirmed, one did not need special Intelligence sources to know that 'they would in fact have fission warheads. To fit a common high explosive warhead on a weapon such as the Scud would be like chartering a jumbo jet to send last week's papers to Los Angeles.

Loose talk about a missile that the Israelis are supposed to have developed, for whose existence there is not a single shred of evidence, is now used in an attempt to justify the deployment of Scuds in Egypt. This merely means that those who have entertained such extravagant hopes about the new and supposed benign policies of the Soviet Union in this "era of detente" are still refusing to face the facts. **The Scud is a clear sign of Russian intent and should be heeded as such.**

DEADLY UMBRELLA

The best-advertised weapon of the war was the SAM-6 Gainful anti-aircraft missile. It is quite new (first seen in 1967) and much more effective than its immediate predecessor, the SAM-3 Goa, since it has a redundant guidance system. If its ground radar is jammed, t h e SAM-6 can still find its target by infra-red homing.

At the same time, the SAM-6 has longer effective range than t h e much larger SAM-2 (V-750 VK), which has been on the scene for many years. But what really made the SAM-2, SAM-3, SAM-6 and the infra-red SAM-7 Grail such a serious threat was not just their design but the fact that the Soviet Union supplied these very costly weapons in numbers that are huge by any standards. It was in respect of these weapons that the tactical effect of the Russian airlift was most important.

The quality and quantity of the Russian weapons supplied to Egypt and Syria in the last year raises an important political question. Secretary Kissinger has assured us that the Russians did not start the war. This may be true, although the evidence is, to say the least, contra-dictory.

But why then did the Soviet Union supply such large numbers of new SAM-6s, SAM-7s, self-propelled quad 23 mm cannon, T-62 tanks and so on to the Arab belligerents in the course of this year? After all, Russo-Egyptian relations were supposed to have deteriorated after the June 1972 expulsion of the Russian advisory/fighting corps in Egypt: Russo-Syrian relations were also deteriorating by all accounts.

Only one explanation seems to be reasonable: t h a t the Russian goal was non-regional — to inflict a bloody wound on Israel in order to punish the Jewish state for its defiant independence and for its role in activating the embarrassing Jewish emigration question in the Soviet Union itself. This is perceived by the Soviet Union as a threat to its internal security and, as such, altogether more important than most foreign policy goals.

The Russians know full well what value there is in Arab gratitude. But they must have also reasoned that pumping weapons into the Middle East would sooner or later result in the spilling of Jewish blood, and that was probably a sufficient payoff for the men in the Kremlin.

As it is, they are probably disappointed, since the loss of j u s t over 2,000 Israelis killed is much less than could have been expected, given the weight of Russian weaponry thrown into the battle.

Above all, the wound inflicted on the people of Israel has been insufficient to cow them into submission. However, the Israelis were in some cases overwhelmed by the weight of Russian hardware (the Syrians alone had more tanks than Britain and France combined); in other cases they were outclassed (in Sinai one can see the Russian radar-assisted quadruple 23 mm AA gun system, ZPU-23 mm Gun Dish, mounted on modern tracked chasses, alongside the twin 20 mm AA guns of the Israelis mounted on 25-year-old half-tracked carriers).

But in war the human element is as important as it ever was and the stolid courage of the Egyptian infantryman did not suffice; in 1973 even more than in 1967 the Egyptians were saved in extremis only by the manipulated cease-fire procured by the Soviet Union.

(Edward Luttwak is the author of "Coup D'Etat," "Dictionary of Modern War," and a forthcoming book on Middle East defence. This article was written for the "Near East Report," Washington.)

VISIT HOLLAND

To the Editor of The Jerusalem Post
Sir, — I'm now on my ninth visit to Israel. My itinerary was planned so that I would spend a week in Rome on my way home. However, in view of the stand Holland is taking against the Arab blackmail, I'll spend my week in Holland instead of Rome.

MAX NOSANCHUI
Tel Aviv (Southfield, Mi.), Dec. 6.

Volunteers in J'lem
help families of war victims

Jerusalem Post Reporter

A volunteer centre has been set up in Jerusalem to assist the families of the hundreds of residents killed, wounded or missing in the war.

The centre is seeking volunteers who can drive relatives to visit wounded Jerusalemites recovering in rest homes around the country, baybysit with children or otherwise assist. The centre is run by a group of persons formerly connected with the volunteer office at Hadassah Hospital during the war. "We had a tremendous turnout of volunteers then," said Tami Abramovitz, an occupational therapist who had helped run the office, "and some of us thought it was a pity to waste it.

"The Defence Ministry provides money and social services to the families of dead and wounded But it doesn't send anyone to a widow with five children to help her shop, or just to have a cup of coffee with her. We're looking for families who can take a family like this on an outing, or students who can help children in these families with their studies. If a widow has to go to the hospital for an X-ray, we'll find someone to drive her."

The volunteers include lawyers who will assist families with legal problems and economists who will advise them on financial problems, including the investment of compensation funds. Plumbers and other skilled volunteers will help with household problems.

The volunteer centre — known as Ayala (acronym for the Hebrew name Jerusalem Association for War Victims) — can be contacted by volunteers or persons requiring help, from Sunday to Thursday from 4 to 8 p.m. at telephone 222810. It is located in the old Beit Ha'am Building at 70 Jaffa Road in the premises of the Council for the Prevention of Traffic Accidents. Mrs. Abramovitz said the centre is coordinating its efforts with the social workers of the Defence Ministry and the Jerusalem Municipal Emergency Headquarters in order to prevent duplication.

THE RENASCENCE OF the Hebrew language is one of the great miracles of modern times. Not spoken for over 17 centuries, the Hebrew language was considered a dead tongue. It could be read in the ancient Scriptures and in literature, but orthodox Jews considered *lashon ha-kodesh,* the "holy language," too sacred to be employed in the ordinary pursuits of life.

Other nations, notably the Irish, have tried to revive their ancient tongues. None have quite succeeded. Gaelic has remained, for the most part, the province of a few scholars. Although there are some sections of Ireland where Gaelic is the dominant language, Gaelic has never succeeded in dominating Irish life. In Ireland's capital, Dublin, English is the prime language. Few Dubliners speak Gaelic.

The revival of Hebrew as a spoken language was due largely to the efforts of one man, who succeeded during his lifetime in attaining his goal. That man was Eliezer Ben Yehuda.

Today, everybody in Israel speaks Hebrew. How did this come about?

Eliezer Ben Yehuda was born in Lithuania into a family by the name of Perelman. He was brought up by his uncle, who although an observant Jew, recognized the value of secular education. The uncle saw to it that the young boy learned subjects which permitted his entrance into the Dvinsk Gymnasium from which Eliezer graduated in 1877.

Ben Yehuda believed that the Jewish people should establish their own community in Eretz Israel, but he became convinced that in order for the Jews to become a united people in their own land, Hebrew would have to be revived as a spoken tongue, the tongue their children would grow up with.

In 1881, Ben Yehuda arrived in Jaffa. On the way, he and his wife made a pact. They decided that theirs would be the first Hebrew-speaking home in

---

Eight injured in Hebron grenade blast

Jerusalem Post Arab Affairs Reporter

Eight Hebronites, including a policeman, were yesterday wounded in a grenade attack. The assault marked accelerated terrorist activity in different parts of the West Bank where widespread subversive elements are organizing support for the Palestine Liberation Organization (PLO).

The incident was the fourth in the region in less than two weeks, after grenade attacks in the Old City of Jerusalem and Nablus, where the Military Governor was seriously injured.

Yesterday's attack took place in the central marketplace of Hebron. A local resident was shot last Friday nearby in an exchange of fire between security forces and a group of saboteurs.

The terrorist activity on the West Bank corresponded with undisguised political ferment, which this week led to a security crackdown all across the West Bank, after four years of virtually complete quiet. The security crackdown earlier this week included the arrest of scores of subversive elements, the blowing up of a number of houses, and the deportation to Jordan of seven West Bank notables and an East Jerusalem lawyer.

The expulsions were yesterday protested in a number of West Bank towns, including el-Bireh, whose mayor Abdul-Jawad Saleh was among this week's eight deportees. Women there yesterday staged a sit-in strike at the city hall in a demand for the repatriation of the mayor.

(King Hussein last night met the eight deportees and discussed the West Bank situation with them.)

The sudden political ferment in the West Bank came as the pro-PLO elements tried to stage a show of strength before next week's Middle East peace conference. The terrorist movement hopes to ensure a predominant representation there.

The pro-PLO activity on the West Bank has been reflected in sabotage attacks, distribution of leaflets calling on local Arabs to stop working in Israel, and calls for civil disobedience against the authorities.

Tel Aviv youth give menora to Dutch 'sisters'

A solid silver *Menora* — a gift from the Tel Aviv Municipal Youth Council to the youth of Tel Aviv's Dutch sister city Groningen — was presented in Jerusalem yesterday to Netherlands Ambassador Gerrit Jongejans.

Presenting the gift, Municipality youth department head Binyamin Fortis said it was a mark of appreciation to Holland in the current struggle. "The *Menora* symbolizes Israel's struggle—few against many — and also the miracle whereby great light and energy were produced from a small amount of oil," he said.

Mr. Jongejans expressed his thanks.

The *Menora* was made by Yoav Ben David of Bezalel art and design academy in Jerusalem. El Al has undertaken to fly it to Holland free of charge. *(Itim)*

PRACTICAL SYMPATHY

To the Editor of The Jerusalem Post

Sir, — There is a school in West Berlin called the "College Francais," founded some 300 years ago to serve the Huguenot Community (Protestant refugees from Catholic France) and since then one of the outstanding schools in Germany.

As an alumnus of that school, I just received a circular from the Alumni Club, addressed to "Old Collegians" all over the world.

After expressing solidarity with Israeli and Jewish members during the recent war, the circular goes on to solicit generous contributions to a special fund set up by the club for the reconstruction of kibbutzim that were damaged during the first days of the war. In conclusion it says: "Let us hope that what will be built with our help, will never be destroyed again."

SHIMON YALLON
Jerusalem, December 5.

IPO OFF FOR GOOD-WILL TOUR

LOD AIRPORT.— The Israel Philharmonic Orchestra left yesterday for a one-week good-will concert tour in England, Belgium, Holland and West Germany.

Abe Cohen, secretary of the IPO, told "Itim" that the orchestra had originally been invited to give a concert in London on behalf of the Jewish National Fund. It was later decided to extend the tour to include the other countries, especially Holland, "as a gesture of thanks to the Dutch people for their support of Israel."

The IPO will give five concerts in its week's tour of the four countries. In London, Daniel Barenboim will conduct with pianist Artur Rubenstein as soloist. *(Itim)*

Hebron mayor sees Syrian PoWs

Hebron Mayor Sheikh Mohammed Ali Ja'abari yesterday visited the Syrian prisoners of war held in Israel and told them he hoped that Syria would soon release the Israeli prisoners of war so that all should be able to return home.

After having been assured by the Syrian prisoners that they feel well and are treated well, Sheikh Ja'abari also expressed the hope that Syria would treat the Israeli prisoners the same way.

TOURISTS REPORT NO SIGNS OF WAR IN EGYPT

Jerusalem Post Reporter

HAIFA.— Nearly 400 British tourists arrived here for a day-long visit aboard the Greek passenger liner, Delphi, yesterday morning. The ship, chartered by the Clarksons travel company of London, is on a Mediterranean cruise and arrived from Beirut.

Before going to Beirut, the ship had called at Alexandria for two days at the beginning of the week. She was the first ship to come here from Egypt since before the war.

Some of the passengers told *The Post* that "on the surface" everything seemed quite normal in Egypt. They had travelled to Cairo, and stayed there overnight and also visited the pyramids. "We encountered no difficulties, and if we hadn't known that there had been a war, we'd never have guessed it," they said.

In Beirut they had visited the Casino de Liban on Tuesday evening and watched the floor show. The famous casino "was packed," they said, and they enjoyed the show. "There's nothing like it in London, nor for that matter in Israel. But you've got the holy places and wonderful fruit," they noted.

The Delphi will come again for a two-day stay on Christmas Eve, when another cruise ship, the Ithaca, is also due for a Christmas visit. No other cruise ships are expected for Christmas, though the Tourism Ministry has announced that six, bringing 2,500 tourists, would arrive.

Three more cruise ships are expected after Christmas, on December 27, 28 and 29.

PLEA FOR UNDERSTANDING

To the Editor of The Jerusalem Post

Sir, — An Arab nurse from the administered territories wrote to me recently, — "I am sorry for that war. I hope that one day we will live together in peace. You can't believe how much I suffered in those days, feeling sorry for the young soldiers from both sides who were killed instead of living nicely together."

The territories administered by Israel are achieving prosperity and a higher standard of living than any other Arab country. This must be obvious to many Arabs after six years of experience with Israel. The future which awaits them under King Hussein's rule is easy to imagine on the basis of 19 years' experience. What Arafat would do for them is hard to guess. Why don't they voice their opinions when outsiders meddle in their affairs and claim to speak in their name? Why don't we help them to express such opinions when the enemy is inventing stories about Israel's mistreatment of the Arabs under our rule?

DEVORA GOLDGRABER
Jerusalem, December 4.

Booby-trapped radio found and dismantled

Jerusalem Post Reporter

NETANYA. — A booby-trapped transistor radio was discovered and dismantled yesterday morning near Moshav Tenuvot, not far from where another booby-trapped radio blew up earlier this week.

The radio was found in a field by a member of the Tulkarm-area moshav. Remembering that an Arab woman working at neighbouring Moshav Nitzanei Oz had been wounded in the face and hands on Monday when she turned on a radio she found in a field, he did not touch the transistor but instead called police.

Police yesterday repeated their warning to the public not to pick up or touch any tempting object — radio, toy, candy-box or whatever— they find left lying about, and to call police instead.

FIRST PUT OUT

Dr. Henry J. Kissinger, the American Secretary of State, was no stranger to Israel in the years before the Yom Kippur War. On two occasions he lectured in Jerusalem to the Israel Defence College, when it was headed by Aluf (Res.) Uzi Narkiss (right), and a firm friendship developed between the two men. When Narkiss visited Kissinger in the White House in 1969, a "Life" correspondent, David Niven, recorded the conversation, from which it appears that Kissinger's view was prophetic. PHILIP GILLON discusses Kissinger with Narkiss, and also recalls some views held by the philosopher-statesman prior to the war.

THE ARTICLE by David Niven on Kissinger was headed "Autocrat in the Action Arena"; it appeared in "Life" on September 15, 1969. It included this passage:

One day his visitor was an old friend, Uzi Narkiss of Israel. Once Narkiss had been a student at the International Seminar at Harvard which Kissinger ran every summer; more recently, he had been commanding general of the troops that took Jerusalem. He had left the army, so his visit was entirely unofficial — and yet, each man was near the heart of his own government and the quiet, easy conversation had a certain meaning.

"Henry," Narkiss said, "the thing that we have learned is that there are many problems that have no solution, that people must live with. The Middle East is such a problem."

"Yes," Kissinger said, "but that does not mean that what is without a solution will remain unchanged."

There is a kind of shorthand in such conversations. "Of course," Narkiss said, "but Israel will stay a long time in the territories it has taken. It will stay as long as it likes."

"No. For a while, yes; for a year or two —"

"Fifteeen years."

"Oh, I doubt it. I think the world climate will not permit it." Kissinger paused. The sun was pouring in his windows. There were prints on the wall, and the furniture, though new, looked pedestrian and uncomfortable. Narkiss was frowning, but Kissinger's face was calm and inscrutable as he went on.

"The issue here is to be sure that the U.S. and Israel do not find themselves on one side against the world and that a general world war does not result. The question before Israel is whether it can trade some of its physical superiority for some political legitimacy. Normally a good agreement leaves both sides happy. In the Middle East, it is when both sides are equally unhappy. Ideally a good settlement leaves no reason to attack. In the Middle East, it would be when both sides were unable to attack..."

UZI NARKISS recalls that, in 1964, when he was head of the Israel Defence College, he decided to enlarge the scope of studies at the College by familiarizing students with world problems. Abe Harman, then Israel's ambassador to Washington, found funds to send American experts to address the College. One of these experts was Dr. Henry Kissinger, then a professor at Harvard and former adviser to President Kennedy on national security, who came to the College in Jerusalem twice. He lectured at length on world problems, such as U.S.-U.S.S.R. relations, and the effect on foreign affairs of nuclear arms.

"The third time he came to Israel was immediately after the Six Day War," recalls Narkiss. "At the time, I was commander of the Central Command, and I took Dr. Kissinger all over the West Bank. After I left the army, I went to call on him in his office in the basement of the White House. He came out to the anteroom where I was waiting, and shouted, 'Hi, Uzi, Come in!' When I sat down, another man came in as well. Kissinger introduced him as David Niven, a journalist from 'Life,' and asked if I'd mind Niven listening to our conversation. I said, 'Of course not, I've got no secrets'.

"The article in "Life" is substantially correct. We spent most of the time discussing how long Israel could hold the areas. I claimed that we were strong enough to hold them indefinitely. He said that he agreed with me from the military point of view, but said that I could not disregard the political aspect. The world, he maintained, would never agree to Israel remaining in the occupied territories for an extended period.

"His point was that the time would come when the Middle East situation might lead to a world conflict, or at least to a confrontation between the United States and Russia. Russia supported the Arabs, America supported Israel. If war started, the two superpowers would face each other on behalf of their friends.

"I told him that it was good news that America was so committed to Israel; I hadn't been so sure. But I said that I doubted whether Russia would interfere actively on behalf of the Arabs, unless Israel crossed the Canal or threatened Cairo. He agreed that Russia wouldn't enter a war directly unless we crossed the Canal. But he said that the present situation couldn't be allowed to persist — the potential danger was too great.

"I suggested that we lived in a time when there were many problems without solutions — I mentioned Vietnam and Berlin — and said that the world just had to learn to live with them. He still insisted that the Middle East was in a different category."

It seems, I point out to Narkiss, that he was wrong, and Kissinger was right.

"Not only I — many other people. He was right in his forecast, certainly, but this doesn't mean that his solutions are right. Can we say that he succeeded in Vietnam? Incidentally, the next time I was supposed to see him in America was Christmas, 1971, but that was just when the North Vietnamese began the 'Tet Offensive.' When I phoned him, he said that he was very harassed because the North Vietnamese had nearly captured Saigon, and he would only be able to see me after the offensive had been stopped. On a short-term basis, he succeeded in getting a temporary peace in Vietnam, but

THE FIRE

we still have to see how it works out over a longer period."

I note that some critics of Israel have alleged that Kissinger made his prophecy of what was needed in the Middle East — both sides being equally unhappy and unable to attack — come true, by slowing the airlift and by forcing Israel to accept a cease-fire when she did not need to do so. Does he think that there is any truth in these allegations?

"I don't know — you must ask Golda or Dayan or Eban. But, remember, he warned us before Yom Kippur."

Does he think that it is good or bad for Israel that a Jew is the American Secretary of State?

"When Kissinger was nominated Secretary of State, many people asked me that question. In my opinion, Kissinger is capable of being absolutely objective — he won't favour the Jews, and he won't lean over backwards to favour the Arabs. His Jewishness is completely irrelevant. His one major criterion is — what is in the interests of the United States?

"He has a remarkable and rare intellectual faculty which enables him to be very objective and detached, to be completely uninvolved, to consider a problem, as it were, from a distance. Israelis may not be satisfied with this — we would prefer somebody subjective, identified with us. Kissinger looks at things from a worldwide point of view which is not necessarily pro-Israel. We would prefer a different approach, closer to our own — we have the right to hope for this, but we don't select the U.S. Secretary of State."

Narkiss does not know whether there is such a thing as the Kissinger doctrine. He thinks that Kissinger's approach is primarily pragmatic — first putting out the fire, then seeing about rebuilding the house. Kissinger does believe, Narkiss says, in moving step by step, a little at a time, and trying to prevent the parties standing still. This way, he thinks, they can be jogged closer towards a settlement, and not allowed to

dig their heels in entrenched positions from which they refuse to budge.

THROUGHOUT THE years, Kissinger made it clear that his Middle East doctrine — if it exists — involves getting the parties concerned to negotiate with each other, America serving only as a sort of prod. There has never been any suggestion that he believes in a peace imposed by the super-powers on reluctant Arabs and Israelis. Since a policy of imposed peace would involve correspondingly substantial guarantees, the reluctance of a Vietnam-weary government to

impose it is hardly surprising.

If the Jews were doubtful about the desirability of a Jew becoming Secretary of State, the Arabs were furious about the appointment. Ihsan Abdul-Kuddous, editor of Egypt's "Akhbar el-Yom" wrote in September, 1973, that "talking to Kissinger was like talking to Israel, because he is a Jew." And Beirut columnist Salim Nassar of "Al Hawadeth" described poor Henry as "the Rasputin of the White House."

Giving evidence before the Senate Foreign Relations Committee in September, Kissinger reaffirmed that the U.S. "cannot substitute for some form of negotiation... but it is prepared to be helpful," if the two sides decide to talk to each other. "It is the view of the Administration that both sides must make some move."

He planned to discuss possible moves at the U.N. General Assembly in October. But, by that time, Yom Kippur had come and gone.

Aluf Uzi Narkiss.

PHILIP GILLON

A PALESTINIAN SOLUTION?

A lasting peace depends on cooperation between Israel and Jordan

IN less than a week the moment of truth will dawn for both Israel and the Arabs as they face each other over the Geneva conference table. No longer will they be able to hide behind words about integration or liberation of territories, about secure or recognized borders, and similar slogans concerned with land rather than people. They will have to realize that their conflict cannot be solved at all by redrawing Israel's frontiers so long as every frontier is bound to become a front. They will therefore be forced at long last to discuss the crucial issue.

In the past this issue has been deliberately sidestepped by most Arab governments for strategic reasons — in order to deal with it at a later stage; while Israel has shunned it for psychological reasons — hoping that it would evaporate as time went on. Instead it has escalated and is now coming to a head. In official parlance it is called the question of Arab recognition of the State of Israel. But in fact it is identical with the Palestinian question: "Restoration of the full rights of the Palestinians" is obviously tantamount to the destruction of Israel, whether or not this is explicitly stated.

That this stark fact can be overlooked by many people in this country (and abroad), that support for a Palestinian nation or state is to be found in Jewish quarters, is due to a widespread double delusion. First, people in this country — understandably — tend to see the Palestinians in their own likeness, as a separate entity, eager to keep its identity. They do it in plain disregard of statements to the contrary, which show that the non-Jewish residents of Israel consider themselves as Arabs, more so perhaps than, say, the Egyptians or the Syrians, who have besides their Arab language and heritage also their separate states, institutions, etc. Whether a state carved out of Israel will be called Falastin or otherwise, it is bound therefore to become a link in the Arab total offensive against the Jewish state.

When Israel and the Arabs face each other at Geneva next week, they will no longer be able to hide behind slogans concerned with land rather than people: the conflict cannot be solved by redrawing Israel's frontiers, as long as those lines are bound to become a front, writes **DR. MOSHE ATER**, The Jerusalem Post Economic Editor. We should forge an alliance with those Arab quarters who are similarly opposed to the PLO's plan to "restore Palestinian rights"—on the ruins of the State of Israel.

Return to homes

Secondly, people here — again understandably — tend to think of Palestinians as the non-Jewish inhabitants of this country, forgetting that this notion is quite different from the one entertained by the PLO, which is acclaimed as representing the Palestinian nation. When Arafat and other terrorist leaders talk about "restoration of the rights of Palestinians," they have in mind not more autonomy, nor even full sovereignty, for the West Bank or the administered areas, but the return to previous homes and properties of refugees now living in camps and cities in the Gaza Strip, in Jordan, in Lebanon and in Syria, a total of 1.5 million people by the PLO's reckoning. They take for granted that this return must be accompanied by the ousting — peacefully or otherwise — of the Jewish "invaders." Only thus is the "secular, democratic" Falastin state to be created — leaving little to the imagination as to how this is to take place.

It is frequently argued that some people in, say, Nablus or Hebron consider Arafat's views too extreme. Or that in many cases ties of trust and friendship have developed between Jews and Arabs, which may strengthen in course of time. However, these arguments are beside the point. What matters is not whether or not Jews and Arabs can co-exist peacefully (that they can has been amply proved by what has been going on in the administered territories during the past six years, notwithstanding some mishaps), but whether this country (however demarcated) belongs to the Jews or to the Arabs (however labelled).

Hitherto both the government and the public in Israel have adopted in this respect a schizophrenic attitude. On the one hand, it has been insisted that Israel is, and must remain, a Jewish state. On the other hand, it has also been stressed that Arabs here have national rights (i.e., collective and separatist, as opposed to civil rights as individuals) equal to those of the Jews. Now this contradictory attitude must at long last come to an end. It must be realized that recognition of Palestinian national (Arab) rights to this country cannot be reconciled with the existence of the Israel (Jewish) state.

Loyal minority

Israel was established in order to provide a national home for the Jewish people, with other inhabitants accepting this rule as they did Turkish or British, and becoming a minority of loyal citizens; or moving to the adjacent countries, where they would find language, social and economic patterns akin to their own. National adjustments and migrations on a much bigger scale, and under harder conditions, have been — and are still — going on in many countries. The ingathering of the Jews in Israel is itself the best example of that. The PLO may oppose Zionism, try to put the clock back and to restore Israel as an Arab country. But if Israel is to survive, these claims must be rejected outright, the PLO's attempts foiled, and no doubts left about the state's Jewish identity.

Such a clarification may sound a knell to the forthcoming Geneva conference, for it would show that Arab recognition of Israel, and genuine readiness to live with it, does not depend on any amount of territorial concessions. Of course, complex maps can be drawn up with complicated boundaries, corridors, enclaves, demilitarized zones, leased bases, UN cordons, and much else. But the most they can achieve is to freeze for a while a momentary situation, i.e., to turn a blind eye to the developments in the countries concerned—and elsewhere; indeed to obstruct these developments. No map showing a sovereign State of Israel will be approved by the PLO, except as a promising stage for another onslaught.

Does this mean that there is no hope for a peaceful settlement? Perhaps. But a chance is still left if it is at least understood that lasting peace will have to run contrary to the "Palestinian" programme; that the PLO will fight it tooth and nail; and that a start towards settlement can be made only by forging an alliance between Israel and Arab quarters similarly opposed to the PLO's "restoration" of the refugees. Which obviously leaves us alone with Hussein's Jordan. Would Hussein cooperate in such a scheme, intended to maintain a viable Israel state associated with his Arab kingdom? It is in no way sure. But neither is it to be ruled out. For such a scheme would have great advantages for both parties, and a fair chance of success against heavy odds.

These odds are too obvious to need elaboration. Jordan is an Arab, Moslem country. Its government is a military dictatorship, far different from this country's democracy. Half of its population stem from what is today called Israel, including a substantial number of refugees still in camps and resentful of the Jewish state. King Hussein supported the Arab attacks on Israel both in 1967 and this year. He would, of course, like to regain the West Bank, and to expand his domain at Israel's expense.

However, Hussein probably also understands that the growing Soviet influence in the Middle East is not working in his favour; that if Israel is eventually carved up, Jordan's chances of survival would also be slim; that he may not always be in a position to quell a terrorist revolt against his regime, as he did in September, 1970. Israel is the only neighbouring state which he need not fear, because Israel would be interested in a strong Jordanian ally. On the other hand, and for the same reason, he ought to be interested in a strong Israel state Another link is provided by the joint American — financial and armament — support. And — last but not the least — an association with Israel could put Jordan on the path of rapid economic growth. Old Palestine refurbished as an Israel-Jordan alliance and common market

could become the economic hub of the Middle East region.

No urgency felt

All of this is evident enough. And the idea of Israel-Jordan cooperation has indeed been broached time and again. Though it has never made headway, perhaps because it used to be considered only one of several alternatives available. Or because no urgency was felt to achieve a lasting settlement. But probably also because it has been dealt with piece-meal, and never allowed to reach major proportions. Even so trade over the "open bridges," the "summer visitors" tourism, and joint financial arrangements have been considered beneficial for both parties concerned, and have been kept going despite political tensions.

Much more dramatic effects could be achieved within a relatively short time by bold expansion of these unorthodox initiatives; by liberalization of the trade flow between the two countries; by opening Jordan to visitors and traders from Israel; by facilitating transit traffic to and from Jordan through Israel ports and vice versa; by launching joint development projects—especially in fields dependent on large scale production units, such as water desalination, atomic power, heavy industry plants; by mutual assistance in agricultural settlement and export promotion; by raising joint loans abroad; and eventually by creation of a joint currency. Dreamlike though such a programme looks at this moment, there is no reason why it could not be carried out once the two countries decide to stand by each other.

That this programme, if implemented, would greatly increase the prosperity, indeed the well-being, of both Jews and Arabs in the two countries concerned, can be taken for granted. Nevertheless, it would be childish to make its implementation depend on popular support, so engrained is — for the time being — mutual suspicion of Jews and Arabs, so remote from today's reality is the prospect of their peaceful co-existence. It would be foolish even to attempt to press people accustomed to fight each other to clasp hands and forget their dissimilarity before a basis of common interests has been created which can serve as a corner-stone for mutual trust.

Let support develop

It would take a long time for the Arabs living in Jordan (and in Israel too) to give up their dream of destroying and looting the Jewish state; to replace the prospect of "restoring" pre-Mandatory Palestine by that of a progressive, modern, bi-national one; to replace Pan-Arab sentiments harking back to the

Moslem conquest by a sense of genuine Palestinian loyalty. It would take a long time for the Jews to overcome their fear of genocide and discrimination, so as to trust the Arabs turned reluctantly into their allies. In the foreseeable future both nations will therefore cling to their separate states, even though the latter may be loosely linked. If the above programme is to succeed, it must therefore be imposed from above, letting popular support develop gradually, as a by-product of the two states' decision to join forces and economic resources.

To that end a start ought to be made by a mutual defence treaty. Israel and Jordan should pledge each other military assistance against any aggressor violating their borders. This should be accompanied by an agreement for mutual help against subversive internal activities. The next obvious step would be close consultation in matters of foreign policy. Along with this would go setting up of joint boards or agencies for gradual coordination of customs tariffs, transport fees, fiscal and monetary policies, etc., for dismantling of barriers to permit a free flow of merchandise and people, and for launching joint development projects. That would include also machinery for settling the vexed question of Israel-Jordan borders, which, however, would by then lose much of its current gravity — with recourse to a condominium envisaged as the ultimate resort for the hardest cases. Eventually, a joint federative capital could be established, say, in East Jerusalem.

None of these steps would infringe the sovereignty of either Israel or Jordan, except in so far as agreed by both of them. Their joint projects and policies would therefore require the mutual consent of both governments. This would involve a fairly awkward procedure, and probably a lot of red tape, in particular at the beginning. However that is the way the European Common Market developed and the E.E.C. grew out of the military NATO alliance.

It might be argued that if cooperation between Israel and Jordan is a good thing, it could proceed without such dramatic gestures as a military pact and a federative goal. However, one has to keep in mind the forces — both external and internal — that would doubtless be set in motion against the scheme outlined above. It would be opposed by Syria, which still clings to its dream — originating from the Ottoman regime — of turning both Jordan and Israel into its southern provinces. By Egypt, which needs imperial escapades to offset popular dissatisfaction at home. By Lebanon, anxious to keep its role as a financial centre of the Middle East. By Moslem countries outraged at the sight of Hussein making peace with infidels. And, of course, by the PLO and by the Soviets, afraid of their thrust to the Middle East being stemmed by the new consolidation. It would therefore need massive support from the U.S. and from other western countries anxious to put an end to the Middle East tension. And in order to make that support effective, the scheme would have to offer it a firm rallying point.

Moreover, the scheme would need a firm commitment of the states concerned in order to provide a framework for the envisaged development. Even old-established binational states — such as Belgium and Canada—are ridden by tensions stemming from language and cultural differences. The tensions are likely to be greater in a country which is still in the throes of dynamic development which is subject to strong economic, social, national pressures, and is facing tasks which cannot be accomplished without major changes. Absorption of Jewish mass immigration, re-settlement of Arab refugees crowded in the Gaza and Jordan camps, modernization of Arab subsistence agriculture, industrial development, urbanisation, rapid advance of new social strata and cultural patterns — none of these processes can take place without friction, conflict, grievances and resentment, which may easily become explosive when allied to national tensions.

A new leaf

The temptation — but also the danger — in such a situation is to avoid change, to slow up progress, and to obstruct it by partitioning the country. This is, broadly speaking, what has been suggested to date under the term of peaceful settlement. An alliance, and an eventual federation, of Israel and Jordan may turn a new leaf in this respect by providing a wider scope for solving the local, partial problems, because in a wider context the importance of such issues is likely to decrease, and more ways and means are likely to be available for counter-balancing the gains and losses of various issues. However, in order to make that sure, the scope and the goal of the envisaged development should be clearly stated.

Naturally, the scheme outlined above would impose considerable strain on the two nations involved. The Jordanian people would have to break away from medieval Pan-Arab fantasies and to constitute themselves as a separate nation. The Jews, closely attached to the West, would have to adjust themselves to their oriental environment. However, both would find ample reward not only in increased safety and material progress, but also in greater freedom of action and in new horizons. Whether the eventual federation would be called Falastin or Greater Israel is irrelevant. What matters is that if successful it could be called both. And that no other alternative for peaceful settlement is so far visible.

Palestine. Although between them they knew several languages, they decided that henceforth they would speak nothing but Hebrew. Their first son, whom they named Ben Zion (son of Zion), was brought up hearing only Hebrew. This boy, later known as Ithamar Ben Avi, became the first modern Hebrew-speaking child.

In Palestine, Ben Yehuda supported himself by teaching, but imposed one condition. No matter what subject he taught, he insisted on teaching it in Hebrew.

Ben Yehuda's campaign for teaching in Hebrew was at first greeted with derision and disbelief. Even well known scholars who supported the general concept of the revival of Hebrew—scholars such as Ahad Haam—were not prepared to follow such extremism.

Ben Yehuda was adamant: He wrote:

"If we want our people to survive, if we want our children to remain Hebrews, we must train them in the Hebrew language. We must make our sons and daughters forget the corrupt foreign dialects which tear us to shreds."

His method of teaching Hebrew in Hebrew became known in schools throughout the world as *Ivrit b'ivrit.*

From the field of Mars straight to the grove of Academe. On the opening day of the Hebrew University, this young Army Reservist goes to an afternoon class with the contemporary equivalent of both sword and pruning hook.

RESTORING EVERYTHING TO EVERYBODY
History is a damned shame

By JOHN CROSBY

I HAVE read with mounting indignation an article about how the white man wrecked Hawaii's lovely primitive culture. Captain Cook has much to answer for. The white man brought syphilis (did we give the Indians syphilis or did they give it to us? I keep hearing conflicting stories). Also, smallpox, leprosy and high blood pressure. To say nothing of high rise apartment buildings, hot dogs, and Liberace. Ugh!

It's the same old story as that of the Red Indians of the American plains. In place of all the tall grass and buffalo, what do we see — syphilis, the common cold, and Chicago. All of you out there whose heart goes out to those poor Red Indians and those miserable brown Hawaiians, hark. Help is at hand. We have formed a protest group called History is a Damned Shame — HIDS — and our noble purpose is to right these wrongs. And many other wrongs. In fact, all of them.

Our great aim is to restore the land, and heritage and culture not only to the Indians but to everybody. We are starting right here in England. As we all know, England has been invaded by *everybody* — the Romans, all those Germans like the Angles and Jutes and Saxons, to say nothing of those permissive Danes and after, the morally decadent French — each bringing along his diseases and terrible food and appalling habits.

Each one enslaved the poor Briton, first giving him syphilis, of course, and then robbing him of his lovely primitive habits like painting his body blue and replacing them with disgusting continental customs like bathing. Ugh! Little by little these foreigners have taken over the whole island. Today what few Britons are left are cowering in Wales talking British which is now called Welsh which hardly anyone understands, including the Welsh.

Now what HIDS proposes to do is to restore this land to its rightful owners, and drive all those Frogs and Huns back to where they came from. We'll tear down all these excrescences they disfigured the island with — like London. Ugh! Did you know that every house that is put up obliterates an average one-sixth of virgin soil? What's more, virgin soil that belongs to someone else.

After we restore Britain to the British, we here at HIDS plan to press forward. The next great step is to restore the more ancient lands to their rightful owners. Now as we all know — or perhaps not, as the case may be — Egypt has been very recently (barely 1,500 years ago), over-run by a bunch of rank outsiders called Arabs, who were the last to get there, although they now act as if they own the place. It had previously been picked over by the Greeks and Romans, each wave of invaders destroying the ancient culture and obliterating the old landmarks. Not a single pyramid has been built in Egypt in over 1,000 years. Did you know that? The original Egyptians who are now known as Coptic Christians have been reduced to a tiny percentage of the population, alas.

Our task is to restore the Egyptians to their heritage and send those Arabs — all 100 million of them — back to Arabia where they came from. Then we are going to tear down all those rotten modern buildings and put up some decent sphinxes again and start fashioning skirts out of grass as God intended them.

After Egypt, we propose to undertake our last and greatest task, the restoration of China to the Chinese. China, as we know, was raped, plundered and occupied by wave after wave of Mongols until today you can hardly find a true Chinese anywhere at all, except for some parts of San Francisco. The Mongols tore down a perfectly good civilisation and erected that monstrosity they have now. Why can't people leave things *alone?* Why aren't people happy with the way things are? Always changing things around. Always bringing in all those modern diseases like syphilis when the ancients had perfectly nice old diseases like dropsy and bubonic plague.

Our plan is to send all those Mongols back to where they came from. And where was that, you ask? Well, they came thataway. Over the mountains, I believe. Actually, the problem of what to do with the 200 million American and 800 million Chinese and all the others now squatting on lands that clearly don't belong to them is occupying some of our best minds here at HIDS. They think a lot, that group. You just keep the money rolling in and we'll keep on thinking, here at headquarters, you can rest assured of that.

To turn to less pleasant matters, you may have heard that HIDS lately has been torn by dissension. A group of Moderates (moderation is the death of idealism, I always say) has sprung up, who are trying to propagate the heresy that History is no longer A Damn Shame after 400 years.

It is their preposterous notion that all those Huns who took over this island 1,400 years ago have since settled down and become proper English gentlemen, hunting the fox, drinking tea, swallowing their diphthongs and all that.

An even more heretical group — Moderate Moderates they call themselves — claim that history is all right after only 100 years, which would legitimise North America, God forbid. And now we have this radical fellow Enoch Powell preaching the even more radical heresy that everything would be all right if we only sent back the Pakistanis to where they came from. What an idea!

Let me remind you I alone am the True Prophet. Just keep those contributions rolling in to my yacht which is a registered off-shore corporation, safely out of reach of the income tax people — them and their silly questions. The income tax itself, need I remind you, is a disgusting foreign idea. The Druids never had any such thing. Just you stick to me, folks, and I'll liberate you not only from the income tax but from income itself. You'll be free as birds. Won't it be loverly?

284

FROM STRENGTH TO STRENGTH WITH THE ALMIGHTY!

ישראל בטח בה' !

For a small moment have I forsaken thee; but with great mercies will I gather thee.
Isaiah, 54

During a distraction, when the enemy's preparations were not correctly assessed, on Yom Kippur we were subjected to a heavy surprise attack on the Golan Heights and at the Suez Canal. Despite the unusual strength of the enemy and the broad political support he received, he did not achieve his objective. With the help of the Almighty, the Jewish defence army defeated him, striking him hard.

THERE IS NO JUSTIFICATION FOR THE DEPRESSION NOW AFFECTING MANY PEOPLE. FOR WE HAVE SEEN MANY TIMES THAT THE ALMIGHTY IS IN ZION AND WILL NOT ABANDON HIS PEOPLE; HE WILL NOT FORSAKE WHAT IS HIS.

The war did begin with a serious setback. But just as all our victories were unnatural, so this time our failure was unnatural. This failure was no doubt to remind us that we had not made the required contribution from the miracles from which we had benefited up to now, and to mend our ways and return to the Almighty and to our Tora.

The depression among some sections of the public has its origins in leftist and Cnaanite circles, which are sowing confusion and discouragement among the members of the public. These circles are completely barren of any Jewish faith, and view events in the light of criteria which are in contradiction to the Tora-historical truth that WE ARE NOT AS OTHER PEOPLES.

Let us shake off the outlook of the Cnaanite and leftist "progressives," which is the source of all evil affecting our people. Let us strengthen ourselves in our faith, follow after our Jewish consciousness, and look in hope and with good courage to the future.

> *"for my salvation is near to come, and my righteousness to be revealed."* Isaiah, 56, 1

There is no security without faith.
Put your trust in the people with faith.

VOTE
TORA RELIGIOUS FRONT
Agudat Yisrael — Poalei Agudat Yisrael

חזית דתית תורתית

אגודת ישראל   פועלי אגודת ישראל

ודתיים בלתי מפלגתיים

285

ON DECEMBER 31 YOU WILL DECIDE THE FUTURE OF THE STATE – YOUR FUTURE YOU WILL DECIDE –

BETWEEN a prospect of peace with our neighbours

AND the road leading to unceasing war

BETWEEN a policy of close friendship with the U.S.A.

AND adventurism endangering this friendship

BETWEEN a policy of striving for peace and the strengthening of our security

AND the "not one inch" mentality

BETWEEN willingness for territorial compromise and the acceptance of defensible borders

AND the approach which disregards realities in the region and the world

BETWEEN a checking and adaption of policy to changing circumstances

AND the inability to learn and change

BETWEEN the declaration of peace and security as central aims

AND the preferring of the Areas to peace

BETWEEN the wish to maintain the Jewish character of Israel

AND willingness to add a large Arab population

BETWEEN readiness to maintain friendly relations with a Jordanian-Palestinian state

AND the ignoring of the existence and aspirations of the Palestinians

BETWEEN preparedness to go to a peace conference at any time, without prior conditions

AND the creation of difficulties, likely to doom the conference to failure before it starts

STRENGTHEN THE CAUSE OF PEACE AND SECURITY

Give them your vote and strengthen their voice

VOTE EMET Hama'arach/Israel Labour Party-Mapam

SNOWS OF HERMON

THE SOLDIERS encamped here at the ski-slope on Mount Hermon are fortunate in having the new American heated tents. The patent is simple enough — a paraffin stove with a chimney emerging through a hole in the top of the tent — but they work wonderfully well and the men say they can sleep in them in their singlets and trunks. These tents are not yet much in evidence elsewhere on the Golan.

Higher up the Hermon, at the Israeli fortified position which was overrun by the Syrians on the first day of the war, the Defence Ministry is installing an advanced system of heating and air-conditioning for the underground bunkers which comprise the fortress. A similar though less elaborate heating and air system that existed there before the war was wrecked by the Syrians, who held the position for two weeks.

The other pictures were taken on the "Syrian Hermon" — strongholds which Israeli forces took from the Syrians in the last days of the war. Here conditions are much harsher, with snow falling almost nightly upon the bunkers and trenches.

Until this week, the troops stationed here ate only cold combat rations, but now rudimentary cooking facilities have been provided. There is still no heating in these positions, although the army has promised that stoves will be installed shortly.

Provisioning these positions is done by helicopter or tracked vehicles only, since there is no approach road for regular transport.

The men stationed here have by now all been supplied with heavy winter equipment, especially padded snow-suits and waterproof boots. Elsewhere in the Golan, where snow is infrequent and night temperatures are usually slightly above freezing, there are still shortages of some winter equipment. (Photos: I.P.P.A.)

But Ben Yehuda was not satisfied in teaching Hebrew just in schools. He wanted Hebrew to be the general language of conversation among adults, as well as among children. In 1883, he organized a society called *Tehiyat Israel,* which meant "The Revival of Israel." The members of this society pledged that they would speak to one another only in Hebrew, even in marketplaces and in the streets.

The following year, Ben Yehuda founded another society which he called the *Safah Berurah,* or the "Pure Language Society." Its purpose was to popularize the Hebrew language and its conversational usage. Hebrew, Ben Yehuda held, lacked elasticity. It was bound by its archaic structure. It needed new forms, new life, some looseness. Moreover, there were no textbooks for most subjects written in Hebrew.

In 1890, Ben Yehuda, with some like-minded associates, founded the *Vaad Ha-Lashon,* which means "The Committee for the Language," which he presided over until his death. Since Hebrew had for so many centuries been abandoned as a conversational language, it lacked words for many new things unknown in biblical days. Ben Yehuda's new committee would pass judgment on the validity of new Hebrew words.

The achievements of this prodigious man fall into four divisions. First: He was responsible for the revival of spoken Hebrew. Second: He implemented the creation of a simple popular style in Hebrew literature, and downgraded the use of inflated rhetoric. Third: He was the first to make a systematic practice of coining Hebrew words. Fourth: He compiled the first complete dictionary of the Hebrew language.

This dictionary consists of 17 volumes. Ben

Israeli soldier in zero weather gear.

SABBATH—No Publication

Going on leave from Egypt.

3 religions in Jerusalem donate blood to PoWs

By GEORGE LEONOF
Jerusalem Post Reporter

A group of 25 Jerusalemites — Moslems, Jews and Christians — donated blood Wednesday morning for transfusion to wounded Israel and Egyptian war prisoners who are to be exchanged under the auspices of the International Red Cross.

The donors were members of the Meditran association for the enhancement of cultural and social relations in Jerusalem. The donations were given at the blood bank off Via Dolorosa in the Old City. The majority of the group were Christians, Lev Schwartz, one of the founders of Meditran, told *The Jerusalem Post* yesterday. "We have more than 50 donors registered so far. Others will follow."

He said, "It is our objective, both as an organization and as individuals, for Jew and Arab to live together in a relationship more enduring than armistices and stronger than treaties."

Meditran was founded more than two years ago, establishing its headquarters in Rehov Hanevi'im, near Damascus Gate. The organization, which has no membership drive, today counts about 200 Jewish, Moslem and Christian members.

Its other activities on behalf of soldiers includes visits to wounded and collection of gifts for war prisoners both here and, through the International Red Cross, in Egypt.

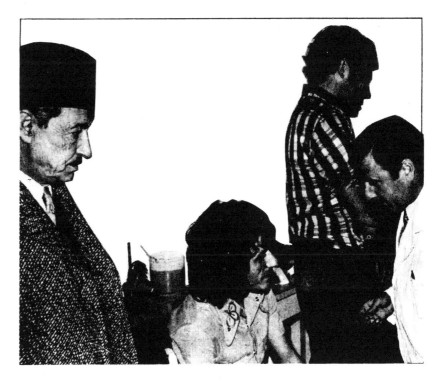

Moslem, Jewish and Christian members of the Meditran organization giving blood in Jerusalem for Israeli and Egyptian prisoners of war.
The men in the photograph are from left to right, Salim Nammari of Wadi Jhoz, Norman Lytle, a Baptist minister, Samir Baden Sharaf, associated with the blood bank located off Via Dolorosa in the Old City.

Yehuda saw the publication of five of these volumes during his lifetime.

The man was remarkable for his utter single-mindedness. When he visited the United States several times on his scholarly studies, although he knew English, he would not permit himself ever to talk English. For him, it was a matter of discipline. He would board a streetcar, and would ask for his change in Hebrew.

So successful was Ben Yehuda's campaign that in

A STATEMENT OF CONCERN

By Foreign Professors Visiting in Israel During 1973-74

Israel and its Arab neighbours are in an uneasy state of cease-fire while both sides bury the dead of another costly conflict. We can testify from first hand experience that this war came as a complete and shocking surprise to Israel on the holiest day of the Jewish year, breaking a cease-fire in violation of all the tenets of international law.

As visiting members of the academic community, who represent a broad spectrum of views, we welcome all efforts towards a just and durable peace. We should like to express our views on some factors that may effect these efforts towards peace.

1. We affirm our belief that lasting peace can only be attained if the Arab states acknowledge Israel's right to exist and are willing to enter into relations with her. The repeated Arab demand for a return to pre-1967 boundaries is a tactic in an overall strategy for the destruction of Israel and is not a basis for peace but a prelude to future wars.

2. Mindful that permanent recognized borders between Israel and the Arab states did not exist between 1948 and 1967, we believe that peace will be durable only if Israel is guaranteed recognized borders that will permit her military security in light of the lessons learned from the Arab surprise attack.

Security guarantees by other nations, even great powers, who must inevitably pursue their own national interests, are no substitute for boundaries that will enable Israel to defend herself.

3. The nations of the world—above all the great powers—must act responsibly to help achieve and maintain peace. The Middle East must not be made into a proving ground of new weaponry, nor should outside powers encourage hatred and war. These nations should recognize at last that surrender to blackmail of any sort only leads to further blackmail.

4. "Evenhandedness" and "neutrality," while desirable in many instances, must not become anti-Israel measures. Israeli prisoners of war must be accorded the same protections as Arab prisoners. Israeli ships must have the same freedom of navigation as other ships. Moreover United Nations forces composed of troops from nations which do not maintain relations with Israel cannot be considered "neutral."

5. The Arabs of Palestine should be able to work out a just and equitable settlement of their differences with Israel. The last six years have shown that the two peoples can live side by side peacefully and constructively and this should serve as a basis for the future.

We recognize that both sides

in the conflict will have to make some compromises if peace is to be attained. All too often international declarations make demands on only one side, namely Israel. An atmosphere in which compromise becomes possible can be created only if each party is able to feel sure that the other is acting in good faith. We call on both sides to make a new and sincere effort to find a way to a lasting peace settlement.

1922, the Palestine mandate accorded Hebrew recognition as one of the three official languages of the country, along with English and Arabic. From then on, Hebrew was used on coins, stamps, and official documents. And within the Jewish community, the use of Hebrew was stressed as a patriotic activity.

I recall that in 1925 while I was walking along the streets of Tel Aviv talking to a companion in English, I was approached by a young man who handed me a sticker. The man was one of the members of a society called *Gedud Maginai ha-Safah,* which means "The Legion for the Protection of the Language." This society had been founded two years earlier, in 1923, to discourage Jews from continuing to speak their native tongues, especially Yiddish. The sticker which the young man gave me said: *"Ivri! Dabair Ivrit!"* Translated, this means "Jew! Speak Hebrew!" Buttons were also distributed in this manner. A campaign went on all through the country with the goal of converting all newcomers to the use of a common language.

By 1948, some 25 years after the founding of the

Legion for the Protection of the Language, the campaign had succeeded to a point where 80 percent of the Jewish population of Israel spoke Hebrew. When the State of Israel declared its independence in that year, 54 percent of the native population knew no other language except Hebrew; it was their sole language of communication.

Many immigrants were coming into Israel from all countries of the world, and a new campaign to conduct intensive Hebrew courses for newcomers was introduced. The institution under whose auspices this program was undertaken was called *Ulpan.* Ulpan trainees generally learn the rudiments of Hebrew in a crash course of two or three months. A good working knowledge of the language, with the ability to read and write, normally takes a year.

In 1954, by act of the Knesset, Ben Yehuda's committee, the Vaad Ha-Lashon, became the Academy of the Hebrew Language. This body is empowered to determine correct and grammatical Hebrew usage. Fiats of the Academy carry official status.

100 JERUSALEM WOMEN HELD

Ramallah school closed for subversive activity

Jerusalem Post Reporter

The Ramallah District military governor yesterday closed down Bir Zeit College near Ramallah until further notice, for serving as a centre of agitation and subversive activity. In Jerusalem, police briefly detained 11 of a group of over 100 East Jerusalem women who staged an illegal march protesting last week's expulsion for subversion of eight West Bank and Jerusalem notables.

The 250 students at Bir Zeit College have staged strikes several times on nationalist grounds, the most recent being last Wednesday, when they and some of the faculty demonstrated on campus in support of the terrorist organizations. For several years they have brought out an illegal pro-terrorist newspaper called "al Radir" (the Little Stream).

After the I.D.F. raid on terrorists in Beirut they staged a demonstration in memory of the three terrorist slain there. (One of the three, Fatah spokesman Kamal Nasser, was a cousin of the college's principal.)

The military government spokesman, Rav-Seren Rafael Horowitz, said yesterday that the college administration had been warned several times, but that the "irritating and inciting atmosphere" had not been stopped. He noted that several Bir Zeit students have been arrested in the past for taking part in terrorist activities.

The Bir Zeit College is a private two-year junior college owned by the Nasser family of Ramallah. Seventy of its students are girls

In the Jerusalem incident, over 100 women staged a sit-down at 11 a.m. near the Red Cross office in East Jerusalem's A Zahra Street. A delegation of strikers met the Red Cross representatives and demanded the return of the eight men expelled.

At about noon the women moved down A Zahra Street bearing placards protesting the deportation. They were met at Salah Eddin Street by policemen, who asked them to stop. When they refused, the police arrested 11 in the front ranks, among them the wife of ex-Jordanian Defence Minister Anwar Nusseibeh and the wife of one of the deportees, Jerusalem attorney Abdul-Mohsin Abu Maizer.

The Jerusalem police spokesman, Nitzav-Mishne Avraham Turgeman, said yesterday that the police used no force and that the arrested women had been questioned and then released at 3 p.m.

Two other sit-downs were held yesterday in Nablus to protest the deportations, at the Municipality and at Najah College. Former Nablus Mayor Hamdi Kan'an, who had earlier been reported to be in Beirut, took part in the sit-down at the Municipality.

Informed sources on the West Bank told *The Post* that the Palestine Liberation Organization is about to call a Palestinian conference for next month in Cairo. It is believed that about 160 West Bank and East Jerusalem representatives will be invited.

In dismissing the appeal, the Supreme Court stressed the gravity of the offence.

Scholars warn Israel not to give up security

Jerusalem Post Reporter

TEL AVIV. — A group of 74 visiting scholars from foreign countries — all but four from the U.S. — yesterday published a declaration to stress that security guarantees, "even by great powers," were "no substitute for boundaries that Israel can defend herself." The statement was timed to coincide with the visit of Secretary of State Henry Kissinger.

The professors, who are here on study and research missions organized by the American Professors for Peace in the Middle East, warned that "even-handedness and neutrality" could cover up measures detrimental to Israel. They said that to achieve peace, both sides in the conflict must make concessions, but the basic requirement for peace is that the Arabs recognize Israel's right to exist.

American Professors for Peace in the Middle East, founded in 1967, has 16,000 members in American universities.

The masthead of the illegal newspaper "El Radir" put out by the students of the Bir Zeit College near Ramallah. This issue included an article in praise of Kamal Nasser, the Fatah spokesman killed in Beirut last year, who graduated from the school in 1941. The title of the article, reproduced above, is: "Kamal will shed his light even in death."

Army ruining bulldozers, 'and their owners as well'

By YA'ACOV FRIEDLER
Jerusalem Post Reporter

HAIFA. — Spokesmen for owners of heavy earth moving equipment complained on Friday that the Army is ruining their mobilized equipment through unprofessional use, and ruining them by the low rates it is paying.

All the machinery has been mobilized since the start of the war, said spokesmen for the 120 members of the organization of owners in the North. This encompassed some 300 pieces of equipment, out of a total of 800 in the whole country.

They noted that heavy earth moving equipment is the only field in which the Army relies virtually exclusively on civilian-owned vehicles, and that their machines were called up at once. So far they had not yet been paid a single agora, but the banks, including government-owned banks, had refused to

delay payment of the interest due from them, as all still owed large sums on the equipment, which cost as much as IL800,000 for the giant D9 Caterpillar bulldozer.

The spokesman charged that the Army was not maintaining their expensive equipment properly, and that many machines were breaking down as a result, besides those which were hit by enemy action, as they are being deployed in the very front lines, fortifying positions and helping the troops to dig in. This lack of elementary care, such as changing oil or air filters, contrasted to the very thorough care given to the Army's own tanks and vehicles, they said.

Their efforts to try and reach their equipment at the front (most of it is deployed in the Golan Heights), and help the soldiers maintain it, had been rejected by the Army. As a result of the poor maintenance, wear and tear was

very high, especially in the Golan where those operating on the hard basalt stones needs special skills, which the soldiers lack. They had also tried to persuade the Army, for efficiency purposes, to deploy the equipment with their original operators, but this too had been rejected, as the operators were serving in their units.

As a result the efficiency of exploitation was also "extremely low," and "our machines are doing no more than 20 per cent of their capacity, although in the Golan they're racing against time to get the forward positions linked up before the deep winter sets in." Another result would be, when the war finally ends, that there would be a shortage of earth moving equipment in Israel for road-building and housing-construction needs, as the ruined equipment would take at least a year to replace, due to the lengthy delivery time.

U.N. condemns 'alliance' of Zionism, racism

UNITED NATIONS (UPI). — The General Assembly on Friday voted 63 to 32, with 22 abstentions, to condemn "the unholy alliance between Portuguese colonialism, South African racism, Zionism and Israeli imperialism."

The condemnation came in an amendment to a resolution to tighten the military, cultural and commercial isolation of South Africa. The resolution itself was passed 88 to 7, with 28 abstentions.

The amendment linking Zionism to racism was submitted by Burundi at the last minute and caused a lengthy procedural debate which extended the Assembly's morning session after hours.

Israel Ambassador Jacob Doron said before the vote that the "Arab propaganda machine reached new depths of immorality" with the amendment. "This Arab propaganda warfare, which makes a mockery of U.N. procedure, goes unabated even a few days before the forthcoming peace conference in Geneva."

Israeli officer says Gamasy is 'gentleman'

An Israeli officer who took part in the talks at Kilometre 101 said in a radio interview on Friday that Egypt's new Chief of Staff, Lt. General Mohammed Gamasy, who led the Egyptian delegation at the talks, proved to be a "pleasant-mannered gentleman" who took meticulous notes.

Tat-Aluf Aharon Avnon, who was recently placed in charge of Army information, said Gamasy seemed to him "a balanced, cool and highly intelligent individual who always knew when to say 'yes' and when to say 'no.'" On informal occasions, over a cup of coffee, Gen. Gamasy unbended, smiled warmly and admitted to spending restless nights before the meetings and before taking important decisions, T/A Avnon said.

A gift for General Gamasy — an Arabic translation of the Jewish Bible — was handed over yesterday by an Israeli liaison officer to his Egyptian counterpart at the site of the broken-off Kilometre 101 talks west of Suez.

The silver-embossed volume, containing the ancient translation by Rabbi Sa'adya Gaon, was sent by Gen. Gamasy's opposite number at the talks, Aluf Aharon Yariv. The book was donated by Social Welfare Minister Michael Hazani; Aluf Yariv was prevented from handing it over personally by the breaking off of the talks.

IMMIGRATION actually increased during the war, and totalled 15,000 in the last three months, Absorption Minister Natan Peled said yesterday during a visit to the absorption centre in Arad.

GIVE THEM A LIFT-
GIVE THEM MORE TIME AT HOME.

DUBEK LTD.
Cigarette Manufacturers

Soldiers on the Golan visited by an
army entertainment troupe.

Rabbinate proclaims special prayers today

The Chief Rabbinate has proclaimed today, Kislev 22, as a day of general prayer in Israel and the Diaspora.

The Rabbinate called on Jews everywhere to congregate in their synagogues at 4 p.m. and houses of study for the reciting of special prayers "in these days of national emergency and on the eve of the peace conference."

The *Minha* (afternoon) service should be preceded by the recitation of Psalms 2, 20, 35, 83, 121, 123, 129 and 130, and the *"Heyay im pifiyot"* prayer from the High Holy Day *Mussaf* service. *(Itim)*

Soldiers give up leave to help Golan settlers

Jerusalem Post Reporter

TIBERIAS. — A unit of reservists who got their first leave yesterday after fighting the Syrians decided to devote their leave to helping the settlers of Merom Golan pick their potatoes — to thank the settlers for the way they had treated them during the war.

The women and children of Merom Golan, in the northern part of the Golan, were due to return to their homes yesterday.

On Wednesday the men of Kibbutz Mevo Hamma, in the southern part, welcomed their women and children back with flowers and singing. They also completed their cotton harvest with the assistance of settlers from the Jezreel Valley and reserve units. The women and children of Neot Golan also returned home on Wednesday.

'Playboy' magazines for the troops

A special surprise package is on its way to Israel from the United States: 3,000 copies of the latest issue of "Playboy" magazine to be distributed among the frontline troops.

The magazines are being sent as a special Hanukka project sponsored jointly by the wife of the President, Mrs. Nina Katzir, and American Ambassador Kenneth Keating.

The magazines are expected to turn frontline-dugouts into the most lavishly pinup-decorated martial installations in Israel's history.

A vision of Europe united behind Israel

By LILI BAT AHARON
Jerusalem Post Correspondent

BRUSSELS. —

On the eve of the Copenhagen Summit of the European Nine, a French political leader last week called for solidarity on the part of Europe as the only means to combat its present energy, financial and political crisis.

Speaking in the framework of the Grandes Conferences Catholiques of Belgium, Jean Lecanuet, President of the Centre Democrate opposition party of France, painted a picture of a Europe which, if it wants to continue free and democratic, must pull itself up by its unified bootstraps to create and assert a personality of its own. A Europe, which, he stressed, must stand with Israel in its demand for secure and recognized borders in a land "in which the Jewish people lived, as we all learned, already 4,000 years ago."

The conference, held under the auspices of Belgium's highest ranking Catholic, Cardinal Suenens, was attended by some 1,200 young and older Belgians who packed the hall of the Palais des Beaux-Arts to listen to an analysis of the current situation and suggestions of how to overcome it.

The energy crisis is already felt by an increasing number of Belgians. In addition to carless Sundays, hailed by many not as a plague but as a tacit blessing which has brought back the simpler pleasures of life to an over-industrialized society, homes are underheated, the use of hot water is limited, pre-Christmas streets are poorly lighted. A number of factories have closed down or have cut down on their labour force.

European solidarity, M. Lecanuet continued, is necessary, indeed essential, not only vis-a-vis oil, but in other economic fields resulting from the energy crisis. He advocated a united programme of European planning in the spheres of textile production, the petrochemical industry, manpower, and the conversion of capital to other activities.

"The problem is urgent," he warned. "The situation is serious and the solution must be found now. The Copenhagen summit will have to come up with concrete replies."

For with economic reduction might come cultural destruction. "When a people loses its economic stature, it also loses its spiritual creativity," said the man who describes himself as "refusing to slide into the right and a fighter of the left."

"We have to have the courage to look facts straight in the face," declared M. Lecanuet. "The time has come for politicians to tell the truth. Is Europe in a crisis of abdication? Or will Copenhagen launch us on the road to unification?

"I said this in the French Assembly, and I repeat this now. I do not agree with the Arabs' use of oil as an arm to be used as blackmail. As soon as you give in to pressure, you find yourself in a mess from which you do not know how to get out... I am ashamed that the sacrifices some of the European countries must make are not being shared by the whole European Community. I do not want France to become the oldest daughter of Islam."

World Jewry's powerful response

Geoffrey Wigoder's **JEWISH SCENE**

THE shock of the Yom Kippur War has been as traumatic in World Jewry as inside Israel.

The initial response was powerful. The fact that the attack came on Yom Kippur made Jews especially angry, while for those who followed the U.N. sessions the interchangeable use of "Israeli" with "Jewish" engendered an added element of identification.

The manifestations during t h e War ran along lines similar to those in 1967. The immediate response was to give money, and sums that seemed fabulous in 1967 were now trebled or quadrupled. The communities that responded most impressively were England and Switzerland. The type of stories that one had heard in 1967 were again heard — ranging f r o m enormous gifts from individuals to examples of real self-sacrifice on many levels. One man who gave his savings of $300,000 in Bonds said, "As a child, I asked my father what he had done to prevent the Holocaust. I never got an answer. I do not want to be unable to answer *my* children."

Jewish identification

One phenomenon of 1967 that was not repeated was the emergence of many individuals who identified themselves as Jews for the first time. This time there was little fresh identification. On the other hand, there was far greater involvement of the younger generations in fundraising. Couples in their '30s a n d '40s came forward and students on campuses collected money (Jewish students in the U.S. raised $750,000 in the first few weeks).

Younger groups also responded by volunteering. Over 50,000 applied to come to Israel but, unlike 1967, there was strict selectivity and only a few thousand were accepted — according to their skills and on condition that they pay their way and agree to stay at least six months. This caused a great deal of frustration among would-be volunteers abroad but was felt to be preferable to the frustrations felt by many once they had arrived in Israel in 1967. F o r university students, it should be noted, volunteering in 1973 at the outset of the academic year generally represented a far greater sacrifice than those who offered to come in June 1967—during their vacation.

Other people found different ways of identification. Blood banks found a wide response although the blood contributions were often not transferred to Israel but held in reserve. Once the situation stabilized, many groups began to visit Israel both to demonstrate their solidarity and to help the badly-hit tourist industry.

The other major sphere of Jewish response has been political. Jews have done everything possible to rally support for Israel in the various countries where they live. In certain countries, this has meant standing up against government policies. For the Jews of France this is no novelty as they have been trying to dissuade their government from its pro-Arab policy for six years, but for the new generation of British Jews this was a fresh experience. In all countries, t h e organized Jewish community h a s stood solidly behind Israel and even if government policy has not been changed, the extent of popular support for Israel — especially in Western Europe — is in no small way due to the public relations activities of the local communities.

For the Jews of the U.S. the boot was on the other foot. They had no cause to oppose governmental policy — on the contrary, they saw their task as strengthening the official policy and buffeting any dissenting influences. This caused its own dilemmas as many Jews who were highly critical of Nixon over t h e Watergate affair felt obliged to mute their views in the light of the Middle Eastern situation. Official Jewish organizations responded to an Administration appeal and asked Senator Jackson to freeze his amendment refusing Russia i t s "most-favoured nation status" — an appeal which Jackson indignantly rejected.

Israel's image

To a large extent, Israel is now suffering from the image it projected of itself — and this is as true abroad as at home. In 1967, although Israelis felt completely confident, Jews abroad were fearful for Israel's survival. Since then, we have appeared supremely sure of the deterrent effect of our own strength. At the same time the Arab campaign depicting Israel as an aggressive occupier has borne fruit. Although many Jews early in the War realized the extent of the danger, many of the less committed remained unconvinced. The Arab line that they are seeking only the return of territory lost in 1967 is widely believed (and Israel information is still inadequate in countering this claim by showing what we believe to be the Arabs' real long-term objectives). Christian response has also been lukewarm, partly for the same reasons. As in 1967, Jewish appeals often failed to evoke a response among Christians although the Christian silence was probably less marked in 1973 than in 1967. But, again, part of the weakness of the Christian attitude has been due to the acceptance of the Arab thesis that they were only fighting to get their own lands back.

A further complication that is becoming progressively problematic is the oil crisis. This contains a strong anti-Israel and anti-Semitic potential. It is true that it can also redound against the Arabs, who are being seen in many quarters as the villain of the piece but already voices are being heard blaming both Israel and the Jews for the problems that have arisen as a result of the fuel shortage.

Russian Jewry has continued to stand heroically although the environment has been even more poisoned than previously. Activists have refused to be silent — they sent cables of support to Israel, they demonstrated in Moscow for the right to join the Israel army, they protested to the Russian news agency Tass over its prejudiced reporting, and even demanded the right to send blood to Israel. Most remarkable, emigration to Israel reached record numbers in the War period (partly because those who received exit visas decided to use them immediately for fear of their revocation).

No reports have been received of anti-Jewish outbreaks in Arab lands, although in some cases these were averted only by the intervention of the authorities. Previous Arab-Israel conflicts had been the signal for physical attacks on Jews and it was feared that these might have been repeated on this occasion.

Effect on apathetic

After the Six Day War, there were Jews who expressed themselves as indifferent or even hostile to the State of Israel. Among those who were hostile (notably in New L e f t circles), little has changed as a result of the War. But among those who were apathetic or who were beginning to veer away, there has been evidence of a turning towards Israel.

As in 1967, the War has brought Israel and World Jewry even closer together. The realization of Israel's vulnerability and growing isolation has posed a new challenge to the Jews of the world and their reaction as well as the new realities being faced inside Israel have emphasised the element of interdependence as the basic underlying factor in the relationship between Israel and World Jewry.

Kibbutz Grat was hit by a Syrian missile.

De Beauvoir hits Syria for 'inhumanity'

PARIS (INA). — France's well-known author and philosopher, Simone de Beauvoir, yesterday decried the "inhuman behaviour" of Syria in its continued refusal to turn over to the Red Cross a list of Israeli prisoners it holds captive.

In a special article in "Le Monde," Miss de Beauvoir condemned Syria's "gratuitous cruelty" and said that if Damascus continued "to step on the laws recognized by all nations to limit the horrors of war, then it deserves to be called 'barbaric'."

She said the "vindictive obstinacy" on the part of Syria runs completely counter to the rest of the Arab world's campaign since the outbreak of the October war to improve its rather negative world image. She referred in particular to Egypt's efforts to show the world it was treating its PoWs humanely.

Miss de Beauvoir concluded with the plea that if "Syria refuses to heed the protests of its enemies, perhaps the Arab world could make Damascus listen to reason by convincing the Syrians of the great damage they are doing to the Arab cause in the world."

Culture tent for tank battalion
Jerusalem Post Reporter

BEERSHEBA. — A tank battalion adopted by the David Ben-Gurion University of the Negev has received a "culture tent" for the use of its men in the front lines.

The 6 x 4m. all-weather, multi-purpose tent can be assembled in 20 minutes and is designed to serve forward units as a cultural centre. It seats 40 on comfortable cushions.

CHRISTIAN CONCERN FOR WAR DISABLED IN ISRAEL

HANUKKA/CHRISTMAS APPEAL

A difficult time lies ahead for a great number of young men wounded in the recent battles. Many of them will continue to suffer from this war for years to come, both physically, emotionally and spiritually, and will require a lengthy and expensive period of healing and rehabilitation in order that they may resume their place in life and society.

Sharing the sorrow and anxiety of the country in which we live for these victims of war, the Christian community of Israel is invited to express compassion and brotherly concern through a voluntary contribution towards their rehabilitation. A committee of members of the Christian community of Israel has been formed to help in the collection of these necessary funds, and to assist in their distribution in close cooperation with the appropriate authorities. Overhead expenses are being borne by members of this Committee.

Contributions should be sent to:

"Christian Concern for War Disabled,"
P.O.B. 249, Jerusalem, Israel.

We believe that Christian institutions, churches and organizations, as well as groups and individuals living abroad, will also wish to contribute to this rehabilitation. It is our expectation that Christians and churches in other countries of the Middle East will find ways to help within their society in the similar rehabilitation of those who have been disabled by this war.

Canon Roger G. Allison	Christ Church, Jerusalem (Anglican)
Brother Dr. Marcel Dubois, OP	Superior, St. Isaiah House, Jerusalem
Rev. W. Gardiner-Scott	St. Andrew's Church of Scotland, Jerusalem
Abbot Dr. Laurentius Klein, OSB	Abbot, Dormition Abbey and Chairman, Ecumenical Theological Research Fraternity
Rev. Roy Kreider	Chairman, United Christian Council in Israel
Rev. Norman Lytle	Baptist Minister to students in Jerusalem
Father Jean Roger, AA	Chaplain, Catholic community, Beersheba
Father Daniel Rufeisen, OCD	Catholic priest, Mt. Carmel, Haifa
Rev. Coos Schoneveld	Executive Secretary, Ecumenical Fraternity
Rev. Magne Solheim	Lutheran Pastor, Haifa
Rev. Alexander Wachtel	Convener, Jerusalem Ministers' Fraternal and Chairman, Church of the Nazarene in Israel
Rev. Dr. G. Douglas Young	President, American Institute of Holy Land Studies, Jerusalem

Sapir declares economy now 'vigorous'

Jerusalem Post Knesset Reporter

Finance Minister Pinhas Sapir yesterday persuaded the Knesset to refer to Committee two Likud motions for a debate about the need for economic and social reform measures, to help the nation cope with the extended emergency.

He said that the economy's "present vigour" during an extended emergency, was proof that the Government had planned its investments wisely and well.

The war had caught the country with large stocks of staples, he said, which had not shrunk in the past three months. Rationing had not been necessary

200 in French Parliament cable support

Over 200 French parliamentarians from the Franco-Israel friendship groups on the Senate and the National Assembly yesterday cabled Knesset Speaker Israel Yeshayahu, expressing their solidarity with Israel.

The message, signed by General de Benouville in the name of 127 Deputies of the Assembly, and Pierre Gigaud in the name of 81 Senators, expressed support for Israel's right to secure and recognized borders, and noted that foreign governments' polices towards Israel were totally governed by interests of strategy and oil — not of justice.

"ARAB" LANDS

To the Editor of The Jerusalem Post

Sir, —

The Arabs vowed to annihilate our State and repeatedly attacked us. We struck back in self-defence and occupied territories as a result of wars which we did not start. Are there two international moral standards, one for Russia and her satellites who are allowed to keep lands of vanquished Germany, and another for Israel who has no right to even a single square inch in retaining territories?!

DR HERBERT COHN

N.B. I am sick and tired of the reactionary stand of *The Post*. I have cancelled my subscription.

Ashdod, December 8.

THE HOLIDAY OF HANUKKAH celebrates the victory of the Jews over the Greeks. It is an annual eight-day festival, and is known as the "Feast of Lights." Josephus, whose history of Hanukkah is based on the first book of Maccabees, does not mention the term Hanukkah. His narration simply concludes, "From that time onward unto this day, we celebrate the festival calling it 'Lights'."

The feast of Hanukkah, which falls on the 25th day of the month of Kislev, was initially celebrated in the year 165 B.C.

Today, in Israel it is customary for the Chief Rabbi to proceed to the Western Wall, which marks the site of the ancient Temple, and light the first Hanukkah candle of the huge candelabrum which is set up at the Wall for the holiday. During 1973, this honor fell to Rabbi Goren, who performed the ceremony.

During Hanukkah, many public buildings are lit up in celebration of the holiday, and each light of a giant candelabrum atop the Knesset Building is illuminated day by day during the entire festival.

In commemoration of this holiday, a torch relay is held, starting out from the town of Modin. Young

THE 2,137th HANUKKA

TONIGHT Jews will light the first candle ushering in the 2,137th annual Hanukka celebration. The festival celebrates the victory of the Jews of Judea, led by the Hasmonean-Maccabean father and five sons, over the Greek Seleucid Syrian occupiers of the country.

This was not a mere political-military struggle and victory. At the outset, the Seleucids had allowed the Judeans almost complete communal autonomy, more than nearly all the subsequent occupiers of this country, perhaps even more than the British Mandatory Government.

The Hasmonean-Maccabean Revolt broke out when the Seleucids decided to Hellenize the Jews by force, to compel them — as the rulers of all the other sections of the Greek Empire had done with the other conquered peoples, with almost total success — to become Greeks by giving up their own religious, social and cultural ways and adopt those of Greece. The Jews, with a culture, religion, literature and way of life of their own going back nearly 2,000 years — one based on the view that life has meaning; Man has dignity; and all people are equal yet are different — found Greek culture and religion, based on the worship of whimsical gods and goddesses to whom life was an Absurd, repugnant. And so, after at first submissively becoming history's first religious-cultural martyrs, the Jews rose up in history's first recorded revolt for religious-cultural freedom.

Jewish religious tradition plays down the purely political-military aspects of the Hasmonean Revolt, emphasizing the myth of the cruse of olive oil: after the Hasmoneans cleared the Temple of the idolatrous fixtures which the Greeks had installed there, they found only one cruse of ritually pure olive oil for lighting the Temple Candelabrum — oil enough for only one day's burning but which miraculously lasted eight days.

In recent times, especially since the rise of Zionism, Jews again began to study and appreciate the military aspects of the achievements of our Hasmonean forerunners — a small but plucky and resourceful band of guerrillas leading their countrymen in successful resistance against some of the best Greek soldiery sent to Hellenize or destroy them. But to commemorate their victory, all Jews — religious or otherwise — light the Hanukka candles: one on the first night of Hanukka, two on the second and so on to eight on the last night.

We will light them again this year, and sing of the ancient victory of the human spirit over the worshippers of gold and silver and sameness; we will light them, and sing of the victory of the olive oil feeding the wicks to spread a glow of light and warmth to banish the darkness and cold into which the petroleum-idolators wish to plunge the world, of the ultimate victory of human dignity and differentness over those who would press all humanity into a slavery of sameness.

Credibility of African independence at stake

AFRICA BECOMING A TOOL OF THE ARAB STATES

By GODWIN OGOWA

I DO not write to curry favour. I am not on the propaganda payroll of any government. The issue of Africa and the Middle East has always dizzied my mind. If I were in Cairo, I would write. If I were in Libya, I would write. If I were in Uganda, I would write. So let no critic be under the misconception that I write because I am in Israel. I cannot continue to remain silent on an issue that burns my heart. Even though I know this article can have no effect on Africa, at least I will be satisfied that I have on the long run voiced it out.

I am at a loss to know why a conflict in the Middle East should take precedence over Rhodesia and South Africa on the agenda of the Organization of African Unity. Is it because these two countries are not Arab? Is it because they are Black Africa?

Unfortunately it is true that the black race is always put in second place even in what is supposed to be its continent. The OAU is now showing itself purely as an Arab instrument — a forum where the white African countries (the Arabs) come to impose their will on their black counterparts.

The Arab nations do not identify themselves as pure Africans. This is evident in their apathy towards the problems of Black African nations.

If the current wave of anti-Israel feeling in Africa is a resolution of the OAU, then the organization is presenting a united front in the wrong direction — unless, of course, the initials "OAU" mean "Organization for Arab Unity."

The involvement of some personalities in this anti-Israel epidemic in Africa leaves me in doubt as to the credibility of African independence. The whole affair is assuming the dimensions of mob action. It is a pity that pragmatic African nationalists are either dead or have been put out of action by the Arabs or their Moslem sympathizers. It is a matter for deep sorrow that Africa has descended to the level of being "teleguided" politically by such "brains" as Idi Amin and Gaddafi.

Face reality

If African leaders want to face realities they should advise their Arab overlords to come down to earth. The Arabs have fought four wars in their mad bid to drive the Jews into the sea, only to lose more of their lands. They should now understand or be advised to understand that the Middle East problem can never have a military solution. What military solution do they expect — the extermination of the people of Israel? Does it mean that the Jews should not have a place under the sun? One of these African mentors should have had enough courage to advise the Arabs to acknowledge the obvious existence of Israel.

I concede, however, that the position of these puppet leaders in Africa can be justified. If the deadly Arab weapon of oil can silence the members of NATO, what effect can one expect it to have on Africa with her fragile economy?

General Mobutu of Zaire is aggrieved about the fate of his Palestinian brothers in the Middle East. Idi Amin is seething with rage that Israel should be allowed to exist. The Africans in the white enclaves of Rhodesia and South Africa are not Mobutu's brothers. The existence of a white "apartheid" government in Black Africa does not perturb Idi Amin. The attitude of Togo, Chad and a host of unviable little countries in Africa can be vindicated. The promise of a million dollars from Gaddafi or Iraq can alter the strongest policies of these poor countries.

Nigeria broke relations with Israel on the grounds that civilian populations in Egypt were attacked. What a sudden show of consideration for civilians in times of war. It was this country which hired Egyptian pilots to massacre civilians during her war with Biafra. "Starvation of civilians is a legitimate instrument of war" was said by Nigeria's Obafemi Awalowo during the same Biafra episode.

That Zambia's Kenneth Kaunde was infected by this current epidemic reveals the Arab influence in Africa. Kaunde's outspokenness and independent ideas won him the love of many young Africans. But, alas,

what is the effect of these qualities without a strong economic backing. The leaders of these African nations which have broken ties with Israel should search their minds more deeply. They should ask themselves whether they were actually satisfying their conscience by this act or whether they were just dancing to the tune of Arab domination in Africa.

(Mr. Ogowa is a Nigerian student who has been working as a volunteer at Kibbutz Shadmot)

Dutch to be inscribed in Golden Book

A public committee headed by Justice Moshe Landau has been set up to raise money to get the people of Holland inscribed in the Jewish National Fund's Golden Book.

Contributions may be made through the United Israel Appeal office, 11 Herman Shapiro, Tel Aviv, Tel. (02) 287111.

In another show of appreciation to the Dutch people, the Tel Aviv committee of the Israel-Holland Friendship Society has sent blue-and-white holiday candles to members of the organization in Holland.

Appeals to Arab wives

Jerusalem Post Reporter

Sixty women leaders from Israel, the U.S. and Canada meeting at the Knesset yesterday called on "the mothers and wives in Syria and Egypt to prevail on their governments to meet with Israelis at the peace table to end the bloodshed of the past 25 years."

The group included a visiting delegation from the Women's Division of Israel Bonds and members of the Council of Women's organizations in Israel.

boys and girls, in turn, carry a lighted torch from the town where the Maccabees initiated their revolt against the Greeks all the way to Jerusalem.

This is a most joyous holiday in Israel, and is celebrated far and wide, regardless of the particular religious inclination or religious intensity of the celebrants. It is considered by many to be a folk festival. During the celebration, gifts are exchanged, especially gifts for the young. It is customary for children to play with spinning tops, which are called *s've-vo-not;* and mother makes it a point to serve *latkis,* or pancakes made of potato batter, as well as a dessert called *suf-ga-ni-yot,* which is something like a doughnut.

The word literally means *sponges.*

During Hanukkah of 1973, the Egyptian front was comparatively silent. Only the Syrian front still remained in eruption, but comparatively stilled. Throughout Israel during 1973, the Hanukkah mood remained somewhat somber, certainly less jubilant than in former years.

· One of my trips to Israel coincided with the Hanukkah season, when I visited the home of my friend, Saul Eshel. His young twin sons were each given his own hannukiah[1]. Each evening, each boy ceremoniously lit one

1. A candelabrum holding eight candles used for the celebration of Hanukkah.

One-third of students still mobilized
Universities to open Sunday

**By SARAH HONIG
and ERNIE MEYER**
Jerusalem Post Reporters

The country's universities will open on Sunday — two months late — but an estimated one-third of their 45,000 students will not be able to attend classes. They are still in the army.

Teams of university lecturers are now touring the various army camps and bases in an effort to speak personally with every registered student who is still mobilized, Tel Aviv University Rector Shlomo Simonsohn said yesterday. These teams, which include faculty members from all the institutions of higher learning, will explain what general arrangements are being made for helping the students make up for lost time and material. They will answer questions and put the students in touch with others who can offer them individual assistance.

The mobilized student will be given forms to fill out with his personal requests for books or for individual counselling. The forms will arrive at the campuses within a matter of days, Prof. Simonsohn says, and replies will be speedy.

The Rector said all lectures would be recorded, transcribed and mimeographed for mobilized students. In addition, all lectures will be repeated during the spring and summer terms, assuming there are enough rotations in reserve duty to enable students who miss the fall and winter terms to attend classes later on.

"We are aware that one cannot sit in a tank across from Ismailya and study normally from mimeographed lecture transcripts, and we are not trying to delude the students," Prof. Simonsohn said. "The aim here is to enable the student to do as much studying as he can, to minimize his losses."

The proportion of mobilized students differs in the various universities, and in the faculties within those universities, so no one knows exactly how many students to expect in a given lecture. It is assumed, however, that the Technion — 90 per cent of whose student body is male — will have a higher absentee rate than Tel Aviv or Bar-Ilan University, for instance.

HEBREW UNIVERSITY

A Hebrew University spokesman said this week that about half the institution's students are believed to be mobilized. The proportion ranges from 70 per cent in the Faculty of Agriculture to 30 per cent in the Faculty of Arts. Although many junior lecturers are also in the army, the spokesman said, H.U. does not foresee any serious shortage of teachers. (One exception may be the Medical School, where 75 per cent of the clinical lecturers are still mobilized.)

The Hebrew University's largest faculty, the Faculty of Arts, has felt the war less than many other disciplines, since 65 per cent of its students are women and it has a large number of overseas students. Over 1,000 of its students, however,

are still mobilized, as are some junior lecturers.

MEDICAL SCHOOL

Dean Aharon Beller of the Medical School estimates that 60 per cent of his students will be on hand at the opening of the school year. The 40 per cent still mobilized, however, will be given every opportunity to complete their year. "We have no illusions that one can study medicine while in the front lines, therefore we will concentrate on helping students while they are home on leave. No matter how short that leave, students will be admitted into their classes," he said. The material missed will be taught to small groups or even to individuals.

The school day will be lengthened to last from 8 a.m. to 10 p.m. and the school week extended over six days, Dean Beller said. He added that he is negotiating with the army to grant all medical students their leave at the same time, so as to enable the University to teach them in groups.

The most difficult problem is that of the first-year students, Prof. Beller said.

The faculty knows where each one of its students is serving and Prof. Beller and other teachers have visited many of their students in the lines.

Of the 300 dentistry students at the H.U. — which has the only dental school in the country — 40 per cent are still mobilized, many serving in combat units. Some 25 per cent are women.

SIMONE DE BEAUVOIR

Syria's PoW policy:'inhuman attitude'

By JACK MAURICE
Jerusalem Post Correspondent

PARIS. — LAST Monday "Le Monde" published an article by Simone de Beauvoir attacking Syria over the prisoner-of-war issue.

The full text of her article (refered to briefly in Tuesday's *Jerusalem Post)* was as follows:

"There is war, then peace, or at least a lull, a truce... the sound of firing dies down, and both sides bury their dead and tend their wounded, the prisoners go home. Over and above these bloody conflicts, the nations re-establish a kind of human barter.

"It is this ancient tradition that the Geneva Convention transformed into international law. Israel pledged immediately to conform to it. After some beating about the bush, Egypt consented to an exchange of prisoners. Syria has refused.

"Israel has given the Red Cross a list of its prisoners and has allowed regular Red Cross visits. Syria has given no names of captive Israelis and has not authorized anyone to check on their treatment.

"Why this inhuman attitude? On the Golan Heights, the tortured bodies of Israeli soldiers have been discovered. However dreadful these explosions of hatred may seem, they are imaginable in the height of battle.

"But, how can we understand a government that in cold blood inflicts on young and unarmed boys the anguish of an imprisonment whose issue remains shrouded in doubt, a government that condemns hundreds of families to uncertainty and waiting?

"Syrian soldiers received orders to make the identification of dead Israelis impossible or at least very arduous, the aim being to shake the enemy's morale and thereby diminish his striking power.

"Today the fighting is over, and if in Israel the nightmare of the prisoners' families were, too, the face of history would not be changed for all that.

"There is no greater anguish than not knowing whether a loved one is living or dead: Damascus' silence seems all the more cruel as it serves no one.

"Syrian leaders do not sympathise with the tears of Israeli mothers. But do they care about Syrian mothers, over 500 in fact, whose sons they could bring back by just one word?

"But these mothers do not share the same torments as Israeli mothers because they know their sons are alive and well. It is likely, however, that they miss them just as much. Their government prefers to deprive them of the joy of having their sons back rather than forgo the opportunity to break some Israeli hearts.

"Cannot these Syrian mothers protest against the useless cruelty of this choice and persuade Syria's leaders to change their line of conduct?

"This is not a political choice. It is not incompatible both to side with Syria against Israel and still insist that it stops violating the Geneva Convention.

"At the start of this latest war, the Arabs sought to wipe out a certain unfavourable image of themselves and replace it with a better one. The Egyptians in particular went all out to convince the world that they were giving their prisoners the best possible treatment. Syria's stubborness is in flagrant opposition to this aim.

"If the Syrians remain unmoved by the protests of their enemies, then perhaps they would heed their friends if the latter point out the great damage Syria is causing to its own cause in international public opinion.

"If Syria goes on trampling on the rules respected by all nations to limit the horrors of warfare, then their action can be summed up in only one word: barbarism."

AN ARAB VIEW:

Peace is not being friends

A leading Egyptian journalist has warned his readers that the Israel vision of normal peaceful relations with its Arab neighbours is not at all what the Arabs themselves have in mind. Sallah Jowdat, writing in a recent issue of the magazine "Al-Mussawar," said that a normal, neighbourly peace — "sulh" in the full sense of the word—could come about only "if the Jews of Palestine... live together with the Arabs of Palestine in a secular state with no racialist characteristics whatsoever, and within the numerical proportions that existed before 1948."

Only if the Jews who arrived after 1948 returned to their countries of origin, leaving solely the pre-48 Palestinian Jews and their children in the country alongside the Palestinian Arabs — only then could the term *"sulh"* — perhaps— be used, Mr. Jowdat explained.

He wrote that Arabic has two words for the English "peace" — *"sulh"* and *"salaam."* After 1967, he recalled, Premier Golda Meir had said that she wanted *"salaam"* to prevail so that she could drive in her car to Cairo or Damascus and go shopping there.

He warned that the Geneva conference might confuse the two terms *"sulh"* and *"salaam"* — but as far as the Arabs were concerned this was to be strictly a *"salaam"* conference, not a *"sulh"* conference. If Israel agreed to withdraw totally from all the Arab lands that it had taken in 1967, and also to restore the rights of the Palestinian people — then on that basis the war and the armed struggle could come to an end.

But that would not mean that Mrs. Meir would then be able to go shopping in Cairo or Damascus or Amman — which would imply the existence of diplomatic relations between Israel and the Arabs, as well as economic and human ties. "We rejected that when we were beaten and impotent. How much more so do we reject it now when we have conquered our defeat and approached the margin of victory?

"Now we are able to attain peace by force of arms — but we have preferred to try first to attain it through diplomacy. Perhaps the efforts of the entire international community will succeed in bringing Israel back to its senses, so that it returns to the 1967 lines and restores the rights of the Palestinians. Then there will be *"salaam"* — but still not *"sulh."*

Rabbi Shlomo Goren, Chief Rabbi of Israeli Jewry, lights the first Hanukka candle at the western wall.

GOREN LIGHTS FIRST CANDLE

Chief Rabbi Shlomo Goren lit the first light of Hanukka at the Western Wall yesterday, comparing the bravery of Israel's soldiers during the Yom Kippur war with the feats of the Maccabees.

The ceremony, in the waning light of the setting sun, was attended by many Jerusalemites, soldiers on leave, bereaved families and tourists, who uttered a thunderous "Amen" as Rabbi Goren recited the Hanukka and "Sheheheyanu" blessings.

The Chief Rabbi sent his greeting to the soldiers of Israel standing guard at the front and wished the wounded a speedy recovery and a speedy return to the prisoners of war still in enemy captivity.

In another ceremony, the traditional torch was kindled yesterday at Modi'in — the burial ground of the Maccabees — and relayed to Lod Airport by runners of the Young Maccabee organization. There, basketball star Tal Brody handed the torch over to an El Al captain who will fly it to the U.S. and other countries which have Maccabee sports organizations.

The "Torch of Courage" — to commemorate those who gave their lives for the freedom of Israel — was kindled yesterday atop Mount Hermon and carried in relay by hundreds of youngsters to towns and settlements throughout Western Galilee. The runners congregated in the afternoon at the monument to the fallen soldiers of the Yehiam convoy, which was all but annihilated in an ambush during the War of Independence.

ARABS AND SAMARITANS

To the Editor of The Jerusalem Post

Sir, — Reference is made to Sarah Honig's article about the Samaritans (December 7).

As a Nablus citizen, I always looked to the Samaritans as brothers and have never regarded them as a foreign element. The relationship between the Arab citizens of Nablus and the Samaritans was always friendly and never faced difficulties.

The writer of the article depended in her quotations on a Holon Samaritan. If she wanted to be more objective and fair, she should have asked the Samaritans of Nablus themselves.

The Arab citizens will never forget the stand of the late High Priest of the Samaritans when he told the leaders of the Israeli Army which occupied Nablus during the June War that the Nablus citizens had always embraced the Samaritans in the same way a mother embraces her children.

What annoys me in said article is the pessimist view that "if a Palestinian State were established, the remaining Samaritans in Nablus would be in the same position as Jews were in Nazi Germany." I want to remind the writer that the Arabs have never been persecutors in their history, even to their enemies. If this is their attitude towards enemies, how will it be then towards their Samaritan brothers?

SA'ID M. KANAAN
Nablus, December 8.

PRESS RESTRICTIONS

To the Editor of The Jerusalem Post

Sir, — In your issue of December 7, Forest A. Broman made a very valid point. But I wonder if your readers are aware how bad the situation is.

Since Sunday, December 2, foreign correspondents have in effect been banned from visiting either the Golan Heights or the Sinai battlefronts. Up to today, Friday, December 7, the military spokesman's office in Tel Aviv has refused all applications from foreign newsmen to visit either front. No explanation has been given for this new policy.

But the Defence Minister, Moshe Dayan, has confirmed that such a policy does exist. When asked by a newsman before leaving for the U.S.: "Do you intend to allow foreign correspondents to visit the front lines or is this going to be a permanent ban," he replied, "I think that foreign and local correspondents have visited the area and talked to our soldiers, and our soldiers talked to them, well let us say a lot *and about enough.* Of course, if there is any military event, we shall allow correspondents to cover that." Daily breaches of the cease-fire apparently do not rate as "military events."

This is a reversal of the policy which has always given Israel such credibility abroad — free and open access to the press. However, it virtually kills TV coverage on the front lines.

What is more alarming is that the Israeli press, which champions press freedom as much as the rest of the world's news media, has not even bothered to tell its readers that such a ban is operating.

PETER LYNCH
Tel Aviv, December 7.

---

additional candle by himself on his own candelabrum. The older daughter, then fourteen, shared the family *hannukiah.*

The boys reveled in the joy of possession, and made a big fuss about the fact that each of them, though only ten at the time, had his own candelabrum. Saul told me that this was not unusual in Israel, and that other families with whom he was acquainted followed the same course.

KISSINGER...AND THE SALAMI POLICY

the Russians' insidious "Salami Policy." Cut away ... cut away, little by little, so that the other nation doesn't fully realize how steadily it's losing ground.

Allow the Egyptian Third Army to be resupplied.

Retreat to the Mitla Pass?

Surrender Sharm e-Sheikh?

And ... where will it STOP ? !

Likud says we must be strong in our pursuit of peace. Must seek peace, not through rampant concessions, not through makeshift arrangements. But through face-to-face negotiations with the Arab states.

Likud is for peace. Not piece-by-piece giveaways.

הליכוד

VOTE

גח"ל, הרשימה הממלכתית, המרכז החפשי
תנועת העבודה למען ארץ ישראל השלמה

LIKUD

Gahal, The State List, The Free Centre, The Movement for a Greater Israel

THE LABOUR PARTY ACADEMICIANS' GROUP AND SYMPATHIZERS

CALLS ON ALL ACADEMICIANS to join ranks behind

Hama'arach and to form an opposition to the extremist "not one inch" brigade, since this approach is liable to drag the country into further wars and destruction.

We believe that, after the elections, the Ma'arach leadership will be able to lead the people to peace, while maintaining a resolute stand against pressures and the erosion of our just security demands, and that it will also be able to preserve human rights and further advance the social achievements of the workers.

The Academicians' Group demands and will continue to demand that the new government be made up of the best people available.

We welcome the new political awareness among academicians, and call on them to work with us, in order to increase our voice in Hama'arach, to ensure that discussions in the Party's institutions are meaningful, and to bring into the discussion forum a broad range of academic groups, which can contribute advice and support to the Labour leadership.

The Academics' Group warns against the dangers of not voting in the elections. This is liable to produce political instability, the result of which would be the payment of a heavy price to the secondary and small parties.

המערך / מפלגת העבודה הישראלית · מפ"ם

'EMET' Hama'arach/Israel Labour Party-Mapam

Access denied to foreign press

To the Editor of The Jerusalem Post

Sir, — The "personal opinion" column by Zeev Schul in Tuesday's issue of *The Jerusalem Post* carried the headline "Foreign Press Favoured. Unhappy Israeli Newsmen Denied Access to Soldiers."

If I may coin a contradictory phrase this headline is an accurate inaccuracy.

It is accurate that Israeli newsmen are denied access to soldiers. It is not accurate that the foreign press is favoured. Only the visiting luminaries of the journalistic fraternity are given favoured treatment. The resident foreign newsman who does a day-in, day-out job of covering the Israeli story is hamstrung at every turn.

There is a good-sized press corps in Israel which over the years has demonstrated its commitment to telling the Israeli story truthfully and let the chips fall where they may. These newsmen represent all the major news agencies, newspapers, television and radio networks in the free world. When they speak, hundreds of millions of people listen. Israeli officials and military authorities may speak truthfully, but it is a fact of life that what an official says is often considered to be biased. However, when a free and unrestricted journalist asks questions and reports the truth as he sees it, his report has an impact.

Therefore, if right and truth are on Israel's side, the way to explain that rightly and tell that truth is through the press. But the press cannot do its job if at every turn it is prevented from seeing for itself and talking to people.

The Israel Defence Forces, and the Army Spokesman's Office, are concerned about military security. This is natural. However, preventing security breaks is the business of censorship, not of the Army Spokesman's Office. I, personally, and most of my colleagues in the resident foreign press corps, do not want to know Israel's military secrets. Knowing them would make me nervous and I wouldn't know what to do with them. My colleagues and I only want the opportunity to report what is publishable. In addition, it is a matter of record that the only violations of censorship regulations in recent years have been by visiting foreign newsmen who came in, grabbed a story and published it after leaving Israel. Resident foreign newsmen have not got that possibility.

Therefore, when the Army Spokesman's Office, undoubtedly acting under orders, frustrates the freedom of the press, prevents newsmen from visiting the fronts, issues orders forbidding interviews, and has favourites among the press corps, it is engaging in the worst kind of news management, in what can only be described as self-serving political censorship.

The solution to the problem is for the military authorities to accept the basic philosophy that truth is their most potent weapon, and the best way to tell that truth to the Israeli public and the world is to let the free press do its job.

DAN BLOOM
CBS Bureau Chief
Tel Aviv, December 18.

Complaint to U.N. against Lebanon for bus shooting

Jerusalem Post Diplomatic Correspondent

Israel complained against Lebanon to the U.N. yesterday in the wake of Monday's shooting attack on a bus at Shomriya, near the Lebanese border. The complaint stressed that it had been only by chance that there had been no casualties from the shooting, which had been carried out in broad daylight.

The complaint asserted that the Palestinian terrorist organizations continue to enjoy full freedom of action and freedom of movement in Lebanon and are able to maintain bases there and conduct propaganda activities without hindrance.

A proven killer of innocent airline passengers, such as George Habash, leader of the Popular Front for the Liberation of Palestine, is invited to appear on the radio in Lebanon and make public statements from other platforms, the complaint stated.

THE MIDDLE EAST

To the Editor of The Jerusalem Post

Sir, — For an unbiased look at the Middle East before the Balfour Declaration, let us examine the 1911 Encyclopaedia Britannica.

Under the heading Jerusalem we find: "The population in 1905 was about 60,000 (Moslems 7,000, Christians 13,000, Jews 40,000)."

Is this the Arab Jerusalem before 1948 that the Arabs want?

Even more illuminating is the material on "Barbary Pirates" which includes the following: "The first half of the 17th century may be described as the flowering time of the Barbary Pirates . . . all traders belonging to nations which did not pay blackmail in order to secure immunity were liable to be taken at sea. The payment of blackmail, disguised as presents or ransoms, did not always secure safety with these faithless barbarians. The most powerful states in Europe condescended to make payments to them and to tolerate their insults.... The continued existence of this African piracy was indeed a disgrace to Europe. for it was due to the jealousies of the powers themselves. France encouraged them during her rivalry with Spain; and when she had no further need of them they were supported against her by Great Britain and Holland. In the 18th century British public men were not ashamed to say that Barbary piracy was a useful check on the competition of weaker Mediterranean nations in the carrying trade . . . An extensive list of such punitive expeditions could be made out, down to the American operations of 1801-5 and 1815. But in no case was the attack pushed home, and it rarely happened that the aggrieved Christian state refused in the end to make a money payment in order to secure peace. The frequent wars among them gave the pirates numerous opportunities of breaking their engagements, of which they never failed to take advantage.... Lord Exmouth . . . in combination with a Dutch squadron under Admiral Van de Capellen administered a smashing bombardment to Algiers. The lesson terrified the pirates both of that city and of Tunis into giving up over 3,000 prisoners and making fresh promises. But they were not reformed and were not capable of reformation, Algiers renewed its piracies and slave taking, though on a smaller scale . . . The great pirate city was not in fact thoroughly tamed till its conquest by France in 1850."

Has anything changed?

HARRY J. LIPKIN
Professor of Physics
Weizmann Institute of Science
Rehovot

Rehovot, December 10.

'Keep talking and stop shooting'

GENEVA STAGE IS READY, BUT PEACE STILL REMOTE

**By ARI RATH
and ANAN SAFADI**

Jerusalem Post Correspondents

GENEVA. —

THE stage is set. The leading actors are already on the scene. But the main theme of the play — "Israeli-Arab Peace" — still seems as remote as ever. After days of tough bargaining, exercises in futility and diplomatic winds blowing hot and cold, the official word was finally out: the Middle East peace conference would open on Friday morning.

The intricate phrasing of the joint Soviet-American letter of invitation could stand up very well to any work of Talmudic sophistry. It managed to find a redeeming formula distinguishing between U.N. auspices and Soviet-American co-chairmanship of the conference and tried to solve the thorny problem of Palestinian representation by saying that the parties had agreed to discuss the question of "other participants from the Middle East" during the first stage of the conference.

But even then, Syria, one of the Middle East's most ferocious and savage belligerents, has decided to stay away from Geneva, at least at the opening stage, making it a rump conference at the start.

The magic formula that was to bring Israel, Egypt and Jordan to the negotiating table is there. But can peace after four bloody wars and over 50 years of Arab hostility really be attained through magic formulas?

Geneva does not seem to bode well for the successful outcome of a peace conference.

Despite its magnificent setting, the marble-walled Palais des Nations — former seat of the defunct League of Nations — has a tradition of failure to achieve anything even resembling peace. Certainly the city on the shores of picturesque Lac Leman, surrounded by the towering, snow-covered Alps, topped by Mont Blanc, is an attractive gathering place for international delegations, even in winter, when the weather is crisp and sunny. But the labyrinths of the 18-kilometre long Palais des Nations corridors, with their Kafkaesque atmosphere, seem a more indicative omen than the beautiful scenery.

The Council Chamber, where the peace conference is due to open this morning, witnessed three months of futile diplomatic bargaining, yielding results merely on paper, during the 1954 conferences on Indochina and Korea. The marble bas-reliefs over its entrance door, with the inscription "Here is a great work of peace in which all can participate," and the wall-paintings inside, depicting Justice, Strength, Peace, Law and Intelligence, do not seem to inspire delegates who come with preconceived ideas. Will the Middle East conference be an exception to the rule and at last do justice to Geneva's reputation as the "City of Peace?"

Probably not, if one is to go by some of the arrival statements here and by what has been said in the last few days by President Sadat of Egypt and by spokesmen for the Palestine Liberation Organization, which the Arabs claim to be the only legitimate representative of the Palestinian people.

Total withdrawal

Egyptian Foreign Minister Ismail Fahmy said on his arrival here that he would "strive with determination to bring about the total withdrawal of Israel from occupied Arab territories, and to restore their national rights to the Palestinians." What these national rights are, was spelled once more on Tuesday by the P.L.O. Geneva representative, Daoud Barakatt: the disappearance of Israel as a political entity and the creation of an Arab-Jewish democratic republic in what was once British Mandatory Palestine.

But one was able to find some solace in the fairly moderate statement made on arrival by Soviet Foreign Minister Andrey Gromyko, who, although consistently refraining from calling the conference a peace conference, said that the Soviet Union would show "goodwill and realism to arrive at a good decision," and would "do its best to guarantee the success of the conference."

Perhaps the Soviet Union has come round after the October War to accepting the American principle as summed up once by Joseph Sisco — "Keep talking and stop shooting." Be that as it may, one thing seems certain — Russia will not let the U.S. arrange a "Pax Americana" in the Middle East.

Whatever is decided will have to be done with the full consent of the Soviet Union.

Knesset

By DAVID LANDAU and ASHER WALLFISH
Jerusalem Post Reporters

The Knesset exploded into angry uproar twice during the political debate yesterday, with accusations of "blood libel" and "brazen impudence" flying between the Alignment and Likud benches.

The Alignment's Haim Zadok sowed havoc in the Likud ranks with a scathing display of the trial-lawyer's rhetoric. He challenged the opposition party to take a clear stand on the Geneva conference and on the territorial question — and exposed evident unclarity and dissent in the Likud camp on these vital issues.

Earlier, Likud leader Menahem Begin had triggered a flurry of heckling and counter-heckling when he accused the Alignment of "blood libel.' He said the Alignment sought to drive a wedge through the heart of the nation, dividing it into those who seek peace — and support the Alignment — and those who want war — and vote for Likud. This was a blood libel reminiscent of the worst manifestations of historical antisemitism, the opposition leader said. There was not a Jew in Israel who did not pray and yearn for peace.

The loudest heckler was Health Minister Victor Shemtov (Alignment-Mapam). "You bring us to war!.... You are interested in war!" he shouted at Begin and at the Likud benches.

ACCUSED OF DEMAGOGUERY

Yisrael Kargman (Alignment-Labour) called Mr. Begin's accusation "drivelling demagoguery," and Yitzhak Ben-Aharon (Alignment-Labour) demanded that he withdraw the phrase "blood libel." The Speaker Yisrael Yeshayahu, who soon lost control of the proceedings and pounded ineffectually with his gavel, also called on Mr. Begin to retract that phrase — but the opposition leader refused.

Haim Landau of Likud shouted that in 25 years of Labour's ostensible quest for peace the country had suffered five wars. Mr. Begin himself recalled that Mapam leader Meir Ya'ari had stated publicly that the "Allon Plan" would not bring peace. What then would it bring? he asked rhetorically. "War and war and war."

Mr. Begin said that whereas the Prime Minister had spoken in her address first of the Geneva conference and only then of the Geneva Convention, he would invert the order — and he called on the Government to do likewise. Israel's delegate at Geneva should demand, when the conference opened, that the very first item on the agenda must be the fate of Israel's prisoners in Syria.

The Government should urge the International Red Cross to convene a special meeting of its membership on this issue — or at least to send an emergency letter to all its membership alerting them to Syria's refusal to obey the Geneva Convention.

Mr. Begin attacked the Government for not having linked the fate of the PoWs in Syria to that of those in Egypt — especially when Egypt's Third Army was at Israel's mercy, needing food and water.

He criticized the Government for agreeing to participate at the peace conference on the Sabbath. It was not merely a matter of religion but of national pride. There were at least 50 members of the Knesset who, were they given a free vote on the subject, would support his position on this. It was still not too late to instruct the delegation at Geneva not to take part in the conference until the Sabbath ended.

BEGIN SCORES GOV'T

As to the conditions under which Israel was going to Geneva, Mr. Begin charged that the Government had yielded on all its declared demands. It had yielded on the question of auspices, having at first demanded that the UN role be kept to a minimum and now agreeing to UN auspices and Dr. Waldheim's chairmanship of the opening session.

(On this point, Mr. Zadok and other Alignment speakers reiterated the Government's position — which had been stated by the Premier — that it would not negotiate with the Palestinian terror organizations at any stage of the conference.)

On the substantive issues, Mr. Begin stressed his view that it would be suicidal to "re-divide western Eretz Israel," putting every town and village in Israel within range of hostile Arab artillery and rockets.

Uproar over Geneva

YESHAYAHU UNNERVED

Mr. Begin sought to end with a quotation from the Book of Maccabees, but was interrupted by Speaker Yeshayahu who urged him to finish. This unprecedented behaviour by the Speaker to the leader of the Opposition caused renewed uproar on the Likud benches — and raised eyebrows on the Alignment side too. Mr. Begin said he would ignore the Speaker's interruption and read the three-verse quotation as he had planned.

Mr. Zadok, who is chairman of the Foreign Affairs and Defence Committee, said Israel was going to Geneva without illusions, but in the hope that the conference might mark an historic turning point. There was no need to fear UN auspices. The talks at Kilometre 101 had been under formal UN auspices — but this had not disturbed their progress.

Having made these remarks, Mr. Zadok weighed into the Likud. Mr. Begin, he said, took the easy way out. He pointed up the dangers and problems of the Geneva conference — without answering the key question: was he, in the circumstances that existed today, in favour of going to Geneva?

Yigal Horowitz of the State List shouted that Likud was in favour. Mr. Zadok replied that he had yet to hear that from Mr. Begin himself.

Was Likud's policy "not to yield an inch" as regards the West Bank? Mr. Zadok now asked. This brought an assortment of shouted responses, not all of them consistent and some of them irrelevant. Haim Landau exclaimed that the Alignment policy was to cede Jerusalem to the rule of El Fatah. This, he said, was what the Alignment meant by its quest for peace — and that was "brazen impudence."

ZADOK THRUSTS

Speaker Yeshayahu called for a retraction of that phrase, but Mr. Landau refused to retract, pointing out that it was Biblical.

Premier Meir and her Deputy Yigal Allon were in their seats enjoying the opposition's obvious discomfiture.

Mr. Zadok launched in again. There were three basic questions: Was Likud ready for territorial compromise with Jordan?; Did Likud accept Security Council Resolution 338 as Israel interpreted it?; Did Likud accept Security Council Resolution 242 as Israel interpreted it?

The shouted answers on this too were varied and various.

Mr. Zadok urged that all Likud members who could answer "Yes" to the three questions could "repent and join the peace party." This brought renewed shouting about war parties and peace parties.

If, however, Likud's answer was "No" — then for Likud to claim that it was in favour of going to Geneva was just a bluff, to earn electoral popularity.

"Our way," Mr. Zadok concluded, "there is no certainty of peace. Your way, there is certainty of no peace."

Mr. Begin himself was out of the Chamber throughout this speech. He was putting the finishing touches to the Likud's election platform, to be published today.

Yitzhak Raphael (National Religious Party) said that for Israel to go to Geneva, without knowing just how much U.S. support it could count on, could lead to difficulties later on. The echoes of Dr. Kissinger's latest visit had aroused fears that he and Israel were not on the same wavelength.

RAPHAEL WARNS

Dr. Raphael said his party regarded Resolution 242 as referring to an agreement with Egypt; but it had no relevance, as regards territorial compromise, to Judea and Samaria. Hebron, Jericho and Bethel were sacred sites, he said, not only Jerusalem. And the Jordan River must be made into the permanent border between Israel and Jordan for security reasons. On the other hand, Israel would have a great deal to offer to Jordan, as long as this offer did not include parts of Eretz Yisrael.

Yaacov Hazan (Alignment-Mapam) said he was not very happy about the Soviet Union being one of the sponsors at Geneva. But Geneva might open up possibilities of re-establishing diplomatic relations with the Soviet Union. This was because the Soviets would be at a disadvantage at Geneva vis-a-vis the United States, which could talk to the Arabs and Israel alike. Moscow's pragmatic policy might dictate a resumption of ties to gain greater influence on the course of the conference.

Other speakers made the following points, among others:

★ Shmuel Tamir (Likud-Free Centre): Israel has been willing to be dictated to, in connection with the timing, the procedures and the agenda of the Geneva talks, in a way which ill befits a sovereign state, and which should give grounds for much apprehension about this country's future.

★ Shmuel Mikunis (Moked-Communists): It is not too late for us to create some democratic framework for the Arabs of the occupied territories, so that they can elect governing bodies in time for the Geneva talks — to attend and to negotiate with us.

★ Gideon Hausner (Independent Liberals): If the Geneva talks continue, all the Ministers in the post-election Cabinet must adhere to the principle that possession of territories is not enough to prevent war, and must follow a common peace programme.

PORUSH ON SABBATH

★ Menahem Porush (Agudat Israel): We would win greater respect in the eyes of the Jewish people and of the Gentiles, if we did not attend the Geneva conference on the Sabbath.

If the Arab demands at Geneva endanger our existence, we are all united in rejecting them.

★ Kalman Cahana (Poale Aguda): I fear that some of the Israeli personalities sent to Geneva as advisers and information experts are very far from insisting on our unshakeable rights in the Land of the Patriarchs. There are too many Israelis in Geneva who are ready to make concessions over Judea and Samaria.

"Israel wants to live" is the headline on this Dutch poster designed by Otto Treumann. The bottom line reads "United Jewish Appeal, Postal Account 23434." This poster was distributed throughout The Netherlands to collect money for Israel. The artist, the papermaker, and the printer each contributed his services without remuneration. The artist and his wife sent a copy to their friends in Israel, and wrote "We send it to you as a token of Holland's support in Israel's struggle to prove to you that you are not alone."

OTTO TREUMANN, a graphic artist of great imagination and technical skill, earned an international reputation in 1970, when he received the David Roell award of the Prince Bernhard Fund in recognition of his achievements in the art of poster design. Together with George Him, Treumann designed the beautiful and well-known symbol on the El Al planes. *(See page 387.)*

He has been a consultant to the Bezalel Academy of Art and Design. Last spring, for the second time, Treumann served as a member of the jury which selected the prize-winning books in the Israel Museum International Art Book Contest.

DUTCH CHURCHES SUPPORT ISRAEL

To the Editor of The Jerusalem Post

Sir, — The letter written by Annette van der Schaaf and ten others (December 2) creates a false impression of the stand taken by the Dutch churches with regard to the Yom Kippur War. To the best of my knowledge there has not been any "official announcement of the Dutch churches saying they do not want to support Israel." Since this letter was written (on October 21) some significant declarations have been made by Dutch churches. One of these was issued by the oldest and biggest Protestant church in the Netherlands, the Netherlands Reformed Church.

In the statement (in the form of a letter to a number of Dutch rabbis) the Netherlands Reformed Church clearly states that it feels itself essentially connected with the Jewish People not only because they are historically interwoven, but because this connection is anchored in the Church's confession. It is further stated that this connection has political consequences and implies the full recognition of the right of existence of the State of Israel, as the Jewish People cannot be thought of separately from the State of Israel. It is also stated that peace and justice in the Middle East can only be achieved when Israel can live within secure, internationally recognized and protected borders. If mention is made of the Palestinian refugees, this cannot in any way be interpreted as lack of support for Israel.

REV. COOS SCHONEVELD

Theological Adviser in Jerusalem of the Netherlands Reformed Church

Ein Kerem, December 4.

Peace — it's official

GENEVA (AP) — The name "Peace Conference on the Middle East" for the first time appeared on an official document of the United Nations yesterday.

It was on a document giving the provisional participants at the parley.

There were no "peace" prefixes in officially designating previous conferences aimed at negotiated settlements of conflicts in Indochina, on Korea and on Laos. None of the previous conferences brought real peace.

U.N. sources said they assumed the designation had been mutually agreed upon by the parties to the conference. U.N. Secretary-General Kurt Waldheim said earlier the name was being used in "working language" but that there was "no official baptism."

Moshe Dayan in his Tel Aviv office.

While most of the governments of the world fall over each other in their haste to toe the oil line, thousands of people have written to Israel's Premier, Golda Meir, to assure her that they support Israel in her struggle for survival and are deeply ashamed of their own politicians. PHILIP GILLON makes a selection from letters that she has received in recent weeks from all parts of the world.

ISRAELIS TEND to think of themselves as b e i n g without friends in the world, with the possible exception of the United States and the certain exception of World Jewry. But, if the letters received by Mrs. Meir are any indication, the "little man" and "little woman" are thinking along the right lines.

The British seem to feel particularly bad about the policies of Prime Minister Ted Heath and his Foreign Secretary, judging from the number of letters they have written to Mrs. Meir (with copies, I hope, sent to their members of Parliament).

Thus, Mrs. Joyce Beckley, of Middlesborough, writes:

"What a price has been paid for Egyptian oil! The cost of this cannot be measured against the anguish and understandable anger of your people.

"I want you and your people to know how I and my friends feel about the attitude of the British Government and its heartless decisions. The heart of Britain, that is, the little people, are not in this thing against Israel. We know to our shame that our Government has betrayed the Israelis. There is no getting away from this fact, which stares us accusingly in the face.

"England — the land of the free standing against all the oppressors of the little countries and their people. This *was* once what my community stood for in

the eyes of the world, ridiculed maybe, but betrayed never! I am very sad to say, this is no more: all has been lost to us by a handful of creepers who have the gall, even now, to call themselves Christians...

"Maybe my country would benefit if it were governed by women. You as lady Prime Minister of Israel set us an example...

"What h a s happened to England and its people I do not know. All I do know is that at this moment I feel no pride in being English.

"The world is sick indeed."

Mrs. Marjorie Hillhouse, of Wallasey, Cheshire, comments:

"We in Britain have been following the progress of your wonderful soldiers and t h e people of Israel with great admiration. My family and I and everyone I talk to in my town are with you in everything you do, in your fight for your land, peace and freedom... Be brave at all times. Whatever decisions our leaders may make, we in England are your staunch supporters. Please tell your soldiers that they are wonderful, and you yourself a brave and wonderful woman."

Mrs. A. Kempson writes to say that she and her husband, of Chessington Zoo, Surrey, have agreed that Mrs. Meir is "a second Winston Churchill. I want you to know we and all the people we know feel this way."

From a man serving with the

Meir

BERLYNE

Royal Air Force in Cyprus, came this protest:

"I write on behalf of my working colleagues and myself, members of the British Royal Air Force, to express our deep disgust at the manner in which our government has treated your nation... I feel sure that we express what the *majority* of British people the world over feel. Unlike Sir Alec Douglas-Home, we feel that Arab oil (or lack of it!!) is no excuse for stabbing a friend and ally in the back, and feel deeply ashamed that we are prevented by military discipline and a hypocritical attitude on the part of our political leaders from rendering you the assistance that we feel is your right.

"A mere ten years ago, I personally could hold my head high (with certain reservations) and proclaim myself *proud* to be British. Our word was our bond, to use an old cliche; now it would seem that our word and our contracts are worth nothing, thanks to continuing governments that ignore the will of the people whom they govern.

"I beg your forgiveness and crave your indulgence on o n e point; that you will, in some way, understand and make it clear to us, the British people in the street and the British military personnel, that our moral backing of your country is understood and appreciated by y o u r people, even though we are pre-

vented by our weak political leadership from rendering you *material* help in your struggle against the Arab nations.

"In conclusion, we pray for your continuing survival as a nation, and offer our sympathy and condolences to the families of all those brave Israelis who have fallen in battle to preserve the freedom of the J e w i s h nation..."

The strangest letter of all those Mrs. Meir received was written by Mrs. Olga Wood, of Coventry, and despatched on October 2, four days *before* the outbreak of the Yom Kippur War. Mrs. Wood describes a vision she had of two Arabs stealing into a cave below a hill and blowing it up with an atomic bomb: the hill, she writes was the "Heights of Golan," and she urges Mrs. Meir to take exceptional precautions to protect the Golan accordingly. Alas! The letter only reached Israel after the war had broken out — even assuming that Mrs. Meir might have acted on the warning.

THE FRENCH also feel that their government's attitude is deplorable. Nobody could be franker than Romain Gaubert, Honorary Magistrate, of Paris, who writes:

"I am an anti-Semite, not in my blood, but, as Maurras would say, on principle, being deeply re-

ligious and on the extreme right wing. Nevertheless, I must express to you my deep admiration for Israel, because of the pride, energy and courage it has displayed in the midst of universal cowardice. I am also an anti-feminist, because I think woman's essential function is guarding the home and consoling the afflicted, but I salute you, the foremost 'man of our time.' I am ashamed of France and the West, who have let themselves be dominated by the Arabs. We should not allow pirates and robbers to ration us and hold us to ransom. We discovered the oil and developed it. Economically they are n o t independent; we should cut their links. Let us be united in solidarity and we will be able to defeat even the Soviets."

Verne Oulens, also of Paris, a writer of both prose and poetry, recipient of numerous diplomas and awards, urges Mrs. Meir to be firm:

"Since you gained the military victory, the Russians have been pressing you to accept the cease-fire. Had the Arabs encircled your army, they would never have agreed to supply it, but would have insisted that you surrender. The Russians would have awaited your total destruction before asking for an end to the hostilities. So, if the war should start again, go on to the end. The Russians will threaten you, but will not dare to intervene

because of the Americans.

"Do not let Dr. Kissinger lull you, hold fast, it is you that have the knife by the handle. Give up as little as possible, because your enemies will never keep their promises. You have bargaining powers and defensible borders — hold fast, hold fast, hold fast!"

Mrs. Grete Engkilde, who describes herself as "a common Danish mother," writes that she is thinking of and praying for Mrs. Meir and her people day and night.

"It looks as if God has forgotten you, but I am quite sure He has not, and never will. Don't think Israel is alone in the world, you have lots and lots of friends who are thinking as I am and praying for you."

Mrs. Engkilde sent 1,000 kroner to the fund for Israel.

Dr. Jan Eric Sundblad, a dentist of Tibro, Sweden, explains:

"I am an ordinary Swede and not of Jewish ancestry. My English is lousy and hopefully understandable. What I want to express is the support of myself and many of my friends in your struggle. The blackmail in oil-business executed by the Arab nations is of the lowest order, and you have more support around the world than is made public. The cold and harsh winter ahead of us here in the north is a small price to pay for the support of your brave people."

Dr. Sundblad adds in a postscript that he would like to participate in Israel's fight for freedom and peace more actively. "If you ever need the services of a dentist, I am both eager and willing to help."

From Brussels, Madame Aline Norteso Molitor writes:

"I am only a housewife, mother and grandmother. I know nothing about the intricate ways of politics, but I have to tell you how I feel, and how millions of other simple people of Europe must feel today after the resolution taken by the nine ministers of our countries in Brussels. When I heard the news on the radio, I felt physically ill."

A similar reaction was described by Miss Hoony Krygsman, of The Hague.

"Allow me to offer you my apologies for the characterlessness of my government. I am ashamed and indignant. I do hope that you will accept it when I tell you that in my surroundings a lot of people agree with me, and that we are loyal to Israel, the state, the country, the people, *their* rights. We also feel very sorry that we cannot help you, dear Mrs. Meir, to get relief from the heavy burden of the responsibility that you have to bear. How very tired must you be since the 6th of October!"

A GREEK, Angelo Athanassekos, running a restaurant, "The Three Hours," in New York, compares the present time to that period in history when the Turks and the Egyptians "sent forces to burn the Peloponnese." He goes on:

"I am 42 years of age and I know that you cannot use me in your fighting lines. However, if I can be of service in any other capacity you need only to call upon me. One way I believe I can help is to pledge the profits on one night's sales per week from my small restaurant in New York. I have contacted the United Jewish Appeal to arrange that this money be sent to you (little as it may be). I pray that this small gesture will help in some way to keep the people of Israel free to continue their fantastic job of building a nation."

A young but firm supporter is John Pirnot, of Omaha, Nebraska, who explains that he is 13 years old, and sends a picture of himself. John writes:

"It is difficult for someone as young as myself to understand why one nation of people should have to struggle against all odds to maintain the right to live freely in their own country, but I know, Madame Premier, that it has been that way for hundreds of years now. There is no other people in history to be tried as the people of Israel have been tried.

"I don't know how you people keep maintaining your courage and your pride, but it is a marvellous thing for the young people of the world to see. I am Christian by faith, but that has nothing to do with whether I side or do not side with the people of Israel.

"I don't know enough about the politics of war yet to know what is really just or who is really at fault, but I do know enough to say that the people of Israel have suffered enough and fought enough and have risen up enough to be declared a nation of people that deserve to live in their own land with the dignity that they have earned."

Mrs. Golda Meir, Premier of Israel.

ON THE OPPOSITE PAGE there is a letter from a boy of thirteen who lives in Omaha, Nebraska. Because this letter is buried in a mass of other material, there is a strong possibility that the reader of a book of this kind, where there is so much to read, might overlook it.

But the letter really doesn't bear overlooking. In fact, it bears repetition.

John Pirnot writes to Golda Meir:

It is difficult for someone as young as myself to understand why one nation of people should have to struggle against all odds to maintain the right to live freely in their own country, but I know, Madame Premier, that it has been that way for hundreds of years now. There is no other people in history to be tried as the people of Israel have been tried.

I don't know how you people keep maintaining your courage and your pride, but it is a marvellous thing for the young people of the world to see. I am Christian by faith, but that has nothing to do with whether I side or do not side with the people of Israel.

I don't know enough about the politics of war yet to know what is really just or who is really at fault, but I do know enough to say that the people of Israel have suffered enough and fought enough and have risen up enough to be declared a nation of people that deserve to live in their own land with the dignity that they have earned.

321

RETURN TO RAMAT MAGSHIMIM

LIKE A MAN returning to the scene of a crime he has witnessed, I was back roaming the Golan Heights the other week, visiting a settlement that had been hit by the Syrians during the recent war, and meeting friends who were still stationed at army camps and guard posts along the cease-fire line with Syria. Something went wrong with my car on the way — a red light signalled a timely warning — and I was advised to drive slowly and carefully to a nearby village for repairs.

"They've got a garage out there in Ramat Magshimim," said a young soldier who stopped his vehicle for a moment next to mine. "It's a garage for tractors, not cars, but I figure they'll be able to help you."

Engine trouble is usually treated in this land of ours as a major tragedy, which should leave the car owner disconsolate and heartbroken But my response at that moment was one of elation. The notion that I could enter Ramat Magshimim without hindrance, just like that, merely to avail myself of its garage, struck me as bold, even extravagant. Could it really be, I asked myself, that this p l a c e, Ramat Magshimim, was a regular settlement, whose members w e r e going out to work the fields and water, whose children were hurrying off to kindergarten and school in the morning, whose families were gathering for dinner in the evening — and in whose garage one could fix up a tractor (and maybe even a private car) ? This simple vision of normal daily life was wonderfully out of keeping with my earlier impression of Ramat Magshimim; and it seemed worthy of celebration.

It did not take me long to realize that I was not alone in sensing a kind of atmosphere of celebration about my arrival at the settlement. Menahem, who is in charge of crop cultivation, climbed down from his tractor to greet me at the door of the garage. He shook my hand warmly, and asked, laughingly, "So you've come *back* to spend the night with us, eh?"

It was Monday, October 8, the third day of the Yom Kippur War. All that day I had visited Jordan Valley strongholds talking to soldiers whose only task it was to be ready for any eventuality — and to wait, wait and wait, hoping that nothing would happen in their sector of t h e border. Towards evening I decided to go north, in order to join one of our fighting units which were then engaged in beating back the attack of the invading Syrian armour.

I reached the Ein Gev road after dark, and from there I turned east to climb the steep hill which leads to the Golan Heights. My first encounter with the Golan was the smell of scorched fields. The roar of heavy guns echoed in the distance, and their red glow streaked across the sky to disappear behind the northern horizon.

I drove up slowly, without car lights, groping my way through the enveloping darkness, with the bright moon, scarred though it was by exploding shells, as my guide. Suddenly, by the roadside, I spotted a deserted Syrian tank. I flashed my torch: it had been a direct hit, the turret blown right off, the body a blistered hulk.

FROM THEN on this was the scenery: on both sides of the road, tanks, armoured cars, jeeps, reconnaissance vehicles in serried ranks, some torn up and burnt out, some abandoned in evident haste by their fleeing crews. There was even a motorcycle topped by a boat, turned upside down. At one point I came across a Syrian soldier in camouflage uniform spread-eagled by the roadside. Little fires kept crackling in the thorny fields, bursting now and then into huge flames, and the heavy air of raging battle was still around.

Some distance from the moonlit road to the left, a row of small houses was silhouetted against the dark. A little light seemed to be shining from a window. It turned out to be only the reflection of the flashes of furious guns out in the battlefield.

This was Ramat Magshimim, one of several Golan Heights settlements evacuated, as I already knew, at the very start of the war.

I left my car near one of the houses, determined to find shelter for the night inside.

That, however, was easier said than done. The place, now a virtual ghost town, gave me an eerie, scary feeling. By the front door of the house, an enemy shell had burrowed a deep hole in the ground. Shrapnel had nibbled at the walls, and broken glass was strewn all around, outside as well as inside.

As I stepped carefully inside, making my way through the debris of window glass, blocks of cement and fallen blinds, I realized that I had walked into a kindergarten. The walls were hung with children's colourful pictures and decorations, — lots of flowers, and lots of tractors — and the furniture was all of lilliputian dimensions. In the dead of night, it suddenly seemed that I was actually hearing the voices of children: were they coming from the next room, or from the

depth of a shelter downstairs? I shivered.

The house nearby had not been damaged. The door was open, the blinds still up. For a moment it seemed that someone would just have to answer if I rang the bell; but the bell would not ring. There was no electricity, and no water — and no people. The television set, turned off, was standing, shamefaced, in the corner, and on the table was a half-empty glass of tea. The sink was overflowing with unwashed dishes.

And on one of the children's beds, a book still open where children had stopped their reading — with a poem about Nina Ktina, the little hare. "So back they settle in the chariot/And home they drive in silence./Nina is a bit tired... Then, suddenly —/Her eyes close... and she falls asleep..."

Along with Nina, I let myself fall asleep for a couple of hours, unmindful of the muffled pounding of the guns farther away, and the fearful wailing of a lonely cat under my window.

AT CRACK OF dawn I leaped from my unknown host's bed, carefully folded the blankets, helped myself impertinently to some of their left-over cheese and tomatoes, and sallied forth to the front. Soon I linked up with a convoy of ammunition-laden trucks, then overtook them to join up with one of our fighting units which was engaged in fierce battle with the Syrians. Oddly enough, the closer I got to the line of fire, the safer I felt: it was already daylight, and I was among friends. I was no longer alone. We were all in it together, and whatever happened, we would help each other, even under fire.

News of war travels fast, but it was only after the war that I learned, to my consternation, I had not been the only visitor to Ramat Magshimim after its evacuation. In between, and until not long before my arrival, a crack Syrian unit, probably commandos, had been there. Thus, Ramat Magshimim can claim the dubious honour of being the only Golan settlement to have been occupied by the Syrians during the fighting. I can't really say I missed them — a meeting between us could have been, not to put too fine a point on it, somewhat unpleasant.

As I was told when I visited the settlement soon after the cease-fire, Syrian troops entered Ramat Magshimim on Sunday afternoon, and stayed there about 30 hours. When they left, on Monday night — just a few hours ahead of me — they took some suitable "souvenirs" from the synagogue of this religious mo-

shav: the silk curtain of the ark, and a few Tora scrolls. The following day, they divested themselves of the loot to ease their retreat before our army; the curtain and the scrolls were recovered, and restored to Ramat Magshimim.

The community received their evacuation orders while they were nearly all in the synagogue, fasting and praying, at noon on Yom Kippur.

The orders had to be obeyed — this much was obvious to all — despite the fact that that meant cutting prayers short and travelling in the middle of the holiest day of the year. It was a matter of *pikuah nefesh* — saving life; but one halachic question remained: how much were they allowed to take with them on the bus, without violating the sanctity of Yom Kippur?

This was a question for the rabbi, and he gave his answer immediately and forthrightly: food and clothing for the little ones, and anything that actually pertained to *pikuah nefesh* could be taken, but nothing more. So it was decreed, then, and so they did.

They boarded the bus — and at that very moment Syrian artillery began shelling the settlement. Men, women and children dashed off to the underground shelters. There they stayed for several hours, while shells rained on their houses above.

Only after dark was there any let-up in the shelling, and this was exploited to get the women and the children back into the bus — which had been hit by shrapnel and its windows smashed to smithereens — and away from the Golan.

The men were evacuated late at night, during another lull between bouts of Syrian shelling. They left behind empty and mostly shattered dwellings, miles of badly damaged water pipes, thousands of dead turkeys and dozens of slaughtered cows.

This is what they came back to, a few days later, even while the war was still raging beyond the old cease-fire lines. Immediately, they set about putting the settlement to rights. Not long after they were joined by the women and the children. Already they have rebuilt their houses, and repaired the water pipes, and are on the way towards replacing their livestock. Already, they are almost back to normal.

Pretty soon, they will even have learned how to fix up a private car that broke down on the way to the settlement.

Kissinger:

Historic chance for peace

GENEVA (AP). — *Following are excerpts from the speech by U.S. Secretary of State Henry Kissinger.*

"We are convened here at a moment of historic opportunity for the cause of peace in the Middle East, and for the cause of peace in the world. For the first time in a generation the peoples of the Middle East are sitting together to turn their talents to the challenge of peace.

"All of us must have the wisdom to grasp this moment — to break the shackles of the past, and to create at last a new hope for the future.

"Two months ago what we now refer to as the fourth Arab-Israeli war was coming to an end. Today, there is the respite of an imperfect cease-fire, but the shadow of war still hangs over the Middle East. Either we begin today a process of correcting the conditions which produced that conflict, or we doom untold tens of thousands to travail, sorrow and further inconclusive bloodshed...

"From two recent trips through the Middle East I have the impression that people on both sides have had enough of bloodshed. No further proof of heroism is necessary, no military point remains to be made...

"What does each side seek? Both answer with a single word: peace. But peace has of course a concrete meaning for each. One side seeks the recovery of sovereignty and the redress of grievances suffered by a displaced people. The other seeks security and recognition of its legitimacy as a nation. The common goal of peace must surely be broad enough to embrace all these aspirations.

"The question is not whether there must be peace. The question is how do we achieve it. What can we do here to launch new beginnings?

"First, this conference must speak with a clear and unequivocal voice: the cease-fire called for by the Security Council must be scrupulously adhered to.

"Prior to last October the U.S. did all it could to prevent a new outbreak of fighting. But we failed because frustration could no longer be contained.

"...We recognize that the cease-fire remains fragile and tentative. The U.S. is concerned over the evidence of increased military preparedness in recent days. A renewal of hostilities would be both foolhardy and dangerous. We urge all concerned to refrain from the use of force, and to give our efforts here the chance they deserve.

"Second, we must understand what can realistically be accomplished at any given moment...

"Based on intensive consultations with the leaders of the Middle East, including many in this room today, I believe that the first work of this conference should be to achieve early agrement on the separation of military forces, and that such an agreement is possible...

"Third, the disengagement of forces is an essential first step — a consolidation of the cease-fire and a bridge to the 'peaceful and accepted settlement'...

"Peace must bring a new relationship among the nations of the Middle East — a relationship that will not only put an end to the state of war which has persisted for the last quarter of a century, but will also permit the peoples of the Middle East to live together in harmony and safety...

"A peace agreement must include these elements, among others: withdrawals, recognized frontiers, security arrangements, guarantees, a settlement of the legitimate interests of the Palestinians and a recognition that Jerusalem contains places considered holy by three great religions.

"Peace will require that we relate the imperative of withdrawals to the necessities of security, the requirement of guarantees to the sovereignty of the parties, the hopes of the displaced to the realities now existing.

"The conference's final objective must be the implementation in all its parts of Security Council Resolution 242 passed in November 1967," Dr. Kissinger said.

"We believe that there must be realistic negotiations between the parties. While peace in the Middle East was in the interests of all, it was the people of the area who must live with the results.

"It must in the final analysis be acceptable to them. Peace cannot last unless it rests on the consent of the parties concerned."

"Our backdrop is a war that has brought anguish and pain, death and destruction, a war that has been costly to both sides, that has brought neither victory nor defeat, that reflected the failure of all our past efforts at peaceful solutions.

"We do not embark on this task with false expectations. We do not pretend that there are easy answers. A problem that has defied solution for a generation does not yield to simple remedies...

"In the months ahead we will examine many problems. We will discuss many expedients. We will know success — and I dare say we shall experience deadlock and despair.

"The American attitude is clear. We know we are starting on a journey whose outcome is uncertain and whose progress will be painful. We are conscious that we need wisdom and patience and good will. But we know, too, that the agony of three decades must be overcome and that somehow we have to muster the insight and courage to put an end to the conflict between peoples who have so often ennobled mankind..."

Gromyko:
Fate of world at stake

GENEVA (Reuter). — Soviet Foreign Minister Andrei Gromyko warned that if peace did not come to the Middle East the fate of the whole world could be at stake.

In his statement at the opening of the Middle East Peace Conference Friday, he said that any document drawn up by the meeting must contain clear-cut commitments by Israel to withdraw from territories occupied in 1967.

It was essential to ensure for all the peoples of the Middle East the right to live in peace and security, Mr. Gromyko said. This also referred to Israel, and it also assumed that justice would be assured for the Arab peoples of Palestine.

He said documents drawn up at the conference must be given the force of international law. If necessary the Soviet Union was ready with other states to take on itself important responsibilities.

Mr. Gromyko spoke of the possibility of demilitarised zones and the use of international personnel in the area, but emphasized that this should be decided on conditions that were mutually acceptable to the parties.

Mr. Gromyko warned that the fire of war in the Middle East might flare up at any moment. "Even as I speak the smell of gunpowder and burning still hang over Sinai and the Golan Heights," he said.

He pledged the Soviet Union's determination to do everything in its power to see that the conference proceeded in a business-like and constructive fashion.

"The intolerable situation in the Middle East created by the policy of Israel cannot go on any longer," Mr. Gromyko said.

"From time to time, tension in this region has spilled over into open military conflict, and each time the fate of the entire world has been at stake... There is hardly any doubt that new military and bloody conflicts in the Middle East will take place in the future as well unless the root causes of the tension that reigns here are eliminated."

Mr. Gromyko warned Israel that any hopes of retaining occupied territories by relying on force had no future.

A reliable settlement in the Middle East was being helped by the positive steps towards relaxation in the world as a whole, including the end of the war in Vietnam, the settlement of postwar problems in Europe and normalisation of relations between states with different social systems on the basis of peaceful coexistence.

"In the light of all this the continuing Middle East conflict, even though military actions have halted, appears as an inadmissible anomaly," he said.

Mr. Gromyko said commitments assumed by the parties in the Middle East within an international framework would be the best guarantee of their mutual security which could only be founded on trust and cooperation under treaties.

"If the need arose to give additional weight to the agreements, the Soviet Union, taking account of the desires of the interested parties, is ready together with the appropriate other powers, to assume suitable commitments for itself.

"Here the Security Council can say its prestigious word. The main thing is that the political settlement in the Middle East should be truly durable."

"Certain other measures in this direction are also conceivable, especially the question of establishing on a basis of reciprocity demilitarised zones in several sectors, and the temporary development of international personnel in individual regions."

"It is essential that this should be decided on conditions mutually acceptable."

"Given agreement on the chief problem, such questions in our opinion would not be an obstacle to a general settlement," Mr. Gromyko said.

"For all its difficulties the Middle East problem is solvable," he said, warning of the dangers of delay.

Fahmy:
'Other means' if talks fail

GENEVA (Reuter). — Egyptian Foreign Minister Ismail Fahmy told the Middle East peace conference on Friday his country had come to Geneva to restore a just and durable peace to "our ravaged and embattled region."

If Israel did not comprehend the deep significance of this gathering, the Arab countries would have to resort to "other means" to liberate their lands and restore the legitimate rights of the Palestinians, he said.

Fahmy said there were five basic essentials for peace in the Middle East:

● Total withdrawal of Israeli forces from Arab territories occupied since June 1967.

● Liberation of the Arab city of Jerusalem and non-acceptance of any situation which may be injurious to complete Arab sovereignty over the holy city.

● The exercise by the Palestinians of the right to self-determination and to live in peace and dignity.

● The right of every state in the region to enjoy territorial inviolability and political independence.

● That there be international guarantees of the major powers or the United Nations or both as an added safeguard to international peace and security in the area.

"These essentials for peace are in conformity with and fully reflect the decisions taken at the Arab summit last month in Algiers," he said.

Fahmy said there can be no Middle East peace until Israel ceases "trying to convince the world that peace can be based on conquests and military domination."

He said there also can be no just and durable peace unless Israel adheres to what he described as "certain norms" — no expansion by force, no acquisition of foreign territories by force, no threats against recognized international boundaries, no infringement of sovereignty and no denial of the inalienable rights of the Palestinians.

"Egypt's determination to work for peace equals its determination to see that all its land, that all Arab land is liberated and that the Palestinians enjoy the right to their territory and to live at peace."

At the afternoon session of Friday's talks, Fahmy delivered a scathing attack on Israel, accusing Abba Eban of using the event for propaganda purposes.

In an unscheduled speech, he said Eban was "playing to the gallery" and "catering for home consumption" because of the Israeli general elections.

Fahmy said that during his own address to the conference he had "used the facts and nothing but the facts."

"It was not in need of the procedures which the Foreign Minister of Israel chose because I do not need to speak here for home consumption and because I do not have any election campaign that is going to take place in a few days in my country."

The Egyptian Foreign Minister said that Israel now found itself completely isolated because of its "behaviour against the Arab community, the Arab countries and against the Palestinians."

Fahmy said that Eban had "tried to belittle the intelligence of the conference by distorting facts."

He then detailed a list of Israeli attacks which he said had been carried out on the Arab people. These had culminated with raids on Syria and Lebanon and the "mass murders" of some Palestinian commandos, he said.

He also said that the atrocities carried out by Palestinian terrorists were the acts of "desperate men which Israel subjugated by force in 1947" and that they were "entitled" to act in this way.

Eban:
No return to 1967 lines

GENEVA (AP). — Following are excerpts from Friday's speech by Foreign Minister Abba Eban at the Mideast peace conference:

"...Today at last, a new opportunity is born. No wonder that this conference opens under the burden of an immense expectation...

"To achieve its aims, therefore, this conference must reverse the whole tide of recent history...

"Israel comes to Geneva in the conviction that there is room for innovation, initiative, choice...

"The crisis of the Middle East has many consequences — but only one cause. Israel's right to peace, security, sovereignty, commerce, international friendships, economic development, maritime freedom — indeed its very right to live has for 25 years been forcibly denied and aggressively attacked.

"And the emotional assault on Israel goes far beyond the political context... It leads to a copious literature that gives lavish endorsement to the Nazi anti-Jewish myths. It nourishes a conspiratorial theory of Jewish history. It explodes into the mutilation of Israel soldiers in the field. It includes the murder and torture of Israeli prisoners. It has culminated most recently in Syria's sadistic refusal to carry out the Geneva Convention on the treatment of prisoners of war...

"Beyond these transitional steps we should have a clear conception of our objective. Israel's aim at this conference is a peace treaty defining the terms of our co-existence in future years... Peace is not a mere cease-fire or armistice. Its meaning is not exhausted by the absence of war. It commits us also to positive obligations which neighbouring states owe to each other by virtue of their very proximity and of their common membership in the international community."

Mr. Eban proposed that Egypt and Israel pledge at the conference to observe the present Middle East cease-fire on the basis of reciprocity.

"I give that pledge on Israel's behalf. The maintenance of the cease-fire is an indispensable condition for any useful negotiation.

"Israel's aim at this conference is a peace treaty defining the terms of our co-existence in future years."

Mr. Eban said the treaty should contain an agreement on boundaries, adding:

"The decisive test for Israel will be the defensibility of its new boundaries against the contingency of attacks and blockades such as those threatened and carried out in 1967 and 1973.

"Permanent boundaries must be negotiated with the utmost precision and care... there cannot be a return to the former armistice lines of 1949-67.

"They proved to be inherently fragile. They served as a temptation to an aggressive design of encirclement and blockade from which Israel broke out in 1967 after weeks of solitude and peril."

Mr. Eban said security arrangements and demilitarized areas could supplement the negotiated boundary agreement, but not replace it. The problem of refugees could be resolved by cooperative regional action with international aid. At the appropriate time Israel would define its contribution to this effort.

"We shall propose compensation for abandoned lands in the context of a general discussion on property abandoned by those who have left countries in the Middle East to seek a new life."

He added: "Our negotiation with Jordan will define the agreed boundaries and other conditions of coexistence between two states occupying the original area of the Palestine Mandate — Israel and a neighbouring Arab state.

"We declare our opposition to the explosive fragmentation of the area between three states in the region between the desert and the sea where there are, after all, two nations, two languages, two cultures, not three."

Mr. Eban said Israel would support a proposal to discuss with Egypt an agreement on disengagement of troops of both countries along the Suez front as first priority when the conference resumed in the new year.

He described Jerusalem as "Israel's capital, now united forever," but said Israel did not wish to exercise exclusive jurisdiction or unilateral responsibility in the holy places there of Christendom or Islam. These should be under the administration of those who held them sacred. Israel would be willing to discuss this principle and agreements on free access and pilgrimage.

Mr. Eban accused both Syria and Egypt of killing Israeli war prisoners after capture. He said that Israel had told the International Red Cross Committee in Geneva of 42 cases of prisoners killed in Syrian hands and 28 while held by Egypt.

After describing Syria's absence from the conference opening session as "regrettable," Mr. Eban said: "Frankness and indignation compel me to state that Syria has not yet qualified for participation in this peace conference. It continues to inflict perverse injury on prisoners of war and their distraught families in contavention of the Geneva Convention. This barbarous violation of human decencies continues unchecked."

SYRIAN TORTURE

Mr. Eban said Syrian treatment of some Israeli prisoners was too harrowing to narrate. "But we know that helpless prisoners of war are shackled and then mudered in cold blood. They are tortured and maimed, beaten and dishonoured. By withholding lists and refusing Red Cross visits the Syrian Government creates wide circles of uncertainty and anguish amongst hundreds of families and thousands of citizens."

He called for an urgent reply by Egypt to Israeli requests for information on additional missing prisoners and repatriation of bodies of dead soldiers.

Mr. Eban challenged the right of the Palestine Liberation Organization to be represented at a later stage of the conference, and described it as "a driving force in the wave of permissive violence that has carried the effects of the Middle East conflict across the world."

Mr. Eban urged restraint by "governments outside the area who may be tempted to think that they know the exact point of balance at which the interests of the parties can be reconciled."

Obviously aiming at Moscow, Mr. Eban added, "we cannot ignore that one of them sparked the arms race, identifies itself exclusively with our adversaries and feels no balancing necessity to concern itself with Israel's welfare or destiny."

SABBATH—No Publication

Newsmen watch the continuing talks at K.M. 101
on the Egyptian side of the U.N. encampment.

NO TIME TO GAMBLE

THE preliminaries for the disengagement talks in Geneva seem to have gone well enough. On the face of it the talks can only favour Egypt at every step.

It is aimed at nothing more or less than the withdrawal of Israel forces from what the army has come to call 'Africa' and the creation of a buffer zone between the two Egyptian armies now positioned east of the Canal, on the edge of Sinai. These are the Second Army, still in fighting shape and able to receive supplies from Cairo, and the much-battered Third Army, that now receives limited supplies under Israel supervision.

Certainty that there will be no more shooting will come only with the disengagement. If this also includes some agreement on the types and sizes of Egyptian forces to be maintained east of the Canal, the lop-sided bargain may still be entirely acceptable to us. It was the search for security that originally took us to the Canal, and we shall not stay there if security can be achieved in some more permanent and promising form. The Canal itself is not worth one single life to us.

The position on the Jordan is different. There is no confrontation of forces there, no shooting or particular danger of shooting. The bridges have been open across the Jordan for almost six years and in recent years the traffic across them has been operated and supervised by tacit and sometimes explicit agreement.

All we ask for on the West Bank is that it shall not become a state hostile to Israel, infiltrated by terrorists warring amongst themselves and competing in attacks against us. The thin line of forces deployed along the Jordan for this purpose at present were able to preserve a tenuous peace despite the Yom Kippur War.

PEACE

By LEA BEN DOR

An Israeli soldier checks the contents of supplies going to the encircled 3rd Army.

A good deal of noise and vituperation has already come out of Geneva, spiced with malice, mistakes and plain lies.

What exactly does Jordan Foreign Minister Sami Rifai mean when he declares that in 1948 Israel attacked the Arab states? As the Mandate ended on May 15, 1948, and the last of the British forces withdrew, a wholesale attack was launched on the planned Jewish areas, and Jordanian guns shelled Jewish Jerusalem mercilessly for a month, while other Jordanian regular and irregular forces cut off its communications with the rest of the country. That is 25 years ago, and no doubt some newsmen in Geneva don't remember what happened.

The speech was venomous; it demanded withdrawal and disengagement and the right to Arab Jerusalem. The right to *Arab* Jerusalem? In some backhanded fashion is that not also implicit acceptance of Israel in the rest of the city? Despite the venom and the demands on behalf of the Palestinians there is nothing there that would absolutely preclude some form of co-existence with Israel.

There is co-existence at present: even the bridges remained open and traffic across them from Jordan to Israel and back continued all through the war, despite the two dozen tanks that joined the fighting in Syria, only to be destroyed by Israel. An optimist might say that the extra ferocity of the speech was in part a matter of airing the frustration over Jordan's decision to keep the peace over the past six years, or even a cloak for their lack of desire to fight Israel.

—HALF-AND-HALF

The Egyptian Foreign Minister Fahmy's speech came in two halves, programmatic in the first, and wildly abusive to the point of being incomprehensible in the second. Why should he insult Israel Foreign Minister Eban, for instance, who made a very carefully composed, conciliatory, eloquent speech by saying it was addressed to the gallery and mere electioneering? Apart from being nonsense it is the kind of insult that is commonly traded between rivals inside a country and not the foreign ministers of countries at war with each other.

Mr. Eban represents a country that has been seeking peace since long before its formal existence, and speaks accordingly. Supposing there were a decision in Egypt to aim at some form of long or medium-term detente and mutual accommodation, it would still be totally out of character for Mr. Fahmy to turn up in Geneva all ready and prepared with dulcet phrases of good will. First of all, he must set his demands at a maximum, a common practice, and not only in oriental markets. Secondly, he must avoid criticism and possible interference or pressure by Arab extremists like President Gaddafi of Libya. And in any case it is an Arab custom to denounce Israel that will not easily be shed whatever happens.

Such an interpretation of the verbal fireworks at Geneva corresponds to the thinking on President Sadat's general strategy for Geneva in some well-informed security circles.

There is evidence, it is considered, that Sadat was anxious to go to Geneva, well beyond his immediate and urgent concern for a disengagement of forces that will put an end to his dilemma over the crumbling Third Army.

Instead of speeding on the conference, Sadat might have tried to dig his toes in and demand Israel withdrawal to the mythical "line of October 22," that is, the reopening of a road by which the Third Army could be supplied with military requirements in addition to the food it is now getting through Israel. There was at least a reference to discussion of this issue in the cease-fire agreement and if Sadat was interested in nothing except the rescue of the Third Army he might have preferred to press for this, perhaps even trying to mobilize the Soviet Union and the Security Council to come to his aid.

Again, when Dr. Jarring presented his celebrated proposal for Israel withdrawal and suggested it should be discussed at Rhodes, Sadat said he would go to Rhodes only if Israel committed itself in advance to total withdrawal in the event of agreement — though it is not clear what there would have been left to discuss.

Now, he has not only not asked for a prior commitment, but has not reacted directly to the fact that Israel has said it will *not* withdraw to the lines of 1967.

He did not plan it that way, but Syria's last-minute unwillingness to produce the lists of Israeli prisoners it holds created another problem for him. If Syria had put in an appearance in Geneva without the lists, we would have walked out, according to the decision announced, and the conference might have been still-born. The simplest guess is that Sadat told the Syrians to stay away, perhaps promising to take care of their interests, just to make sure the conference would at least start.

★ ★ ★

ALL of this, taken together, however, does not mean that Sadat is ready to put his signature to a peace treaty. It is doubtful, informed circles say, whether he could afford to do that even today, with Gaddafi glowering from Tripoli and President Assad of Syria describing the whole peace talks as a waste of time. Long-standing political and territorial disputes are not settled by two quick signatures on a piece of paper, however handsomely engraved. Sadat wants the Third Army restored to freedom of movement, he wants the Canal re-opened — and has already asked foreign firms for estimates of costs — he wants to be the man who won this victory for Egypt. He could commit himself to ending hostilities without a treaty. Cairo columnists have been busy explaining the difference between the no-shooting of *salaam* and the full brotherhood of *sulh,* illustrating it with the terrible threat that even after an agreement Mrs. Meir will not be able to do her shopping in Cairo.

If Sadat is willing to give only part of what is asked, instead of normal relations to reinforce the original paper agreement, then he will presumably receive only part of what he wants. This could well mean that any Israel withdrawal agreed upon is not as large as he demands, or would be carried out in stages as peace becomes more

solid and border security less important. That would take us back somewhere in the direction of the earlier proposals for an interim solution.

Why should Sadat accept something now that he previously refused?

Because now, at this moment, he can still tell the Egyptian people that they have won a great victory. But the euphoria over this victory is likely to evaporate within a few months, when it is discovered that despite the great mass of new weapons, the careful preparation and the successful surprise attack the Egyptian armies did not really get far towards recapturing Sinai for Egypt. According to this reading of the situation, Sadat would like to regain the Canal and at least a good slice of Sinai, eliminate the need for further wars — and be able to claim that it was the result of his own military action together with his effective tactics at Geneva, and to do this without having to be too grateful and beholden to the Russians, the Americans Syria and the Arab oil states. They might all wish to give him too much advice later.

SEVEN DAYS TO GO—AND

40 per cent undecided

Jerusalem Post Political Reporter

TEL AVIV. — Forty per cent of the electorate have not yet made up their minds who to vote for in the Knesset elections next Monday, according to the latest poll conducted by the Institute for Applied Social Research and the Communications Institute of the Hebrew University.

The poll, conducted on December 17-18, was restricted to the Jewish urban population, and did not include the army.

The pollsters found that, of those who have decided, 50 per cent will vote Alignment, 29 per cent Likud, five per cent for the N.R.P., four per cent for Shulamit Aloni's Civil Rights list, three per cent for the ILP, two per cent for Moked, two per cent for the Aguda bloc, and one per cent for the Panthers. Other lists got less than one per cent each.

Alignment circles have confirmed reports that polls commissioned by them show that they will get 50 seats in the 120-seat legislature and the Likud 38. (In 1969 the Alignment won 56 seats and the Likud, 31.)

Compared with a similar poll conducted last week, the results show a two per cent decline for the Likud and an 11 per cent decline for this party in two weeks. The Alignment is on the same level as it was last week, and 10 per cent higher than it was two weeks ago.

Holland picked as site for WJC meeting

AMSTERDAM (INA). — The Netherlands has been chosen as the site for the Tenth World Jewish Congress, as a token of Jewish gratitude for Netherlands' friendly attitude toward Israel during the Yom Kippur War.

The Dutch representative to the WJC, Isaac Zadoks, said the decision was made after consultations with Premier Joop den Uyl, Queen Juliana's private secretary and Victor Marijnen, Mayor of The Hague, where the congress will take place.

Mr. den Uyl and Mr. Marijnen told Congress secretary Gerhard Aieger they were very pleased with the decision to hold the congress in their country. The congress is scheduled for April 23 to May 6, with delegates from 64 countries expected to attend.

Hague police authorities have assured Mr. Zadoks that sufficient security measures will be taken during the congress.

'OBSOLETE BEHAVIOUR'

To the Editor of The Jerusalem Post

Sir, — Your issue of December 7 carries a front page report from Oslo, Norway, to the effect that six suspects, including two Israelis, are expected to go on trial on January 7 for the murder of a Moroccan who was alleged to have been associated with the Black September terror organization.

Efforts are no doubt being made to provide the accused Israelis with adequate legal counsel so as to afford them the best available defence. This is an obsolete and archaic way of looking out for the interests of these defendants, regardless of their innocence or guilt. According to modern accepted norms of international behaviour the thing to do would be to hijack a Norwegian airliner and bargain its release against the release of the Israeli defendants. Or would the world scream if *we* did it?

JULIUS I. FOX
Kfar Shmaryahu, December 7.

OIL WEAPON

To the Editor of The Jerusalem Post

Sir, — I would like to suggest a somewhat different interpretation of the oil embargo than the one commonly accepted. The aim of the oil weapon, according to my interpretation, is not to move Israel by proxy leverage, but rather the outright economic exploitation and political domination of the industrialized world by the Arabs behind the smokescreen of a war against Israel. After all, what easier way is there to coax western Europe into contributing so selflessly to its own demise, if not by presenting the product in the ultimate anti-Jewish design?

It is not difficult to project the mental state of the Arab leaders as they approach this conflict. Their history of statecraft is a continuing record of power confrontations and subversions (largely intramural, although this fact is irrelevant), substantially unencumbered by even the pretence of constructive social accomplishment. The lessons of colonialism also may not have been entirely lost, and why can't the positions be reversed? As covetous eyes focus on the wealth and power of Japan and Europe, one might easily rationalize "All this was built on the basis of our oil..." The easy increases in the price of oil satisfy the demand for economic tribute that a colonial power exacts from its colonies, but the prospect of political domination as well must be tempting. France, England and Japan already taken, not a bad start. As for Russia, the historical parallel between recent events and the late 1930s is difficult to dismiss. Then, as now, the Soviets saw fit to support a belligerent power that was fundamentally and demonstratively hostile toward it.

It should not take very long for events to prove or disprove this interpretation, for arrogance typically overreaches and unmasks itself (assuming that it hasn't already done so). And, to the extent that its validity is established, we can take some satisfaction from the fact that our struggle has not been simply the defence of a small country from annihilation (a worthy enterprise in its own right, of course). Rather, we will have vaulted into a position of leadership in the epic confrontation of global forces — a role for which history has not left us unequipped.

NORTON C. LEVINE
Tel Aviv, December 10.

SOLIDARITY FROM OVERSEAS

Erika Gidron

A NEW type of tourist is beginning to arrive in Israel. Overseas organizers are now expressing their amity for the people of Israel by sending solidarity groups to tour the country. The first such group — 31 Swiss postal workers — arrived recently for a 14-day stay; similar groups are on their way from France and Holland. More are expected to arrive in the coming weeks.

Solidarity of another sort finds its expression in daily arrivals of overseas volunteers, coming to supplement Israel's depleted labour force, from which many remain mobilized to man the ceasefire lines.

Some 2,000 volunteers, individuals and groups, have come so far. Hundreds more have registered with Jewish Agency offices abroad and are waiting to be called, in case of need. Applicants are carefully screened and selected according to the needs of the local labour market. They must be prepared to find their own fare and to remain in Israel for not less than three months.

Among the first to volunteer their services were doctors, surgeons and operating theatre nurses, most of them from the United States. For the first two critical weeks of the war they worked side by side with Israeli medical staff, putting in 18-hour shifts in the struggle to save the lives and limbs of the wounded.

Therapy of a different kind was provided by Danny Kaye, who interrupted a world tour on behalf of the U.N. International Children's Emergency Fund to volunteer his own inimitable brand of humour to hospitals throughout the country. He was only one of a group of world-renowned performers and musicians who came, for the second time in six years, to give of their time and talents.

As in June, 1967, the first to arrive were Daniel Barenboim and Pinhas Zuckerman, followed by Isaac Stern and Zubin Mehta. Quipped Mehta, on his way to the northern front: "This is the one time I'm likely to set foot on Arab soil. If the Arab boycott office only knew!"

Although most volunteers are directed to kibbutzim to help out with the citrus harvest — some recent arrivals were recruited to help staff essential non-military industries, including bakeries and food-processing factories.

The war and the weather combined to produce a new problem: icy blasts of cold northeast air blowing in direct from — where else? — Russia, caused a sudden drop in temperature. One group of young American volunteers, eager to help Israel's war effort, found themselves standing among stacks of long johns, folding and packing warm winter underwear urgently needed by Israeli soldiers shivering atop Mount Hermon in summer fatigues.

THE EXPERIENCE of individual volunteers have already become legends. There was the American professor, an expert in water desalination currently at Beersheba University, who set off for the Suez Canal in a small delivery van to distribute cigarettes, candy and gift packages to soldiers serving in frontline units. On the way he stopped to give rides to soldiers returning to the front. Somewhere in Sinai he and his vehicle, bristling with fierce-looking soldiers in the front and candy bars in the back, picked up another hitchhiker: an Egyptian intelligence officer who, in the swirling Sinai dust and amid the general confusion of battle, assumed that he had stumbled into an army patrol.

Currently making the rounds is the story of the Tel Aviv ice-cream vendor who almost ended up delivering his wares to the Egyptian Third Army. Too old for active service, he packed his entire stock in a truck and headed south, collecting transistor radios, toilet articles, gift packages and mail for soldiers on the way. He also bought 10,000 postcards, and while the boys were enjoying the unexpected ice-cream treat, made each one write a few words home. In this way he went from one tank unit to another until he suddenly came under artillery fire. Not certain of his direction, and not daring to stop, he drove straight on and almost ran into an outpost manned by Egyptian soldiers before turning back and speeding for home. "I didn't bother to stop and explain," he says. "And I don't even know how to say ice cream in Arabic."

From the edge of catastrophe to triumph

LONDON. — On Monday, October 15, there was feverish activity on the Israeli side of the Suez Canal. Aluf Arik Sharon had at last been given permission to cross the Canal.

Sharon had planned the operation three years before, during the war of attrition. It was called Operation Gazalle and involved a task force crossing the Canal with the aim at the time of knocking out the anti-aircraft missile batteries on the west bank of the Canal.

The "Sunday Telegraph," in reporting this, says that Sharon had prepared with immense care, leaving weak points in the high sand walls which the Israelis erected along the bank of the Canal so that his tanks could break through quickly to cross the water. He had marked the weak points with red bricks.

Ironically, the Egyptians had encountered the most difficulty in this sector, because the sand was gritty and cohesive and had not broken down when water jets were used on it.

Sharon's task force, an "ugda" combining units of various arms — artillery, armour, mechanised infantry and paratroops — started to move as it grew dark at 17.00 hours. Eight hours later they were across the Canal in the midst of a devastating battle which lasted until midday on Tuesday, October 16.

Sharon released three reinforced brigades on the night of the crossing. One moved north in an offensive feint against the Egyptian Second Army, another swept down to the shore of the Great Bitter Lake and then turned south (using the lake to protect its flank while it pushed the Third Army south), while the third headed for the Canal where it made a smart right turn and pushed the Second Army north.

In support he had a brigade of artillery, along with heavy artillery, self-propelled guns and heavy mortars. He also had bulldozers and tankdozers and Sherman tanks converted into battlefield ambulances and yet other tanks with cherry-picker arms mounted on them to raise artillery observers over the battlefield. Behind him, lurking in the safety of the hills, was the "ugda" of paratroops and tanks with rubber rafts lashed to half tracks ready to make the crossing led by Aluf Avraham Adan.

"By 01.00," Sharon told the "Sunday Telegraph" reporters, "the bridgehead was established and the first tanks moved across at 06.00. By midday we had destroyed six batteries of Sams and 20 tanks. And that was the end of the operation."

BLOODIEST FIGHTING.

It was not, of course, as easy as that. While the tanks shoving back the Third Army had a comparatively easy job, those assigned to push the Second Army north found themselves involved in the fiercest, bloodiest fighting of the whole war.

The men who bore the brunt of this fighting were once again Col. Amnon Reshef and his 14th armoured brigade. Reshef recalls that night: "The brigade moved quietly down to the lake and were turned north along the Canal road, tank by tank. There were swamps on one side and irrigation ditches on the other. We went in three prongs, with the left hand one running along the Canal. We caught them completely by surprise until they woke up and started shooting at the tail of the column from only forty metres range... They cut us off and the road to the Canal was blocked by fire from the flank.

"They stopped our bridging equipment and the paratroopers from coming down. I assigned one battalion to move back to clear the blockade and evacuate our wounded. The moon came up at 23.30 and lit up a desperate battlefield. Everything was in confusion. One tank commander spoke to me over the radio and told me he could not traverse his gun because an enemy tank was too close. I ordered him to open fire with his machine gun and from point blank range he hit the fuel tank and destroyed it."

It was not until the following morning that they were able to clear the Egyptian position. The "Telegraph" writer saw twenty-five burnt out Patton tanks in this area, lying muzzle to muzzle with Egyptian T-55s.

Meanwhile, the front of Reshef's column roared on. "There was so much equipment we did not know what to shoot at," he recounts. The range was very close. There were anti-tank guns, field guns, and Sam missiles, all facing the Pattons as they pushed along the Canal.

Reshef sudenly saw five tanks on his flank at 50 metres range — by this time the battlefield was lit up by the moon and the burning armoured vehicles. At first he did not know if they were friend or foe. He recognized them as enemies when they were only thirty metres away. Within fifty seconds there were four fires. "I don't know what happened to the fifth."

The Israelis call this the "Battle of the Chinese Farm," because on the edge of the battlefield there is an experimental farm. It was built by the Japanese, but when it was captured in 1967, the Israeli soldiers found documents written in a mysterious language they thought was Chinese.

EGYPTIAN COUNTER-ATTACK

The Egyptians counter-attacked the next day and pushed the Israelis back. For a short while it seemed as if they might close the bridgehead, but when the fighting was over, the Israeli tanks had held on and had caused such destruction that even after the usable Egyptian tanks had been towed away, there were still 108 left on the battlefield, completely destroyed. Sharon told us with grim satisfaction: "We knocked out 360 tanks, and that will keep two Russian factories working for two years."

Sharon lost 100 killed and 300 wounded at the bridgehead. At one stage the bridges came under fire from a Katyusha rocket battery. The Israelis could not understand

A report from our London Correspondent DAVID LENNON on the third instalment of the history of the Yom Kippur war as seen by "The Sunday Telegraph"

where these rockets were coming from but laid their mortar sights on the trajectory and when dawn broke the sights pointed directly to the African Glen, a 15,000-ton American freighter, one of those trapped on the lake since 1967. The Israelis called up their aircraft and bombed and rocketed it. As it settled in the water, the Egyptian rocketeers abandoned ship.

The Egyptians had been taken completely by surprise by the Israeli crossing. The Egyptian staff did not know the extent of the Israeli incursion for at least 36 hours after it had taken place.

Sharon told the "Sunday Telegraph" men, that if he had been allowed to carry on, he would have polished off the trapped Third Army in two days, and the Second Army would then have been forced to withdraw across the Canal or face a similar fate. It would have meant a defeat for the Egyptians even more humiliating than that of 1967.

Once the situation became clear to President Sadat he told Moscow that he wanted a cease-fire as soon as possible, and he also restored relations with America in the person of Dr. Kissinger in order to achieve his aim.

ASSAD LESS KEEN

President Assad of Syria was much less keen on a cease-fire, but the Russians began putting the pressure on Syria with threats to cut off military supplies. Reluctantly Assad agreed to order a cease-fire.

In the desert the cease-fire broke down almost immediately. The Israelis raced for Suez and down the gulf to the port of Adabiya. They tried to take Suez but were repulsed in bloody, hand-to-hand fighting in an operation which many Israelis regard as vainglorious and useless — a waste of lives.

In those 19 days of fighting the Arabs had shattered the myth of Israeli invincibility and had demonstrated several flaws in the Israeli command structure and weaponry. They had regained their pride, but in the end they had kept that pride only because they had not been told what had happened.

They did not know the appalling danger created for them by the outrageous brilliance of Sharon. And however much one may praise the newly revealed bravery of the Egyptians and the Syrians, it must never be forgotten that the Israelis changed the game completely.

From being within an ace of catastrophe, they came within one trump of absolute victory, a trump played by both the Russians and the Americans, because neither of the superpowers could afford to see the Arabs humiliated yet again.

Poll shows U.S. pro-Israel sympathy up

NEW YORK (INA). — The latest Gallup Poll has shown that sympathy for Israel in the U.S. has grown rather than diminished since the October war and subsequent Arab oil boycott. The "New York Times," publishing the results of the poll yesterday, reported that a check around the country by its correspondents "found no significant expression of anti-Jewish sentiment despite apparent efforts by groups and individuals to fan a reaction against Jews in the U.S."

The poll was taken between December 7 and 10. It found that among the 1,514 persons aged over 18 who were interviewed in 300 locations, 54 per cent favoured Israel in answering the question, "In this trouble, are your sympathies more with Israel or more with the Arab states?"

The number favouring Israel was up from the 47 per cent who supported Israel in a poll taken between October 6-8.

IT IS DECEMBER, 1973, my wife and I are in Israel. We have arranged to see Dale Atkins, a former teacher at my wife's school. Dale had gone to Israel to work with deaf children. She soon found herself caught up in the War.

Now Dale bounces into the room in our Tel Aviv hotel. She is young, beautiful, twenty-six, and bursting with the excitement of seeing old friends.

In the course of an afternoon, she spills out an endless stream of reminiscence. Every one of her friends, both male and female, have become closely involved in the War. Her friend, Yossi, had been badly wounded. When she went to see him at the hospital, he was so covered with bandages he was not to be recognized. But Yossi's mother was smiling, because Yossi was alive.

Yossi was a pilot. He had been shot down on the Sinai front. His buddy had been killed under his very eyes. The shock was almost too much for the young boy to bear, and his family feared for his mental health.

Yossi spent two weeks in the hospital; but they couldn't hold him down, and he went back to the front. As Dale put it: "The wounded want to fly again. Most of them rush back to the front. It's impossible to keep them at home."

Among other things, Dale told us about the family in the town she'd been working in, the village of Yeroham. This family had come from Morocco, and had taken literally the Biblical commandment to increase and multiply. The parents had reared a family of thirteen children. Eleven of the thirteen were now off in the War. Of course, the girls weren't fighting, but they were away from their usual pursuits at home, involved in war work.

But what Dale was most voluble about was the psychic effect of the War on the young soldiers. She said that the syndrome of war had torn these young kids apart. In some cases, it had just about sucked out all the gentleness that had been in them. Before they had left, these boys, she said, were innocent, open, and had never felt real hate. They certainly had never spoken in terms of hating the enemy, nor in terms of despising the Arabs.

After they had seen some of their closest friends destroyed by gun fire, their attitudes abruptly changed. They now felt the Arab was a personal enemy. They felt uncontrollable surges of revenge against those who had started this brutal, senseless

335

WE SUPPORT LIKUD

A Public Appeal by Professors, Scientists

and University Faculty Members:

All of us have reached the conclusion that the Ma'arach Government bears responsibility for the most grave moral, social, economic, political and even security failures and blunders.

It is our duty to state publicly that the present government is not capable or entitled to lead the country. There must be a change of national leadership through the democratic process, just as in every other free country.

The situation demands a Government of National Unity to face the trials and dangers of the future.

Therefore, we the undersigned, notwithstanding our different opinions, call upon the citizens of Israel to give the Likud a mandate to form a Government of National Unity, to include men of experience, talent and ability.

Prof. Yohanan Aharoni
Archaeology, Tel Aviv Univ.

Prof. Gedalyahu Alkoshi
Hebrew Literature, Jerusalem

Prof. Moshe Amit
Ancient History, Jerusalem

Prof. Moshe Arens
Aeronautics, Haifa and Tel Aviv U.

Prof. Adi Ben-Israel

Prof. Chava Lifshitz
Chemistry, Jerusalem

Dr. Baruch Margalit
Bible, Haifa Univ.

Sarah Minster, M.A.
Philology, Jerusalem

Prof. Zvi Neuman
Medicine, Jerusalem

Prof. Joseph Otterman
Space Science, Tel Aviv Univ.

Jewish students from U.K. pick fruit over Xmas

Some 200 Jewish college students and high schoolers from Britain have given up their Christmas holidays to come here and help with the citrus harvest, the Youth Department of the World Zionist Organization announced yesterday.

Department deputy director Maurice Zilka said the volunteers were picking and packing the fruit alongside Arab workers, doing an eight-hour day in the groves, and learning Hebrew for two hours every evening. They were staying at two hotels in Netanya, he said.

Zilka said the fruit-pickers did not come under the category of regular volunteers from overseas, since they had come to Israel just during the holidays.

The fruit-pickers pay their own air fares — like regular volunteers.

Likud probe reports:
No shelters for 40% of Tel Aviv pupils

By SARAH HONIG
Jerusalem Post Reporter

TEL AVIV. — The Likud's candidate for mayor, Shlomo Lahat, charged yesterday that no shelters are available for some 25,000, or 40 per cent, of the city's school children. Mr. Lahat based his charge on the results of an investigation carried out for him by one of Tel Aviv's largest detective agencies, Modi'in Ezrahy.

According to the report released here yesterday, 30 per cent of the city's schools have no shelters at all: In 22 per cent of the other schools the shelters are too small for even half of the pupils. This is not the case only in old schools, but even in some new ones such as the school in Neve Avivim, the report said.

Ten per cent of what are called school shelters are not really *bona fide* shelters but are improvizations such as corridors, or classrooms with windows blocked off by defence walls, the report went on. Of the good school shelters, only 75 per cent are ready for immediate use. The others are used as cafeterias, gyms, shops, libraries or clubs.

Of the schools with no shelters at all, some 40 per cent are close enough to public shelters to rush the pupils there in case of emergency. But this still leaves 20 per cent of the city's 340 schools with shelters neither on the premises nor close by according to the report.

As for the rest of the population some 20 per cent, or 72,000 people are without shelters, the report said. But during work hours the number of people in this city is more than doubled, it pointed out. Thus, the 72,000 shelterless Tel Avivians are joined by more than 300,000 persons who come here to work, shop or study.

The incumbent municipal administration agrees that not all is as it should be, but maintains that when it comes to shelters Tel Aviv is better off than any other city, as 80 per cent of the population are covered by shelters.

Students may be called up to essential jobs

By YAACOV FRIEDLER, Jerusalem Post Reporter

HAIFA. — The Labour Ministry is considering schemes to employ the 45,000 students who are not on military service in essential jobs.

Labour Minister Yosef Almogi said yesterday that the jobs considered essential are in citrus packing, in hospitals and in social work and possibly in certain industrial jobs. If it is found that the students — men and women — are needed, the Ministry would ask them to volunteer for the work.

Mr. Almogi said he had decided on the scheme after visiting the troops at the front this week. Students who have been mobilized were grousing that the burden of the war was not being fairly shared, and that their colleagues in the universities were in fact able to study as "though nothing had happened."

The Minister thought it extremely important that everything be done so that the battle front and the home front share equally in the war effort. economically and socially.

'YOU WERE THE ONE WHO GAVE ME WATER

Proof for Swedish journalists: Syrian wasn't 'bumped-off'

By ZEEV SCHUL
Jerusalem Post Reporter

THIS week's Christmas issue of a popular Stockholm weekly, called whatever the Swedish equivalent for "Look" is, features as its centre-piece the story of Ahmed Jijo, 25, a Syrian tank-gunner (loader) from El Hader village near Aleppo, who is a prisoner alive and well in Israel — and lucky. In better times, Ahmed used to be the owner of a small farm and some head of sheep. But he was mobilized a few years ago — "and they forgot all about me and kept me on."

Ahmed Jijo's story began on the morning of October 12, near Khirbet Arnaba some 3 kms. off the Kuneitra-Damascus road just over the 1967 cease-fire line.

A group of journalists, including a Spaniard, a Swiss and the Swedish representative of the illustrated weekly, were given what conducting officers of the Press Liaison Office irreverently refer to as "the grand tour" of the Golan Heights. At that time a full fledged artillery exchange was still going on north of the area — but also including occasional salvoes straddling the Kuneitra road, including the Khirbet Arnaba area.

The journalists were accompanied by Eliahu Amiel, known to his many friends and acquaintances as "Husie." Husie was to play the main "supporting role" in Ahmed Jijo's life.

There were some charred Syrian T 55 tanks lying a short distance below. From one of them came the sound of a voice. In Arabic. It sounded as if someone had forgotten to shut the wireless off — one of those eerie sounds one does come across on battlefields.

WANTED WATER

The four men clambered across the black lava rocks to investigate. As they did so, they saw something waving at them from underneath the tank. It was the charred hand of Ahmed Jijo, waving back and forth like a pendulum.

Ahmed — in a near-delirium — was talking to himself most of the time. "mayya — bidde mayya" he said... (Water — I want some water).

At first it looked as though Ahmed were trapped beneath the tank but with the help of two husky sergeants fetched by Husie they were able to extricate the man. He looked in pitiful shape. His hands and face were badly burned and one of his legs was also twisted at an unnatural angle.

Husie gave him his water flask. The Syrian soldier raised it to his lips and drained it. Then lay back relaxed and slipped into unconsciousness again.

The two sergeants were arguing. To the journalists, it seemed as if they were arguing about what to do with the man. As one of the journalists was to record: "We were sure they intended to bump him off as soon as they carried him out of our sight. Nobody would pay much attention to another shot in the area which was, after all, still under artillery fire..."

This was also the gist of what one of the team-members of another "Look" party which came to Israel a fortnight or so ago said.

Husie protested. It didn't do much good. He was listened to sympathetically, but without conviction.

So Husie set out on a private search of the military hospitals and prisoner of war camps on his own.

His list of dates and facts eventually narrowed the choice down to half a dozen, and then finally to one Syrian soldier: none other than Ahmed Jijo, who came limping out of cell No. 3 in the military prison the other day to look at Husie and the Swedish journalists.

"I know you. You were the one who gave me the water," he said, *looking at Husie.*

Ahmed Jijo, back on his feet, is a tall, powerfully built man, about 25 years of age. He told the journalists his version of what happened. The Syrian soldiers were never told there was going to be a war. They advanced during the night of October 5.

LEFT BY FRIENDS

"On Sunday at about 7 o'clock in the morning there was a fierce kind of blow on the left side of the tank. Everything was filled with smoke. The tank commander was killed. I opened the turret hatch and tried to get out but there were planes attacking us and much shooting and I slid down and closed the hatch again. But then the tank began to burn and ammunition exploded. I managed to slide out and felt for the first time this terrible pain in my leg, my hands and on my face... the tank stopped burning and I crawled underneath it for better protection."

"About five o'clock in the afternoon that same day two Syrian soldiers walked past. I recognised them. Both were my friends and in the same unit. They would not, however, take me with them and left me only a few unopened tins of beans and biscuits. I couldn't eat the biscuits because my mouth was burned inside as well as outside. I even tried to open those tins with my teeth to get at the liquid. But I couldn't...

"I slept and woke and slept again. And each time I awoke I knew I was going to die. This time or maybe the next... Then you came. I remember you. You gave me the water..."

Ahmed Jijo, married and proud father of a son, hopes to be able to return to his farm soon. He still has one foot in a cast. But it doesn't bother him. And he can't forget the taste of that water — nor the two sergeants who brought him to a first aid station, carrying him all the way in a fireman's grip. That was what the argument had been about — whether they would have to use a stretcher, which was inconvenient in that boulder-strewn area, or "improvise."

"One Israeli sergeant is the equivalent of a platoon. Two are a mass meeting..." the narrator, himself a sergeant, who had served in the north, said.

Kollek at engineers' forum
Israeli care justifies Jewish claim to J'lem

By ABRAHAM RABINOVICH
Jerusalem Post Reporter

Not since the days of Herod the Great has Jerusalem been as well taken care of as during the last six years, Mayor Teddy Kollek said yesterday.

The concern Israel has demonstrated over Jerusalem since it came entirely under Israeli administration in 1967 is one of the arguments justifying its claim to the city, Mr. Kollek said. Other reasons cited by the Mayor: "We were here a couple of thousand years before anyone else; we've been a majority for the past 150 years; and all other religions have other cities which are holy to them." Only as a united city, he said, can the future of Jerusalem be properly planned.

The Mayor was addressing the final session of the Third World Congress of Engineers and Architects. Praise for the current direction of Jerusalem planning was heard from a number of the foreign architects and planners participating. "Mayor Kollek and his planning team are on the right path," said Prof. Harry Mayerovitch of McGill University. "What has been done until now gives me hope for the future."

City Councilman Meron Benvenisti, who holds the urban portfolio on the Municipal Council, said the task of the planner in Jerusalem should be to preserve the contrasts that make for "creative tension." He described these contrasts as the physical one between the desert and the sown, that between spiritual and secular, between Occidental and Oriental, and between Arab and Jew. "The problem in Jerusalem is to keep the balance without letting one overwhelm the other," he said.

City Engineer Amikam Yaffe said the central business district (CBD) should be developed in its present location for the next 15 years at least — instead of being permitted to expand from Mahaneh Yehuda to Binyenei Ha'ooma, as some have suggested, or to create sub-centres in the north or south of the city. "The traditions of people using this area are very strong, and it is not considered desirable to uproot these traditions," he said. He also cited economic and tranportation reasons.

The existing CBD contains 250,000 square metres of floor space. The city planners envision this growing to 1.8 million square metres by 1985.

Prof. Nathaniel Lichfield, planning consultant to the Municipality, said that the topography of Jerusalem would permit a population of 500,000—600,000. When this number is reached, in about 1985 or 1990, he said, the overspill will have to be contained in new towns, smaller satellites, or linear development along the valleys leading from the city.

Squeeze the U.S. even more, says Egyptian paper

CAIRO (UPI). — The semi-official newspaper "Al Ahram" said yesterday that Arab countries should escalate their oil pressure on America and begin a campaign to harass the U.S. dollar, despite the opening of the Geneva peace conference.

"The climate at the opening session of the Geneva conference fully justifies Arab countries in maintaining the use of their weapons of economic pressure against America," the newspaper said.

"The use of these weapons should be escalated, not merely by cutting oil production or raising oil prices, but by using Arab financial deposits to start a battle against the dollar," the newspaper added.

'Jews abroad coming closer to Zionism'

The recent war marked a turning point in relations between Israel and the Diaspora, and Jews abroad are coming closer to the Zionist viewpoint. This was stated yesterday by acting Jewish Agency head Arye Dulzin at the opening of a seminar at the President's Residence.

Mr. Dulzin said that where, before, there had been a sense of partnership, there was now a feeling that the Jews of Israel and the Diaspora formed one people. Jews in many countries had even come into open and daring conflict with their governments over policy during the recent war.

One part of the Diaspora where all is not well — Latin America — was the subject of another meeting in Jerusalem yesterday, of the Zionist Executive and representatives of the world Zionist movement. The meeting, chaired by Mr. Dulzin, heard warnings that the million Jews of Central and South America were on the way to assimilation, and that they could not be turned towards Zionism by emissaries who copy New Left slogans.

Knesset Member Yitzhak Korn told the meeting that 80 per cent of the Latin Jewish students were indifferent or hostile to Judaism and Zionism. The 21,000 Jewish students in Buenos Aires maintain no Jewish activity at all. A revision in educational methods in Latin America was called for, he said.

Several speakers noted the contrasts between Jewish disarray and Arab organization in Latin America. Avraham Shenkar reported that Latin Arabs held a continent-wide conference at Sao Paolo during the recent war to plan propaganda and education work among their millions of brethren.

U.S. PROFESSORS:
Helping Israel's cause abroad

By JUDY SIEGEL
Special to The Jerusalem Post

Taking a lesson from their energetic colleague Henry Kissinger, a former Harvard professor, an organization of 15,000 American university educators is working to influence U.S. government policy and public opinion on the Arab-Israeli conflict.

American Professor for Peace in the Middle East (APPME), whose membership on 600 campuses includes several hundred prominent non-Jews, has just sent its national executive committee to Israel for a two-week fact-finding mission.

"We are the first and only American academic group to insist on direct negotiations among the parties in the area and to demand security for the State of Israel as a prerequisite for any settlement," says Rivke Hadary, director of APPME's Israel office.

"Yet our function is mainly the gathering and distribution of information," she continues, ''and we have sent hundreds of lecturers around the country since the Yom Kippur War. Professors, now more than ever, are in a position to influence government officials."

Despite their unanimity of support for Israel, APPME is not monolithic. "We have no rigid position on boundaries or the status of Jerusalem," says Mrs. Hadary.

"Some of our members believe in a small nation's right to exist, while others simply see the need for a strong democratic state to counterbalance the Communist influence in the area," she added.

Six APPME members met Sunday night for a forum on reactions of the American academic community to the Yom Kippur War and the mood of the campus today. Held at Jerusalem's Diplomat Hotel, the conference was attended by over 300 foreign and Israeli professors, journalists and members of the public-at-large.

Michael Curtis, professor of political science at Rutgers University and chairman of the forum, opened the discussion on a sombre note. "The Arabs' new competence on the battlefield is not the only surprise to come out of the war; so did their amazing aptitude at using public relations to benefit their cause. The clever ads they placed in "The New York Times" and elsewhere seem very convincing to people who aren't sufficiently familiar with the historical facts.

"American blacks are a much more important factor in politics and on campus than before the Six Day War," he continued. "Unfortunately, many of them identify with the Arabs as struggling partners in the Third World."

Prof. J. Leo Cefkin, who teaches political science at Colorado State University, expanded on the topic: "Moderate blacks greatly admire Israeli values and advances, and they want to emulate many of them. But the radicals are almost uniformly opposed to the State of Israel for several reasons. Most Jews are white and therefore the adversary; radicals who feel alienated from U.S. society are opposed to Israel, which they associate with the American government; and those who are proponents of the liberation of blacks feel obligated to support any other supposed liberation movement, including the Arabs'."

Turning more optimistic, Prof. Cefkin said that even though there are few Jews in Colorado and other Western states, most of his colleagues and acquaintances firmly back Israel. "When someone at the university saw anti-Israel propaganda they immediately brought it to me so I could answer it."

Joseph Neyer, who teaches philosophy at Rutgers, asserted that American campus youth will be easily swayed by Arab propaganda unless it is counteracted by their professors.

"The generation in college today is barely old enough to understand the '67 war, let alone all the preceding ones. Many of them see Yom Kippur's as a struggle for territory and not as Israel's fight for survival. Something must be done, not only because theirs will be the American public opinion of the future, but because they are a potentially valuable source of aliya."

The American New Left is delighted with the results of the latest Arab-Israel war, according to Queensborough Community College professor of history George Moutafakis. "They believe the U.S. is an imperialist power with many client-nations all over the world, including Israel, and that the war proved that Israel would have been defeated without American support. Of course they don't refer to the large Soviet airlift to the Arabs that preceded the American flights.

"Writers like Noam Chomsky also continue to emphasize the 'deterioration of Israeli society and values' and that the people can no longer gorge themselves on overconfidence."

According to Prof. Moutafakis, American public opinion is very fragile and erratic.

"We of APPME must redouble our efforts to see that it remains favourable towards Israel."

---

war that had robbed them of their best friends. Dale said that some of her friends admitted that they could hardly recognize themselves at times. They could hardly stop themselves from pouring out their bitterness to her, and they deplored their feelings of bestiality.

As she recounted these conversations, this young girl wept openly. She mourned for their lost youth. Their innocence had been swept away, and Dale was caught up in her own incoherent dirge. She had loved these boys, loved them for their humaneness, for their inner decency. And now she was wondering — had that part of their characters that she had treasured most been irretrievably lost?

During that afternoon, Dale told us many stories of heroism and many harrowing episodes. "My friend Jacob," she said, "saw the pieces of his

The Labor central committee in executive session.

Dry Bones

Rabbis rap President's wife over 'Playboy'

Mrs. Nina Katzir's initiative in sending 3,000 copies of "Playboy" magazine to the troops has run into more opposition from Orthodox quarters. The Union of Immigrant Rabbis from Western Countries has sent public appeals both to Mrs. Katzir (the President's wife) and to U.S. Ambassador Kenneth Keating, who is assisting her in bringing in the magazines, urging them to forgo their effort.

The Immigrant Rabbis' protest follows an appeal from Deputy Education Minister Zevulun Hammer (NRP) to the army not to accept the magazines. Mr. Hammer claimed that their salacious contents would lower morale instead of raising it.

In a cable to Mrs. Katzir, the Immigrant Rabbis' chairman, Rabbi Alexander Carlebach, referred to "Playboy" as literature which cheapened woman's dignity (the magazine offers nude pin-ups). This was not the appropriate gift for Jewish soldiers on Hanukka, the festival which commemorates Jewish triumph over heathen practices.

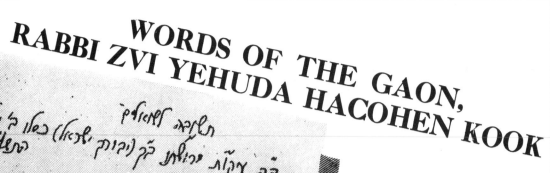

WORDS OF THE GAON, RABBI ZVI YEHUDA HACOHEN KOOK

Following the acceptance and publication of the decision obligating our public representatives in the ב List — on the basis of their traditional sharing of the burden of national responsibility — to reject any concession, G-d forbid, of any parts of Eretz Israel, the heritage of our forefathers, it is now clear and obvious to all Jews who believe in the fulfilment of the word of G-d, his Tora and his mitzvot, through his people and his heritage. That they should vote ב in the coming elections. The ב List stands for sanctifying God's name through the sanctity of our state.

In anticipation of seeing complete salvation in the holy majesty of his great name, which he has bestowed on us, in the eyes of the whole world

Zvi Yehuda Hacohen Kook

VOTE
CHAZIT DATIT LE'UMIT
Hamizrachi — Hapoel Hamizrachi

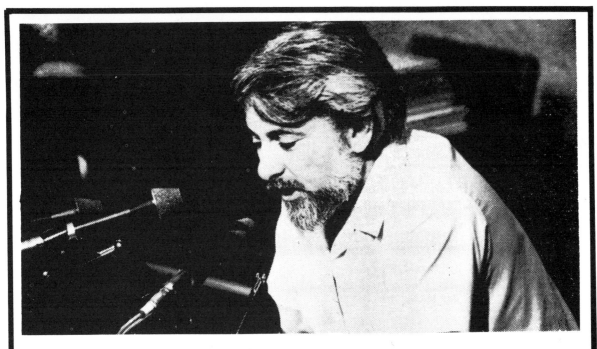

URI AVNERY?
WHAT DOES HE WANT?

Separation of State and Religion... A five-day working week...
Legalized abortion... Civil marriage and civil divorce...
Abolition of travel taxes... A new Ministry for the Protection
of the Environment... Social Housing for young couples...
Air conditioning in all buses and taxis... Equal status for
Reform, Conservative and Orthodox rabbis... Free University
education... The nationalization of the Kupot-Holim and the
creation of a British-style National Health Service for all...
A law for the protection of animals... In short, a modern Israel.
AND ABOVE ALL: PEACE!

ELECTION PROMISES?

No, Uri Avnery promises only one thing: to go on fighting
for the same goals for which he waged fireless fight during
the last eight years in the Knesset. For these items, and for
many more, which have become identified with the name of
Israel's No. 1 independent parliamentarian,

VOTE FOR URI AVNERY!
MERI (HA'OLAM HAZEH)

Geneva and the elections

Even if the Geneva talks do not lead to peace, those who said Israel could not refuse to participate in them were right, Finance Minister Pinhas Sapir told a Histadrut rally in Ramat Gan on Friday.

"For years we said we wanted to meet with our neighbours face-to-face. We didn't expect to clasp hands immediately and sign a peace treaty," he said. "We only wanted to hold negotiations without prior conditions in the hope that through negotiations we would reach an agreement that would bring us peace."

★　★　★

Likud leader Menahem Begin, M.K., speaking at Beit Hapraklit in Tel Aviv on Friday, said the opening speeches of the Arab delegates at the peace conference showed their desire to liquidate Israel in stages.

He warned that if Israel failed to look at reality with open eyes, it would be taken by surprise, as on Yom Kippur, "but the danger would be greater." He said that Israel had to stand firm for two or three years since time was working for her. "Even today we still have friends in the world," he said, "and they will increase when alternative sources of oil are found."

★　★　★

The Geneva conference must not turn into another Vietnam peace conference where "in Paris they talked and in Asia they fought," Interior Minister Yosef Burg told the Commercial and Industrial Club in Tel Aviv on Friday.

He said the Geneva talks will test the true desire of the Arabs for peace and Israel's ability to stand firm and negotiate skilfully.

Gideon Hausner, M.K., told an Independent Liberal election meeting in Petah Tikva on Friday that he hoped the Geneva talks would make progress when they moved behind closed doors without the presence of journalists and TV cameras.

★　★　★

Why Syrians aren't there

DAMASCUS (Reuter). — Syria said on Friday it had decided not to attend the Geneva conference because "there will not be a serious search for a just and permanent peace."

An official statement said, "This is due to Israel's endeavours to divert the Geneva conference to a field of manoeuvres concentrating on side issues in order to block the main goal for which the conference is convened, namely the implementation of United Nations resolutions on Israel's withdrawal from all occupied Arab territories."

Referring to prisoners-of-war, the statement said, "Syria's attitude was clear from the beginning. It replied to Israel's allegations by official memoranda sent to the International Committee of the Red Cross in Geneva. It proved by irrefutable facts that it was Israel which violated the Geneva Conventions and it was she which refused publicly to abide by them through her delegate to the annual Red Cross conference held recently in Iran."

Rifai attacks Israel's 'expansionism'

GENEVA (Reuter). — Jordanian Prime Minister Zaid Rifai, in his speech to Friday's opening session of the peace conference, attacked Israel for its "expansionist policy" and for the damage and destruction caused to the Arab peoples.

He said that the world had watched in silence Israel's armed occupation of Arab territories and its escalating aggression, but that the fighting in October was an Arab effort to turn peace into reality.

Israel should also retreat from its positions inside Syria since Syria's absence from the conference did not prejudice its right to Israeli withdrawal. Rifai said.

"Questions of withdrawal, boundaries, Palestinian rights, refugees, obligations of peace, and the status of Jerusalem are all of common concern and collective responsibility." he stated.

"My delegation therefore is not prepared to conclude any partial settlement on matters we feel are of a joint interest with our Arab brothers at this conference."

Rifai said Israel "does not belong in our environment, and is a stranger to our homeland.

"How could Israel be introduced into the Arab region and live at peace with us as long as it insists on being foreign and hostile," he asked.

He said that in 25 years "Israel has failed to win the slightest degree of love or acceptance by its Arab neighbours. The seeds of oppression that were planted in Arab soil grew up with hatred."

Rifai listed the following among the issues to be decided at Geneva:

● "Israel's complete withdrawal from all Arab territories occupied since June 1967. A programme of implementation and a timetable for this withdrawal should be drawn up and agreed upon.

● "The legitimate rights of the Arab people of Palestine must be fulfilled in accordance with the resolutions of the UN, and the Palestinian refugees must exercise their right of repatriation or compensation in accordance with law and justice.

● "Arab Jerusalem is an integral part of the Arab occupied territories, therefore Israel must relinquish its authority over it. Arab sovereignty must be restored in the Arab sector of the city. The holy places of all the three divine religions must be preserved, protected and respected and free access for all the followers of these three religions must be secure and maintained."

Troops not getting 'Playboy' gift

No "Playboy" magazines will be distributed to soldiers after all, it was announced yesterday.

The President's wife, who had organized the scheme together with the U.S. ambassador, said yesterday through the Government Press Office that the shipment of "Playboy" had not arrived and the magazines would therefore not be given out.

When the plan was announced last week it met with criticism from the National Religious Party, on the grounds that the nude photographs contained in the popular American magazine would "impair the moral fibre of our soldiers." The President's wife was also criticized for taking part in the operation: author Moshe Shamir wrote in "Ma'ariv" last week that it was in poor taste for her to lend her name to such a project.

Arab war to last for 'generations'

KUWAIT (AFP). — The Kuwaiti army chief of staff, General Mubbarak Abdallah al-Jabr al-Sabah, said yesterday that the Arabs' war on Israel would go on for generations, because "there can be no co-existence with a foreign entity whose aspirations endanger our religion and community."

Gen. al-Sabah was being interviewed by a Kuwaiti newspaper. He added that Kuwaiti soldiers were now stationed on both the Syrian and Egyptian fronts.

Rubinstein plays for Israel

The great Artur Rubinstein gave his services free to the concert by the Israel Philharmonic Orchestra earlier this month at London's Albert Hall in aid of the Jewish National Fund. Rubinstein has *always* returned the fees he has earned from IPO concerts, and the money has been used by the orchestra management to endow the Rubinstein Chair of Musicology at the Hebrew University.

For a pianist only a few weeks from his 88th birthday, the ability simply to play all through Beethoven's Emperor Concerto is miracle enough.

Over 7,000 patrons paid up to £150 for a ticket, but there was no festivity or salutation — and no banners, no fanfare, no speeches, no encores. *(Jewish Chronicle)*

Golan search for missing men

More than 100 Israeli soldiers are conducting an intensive search of the Golan Heights for the bodies of men missing since the outbreak of the war.

The bodies of several hundred Syrian troops have been found, "Yediot Ahronot" reported.

It did not say if the remains of any Israelis had been found.

"Yediot" and "Ma'ariv" said the searchers were aided during early stages of the operation by Syrian prisoners of war, who were brought to the area from camps inside Israel.

The Syrians were recruited, "Ma'ariv" said, "after they reported that they were witnesses to the death of Israel soldiers and could indicate the places where they fell."

The bodies of Syrian soldiers found in the search have been interred in a special plot, with each grave identified by the soldier's name and identification number.

Carless Sabbath would upset status quo—Peres

Jerusalem Post Knesset Reporter

Transport Minister Shimon Peres rejected the idea of making the Sabbath a compulsory carless day for drivers, on the grounds that this would upset the *status quo* on religious affairs (maintained between Labour and the NRP) and constitute a form of religious coercion which the Coalition had never entertained.

Mr. Peres said that observant M.K.s had objected to laying up their cars from Friday afternoon till two a.m. Sunday morning. That was why it was decided the Sabbath carless day would be from sundown Friday to sundown Saturday.

The carless day scheme is supposed to alleviate the fuel crisis but not to alter the *status quo*, Mr. Peres said. If Israel had public transport on the Sabbath the way other countries have it on Sunday, he said, the matter would look vastly different. However, a proposal now to introduce Sabbath transport would only cause domestic strife.

Later, the House also moved to Committee a motion by the Poale Aguda urging against the immediate introduction of winter time, on the grounds that this would prevent early morning prayers in the dark, and cause especial sorrow to the thousands of mourners who wished to say the *Kaddish* for the dead of the Yom Kippur War.

Interior Minister Dr. Yosef Burg, replying, said he was sure the Government would give due consideration for the wishes of worshippers before taking a final decision about shifting the clock.

Over 30 per cent of this country's drivers chose Sabbath as their carless day, he said — a fact that will be enough to alter the image of the Sabbath in Israel.

Chief Rabbinate of Israel

APPEAL TO THE
JEWISH PEOPLE
IN ISRAEL AND THE DIASPORA

"It is even the time of Jacob's trouble; but
he shall be saved out of it" Jeremiah 30,7

FEARFUL DAYS, days of grief and suffering, have been Israel's lot since enemy forces, with tanks and planes, attacked our defence posts on the Golan Heights and our bunkers at the Suez Canal, at the height of the holy Yom Kippur ritual, drenching Israel's borders with blood and fire, and a frenzy of murder and barbarity.

The soldiers of Israel, standing before their Creator in fasting and prayer, with the aid of the Almighty, with their very bodies and the strength of their spirit, stopped the enemy columns of tanks and infantry, which were armed with sophisticated Russian weapons, and which poured in on them like a flood, bent on destruction and evil, saying, "Come, and let us cut them off from being a nation; that the name of Israel may be no more in remembrance."

WERE IT NOT FOR THE ALMIGHTY, when all the Arab peoples rose up to destroy us, Israel would not have had the strength to withstand the onslaught; blessed is the Lord who saved us from them.

The wonders and miracles of the Almighty were revealed to all, at the height of the war and afterwards — by the grace of the Lord, in the course of a few days, we changed our role of the pursued to that of the pursuers, from humiliation to victory. We saved ourselves at the cost of much blood and many losses. More than two thousand heroes lost their lives, and thousands of fine men were injured in this bloody war, fighting with every ounce of strength they possessed. And even now, we find ourselves in the face of difficult military and political confrontations, the results of which none can foresee.

At such a time, we must subject ourselves to a strict moral stock-taking, "Let us search and try our ways, and turn again to the Lord." We must ask ourselves, On whose account and for what reason has this terrible judgement been applied to us? Perhaps we were guilty in the sight of heaven, at a time when we were drunk with victory after the Six Day War; perhaps we then thought that what we gained had been achieved with our own strength. Or perhaps the moral and social lowering of standards, civil hatred, and the throwing off of faith which have become widespread in our life, perhaps these have upset the special relations of the Jews with the Almighty, as it is written, **"YE SHALL BE A PECULIAR TREASURE UNTO ME ABOVE ALL PEOPLE: FOR ALL THE EARTH IS MINE."** Perhaps it was this that brought about a weakening of our spiritual superiority.

We have been warned about such a thing in our holy Tora: **"WHEN THOU ART IN TRIBULATION, AND ALL THESE THINGS ARE COME UPON THEE, EVEN IN THE LATTER DAYS, IF THOU TURN TO THE LORD THY GOD AND SHALT BE OBEDIENT UNTO HIS VOICE."** The very eminent Maimonides ז"ל has stated our obligation to maintain faith in times of trial; he said: "And this is the way of repentance; when you are afflicted with troubles, you cry out and lament, but all know that 'troubles have been brought on you for your wrongdoing, as it is written 'Your iniquities have turned away these things.' And this is the means of ridding yourselves of troubles; but if you do not cry out and lament, but say 'This thing came on us because this is the way of the world, this misfortune happened by chance, — it would be ugly conduct, and you would sink down in your own iniquities."

In these stormy days, how much more does this apply! Surely it was the hand of the Lord that stirred up our hearts to devote ourselves to repentence. For did it not all happen in the middle of the great and awe inspiring Yom Kippur; to quote the immaculate language of Maimonides ז"ל, "That is the time for repentence for all, for the individual and for the many, it is the end of forgiveness and pardon for Israel."

BROTHERS AWAKE! Have regard for our souls, cease from civil strife. **UNITE** as one man for the sake of our people, our Tora, and our enemy-surrounded country. Put away civil hatred from your hearts; let every man help his companion and encourage his brother to be strong. Trust in the Creator of the world will be planted in your hearts; you will gain confidence that the word of the Lord, as spoken by his prophet, will be fulfilled: "Keep ye judgement, and do justice: for my salvation is near to come, and my righteousness to be revealed." Increase your observance of our holy Sabbath, and deepen in your hearts the three profound loves: Love of the Lord, Love of the Tora, and Love of Israel, its people and country.

As our Sages of blessed memory taught: Israel will not be redeemed until it becomes one community, as it is written, "In those days, the house of Judah shall walk with the house of Israel, and they shall come together out of the land of the north to the land that I have given for an inheritance unto your fathers."

And it is a fundamental principle of our faith that, when we are on the road to redemption, there is no going back. As our Sages of blessed memory said in Midrash Shoher Tov: I will lift up mine eyes unto the hills, from whence cometh my help, as David sang in a Song of Degrees. Since you have allowed us to ascend, we shall not descend; since you have saved us from the rule of Esau, we shall not return to oppression; as it is written, "And saviours shall come up on Mount Zion to judge the mount of Esau; and the kingdom shall be the Lord's."

And regarding the peace conference between Israel and her neighbours, which is about to start, we would say: remember the words of prophecy of Joel, **"FOR, BEHOLD, IN THOSE DAYS, AND IN THAT TIME, WHEN I SHALL BRING AGAIN THE CAPTIVITY OF JUDAH AND JERUSALEM, I WILL BRING THEM DOWN INTO THE VALLEY OF JEHOSHAPHAT, AND WILL PLEAD WITH THEM THERE FOR MY PEOPLE AND FOR MY HERITAGE ISRAEL, WHOM THEY HAVE SCATTERED AMONG THE NATIONS, AND PARTED MY LAND."**

To the representatives of Israel at the Conference, we would say **BE STRONG AND OF GOOD COURAGE**; may the Lord of your people defend in righteousness and with strength our age-long rights to our surrounded country, and Judah will be in Jerusalem forever. The Lord who dwells on high will put wise counsel into the mouths of those attending the Conference, in order that security and peace be brought to our borders, "And my people shall dwell in a peaceable habitation, and in sure dwellings; nation shall not lift up sword against nation, neither shall they learn war any more."

DEAR BROTHERS! Strengthen ye the weak hands, and confirm the feeble knees. Say to them that are of a fearful heart, Be strong, fear not: your God will come and save you. No weapon that is formed against thee shall prosper; and every tongue that shall rise against thee in judgment thou shalt condemn. There will be peace in our land, a just, honourable and durable peace, as it is written, "The Lord will give strength unto his people; the Lord will bless his people with peace."

WE SHALL ACT IN THE NAME OF THE LORD AND WE SHALL PROSPER

CHIEF RABBINICAL COUNCIL OF ISRAEL

E. Jerusalemite jailed 4 years as spy for Jordan

An East Jerusalem man was 'this week sentenced to four years' imprisonment for agreeing to spy for Jordanian Intelligence.

The Jerusalem District Court was told on Tuesday that Mahmoud Abed Salim, a self-styled journalist and artist, visited Jordan last May where he was recruited by Jordanian Intelligence. He agreed to furnish information, particularly concerning the purchase of land in East Jerusalem by Jews and the names of Arabs who "collaborated" with the Israelis.

He was arrested at Allenby Bridge before completing his first assignment, with five films of the Israeli Independence Day parade in his possession.

The Court said it was taking into account Salim's clean past and the fact that he had not succeeded in giving any information to the Jordanians. *(Itim)*

Six Egyptians surrender, tired of waiting for Israel to leave

POST Military Corrsepondent

TEL AVIV. — Six Egyptian soldiers who had hidden out in a bunker north of Suez since the cease-fire, two months ago, vainly waiting for Egyptian troops to retake the area, surrendered to an Israel Army patrol on Monday, unkempt, bedraggled and exhausted.

The six had skillfully camouflaged their hide-out and ventured out only at night in order to replenish their water supply from some nearby water tanks. They had lived off a stock of Egyptian battle rations and lentils, hoarded in their bunker and, when they surrendered, still had ample supplies.

The soldiers gave up hope when they realised that Israel troops in the area were securing their positions and digging in, obviously preparing for a long stay, instead of withdrawing from the west bank as the Egyptians had expected.

Only 16% think Arabs want peace

Only 15.78 per cent of Israelis believe that the Arabs want a lasting peace, even in light of the Geneva Conference, a poll taken last week shows.

The Dahaf organization had asked a sample of 1,199 Israelis whether, in the light of the Geneva Conference, they now believed more in an Arabe desire to come to a lasting peace agreement with Israel. Some 65.74 per cent said they did not, while 18.47 per cent either gave qualified answers or didn't know.

AFRICA AND GENEVA OVERSHADOW LOCAL CONCERNS

Battles for mayoralties rage on, but the public isn't listening

By SARAH HONIG
Jerusalem Post Reporter

THE forthcoming municipal elections are an unmistakable casualty of the Yom Kippur War. Public relations experts and campaign managers are desperately engaged in frantic last-minute resuscitation attempts.

But the patient is scarcely responding. The public is simply uninterested. Thus the campaign which, despite the fact that it started with a bang, had from the outset failed to generate any excitement, is about to conclude with a pitiful whimper. Try as the public relations experts may to salvage some of the enormous expenditures in campaign funds prior to the war,

it can already be said at this late date that they have dismally failed.

It's not really their fault, either. I found a good indication of just how unconcerned the public is about local politics in these turbulent times, when I stopped passers-by in some of the streets of Tel Aviv's satellite towns. I asked them what they think about their candidates. Many knew who the present incumbents were merely because they have been there for a number of years. But most could not name their challengers, much less pinpoint the issues around which the campaign is being waged.

The question of whether peace will emerge from Geneva and fears that Israel may be sold

out there, overshadowed by far internal local affairs. The municipal campaigns had become dull sideshows which have gone largely ignored.

With everyone's attention focused on "Africa" and Geneva it's pretty hard to get excited about traffic congestion, urban development policy, garbage collection, litter-bugging, sewage unions, municipal parks and centre-of-town eyesores. "These should be our biggest problems," one Tel Avivian said to me recently with a wry smile and a loud sigh.

Funny, but not very long ago we really thought that they were.

friend blown up all over the battlefield. Frantic, he ran out and gathered up all the pieces of the body he could find. He wanted to be sure that his friend would be back together again, and would be accorded a decent burial. He would go to see his friend's mother and bring her her son's remains. He told me that the two of them had been standing together on the battlefield. A shell exploded and he had been clutching his friend's leg, when the boy was hit. He tugged at the leg, but his friend wasn't there. It was just the leg. Jacob was twenty-two; his friend was about the same."

Dale said Jacob had been obsessed with bringing back his friend's blown-off leg. She had sat appalled, and had listened in uncomprehending belief. "I know," said Jacob, "that he would have done the same for me." Still she hadn't quite understood. How can one comprehend another's brush with death?

Perhaps, Jacob was responding to some powerful subliminal tug. Orthodox Jews believe that some day there will be a resurrection, and that the bones of all the buried will arise from their graves, and will march, under God's command, to the land of Israel, and to the glory to come. Reared in that tradition, Jacob unconsciously reacted. He knew it was Orthodox custom to bury any dismembered parts of the body along with the corpse. Therefore, he had considered it his sacred duty to gather up as many parts of his friend's body as he could find. "He would have done the same for me," Jacob had told Dale.

French Socialist leader: 'Major political forces support Israel'

By MARK SEGAL

Jerusales Post Reporter

ROBERT Pontillon is Deputy Secretary of the French Socialist Party for international affairs and Chairman of the Middle East Committee of the Socialist International. Here on a visit, he is amazed that Israelis believe this country is isolated. "You must differentiate between governments' attitudes and that of the major political forces in various countries and broad public opinion."

Even in the European Economic Community, only the governments of France and the United Kingdom are against Israel, while the EEC as a whole is sympathetic, M. Pontillon explains. He notes that in a recent public opinion poll conducted in France, 70 per cent came out for Israel and against the French Government's line. As for the political parties — some 80-90 per cent of his Socialist Party were as close to Israel as they have always been. Even the Communist Party — with whom the Socialists have an electoral alignment — which usually clings to the Soviet line, has internal problems in regard to the Yom Kippur War, and he knows that many Communists were against the official party line.

The Centre Party — led by M. Lecanuet—is entirely pro-Israel. Inside the government itself there is disagreement with the Gaullist line. Independent Republicans or "the Giscairdists" (as they are known) are close to Israel, M. Pontillon says, and even many Gaullists are friendly. The majority of people in France feel closer to Israel than to others, he says.

Stressing M. Mitterrand's continuous interest in Israel, M. Pontillon revealed that last Thursday the French Socialist Party leader had written to the Ambassadors of the Soviet Union and Syria in Paris expressing his concern about the fate and treatment of Israeli prisoners of war in Syrian hands. The French public was suitably informed of the matter, he said. Moreover, M. Mitterand had refused to meet Col. Gaddafi during his state visit to France.

Arab contacts

M. Pontillon has good contacts in Arab capitals too, it turned out. He was in Egypt in September and just before coming here met a leading member of Sadat's Arab Socialist Union Party in Paris.

"It is my impression that there is much good will in Egypt for a peace settlement. They have acute internal problems... But you know the Arabs are often captives of their own declarations," he said, adding that in various spheres Egypt has fewer problems than other Arab countries.

Asked whether it was his impression that Sadat was sufficiently well-entrenched in power to make a settlement, the French Socialist believed that the Egyptian President was strong enough to do so and that he needed peace in order to solve his internal problems. Moreover, the military budget took up half the national resources as the Egyptians had to pay the Soviet Union for arms. It was also his impression that the Soviets were not very popular with the Egyptians, who seem to be aware of the high price they will have to pay for Soviet aid.

"It seems to me that the Egyptians wish to avoid being too close to either the Soviets or the Americans but wish to look to Europe as a third power."

A myopic sheikh toys with the fate of humanity

'GUNBOAT DIPLOMACY' IS NO ANACHRONISM

By Irving Kristol

IF it weren't so very sad, it would be funny. Rather like one of those pleasantly dotty British movies of yesteryear. One can see it now: Sir Alec Guinness playing the part of an obscure myopic Arab sheikh who, through a freak accident, and with the unwitting connivance of some frantic, intricate, and utterly self-defeating diplomacy by the Great Powers, is miraculously transformed into what German philosophers used to call "a world-historical figure," deciding the fate of nations and the future of the human race.

The movie would end happily, of course, with our unheroic hero bringing an unwonted reasonableness into the mad game of international power politics, thereby saving common men all over the world from the absurd manipulations of their governments. Alas, life never does imitate art quite so faithfully. King Faisal is surely a man of many qualities, but one may doubt he is up to filling this particular role.

The 20th century has witnessed more than its share of bizarre events, but the current oil crisis must rank near the top of the list. Here is a mini-power — in truth, a minuscule mini-power — which, in alliance with a few microscope sheikhdoms, is wrecking the economies of Western Europe and Japan, causing grave economic distress to the United States, and demanding that all of these populous and powerful nations reshape their foreign policies to suit its tastes.

> "The victims' response to blackmail makes Arab oil policy seem rational."

The question of whether these foreign policies are right or wrong is in this instance beside the point. What is at issue is not the relative merits of the Israel vs. the Arab case, but rather whether such nations as the United States, Japan,

Britain, France and Germany are, in any significant sense of the term, great powers at all. For if this kind of oil blackmail can be effective in the case of Israel, why can it not be equally effective with regard to other matters the Arab nations decide to get exercised about — say, the situation in Greece or the existence of American naval bases in such traditional areas of Arab concern as the Mediterranean or the Indian Ocean? It might be said that the present regime in Saudi Arabia is basically pro-Western and is not likely to engage in such hostile policies. True enough. But Arab regimes have a way of coming and going, and it is not so hard to imagine a King Faisal being succeeded by a Colonel Gaddafi. Meanwhile, of course, the oil and the potentiality of blackmail remain.

In all fairness to the Arabs, and to their unquestionable distress at the misadventures they have encountered on the battlefield, one can understand their yielding to the temptation to use oil as an instrument of foreign policy. One can understand it, that is *up to a point*. A little blackmail is nothing new in international politics; but there is such a thing as due proportion. If Saudi Arabia and those other sheikhdoms with such forgettable names had cut back *slightly* on oil deliveries so as to cause a degree of inconvenience to Europe, the U.S. and Japan — as a kind of reminder that Arab sensibilities were deserving of more attention than they were getting — that would be comprehensible. Or if they cut back oil outflow sharply *but temporarily*, that too would be the kind of symbolic action that would be comprehensible.

> "Smaller nations are not going to behave reasonably—unless it is costly to them to behave unreasonably"

What is not comprehensible is the apparent Arab belief that they have both the right and might to use their

oil to destroy the economies of Western Europe, the U.S. and Japan to "bring these countries to their knees," as the Arab press puts it. And what is least comprehensible of all is the apparent impotence of these same nations in the face of such extreme behavior. One would think the Arabs had taken leave of their senses were it not for the fact that their victims are responding in such a way as to make Arab policies seem so rational.

The relations among nations are governed by a few fragile covenants which we call international law, by some vague consensus of world opinion which we call international morality and, above all, by common sense. What is in violation of international law or morality is not always easy to say; clever lawyers and ingenious sophists can usually make a case for practically anything they set their minds to. Common sense, on the other hand, is a much clearer and surer guide. Thus, there is nothing in either international law or morality which prohibits the Russian fleet from sailing up and down our Eastern coast at a distance of, say, 30 miles. That it doesn't do any such thing — that such behavior is unthinkable — is a function of common sense; one great power does not behave in such a provocative way toward another unless it is eager to go to war.

It is essentially these same prudential considerations which govern the relations between great powers and smaller ones. Small powers do not flagrantly offend large powers lest they suffer some undesirable consequences. And a great power does not simply dictate to a smaller and weaker power because this would cause the latter to seek the protection of some other great power. This kind of prudential self-restraint, derived from common sense considerations, is — and always has been — the basis of international stability and world order, to the extent that they exist. It has also been — and will forever be — the basis of "the right to self-determination" by the small and the weak.

Obviously, this web of international relations imposes restraints — frequently irksome restraints — upon everyone. No nation is free to do exactly as it pleases. Capricious and arbitrary — or merely imprudent — actions run risks and exact penalties. No nation is even free to claim all of its "rights," though these be enshrined in various solemn documents of the United Nations. Finland is not going to exercise its theoretical right to join NATO, just as Cuba has not exercised its theoretical right to join the Warsaw Pact. The United States is not going to intervene in Argentina to protect the lives and property of American citizens there (though under international law it properly could); China is not going to intervene in Indonesia to protect the lives and property of Chinese citizens there. And so on and so on — that's what makes the world a livable place: common sense and prudence and self-restraint.

All of this would be so platitudinous as to be not worth the saying were it not for the fact that, over these past couple of decades, common sense in international affairs seems to be a commodity in ever shorter supply. This is especially true for the smaller nations, which have become extraordinarily careless and carefree in their behavior. To some extent this may be a consequence of the existence of the United Nations, where smaller powers have been given both voice and vote out of all proportion to their power. Insignificant nations, like insignificant people, can quickly experience delusions of significance when they read about themselves in the "New York Times." But more important, I should say, has been the legalistic-moralistic-"idealistic" mold into which American foreign policy was cast after World War II — an exercise in which both our "anti-imperialist" liberal establishment and that paragon of self-righteousness, John Foster Dulles, participated with immense enthusiasm.

It was as a consequence of this exercise, for example, that the idea of "aggression" was defined to encompass only the first movements of troops across a border — and, conversely, such a transgression of borders automatically came to be defined as "Aggression." Even textbooks in international law had never, up to that time, been so simpleminded, recognizing all sorts of circumstances in which "preemptive" or "retaliatory" military incursions were legitimate. It is because we insisted on being so absurdly simpleminded that there was such anguished debate in this country over the question of whether the Vietcong were acting as part of a "foreign" invasion of South Vietnam or were an indigenous group involved in a civil rebellion. A sillier controversy cannot be imagined, and only seemed to make sense because it was so widely assumed that the United States had no "right" to interfere in another country's civil war. But there is nothing inherently immoral

in not intervening. Besides, for a great power, non-intervention in a civil war elsewhere is as much an "active" policy as intervention — as anyone old enough to remember the Spanish civil war will affirm.

So far as the Middle East is concerned, the key event was Suez, 1956. By any common sense reckoning, and even by traditional articles of international law, Britain, France and Israel had every right to occupy the Suez Canal — an international waterway—and reopen it to international traffic. True, Egypt "owned" the canal, just as Saudi Arabia "owns" its oil. But ownership confers obligations as well as rights — including the obligation not to abuse one's rights of ownership to the extreme detriment of others. Where this obligation is not voluntarily recognized, such recognition may be properly imposed. That was sufficient justification for the Suez expedition.

Moreover, it was foreseeable even then that, if "canal blackmail" were tolerated, "oil blackmail" would surely follow. As "The Times" of London said in an editorial on August 1, 1956: "If Nasser is allowed to get away with his *coup* all the British and Western interests in the Middle East will crumble... The great oil works and fields of the Middle East are one of the main foundations of Britain's and Western Europe's industry and security. Anyone who thinks that a victory for Nasser would not encourage other extremist demands against the oilfields — and against strategic bases — should confine himself to tiddlywinks or blind man's buff."

> "Gunboat diplomacy is anachronistic today, and not very effective in the end."
> ——"Time"

Had the expedition been successful, there probably would not have been any Arab-Israeli wars in 1967 or in 1973, and there would be no oil boycott today. And it would have been successful had we not intervened against it. The Russians, at that time, could not have intervened if they had wanted to; and it is by no means clear that the Soviet government — which has a keen appreciation of other nations' interests — really wanted to. It was our decision that was crucial. And we deserted our allies while reading them a sermon. The days of "gunboat diplomacy" were over, we piously (and hypocritically) told them. We forgot to tell them that

the days of "oil diplomacy" were about to begin.

In truth, the days of "gunboat diplomacy" are never over. (The Russians understand this, which is why they are busy building so many of them.) Gunboats are as necessary for international order as police cars are for domestic order. Smaller nations are not really worried about American atom bombs, any more than the Mafia is. And smaller nations are not going to behave reasonably — with a decent respect for the interests of others, including the great powers — unless it is costly to them to behave unreasonably. In 1956, the United States in effect took away Europe's gunboats. We didn't substitute our own — we just decided that gunboats were an anachronism in our enlightened and progressive era. Now, we are vexed at the "contemptible" way — I am quoting a very high State Department official — in which our European allies are succumbing to Arab blackmail. It is indeed contemptible. But it is not so clear we have earned the right to say so.

Mr. Kristol is Henry Luce Professor of Urban Values at New York University and co-editor of the quarterly, "The Public Interest."

Events beyond Anwar Sadat's control forced a drastic revision of his original scenario for a Middle East peace conference. The choice before the Egyptian President now is to renew hostilities — in the hope of realizing his war aims — or to settle for a genuine compromise in Geneva. DANIEL DISHON examines the chances of Sadat's opting for a compromise.

SADAT AND GENEVA

THE FIRST plenary session of the Geneva Peace Conference has met. The ritual speeches of the public opening ceremony have been made. Procedures for the next stages were agreed upon behind closed doors. The diplomats have now taken time off and left it to the military negotiators to continue, in the solemn surroundings of the Palais des Nations, where they left off in the wind-blown tent on the Cairo-Suez road.

In the breathing space between the ceremonial and the substantive phase at Geneva, it is worthwhile turning back for a moment to examine what we know of the scenario the Egyptians originally had in mind for the conference. For this, we have the evidence of two major occasions: Sadat's one wartime speech (October 16) and the Algiers summit conference (November 27-28).

Sadat's speech is of special significance because it was made at what he considered the height of his success. On October 16 the IDF was already across the Canal and had initiated the movement which was to reverse the fortunes of war on the southern front. But Sadat was as yet unaware of the gravity of the threat. The speech thus unfolded Sadat's thinking in its pure state, as it were; it set forth what, at that moment of apparent triumph, he expected to be translated into reality. We are therefore entitled to regard it as particularly revealing and authentic.

The speech contained a five-point "peace programme" which said:

1. "We are fighting, and shall fight, in order to liberate the areas occupied by Israel since 1967, and to find a way to restore the legitimate rights of the Palestinians. In this matter (i.e., the matter of the Palestinians), we cling to our obligations under the resolutions of the U.N., whether of the Assembly or the Security Council."

2. "We are ready to accept a cease-fire on the basis of Israel's immediate withdrawal from all occupied territories..."

3. "We are ready, after the completion of total withdrawal from the said areas, to participate in an international peace conference at the U.N..."

4. Egypt is ready to take immediate measures to clear the Suez Canal.

5. Egypt rejects all "vague promises" or "flexible definitions" (an allusion to the contradictory interpretations of Security Council Resolution 242).

The salient points here are the following:

● Withdrawal to the lines of June 4, 1967, is the automatic right of the Arabs. It is not a matter for discussion (the peace conference is to start only *after* withdrawal is completed), nor do the Arabs owe Israel a political price in return for it. According to this scenario, Israel's "reward" for withdrawal is not peace, not even a settlement including security arrangements or a declaration of non-belligerency, but only a cease-fire. (So much for those who argued that, between 1967 and 1973, Israel could have had either territories or peace. Obviously, the choice was between "territories but not peace" or "no territories, but no peace either.")

● Since withdrawal would be completed before the peace conference convened, the only possible subject left to be discussed at it would be Egypt's second war aim: the restoration of the right of the Palestinians. Withdrawal to the 1967 lines would satisfy the formal claims of the neighbouring states. In order to satisfy the Palestinians, too, the area of Israel would have to be narrowed once again. This would be the task of the conference.

Sadat's reference, in this context, to the U.N. resolution on Palestine, reveals that he is thinking of the partition boundaries as laid down by the U.N. in 1947. Even these however, would only be a staging post on a road of which at least two further stations have been mentioned by Egypt. One is the long-standing argument that Eilat and the Southern Negev do not belong to Israel (because they were taken possession of *after* the 1949 armistice agreements). The other, more novel idea (proposed to the Palestinians by Cairo's "Al-Ahram" on November 3) is to take up the cause of the Israeli Arabs — presumably in a manner similar to the use made of the Sudeten Germans for the dismemberment of Czechoslovakia in 1938-39.

THE SECOND of Egypt's war aims, that of "restoring the rights of the Palestinians" was reformulated — in more extreme terms — at the Algiers summit.

The Algiers resolution does not speak, as Sadat did on October 16 of the "legitimate rights" of the Palestinians (i.e., those anchored in the 1947 partition resolution) but of their "national rights." Presumably, this means that the people called Palestinian has the "national right" to all of the country called Palestine. If, however, there were any doubts about how to interpret the difference between "legitimate" and "national" rights, these were resolved by two further statements made at the summit by the Secretary-General of the Arab League, the former Egyptian Foreign Minister Mahmud Riyad: that Yassir Arafat's Palestine Liberation Organization (PLO) was to be the only legal representative of the Palestinians; and that the exact meaning of "the rights of the Palestinians" would be defined by the PLO.

The PLO's definition is perfectly well known. It is laid down in the Palestinian National Covenant of July 16, 1968, which speaks of "Palestine in the boundaries that existed at the time of the British Mandate" as the "homeland of the Palestinian Arab people" and states that "the establishment of Israel is fundamentally null and void."

The stages of Egypt's original scheme were thus: a) an Israeli withdrawal from the 1967 territories in return for a cease-fire; b) withdrawal from the 1967 to the 1947 border lines, in return, presumably, for some promise of non-belligerency; c) "restoration of the rights of the Palestinians" *as defined by the PLO*.

Thus peace would be achieved; not, indeed, peace with Israel but, rather, a peaceful Middle East with no Israel to disturb any Arab mind.

SO MUCH for the original scenario. It is a measure of the IDF's success in turning the military tide that the process envisaged by Sadat only ten weeks ago has been rendered illusory on every count. Neither the present cease-fire nor the Geneva conference fits his prescription; the Suez Canal can still not be reopened without a move by Israel; and the ambiguities of Resolution 242 hang over the Geneva conference as much as they did over Jarring's mission.

These departures from the original script were brought about by the imperatives of the military situation. Egypt has shown sufficient tactical flexibility to adjust to the new si-

tuation, different though it is from Sadat's triumphant presentation in mid-October. But is this a matter of tactical shifts only, with the ultimate aims remaining as they were? Or has the wartime euphoria been recognized as such and have the sights been lowered accordingly?

At the moment of writing, it seems too early to say. Conceivably, the Egyptians still believe that they hold cards strong enough to steamroller Israel into complete withdrawal on political terms, and under security conditions, which would not make it too difficult to move on to further stages of Israel's gradual dismemberment. The combination of Soviet support, all-Arab backing (including the wielding of the oil weapon), Israel's assumed fear of another war, her diplomatic isolation, her internal dissent, and America's desire to get back into the Arabs' good graces — all these, as assessed by Egypt, may well nourish the hope that developments may still take the course originally charted, though perhaps more slowly than expected. Certainly there was no word in Fahmy's speech to hint at the contrary.

Yet, the moment must inevitably come, at some stage or another of the Geneva conference, when Sadat will have to realize that the original scenario is not being followed: Israel has not been weakened that much (either militarily or in its determination to survive); the oil weapon may back-fire; diplomatic pressure has its limits; the U.S. will not wish to co-author a script of this kind; the steamroller will come to a halt. The really crucial question about Geneva is not so much what the Egyptians wanted in the first place as what they will decide to do when they realize that they cannot have what t h e y wanted.

FORGOING ANY further attempt at prophecy, at least for the time being, I should like merely to set out the alternatives and dilemmas which will then face Egypt.

The basic choice will be between renewing hostilities with the object of realizing the original war aims, or settling for a compromise.

The decision to go to war again may well prove even harder in the future than it did in the past. Just as the IDF knew after 1967 that a strategic *coup* of the kind which caused the elimination of the Arab air forces in three hours could not be repeated, so the Egyptian command must now realize that it cannot expect to achieve real strategic surprise a second time. Furthermore, the international situation may not

again be so favourable and the presence of U.N.E.F. may cause some embarrassment.

Against this, however, there is the lesson drawn by Egyptian War Minister Ahmad Ismail Ali (in an interview with Mohammed Hassanein Heykal after the war) that a meticulously planned and well-rehearsed operation will indeed succeed. There will also be the memory of how close Egypt came to a major victory in October. So why not try again — a little harder?

Compromise produces difficulties of another kind: if it involves territorial compromise, it will create Egyptian domestic opposition; if it involves compromise over the status of the Palestinians, it will weaken Egypt's inter-Arab standing and expose her to charges of having betrayed the all-Arab cause. Egypt's first aim must therefore be to disguise the nature of any compromise solution by not calling it a settlement, let alone peace. In order to be acceptable, it must be described as "provisional."

SUCH A SETTLEMENT can take two forms: a partial settlement which gives each Arab participant some limited satisfaction in return for partial security arrangements (demilitarized areas, U.N. buffer zones, etc.); or a settlement which in effect comes close to a separate solution of the Egyptian-Israeli dispute to the exclusion of the others.

Is a separate, Israeli-Egyptian, solution then the more probable? Some indications point that way. At every turn during and since the war, Egypt has in fact acted according to the narrow Egyptian national interest, without consulting her Arab allies and backers, and has then sent out special emissaries to explain the steps already taken. This is true of the acceptance of the cease-fire, of the decision in principle to resume diplomatic relations with the U.S., and of the very mention of a peace conference in Sadat's speech on October 16.

A merry Christmas for Jamil Shalhoub

By YA'ACOV FRIEDLER
Jerusalem Post Reporter

HAIFA. — It was a really merry Christmas for Jamil Shalhoub, yesterday morning. He, his wife and their six children were celebrating the Greek Orthodox feast by the illuminated Christmas tree in their spacious Hadar Hacarmel flat, when I informed him that he had been elected to the City Council. He is the first Arab Councillor here since 1948.

The smiling, stoutish, 45-year-old lawyer, who got his degree from the Hebrew University in 1959 and speaks fluent Hebrew, was elected on the Alignment ticket although he is not a party

Jamil Shalhoub

member. The soldiers' votes, counted on Sunday night had given the Alignment its fifteenth seat and brought Mr. Shalhoub into the Council.

Born in Haifa to a family of Lebanese descent, he has many relatives in Syria, where one, Dr. George Shalhoub, was a cabinet minister in 1959; in the Lebanon, where some are members of the Greek Orthodox clergy, and in Egypt. The Egyptian film star, Omar Sharif, is a second cousin, he told me.

Mr. Shalhoub said he felt he had a double task to carry out on the Council — as a resident of Haifa to help the city develop and regain its pre-1948 importance, and as an Arab to help improve the living and education standards of the Arab community. And combining the two, to cement "the good Jewish-Arab relations in Haifa, and impress on those Arabs, and Jews too, who still have doubts, that the Arab citizens are citizens of the State of Israel, in every sense of the word."

He considered Haifa "the capital of the Arab residents of the northern part of the country, where 60 per cent of all Israeli Arabs live. Haifa is geographically close to Jenin and Nablus, and their merchants should deal with Haifa and not with Tel Aviv or Netanya." He would also work for the development of trade and tourism in Haifa.

He noted that Haifa has some 22,000 Arab residents of whom 7,000 voted. Of these about 2,700 voted for the Rakah New Communists, ("Thanks to Shalhoub, Rakah lost many Arab votes to the Alignment in Haifa," a young Arab who had come to wish him a merry Christmas told me;) and over 300 for the Likud. "That means that 4,000 voted for the Alignment and put their trust in me. I hope not to disappoint them."

The most urgent task was to assure decent housing and living conditions for those Arabs still living in "sub-standard and crowded conditions" in Wadi Tini, Halissah and Wadi Nisnas. He suggests that a big high-rise building be built in Wadi Nisnas, complete with shops and community facilities, in which practically all the wadi residents might be housed. He would also try to assure housing for young couples and large families among the Arab residents in the public housing schemes built for the purposes.

THANKS TO THE DUTCH

Hundreds of boys and girls will distribute orange-shaped lapel tabs to passersby in the main cities today, in another gesture of friendship to the Dutch people.

The tab shows a windmill and the slogan, "The Israeli People Admire the Dutch Nation." The distribution is sponsored by the Public Committee for Appreciation of the Dutch Nation, in conjunction with the B'nai B'rith youth movement.

Ismail: 'We've got 'em cornered'

CAIRO (UPI). — War Minister Gen. Ahmed Ismail said yesterday the Israelis have placed themselves "in a corner" by establishing a bridgehead on the Suez Canal's west bank during the October war.

"No man in his senses could have launched this operation because he voluntarily placed himself in a corner," Ismail said.

The general, who is commander-in-chief of the armed forces, was addressing a group of Egyptian emigrants who came to Cairo for their Christmas holiday.

Ismail said Egyptian troops were surrounding the Israelis from all directions on the Canal's west bank.

"Any pressure on the Israeli bulge will make it collapse," Ismail said.

"I would like to assure you that the enemy forces are in trouble, not us," he told the emigrants.

He said the Israelis suffered great losses in men and equipment during offensives across the Canal, but continued the attack "because it was a psychological more than a strategic or military operation."

Ismail denied Israeli claims that the Egyptians were assisted by Soviet advisers during the planning or execution of the October war.

"We were assisted by no one," he said. "There were no Soviet experts or troops with us during the planning or execution of these operations."

Addressing the same gathering, Maj.-Gen. Hassan el-Greitly, the army's chief of operations, said Egyptian troops now are fighting a war of attrition.

Israeli reservists continue to be mobilized, and this is having an adverse effect on the Israeli economy, he said. "We do not want the enemy to escape from this situation.

"What we are doing now is the attrition of the enemy, because for us the war has not ended at all," he said.

The fact that Egypt is taking part in the Geneva Peace Conference has no effect at all on the armed forces, he said.

"Our mission is to liberate occupied lands and, in our view, this can only be accomplished by force," he said. "We are awaiting the order to complete our mission."

In his one-hour address, Ismail said token forces from Algeria, Morocco, Tunisia, Kuwait and Sudan took part with the Egyptians in the October war.

Marksmen deployed to hit Egyptian snipers

Jerusalem Post Reporter

TEL AVIV. — The army has deployed snipers on the Suez Canal front to pick off Egyptian snipers who have been shooting Israeli soldiers during the ceasefire, the army weekly "Bamahaneh" disclosed this week.

After the Egyptians made a nationwide appeal for expert marksmen to volunteer their services on the front line, the army called out its own highly trained snipers (who served with the infantry during the war). These men are charged with picking off Egyptian snipers.

Two of the Israeli snipers were interviewed in "Bamahaneh." They noted that the Egyptian snipers prefer a lone soldier as their target, and always aim for his head.

The snipers are usually well hidden — in a treetop or an abandoned building, for instance — and rarely venture more than a single shot.

"The trick is to fire and vanish," one Israeli sniper said. "The muzzle flash might give you away, and one must always assume he is facing at least his equal."

A sniper's job demands patience and composure, the two told "Bamahaneh." He must detach himself completely from his environment as he observes his target — often for long hours on end — and wait for a chance to take his shot. Since his target is an enemy sniper, he will only get a very brief view of that part of the Egyptian's head which he sticks out just as he is about to take his own shot, they said.

ORT: STRIVING TO KEEP AHEAD

Helga Dudman

IT IS BY NOW a cliche that, in facing Arab armies, we have always relied on a "training gap" — the fact that the individual Israeli has a far higher level of technical competence and resourcefulness than the individual Arab, and that this is the k e y to our security in the face of overwhelming numerical superiority in manpower and equipment.

Cliche or not, "the last w a r proved this to be true, as never before," the Director of Ort in Israel, Mr. Joseph Harmatz, told me recently. "We must prepare ourselves for increasingly sophisticated military technology. And we are already doing so."

At the same time, he warned, "But we are also finding out how poor we are — poor, among other things, in really modern teaching equipment. We just don't have the money for it."

Mr. Harmatz has a first-hand opportunity to evaluate developments in military equipment, since Ort's diversified training programmes include those in which students — and, of course, graduates — are assigned to the army's technical branches. The results are more than interesting. Thus, anybody in a position to compare the design of an American tank with that of a Russian one will see that the former is built with the welfare of its occupants in mind: it is roomier, more comfortable, rides m o r e smoothly, and thought has been given to such matters as soundproofing. But all this is at a certain cost of military effectiveness. For instance, the American tank — vis-a-vis the comparable Russian opposite number — is heavier and taller, which makes it an easier target, especially on a desert plateau.

Optical sights provide another example of the difference between Russian and Western concepts of military design. Those made in America are highly accurate, but require calculations by the men using them. By contrast, sighting devices manufactured by the Russians involve only a simple act of lining up the target, but are less accurate. What they lack in accuracy is made up for by the quantities used.

"The Egyptian and Russian concepts of men and equipment — the view that both are expendable, and are available in great numbers — turn out to be well suited to each other. It is an appropriate partnership," said Mr. Harmatz. (Incidentally, the name "Ort" comes from the Russian; it is an acronym for the Russian "Society for the Promotion of Handicrafts, Industry and Agriculture," and the organization, which is now an international one, was founded in Russia in 1880. But Ort's outlook today is purely Western, with stress on a high level of individual training and competence.)

SO MUCH FOR the philosophical viewpoint, which emerges logically from the daily work of Ort in Israel — running a chain of technical high schools and colleges, f a c t o r y and apprenticeship centres and programmes, and adult training courses now involving over 40,000 students. T h e Ort network is, of course, only one aspect of the country's vocational education, which also includes Amal, Youth Aliya, t h e armed services' technical schools, and so on.

During the recent war, as often reported at the time, the country's vocational school students, from all these streams, performed many jobs on the industrial front. The 1967 call-up regulations permit mobilization of second- and third-year vocational students (but not — and this may come as a surprise — senior students in regular academic high schools).

Of the 25,000 11th- and 12th-grade students in the vocational schools throughout the country, 15,000 were found suitable for needed jobs, and of these, 5,000 were actually sent to factories and other establishments, to replace regular workers who h a d been called up by their army units. (These figures do not include efforts by other students within other frameworks, such as Gadna or direct volunteer work.)

"With all the criticism of things that went wrong, it is perhaps overlooked that industry continued to run very well," said Mr. Harmatz. "The productive sector worked beautifully. W h a t broke down was transportation." For example, in an essential area such as electricity, "the Electric Corporation had hundreds of its men called up. Their jobs were filled in some cases by retired workers, but also by third- and fourth-year technical students. And as everybody knows, there were no breakdowns."

Golda is 'Sun's'
Woman of the Year

LONDON (INA). — The newspaper "Sun" devotes an entire page to a profile of Golda Meir, whom it names as the 'Sun's' "Woman of the Year."

The profile says: "No woman alive has done more to earn this description. Like the late Pope John, Golda was first described as a caretaker, a temporary expedient, but turned out to be something very much more. She started off as a footnote and ended up as the 'Title of the Book'."

The 'Sun' continued: "The battle she fought in October was the gravest of her life, surrounded as she was by brilliant but acrimonious generals. There were blunders. Golda may be held responsible for them. But this old lady has survived — and so has Israel. Who else could be our Woman of the Year?"

In the U.S., Mrs. Meir has been named the "most admired" woman of 1973 in the annual poll taken by the Gallup organization. She received more than twice as many votes as the next highest woman, Mrs. Pat Nixon, wife of the President. Mrs. Meir was first in the poll in 1971 and second last year.

Youth Aliya students training at the electronic laboratory at an Ort school.

Even
a responsible
Government
can err

But
to elect
an irresponsible
Government
is to err inexcusably

Support the cause
of peace and security

THE EVENTS
OF YOM KIPPUR...

THE EVENTS OF YOM KIPPUR — make it essential to introduce correct procedures for government, ensure that decision making is democratic, that parliamentary control of government is observed, and that disaster-fraught kitchen politics are avoided. In short, we must have a written constitution.

THE EVENTS OF YOM KIPPUR — indicate the need for retrenchment and economy in government and public institutions, the limiting of government spending for nonsecurity purposes, reform of the tax system, and the prevention of favouritism and discrimination.

THE EVENTS OF YOM KIPPUR—Call for a just distribution of the economic burden between those called up and those at home, the rehabilitation of the businesses of those called up, special priorities, incorporated in a law, for released soldiers, the call up of yeshiva students, who are at present excused army service, and the introduction of service in a labour corp for young women who do not serve in the army.

THE INDEPENDENT LIBERALS
WILL FIGHT FOR THIS

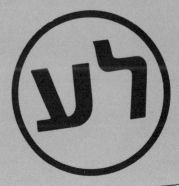

Fringe parties fight for votes

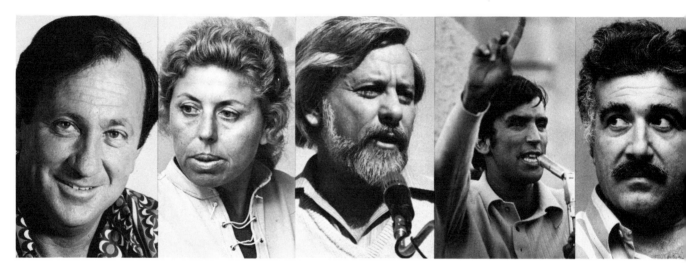

PE'IL   ALONI   AVNERI   MALKA   COHEN

MOKED, CIVIL RIGHTS, MERI, AND TWO PANTHER LISTS

By MARK SEGAL
Jerusalem Post Political Reporter

ALTHOUGH the main political parties have dominated the media in the short but bitter 1973 election campaign, several smaller lists on the fringes are fighting hard for the voters' support.

The newest of them all is the Civil Rights list of Shulamit Aloni; our interview took place in the bustling if tiny rooms of the office of Ram Ron, former Israel Military Attache to Washington near the Tel Aviv Sheraton Hotel which is the Civil Rights List campaign headquarters. Mr. Ron is third on the list.

Mrs. Aloni is in good fighting mettle, and she needs it. Lacking money and a machine, she has to travel up and down the country, addressing meetings, sometimes three a day, and is thankful for the understanding shown by her husband and two teenage sons.

She is indignant that the Central Elections Committee decided to keep her name off the ballot slips. Thus soldier voters may not link her voting symbol *resh-tsadi* with her name. "This is another case of the dictatorship of the majority," she says, noting that the present election system (she linked Avraham Ofer and Menahem Bader) is structured to keep out any new force.

She accuses the two main parties of waging dishonest campaigns — "Neither has told the voter which leadership they are choosing ... The Alignment insults the voters' intelligence with its gimmicks. What's this Alignment attack on 'the punishing voter'? Do they mean that the thief should get a prize because he did not murder?

"I tell the voters — help me to help others. We have to fight this system which perpetuates flattery of the powerful, dependence and protektzia. We have to retrieve our old values of integrity from the corrupting influence of this regime, with the individual citizen facing a huge bureaucracy," she says.

A most active group on her behalf is the Electoral Reform Movement (one of its leaders, Dr. Boaz Moav, is candidate No. 2) and if, as she hopes, they win one or more Knesset seats, then her faction will open a citizen's advice bureau at the Knesset with regular receiving hours, as well as regional bureaux. Women's rights will also be one of her interests. Her group favours a dovish foreign policy, tending toward Deputy Premier Allon's view in security matters.

THIS is the third election campaign for Meri-Haolam Hazeh chairman Uri Avneri. When we met in a busy cafe near his Tel Aviv editorial offices, he said he was confident that his reputation as a fighting Knesset member — "as the ombudsman for the people" — had been established.

"I missed only three meetings in my eight years in the Knesset. I have an attendance record ten times better than the average M.K."

But what exercises him now is the question of peace. "We are the peace party, and suddenly we are reading our slogans in the propaganda of other parties. The Alignment, the Independent Liberals and Moked are borrowing our old slogans. When we used to talk of the Palestinians, we were accused of being traitors. I did not enter politics to become only a Knesset member but to further my ideas and if others accept them, I should be happy. But I don't believe them."

Mr. Avneri says 80 per cent of his constituency is now in the army. "We appeal to young, male Israelis just like our magazine, and I think the war has brought many young Israelis to press for peace. After all, the magazine was set up by a group of combat soldiers from the 1948 war."

Asked why he did not combine with Moked, Mr. Avneri blames Meir Pe'il, the No. 1 Moked candidate. "After the war I offered a united peace front and even a surplus vote pool arrangement, but Moked preferred to pool votes with the Black Panthers — and conceal it from their voters."

Mr. Avneri claims Moked is "a typical Communist front effort." To judge by their advertisements, no one would know that their second candidate is that old Stalinist, Maki Secretary-General Shmuel Mikunis, who defended the Slansky trial in the 1950s."

Mr. Avneri claims that Maki is subsidised indirectly by the government, and is used by the Foreign Ministry abroad. Moreover, he charges, Maki is cleverly using Mr. Pe'il to obtain legitimacy and to further their design of eventually joining the Alignment.

Explaining the Meri-Haolam Hazeh slogan "a vote for us is a net vote for peace," Mr. Avneri says if someone votes for the Alignment then "theoretically a third goes to Dayan, a third to the doves and a third to the opportunists. A vote for Moked is half and half. One does not know where Maki will end up, they are so busy trying to get into the Alignment at any cost. If you vote for Shulamit Aloni — well admittedly she did good things in the Sixth Knesset, but nothing about peace. But for us it's 100 per cent for peace."

Mr. Avneri explained : "In practical terms, our vote will not be passive concerning the next government. We will enable the Alignment doves to get rid of Golda and Dayan. I told the Russians and the Arabs at Geneva that they have to strengthen Eban and the doves."

THE head of Moked is a former army colonel. Meir Pe'il at 47 is a popular figure among the left. Entering politics full-time after he was dropped from the Tel Aviv University history faculty, Pe'il brought together five New Left groups drawn mainly from ex-Mapam dissidents like Ran Cohen of Kibbutz Gan Shmuel, almost all of Kibbutz Kerem Shalom and Dan Leon, senior aide to World Zionist Information head Avraham Shenkar. It was named "Blue-Red." He opted for an alliance with the Israel Communist Party, calling it Moked, but Mr. Pe'il says, "they are communists only in name having left the Soviet church years ago." (He vigorously denies the story that he is committed to switch with Mr. Mikunis in two years' time if Moked wins only one seat.)

They refused to join forces with Meri-Haolam Hazeh, mainly because they object to Mr. Avneri, but also because that party is not socialist.

Maki's new ideologist, Raoul Teitelbaum, believes that Moked has taken the "place in the leftist political spectrum vacated by Mapam. Both Mr. Pe'il and Mr. Teitelbaum speak of swinging support behind the doves in the Alignment, specifically Lyova Eliav and Yitzhak Ben-Aharon.

"We will be a ginger group in the Knesset," Mr. Pe'il says. The Moked leader would willingly support a government headed by Pinhas Sapir. "He is a pragmatic man, although I distrust his pro-capitalist tendencies. But he is a practical man and will swing the apparatus our way, if we have sufficient influence." But Mr. Pe'il denied they had made a deal with the Alignment.

He denounces Premier Meir and Defence Minister Dayan, for what he calls 'their irresponsible approach" on the prisoners issue.

"When the Syrians say they want to exchange the Golan Heights for prisoners, they should have shut up and not said we are going to build more settlements on the Golan. Sapir was also wrong to talk about building a city there."

The mention of Moshe Dayan's name makes him mad. Pe'il left the army six years ago bitter at the army's bureaucratization, which, he said, causes a brain drain. "The best minds have left. The average regular army officer is below the national average. This has to be radically changed." He claims that his army career was hampered by his membership in Mapam and the fact that his brother, Oded Pilevsky, is a leader of Matzpen.

"No one said anything specifically about these points, but I know it for sure."

SHALOM Cohen, head of the Israeli Democrats-Panthers, claims to be a crusader for the forgotten poor.

"Geneva is a long way away. The social problems have not simply gone away. For us this is the main issue. As the emergency period lengthens, so the ranks of the poor have grown. The big families whose breadwinners are in the army get only IL600 to IL700 a month, and prices have jumped. These are the new poor, and there is no one who cares about them. Thus they come to us."

Mr. Cohen's group has no money, as is evident from their offices in a run-down building near Tel Aviv's central bus station. Despite all the odds, they made a remarkable showing in the Histadrut elections especially in such immigrant towns as Beersheba and Acre where they now have influence on local Labour Councils.

Most of his supporters are now in the army, he says. This compounded the difficulties of the election campaign, because his list lacks the money for much newspaper advertising — the main channel of reaching the troops. But above all his list forfeited the fireworks that drew attention and votes in the Histadrut election campaign.

"We have abandoned street demonstrations and anything likely to lead to clashes with the police. The nation is mobilized, and the old headline-catching technique is not acceptable today."

The IL100,000 his list gets through state financing has gone on deposits for 27 municipal lists: "So you see we are certainly here to stay as a movement."

Mr. Cohen says his group is challenging Gahal's traditional strongholds in the oriental quarters of the cities, and the Alignment in development towns. This, he said, explains the large amount of money spent on advertising by the competing "Blue-White Panthers" of Eddie Malka, "who was bankrupt just before the elections. And his second candidate, Cochavi Shemesh, we chucked out after he went with Rakah to the East Berlin Communist Youth Festival."

Eddie Malka in turn heads a separate Panther List which he says are the true Black Panthers and he charges Cohen with having sold-out to the Alignment. Malka promises to continue the Panther struggle for the disadvantaged either inside the Knesset (if elected) or outside if they fail to get a seat.

For many people, the *chutzpah* of the Israeli Democrats-Panthers is characterized by their choice of the letter "zayin" as their election symbol. Mr. Cohen notes with a smile: "No one dared pick that letter all these years. We took it because this showed we were challenging Israeli society. We took a dare or if you wish cocked a snook at the established pattern of things here."

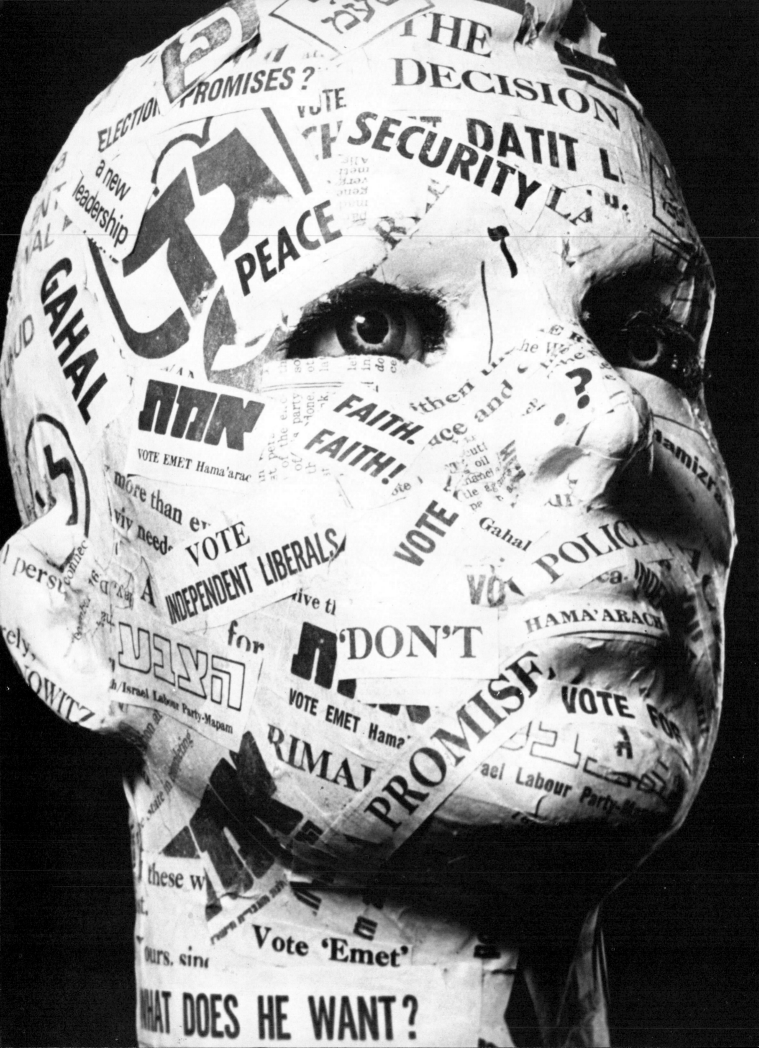

THE POLITICAL SYSTEM in Israel is rather confusing to most Americans. The electoral system, based on proportional representation, is meant to insure minorities some voice in the government. In contrast to the essentially two-party system which prevails in the United States, the political system in Israel is multi-partied. This sometimes results in the formation of a cumbersome and altogether unwieldy cabinet with conflicting interests which would seem to inhibit rather than to promote the smooth management of the State. Nevertheless, Israel's Founders felt that it was necessary in a democratic society that minorities be represented in the government.

In the last general election, held on December 31, 1973, 2,037,478 voters were eligible to cast ballots. Of this number, approximately 79 per cent went to the polls, a rather high percentage of the eligible voters by any standard. These voters had a choice of opting for any of 21 different parties, parties which ranged through an entire spectrum of political beliefs.

The majority party formerly in power, and the largest in Israel, is known as the "Labor-Mapam Alignment." In the December 1973 election, they received over 600,000 votes, thereby becoming entitled to 51 seats in the 120-seat legislative body called the Knesset.

The Labor-Mapam party is socialistic in orientation. Heretofore, the Labor-Mapam had espoused a policy of no compromise with regard to the administered areas captured from the Arabs during the 1967 War. However, in this election, the party went on record as favoring "territorial compromises," calling for peace through negotiation, and for recognition of the national identity of the Palestinian and Jordanian Arabs. This was a drastic change in program. Evidently, the Yom Kippur War had made a dent in some of the intransigent attitudes which Labor had so stubbornly clung to during the past six years.

The ads of the Alignment appear in this volume bearing the indicia of Emet and Maarach, two components of this group.

The second largest bloc of votes was gathered by the Likud, a coalition group which had scathingly chastised the majority government for its failure to call out the Reserves and move armor up to the fronts to meet the surprise Arab attack of October 6. The Likud was bitterly critical of the operation not only of the Army, but of the intelligence service as well.

Although Likud claimed to be willing to effect some territorial compromise, it was the party furthest to the right and opposed "the renewed partition of the Land of Israel." This, in effect, meant that it opposed any withdrawal from the Jordan River borderline. Moreover, Likud stood fast in opposing unwarranted concessions to the Arabs. It pointed out repeatedly that had the borders demanded by the Arabs existed when the Yom Kippur War started, Israel would have been overrun. It also recalled in ringing terms that the promises of the Arabs were not to be trusted, citing the evidence that when the last cease-fire was put into effect after the 1967 War, and the line of demarcation had been set, the Arabs almost immediately advanced their missile sites in blatant defiance of the treaty they had just signed. These violations were reported by American army observers at the time. Despite representations made to both the Russians and the Egyptians, these SAM movements were not rolled back.

Prior to the election, I participated in many parlor discussions with respected burghers who had lived most of their lives in Israel. Some of these were men of property, others were professionals, but all were thinking, responsible citizens. In the talk about the internal political future of Israel, I was surprised to hear so many sober individuals express their deep disappointment with the majority party and their desire for change. Some were now switching their votes to Likud, asserting it was simply time to try a new group. True, some citizens wouldn't vote for Likud because they felt they couldn't put the government in the hands of the extremist Menahem Begin who adamantly insisted that no concessions at all be made to the Arabs. But all, without exception, agreed that the government had failed them, that there had been an unnecessary loss of life and an unnecessary loss of prestige. They felt that their leaders had become complacent. This was the word that was used over and over again. It was felt that the government had been in power so long that it had become somewhat shortsighted and somewhat rigid. All felt that the times required leaders with a new vision and a new voice.

Gahal is one of the component groups of the Likud coalition.

The third largest political party in Israel is the Mafdal National Religious Party which, in the last election, gathered better than 130,000 votes, thereby securing 10 seats in the Knesset. This group represents orthodox religious interests. Its expressed goal is the realization of Israel's historic rights to the whole of the Land of Israel, the

SABBATH—No Publication

Volunteer from England picking oranges in a kibbutz grove.

A SMILE FROM COPENHAGEN

AT THE beginning of November *The Jerusalem Post* published a somewhat bitter piece of mine entitled, "We've Lost the World's Sympathy Again," in which I apologized for having once wrongly suggested that the world would love us only provided we put our heads on the chopping-block.

"One of the harshest lessons of the Yom Kippur War," I wrote there, "is that we won't manage to win people's sympathy and understanding even by being beaten. More than that: the worse our situation, the more obviously just our cause, the lonelier we stand — the more ready they are to sell us out."

The piece was reprinted in a number of papers abroad, and the replies I received from foreign readers included one by a Danish lawyer from Copenhagen, who made an inspired attempt to explain the way things look to a small and shivery nation in northern Europe.

The letter, signed by my correspondent with his full name and address, runs as follows:

"Dear Sir of the Israeli Press!

I have been a fervent admirer of the Jewish People for a long time, which is the reason why I'm taking the trouble to write these lines sitting in an unheated flat early in the morning when I'd rather have stayed lazily in my warm bed. If I'm writing to you all the same it's because I have a feeling you need me.

"Now then, you say you've lost the world's sympathy again, and that everybody's mad at you for having been attacked. With all

respect, I don't see how you can offer such a dubious claim. To begin with, you couldn't have lost the sympathy of all those African states because you never had it. That bunch care for nobody but their own selves, and if anyone had illusions otherwise then I'm surprised at him, to say the least.

"Britain and France, on the other hand, took exactly the stand you expected of them, so there again you didn't lose anything except the good manners which have gone by the board in Europe long since. And I hope you're not seriously claiming you lost the sympathy of the U.S.S.R., etcetera, etcetera the world round.

"As for my own little country, Denmark, the latest public opinion polls show that 83 per cent of its population sympathize with Israel, 15 per cent haven't the faintest idea what it's all about, and two per cent support the Arabs through thick and thin. I'm convinced the picture's the same in all civilized countries.

"NOW GIVE me leave to ask whether you figure it would be any practical use if we here in Copenhagen began all of a sudden to read your buddy Anwar Sadat the riot act for his riotous behaviour. What on earth can Israel benefit from a friend who weakens himself by political statements without having any real power to back them up? Politics is a power-game, my dear sir. A foreign policy without power is, if you'll forgive me, sheer idiocy. I hardly imagine you aren't

aware, for instance, that France's position in face of the Arab threats is a great deal weaker than your own, and that as for Great Britain — its ruling-the-waves days are over. The only one who can stand up to the Arabs is you.

"The Americans could too, of course, if they used their military might, and they may yet come to it one day if they get angry enough and their President feels confident he won't be denounced for it in Europe like for Vietnam. For the time being, though, one had better keep one's big mouth shut when one's dealing with mad guys like the Arab rulers, unless one's a great power such as Israel.

"Please consider, my friend, what'd happen if Denmark were in your position and were attacked from without. Believe me, only the U.S. would be able to save her — perhaps! — and the same goes for every country in the free world you'd like to name. We're not immoral, mind you. We're not scoundrels. We're just weak. And at the present time the weak must pretend to be scoundrels, else they're sat on.

"Let me add, by the way, that we could have pretended worse. Actually we didn't bow to the Arab dictate to cry out against you loud and clear. We just shut our big mouth and played fish, the way a responsible nation should in the Oil Age.

"So don't you tell the Israelis you've lost the world's sympathy because, on the contrary, we love and admire you, and we're trying to help you now more than ever — but quietly, on the sly, because that's the only way in winter. We make believe, if you know what I mean. Like when Colonel Gaddafi demanded that Denmark provide military training for Libyan soldiers, and by agreeing to we did Israel an immense service, seeing that we've got the shortest and lousiest military training in the world...

"That's it. I wanted to try and save a bit of our honour, though I don't expect understanding on your side. More than that: I'm afraid we'll lose your sympathy. Still, that doesn't keep me from sending, through you, my warm regards to the wonderful people of Israel whom we all love.

"P.S. Please don't publish my name. I wouldn't at all care to receive a boobytrapped letter in the mail."

Ephraim Kishon

Translated by Miriam Arad
By arrangement with "Ma'ariv"

365

Two million eligible to cast ballots
HOW TO VOTE

By ASHER WALLFISH
Jerusalem Post Reporter

NEARLY 2,040,000 voters are eligible to cast their ballots in tomorrow's elections for the Eighth Knesset — about 17,000 more than the number originally on the electoral register, when the elections were set for October 30.

Thus the Yom Kippur war, which caused an inevitable postponement of the polls, also gave the franchise to more teenagers — many of them soldiers — whose vote may well be influenced by their experience in khaki.

On the same day, in the same polling station, but in a different ballot box, votes will also be cast for the local authorities. The number of eligible voters for the local authorities is slightly larger, since it includes residents who do not have Israeli citizenship.

The results of the elections to the Knesset also have another meaning, in financial terms. Election campaigns are financed by the Treasury.

Lists represented in the outgoing Knesset receive allocations for the campaign calculated according to their strength in the outgoing Knesset. But new lists get their campaign money back only if they put candidates into the Knesset. So it pays to win in the poll.

★ ★ ★

SOLDIERS serving in the regular Army, or the reserves, vote at special military polling stations. These may be fixed — as in camps, or mobile—for small units in isolated areas.

This year, for the first time ever, scores of thousands of soldiers will be voting, from over an immense area, stretching from points 40 km. from Damascus to 100 km. from Cairo. Three days have been assigned for Army polling — Sunday, Monday and Tuesday. But the Army hopes to get nearly all the votes in by tomorrow midnight. The principle of the secret vote would be impaired if a soldier-voter heard election results on Tuesday morning over the radio and went to cast his vote in line with the general trend.

Soldiers vote in double envelopes. The inner envelope contains the actual slip with the symbol of the Knesset list he favours. The outer envelope contains the voter's name and identity number on the outside. Civilians' envelopes are opened and counted at their neighbourhood polling station. Soldiers' outer envelopes are first checked for authenticity at the Central Elections Committee by computer — and only then are the outer envelopes opened and the inner envelopes passed on to the tellers.

The only Israelis abroad who may vote are Israeli seamen and passengers aboard vessels flying the Israeli flag, provided the vessel contains at least 15 eligible voters. The vessels bring the special ballot box with double envelopes used to the nearest Israeli port or diplomatic mission, so that they can be rushed to Jerusalem in time. Late votes are disqualified. But the seamen started voting a week ago to enable sufficient time to get the ballot boxes to the Central Election Committee.

★ ★ ★

CIVILIAN voters are registered at one of the nearly 4,000 polling stations up and down the country where their particulars appear on a numbered register kept by a polling committee. The polling committees are staffed by representatives of the political parties who check the voters' identity cards and their particulars on the register and observe order in the voting process. They stamp the voters' identity card to prevent him trying to vote again at another station. The polling committee members may not converse with the voters, except to expedite the voting process.

The secrecy of the vote is assured inside the polling booth itself, where the voter chooses the slip bearing the letters denoting the list of his choice, puts it in the envelope given him by the polling committee, and then seals the envelope. He emerges with the envelope to place it in the ballot box. (Or he may emerge earlier than that, to complain that the slips of his choice have disappeared at the hand of some previous voter-vandal.)

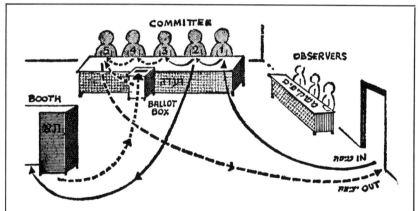

Above is a graphic sketch of a typical polling station, designed to show the voter what to do when he goes in to vote.

Each member of the Committee has a definite task. By following directions the voter will save the time of all concerned.

1) The voter identifies himself by presenting his Identity Card to Committee Man No. 1.
2) He receives an envelope from Committee Man No. 2, enters the booth, puts his ballot into the envelope; closes the envelope.
3) He then returns to the Committee Chairman, No. 3, and deposits the envelope in the ballot box while the Committee members look on.
4) His Identity Card, stamped and perforated, is then returned to him by No. 4 and he leaves the station.
5) Meanwhile, No. 5 strikes his name from the voters' register.

Polling stations are open f r o m seven a.m. till 11 p.m., unless they have less than 350 registered voters — in which case they are open from eight a.m. till nine p.m. It is the results from these smaller stations — in country areas — which come in fastest. But since the patterns they give of the poll are not as indicative of the national trend as the urban stations, the public will only begin to see half-way through the night what sort of a Knesset he can expect.

It will take until a fortnight after election day before the final results are in. They will be published in "*Reshumot,*" the official gazette, together with the names of the successful candidates from each list.

Approximately one out of every twelve eligible voters is a non-Jewish Israeli-Moslem, Christian or Druse. The number of eligible voters from the non-Jewish sectors of the population is some 172,000.

TWENTY-one lists of candidates are competing in the Knesset elections. Thirteen of the lists have Members on the outgoing Seventh Knesset, and eight are new. The 21 lists are fielding a total of 1,065 candidates. Some lists, like the Labour-Mapam Alignment, contain a full 120 names, to tally with the 120 seats in the Knesset, and some contain only a handful, in line with the expectations of the list in the poll.

A list which does not win at least one per cent of the total number of valid votes cast in the poll is disqualified. All the votes cast for it are worthless. The sponsors of a new list forfeit the IL15,000 deposit placed with the Central Elections Committee if the list fails to pass the one per cent blocking percentage.

Meshel calls for law against war profits

TEL AVIV. — The Histadrut will insist on the speedy passing of a law against war profiteering, Acting Secretary-General Yeruham Meshel told a meeting of employees of the Histadrut Executive here on Friday. Mr. Meshel said it was imperative that easy war profits be curbed drastically.

East Bank of the Jordan as well as the West Bank.

A second religious party, called Agudat Poale Israel, gained 60,000 votes in this election and earned five seats in the Knesset. This is an ultra-orthodox group and is concerned almost exclusively with religious issues. The Mafdal group is more secular in outlook than the Agudat Party.

The religious parties favor a theocratic state. They want a government based on Halacha, the body of law embodied in the Bible and the Talmud. The Talmud, written over a period of a thousand years, embraces all the disputations of the rabbis in their schools and academies in Babylonia and Jerusalem. The earliest interpretations of the Talmud date back to around 300 B.C. and continue through 700 years of the Christian Era. The religious parties consider these laws immutable. They believe that the Bible was given by God to Moses on Mount Sinai and, being heavenly ordained, is perfect in every aspect.

Fundamentalists to the last degree, they oppose civil marriage, and fight unceasingly for a strict observance of the Sabbath as a day of rest. For example, they oppose public transportation on Saturday. This, of course, finds little favor with the nonreligious population, who after working six days, look forward to the seventh day as a day of relaxation and recreation through excursions, sports, traveling to the beach and to resorts, and a day for visiting.

Accommodation on this score has been somewhat difficult at times. In the city of Haifa, the liberal element has prevailed, and public transportation is available on the Sabbath. In Jerusalem, and in Tel Aviv, buses cease operation from sundown Friday to sundown Saturday. However, taxis operate, and private modes of transportation go on without hindrance except that, in certain quarters of Jerusalem where the ultra-pious reside, it is considered an affront to drive through their streets on the Sabbath. This is also true in certain other ultra-religious communities, like Bnei Barak, where the overwhelming part of the population are strict observers of Halachic law.

In the past, the Labor Party had formed a coalition government with the religious parties. But in the election of 1973, the religious parties refused to join in a coalition government with Labor, leaving Labor to seek allies elsewhere.

The Independent Liberals scored better than 56,000 votes, and gained four seats in the legislative body. This group favors territorial compromise, and recognizes the rights of Palestinian Arabs to some kind of self-determination, on condition that the Palestinian Arabs are willing to establish peaceful relations with Israel and are willing to recognize the right of Israel to exist as an independent polity.

There are two communist parties in Israel. The New Communists, or Rakah, garnered over 53,000 votes and won four seats in the Knesset. Most of the members of this party are Arabs who have

ARABS HOLD THE KEY
IN JERUSALEM VOTE

By ABRAHAM RABINOVICH
Jerusalem Post Reporter

The outcome of the municipal election in Jerusalem tomorrow depends in good part on several thousand voters who are citizens of an enemy state.

It is the Arab voters of East Jerusalem — almost all of them Jordanian citizens — who may determine whether or not Mayor Teddy Kollek's Alignment maintains its majority on the Municipal Council. Although Mr. Kollek's re-election as Mayor is a certainty, his freedom of manoeuvre will be considerably cramped if he must rely on a coalition.

It was the Arab vote in 1969 which provided the Alignment with the two seats that gave it a 16-15 majority. Some 7,800 Arabs voted then out of 35,000 eligible, a far greater number than anyone expected. This year 43,000 Arabs are eligible.

Mr. Kollek's principal opponent is Likud Deputy Mayor Yehoshua Matza who believes he can add to the six seats his party holds on the Council. Mr. Matza, who had favoured the construction of housing at Nebi Samwil before the war for political reasons, attacks Mr. Kollek for having opposed it on aesthetic grounds. "It's clear now that we were correct," he said. Mr. Matza also condemns the idea proposed by Mr. Kollek of a borough system that would permit extensive self-government to the Arab population. "This is a danger to our sovereignty over Jerusalem," he says.

Mr. Matza has been campaigning extensively in East Jerusalem — which his party ignored in 1969 — and is convinced he will win a substantial vote there despite his nationalist views. A campaign brochure in Arabic shows Mr. Matza against a backdrop of the Dome of the Rock Mosque. It identifies Mr. Matza, who is a 10th generation Jerusalemite, as "a son of Jerusalem" — which may be a hint to the local Arabs that he is better suited to talk to them than, say, a son of Vienna.

In his campaigning, Mr. Matza promises the Arabs full equality and improved municipal services.

The religious parties, which control a quarter of the Council seats, can be expected to maintain their strength. Agudat Yisrael (four seats) and Poalei Agudat Yisrael (one seat) have merged on a ticket headed by Deputy Mayor Rabbi Menahem Porush. The National Religious Party (three seats) is headed this time by Dr. Yosef Goldschmidt, M.K., who has called for the speeding up of Jewish settlement in the city and for the election of an observant Mayor. The Ole Bavel (Iraqi Immigrants) Party, which has one seat, is again fielding a list.

One of the most active campaigns has been waged by lawyer Uri Huppert of the Independent Liberals, which holds no seats at all on the present Council. He has participated in more than 100 *hugei bayit* (parlour meetings). His platform calls for a master plan for dealing with the city's social problems and a borough system which would permit Arabs, Orthodox Jews and other residents to organize their local way of life through borough councils. Mr. Huppert, a former head of the League against Religious Coercion, advocates removal of all traffic barriers around religious neighbourhoods on the Sabbath since the streets are public property, the opening of youth clubs on the Sabbath and theatrical productions on Friday nights.

A new party is Citizens for a Better Jerusalem, headed by Prof. Yaacov Lorch of Hebrew University, whose lists includes students, architects and archaeologists. Its principle goal is to prevent illegal building in the city and to protect Jerusalem's special character. Its campaign has been almost totally neutralized by mobilization, which saw almost all its young candidates and workers called up.

Another list representing the owners of small workshops and Egged co-op members is headed by Victor Saniel.

been wooed by communist propaganda. These Arabs are hostile to the entire concept of Israel. These hard-core communists—Arabs and Jews—simply follow the Moscow line, lock, stock, and barrel. They openly favor the dissolution of the State of Israel, which they claim belongs to the Arabs and should be returned to the Arabs. These Jewish communists are thus, in effect, opting for the liquidation of their country.

The second communist party, which is the equivalent of Israel's New Left, is called Moked. This party scored 22,000 votes and won one seat in the Knesset. Moked believes in the right of Israel to exist, but favors a communist form of government.

A new party which made a surprising showing in the last election was the Citizens Rights Party, headed by Mrs. Shulamith Aloni. This party achieved a vote of 35,000 and won three seats in the Knesset. Its members are involved with social issues, favor the separation of synagogue and State, and decry the power of the rabbis. They wish to wean Israel away from its theocratic moorings and would like to secularize Israel and modernize its administration.

The Party of Progress and Development is an Arab party. It was supported by better than 22,000 voters and gained two seats in the Knesset. Its main thrust is to protect Arab interests. This party supports Israel and does not wish or strive for the

GENEVA Act1:Scene2

Ari Rath

THE LINES on the screen forming the backdrop to the stage are still dim and hardly discernible. The chief actors are still moving mainly behind the scenes. But slowly a pattern is begining to emerge. It is a pattern of talking Middle East business in earnest by the Israel and Arab protagonists under the eagle eyes of the Americans and the Russians.

There will not be any easy and quick breakthroughs, but there will also not be much marking time or indefinite stalling.

If there was anything that came close to breaking some ice, it was in the sphere of Israel-Soviet contacts at the peace conference. The much publicized and extremely cordial meeting last Friday night between Soviet Foreign Minister Andrei Gromyko

and Israel's Abba Eban was a clear pointer in that direction. The meeting ended, at the Russian's own request, in a tete-a-tete talk between the two ministers.

It was also no coincidence that Israel's senior delegate here, Ephraim Evron, paid farewell calls Wednesday prior to returning to Jerusalem, on both the ranking U.S. delegate here now, Michael Sterner, and Ambassador Vladimir Vinogradov, head of the Soviet delegation in Gromyko's absence. Their meeting was the first direct contact between the Israel and Soviet delegations here after last weekend's opening session.

While the Kremlin keeps saying that no solution to the Israel-Arab conflict can come about without the Soviet Union's con-

sent, it also seems to have finally realized that there can be no real peace in the Middle East without its coming to terms with Israel and assuring its security.

It was noted here with interest in this connection that the Labour Alignment had made special reference in its election platform to Israel's readiness to resume diplomatic relations with the U.S.S.R.

But establishing Israel-Soviet contacts in Geneva is not going to be smooth sailing. This was proved by the tough negotiating over the firm objection of both the U.S. and Israel to having the two superpowers, and especially the Russians, take an active part in the meetings of the military working group.

Gromyko is understood to have gone out of his way in attempting to allay Israel's fears and suspicions as to the Soviet Union's role as co-chairman of the conference. He is also reported to have indicated that resumption of diplomatic relations between the two countries, severed by Moscow in June, 1967, would depend on the way the Geneva talks progress. In fact, it was Gromyko who first broached the subject of resuming diplomatic relations.

This week the Russians in Geneva even went one step further. A senior Soviet source made a point of passing the word to the Israelis here that "it should not be assumed that the position of the Soviet Union would necessarily be contrary to that of Israel."

A Protestant's letter to the Pope

To the Editor of The Jerusalem Post

Sir, — On Christmas Day, I sent a letter to Pope Paul VI and I feel that the following extracts may be of interest to your readers:

"Some days ago, Sir, you received in audience a number of African heads of State and discussed with them 'the problem of Jerusalem in Jewish hands.' One of your guests was President Numeiri, of the Sudan, murderer of tens of thousands of Sudanese black Christians...

"The Vatican has not officially acknowledged the existence of the State of Israel... apparently being more interested in 'Holy Places' than in human welfare. But it is true that these 'Places'—a scandal to Christian faith and dignity — do represent a source of excellent profit...

"You should come back to Jerusalem, Sir, and see for yourself that since 1967, and only since then, every Christian, Moslem and Jew has

free access to the Holy Places and full liberty of worship. Even Numeiri, the murderer, would have free access to Israel's Temple Mount.

"Please allow me, Protestant theologian that I am, to quote our Master Jesus, from the Gospel according to St. Luke (21,24) — 'Jerusalem will be occupied by t h e Nations, until the time of the Nations comes to its end.' Thus Jesus himself sees in the amazing events of June 1967 a definite messianic sign heralding his Parousia, the Second Coming, this time to inaugurate the Kingdom of God upon this bloody and beautiful earth, as in Heaven.

"By opposing Israel's messianic history in Jerusalem today, the Nations, and your Vatican, are opposing God's will to lead history to salvation. There is, perhaps, Sir, still a little time left for repentance."

Rev. CLAUDE DUVERNOY,
Dr. Theol, Christian Israeli citizen
Jerusalem, Christmas Day, 1973.

Reserve generals to aid war inquiry

The government-appointed commission inquiring into the shortcomings connected with the Yom Kippur War stated in Jerusalem yesterday that it has held 38 meetings and taken evidence from 26 witnesses so far.

This was the first announcement by the commission since it started work behind closed doors over a month ago.

The commission also announced it had appointed six reserve generals to gather verbal and documentary evidence from soldiers to help it draw its conclusions. They are: Aluf (res.) Yosef Avidar; Aluf (res.) Moshe Goren; Tat-Aluf (res.) Baruch Gilboa; Tat-Aluf (res.) Shimon Gilboa; Aluf-Mishne (res.) Yisrael Carmi; and Aluf Mishne (res.) Yehoshua Nevo.

The commission will in the meanwhile continue to take testimony from witnesses appearing before it directly.

21 lists contesting

Following is a list of the 21 parties competing for seats in the Eighth Knesset, their Hebrew letter-symbols, and (in brackets) the number of seats they won in the 1969 elections.

אמת   **LABOUR-MAPAM ALIGNMENT** (56)

חל/טעמ   **LIKUD** (32), comprising Gahal (26), State List (4, counting Meir Avizohar, who broke away to join the Labour ranks), Free Centre (2) and the Greater Israel Movement (new)

ב   **NATIONAL RELIGIOUS PARTY** (12, counting breakaway M.K. Avner Shaki)

גד   **AGUDAT YISRAEL, POALEI AGUDAT YISRAEL** (6)

לע   **INDEPENDENT LIBERAL PARTY** (4)

רק"ח   **NEW COMMMUNISTS — RAKAH** (3)

רא   **PROGRESS AND DEVELOPMENT** (2) — Alignment-affiliated (Moslem) Arabs and Druse

יא   **COOPERATION AND BROTHERHOOD** (2) — Alignment-affiliated (Christian and Moslem) Arabs

קנ   **MOKED** (1), comprising the Maki Communists and the Blue-Red list

ש   **MERI** (2, counting breakaway M K. Shalom Cohen) — headed by Uri Avneri M.K.

ז   **BLACK PANTHERS** — Israel Democrats (new — headed by Shalom Cohen M.K.)

פ   **PANTHERS BLUE-WHITE** (new)

רצ   **CITIZENS RIGHTS MOVEMENT** (new — headed by Shulamit Aloni)

כך   **THE LEAGUE** (new — founded by the Jewish Defence League)

מס   **SOCIAL EQUALITY MOVEMENT** (new — headed by Avner Shaki M.K.)

רס   **REVOLUTION SOCIALIST LIST** (new — headed by Rami Livneh, now serving a jail term for security offences)

עא   **ARAB LIST OF BEDUIN** and Villagers (new)

סנ   **POPULAR MOVEMENT** (new)

ער   **ISRAEL ARAB LIST** (new)

ענ   **BROTHERHOOD MOVEMENT** (new)

רח   **YEMENITE LIST** (new)

dissolution of the State of Israel. It simply wants to secure better conditions for the Arab minority.

Another party, with more or less the same viewpoint, is the Party of The Bedouin and the Villagers. It scored 16,000 votes and landed one seat in the Knesset. Its name implies its constituency.

The Black Panther Party of Israel has absolutely no alliance with the Black Panthers of the United States. The Israeli party merely appropriated the name because its leaders thought the name would attract attention. Most of the members of the Black Panthers are oriental Jews — Sephardic Jews — who have emigrated to Israel from Iraq, Iran, Morocco, Egypt, Yemen, Tunisia, and other Arab-speaking lands. Their native tongue, in most cases, is Arabic. Some speak Ladino, a Judao-Spanish which dates from the 15th century, and is still spoken by the Jews of Bulgaria, Turkey, and Greece. These Sephardic Jews deem themselves underprivileged and do, in fact, suffer a lower standard of living. To rectify this, they have formed a party of protest which aims to improve their living, working, and educational conditions. In the last election they polled about 13,000 votes.

War that 'unleashed new demons'

The consequences of the war and the possibilities of peace in the Middle East are examined by the "Sunday Telegraph" Here are some points from this lengthy analysis.

Jerusalem Post Correspondent

LONDON. — "Israelis have still not realized how much the world has changed since 1967, when they were both cock of the walk and everybody's darling.

"The October War was very much more than just another round in the 25-year-old struggle between the Israelis and the Arabs, for it unleashed new demons which no one has yet managed to control." The wars of 1948, 1956 and 1967 "simply served to set in motion a long-term Arab campaign to attack again, and this time to take the new Israel by surprise.

"Even before the October War Arab oil money and the power of Islam had already defeated Israel diplomatically in the African continent.

"Even graver than the diplomatic implications is the hard fact which emerges from the war that the Arab nations are among the most powerful in the world. With a super-abundance of manpower and money to spend in the gigantic arsenal of the Soviet Union behind them, Egypt and Syria have developed armies and air forces as powerful as many European ones. Only American support for Israel and the military skill of Israel's army made it possible to hold the Egyptians and the Syrians. And now the Iraqis have comparable resources."

Continuing, the paper says that "what matters today, however, is that Israel is diplomatically isolated, and the full force of world opinion is being brought to bear on her.

"Because of her growing need for Middle East oil and her $3,000m. investment in its production in the Arab countries, the U.S. cannot afford to be anti-Arab."

It is even claimed that Kissinger has paid more attention to the threat to detente than to the danger to Israel.

"President Nixon, in pursuit of American interests, as the need for Arab oil grows, is moving towards a policy of what is called 'even-handedness.' That, basically, is why Israel has been forced reluctantly to the peace-making table at Geneva. And the chances are that she will be forced by the pressure of her one real ally, America, into surrendering territory in the hope of getting a more lasting peace before the next round."

CONDONE TERRORISTS

The "Sunday Telegraph" continues: "Even the activities of the Pales- tinian terrorists played their part in isolating Israel. For, while they were condemned throughout the West — although there were some people even in the House of Commons who were prepared to condone the terrorists' most barbaric excesses — many governments were not prepared to risk their revenge.

"And so, gradually, by genuine concern over the fate of the Palestinians and at Israel's refusal to give up Arab territory, by bribery of African states, by the use of the oil weapon, by terrorism, and by concentrated political and economic campaigns, the Arabs brought about the isolation of Israel, an isolation which, despite the sympathy which might be felt for Israel, is very much a fact, but still one which the Israelis find hard to grasp.

"It is an ugly truth for Israelis to realize that not only has the local war situation changed for them, but also the world has changed for their American friends and emotional sympathizers in Europe."

With Israel's internal problems, and especially the debts facing the economy, "unless some kind of peace under pressure, which must involve boundary changes, can be worked out, the immediate future for isolated Israel is a bleak one. It seems that while the Arabs did not win the war the Israelis cannot win the peace."

The Jewish Defense League polled a little under 13,000 votes. This is the party of Meir Kahane, who came from the United States to Israel where he is, for the most part, regarded as a troublemaker. He has been charged with illicit activities involving the smuggling of arms and use of violence and is currently awaiting trial.

Another minor party is Meri, a left-wing party led by Uri Avneri. This party represents the super-dovish elements in Israel which believe rapprochement between Arab and Jew should be staunchly pursued. In the last election, this party fell just short of gaining enough votes to win a Knesset seat.

The Social Equality Party also barely missed gaining a seat. This party represents the oriental community and is somewhat similar in objective to the Black Panther Party, but not as melodramatic, nor as charismatic.

Other minor parties are: the Party of Cooperation and Brotherhood, which has a strictly Arab list; the Blue White Panthers; the Ahva Party; the Israel Arab list; the Yemenite list; the Revolutionary Socialists, an extreme left-wing party which disavows the Zionist State; and the

Shrill beeps on E-Day minus one

By EPHRAIM KISHON

IF the reader should see a local citizen slumped over a pile of newspapers with glassy eyes and lips mumbling what sounds like baby-talk, let him go over to the fellow and comfort him:

"Only one more day."

The blessed game's been going on since the establishment of the State. At that time the Israeli voter signed an agreement for the distribution of surplus votes in order to keep the status absolutely quo, and in the years after developed an amazing telepathic sense for stopping the clock. The public has one declared aim: to prevent any single party from getting an absolute majority. Accordingly, whenever Mapai appeared too strong on the Israeli voter's radar screen, he put out his hand and with eyes shut took a different slip, while any time the Opposition swelled, his fingers went to the Mapai "aleph." The average voter turned himself into a sensitive electoral computer of the delicate balance.

The Yom Kippur War, however, damaged his transistors, and his antennae have stopped receiving the message. All he gets now is shrill interference noise, such as Ma'arach announcements about the looming threat of a big bad Likud, or Likud promises that it won't set up a Government without the Ma'arach, come what may. No wonder the citizen's scared he'll vote the wrong way and topple the Ma'arach or strengthen it by mistake.

The voter's looking for an ingenuous kind of slip saying "M005" — that is, Ma'arach less five mandates — or "LP," i.e., Likud plus. But sad to say, those aren't available yet for the Choosing People.

Since the Parties didn't publish the make-up of their Governments before the Elections in order to spare us the shock, the Israeli voter is forced to cast his ballot in an entirely unfamiliar way, namely by rational calculation. As a result, according to a recent poll some 40 per cent of the population admit they've no idea who to vote for. The other 60 per cent don't admit it. We're all consumed with envy for the Religious, for the still-not-an-inchers, for the devout withdrawal-nicks, and the Shulamit-Aloni-loners, but the decisive majority can't decide. The average voter hopes that on his way to the polling-booth the fresh winter air will clear his brain, or that once he's inside, the radar will start operating again and his hand'll be pushed towards the necessary letter. For the time being it's shrill beep-beep on the air, and the status quo is in danger.

The little voter sighs: why don't they announce hourly results of the count on Election Day, and then he could adjust the balance with his vote.

★ ★ ★

IT looks like we've no choice but to do a little soul-searching.

Nothing shows the situation of the Ma'arach as plainly as its repeated warnings to us not to punish it. Over the past few years its leaders have acted on the old formula of: "Do you want war? Prepare for peace!" Yet it'd be a mistake to think they made only that one mistake in October. Behind the Egyptians' successful Canal double-crossing there's a long story of slow rot, starting with an economy of white licence-plates and ending with the sunflower-seeds on our cinema floors. The Ma'arach leaders have a considerable part in our becoming a Levantine crowd, though we'll say that for them—that they went about it democratically. On top of that they certainly keep a few talented people on ice, and you can't ignore the fact that they've got Nixon's girl, the one and only Golda who speaks English so you understand. Let's add that Mr. Dayan, too, has been surprising us lately with his revolutionary novelty of telling the truth *before* the Elections, and that the beehive is a-humming with several international whiz-kids in the field of contribution campaigning. And we can't deny that all we lacked in the War was eggs. On the whole the Ma'arach has built us a state that's carelessly slapdash but strong and blooming.

The Likud, on the other hand, has been enjoying the benefit of virginity, though it took a lot of bickering midwives to get the pretty maiden out into the world. You can't separate the Likud from Mr. Begin, who is no doubt the most consistent politician we have — both in his character and in his clothes. Yet it's just this quality, rare as it may be in our sub-tropical region, that makes the public wonder whether Mr. Begin may not prove a captive of his own speeches, and act with honesty and noble faith at times when cunning and manoeuvring skill are called for.

Another horrible thought is that Mr. Begin will pick his Cabinet out of all those photographs of leading candidates in the Likud ads, none of which except Arik's look as if they promised redemption.

★ ★ ★

IF you've read this piece in the expectation that at the end you'd be told whom to vote for you're in for a disappointment. We don't have any magic answer that'll settle such things as how to arrange the tables between the two camps, or how to engage the forces so that Begin recommends Golda for the premiership (quite thinkable, that), and Abba Eban supports the nomination of Shmuel Tamir for Minister of Information (quite, quite unthinkable).

The reader will have to make up his own mind despite his understandable confusion. It won't be easy. Only a few days ago we witnessed a typical and moving scene, when a lady of our acquaintance poured her heart out to us:

"I'm going to do something I never did before!" the poor woman sobbed, "I'm going to vote Likud. I'm scared of Begin, I've always been suspicious of them, and now I'm going to vote for them! I feel awful! What'll I do?"

"Madam," we told her, "shut your eyes and think of your country."

Translated by Miriam Arad
By Arrangement with "Ma'ariv"

Popular Movement.

To achieve a place on the ballot, 750 signatures are required.

The way proportional representation works out in Israel is that a certain number of votes is required to elect a member to parliament. In the 1973 election, that number turned out to be 11,200.

The party delegate who is selected for the seat is the candidate who tops the list of the party. Each party posts a roster of candidates on its list. If the party received, let us say, 25,000 votes, the top two candidates were elected; if they received 65,000 votes, then the top five candidates were elected.

The top candidate of the leading party is then invited by the President to become Premier and form a government. Thus, for many years, the Labor Party received the most votes and its top candidate, Golda Meir, automatically became the Premier designate.

When a Premier obtains an invitation to form a government, he or she nominates the cabinet ministers, and submits their names to the full body of the Knesset for approval. If the proposed cabinet does not gain a majority vote of confidence, then the government cannot function and must be dissolved. Then a new cabinet is chosen.

It can be seen that in order to assure a vote of confidence, a Premier must choose a cabinet from among those parties who agree to support the government program.

The Israeli system of dividing Knesset seats is arranged as follows:

The total valid vote is computed by adding up all

OUR INNER STRENGTH

THE truths of this election have been repeated in the past few weeks to the point of becoming cliches: the choices are unclear, the undecided will decide, the soldiers' vote will be decisive, the polls, this time especially, can't be trusted.

One of the big questions is whether this time, after what has been described as the "earthquake" of the October war, the historic voting pattern that has prevailed since 1949 will be broken. Another is whether the election results will make possible establishment of a government that will be able to muster sufficient domestic consent to seize the opportunities and ward off the dangers awaiting us in Geneva.

There is of course the danger that the Arabs may misinterpret the coalition bargaining that will inevitably follow the elections. Where we see familiar democratic processes, they may see weakness and be tempted to exploit it militarily. Something like this happened in 1967 when Nasser and his Soviet advisers mistakenly believed Israel's internal political fights made it ripe for attack. Hopefully Sadat will not be misled by such illusions, for he would then, like his predecessor, smash into the underlying granite of national unity, which ultimately makes our turbulent elections possible.

There is after all something remarkable about a new nation at war that declines not merely to set aside, but even to postpone the constitutional need to obtain a renewed popular mandate for its government.

That we take the remarkable for granted is the measure of our inner strength. That we have not succumbed — as larger and older nations have — to the pressures for regimentation is the measure of our inner purpose.

And the paradoxical result — so difficult for some to understand — is that this release of democratic turbulence ultimately refreshes and renews national resolve and cohesion.

Admittedly our constitutional arrangements leave much scope for reform. And our party system, locked into the patterns of bossism that arise from proportional representation, is perhaps highest on the list.

Yet even with its creaks and cracks Israeli democracy has withstood the unusual tests which confronted it and helped forge a heterogeneous immigrant nation into one.

As we go to the polls today we will give expression to our present perplexities and to our differing views, but also we shall pay tribute, as only a democratic nation can, to the ties which bind us together.

Creation on the Golan Heights.

the votes cast for all the parties which gained representation in the Knesset. (Votes cast for those parties failing to secure the minimum 1 percent of the vote are simply cast aside — in the December '73 election, such votes accounted for 1.2 percent of the total valid vote.)

This corrected valid vote is divided by 120, the number of seats in the Knesset, and thus the number of votes required for a seat in the Knesset is obtained (as mentioned previously, in 1973 the magic number was about 11,200).

This number is divided into the vote obtained by each party. As a result, each party obtains the number of full seats it received *plus* a remainder or surplus which enters into the distribution of the remaining seats.

In the '73 election, if a party received 15,000 votes, it would receive one seat plus a surplus of 3,800.

By this method, 116 to 118 full seats are distributed, with the remaining two to four seats distributed to those parties having the *largest surpluses*. There is an added rule that parties gaining full Knesset seats may enter into agreements combining surpluses, since the final seats are distributed according to the largest individual *or* combined surpluses. Usually the assignment of the last one or two Knesset seats is not known until the official count is completed and the surplus arrangements made public.

Because the political situation has been so unstable, the electoral system has been called into question. There are now many voices arguing for a change that would effectively bar the proliferation of parties that has bedeviled Israeli politics. By the simple expedient of raising the minimum requirement for representation in the

Hadar Hacarmel tower approved

By YA'ACOV FRIEDLER
Jerusalem Post Reporter

HAIFA. — The Haifa District Town Planning Commission this week gave its final approval for the construction of a 23-storey tower, which will be the city's largest commercial building.

The building, to be called The Haim Tower, will cost IL20m. It will be put up by the Ferber Fur Corporation of New York, in cooperation with the initiators of the scheme, the Kuehnreich Brothers, furriers, of Haifa. It will rise at the eastern end of Rehov Herzl, the main thoroughfare in the Hadar Hacarmel district, on a plot bought from the 20th Century Fox corporation some years ago.

A spokesman for the Ferber Corp. told *The Jerusalem Post* yesterday that they had decided to go ahead with the scheme as quickly as possible, in order to demonstrate their "absolute confidence in Israel's future, notwithstanding the present difficulties." The working plans are now being completed and it is hoped to start construction in the spring and finish within two years. The design is by architect Moshe Oren.

The Haim Tower will have three underground floors for parking, a large fur and shopping centre for tourists, office space, and a 100-room hotel. The promoters expect the tower to revive Haifa trade in general, and in particular reverse the trend of business moving from the eastern part of Rehov Herzl to the western end; and that it will give a great boost to Haifa's tourism activities.

The proposed Haim Tower designed by Moshe Oren, approved for Haifa's Rehov Herzl.

IT OCCURS TO ME / Hadassah Bat Haim

Any excess baggage?

ISRAEL REVEALS TO almost every visitor a different aspect of human behaviour. On the whole, people find what they are looking for. They come with preconceived ideas, confirm them, and go home deeply satisfied with their intelligence and perspicacity. Highly suspicious of any assaults on their opinions, they cleverly reject any contradictory presentations as attempts to pull wool over their eyes. These efforts are always foiled by their cool, experienced appraisals. I have, as a representative of the citizenry, been castigated as a Communist, a Fascist, an oppressor of a helpless minority and a cowardly appeaser of those who avowedly want to destroy us.

Fortunately, most of our guests take a benevolent view of our activities and enough praises have been heaped on me — as a representative of the citizenry — to be rather embarrassing. True, I point out and explain our developments and institutions as if I had invented them myself; but to be personally complimented on my stand on the Canal, and my dogged counter-attack on the Golan, not to mention my sturdy independence, my brave refusal to be bullied and my political acumen is, though well deserved, difficult to answer with becoming modesty.

THE YOUNG American journalist whom I met on her way home is a shining example of everything a tourist should be. Every Israeli she has met is either a hero or

a charmer or both. Cases of overcharging and boorishness she writes off as quaint aberrations of the national character.

She even professes to enjoy the taxi ride, which fills me with terror. The driver, recently released from military service, has not yet adjusted himself to civilian life and charges at every vehicle and all other obstacles on the road as if he were still at the wheel of his tank. However, he is not too preoccupied to ask Karen what she will take for the small portable typewriter she is carrying, as it is just what his daughter needs to further her studies in English. He tries it out with his right hand while Karen leans on his shoulder to instruct him. Naturally he cannot give too much attention to the road, but conscientiously reduces his speed to eighty while he is busy with other matters.

At once a voice from the back informs her that such a machine, new, would cost at least twice what the driver is prepared to give. The gentleman next to him says he is also looking for an English typewriter, as he has a lot of relatives in the States who profess to find his handwriting illegible. A slight diversion now occurs while we discuss the location of his family, because which of us doesn't have cousins in America? When we have all exclaimed about the wild coincidences of the uncle of the baker near the window living not ten blocks away from a dear friend of the lady beside the driver, we debate the ethics of the proposed sale.

Some passengers, now fiercely partisan, insist that Karen should stick out for the highest price, while others feel that the driver has a prior right to purchase. The gentleman at the back, outnumbered, says very well, but he would like to bid for her camera and, having ascertained what is in the small leather case, for the electric hair-dryer, an appliance his wife has always wanted. In that case, asks the lady in the front, would Karen be prepared to part with the attractive shoulder-bag she is wearing? The lady can provide her with a plastic carrier to transfer the contents into.

The bargaining goes on, hotly pursued by everyone but the owner of these desirable goods. She is too busy adding to her collection of vignettes to be published in her home newspaper. At Lod, relieved of any possibility of being charged for excess baggages, she bids us all farewell and promises to come back soon. She has noted down the seven addresses where she can come and stay on her next trip, and assures us that only in Israel could she have had such a wonderful taxi ride.

Knesset to a larger percentage, small splinter groups would be avoided.

In order to secure a seat in the legislative assembly, a party would require support of a greater part of the electorate than it now needs. As a result, there would be fewer parties, and the strength of each party would be increased.

A coalition government would be more feasible and the chances that one party might actually achieve a majority vote would be greatly enhanced.

Many Israelis believe that the times require a stronger government; a change in electoral rules would be the first step towards achieving that goal.

The dispute over when to cross

THE DECISIVE THURSDAY ON THE SINAI FRONT

The "Sunday Times" in London yesterday published the third instalment of its report of the Yom Kippur War. Here are extracts from the report by The POST'S London Correspondent, David Lennon.

Aluf Arik Sharon has implied that he was overruled from the start, and that the position in Sinai through the first week was one of stalemate. "Neither point appears to be correct," the "Sunday Times" claims. It continues:

Aluf Gonen had allowed the Tuesday counter-attack in the central sector as Sharon had been seeking. "The result had been failure and the loss of the 109th Armoured Brigade to Egyptian missiles. And from Egyptian sources it seems that the middle of the (first) week saw a major battle in Sinai in which Sharon lost the site of his Advanced H.Q."

The decisive change on the Southern Front came on the Thursday, when the Egyptian C.-in-C., General Ismail, began to bring over into Sinai the 500 tanks he had held on the west bank of the Canal to protect the rear of his armies. Ismail's apparent intention was to divert some of the Israeli effort from the increasingly hard-pressed Syrians.

Sharon argued that this was the moment to strike across the Canal, and he was supported in his belief by Aluf Avraham Tamir. Their plan was overruled by Dayan, Elazar and Bar-Lev, who wanted to wait for a build-up of Israeli forces in Sinai as men and weapons were released from the Syrian front.

ENEMY ARMOUR

The then O.C. Southern Command, Shmuel Gonen, is credited by the "Sunday Times" with having had the perspicacity to see the build-up of Egyptian armour in Sinai as "the decisive opportunity for Israeli tanks to destroy the Egyptian armour, because the Egyptians in advancing would have to leave the protection of their infantry-borne missile screens." Bar-Lev supported this appreciation of the situation.

On the second Sunday of the war Egypt came out to fight, and as Gonen and Bar-Lev had predicted, this presented the Israeli tank crews with the targets they had been seeking.

"This attack did not come out of a period of calm, for fighting had been more or less continuous since the first day. But it was a dramatic increase in the scale of the Egyptian effort."

With more than 1,600 tanks involved, the battle surpassed the Second World War battle of El Alamein for the amount of armour deployed by the two sides. The main Egyptian thrust was made in the direction of the Gidi Pass. Within an hour the well-dug-in Israeli tanks had destroyed the Egyptian first wave, and when 145 Egyptian tanks rolled forward in the second wave, the Israelis hit them with everything they had.

The "Sunday Times" believes that it is an exaggeration to claim, as Israel does, to have destroyed 250 Egyptian tanks, but the paper pointed out that even Arab communiques confirmed terrible Egyptian losses.

"This Sunday battle had been the most significant mass armoured confrontation of the war. The cautious waiting game policy of Elazar, Bar-Lev and Gonen had been borne out by the result. The scene was now set for them to give the go ahead to Arik Sharon to attempt a bold counter-attack across the Canal. As often happened with Sharon initiatives, the attack did not go exactly as his superiors had intended. It succeeded, but only just."

The forces punching their way towards the Canal ran into much stiffer opposition than expected, and the whole operation fell dangerously behind schedule. "On any orthodox military measurement, Sharon's attempt to establish a bridgehead was a disaster. Starting with a division, he had managed after 16 hours of frantic activity to get a force of rather less than battalion strength across the canal, plus a little armoured support.

NO BRIDGE

"There was no bridge, and because of shell damage done to the bridge sections on the way through, there was no chance of establishing one within the next 12 hours.

"Considering the amount of shoot-ing that had been going on in the whole Tasa—Bitter Lakes—Ismailia triangle since the previous evening, the Israelis had no right even to hope that they still had the advantage of surprise. Had a force in any kind of strength turned up on Tuesday there would have been nothing whatsoever the Israelis could have done about it. To get a division-strength force of her own across the water by barge ferry would have required 1,000 trips.

"What happened next was the result of remarkable ineptitude on the part of the Egyptian army and of behaviour on Sharon's part which his friends would regard as a manifestation of genius, and his enemies as a descent into military dementia.

Sharon decided to "to hell with the bridgehead, the important thing is to get behind the Egyptian lines." When Gonen heard Sharon's plan was to abandon the western crossing site and make off for the Egyptian rear areas, he told Sharon to dig in around the bridgehead and hold it until a new attempt at bridging could be made.

In a radio phone conversation the contradicting views could not be reconciled, and it ended abusively with Sharon shouting down the phone: "Gonen, if you had any balls, I'd tell you to cut them off and eat them."

"With that, Sharon split up his tiny force into raiding parties and sent them out in search of Sam sites, fuel dumps and anything else that seemed to be worth attacking. Slightly awed, one of Sharon's staff said that the army might well respond by kicking Arik out. 'So,' Sharon said, 'I'd join up under another name'."

SKY OPEN

Much of the damage inflicted by his raiding parties was relatively trivial, but by midday, according to Sharon, four Sam missile sites had been knocked out so that a wide area of sky had been opened up in which the Israeli jets could operate without inhibition.

The more remarkable factor was the absence of any Egyptian response, and the "Sunday Times" attributes this to the nature of the command structure of the Egyptian Army.

"**There was no Egyptian equivalent to the incessant Israeli patrol** and reconnaissance activity. Junior commanders simply fought the Israelis as and when they presented themselves, and gave no priority at all to making combat reports. And even divisional commanders — men on the equivalent level to Sharon — had little independence of action. The effect was that there were no real command centres closer to the fighting than Ismail's war room in Cairo. An Egyptian officer, asked after the war who had been the overall field commander, replied that it was Ismail sitting in front of his multi-coloured maps."

It was after dark on Tuesday evening before any Egyptian response came with a properly coordinated attack on the eastern approaches to the crossing point. Late as it was, it nearly succeeded. The Second Army came down from the north, and the Third Army came up from the south to relieve and reinforce the Egyptian infantry holding out in the "Chinese Farm" area.

The bloody battle raged for many hours before the Egyptian resistance at the Chinese Farm was reduced, and the artillery fire at the Canal crossing point slackened enough for the Israeli engineers to get their pontoons in position for their much delayed bridge. Losses continued to be heavy, and the paper quotes the commander of the bridging operation as saying: "Our boys were the target of all the guns and planes in the neighbourhood . . . everybody here lost a friend."

AIR COVER

The limited air cover that Israel was able to give this bridging operation was possible because Sharon's raiders had torn a hole in the Sam umbrella — "and that, perhaps, was the best argument in favour of his defiance of Gonen. Nonetheless, the fact was that a

plan which had originally failed dramatically was essentially being bailed out by the fighting ability of the Israeli rank and file. Around the middle of Wednesday, 30 hours behind schedule, the bridge was in place and the first of Bren Adan's three tank brigades began to roll across."

The bridge and its whole environment remained a perilous place for the rest of the week, but "the Egyptian attacks were more distinguished for their stubbornness than their coordination." On Wednesday night the Egyptians attempted an attack against the growing force established on the western bank, and were badly beaten. "The Israeli initiative west of the Canal did — just — succeed in the minimum political aims of achieving a morale-boosting victory and gaining a significant bargaining counter. Even so, it needed a somewhat cynical Israeli exploitation of cease-fire violations to rub home the victory."

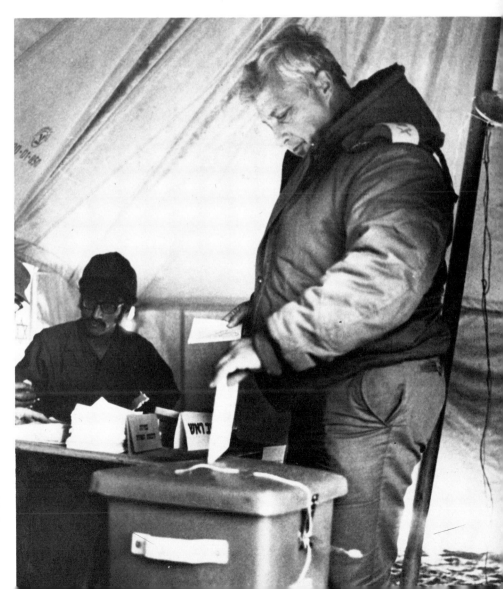

General Ariel Sharon casting his ballot.

Arab radios broadcast *hajjis* chant: 'Liberate Jerusalem'

BEIRUT (AP). — King Feisal of Saudi Arabia yesterday launched the Haj — the world's largest religious festival yesterday with two million Moslem pilgrims chanting "liberate Jerusalem."'

The 69-year-old monarch walked barefooted into Mecca's grand mosque and washed the Ka'aba, the cube-shaped black stone that stands as Islam's oldest shrine.

The roaring chants were clearly heard on Mecca radio as the man who led the Arab oil embargo performed the two-hour washing ceremony in seamless white garments.

Sixteen Arab and African radio stations hooked into the Saudi network for a live description of the annual event that started the week-long rituals of haj, or Moslem pilgrimage.

As "prince of the believers" and "guardian of the holy places of Islam," a religion that claims more than 500 million adherents, it is the Saudi monarch's exclusive privilege to wash the Ka'aba.

Moslems throughout the world kneel and turn their faces in the direction of the Ka'aba, when they perform their daily prayers.

Prophet Mohammed's tomb in Medina, 320 km. from Mecca, is classified as Islam's second holiest shrine. Jerusalem's Al Aksa Mosque and Dome of the Rock, where legend has it that Mohammed ascended to heaven on a winged steed are classified third.

In his traditional address to pilgrims from 63 countries on Sunday night, Feisal urged Moslem nations to join forces in a common struggle to recover Jerusalem.

"We need to bolster our solidarity, our faith in God to stand strong and united against the Zionists, the enemies of Allah," Feisal said.

"Jews have no religious or historic right to Jerusalem... their only shrine, the Temple of Solomon, was removed by the Romans when they occupied Jerusalem... So Israel has no right to remain in the Holy City."

Easier where they came from

Among the first voters to queue up outside polling stations in Ashdod and Beersheba were many Georgian immigrants, most of them voting in Israel for the first time.

Some expresed dissatisfaction with the fact that they had the 21 Knesset lists to choose from. "It was simpler in the Soviet Union, where there is only one list," one of them said.

Sixty-five miles to Cairo. The sign in Arabic reads: "To the right—17 K.M. to Ismalia. To the left—102 K.M. to Cairo."

Dangers at the Geneva talks

THE BITTER AND

There are clear dangers for Israel in the Geneva talks: The relinquishing of territory, the vague formula of the "legitimate" rights of the Palestinians, the possibility of an "imposed solution," and the pitfalls inherent in demilitarization. PROFESSOR BENJAMIN AKZIN argues that these dangers must be clearly perceived in order to put the prospects of an agreement into proper perspective.

HOWEVER important the Knesset elections which have just taken place, they do not change the essential external factors involved in the Middle East conflict, nor, for that matter, do they affect the underlying currents in Israeli society. Now, while the counting of votes is still proceeding, it is well to consider some of these factors which the new government, whatever its composition, will have to face.

After the first few critical days of the Yom Kippur war, a dramatic change for the better occurred in the military situation. The perceptive eye will notice somewhat similarly encouraging, though less dramatic, developments on the hitherto bleak political front.

The first cracks have appeared in the recently established and seemingly solid phalanx of Arab unity. Industrialized nations are beginning to prepare to resist the Arab oil blackmail and to hasten their progress toward independence from Arab suppliers. The developing countries, only recently on their way to becoming satellites of the Arab world, are now perturbed over the effect of Arab oil policy on their own economies and show signs of serious unrest. Arab politicians, more sensitive to outside currents than ever before, have already taken note of these symptoms and have begun to loosen their stranglehold on the world oil market.

Justified suspicion

For all our justified suspicions regarding the Arab countries' ultimate designs on Israel, it does seem that some groups within them have started pondering the alternative of a real reconciliation with Israel's existence. Even within the terrorist movement, despite continuing calls for "the liberation of the fatherland" and the "elimination of the Zionist foreign body from the map of the Near East," hints are now being dropped of their readiness to compromise on the basis of coexistence with Israel. And though it is likely that Israel's destruction remains the long-term objective of the Arab leadership everywhere, the possibility should not be overlooked of the "dynamism of peace" gaining strength in the course of time at the expense of an irreconcilable revanchism. None of this is any cause for reducing our watchfulness, nor is there as yet any reason for rejoicing. But the gloom that has settled recently over so many minds has lightened somewhat of late.

This having been said, let us look at the dangers which seemed near-fatal a few weeks ago and which still represent very real threats. To perceive these dangers clearly may help in overcoming them. Nothing but illusion followed by disillusionment and renewed near-despair would ensue were we to refrain from facing these dangers.

There are a number of danger-spots connected with the Geneva conference. The disengagement talks now under way is one of them. "Disengagement of forces," we might just as well realize, has become a polite euphemism for a one-sided relinquishment of territory by Israel. There is no longer talk of retreating to the October 22 lines. What is being discussed now is a retreat from both the west bank of the Canal and a considerable portion of the Sinai peninsula — and this prior to any conclusion of peace, to any declaration of non-belligerence, to any formal armistice, to any precise commitment on Egypt's side, and even to any concrete evidence of Egypt's intent to prepare for near-peace normality such as would flow, for instance, from preparations to open the Suez Canal for navigation. More exactly, two points are under discussion: how far Israel would retreat into Sinai; and to what extent Egyptian military re-occupation of the relinquished territory would be checked by limitations upon numbers and/or by the presence of foreign troops and observers.

A second threat is that contained in the deliberately vague formula of the "legitimate" or "national" or "integral" rights of the Palestinian people" — all of these adjectives having aready appeared in Arab or pro-Arab sources. While in Israel the debate continues as to whether and what concessions should be made within the 1967 lines, the ground is being prepared on the other side for additional demands when the time comes, with parts of the Negev and Galilee as the next goal. Indeed, it is at that point that Syria appears to be intending to enter the talks. In this connection, I do not even mention the question of who, precisely, would represent the "Palestinians". For the Soviets, the Americans, the Arabs, other than Jordan's present government, and possibly some conservative elements on the West Bank, it has become obvious that sooner or later it will be the terrorists who will mainly represent the "Palestinian people", and it is only a question of prestige and timing whether they will appear in that capacity at Geneva or at a later stage.

Imposed solution

A third threat is contained in the possibility of an "imposed solution." In truth, the distinction between "friendly persuasion," "pressure," and "imposition," is more semantic than real. A degree of pressure is undoubtedly going to be exercised upon Israel, whatever the name under which it will appear (and upon Egypt and Jordan too, if this is any consolation, though this will come from Arab quarters and from

THE SWEET

certain European countries as well, and not only from the Super-Powers). This in itself is not so tragic, for pressures, open or disguised, are omnipresent in international politics, and the balance of various pressures is what makes for international relations. The basic question is not *whether* there will be an attempt to impose a solution, but the *nature* of the solution imposed. That it will not amount to an immediate peace is aready clear. What remains unclear is whether the solution will be meant as a step towards peace or as a prelude to a renewed attempt to assault Israel. And the crucial point is not what the USA or even the USSR mean it to be, but what the Arab world mean it to be.

A fourth danger is connected with the idea of demilitarization, so much talked about of late. The futility of international guarantees has been sufficiently exposed and is now fully understood. What people understand less is that demilitarization is at least equally as futile, and possibly more so. An agreement to limit or to exclude military moves by a given state in a territory acknowledged to belong to it, is essentially unenforcible under modern conditions. To realize this, we need think back not only to the helplessness of Israel in face of the advancement of missile sites by Egypt immediately after the 1970 cease-fire, and contrary to its stipulations, but also to the inability of France (largely because of pressure from Britain) to react to the entry of German troops into the "demilitarized" Rhineland in 1936. It was that experience, incidentally, that played a cardinal role in persuading French politicians, with Flandin and Daladier at their head, that it was no use trying to stop Hitler. What is more, a re-militarization of any demilitarized areas around Israel's borders must be expected to proceed piecemeal: first a company, then a couple of batteries, then a battalion and so on. At no given moment could Israel take decisive action by crossing the border, without incurring universal wrath for "over-reacting" and without being named as an aggressor. To rely on others, whether U.N. observers or international contingents or foreign troops, to stop such progressive re-militarization would amount to placing our hopes once more in those much-vaunted "guarantees."

Among the dangers confronting us, I have not mentioned the possibility, feared by many, of a "sell-out" by the United States or by its prestigious Secretary of State. It is puerile to ascribe such an intention to either. Their good-will towards Israel is unquestionable and, for the time being at least, appears both sincere and firm. But two reservations ought to be kept in mind. One is the famous *"rebus sic stantibus"* clause to which all international policies are subject: that is, a change in prevailing conditions may bring a change in policy. The other reservation springs from the fact that, to the United States, Israel's security is but one objective among many others. It is not exactly expendable, but it may have to be made an object of compromise (and therefore conceivably "compromised" in the other sense of the word) against other equally, or more, important objectives, within the framework of a global policy which allows of compromises. To us, Israel's security is the one primary and vital concern, on a par, let us say, with the concern of Washington that the United States not be abandoned to a nuclear attack.

Sensible solution

Similarly, a temporary cooling-off of Arab-Israel hostilities may appear to the United States a sensible solution, whatever the future prospects, whereas to Israel, a temporary solution makes sense only if its prospects outweigh the risks. To take note of this difference of attitudes has nothing to do wtih "trusting" or "not trusting" President Nixon or Dr. Kissinger. "Trust" is a factor in relations between individuals and has no relevance to international politics.

None of the above means that the Geneva talks and the simultaneous contacts that go on between us, the Great Powers, and various Arab elements, are devoid of hope. They are not. But if we want to extract any possible sweet out of the bitter we must first realize that the bitter is there. The difficulties existing or lurking must be clearly perceived. Wishing them away will only make them more real.

This poster which recently appeared on Swiss automobiles reads "Better without a car than without character."

Mild weather favors this outdoor polling station at an army unit yesterday. The booth partially conceals a half-track.

PALESTINE WAS EMPTY

To the Editor of The Jerusalem Post

Sir, — I was not surprised when, at the opening session of the Peace Conference in Geneva, the Prime Minister of Jordan attempted to show that the Jews are interlopers who came into a Palestine heavily populated by Arabs who, themselves were indigenous to the land. His argument is fallacious and should not be allowed to win by default, as have so many others which, through constant unchallenged repetition have acquired the aura of verity (e.g. the inflated figures given for the number of Arabs who left the country in 1948).

The truth is that the total population of Palestine at mid-19th century was, at the very most, 100,000, including perhaps 15,000 Jews. Proof of the depopulated status of this country during most of the 19th century may be found in statistics in books written contemporarily by Christian scholars liv-

ing here, such as those by Rev. T.H. Horne (1836), Rev. W.H. Thomson (1861), Col. C.R. Conder (1889), Rev. J. Fulton (1900) as well as in U.S. Consular Reports and other sources.

To give one example: According to Bishop M. Russell, in "Palestine, or the Holy Land, from the earliest period to the present time" (1849) the population of the major towns was as follows: Jerusalem, 12,000 (including 6,000 Jews); Bethlehem 1,000-1,500; Hebron, "400 families"; Jenin, 800; Nablus 6,000 to less than 10,000; Nazareth 1,000-1,500; Safad, "600 houses of which 150 were Jewish homes"; Tiberias, "less than 2,000, half Jewish." No figures were given by Russell for the following: Gaza, which was then according to other sources the size of Jerusalem; Acre, with 5,000 in 1861; Jaffa, with 4 to 5,000 in 1836 and 11,000 in 1861; Ramleh, with 5 to 6,000 in 1836 dropping to 4,000 in 1861; Beersheba, Haifa

Jericho, Lod, Ramalla and Tulkarm which either did not exist at that time or were mere "miserable villages." A large-scale map of 1853 by W. Hughes showed few inhabited villages.

Where did the 1,280,000 Arabs in the British Mandate census of 1946 come from? Obviously the great majority of "Palestinians" were themselves immigrants or sons or grandsons of immigrants from other Arab lands, that came to partake of the prosperity generated by the Jews. Entire towns and villages in 1948 could trace their origins to other countries, e.g. Safad (Morocco); Bet Shean (Egypt); Bellad esh Sheikh (Hauran), to name a few. Even during the Holocaust, when the doors of this country were slammed shut in the faces of European Jews looking for succour, the Arab immigration remained unabated.

PROF. R. KENNETH
Rishon-le-Zion, December 24.

FOREIGN MINISTRY UNDERESTIMATED ENEMY

By Prof. Benjamin Akzin

Everybody has been talking about the "lessons of the Yom Kippur War," and many people rightly consider that the state or states of mind prevalent in various sectors of Israeli society during recent years were an important contributory factor both to the initial shock suffered at the outbreak of hostilities and to the deterioration of Israel's image in the outside world.

The basic weakness in our mental attitude has generally been correctly identified as the sin of over-confidence. But the manifestations of this over-confidence were manifold, and not all of them have attracted sufficient attention.

There was the obvious arrogant, brash and strident over-confidence that caused the public to over-estimate our military capabilities and to under-estimate the capacity of the Arabs to improve their military performance. Over-confidence leads to *nonchalance,* to neglect of vigilance and the need to take precautions. This attitude apparently penetrated even our military establishment, and not only its intelligence branch but also the operations and quartermaster's branches. Even the highest echelons of the IDF appear to have been affected. If this were not the case, certain omissions which came to light at the outbreak of hostilities and during the period preceding them would not have occurred.

A similar atmosphere of over-confidence, of facile optimism, of over-estimation of our own skill in diplomacy and an under-estimation of the enemy's diplomatic-cum-propagandistic know-how, characterized our Foreign Ministry. In a way, less can be pleaded in extenuation in this latter case. For, while nothing happened during six years to disprove our optimism in the military field, ominous signs were multiplying to show its baselessness in the fields of diplomacy and propaganda. But the Foreign Ministry preferred to close its eyes to these signs, seeking refuge in a formula that everything was going to be fine.

When discussing the lessons of the past in terms of essential political and personal adjustments, not only the weight of past mistakes should be gauged, but also the capacity of the above two establishments, and of those heading them, to learn from the past and introduce changes in their attitudes and work habits. It is here, I fear, that our diplomatic and information establishment falls short. Our senior military men seem much more flexible than many of our senior diplomats, the contrast sharpening the nearer we reach the top of the two establishments. If the current discussions regarding the personal changes required were to consider capacity to shoulder the tasks of the future, instead of concentrating on responsiblity for mistakes of the p a s t, appropriate consequences could easily be drawn. In saying this, I do not rerer to dovisn or hawkish policy-aims — a matter for the future Cabinet to decide — but simply to the degree to which the men in charge can master the techniques of their trade.

Not being a specialist in military studies, I would not venture to describe the techniques required in that field. But the life-long study of international diplomacy and propaganda convinces me that in diplomacy the major qualities needed are the ability to evaluate a situation correctly, a readiness to foresee its possible variations, sufficient mental flexibility to plan alternative courses, and, of course, skill in negotiation. The latter involves the ability to listen as well as to talk, to combine personal friendliness with steadfastness in adhering to one's own position, to adjust arguments to the character and interests of the other party, and, above all, to conform to the old Roman maxim *suaviter in modo, fortiter in re.* (Freely translated: "an iron fist in a velvet glove.")

In the field of information or propaganda, the essentials are an understanding of the peculiarities of the media and an alertness to the challenges of the hour.

Shortcoming in both fields, long obvious to those in the know, must be corrected; and if the qualities needed to accomplish the two tasks are, as many believe, incompatible, these tasks should be divided between two distinct agencies.

Paradoxically enough, the over-confidence already referred to was largely responsible for what is ostensibly an opposite state of mind: the disillusionment of some of our best minds and most sensitive souls with those basic values of our society that go under the names of Jewish identity, Zionism and Israeli patriotism. Much of this disillusionment is due to materialism and its corruptive by-products, and to the lackadaisical acceptance of those social evils which have taken root among us. If so many of our intellectuals, teachers and artists, university and secondary school students react to this materialism by enjoying its fruits while at the same time despising it, this is an easily understood psychological phenomenon.

But this disillusionment has other roots, too. It is due in no small measure to the assumption of many among us that the State is secure and can be taken for granted, and that, therefore, we can afford to search elsewhere for ideals worth living for. It is in the course of pursuing other ideals — justice to the Arabs, putting ourselves in the enemy's shoes, empathy for supernational brotherhood, and so forth — that the values of Jewish national consciousness, Zionism, and Jewish statehood find themselves downgraded. This inter-connection was blatantly demonstrated by the dramatic manifesto of a group of university professors on the morrow of the Yom Kippur War: their assumption of Israel's invulnerability was suddenly shaken, and as a result their patriotism (a term they previously used almost as an invective) have already reverted to their former postures.

A far deeper re-thinking will be required before those concerned, in many ways the best among us, realize that the continued existence of the Jewish people, of Zionism, and of the State of Israel, cannot yet be taken for granted and that these are still ideals worth fighting for.

The Israel Foreign Ministry delegation to the Geneva Conference, just before it emplaned for its first trip to the talks last month. From left to right: Foreign Ministry Legal Adviser Meir Rosenne, Foreign Minister Abba Eban, Ministry political adviser Shmuel Divon, Assistant Director-General Ephraim Evron, and Director General Eytan Bentsur.

French people support Israel, politician says

Jerusalem Post Reporter

TEL AVIV. — The majority of the French people support Israel, but a change in official policy is not likely before the presidential elections, according to a visiting French politician.

Alain Bonnefoy, secretary of the young guard of Jean Lecanuet's tiny Centre Democrate Party in France, heads a twenty-man delegation which winds up a week's visit in Israel today.

President Pompidou's term of office expires in 1976, "but there are good reasons to believe that elections will be held this year," he said.

France cannot play a positive role in the Middle East, Mr. Bonnefoy said, because she is "tied by her pro-Arab stand."

"But we, and practically all Frenchmen, want Israel to live in peace behind secure borders."

SABBATH LIFTS FOR SOLDIERS

To the Editor of The Jerusalem Post

Sir, — It is indeed meritorious and in the best of good taste, that most motorists have chosen the Sabbath as their carless day.

However, unlike other countries which have introduced carless days, Israel has no public transport on Saturdays and therefore those who least deserve to, are bearing the brunt. I refer, of course, to our soldiers coming home for a few precious hours of leave.

As every motorist knows, there are long stretches of road between towns, especially from the south to Tel Aviv. And it is here that soldiers can be seen gesturing desparingly at the few cars which speed by on Shabbat — unable or unwilling to provide them with desperately needed lifts.

Is there no way in which public transport could be used to assist these young men on Shabbat? Surely the defenders of our nation deserve foremost consideration.

PEARL LEVINSOHN
Netanya, December 23

Daylight saving & religious freedom

By AARON SITTNER
Jerusalem Post Reporter

Orthodox Jewish circles are maintaining their pressure to have the introduction of daylight saving time — scheduled for January 15 — delayed for about two months.

The fuel-saving measure was universally backed when it was mooted in mid-November. Shortly afterwards, however, it became an issue of "religious freedom," as one person put it.

The problem is based on requirements of *halacha* as they concern the times for prayer. A Jew is required to pray three times daily, and must recite each prayer within its own time ambit. These times are not constant, but vary with the position of the sun in relation to earth.

According to Rabbi David Shisgal of the newly formed Committee for Postponement of Daylight Saving Time, March 15 is the earliest date on which the clock could be advanced without causing hardship to persons who wish to pray before going to work.

"This is a basic religious freedom," he told *The Jerusalem Post* yesterday. "Several non-religious Members of Knesset whom we have approached pledged to support us."

He said another dimension has been added to the problem as a result of the war. Many persons who used to shun the synagogue have now become regular worshippers because they have to recite *kaddish* prayer for kin who fell in battle.

The earliest a person may begin his morning prayers is approximately 50 minutes prior to sunrise. In the Tel Aviv area, this would be 5.54 a.m. on January 15, 5.47 a.m. on February 1, 5.36 a.m. on February 15 and 5.21 on March 1.

Rabbi Shisgal said: "Only by March 15, when the beginning time is 5.04 a.m., could the clock be put ahead an hour and leave the religious Jew enough time to pray before starting out to work."

A final decision on the date for introducing daylight saving time is to be made by the Ministerial Economic Committee when it meets on Sunday.

SAMARITANS AND NABLUS

To the Editor of The Jerusalem Post

Sir, — As a Nablus-born Samaritan now residing in Holon, I am gratified with Mr. Sa'id M. Kan'an's personal declaration (in his Reader's Letter of today) that as a Nablus resident he regards Nablus Samaritans as his brethren and that he never considered them a foreign element in Nablus.

Nevertheless, I would have expected that Mr. Kan'an would admit that the Samaritans' lot in the past was far from a happy one, as is particularly evident from the fact that at the beginning of the Arab rule in the seventh century C.E. the Samaritans numbered some 300,000 to 350,000 people, but at the end of the period of Arab domination, in 1917, there were no more than 146 Samaritans left. I would have hoped that Mr. Kan'an would declare that times have changed and that he would promise that in the future the Arabs would not treat Samaritans as they have done in the past, since the historical truth stands in total contradiction to his statements, which paint a picture of Samaritans embraced by the Arabs as a mother embraces her children.

The most important matter, however, is the continuation of the Samaritans' connection with their holy centre (Shechem) and this is free of any political implications. This connection is vital and arises from our very tangible rights all throughout our history and constitutes an absolute prerequisite to our continued existence. We hope that this right will be respected as far as all Samaritans, both from Holon and Nablus, are concerned and that it be respected under any condition and at all times as it has been respected ever since June, 1967.

BENYAMIM TSEDAKA
Editor of A.B. — Samaritan News
Holon. December 20.

BASIC FACTS

To the Editor of The Jerusalem Post

Sir, — I wonder if our Israeli propaganda experts have ever seriously tried to explain the following basic facts to world opinion and first and foremost to Afro-Asian and Communist countries:

1. In their condemnation of imperialism and colonialism, Afro-Asians and Communists should be made aware of the fact that the biggest victim of imperialism is the Jewish people, who were first subjugated and then driven out of their land by the brute force of one of the most powerful imperialist nations in history — ancient Rome. Should this wrong, even if committed 2,000 years ago, not be repaired, especially since its consequences are still being felt today?

2. The Communist bloc, whose very reason for existence is the idea of equitable distribution of the land amongst all men, should fully recognize the monstrous disproportion in the division of land between the Arab and Jewish peoples. Is it not high time to cry aloud in the international forum: "Land reform not only amongst individuals but also among peoples"?

3. The Arabs would do better to think seriously about the truth in the proverb, which has its equivalent in many languages "He who wants all, shall lose all."

HATUMA RAHAMIM
Ashkelon, December 11.

Goren asks Pope to intercede on PoWs

Chief Rabbi Shlomo Goren yesterday asked the intercession of the Vatican on the issue of Israeli prisoners of war in Syria.

The Chief Rabbi asked the Apostolic Delegate in Jerusalem, Msgr. Pio Laghi, to convey his request to the Pope — and the Delegate promised to do so.

Msgr. Laghi paid a visit to Rabbi Goren yesterday.

The Chief Rabbi also asked the Papal See's help on the impasse between Israel and Egypt on the retrieval and burial of Israeli soldiers left dead on Sinai battlefields now under the control of the Egyptian Second and Third Armies.

5,000 volunteers came since war —and most stayed

Jerusalem Post Reporter

Five thousand volunteers have arrived in Israel since the Yom Kippur War.

Mordecai Bar-On, head of the Jewish Agency's Youth and Hechalutz Department, said yesterday that the percentage of those who have dropped out is very low. In a report to the Agency Executive, he attributed this to the close examination of all prospective volunteers in their home countries and the seriousness they have displayed towards their work here.

Except for 600 who arrived here on their own, all have been channelled through the Jewish Agency.

Arye Dulzin, acting Agency chairman, said that the volunteer movement would be widened and given a permanent framework. It will include persons above 30, as well as all levels of education and a variety of professions, he said.

A wounded soldier casting his ballot yesterday at a mobile balloting station at the Sheba Hospital.

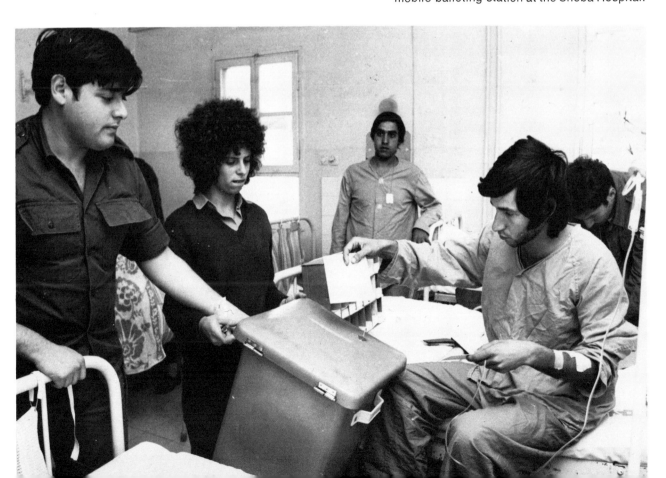

Oil blackmail, only a beginning

The dire picture of the world painted by the economist Thomas Malthus, at the end of the eighteenth century, may apply to the world today where the energy crisis has accented the significance of limited natural resources, writes Professor F. de Körösy, of the Negev University Research and Development Authority.

THE energy crisis has made the world aware that the "affluent society" has been living in a fool's paradise.

It had been warned by Malthus as early as 1798 that continued increase of the world's population would end in overcrowding, and eventual starvation, but for years his warning seemed to refer to so distant a future as not even to be true.

Today it is clear that the Malthusian theory applies to commodities, as well as space. Time and again calculations have been published showing how long resources of coal, oil, iron and practically everything else are likely to last. Obviously, they would last longer at the consumption level of Nigeria than at that of the United States, but eventually they would disappear. The world is now becoming concerned about its fossil fuel sources, coal and oil.

All in all, the long-term energy situation may not be altogether hopeless, but is still very far from being solved. The short-term problem is that we have got accustomed to the very comfortable use of oil, and have neglected coal and other possible energy sources such as oil-shale. Furthermore, at least half of the oil today comes from the Arab states and may easily come under Russian domination. As we have seen, shortage of energy will also quickly lead to a shortage of most other commodities which can only be isolated, enriched and manufactured with energy.

All this could easily happen before the Malthusian situation is reached. In peace and with international cooperation, resources could last longer, but eventually the world population may have to decline to the level determined by utilizable solar energy. When shall we get that far? Nobody knows. Evidently reserves of one commodity will last longer than reserves of another and evidently we could do better with cooperation than with enmity, blackmail and war. And the sooner we begin to limit or even decrease world population, the better.

Up to now, all these terrifying prophecies have not come true because new sources of energy and of valuable commodities have been brought to light. It was this which gave us the feeling of false security. We thought that there was no real problem and that this process could last for ever. It cannot. The law of conservation of matter is valid and the law of continuous loss of useful energy is also true. The only question is, when will a critical shortage of an essential commodity be reached?

The energy crisis we have just entered upon is still far from eventual shortage of an essential commodity. However, it is the first time we experience the macabre feeling it creates and it is high time we began to think about it in global dimensions.

Time to breathe

New oil sources have been found in different parts of the world. They only have to be developed to give us renewed time to breathe. The use of nuclear fission energy is scarcely at its beginnings and the problems of fusion energy, though unsolved at present, could perhaps be solved in the not too distant future. Solar photo-electric cells seem very attractive, but are too costly at the average daily energy influx of about 0.2 kilowatt per metre square, i.e., the energy consumption of a 200 watt light bulb.

The population can perhaps be stabilized before a too serious Malthusian situation is reached. The writing, however, has appeared on the wall and it may be the last time we are free to make decisions.

As things stand today the western world is spoiled by comfort and the most comfortable source of present day energy happens to be in Arab hands and is to a large extent already manipulated by Russia. The oil-controlling nations have begun to blackmail the free world. The decline of imperialism in the West and its awakening in the East has led to the nationalization of oil companies and a rapid rise in oil prices. Money flows towards the oil wells and much of it is not even made use of there. It ruins western currencies and allows an unprecedented import of arms.

Unluckily for us, it has also led to political blackmail, in the first instance turned against Israel. Blackmail may be turned in the future against practically anybody. Governments could be overthrown, political systems changed, incommensurate prices in money or commodities extorted in exchange. Only the most short-sighted of western politicians fail to see this clearly, but most of them keep silent about it for fear of making it come true. Suppose only for argument's sake that Israel could be wiped off the map in the course of the "peace talks", Russian-Arab blackmail would continue, as happened with Hitler's aggressions after Munich. The free world will have to make a stand or collapse.

A stand for what? For an equitable, just price of oil? Here we encounter an essential theoretical difficulty. Even if political blackmail is ruled out, what is the "just" price of oil? Actually, what is the just price, the value, of anything? We have no answer.

Should we fall back on the capitalist definition of value on a free market? Not in a monopolistic situation in which a market has ceased to exist. The moment one group possesses something that has become vital for others who do not have it, that group can squeeze anything from the latter.

We have not yet quite reached this situation, but we are much nearer to it than we would have thought possible two years ago. Not having even a theoretically correct answer makes a situation very bad indeed. Theoretical solutions are generally not quite true but they are often a tolerable first approximation to an answer. The first solution may work until a second approximation is worked out. But what if even to start with there is no answer? We are at an impasse.

Human nature being what it is, there is no reason to be optimistic. Nobody is going to be willing to starve just because an opponent power or an agglomeration of countries is withholding a vital commodity in order to strangle it. During its successive years of bad harvests Russia was not willing to starve, and squeezed food out of America. For the West today oil may be just as important.

A first hit-back could, of course, be a counter-blockade of food and essential products by the industrial civilizations. But because of their low living standards, some Arab countries could go a long way on the road to hunger without submitting, especially if the masses and not the leaders are hungry. Still, it

might possibly work if the West were not too civilized and used this weapon quickly. Soon it could be too late.

The other, more terrible but historically more usual solution would be a military occupation of the oil wells by the powers who need it. This might trigger off an atomic war, because the Russians evidently plan a less military kind of infiltration of these countries. Fear of an atomic disaster would only work, however, so long as hope of survival itself survives.

Once more we have arrived at a problem which is unsolved even in theory. To whom does oil, or for that matter any natural resource "belong?" Shepherds drove their sheep, goats and camels along the sparse vegetation of deserts, until geologists and engineers came from far away and found oil under their feet. At first the shepherds did not even know how to use the oil. More engineers came, wells were drilled and the shepherds began to learn how to work them and their grandchildren studied engineering. Contracts were agreed upon to divide up the proceeds. They may have been just or unjust but they have been torn up in our days anyway and the endless extortion has begun. How can we find a "just" contract in such cases? The stage seems to be set for a major war, perhaps a world war, for resources. Oil is only the beginning.

Goodwill required

A peaceful solution would obviously be preferable, but would require an enormous reservoir of goodwill all round for its achievement. Even-

tually, if we do not blow ourselves to smithereens before, it will be necessary to establish an international board to supervise both natural resources and population densities. And even though neither the United Nations nor its Security Council afford us much optimism about the functioning of such organisation, it is necessary.

We may be given a period of grace in a few years' time. The Western powers will have opened up Alaskan, North Sea and Indian Ocean oil reserves and the acute monopolistic situation of the oil sheikhs will crumble. Neglected fossil fuels will be used, atomic energy plants will be built everywhere in spite of the hazards involved.

Israel has been the first, but will not be the last, victim of this new blackmail by natural resources. We shall have to withstand enormous pressures in order to survive the next four or five years until the monopolies are broken and some Western eyes are opened to what is going on. Then we and the world can stumble on towards the next blackmail crisis. Let us hope that it will not be played out again on our backs.

As long as we have no better theories, perhaps we and the world would be best advised to try to follow the Talmudic precept: "Do not unto others what you would not want them to do to you."

WHEN I GRADUATED from Columbia College in 1925, practically all the young intellectuals I knew were hovering on the fringes of the Communist movement. Only one or two were card carrying members, but almost everyone else was, at least, emotionally involved with this new force that was believed to represent a new hope for mankind. Most liberal circles, and certainly most liberal magazines took the attitude of "Let's give them a chance. What the world has done to date hasn't turned out to be quite so wonderful; so let us see whether this new system might produce something nearer to the heart's desire."

The attitude, then, towards communism among the college group of my day was one of permissiveness, encouragement, open-

mindedness, and above all, hopefulness.

Many of my friends and acquaintances would go to cocktail parties, meetings, and smokers where funds were raised for the support of Communist endeavors. The Daily Worker was going strong. The Communist Party was led by Earl Browder, but had many Jews within its ranks.

In 1925, I made my first trip to Palestine, in 1927, my second trip. Both were extended stays, covering more than a year. During 1927, I visited Hebron, and took occasion to drop in on the Hebron Yeshiva. This academy, the Slobodka Yeshiva, had been transferred from Lithuania to Palestine in 1925. Here I met boys who were more or less my own age, some still in their teens, some in their early twenties. All were students diligently engaged in

And it shall come to pass,

that as you were a curse among the nations,

O house of Yehuda, and house of Israel;

so will I save you, and you shall be a blessing :

fear not, but let your hands be strong.

These are the things that you shall do;

Speak every man the truth to his neighbour;

execute the judgment of truth and

peace in your gates :

and let none of you devise evil in

your hearts against his neighbour...

saith the LORD

Zechariah 8

The above paid ad was placed by an anonymous person, as a gesture of comfort to his countrymen.

JEWS IN ARAB LANDS

To the Editor of The Jerusalem Post

Sir, — I feel that the suffering of Jews in Arab countries has not been given sufficient world wide publicity. Now that the Government of Israel is starting a campaign to show the world a little of what has been done to Israeli prisoners-of-war, the opportunity might be taken to stress that it is not only the Israeli soldiers who have suffered at the hands of the Arabs but also their own citizens, Jews from their countries, who were born there and lived there for many generations.

It is ironical that the Egyptians talk about their Arabs in Israel, who of course live better now than ever before, while the Israeli Government is silent about the Jews in Arab lands who are really suffering.

S. SPECTOR

Jerusalem, December 12.

BEN-GURION STREET

Sir, — May I suggest that Allenby Street in Tel Aviv and Haifa be renamed Ben-Gurion Street. These two streets are important enough so that the name of the founder of the State won't be diminished. On the other hand, it is high time that we got rid of those remains of British colonial rule and start honouring a national hero instead of a foreigner.

BENJAMIN DOUKARSKY

Jerusalem, December 15.

To the Editor of The Jerusalem Post

Sir, — The time has finally arrived, I believe, to rename King George Street in Jerusalem. With the recent passing away of David Ben-Gurion, the architect of the modern State of Israel, it would be most fitting and appropriate to have this main thoroughfare renamed in his honour.

Also, Allenby Street in Tel Aviv could be fittingly renamed in David Ben-Gurion's memory.

TZVI (HERSHEL) TOREM

Jerusalem, December 28.

Jerry Chervin (wearing hat, center) and Rabbi Shlomo Mersel at the newly inaugurated field yeshiva near Kuneitra.

'Field yeshiva' at Kuneitra warms body and soul

By DAVID LANDAU
Jerusalem Post Reporter

Jerry Chervin yesterday made the last of a series of 33 "Bible and Booze Express" trips to the Golan Heights, handing out his 613th pair of tefilin to an officer serving in occupied Syria. The number is symbolic — there are 613 *mitzvot* in Jewish law. Last week Chervin, an American immigrant living in Jerusalem, gave the 525th pair to none other than Chief of Staff David Elazar whom he met on Mount Hermon. Rav-Aluf Elazar said he had read of "Jerry's" private spiritual-and-temporal-welfare efforts for the troops, and praised them warmly.

Last week too Chervin inaugurated, together with the Ministry for Religious Affairs, a small "field yeshiva" near Kuneitra. The Ministry provides the Talmud books and other religious requisites, and Chervin supplies vodka and brandy, warm socks and gloves, as well as Psalters and prayer books.

The yeshiva has a nucleus of students from among units of yeshiva tudents serving in the locality, but the idea is for any passing soldier to drop in and warm body and soul.

Accompanying Chervin was Rabbi Shlomo Mersel, principal of the Horev School in Jerusalem who gave a lecture at the field yeshiva. The girls at his school knitted balaclava hats for the troops in the Golan with wool which Chervin supplied — and Chervin then ferried the hats up north, together with his other goodies, acquired with the help of contributions from local and American friends.

In his 33 trips, Chervin and his "junior partner," Dr. Arthur Levinson of Hadassah Hospital, have covered 13,000 miles in Chervin's car which was new before the war broke out and is now a good deal the worse for wear.

Apart from tefilin, food, drink and clothes, Chervin handed out three television sets: one to the Mount Hermon garrison, one at Mazra'at Beit Jann and one at Tel Shams.

The field yeshiva's name — seen on the wall behind the students — is *"safra vesayfa"* — "the book and the sword."

393

Kuwait's refusal to try murderers

A "New York Times" editorial yesterday said: "As the Government of Kuwait continues to resist world-wide demands for a proper trial of the five Arab terrorists who murdered 32 innocent persons in recent criminal acts of air piracy, an international agreement to deal with such obstruction of justice becomes more urgent than ever.

"... Attempts by the International Civil Aviation Organization to deal with the problem have been persistently sabotaged by a line-up of Arab and African nations, abetted and supported by France and the USSR."

THANKS TO THE DUTCH

Jerusalem Post Reporter

TEL AVIV. — A man who wants to remain anonymous yesterday parted with two rare old books in token of respect for the people of Holland.

A Latin version of the Bible, printed in Amsterdam in 1712, was handed to the Honorary Dutch Consul, Joseph Voet, for transmission to the National Library of Holland, and a book of verse by Luyken, also printed in the 18th century, was presented to Pit Bosboom of Amsterdam, who, as a member of the Dutch resistance, saved a thousand Jews from the Nazis during the Second World War.

The ceremony was held at the office of Hillel Seidel, chairman of the pro-Holland Committee, at the Histadrut Executive. It was attended by representatives of the persons saved and of the Abrams Institute for Crippled Children, which Mr. Bosboom has been helping for years.

President Katzir, first to vote at the Moadon Ha'oleh, in Talbieh, Jerusalem.

---

the study of the Talmud. These were youths wedded to Tora study. Some had come from the United States, some from Canada, some were born in Palestine. It would be hard to find a group that was less politically minded, or less practical minded for that matter, than this small group of dedicated young men.

In 1929, Jews throughout the world were outraged by news of the massacre in Hebron. Arabs had cold-bloodedly slaughtered men, women, children and the aged. Among the 77 dead and 80 wounded were many of these same young men whom I had visited with and talked to. In their mad frenzy to eliminate the Jew, the Arab rioters had

Americans feel their talents under-utilized

By JUDY SIEGEL
Special to The Jerusalem Post

Forty young adults from the U.S. and Canada met this week with 73 of their Israeli contemporaries and concluded that their talents are being seriously under-utilized for the benefit of Israel.

Spurred on· by the young guard of several Israeli political parties, the Youth Leadership Division of the World Zionist Organization invited the up-and-coming intellectuals, businessmen and professionals to visit Israel for eight days. The aim of the discussions, which ended at Jerusalem's Tadmor School last night, was to find ways of cultivating a young Zionist leadership abroad and to make personal and practical contacts between Israeli and Diaspora Jewry.

Hardly a homogeneous or likeminded group, the visitors ranged from a 30-year-old wholesale shoe salesman to a long-haired teacher of Jewish consciousness at a California university and a lawyer-lobbyist for American consumer advocate Ralph Nader.

"We Americans have so much more to give than just money," the young lawyer told his Israeli counterparts. "Informal and nontraditional channels must be opened up between the two sides. If we had contacts here who would give us a shopping list of things the country could use and report when they arrived, we'd begin to minimize Israel's feeling of isolation from the outside world."

Knesset Member Dr. Yehuda Ben-Meir (NRP) agreed that young Jews are not being adequately mobilized to help Israel. "The reason," he explained, "is that they feel alienated from status quo institutions like the Presidents' Conference, that don't represent them and are not encouraging young leaders to help with the job."

"I don't think most young Americans know much about Israel or even feel close to her," interjected Eliot Shimoff, who teaches psychology at the University of Maryland. "How many can name a few of her political parties or describe her way of life?"

Uri Gordon, Israeli chairman of the Young Leadership of the World Labour Zionist Movement, added that the information gap exists on both sides. "Our parents had strong ties with the outside world because many of them were immigrants. But there is a danger that the new generation of sabras will grow up in Israel with no ties to Diaspora Jewry."

He urged the formation of a worldwide, non-party movement of young Zionists who would advocate a programme of aliya, volunteerism, the study of Hebrew and meaningful Jewish education.

During the course of the day-long session, the Israelis and Americans exchanged names and addresses, promising to keep in contact and to ensure that the youthful dialogue would blossom into practical help for the State of Israel.

NORWEGIAN SUPPORT
To the Editor of The Jerusalem Post

Sir, — As a student of history, I do not hesitate to predict that when this epoch is reviewed and appraised at some future date, the rebirth of Israel will stand out as the greatest and most glorious event of the century.

Like all crucial turns in history, the reconstruction of the Jewish State on its old soil cannot be achieved without struggle, bloodshed suffering, and — indeed — some injustice. The Yom Kippur War was only part of this pattern.

As a European friend of Israel, I often feel sick at heart when I see the European lack of knowledge and understanding, and their short memory about events in the Middle East. The European of today seems to be more concerned about his filthy oil problem, his standard of living and his barren materialism. For some years European opinion has been effectively thwarted by leftist propaganda, aided — alas — by returning UNTSO generals who have enthusiastically offered their patent "solutions" to all the problems in the area.

Something must be done to open the eyes of the Europeans before it is too late. I am afraid that your *real* friends in this part of the world are woefully few. This can and must be changed. But for the time being, the people of Israel are terribly alone with their great historical task.

May you keep your spirit and strength, whatever happens in Geneva, on the battlefields, or elsewhere.

ARNE HAUGAN
Major General, Norwegian Army
Bodo, Norway, December 26.

Battle of the airways

Philip Gillon

DURING THE Yom Kippur War, the Division for Broadcasts Abroad and to Immigrants of the Israel Broadcasting Services—the cumbersome title has replaced *Kol Zion Lagola* — broadcast 22 programmes a day, working round the clock. Victor Grajewski, the Director, claims proudly that at one stage, El Al and his Division were the only links between the Israelis and the world, apart from those provided by foreign correspondents. He has hundreds of letters to prove his claims.

Thus Howard Picker, of Albany New York, wrote on November 7:

"We in America are extremely anxious to hear Israel and urge you to develop this medium. The broadcasts of our detractors are more powerful than ours and the news here is often inaccurate. We find it difficult to comprehend why Radio Cairo is so much more powerful than Radio Israel. We Jews should not let this happen. America should be inundated with broadcasts from Israel by short wave. This is a battle that also must be fought."

The position in fact is that the United States is the worst served country as far as short-wave broadcasts from Israel are concerned. Part of the problem is that short-wave reception went out of fashion with the advent of the transistor: nevertheless, Mr. Grajewski claims, there are many millions of Americans with short wave sets just gasping for full programmes from Israel.

At present, news from Israel is broadcast on medium waves by station WEVD in New York to which *The Jerusalem Post* tele-

phones a four-and-a-half minute news review four times a week which is broadcast at 8 p.m. EST. Mr. Grajewski provides WEVD with a 20-minute taped Hebrew programme twice a week, as well as other taped material. But WEVD, known as "the ethnic station" because it carries many foreign language programmes, is confined to New York.

The programmes broadcast in English in Israel, at 1.30 p.m. and 8.30 p.m. local time, are relayed to America — but are heard there at 8.30 a.m. and 2.30 p.m. EST time, very unsatisfactory hours indeed.

Mr. Grajewski maintains that what is needed for radio contacts with the U.S. is short-wave broadcasts of something like 30 minutes a day, broadcast from Jerusalem at three or four in the morning, which means that they could be heard in the U.S. at 10 p.m. EST, a good listening hour for eager auditors.

AS PROOF of the interest taken by Americans in reports emanating from Israel, he quotes the fact that, in one of the programmes relayed to the U.S., mention was made of the need for transistors for soldiers at the front. This resulted in offers of 10,000 transistors.

Radio Cairo is certainly not niggardly in its use of the air waves. It broadcasts in 48 languages, and has an English programme lasting eight hours a day that can be picked up with ease anywhere in the world. Compared with this, Israel provides a regular one hour in the evening to Europe and South Africa, with a possible addition sometimes of another 45 minutes.

N.J. Pines, of the Department of Political Studies, University of the Witwatersrand, Johannesburg,

wrote a letter on October 23 of mixed praise and criticism:

"I am writing to congratulate you upon your superb coverage of the current Middle East crisis. Like Israel herself, your broadcasts stand out as beacon of light radiating truth and reflective of the same humanity and hope of all that is decent in this duplicity-governed world.

THE VALUE of the short-wave transmissions to the U.S.S.R. is of course well known: Victor Grajewski maintains that the Voice of Zion has contributed substantially to the development of the Russian Jewish revolution since 1967. So potent was the influence of the Israeli radio that there has been heavy interference with the programmes. This, together with the desire to reach the Jews in South America, led to the building of the powerful new transmitters. When, during the Yom Kippur War, Jerusalem broadcast that plasma was needed for wounded Israeli soldiers, dozens of Russian Jews offered blood, although it was not clear how they could deliver it.

The languages used by Israel for overseas broadcasts are English, French, Hebrew (and easy Hebrew), Russian, Rumanian, Yiddish, Ladino, Mograbi, Georgian, Hungarian, and, in recent weeks, Spanish. This is an impressive list, although it cannot compare with Radio Cairo's formidable 48 different tongues telling the tale of Egyptian conquests and wrongs to the entire world.

MR. GRAJEWSKI'S argument is that the great transmitters now installed are idle for several hours a day. The installation cost millions — using them for broadcasting around the world and around the clock, would involve a comparatively small budget, which he estimates at a few hundred thousand pounds a year. He has a trained and dedicated staff which worked long extra hours in the war, and is willing to take on the Egyptians over the air.

The picture that emerges is that the Foreign Division is the Cinderella of Broadcasting House, and that its operations are looked on as being of marginal importance. The explanation of this attitude lies in the history of the division. *Kol Zion Lagola* was introduced by the Jewish Agency primarily as a medium to inform the Diaspora of what was happening in Israel, and, it was hoped, to inspire them with a fervent desire to pull up their stakes and move to the Promised Land. To this day the bulk of the budget comes from the Jewish Agency. Its most dramatic success, the contact with the Russian Jews, is a Jewish Agency achievement. The decision to extend the service to reach Latin America in Spanish was also an Agency one, bound up with the desire to promote aliya from the countries concerned.

But the position has changed considerably in recent years, certainly in recent weeks. Radio is the cheapest, quickest and most effective way of presenting a country's point of view. Even allowing for the reluctance of the Israel Army to let any correspondents, local or foreign, find out what is happening, there are many matters about which Israel is willing and even anxious that the world should be informed. A complete change of attitude to broadcasting seems to be necessary: it is a great pity that the air waves are being lost by default to the Egyptians.

Revamp information policy

To the Editor of The Jerusalem Post

Sir, — Alongside the present Commission of Inquiry investigating the setbacks of Israel at the beginning of the October war, would it not be constructive to investigate the shortcomings of our Foreign Ministry since 1967?

The Prime Minister said in one of her speeches soon after the war started that we did not want to attack first because of world opinion; we held back and, to our great cost, we were attacked by our neighbours...

This great sacrifice by Israel has now been forgotten by most of the rest of the world, and overshadowed by ensuing events. Why?

As a foreign correspondent, I must say that the Israeli propaganda machine (which should be the direct responsibility of the Foreign Ministry) seems to be almost non-existent.

From the evidence at hand, it seems that the Foreign Ministry did nothing to salvage any sympathy that other nations might have felt for us.

From March 30, 1972, up to the outbreak of the war, nine African nations severed their diplomatic relations with Israel. Was this not a sure sign that something was in the wind? Could the Foreign Ministry not have done something to prevent another 20 African countries from severing their ties from October 6 until the present time?

At present, there are two expert Arab diplomats travelling the globe explaining to the freezing populations of Europe and America why they are cutting off oil supplies. What are the Israelis doing?

In 1967, the pre-emptive strike by Israel influenced most of Europe and the world to support the Arabs. What has been done to reverse this position now that the Arabs have struck at us first?

Where are the necessary teams of Israeli diplomats explaining Israel's position to the rest of the world? The only report I have seen of Israeli diplomacy was buried on page three of your paper on December 3. A three-man delegation of Tel Aviv University professors had left for the U.S. "to explain Israel's position in the current stage of the Middle East conflict." We are all aware that America knows our position; it is our friend and anyway we already have plenty of good spokesmen in America. But what of France, England, Japan, etc.? Why not send teams to these countries where they are really needed? We should be on the front pages of the world press not only for our military efforts, but also for our diplomatic ones.

I strongly suggest that we get rid of the "dead wood," so widely talked about in the Foreign Ministry, and start training some go-ahead people for this mission.

The lack of accurate information given to foreign correspondents even in peace time, and the disgraceful organization of press coverage for major news events, is a well-known fact and something must be done to correct this now. Proper handling of foreign journalists is essential to an all-out diplomatic battle.

Print the pictures of the Syrian massacre. Give out the stories of torture of our PoW's in Egypt through an official channel, instead of leaving it to leaks from the Defence Ministry. Explain to the people of Holland why they are short of oil and don't leave it too late so that they might change their minds.

Let us draw up a plan for the Common Market countries to boycott the Arabs economically, since they are unable to do it themselves. Let us tell Europe who is blackmailing them and why, before it's too late and we are forced in Geneva to give up the territories or, worse, we are forced to prove ourselves on the battlefield again.

S. M. GOLDSTEIN
Tel Aviv, December 4.

This letter was sent for comment to the Ministry of Foreign Affairs on December 11, but no reply has been received as yet. — Ed. *J.P.*

OCTOBER WAR DIDN'T SPUR ALIYA

Katzir proposes forum to increase links between Diaspora and Israel

Geoffrey Wigoder's
JEWISH SCENE

THE establishment of an advisory council working under the auspices of the President to act as a forum on the spiritual and cultural links between World Jewry and Israel has been proposed by President Katzir. He was speaking at the close of a three-day seminar on "World Jewry and the State of Israel: The Yom Kippur War" held at the Presidential residence and chaired by Professor Moshe Davis of the Hebrew University's Institute of Contemporary Jewry. •

By all accounts the Jewish masses reacted impressively during the Yom Kippur War. Prof. Shlomo Avineri of the Hebrew University said, "1973 proved the centrality of Israel — for better or worse" and Prof. Ernest Krausz of Bar-Ilan University spoke of "a shared sense of peoplehood." This was borne out by the reports from some of the participants from other countries — Prof. Chaim Perelman from Belgium stated that the relationship to Israel is the only unifying element in Jewish life in his country, while Prof. Adolphe Steg, president of the Representative Council of Jewish Institutions in France (CRIF), was prepared to say that the events of the past few months have meant the end of assimilation in France.

Of course, recent developments should not be viewed in isolation. The natural tendency is to compare what happened in 1973 with 1967. The general feeling is that 1967 was more of a traumatic experience in the Jewish world than 1973 ("1967 was decisive—not 1973, said Rabbi Mordecai Waxman from the U.S.). 1973 had a *deja vu* quality—a Second Seder anticlimax. To many, the sense of urgency did not come through. In 1967, Jews feared for the very future of Israel for the weeks preceding the War and for the first day. In 1973, when the danger was in fact much greater, this never got through. As one speaker said, "For the first few days, when there was real danger, we were fed by the image project-

ed over the last six years and by the confident statements of your generals. When we did get round to understanding the danger that had developed, the major threat had passed."

One war

It was Mr. Avraham Harman, President of the Hebrew University, who added a further perspective when he asked, "Why this concentration on comparisons with 1967 — why not with 1948?" Dr. Kissinger's reminder at Geneva that this has been One War since 1948 (and indeed its roots go back much further) is timely in this context. Israel-Diaspora relations cannot be analysed in sections but require historical examination in their fullest perspective — with each point of reference leading back to an earlier one. Certainly 1948 saw the Jewish reactions emerging into exactly the same frameworks that made such impressions in 1967 and 1973 — the tremendous upsurge in economic support, the volunteering movement (Machal), the intense political lobbying and the acutely heightened Jewish identification both in the Western world and the U.S.S.R. as well, of course, as the beginning of mass aliya. What has happened since — including as a result of the Yom Kippur War — has been a continuation or renewal of existing processes.

Ephraim Katzir, President of Israel.

Considerable attention at the seminar was paid to reactions in intellectual circles. The picture that emerged was at times contradictory (Prof. Marie Syrkin of the U.S. characterised it as ranging "from muted concern to indifference," whereas Prof. Emil Fackenheim of Canada found that "this time Jewish professors did not hesitate to approach their non-Jewish colleagues on Israel's behalf").

Arab propaganda

But the general picture was of the successful impact on intellectuals — Jews and non-Jews — of the Arab propaganda line since 1967. The disappearance of the threats against Israel's existence and their replacement by the stress on regaining lost territory, together with arguments for the Palestinians' right of self-determination, attracted considerable sympathy. The concept of the "Third World," with Israel manoeuvred outside, is highly popular. Speaker after speaker referred to "apathy," with Professor Maurice Freedman of Oxford saying that for many, Israel is at best "boring." The New Left, which seemed to offer a challenge in the late 1960s, has collapsed — but it has left a legacy in that much of its ideology has been absorbed and provides axiomatic premises for today's intellectual thinking. Professor Freedman commented that Israel is now seen as too developed to qualify for sentimental attachment and is no longer an object for sympathy as it used to be in the past.

Several speakers alluded to Israel's information policies. Professor Freedman said "Intellectuals will not believe that the right is all on one side. The Arabs have a case and the intellectuals are alienated if you try and tell them that Israel is right in all respects." In any case, he added, an image of toughness and military efficiency is not what attracts today's intellectuals. Others pointed to the information dilemma — should we project Israel as strong or weak? In fact, this dilemma is no novelty. Israel has to speak to several destinations and inevitably some will be unsatisfied. For example, it has been suggested that the confident statements were made by the generals during the first days of the War in order to pull the wool over Jordan's eyes and deter her from entering the War. I do not know if this is true or not — but if it were, it would surely be justifiable even though it meant we were unable to whip up a full measure of support in the outside world and lost some of our credibility image.

It was suggested by Prof. Daniel Elazar of Bar-Ilan and Temple Universities that the events of the War had led to a greater polarization within the Jewish community. Those who had been committed were now more committed; those who had been apathetic were now more indifferent. There was little evidence of Jews abandoning the positions where they stood before the War. Speakers who referred to the situation in the U.S.S.R. came to similar conclusions.

There were no signs that 1973 — unlike 1948 or 1967 — had given a fillip to aliya. Professor Freedman, for example, commented, "The English community finds itself increasingly isolated by its support for Israel — this will express itself in increased contributions but not in increased aliya." It was the Israeli and not the overseas participants who raised the issue of aliya — with Walter Eytan calling it the "basic link between Israel and World Jewry" that comes as the result not of a one-time operation but of a long educational process and Moshe Rivlin of the Jewish Agency decrying the fact that before the State modern historical periods in this country were reckoned by periods of aliya but since 1948 they are reckoned by wars.

The issue of the memory of the Holocaust, which appeared so prominent at the time of the Six Day War, did not crop up naturally in the discussions and was only injected by those scholars with a special interest in the subject. As Rabbi Waxman put it: "1967 had as its framework the Holocaust; 1973 had as its framework the Six Day War." On the other hand, S. Yizhar pointed to the fact that of all the peoples in the world, it is only the Jews who live in fear of a *churban*.

It was S. Yizhar, presenting the discussions in the subcommittee on the implications of recent events for Israeli education (vis-a-vis the Diaspora), who reported that difficult questions were today being asked among Israel's troops. "Why do I have to be a Jew? Why can't we live like any other people?" This questioning of identity parallels that which has been heard in World Jewry for some time and brings together young Jews here and abroad in the same self-questioning — with a parallel, and often identical, challenge to Jewish education.

Supplies for the encircled 3rd Army cross the Canal.

CHRISTIAN COMMENT

CONCERNED CHRISTIANS

THOUSANDS OF CHRISTIANS from many lands have come on pilgrimage to Israel since the Yom Kippur War. Their motivations have been varied and uniformly admirable, and they are especially welcome at this time, when the timorous might well have thought such a visit inopportune.

As well as those coming in a spirit of pilgrimage, Christians have come from various countries to identify with the people of Israel, to demonstrate by their presence their deep concern over the turn of events, and to learn at first hand the many aspects of the current situation.

One of these visits was initiated by a group of rabbis from Boston, Mass. who invited the Christian clergymen of their city to join them on a tour of Israel so that they might see the country through Jewish eyes. They prayed together, broke bread together, and shared together in a series of consultations with religious leaders of all the monotheistic faiths. The discussion on these shared experiences showed them to have been profitable and enriching to both groups. At the closing session, the Christian participants were able to say that they now had a fuller appreciation of the link between people and land, while the Jewish participants affirmed that they found their own views broadened by exposing their history, their ethos and their passions to their Christian brethren.

The Rev. James Wall, an American Methodist minister, is editor of "Christian Century," an influential magazine enjoying worldwide distribution. In the dual capacity of religious leader and journalist, Mr. Wall arrived at the independent conclusion that he needed to come to Israel to see for himself, rather than rely on official propaganda.

He did things he had never done in his home town, such as

Oikoumenikos

studying the Hebrew prayer book with a university scholar; he heard the personal story of a victim of the Holocaust, learned about new dimensions in the Jewish-Christian dialogue, saw refugee camps for himself, and heard testimony from Jews and Christians on how living together improves mutual understanding. As he was leaving the country, this celebrated journalist said something so simple that it was profound: despite the fact that he had been studying Middle East problems for years, he never really understood Israel until this, his first, visit.

Another unusual visit was that of an interfaith group from Springfield, Mass. This homogeneous group of clergymen who share the problems of their home city, now shared the experience of seeing Jerusalem together. After a series of joint visits, during which the exchange of reactions greatly enhanced the meaning of what they saw and heard, they separated according to profession for a two-day exploration in depth of issues and ideals of special interest.

Finally, mention must be made of the study group sponsored by the Graymoor Ecumenical Institute of New York and led by Father Charles Angell, a leading Catholic ecumenist. Before leaving New York on this tour, Father Angell said:

"My concern is for all the people of the Middle East, but the cause of Arab Christians and Muslims is not served by beating war drums, nor by fostering the illusion that somehow Israel will disappear from the earth. I am particularly alarmed by the tendencies of some Christians to

walk away from a depressing situation. Apparently some fair-weather friends are willing to turn their backs on the people of Israel, whose very existence is at stake. I hope our small project will indicate that this is not a universal attitude."

ONE OF the Israelis who visited Christians abroad was Professor Shemaryahu Talmon, Professor of Bible at the Hebrew University. He was invited by the University of Munich, together with Professor Benyamin Uffenheimer of Tel Aviv University, to take part in a theological symposium on "Common Bible, Different Religions: The Meaning of the Old Testament for Judaism and Christianity Today." He used the opportunity to attend the meeting of the International Consultative Committee of Organizations for Christian-Jewish Co-operation as well as meetings between leaders with representatives of the World Council of Churches (W.C.C.), and later, with prominent Catholics of the International Catholic-Jewish Liaison Committee. Oikumenikos asked Prof. Talmon what subjects had been discussed at these meetings.

"At all of them, of course, discussions on the Middle East situation were very prominent; they also dealt with means of fighting anti-Semitism and anti-Israel attitudes among Christians. There were also discussions on basic issues, for instance, about the contribution that Judaism might make to the realization of the ideal of world community.

"It was agreed that the consultation between W.C.C. leaders and prominent leaders of world Jewry planned for October, 1974, which would probably be held in Jerusalem if the security situation permits, would be devoted to the theme, "The Role of Power in the Mutual Relations of Communities in the Christian and Jewish Traditions.'

"The W.C.C. leaders undertook to investigate the possibility of softening the anti-Israel attitude of Protestant Churches in the Arab countries of the Middle East, and to look into the charge made by Jewish participants of rising anti-Semitism in Church circles in Africa.

"They promised to take action in connection with the prisoners of war in Syria through their representatives in the Arab countries and through the United Nations. Earlier, two staff members of the W.C.C. had visited two Israeli prisoners of war in Syria, and reported that they were in good health.

"The same questions came up in the meeting with the Catholic Committee, penetrating discussions, in an atmosphere of friendship and cordiality, on questions such as the historic right of the Jewish people to the land of Israel, the status of Jerusalem, the religious foundation of the State of Israel. As Jews, we found a great readiness among our Catholic counterparts to consider our standpoint and to accept this as a basis for further discussions. As far as Jerusalem is concerned, we got the impression that the Vatican had in fact dropped the idea of internationalization of the city."

Prof. Talmon was deeply impressed by the atmosphere of the discussions he had during the theological dialogue in Munich.

"It was a very valuable and frank meeting, a true exchange of theological viewpoints on a high intellectual level, and I have the feeling that this could almost serve as a pattern for what I would consider as the right setting for Jewish-Christian dialogue. Prof. Uffenheimer and I tried to highlight the continuity of Jewish religion from biblical to modern times, against the Christian view which differentiates between biblical Israel and post-biblical Judaism, implying that the development of Judaism after the coming of Jesus goes in a completely different direction. Both sides were prepared to take up the points which were raised by their counterparts and to start on a new investigation."

To illustrate his impressions of the attitude of European Christians to Jews and Judaism, Prof. Talmon described what happened at one of the meetings he attended on Jewish-Christian cooperation.

"I asked several participants whether they met Jews in their daily life. I was rather surprised to discover that some of them had not met Jews for a long time, and had only now met any from Israel for the first time. So one might say that they did not relate to Jews in the context of daily relations. I feel that there is a certain danger in this, because Judaism is identified with Israel, and often with Israeli Government policy, and it is forgotten that Judaism comprises much more than the State of Israel.

"This makes the political dimension an overriding one in the contacts between Jews and Christians. In this connection the influence of the modern 'liberation theology,' which sees Christianity as basically a movement for liberation of the oppressed is strongly felt. The Palestinian movement is easily seen as a liberation movement, with Israel as the oppressor. Such an oversimplification of the case may

backlash against Jewry and Judaism."

To avoid this, Prof. Talmon felt that there needed to be a re-emphasis of the basis of modern Israel, namely Zionism as a liberation movement.

"It should also be noted that in the Churches there is a quest for new societal models, and I think it is very important to stress that in the whole of the Middle East only Israel presents a valid attempt to create a new society.

"I met with rather strong criticism of Israeli Government policy," Prof. Talmon went on, "and I found it very important to get across that Israel is not a monolithic society, and to point out that some of the criticisms voiced by Christians are shared by a good many Israelis who do not necessarily identify with the extreme left or the extreme right. I must honestly say that the unqualified backing of Israel by very right wing groups like the Axel Springer press empire is a liability, and therefore the more understanding we can find among leftist oriented Christians the better it is.

"I habitually asked my interlocutors, when they attacked me about the legitimate rights of the Palestinians, if they also considered the legitimate rights of Israel, and whether attacks similar to those launched on me were also launched against Palestinians who came to speak to them. If criticism is expressed against the background of an essential acceptance of Israel, it should not be considered a disaster."

Notwithstanding some criticism of Government policy, said Prof. Talmon, his impression was that rank and file Christians were basically sympathetic to Israel. Things were quite otherwise when the hierarchy and Church leadership were concerned.

"CHURCH leaders are concerned with repercussions of their decisions in higher quarters, and the more exalted the Church leaders, the more conscious they are of their constituencies in different parts of the world, especially in the Arab world and the Third World. Sometimes one gets the the impression that political expediency is the overriding consideration.

"Further, I noticed that the hierarchy tends to maintain a stronger missionary stand towards Judaism than does the rank and file. An important element is the influence of the new concept of liberation theology which I have already mentioned. This type of theology is not found among the average church-

goer, but among students and the higher echelons. However, I feel that this movement has already passed its zenith. Moreover, people who wave the banner of Third World liberation feel somewhat uneasy at suddenly finding themselves in the company of countries like Saudi Arabia."

Asked to give some indication of the possibilities of further co-operation between Christians abroad and Israel, Prof. Talmon chose a concrete example.

"Next year, the International Consultative Committee of Organizations for Jewish-Christian Co-operation will deal with the problem of the 'guest workers' in Western Europe, and young Israelis will be invited to be present. This serves a double purpose: on the one hand Israelis will be able to share with Europeans their experience with the Arabs working in Israel, which is not dissimilar to that of the guest worker; on the other hand, they will be able to learn of some of the risks and problems brought about by the presence of large numbers of workers who are not integrated into the society within which they work.

"These and other initiatives," concluded Prof. Talmon, "h a v e strengthened me in the belief that the situation in relations between European Christians and Israel is by no means as bad as was feared in the period of our anguish during the recent war."

THANK YOU, UNCLE SAM

To the Editor of The Jerusalem Post

Sir, — To paraphrase Winston Churchill, "Never have so few received so much from so many!" I am referring, of course, to the recent decision of the U.S. Government (Congress and President) to provide two billion dollars in aid to Israel. Thus, every man, woman and child in Israel is receiving over $700. Particularly since the end of World War II, the U.S. has been known for its largesse, but never to this degree.

We here in Israel are proud that we always pay our debts, hence, we now have a new obligation of about $300 per person for the part which is a loan or credit — a sobering realization that should cause both our Government and us individually to tighten up our belts and act accordingly. And those long-faced "doubting Thomases" in our midst must recognize that actions speak louder than words; every action of the U.S. Government has been that of a true friend, regardless of the convoluted social and political processes through which the decisions have been reached. As of this date, every Israeli can only say: "Thank you Uncle Sam. Thank you, Senator Jackson. Thank you, Mr. and Mrs. America!"

ARTHUR E. HOFFMAN
Colonel, U.S.A.F. (Ret.)
Jerusalem, December 31.

Beduin MK won Galilee, Negev votes

By H. BEN-ADI
Jerusalem Post Reporter

BEERSHEBA. — Israeli Beduin were yesterday streaming to a villa five kilometres off the Arad-Beersheba road to congratulate their first Knesset representative in 25 years of statehood, Sheikh Hamad **Abu Rabeya.**

Sheikh Abu
Rabeya

The more than 17,000 votes Sheikh Abu Rabeya's new Alignment-affiliated list of Beduin and Arab villagers won in Monday's election not only put him in the Knesset; because of a vote-sharing arrangement they also assured the return of Alignment-affiliated Deputy Communications Minister Jaber Mu'adi (who ran second on the Progress and Development list).

The win also means that Sheikh Abu Rabeya will now get a telephone.

One result of his election means that Communications Ministry staff will now have to string a line the 15 kms. from Arad to his villa in order to install a telephone. There is none now in the M.K.-elect's area.

The 44-year-old sheikh, between receiving well-wishers, told *The Post* yesterday he had set up the list because Beduin felt the Israeli Arab list they formerly voted for was ignoring their interests. These included more schools, medical service and permanent housing for Beduin, and a final settlement of the land question that has been hanging fire for 25 years.

He said he was especially happy to have strengthened the ranks of the Alignment with the two more Knesset seats his victory assured it, and hoped this would help bring genuine peace.

Opposition leader Menahem Begin (standing fifth from the left) stands patiently and confidently in line at his neighborhood polling station in Tel Aviv.

SABBATH—No Publication

Soldiers using the dining hall as a polling booth.

entered the Hebron Yeshiva, and had put to death everyone they could lay their hands on. The British, as usual, had given passive assent to the atrocity. No question had been raised by the Arabs as to whether the young men they had killed were or were not political agitators. They happened to be Jews, and that was enough to justify their being killed.

I was enormously upset by this news, but not nearly as upset as when, the following day, I read that the New York Communist Party had sent a telegram of congratulation to the perpetrators of the massacre stating that the Communists in America supported their efforts to oust the imperialists, applauding the steps the Arabs had taken to rid themselves of the exploiters. I was

appalled that a group of so-called idealists, people who claimed their goal was to improve life for mankind, could condone such cold-blooded murder.

In a lightning flash, I saw exposed the whole shabby fabric of Communist pretension. It was clear to me that the New York Communist cared little or nothing about the lives of the poor boys who had been killed, and I suspected that they probably cared just as little for the so-called rights of the Arabs they were cheering.

When I questioned some Communist supporters about this telegram, I was told — as I would be told for a number of years thereafter — that the means taken were justified by the end in view. To promote their cause, Communists had to take advantage of

---

GADDAFI BEHIND ARAB TERROR, SAYS 'THE TIMES'

By DAVID LENNON, Jerusalem Post Correspondent

LONDON. — The group of Arab terrorists responsible for most of the recent outrages was formed and financed by the Libyan ruler, Col. Muammar Gaddafi, who has also been involved in the financing of many terrorist organizations in different countries, according to a report in "The Times" on Friday. Other papers have discounted the report as being professional intelligence "disinformation."

"The Times" says that in April this year Gaddafi invited renegades from the Popular Front for the Liberation of Palestine to Libya, where he put them into training camps under his personal direction. The new group was formed on April 9 and is called the National Youth for the Liberation of Palestine.

Its first operation were the Nicosia attacks on an El Al plane and the Israel Ambassador's residence. The same group was responsible for killing four people and wounding 55 at Athens airport on August 5. Five members were arrested in a flat near Rome airport exactly a month later by the Italian police, who found two portable anti-aircraft missiles, intended for use against an El Al plane.

The massacre at Rome Airport in mid-December was also the work of the same organization. This plot, in which 32 people were killed, was also planned in Tripoli.

It is the five terrorists who carried out this crime, now being held in Kuwait, who revealed Col. Gaddafi's connection. As they told the story their weapons and support equipment were delivered in the Libyan diplomatic pouch and a Libyan diplomat

personally sent off the five terrorists with final orders from Madrid to Rome.

A macabre touch was that Gaddafi offered the group a bonus of £250,000 (IL2.5m.) in the form of insurance payable to their families in the event of their unexpected deaths. He promised to organise additional terrorist operations to free them if they were jailed. He is now rumoured to be putting pressure on the Kuwaiti government and on the P.L.O. to allow them to travel to Libya.

The terrorists questioned in Kuwait also revealed that other groups financed by Gaddafi are now moving in various European countries. This ties in with reports from Brussels about Gaddafi's financing of other terrorist groups.

There is apparently neither consistency nor discernible pattern behind the Libyan leader's support of organizations in different countries. Gaddafi's regime has allocated £45 million to Black September and £20 million to other fedayeen groups. Libyan aid has also included £1 million in military aid and possibly training to the Irish Republican Army, some £10 million to the anti-Ethiopian Eritrean Liberation Front, and to opposition groups in Syria (£1.3m.), Somalia (£500,000), the Peoples Democratic Republic of Yemen (£1m.), Chad (£1.2m.), Morocco (£2m.), Tunisia (£1m.), Thailand (£300,000), the Philippines (£2m.) and Panama (£1.5m.).

At least two of the countries against which Gaddafi is financing opposition groups are themselves in receipt of Libyan assistance: Syria and Lebanon. They were reportedly shocked when they heard the news through diplomatic channels.

Italians ired by boycott warning

The demand by the Arab boycott office for the dismissal of the editor of "La Stampa," who is Jewish, is absurd, the Turin newspaper said in an editorial yesterday.

The Arab boycott office has threatened economic reprisals against Italy's biggest private company, the Fiat motor concern — which controls "La Stampa" — unless Dr. Arrigo Levi, 47, its editor, is dismissed.

The threat, which has been widely condemned here, followed the publication in the newspaper of a satirical article highly critical of the Libyan leader, Colonel Muammar Gaddafi.

The Arab demand raised a furore in Italy, heavily dependent on Arab oil for its energy. The Journalists' Union and most politicians came to the defence of Levi.

The editorial yesterday, signed by deputy editor Carlo Casegno, said the decision to make the dismissal demand was reached by a conference of Arab ambassadors in Rome last month.

The ambassadors "have committed a resounding error and damaged the image of their countries with Italian and international public opinion," the editorial said.

In Rome, a television skit mimicking Gaddafi scheduled on a national programme for last night, was scratched, apparently for fear that the Libyan leader may take it seriously and lodge new protest against Italy. The daily "Corriere Della Sera" wrote that the national television dropped the play "for fear of new absurd demands by the Libyan President."

In Cairo, the head of the Arab League's anti-Israel boycott office denied that his office has specifically demanded the dismissal of Levi.

Mohammed Mahgoub, director of the Damascus-based boycott organization, who is now in Cairo, said, "Levi has been printing anti-Arab reports systematically in his paper. What we did was to ask the Fiat company to take measures to put an end to this otherwise its interests in the Arab countries would be exposed to danger."

(Reuter, AP, UPI)

Call for Arabs to boycott M & S

CAIRO (AP).— A boycott of goods from the British Marks and Spencer store chain was urged yesterday by the influential Cairo newspaper "Al Ahram." The paper called for all Marks and Spencer products on sale in Arab markets to be confiscated and for the sellers to be fined.

Sieff, the company president, is presently recovering in hospital after being shot in his London home last week by a gunman.

The stores of Marks and Spencer are the "first target' of Arabs, including Egyptians who visit London... we should not hide this bitter fact," "Al Ahram" said. Despite the fact these stores are on the blacklist of the Arab Boycott Office, their products are flooding Arab and Egyptian markets, the paper said.

Edward Sieff, President of the prestigious London department store, Marks and Spencer.

Driver, Not everyone can serve at the front but everyone can give a lift to soldiers from the front!

EFFECTIVE VOLUNTEERS

To the Editor of The Jerusalem Post

Sir, — Aluf Meir Amit (December 27) is not entirely correct when he states that the new organization which has been formed to counteract Arab oil propaganda must enlist *only* professionals, because he has "little faith in well-meaning volunteers." One need merely l o o k at the daily newspapers in the United States and Great Britain, for example, to appreciate the talent displayed in the letters-to-the-editor columns on behalf of Israel. M o s t are voluntarily submitted and serve as very effective counterweapons. They are often beautifully written, always timely and to the point, and their sincerity is beyond dispute. Last but not least, they don't cost any money, and give the writer (whose numbers are unlimited) a sense of direct participation in a cause dear to his heart. The effectiveness of the so-called "volunteer," therefore, must not be underestimated.

The afore-mentioned is not to say that such an organization should not be *run* by professionals. It should be! But it shouldn't, for heavens sake, exclude us "amateurs" from its efforts. There are tens of thousands of persons all around the w o r l d waiting for some organization to tell them what to do, when to do it, and how to proceed. Ours could, conceivably, become the largest counter-propaganda corps in t h e world, if skilfully handled. Israel has more friends than she realizes, and they're at her beck and call!

LUCI R. BLAU
New York, January 5.

Labour 51, Likud 39 after final tally

With all votes counted yesterday afternoon, and surplus votes allowed for, the final distribution of the 120 seats in the Knesset is as follows:

List	Seats	List	Seats
Labour-Mapam Alignment	51	Citizens Rights (Aloni)	3
Likud	39	Progress & Development (Arabs	
NRP	10	affiliated to Alignment)	2
Aguda — Poale Aguda	5	Moked-Maki	1
ILP	4	Beduin & Villagers (Arabs	
New Communists (Rakah)	4	affiliated to Alignment)	1

In calculating the distribution of mandates, the first step was to set aside the votes cast for eleven lists which failed to gain the required minimum of one per cent of the ballots.

The remaining valid ballots were divided by 120, giving a quotient per Knesset seat of 12,473 votes. The number of votes won by successful lists were divided by this quotient to give first-round distribution.

Three seats were left unoccupied after the first round.

These three were then distributed according to the new Bader-Ofer rule, which favours the largest parties. The Likud got two of them and the Alignment the third.

Had the three free seats been distributed according to the number of surplus votes (the previous criterion) they would have gone to the Likud, Moked and the ILP in that order. This is illustrated in the table below.

List	Distribution of seats after first round	Final distribution under previous surplus system
Alignment	50	50
Likud	37	38
NRP	10	10
Aguda	5	5
ILP	4	5
New Communists	4	4
Citizens	3	3
Progress Development	2	2
Moked	1	2
Beduin and Villagers	1	1
	117 seats	120 seats
Still vacant	3	
Total	120	

Kibbutz needs aid for potatoes

KUNEITRA. — Ein Zivan, on the Golan Heights, stands to lose 150 tons of valuable seed potatoes if it does not find volunteers to pick them soon, the kibbutz said yesterday in an appeal to high school students.

Ein Zivan representative Nico Berlin said part of the crop, destined to replace expensive imported seed potatoes, had already been lost. He complained that the army was keeping key men whose release had already been approved, and said that yield had dropped to 2.5 tons per dunam from an expected 3.5 tons per dunam due to lack of care during the war.

Whatever the fate of their potatoes, however, Golan and Lebanese-border settlements are already getting war-damaged buildings repaired under a IL5.5m. appropriation channelled through the Housing Ministry. This was announced Friday by the ministry, whose Rural Building Department is handling the work. *(Itim)*

Champagne toast to a new Government. Golda Meir, Premier designate; Ephraim Katzir, President; and Yigal Allon, Deputy Premier.

44% in Belgium poll would act against Israel

BRUSSELS (INA). — According to a recent public opinion poll, 44 per cent of the Belgians favour countermeasures against Israel in order to solve the energy crisis.

The poll, conducted by the two newspapers, "Le Soir," and "De Standard," shows that 31 per cent believe the world should exert pressure on the Arab nations in order to ease the oil situation.

The remaining percentage expressed "no opinion."

The poll also included a breakdown of the opinions of the Flemish-speaking and French-speaking populations, 51 per cent of the Flemish speakers favour countermeasures against Israel as compared to 37 per cent among the French speakers.

The Belgian poll results contrast sharply with those of a similar poll in the Netherlands recently. Despite the total Arab oil boycott, a large majority of the Dutch supported Israel and indicated the Dutch Government should not give in to Arab pressure.

Assad: Arabs will win in future

DAMASCUS (UPI). — The Arabs should revise their military strategy in accordance with experiences gained during the October war, President Hafez Assad said yesterday.

Addressing officers at an unidentified air force base, Assad said the good performance of the Arabs in that war should assure them of victory against Israel in the future.

Damascus Radio said the President, who is an air force officer himself, was accompanied on his visit to the base by Defence Minister Maj. Gen. Mustafa Tlas and Air Force Commander Maj. Gen. Naji Jamil.

Assad told the officers: "Your heroism and courage have destroyed the illusions of the enemy and forced him to revise his strategy..."

The achievements of the Arabs in October, he said, "make the possibilities of victory in the future greater and speedier."

Pope bids for voice in fate of Jerusalem

By PEGGY POLK

VATICAN CITY (UPI). — Pope Paul VI wrote in a private memo before making his 1964 pilgrimage to the Holy Land that he hoped the visit would reawaken Roman Catholic desire for "guardianship" over its most sacred shrines, the official Vatican newspaper said at the weekend.

"L'Osservatore Romano," marking the 10th anniversary of the pilgrimage, published the text of the hitherto unknown notes which it said the Pontiff wrote by hand on September 21, 1963, three months after he was elected spiritual leader of 600 million Roman Catholics.

Coming during the current Middle East Peace Conference in Geneva, the disclosure served to underline the Pope's strong determination for a voice on the future of Jerusalem and the Holy Places, Vatican sources said.

DESCRIBES AIM

Describing the aims and character of his intended pilgrimage, which was not announced to the world until two months later, the Pope wrote:

"Such a visit would have to be for the aim of rendering honour to Jesus Christ, our Lord, in the land that his coming to the world has made holy and worthy of veneration and of guardianship on the part of Christians.

"Subordinated purpose of such pilgrimage is the moral defence of those Holy Places. It is the reawakening of Catholic interest for the guardianship that the Catholic Church cannot evade to desire for them and to exercise there," the notes said.

The Pope went on to list as other aims an entreaty for Middle East peace, meetings on Christian unity and "the hope of finding some convenient form of approach" to Moslems and Jews to whom the land also is holy.

SEARCH FOR UNITY

During and after the Papal visit to the Holy Land in January 1964, the Vatican emphasized its religious nature and the Pope's search for Christian unity in talks with Patriarch Athenagoras of the Eastern Orthodox Church. Roman and Eastern Orthodox Catholics had not met since the split between the two churches in 1054.

The Holy Land figured prominently in the Pope's Christmas address to the College of Cardinals on December 21, 1973.

In it he spoke of the "duty" and "right" of the Church "of working to ensure that any possible solution touching the status of Jerusalem and the Holy Places in Palestine should take into account the exigencies of the special character of that city..." But he carefully refrained from spelling out the Church's goals.

The next day, a delegation of African leaders — including Emperor Haile Selassie of Ethiopia, a Coptic Christian, and President Ja'afar al-Numeiry of the Sudan, a Moslem — visited the Pope to express their united view that Jerusalem "should not be under the exclusive control of any one religion."

They urged a solution to its status on the basis of resolutions by the United Nations which in 1974 called for internationalization of the city.

War 'not ended' with Israel

CAIRO (UPI). — Egypt's war against Israel has not ended, and the mission of the armed forces is to liberate all occupied Egyptian territory, War Minister Gen. Ahmed Ismail said yesterday.

The Middle East News Agency said Ismail, who is commander-in-chief of the armed forces, made the statement during a visit to Egyptian troops in Sinai.

every opportunity to gain a forum, gain attention, gain support. Truth might be a casualty. No matter. Truth didn't count. The only thing that counted was to build up the Communist movement. To hasten the advent of a better world, a little perfidy was justified.

I knew then that the Communists were corrupt. They loved Mankind but hated men. I knew then that they would stop at no trickery, no matter how low, to achieve their ends.

Unfortunately, it took some of my acquaintances ten years more — in some cases, twenty years more — to learn the same truth. They were reluctant to abandon their *idée fixe*. They had a deep emotional investment in the Communist ideal, which they guarded as zealously as any religious convert. Their attitude, for the most part, was "My mind is made up. Don't confuse me with the facts." And so, until Krushchev came along and himself denounced Stalin as the butcher he was, some of these people, friends of my youth, kept their faith and hewed to the Communist line until utterly overwhelmed by the facts of history.

We find the same phenomenon today in Israel, where a small group — about one percent of the population — adheres to the Moscow line. The Rakah Political Party defends the pronouncements of Brezhnev, Gromyko, *et al*, hook, line and sinker — managing somehow to ignore the patent fact that the Russians mean to destroy *their* kin, and *their* kith along with the political state of Israel.

By and large, however, the Israeli recognizes that his arch-foe today is Russia. It may be true that the Russian, despite the anti-semitic bias which lies deep in his background, has no built-in ineradicable hatred of Israel, as does the Arab. Russian policy in the Middle East is based on economic and political motivation. But the difference between Russian enmity and Arab enmity is: whereas Arab enmity is implacable and cannot be dealt with on any rational or practical basis, it is the Russians who have the power. And this power is being exercised with a lavish hand against Israel. Israel, though not officially, recognizes the threat of Russia. For one thing, the Israeli Army does not accept Communists in its ranks, regarding such men as potential traitors.

During the Yom Kippur War, orders delivered in Russian were picked up by Israelis on the radio. Apparently, Russian advisers were in communication with each other, directing the flow of arms to the Arabs, directing the strategy, the logistics. Notes, written in Russian, were found in captured bunkers. The Russians seem to have made extensive preparations to remain in both Syria and Egypt during the War. A captured mail bag, shown on page 43 of this book, simply emphasizes the extent of these preparations, right down to the last detail.

The extent of Russian participation is well known and beyond cavil. What is not generally noted in the world press is the Russian indifference to

Malaysia won't host Israelis

KUALA LUMPUR (Reuter). — Malaysia has changed its mind about replacing Japan as host of the third Asian amateur tennis championships in March because of Israel's possible participation, informed sources said here on Saturday.

While the Malaysian Government has no objection to sending athletes to compete against Israelis abroad, its current policy is not to host any event in which Israel is represented.

Mr. V. Rajaratnam, secretary of the Malaysian Lawn Tennis Association, said a cable had been sent to the Asian Lawn Tennis Federation on Friday on Malaysia's decision not to host the championships.

THANKS TO TOURISTS

To the Editor of The Jerusalem Post

Sir, — We would like to thank, through your column, the tourists who sent us gift packages through the Israeli Government Food Ltd. of Lod Airport.

Needless to say how welcome the packages have been to us, stationed so far away from home. It is good to know so many people care.

AMI ELBILIA

Sinai, December 23.

INDIVIDUAL PROPAGANDA CAMPAIGN

To the Editor of The Jerusalem Post

Sir, — Most Israelis agree today that not enough effort is made to explain Israel's position abroad. During the Yom Kippur War, I was so angered by British coverage of the Middle East situation that, on impulse and much against my nature, I took up my pen and began to write. I wrote to the B.B.C. and to British papers, stating Israel's case and her desire for peace. I was surprised when one letter was broadcast and another published. In answer to the published article, I received many letters from non-Jews abroad expressing their sympathy for Israel and a desire to help in any possible way.

I started this letter campaign by writing to my old local paper, "The South Wales Echo," which has a circulation of about 750,000. After encouraging results there, I wrote further afield to national papers and magazines.

Such articles and letters did not take up a great deal of my time and I believe that all Israelis who have contacts abroad should bombard newspapers with letters. Teachers can write to educational magazines, housewives to women's magazines, etc. I think that letters from ordinary citizens have more effect than cold professional reports on the political scene.

BRENDA LANDES
Kibbutz Bet Haemek, January 4.

ATTITUDE TO JAPAN

To the Editor of The Jerusalem Post

Sir, — The subject of a possible Jewish counter-boycott against Japan was discussed in your November 27 weekly edition and also in the local press. I wish to offer a few suggestions from the point of view of one who has spent a number of months in Japan but is not an expert.

1. Any boycott should be applied simultaneously to all countries known for their anti-Israel policies. The Japanese are asking hard questions about why the U.S. State Department publicly criticized *their* recent move after years of official silence toward British and French mischief-making that went beyond mere words. A boycott against Japan alone would give the impression that the Japanese are being singled out as scapegoats because of their vulnerability and racial prejudice. My suggestion is to apply boycott measures in inverse proportion to Arab oil cutbacks to the country concerned.

2. The boycott should not apply in Israel or to companies which have defied Arab boycott threats in dealing with Israel. It would be foolish to penalize Israel's friends in Japan or to add the threat of a customer boycott to the existing obstacles to trade with Israel. Conversely, letting companies get around the boycott by selling through Israel might be a good way to induce them to do business there.

3. Economic measures will be of limited value unless accompanied by a serious effort to enlighten the Japanese public as to the elementary facts about the Middle East situation and explain Israel's position. Economic pressure is not the only problem. The propaganda battle here is being lost to the Arabs by default. The presentation of counter-arguments will require a more solidly based and sophisticated approach than is frequently in evidence in Western countries, where the public's sympathy is all too often taken for granted.

4. Travel by Jews to Japan should not in general be discouraged. It would only serve the Arabs' purposes to allow this issue to inhibit contact between people, particularly in Japan where personal contacts are all-important. Constructive contact between Jews and Japanese should be continued, and even expanded to offset the Japanese Government's plan to increase contact wtih Arab countries.

5. We cannot ask the Japanese to reduce petroleum consumption unless the Jewish community changes its own wasteful ways. Regretfully, the Jewish Community Centre is one of the most overheated buildings in Tokyo despite the current crisis.

6. Consideration should be given to positive uses of the economic weapon, perhaps preference in contracts to companies which invest in or trade with Israel, and sharing of energy-saving technology. The Japanese would be particularly appreciative of efforts to find a solution on the basis of cooperation rather than confrontation.

7. If drastic measures become necessary, the need for them should be recognized as the result of failure of past policies. The chronic neglect of Asia by world Jewry should be a prime target for reappraisal.

8. Protests to Japanese consulates have had a restraining effect. But the Japanese seem to think that support for Israel is strictly because of Jewish influence. Protests from non-Jews should be clearly identified as such.

HAROLD SOLOMON
Tokyo, December 10.

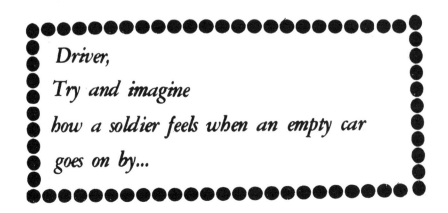

Driver,
Try and imagine
how a soldier feels when an empty car
goes on by...

SOLAR ENERGY

To the Editor of The Jerusalem Post

Sir, — Most of the solutions to the current power crisis are long-term projects, such as nuclear power, geothermal power and off-shore oil-wells. One obvious solution can be implemented immediately, using existent technologies. Solar energy is the one source we in Israel possess in abundance.

I operate a night-heated electric hot-water system, which consumed 3,000 kilowatts of electricity during the year 1972. I would gladly convert to a roof solar-heating unit if (a) it were immediately available and (b) at a price comparable with the annual electricity bill (around IL120). If another 100,000 homes were converted to solar energy, the country would benefit by a reduction in electricity consumption of 300 million kilowatts, which corresponds to an annual saving in fuel oil of some 100,000 tons.

Of course the Israel Electricity Company would suffer a loss of income and the sky-lines of our cities would become even uglier than they are now, but we would benefit by reduced air pollution caused by the burning of 100,000 tons of oil. *S.J.W. PLEETH*
Haifa, December 20.

FOREIGN PRESS

'When terrorists have a free hand'

Anyone who wonders why airline terrorism and hijacking persist would be well advised to look at a box score compiled from a "New York Times" of such events since 1968, the **Wall Street Journal** said in an editorial on Friday. The paper continued:

Of some 71 Arab terrorists who have committed some crime against air travellers or airlines in that period, 53 have gone free either through escape, rescue by other terrorists or by merely being released by their captors. Four have been killed in action and 10, including five who killed 31 persons on Pan Am and Lufthansa airliners last month, are being held. Those five are being held in Kuwait, which apparently may turn them over to Yasser Arafat and his Palestine Liberation Organization for trial.

If Mr. Arafat does get them and actually hands out a sentence, he will be doing more than most established governments have done. Of the 71, only four are serving a sentence. The 71, incidentally, doesn't include those involved in three of the listed incidents, where the number of hijackers was not ascertained.

But the terrorists' victims have paid dearly. Forty-one are dead and 80 were wounded. That's not to mention the damage to airliners and other property.

As we said, if anyone is wondering why terrorism persists it helps to look at the box score. The terrorists are winning and the weak-kneed or cynical governments that should be dealing with them are losing.

---

violations of all the normal codes of international behavior. When Syria exercised psychological cruelty in refusing to divulge the names or the number of prisoners they held, when Syria flouted every convention of civilized man in regard to the rules of war by not permitting even the International Red Cross to visit these prisoners, not a single note of disapproval was voiced by the Russians. Other nations prodded Syria to at least release the names of the prisoners.

Moreover, the Russians abet the Palestinian guerrillas. The Russians travel recruits from Kuwait to Russia to train them in Russia as infiltrators. They indoctrinate them for several months in training camps. They then supply these guerrilla groups with machine guns, mortars, and small arms before sending them back to Syria, to Lebanon, and to other Arab countries from whence they can proceed to kill women and children. The Russians bankroll much of the movement.

It is clear that Russia knew that the Yom Kippur War was being planned, and withheld this information from its détente partner. And after the War started, it was Russia who called on every one of the Arab countries to support the Arab war effort—not with money, not with munitions, not with medical supplies — but by sending troops to the Syrian and Egyptian fronts. Russia made every effort to escalate the War. It was only when the Israelis were succeeding in defeating the Arabs that Russia began calling for a cease fire.

Russia's interests in the Middle East, always profound, are even stronger today. For Russia, control of the Middle East means control of the world's major oil supply, ergo, control of the very source of capitalist energy.

For Russia, control of the Middle East means control of the Suez Canal, the pathway to the Indian Ocean. Control of the Levant means a linkage between Russia's Mediterranean fleet,

New KGB offensive against Jews

> "In early October, the KGB took advantage of Jewry's preoccupation with Israel to launch a new campaign of oppression. Alexander Feldman who was sentenced to three and a half years 'strict regime' on a charge of malicious hooliganism is a prime example of this new policy," writes Colin Schindler, editor of a weekly bulletin published in London, "Jews in the USSR—Latest Information."

Solidarity with Israel

The Yom Kippur War had an electrifying effect on Jews in the USSR. Messages of solidarity with Israel were sent from the remotest Jewish communities in the USSR. For example, a group of eight Jews from Tallinn, the capital of Soviet Estonia, who had not until then been active, sent the following message to President Katzir: "In these anxious days, our hearts are entirely with our people. We regret very much that it is impossible to be with you, but we hope that the hour is not too distant when our energies and skills will serve to strengthen and develop our land."

Some of the younger Jews preferred a more demonstrative method of showing their feelings. As the war entered its second week, three Moscow Jews staged a demonstration outside the offices of the Central Committee of the Communist Party. They paraded up and down with placards which stated: "We consider ourselves to be Israeli prisoners-of-war in the USSR, and we demand to be granted exit permits or to be put in a Soviet prisoner-of-war camp." Within minutes they and the five Western correspondents who were reporting and filming the demonstration were arrested.

As the war progressed, Soviet Jews showed their support in other ways. Sixteen Jews from Tbilisi and Leningrad sent a telegram to President Nixon asking him to give arms to Israel to balance the enormous help given the Arabs by the USSR. New applicants for emigration showed their disgust at the Soviet Union's attitude towards the conflict by requesting Israeli citizenship. As in many other countries, hundreds of Jews volunteered to give blood to Israel. The Soviet Red Cross categorically refused to take blood which would go to Israel's wounded. However, announcements were made in colleges and universities that students should give blood to the Arab cause.

In particular, the biased and distorted coverage of the war by Tass and other news media annoyed Soviet Jews.

The "neutral" statement of the nine EEC countries designed to appease the oil-producing Arab states angered five Jews in Tallinn. In a letter addressed to "Citizens of the Common Market countries," they pointed out:

"The policy of closing your eyes to the denial of the Arab countries to recognize the right of Israel to exist certainly contributed to the four Arab-Israeli wars. In the end, even this attitude succumbed in the face of economic sabotage and threats of terror. Your silence will be interpreted as support for that sabotage and that terror. Your government has sold itself and its morality for a tanker of oil. It is possible that you, too, will bury your convictions in return for a gallon of petrol. Remember Munich 1938 and what followed."

In early October, the KGB took advantage of Jewry's preoccupation with Israel to launch a new campaign of oppression. Alexander Feldman who was sentenced to three and a half years "strict re-

gime" on a charge of malicious hooliganism is a prime example of this new policy.

Feldman had been told a number of times by the KGB that he was "abnormal," and as early as September, a friend was told that a case had been started against him. Everywhere Feldman went he was shadowed by KGB agents. He felt that his arrest was imminent. In view of this situation, Feldman made sure that he would not put himself into any sort of compromising position which could lead to a fake charge. One way of doing this was to be accompanied by a bodyguard of friends who would be witness to any provocative incident.

Trap is set

On Simchat Tora, Feldman attended the service in the synagogue and walked home with friends. At seven in the evening, he said goodbye to them and began to take the road to his home, a few minutes away. Feldman was followed by two male students and a young woman, who then ran ahead and hid in some bushes. As Feldman approached, the girl, in true Victorian melodramatic fashion, jumped out screaming, carrying a rather large cake, which she deliberately dropped. The two students ran after Feldman, pounced on him and arrested him in the manner of good Soviet citizens.

They then threw him into the car of the deputy head of the Investigation Department of Kiev's Darnitsky region, who was waiting for the incident to take place before he started up his car so that he could just pass by. At the police station, Feldman was offered a choice: He could either be charged with assaulting the girl or attempting to rape her.

The assailants were part of the trap set to catch Feldman. The girl described herself as a kindergarten teacher, but had not taught in Kindergarten Number 505 in Kiev for at least three months. Her present place of employment was not revealed even in the courtroom. The two students were enrolled at the Institute of Jurisprudence, but turned out to be police cadets studying law.

Plans were made to keep the trial as secret as possible. It was postponed once and was finally held in the hall of a club belonging to a car factory and not in the scheduled court room.

Despite a three-metre high fence around the factory, militia were posted all around the perimeter. Feldman's family and friends were barred from entering. The only people permitted to witness the proceedings were plainclothes KGB agents and militiamen who were brought to the factory gates in two coaches. Some of the latter were recognized as having been present at the Babi Yar service in September while others were known for their provocations outside the Kiev synagogue. In this atmosphere, the Kiev court sentenced Alexander Feldman to three and a half years for an act of malicious hooliganism that he never committed.

In addition to "hooligans" and "parasites", the KGB searched in vain for Jewish alcoholics. Ida Nudel, a well-known Moscow activist, went for a check-up one day for her heart complaint. By chance she glanced at her medical card and saw she was labelled as an alcoholic. In Soviet terms, this can be interpreted as a sign of abnormality, curable by a period in a psychiatric clinic. A strange accusation for a woman whose closest contact with alcohol is a glass of *kiddush* wine on Shabbat.

Then there was the case of the Jewish carpenter from Derbent, Petya Pinkhasov. He was arrested on an embezzlement charge after he refused to give up his idea of emigrating to Israel. He was sentenced to five years imprisonment in November. And Leonid Zabelishensky who got six months on a parasitism charge in Sverdlovsk in December.

By a return to oppressive methods, it is clear that the KGB wants to frighten the Jewish masses by persecuting the few activists. In the past a policy of trial and arrest has proved futile because many Jews have considered the risk worth taking. In addition to those who left in 1973, there are still many thousands of Jews sitting on their suitcases, waiting to leave. In addition, the Soviet Union's desire for acceptance into the international community and its ardent overtures for detente are likely to be sharply rebuked by the West if persecution of Jews continues.

The Soviet Union's recent ratification of the U.N. Declaration of Human Rights shows that freedom of emigration is not the internal affair of one state, but of all mankind. How far the USSR will honour its promises in 1974 is anyone's guess, but it is clear that a spontaneous movement like the Jewish one cannot be put down easily or in silence.

Soldiers of the encircled 3rd Army taking supplies across the Suez Canal.

formerly locked up in the Caspian Sea, and Russia's fleet in the Indian Ocean.

In geopolitics, control of the Middle East has been, and continues to be, one of Russia's chiefest aims. Peace between the Arab countries and Israel would render Russia's leverage less weighty. And since Russia aims to be important to the Arabs, the U.S.S.R. must continue — and will continue — to foment differences between the Arab world and Israel.

Russia, of course, would feel humiliated if the Arabs, backed by all the sophisticated weaponry that Soviet technology has devised, were ignominiously defeated.

On the other hand, the United States cannot permit Russia to gain control of this strategic region to its own exclusion. The United States, too, has vital interests in the area. For one thing, the United States, too, needs the oil, and dares not relinquish full control of the wells from whence this oil flows.

Nor can the United States permit Russia to turn the Mediterranean into a Soviet lake. The military threat to Europe, America's first line of defense, would become too dire.

The United Sates wants peace in the Middle East; Russia wants war. And Israel pays for these geopolitical maneuverings in blood.

DAYAN QUOTES BEN-GURION:
'There is no successful war'

By ERNIE MEYER, Jerusalem Post Reporter

A weak peace is better than a successful war, and there is no "successful" war, Defence Minister Moshe Dayan last night quoted the late David Ben-Gurion as saying.

He was speaking at the official function at the Jerusalem Theatre marking the end of the 36-day mourning period after the death of David Ben-Gurion. Mr. Dayan said that Prime Minister Golda Meir could not attend because she was not well.

The audience in the packed hall included President Ephraim Katzir, Cabinet Ministers, Knesset Members, members of the judiciary and members of the Ben-Gurion family. Former President Zalman Shazar also attended.

Mr. Dayan said that Ben-Gurion's faith in Zionism was perhaps deeper than any religious faith. That faith was coupled with great vision and the ability to take action, he said. To David Ben-Gurion any Zionist aspiration was worthless unless it resulted in a personal commitment.

Ben-Gurion also understood Israel's terrible isolation among the Arab nations surrounding it and the greater world beyond, with its ties to the Arab world. That is why he used every opportunity to try and break that isolation; during the Korean War in the early 1950s he even wanted Israel to take an active part, he added.

Mr. Dayan recalled that on his many trips from his house in Tel Aviv to Jerusalem, David Ben-Gurion liked to travel through Jaffa — which reminded him of the past. On occasion he would compare teeming Tel Aviv to ancient Niniveh and between clenched teeth describe its inhabitants as a "people of waiters."

The Jerusalem Symphony Orchestra played an adaggio by Bach and a Tchaikovsky elegy. The reading of a 1918 letter by Ben-Gurion to his wife Paula, a letter to bereaved parents, and a recording of one of his speeches rounded out the one-hour ceremony.

U.S. public still back Israel, 38:7

By IRA SILVERMAN
Jerusalem Post Correspondent

WASHINGTON. — A new national poll reveals that support for Israel has diminished very little since the Arabs employed their oil embargo against the U.S. This news comes at the start of an intensified Arab propaganda effort here.

The poll, conducted by Opinion Research Corporation and commissioned by CBS News, found that 38 per cent of the American people say they sympathize with Israel, in contrast with only seven per cent sympathizing with the Arabs. The remainder either sympathized with neither, or had no opinion. These results confirm the findings of a Gallup poll conducted shortly after the conclusion of the October war.

When asked if they believe that the Arab countries are out to destroy Israel or are just bent on regaining land lost in the 1967 war, 28 per cent say they believe the Arabs want to destroy Israel, but more than half, 52 per cent, say that the Arabs want only to regain their lost land.

The respondents were also told that the Arabs say they will resume oil shipments if Israel returns the occupied territories, and were asked how much pressure the U.S. should put on Israel to give up those lands. Thirty-five per cent said substantial pressure, but 60 per cent said little pressure or none at all.

The survey in addition inquired about the people's views on the Jewish lobby, asking if Jewish groups in the U.S. have too much influence over foreign policy as it affects Israel. Thirty per cent said yes, compared with 48 per cent answering no.

The poll was released as part of a CBS News documentary programme on the lobbying efforts of the pro-Israel and pro-Arab groups in the U.S. The nationally-televised programme evaluated the pro-Israel effort as having been most effective, calling I.L. Kenen, the chief American spokesman for Israel in Washington, "one of the most powerful lobbyists in Washington."

The programme reported that in the past, the Arab lobbyists have had less impact, but are now intensifying their efforts. This new move was highlighted by the visit last month by Saudi Arabian Oil Minister Sheikh Ahmad Zaki Yamani, and will be continued by Dr. Clovis Maksoud, a leading Arab spokesman who arrives in the U.S. today for a three-month propaganda campaign.

Maksoud, a 46-year-old Lebanese Christian, will tour the country on behalf of the Arab League and will be based on the League's Washington office. Maksoud is no stranger to the U.S. having received a law degree in Washington and spoken here on numerous occasions. He has repeatedly advocated that Israel be replaced by a new "democratic-secular" Palestine.

Threat against airlines 'friendly to Israel'

TRIPOLI (Reuter). — Arab states will consider taking economic reprisals against international airlines which they claim have made flights "assisting Israel," the Libyan news agency Arna said yesterday.

The agency said action against them was among issues to be discussed at a meeting of the Arab Boycott of Israel Office due to open in Abu Dhabi on January 14, but did not name the airlines considered to have aided Israel.

The agency quoted the head of the Libyan regional bureau of the Boycott Office as confirming its demand that the editor of the Italian newspaper "La Stampa" be sacked following publication of an article highly critical of Libyan leader Muammer Gaddafi. The economic interests in the Arab world of the Fiat motor concern — which controls "La Stampa" — "will be jeopardised unless firm measures are taken to dismiss the editor of 'La Stampa' Signor Arrigo Levi," he was quoted as saying.

Teachers to do free overtime

Jerusalem Post Reporter

TEL AVIV. — The Histadrut Teachers Union has agreed that those of its members who must now fill in for mobilized colleagues do three hours of substitute work a week on a volunteer basis. This follows a demand by the Director-General of the Ministry of Education, Elad Peled, that full-time teachers donate four work hours per week.

A full teaching post means 24 hours a week.

Mr. Peled further suggested that teachers working an 18-hour week give three extra hours substituting for mobilized teachers; that teachers working 12 hours a week give two additional hours; and that teachers who work a six-hour week add one hour.

The Union, however, agreed only to three additional hours for full-time teachers. It stipulates that any time which the teachers put in over the three weekly hours should be paid for.

AGAINST THE MACHINE

One of the few surprises of the elections was the strong showing of Shulamit Aloni's "Civil Rights" list. MARK SEGAL interviewed Mrs. Aloni this week.

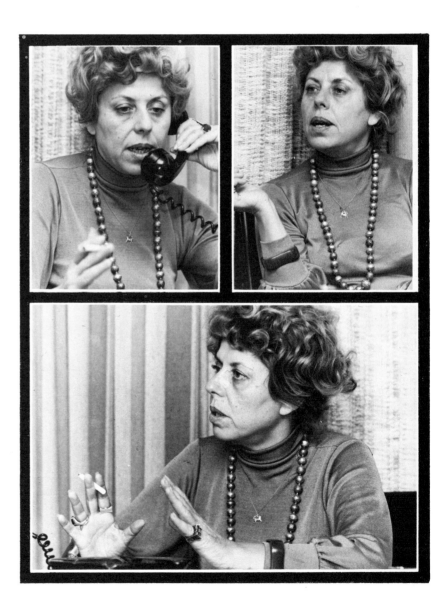

Mrs. Shulmit Aloni, leader of the Civil Rights Party.

THE EIGHTH KNESSET should be an interesting place and one of the most newsworthy of its members will undoubtedly be the irrepressible Shulamit Aloni. Not that she is an entirely new face — she was an M.K. for Mapai in the Sixth Knesset, but, falling out of favour with the party bosses, failed to make the next candidates' list. If anything, she is a controversial figure, and she enjoys that kind of reputation enormously. Having learned from bitter experience the price a politician pays for non-conformity under our proportional election system, Mrs. Aloni has become a convert to the Movement for Electoral Reform.

The success — exceptional by our standards — of Mrs. Aloni's Civil Rights list has been one of the most significant phenomena of these elections. It was my impression after visiting the group's modest offices near the Tel Aviv Sheraton that they are rather bewildered by this sudden increment of power. Three M.K.s puts them on the verge of the big league and already they are at the centre of the political manoeuvring as other parties bid for their support for their favourite schemes.

WAS HER DIVORCE from the Labour Party absolute?

"Perhaps we will become the catalyst that will infuse some democracy into the main party, with primaries and other such measures," was her reply.

As to whether she would join a Labour-led Coalition, Shulamit Aloni said, "It has not been suggested to us, but if our votes can neutralize the religious parties and help enlightened legislation we shall do so. I personally am not tempted by the idea of joining a Coalition government, and wouldn't if it committed us to a line that contradicted our election promises."

As for a parliamentary bloc with the ILP, she noted that most of their programmes coincide and that perhaps by joint action they could effect changes. "But we prefer not to rush to the *huppa*," she cautioned, declaring her willingness for a common front against religious political extortion. "We are offering the Alignment an opportunity to implement its platform with our help," she added, with a twinkle in her eyes.

Mark Segal

Mrs. Aloni is an old hand at this game and her friends are lucky in having someone who knows how to cope quite well with the intricacies of parliamentary tactics. It would seem that she knew exactly what she was doing when she put her list together just in time to slip through the door before the legal deadline for submitting Knesset candidates' lists, back in September. In an election-eve bet among her friends on the likely results, she won the IL200 deposited for the most accurate forecast.

The fact that her list won 3.5 per cent of the army is especially gratifying to Shulamit Aloni, for this is more than all the soldiers' votes polled by the ILP and Moked.

She believes that many women, especially among the educated strata, supported her group, including "rebellious" women in tradition-bound communities.

"That's where our 30 votes in Rosh Ha'ayin come from," she explains. Votes also came in from Arabs and Druse. They had some support in Dalyat el-Carmel and Ussafiya, and 1.5 per cent of the Beduin voters cast their ballots for her list. Why? "They are simply fed up with being treated as vassals whose votes can be bought."

Shulamit Aloni agrees that her list benefited from the protest vote against the Labour Party machine and that the same wave that cast Yehoshua Rabinowitz out of Tel Aviv Town Hall carried her into the Knesset. Though her group's dovish sympathies in foreign and security affairs were no secret, she felt it would be inaccurate to assess her votes as being pro-dovish; rather, her campaign had focused on internal matters, with such slogans as "Aren't You Fed Up?" Though voters were aware that her list was against any link with the Likud, they were more interested in what she was *for*.

"It was a positive vote for electoral reform, for changing our method of government, for women's equality under the law, against bureaucracy and against religious coercion."

SHE IS PREPARED to concede that many people who voted for her list did so both as a personal protest against Golda Meir and "against the Labour Party machine and all it stands for."

Mrs. Aloni says frankly: "The dilemma is how to organize a political movement without getting bogged down in a party machine. We want to be a ginger group, and we realize that a framework is necessary, so we have to think hard how not to fall into the pattern of Israeli political organizations."

She sees it as her duty in the Knesset to help retrieve some of the prerogatives that the Government has taken away from it, "so that it should be a House of Representatives and not just of appointees."

Among her first plans is a revision of the Histadrut pension fund regulations which discriminate against unmarried and divorced members. Then there is Prof. Kaniel's draft electoral reform bill, which calls for dividing the country up into 18 regions, each returning five members, with the remaining 30 M.K.s being chosen from national lists — in fact a blend of the constituency and proportional systems. She intends looking into the Broadcasting Authority and Government management of news. She is going to fight for the replacement of the Authority's director, Shmuel Almog, by someone like Leah Porat, head of the Council of Arts and Culture.

While Shulamit Aloni feels that women are discriminated against in Israel because of prejudices and certain laws, "I personally have nothing to complain about and I have four men at home" (her husband, Reuven, is in charge of developing Sharm e-Sheikh; her eldest son, Dror, 20, is an officer in Zahal; Nimrod, has just started his army service, and Ehud is 14). But she is very much against the divorce law which enables a woman to squeeze money from her ex-husband for the rest of his life.

JOKE POLITICIANS AND OTHER DIVERSIONS

The syndrome that always appears in crises

by Alex Berlyne

This scene, in a 1946 film, describes a universal experience which I call the Dolly Messiter syndrome. Briefly stated, it consists of a crisis situation with attendant *nudnik* complications. You can depend on it, I've found. Whenever you are grappling with an emergency, someone is practically certain to barge in on you with some completely irrelevant nonsense which is guaranteed to distract you during the decisive moment.

Right now, while the nation's future is being decided, *nobody* seems to be minding the store. All our politicians, of every complexion, are engaged in furious horse-trading and the questions of the hour are, apparently, civil marriage, post mortems, army service for religious girls and that old favourite "Who is a Jew."

The ease with which the elected representatives of the people can be distracted from the real issues suggests that they are childish in the extreme. Any parent knows that a bright new rattle can divert a baby's attention from whatever it was that agitated him a moment previously. There is a term used by evolutionists, neoteny, which seems to explain these political antics. It means the prolongation of certain infantile characteristics into adult life.

In some people this phenomenon expresses itself harmlessly in a love of practical jokes well beyond school-leaving age. There are firms like Ellisdon Brothers in England, Feistel in Germany, and Payragric in France, as well as several in Japan, which manufacture these jokes and tricks in vast quantities. Special shops cater to the demand. A few years ago there were twenty or so in London alone, all dedicated to the idea that the stink-bomb is the highest form of human endeavour. One shop, in Great Russell Street, numbers Prince Charles among its clientele. Not long ago he bought several Whoopee Cushions which make a rude noise when sat on. It hardly augurs well for the future of the realm.

The best-selling line in the Tottenham Court Road Magic Shop is the stink-bomb. The going rate is rather stiff, 12p for a box of three, but the proprietor was quoted in a recent article in "The Illustrated London News" as saying that the 20 gross of boxes which he had in stock would only last him until the summer. If you're any good at arithmetic you'll have already worked out that this amounts to 8,640 rather unpleasant episodes which could be traced back to one shop alone.

A leading toy importer tells me that there has never been much demand for these tricks in Israel, "there isn't the tradition, you see." In fact, a number of them are specifically prohibited by law, in order to guard us against their dire effects. Unfortunately there doesn't seem to be any legislation to protect us from the merry pranks and wheezes of professional politicians.

For several decades that I am aware of, the motto of Ellisdon Brothers has been: "Joke spoon (or whatever item they're advertising). Try it on your friends." At this stage in our country's history I was interested to note that one candidate campaigned on a platform of "air-conditioning in all buses and taxis." Perhaps we ought to amend the slogan to "Joke politician. Try it on your friends.."

VIEWPOINT By Erwin Frenkel

WHEN GOVERNMENT FAILS TO SPEAK OUT

FELIX Frankfurter once said that democratic government may be defined as "the government which accepts in the fullest sense the responsibility to explain itself."

It is a definition which can fruitfully be applied to Israel, not to measure its democratic pedigree, but to test the manner in which the government leads. For what Frankfurter had in mind was the responsibility of democratic leadership — the means by which consent is maintained between leaders and the led in a democracy.

Probably he did not consider the queer democratic offshoot which is coalition government, where explanation becomes entangled in contradiction, where the statement of one minister becomes the occasion for a rebuttal by another.

But he probably did have in mind matters like economic policy, the state of the armed forces, relations between the officer corps and government, the health of the head of government, major foreign policy decisions; and perhaps if the U.S. of his day had included it, the loss — by virtue, of an accident — of 15-16 per cent of a government oil company's proceeds.

In Israel, especially the Israel after the Yom Kippur War, such items are no longer subjects in need of government explanation. Because a few generals began to denounce each other through the press, it has been decreed that soldiers of all ranks can no longer talk to newsmen. Because our economic ministers were busy with elections or because they have nothing to say, we do not know what kind of policy is to be adopted to cover the immense costs of war, mobilization, and world inflation. Because of the fluidity of our internal politics, the custodians of the State have watched as a field general engages in coalition negotiations. Because the Government is predisposed to telling as little as possible, it negotiates withdrawal under the euphemism of disengagement. And because withholding news has become an automatic reaction, an explanation of the cause of the fire at Abu Rodeis is denied the Israeli public.

The war has raised many questions. It has made the need for the government to explain itself to its public even more imperative than before. For only by such explanation can public trust be maintained. Instead, there has been silence. It is perhaps most graphically illustrated by the fact that since the elections, not a word has been heard from the Prime Minister and head of the Labour Alignment, stating what the results of the election mean for her policies.

When a government fails to explain itself to its own people, there is no reason to expect that it can explain itself abroad. Those in search of culprits for failings of our information policy abroad would do well to examine causes, not symptoms.

If, for example, disengagement is not presented for what it really is — a daring Israeli initiative for withdrawal into Sinai that could help promote a settlement — we should not be surprised if Dr. Kissinger and Sadat, and not Israel, reap the political credit when our troops move back.

Our leaders will then still be explaining that they gave nothing away, making no sense abroad and no sense at home.

But it is consent and conviction at home, not foreign information policy, which is the prime issue in the government's failure to explain itself. Democratic governments have a responsibility to explain themselves, not in order to satisfy the curiosity of inquiring journalists, as some of our leaders would dismiss it, and not even because of that fine phrase "the public's right to know," but because of the fear of what happens when they don't.

Sharif picks Israelis for bridge circuit

LONDON (UPI). — Egyptian movie star and bridge champion Omar Sharif is doing his bit to help bridge the differences between his country and Israel.

Sharif has chosen Israel's leading players Mori Stampf and Adrian Schwartz as teammates for this month's Cutty Sark international bridge tour of Britain, the organizers announced yesterday.

Special security measures will be taken in view of Sharif's "provocative choice of colleagues," a spokesman for the sponsors said.

English internationals Jeremy Flint and Boris Schapiro are also in the squad, which opens the tour in Glasgow on January 28.

419

Fiat denies Libya turned back tractors

TURIN (AP). — Fiat denied yesterday a report that Libya recently sent back to Italy a shipment of tractors to back up demands for dismissal of the editor of a Fiat-owned local newspaper, "La Stampa."

The report in Rome's financial paper, "Il Globo," said the order to return the shipment marked the beginning of an Arab boycott against the Italian company. The Arab Boycott Office has asked Fiat to fire the Jewish editor-in-chief of "La Stampa" or face economic reprisal. The Boycott Office said editor Arrigo Levi was a "Zionist working against the Arabs."

The threat came after "La Stampa" printed an article ridiculing Libyan strongman Col. Muammar Gaddafi and his philosophy.

The Italian Government, meanwhile, had rejected the Arab request to fire Levi after politicians, Fiat and newspapers had reacted indignantly to the Arab boycott threat.

Fiat said the report in "Il Globo" may be the result of misunderstanding. The company spokesman said that in the past few days part of a load of Fiat trucks and buses failed to pass Libyan customs because delivery papers were not in order owing to new rules the Libyans enforced.

The Fiat spokesman described this as "an episode which has been already solved," and that "there are currently no business relations with Libya in the sector of tractors."

Shumel Garmi who lost about 40,000 Israeli pounds during the war.

RESERVISTS ARE FEELING THE MONEY PINCH

By ABRAHAM RABINOVICH
Jerusalem Post Reporter

OCCUPIED SYRIA. — From his cheerful countenance, one could never gather that Sgt. Shmuel Garmi was approaching economic calamity.

"This war will cost me at least IL30-50,000," he said off-handedly during a chat with a visitor to the Syrian front last week. The sergeant, who is of Yemenite extraction, owns a prosperous diamond exporting firm in Herzliya. Normally every October he travels to Hong Kong to purchase raw gems. This October, however, the 38-year-old reservist did his travelling to the Golan Heights. He went in the turret of a Sherman tank which entered the battle the morning after Yom Kippur and survived some of the bitterest fighting of the war. Since the cease-fire, his unit has remained on the front line.

"This is a veteran unit—most of the men are 35-40," said the tank commander. "We all have families and many of the fellows who are self-employed are really hurting. Those without any capital will be broken. What's good about being up here at the front is that I don't think about the business. All I think about when I get home is eating well and sleeping well. I pass the places where men in our unit were killed during the war and I think *haikar habriut* — the main thing is to be healthy."

As mobilization becomes more protracted, its burden is being increasingly felt by reservists who have been in uniform since Yom Kippur, particularly by self-employed persons whose businesses have shut down. There is growing resentment too over the fact that the burden is being unequally shared between those who have been kept in uniform — usually men in first-line combat units which had experienced heavy fighting and sacrifice in the war — and those who have either been demobilized or not mobilized at all.

"I'm a kibbutznik so I'm not affected economically by mobilization," said a young tank gunner. "But something has to be done to overcome this inequality. Two of our fellows went on leave to Tel Aviv last week and met with some of their friends who were not mobilized. When they came back they said it was like meeting people from a different world. The others did all the talking about 'the situation' and our two boys just kept quiet.

Herzl Shafir (army manpower head) came to our unit last week and listened to our complaints. He said something will be done. I hope it is."

Feelings of inequality even arise among members of the same tank crew over the monthly payments made them (up to IL1,800) by the army and Equalization Fund. "I'm self-employed," said a tank driver, "and I had declared for income tax purposes that I earn IL1,200 a month. So that's what I'm being paid now for reserve duty. Our gunner, who is a bigger liar than I am, declared only IL800 a month. The tank commander, who is a sergeant like me, declared IL1,800. The three of us are all doing the same job here, putting in the same hours and living in the same conditions, yet I'm getting 50 per cent more than the gunner and 50 per cent less than the commander. Don't make any mistake. We love each other and the discipline here is fantastic. Everyone in the unit does his job without having to be told what to do. We're confident of our strength in case fighting breaks out again. But there is inequality and it has to be straightened out."

Enemy Prisoners and

Wounded Syrian prisoners of war talked to members of the Israeli public for the first time this week when a group from Meditran, a Jerusalem organization **working** to promote inter-faith relations, was allowed to visit them in hospital.

It took Meditran — an interfaith group formed in Jerusalem two years ago for the promotion of Israeli-Arab cultural and social relations — six weeks to obtain permission to present the gifts to the wounded of both sides. Finally, last Sunday a delegation of seven, comprising Christians, Moslems and Jews, distributed some 200 individual gift packages containing books, candies, games and toilet articles, at two government hospitals, Shmuel Harofe and Assaf Harofe.

Half the presents, collected by volunteers from residents in both parts of Jerusalem, were earmarked originally for Israeli prisoners in Syria.

Lev Schwartz, one of Meditran's founders, says that all the organization's efforts on this point collapsed in the face of Syrian obduracy. "Neither the International Red Cross nor various other channels through which we acted could make any headway with the authorities in Damascus.

"All of us in Meditran, regardless of nationality or religion, consider the decision of the Israeli authorities nevertheless to permit our distribution of gifts here, the best proof of their deeply humanitarian attitude towards their fellow men. This is particularly gratifying to members of Meditran. Our objective, both as members of the organization and as individuals, is an Arab-Jewish relationship of peace and community stronger than treaties and more enduring than armistices.

"At the same time, we have not abandoned our efforts to secure for Israeli prisoners in Syria at least some of the privileges that we have seen enjoyed by Syrian PoWs here. I must admit that it was particularly moving to me as a Jew

to see how the faces of the wounded men lit up when the two Moslems in our delegation them the traditional Arabic greeting, *Ahlan wa'sahlan bikum;* I could not help thinking how happy our boys in Syria would be to be greeted with a *Shalom aleikhem* in similar circumstances."

THE MOSLEM members of the group, Sali Nammari and Wajeh Nusseibeh, are members of two of Jerusalem's oldest and best-known Arab families.

"Several of the prisoners," Mr. Nammari says, "told me they were sure on being captured that they faced torture and death. Instead, they were given first aid, and quickly transported to hospitals. Now their only complaint is that there are not enough Arabic speaking nurses to talk to."

Two of the 19 prisoners visited by the group related proudly that they had been flown to hospital by helicopter.

Both Moslem members of the delegation later visited Israeli war wounded. At Assaf Harofe Mr. Nammari, a contractor with the British Eighth Army during World War Two, found a "comrade-in-arms" in the person of hospital director Dr. Eliezer Geltner.

One of the soldiers to whom Meditran's purpose was described said, "It's hard to trust the Arabs — they never keep their promises."

"I challenged this on the basis of personal experience," says Mr. Nammari. "I told him that I had married a Jewish woman in 1942, and that when fighting started both in 1948 and in 1967 I happened to be away from home. My Arab neighbours nevertheless did all in their power to ensure that no harm befell my wife, and at no time did she feel

insecure under their protection."

Mr. Nammari has also offered personally to intercede in Damascus on behalf of Israeli PoWs. For this purpose, he recently sent his passport to Amman with a request for a Syrian visa. It has not yet been returned. He has also participated — "very actively," in the words of Lev Schwartz — in a Meditran delegation to high ecclesiastical circles with a request they intercede in Syria on behalf of the PoWs.

According to Mr. Nammari, most of the 19 Arab wounded visited by the group — 12 Syrians, five Egyptians and two Iraqis — were anxious to return home. Most of the Syrians, however, were reticent on the question of an exchange of prisoners. The one notable exception was the pilot, Lt.-Col. Khedr. He said that he was a soldier and knew how to take orders. If his government decided against such an exchange, "it must know what it is doing, and I accept the decision," he told Nammari.

A SYRIAN pilot, both his crushed legs amputated below the knee following the shooting down of his plane over the Golan Heights, praises the medical attention and his treatment generally at the hands of Israelis. But the airman, 36-year-old Adnan Alhag Khedr of Damascus, says he will be ready to continue fighting the Israelis any way he can unless they evacuate Syrian territory.

An Egyptian peasant, wounded and captured on the Suez front only three weeks ago, sobs uncontrollably as he recalls his fears that he would be shot on the spot by his captors. Instead, he was given cigarettes, food and first aid before being evacuated to a hospital. Private Rakheib

Human Beings

Abdul Rahman Rakheib, 27, of el Karomti village, weeps again as he asks why he is not being sent home.

Another *fallah*, 20-year-old Syrian private Habib Ali, from the village of Almuda near the Turkish border, is recovering from a leg wound. A head wound has completely healed, he says, thanks to his speedy evacuation from the battlefield by the Israelis. Ali's expression is still one of wonderment as he mentions that he was in an Israeli hospital two hours after being hit by shell shrapnel on the Golan.

These wounded men were speaking to members of the first organization permitted personally to distribute gifts and to speak with wounded Arab PoWs

GEORGE LEONOF

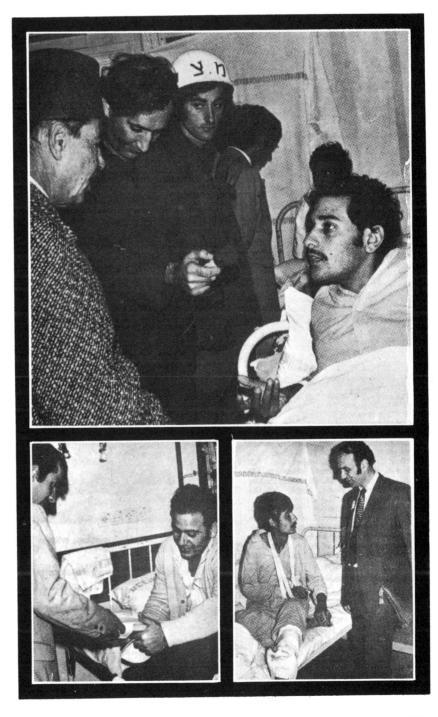

Salim Nammari with Syrian prisoner. (Below, left) Wajeh Nusseibeh presents gift to wounded Israeli. (Below, right) Lev Schwartz, a founder of Meditran, talking to wounded Syrian POW in the hospital ward.

Itzik and his ma, Purveyors to the Troops
The warmest bath-house in Syria

By ABRAHAM RABINOVICH
Jerusalem Post Reporter

KHAN ARNABA, Occupied Syria. — Rain being driven across the grey Syrian plateau by strong winds lashed at four soldiers huddled in a reconnaissance jeep feeling its way through this captured Syrian village early this week. From the porch of a building, a bearded soldier beckoned them in out of the storm and the four raced inside.

What they found was not merely shelter but — by the bleak standards of the Syrian front — a palace of oriental delights. They had hardly had a chance to thaw out in the amply heated building when cups of hot coffee and pieces of home-made cake were thrust into their hands.

The dazzled patrol men were then led to a room shrouded in mist. At one end were shower stalls, at the other a home-made sauna whose heated stones threw up clouds of steam as water was poured on them.

The mud-caked quartet, who had not showered since their last home visit, said wistfully that they had no change of clothing with them. "You don't need any," said their bearded host, "I'll give you clean underwear, a clean uniform and even new boots if you need them." When the men emerged an hour later, fortified by shots of brandy, the rain no longer seemed to matter.

The bath-house of Khan Arnaba has become, for the thousands of men deployed along the Syrian front, an almost dreamlike retreat from a world of mud, cold and shelling. It is not only the heat, the showers and the change of clothing that bring them streaming in but the regular visits by groups of *dodot* ("aunties") from the civilian rear. These are in fact Jewish mothers beefing up the front line with that ultimate weapon — chicken soup. They also bring with them home-made cakes, pies, brandy and other items not normally furnished by the army quartermaster.

The bath-house operation was organized by Lt. Itzik and his mother. Itzik, a Netanya accountant whose normal reserve duty is liaison with UN cease-fire observers, was mobilized towards the end of the Yom Kippur War and told to set up a shower facility for the troops in the northern front. The reservist officer is an old soldier adept at organizing a measure of civilization even on the front line.

Itzik chose as his bathhouse site Khan Arnaba, in the heart of the Israel bulge in Syria. (The village, appropriately, was also the site of an ancient khan which had served travellers on the road between Acre and Damascus.) Commandeering an empty building, he had army technicians rig up shower stalls. "But I saw that this wasn't enough," he explained. "I wanted a place where the men could get out of their dirty clothing and drink something hot." It was the sort of situation in which a man turns to his mother.

Itzik's mother, an energetic lady from Netanya, soon had the local Wizo branch involved. Each Sunday, 180 Wizo ladies each bake a cake and the following morning they are loaded into a van (lent by a Netanya firm) along with large pots of soup, liquor, cigarettes, knitted caps and other supplies. The half dozen ladies who make the trip each week spend about three hours on the porch of Itzik's inn, distributing their wares after heating up the soup and making coffee. Even before they are finished, another group of aunties arrives from Haifa.

"I've got teams of *dodot* up here every morning and afternoon," says Itzik. Groups recruited by him and his mother include Wizo, Rotary and Mizrahi Women from Haifa, Working Mother groups from Netanya and Tel Aviv, and faculty groups from the Technion and Haifa University.

"There isn't any shortage of food here, you understand," says Itzik. "But the fact that the men are handed cake and coffee by some *doda* who has taken the trouble to come up here makes all the difference."

The response of the troops to these visits is so enthusiastic that the chief bath-house attendant, Samal Baruch, is invariably overwhelmed as he tries to maintain order around the serving tables. "I can't stand rudeness," complains the bearded sergeant who normally runs a flower shop in Bnai Brak. He and his three assistants — like him, ultra-Orthodox reservists who had served as infantrymen during the war — rise each dawn to get the bath-house fires going.

If Lt. Itzik had his way they would be working nights too. "If I can get hold of a 16 mm. projector, I'd start a cinema."

A burly tank sergeant emerging from the shower-room this week said he popped over to the bath-house as frequently as he could from his front-line position, not far away. "They've got everything here," he said, "except geisha girls."

Samal Baruch outside the Khan Arnaba bath-house.

ISRAEL IS MELANCHOLY. The Yom Kippur War has left the country washed out.

To their distress, Israelis realize that they are not their own masters, but only pawns of indeterminate influence in a massive tug-of-war between the two superpowers. Had Israel been allowed to play out her role in the Middle East without interference by either the United States or Russia, she could have successfully defended herself against all the Arab armies of the world.

Today, Israel realizes she will not be allowed to do this. In any war, whether it be a preemptive strike initiated by Israel as a defensive action, or a response to a war initiated by her neighbors, Israel will be allowed to go just so far. Whether or not she could or would want to, Israel would never be permitted to conquer Damascus or Cairo; Israel would never be permitted to administer a beating which might render the Arabs incapable of starting another conflict. The superpowers will only tolerate an Israel with clipped wings.

On the battlefields, the war in the Middle East may be fought between Israelis and Arabs; but behind the scenes, the war belongs to the United States and Russia. And neither can allow a definitive victory by either Jew or Arab.

Israel knows that the Arabs intend to fight her, no matter how many times they are beaten. This alone is enough to make the situation pretty grim. What economy can thrive when it is forced upon a course of constant war?

But the outlook is even worse. No matter how

EX-COLLEAGUE QUOTING TAPED BRIEFING

Kissinger thinks Israel is paranoic

Jerusalem Post Reporter

TEL AVIV. — U.S. Secretary of State Henry Kissinger called Israel's insistence on secure and defensible borders "paranoic" when talking freely to his staff on his recent air flight from Europe to the U.S., Harvard University Professor Amos Perlmutter related, on Friday night.

Prof. Perlmutter, interviewed on the radio by Gideon Levari, was quoting from the taped recording of Dr. Kissinger's remarks, which have not been published so far. He said that his old Harvard faculty colleague never used the word "peace settlement" in describing the aims of the Geneva talks. For Dr. Kissinger there was no such thing as "absolute security," Prof. Perlmutter said; rather, the Secretary envisaged an Israeli withdrawal to the 1949 armistice lines, according to his taped talk.

The political science professor quoted from other Harvard colleagues when noting that Zionism or any other ideology of small nations interfered with Dr. Kissinger's concept of a world order based on super-states. Moreover, if it came to a showdown, Dr. Kissinger would prefer the Arab states over Israel because of their monetary power, oil and size. The Harvard professor reflected the view that Dr. Kissinger was now a victim of his own detente scheme with the Soviet Union, and that the media had become hypnotized by Kissinger's coming and going — "for his record has shown he is neither Bismarck nor Metternich, but a fireman rushing around the world putting out fires."

He accused the Israeli leadership of being hypnotized with the Kissinger legend. Asked what would happen if Kissinger sought to pressure Israel into accepting a withdrawal from the Suez Canal without getting anything in return from Egypt, Prof. Perlmutter's advice was, "Stand up to him and he will fold up."

In general, the professor advised Israel to free itself of the Kissinger legend and look to American public opinion, which was sympathetic towards Israel. Israel should also look to the 1976 presidential elections: most of the emerging candidates, whether Republican or Democrat, were activists and, unlike Kissinger, held no illusions about Soviet intentions, the professor said.

The concrete causeway which the Israelis erected over the Suez.

426

stout her military strength, Israel's might is effectively counterbalanced by the Damocles sword of Russian intervention.

It is this realization that has changed the mood in Israel today. The very life of the country and the lives of its people are likely to depend, in large measure, on the good graces of the American government. And those good graces may depend on factors of geopolitik well beyond the control of the Israelis.

When the Biafrans were attacked by the Nigerian Government, many people throughout the world were sympathetic; but very, very few—no matter what their faith, or color, or political bias—really put themselves out to succor the Biafrans. The stark fact is that people fight for their own. Neither Jews nor well-wishers of any faith lost too much sleep over the Biafran cause. The Ibos died like flies, and perhaps here and there, one humanitarian sighed a deep sigh, but no one really ached like the Biafrans ached.

One cannot expect the world to be deeply affected by any imminent erasure of Israel. However deeply well-wishers might deplore such a horrible event, their lives would not be really affected. Only the Jews will be deeply affected. Only the Jews will cry. Only the Jews will be uprooted.

As this book goes to press in mid-July of 1974, we find the Palestinian guerilla organizations clamoring for a seat at the Peace Conference. We also read in news reports that Israeli Information Minister, Aharon Yariv, has conveyed the impression that Israel would be willing to sit down and negotiate at Geneva with the Palestinians provided the Palestinians would cease from making further raids on Israeli civilians, and provided that the Palestinian organization would publicly announce that it would fully recognize the right of Israel to exist as a sovereign state.

It seems obvious that the second demand must be basic. How could the Palestinians expect less? How could Israel agree to negotiate with any group that started by declaring it wished to destroy the State of Israel? Do the Palestinians want Israel to sit down with them at a conference table to determine, in effect, just how they can all cooperate in

THE PERILS OF PEACE

To the Editor of The Jerusalem Post

Sir, — For years, we have been harping on the theme of a permanent peace settlement. At the moment, official thinking goes in the direction of defining peace as a matter of stages, or degrees. Thus, mere recognition of the other side's right to exist is seen as a meagre peace. The quality is somewhat improved with the establishment of diplomatic contacts. Trade relations represent a yet more advanced stage of peace; and near-consummation of the ideal of peace is attained with the free flow of goods and people across frontiers.

The weakness of this approach lies in its being borrowed from the industrial West and — one suspects — its being originally devised for their consumption.

Of course, among highly developed industrial societies, a level of economic interdependence may sometimes be reached which virtually precludes a relapse into war. France and Germany are often mentioned as a case in point. The same is, however, far from true with primitive societies. Here, disruptive forces are usually far stronger than those working in the opposite direction. For anyone in need of convincing, witness the number of unions, federations and common markets which have been established among the Arabs themselves to be dissolved almost as promptly as they were established. These unions hardly go beyond signing the formal instruments bringing them into existence. The reason for this fickleness is obvious. Apart from the desire to unite, there is very little else to be united about. It is, unfortunately, all too likely that a similar fate will befall attempts at economic cooperation between us and the Arabs. Also, our recent experience in extending aid to African states points in the same direction.

There is, of course, nothing wrong in pondering the nature of peace, were it not that the definition is put forward as the measure of the concessions we would be prepared to make.

We have to accept that our region is extremely volatile and, probably, will remain so for many years to come. The belief that a permanent peace settlement can be reached is an exercise in wishful thinking.

What is needed is the evolvement of a policy which takes account of the facts of the region. Before us, there are basically two policy choices. One possibility is to attempt to break out of our isolation and involve ourselves directly in inter-Arab rivalries. Here the choice is between going together with Egypt or helping to contain it.

The other possibility is to maintain our isolation. There are powerful reasons for choosing this position. The consequences of an involvement in inter-Arab rivalries are almost incalculable. An Egypt made dominant through our connivance or support may eventually prove a far more formidable enemy — once our support is no longer needed — than the one we have known hitherto. Owing to the disparity between our military strength and our present numbers, the Arabs stand to gain far more from our involvement than we do. Also, a policy of involvement may pose a threat to the identity of the Jewish state.

All this points not to a change of policy, but to a persistent pursuit of long-accepted principles. The answer to the problems posed by the last war is not a permanent peace settlement, but a greater stress on immigration and economic development. In Geneva, all we can hope for is an arrangement which will ensure us a reasonable period of quiet, and this is all we should be prepared to pay for.

ERLING COHN

Department of Underdeveloped Countries, Tel Aviv University
Ramat Gan, December 18.

Giving up land won't bring peace — Navi

TEL AVIV. — Beersheba Mayor Eliahu Navi on Friday warned Israelis against "deluding themselves" into thinking they could solve the Arab-Israel dispute by returning territories to the Arabs.

The Iraq-born Mayor, who was addressing the Engineers Club here, said the dispute had never been over territories. The Arabs simply saw Israel as a foreign body which must be destroyed. He noted that the Arab states had never been willing to recognize any borders for Israel, not in 1947 and not in 1949.

Mr. Navi said the last war, whether or not it had been aimed at Israel's annihilation, was the most serious of all, because it had shown the Egyptians would do anything — divert their development budget, conscript University graduates and enslave themselves to the Soviets — to wage a holy war against Israel.

"The war has made peace between Israel and the Arabs even more remote," Mr. Navi said, since the Arabs had begun to believe they could wipe out Israel. As long as they believed this there would be more wars.

Mr. Navi said a dispute which has gone on for years cannot be ended with a single signature. But he saw a chance for some kind of arrangement with the Egyptians which could reduce their sense of frustration and permit the Canal to be reopened. Such an arrangement — which would have to involve separation of forces and maximum security for Israel — would give several years' breathing space, during which Arab unity and the oil weapon would lose some of their force.

And, he added, if the Arabs finally came to realize that Israelis are not devils and cannot be wiped out, "perhaps some day we'll be able to visit in Cairo." *(Itim)*

THE GENERALS IN POLITICS

WHATEVER Aluf Arik Sharon talked about with the various party leaders whom he has met in recent days, the very meetings themselves are a cause of concern and have provoked criticism. A general, on active service, who is himself a Knesset Member and leading politician in civilian life should be doubly careful not to give the impression that he is dabbling in politics while still in uniform.

Aluf Sharon maintains that he is not involved in the coalition negotiations. But the persons with whom he met certainly are — and that alone is reason enough for him, in his delicate position, to avoid public contact with them at this time.

But Sharon's behaviour cannot be criticized in isolation, as if it were some unique enormity in Israeli public life. The very real and growing problem of the soldier-politician and his place in our society — a problem exemplified but by no means exhausted by Sharon's case — urgently needs rethinking. Perhaps the new Knesset, with its large number of reserve officer members, will address itself to it.

The problem surfaced when Aluf Ezer Weizman and Rav-Aluf Haim Bar-Lev moved with disturbing speed from the General Staff to the Cabinet. But it certainly existed, beneath the surface, long before that, as officers in their early forties on the verge of demobilization jockeyed for top jobs in industry and finance—jobs which in the Israeli reality are all too often within the patronage of the political parties.

The coincidence of the Yom Kippur war and the election brought the issue to a head, with relatively large numbers of ex-generals, now-politicians, donning their uniforms again. Lacunae were exposed in the relevant laws, but the change-over from politics to the army, and back to politics again, revealed a deeper malaise, not just legal lacunae.

For generals to feud among themselves in the heat of battle is a common phenomenon in many armies. But the manner in which some of the Israeli generals used the press —particularly the foreign press — to air their differences, smacked of politicians playing at politics. And indeed, a few days earlier they had been politicians, sniping at each other across party lines. If there is any truth in the charges that these feuds spilled over into the direction of the war itself, then the army-and-politics problem has crossed the danger line.

Israel has always sought to avoid the creation of an officer cadre set apart from the people as a whole. It has sought to maintain the tradition of its "citizen army," where even the professionals do not regard their military service as a lifelong career but rather as a period of extended national service to be followed by a new career in civilian life.

It has sought, too, to keep its officers — even its most senior officers — young and fresh, by early promotions and rapid rotation of tasks, and above all by early retirement from the army.

These aims were valuable and have paid excellent dividends in the past. But as time passes they lead to scores, and soon hundreds, of senior officers, still intimately connected with the army and ready to resume their service at moments of crisis, moving into the top political and economic posts. In time, this inevitably begins to blur the line between the military and the civilian powers, the line which for all Israel's informality and improvisations, is as vital here as in any other democracy.

What elections meant depends on who's asked

By LEA LEVAVI
Jerusalem Post Reporter

TEL AVIV. — How will the election results affect us over the next four years? The answer depends on whom you ask — as a Wizo symposium on the subject, held in Tel Aviv this week, proved.

Participants in the symposium were Adi Amorai, M.K. from the Labour Alignment, Dr. Zalman Abramov of the Likud and Meir Pail, of Moked.

Dr. Abramov was applauded when he said: "Before the Yom Kippur War I believed in peace initiatives because I wanted to think the Arabs were finally becoming more ready to make peace with us. Today I am convinced that the Arabs do not want peace."

Meir Pail — who aroused both great interest and vociferous opposition—declared: "As a historian, I can tell you that the composition of the Eighth Knesset could be a disaster. Fewer M.K.s are willing to compromise, while at the same time international pressures towards compromise are going to increase. If we compromise voluntarily, of our own accord, we may be able to give up less and to get more in return. But if we wait until the Big Powers force us to give in, we will have to give up more without getting enough in return. If a Minister gets up in the Knesset and says 'The Americans pressured us', all opposition is immediately hushed. Why do we have to wait until the Big Powers pressure us? Why don't we control our own destiny while there's still time?"

A woman in the audience asked him what he was willing to give up. "The Arabs want the situation to go back to what it was before the Six Day War," he replied. "Our leaders seem to want to go back to the situation which existed before the Yom Kippur War. I see a situation in which we meet the Arabs most of the way geographically, but demand in return that they make peace with us."

All participants mentioned the economic and social consequences of the war effort:

Meir Pail observed that money for the war effort has to come from somewhere, "And I'm afraid it will come at the expense of welfare, education, health and other social programmes since cuts in those areas won't be felt as soon, or as sharply, and won't lower the general standard of living as much as cuts in other spheres."

Adi Amorai: "I hope the public will continue the restraint it has shown until now and will refrain from spending money on luxuries so that means of production can be diverted to essential fields, both in the war effort itself and in maintaining the services of the welfare state — including building for slum dwellers, young couples and immigrants."

Dr. Abramov: "I agree with everything Adi said, but I want to add one more thing. It's about time that we started working in this country and getting paid for the work we do, rather than for the fact that we are physically present. There shouldn't be extra people in government offices, factories or anywhere else while workers are desperately needed in other fields."

The women applauded.

LIFTS FOR SOLDIERS
To the Editor of The Jerusalem Post

Sir, — There are several common replies given by motorists when asked why they pass up soldiers waiting at the roadside for lifts. They include: "I'm in a hurry and can't stop." "I have to stop every few kilometres on the road to let them off." "They muddy up the car and upholstery." "I need to have a private conversation in my car."

Every driver when setting out on a journey should keep the seats clear of his suitcase, hat, coat, etc. and store them in the trunk of his car. Every driver should remember what our soldiers did for him during the war and continue to do now, as he lives at his army base away from home and family and job. If it weren't for the bravery of our soldiers, no Israeli would be driving on the roads today.

Our soldiers were in a hurry — to push back the enemy. Our soldiers were muddied and bloodied as were their vehicles of war; our soldiers stopped every few kilometres to assess the situation and push on; our soldiers put off their private conversations for other times.

And empty cars drive gaily by the *trampiada* (soldiers' traffic stops) while long lines of soldiers wait patiently and at the mercy of the goodwill of those at the wheel. This is the thanks they get, rain or shine. What sort of country is this whose drivers need to be exhorted to give soldiers a ride? We really can never do enough for them. Because of them we are alive. Can't we thank them even in this small way?

SUE ZOHAR DESHEH
Jerusalem, December 24.

Driver,

Do what is no more than the minimum for those doing the maximum—

Give Soldiers Lifts !

'Rumania aliya not suspended'

ZURICH (INA).— The Chief Rabbi of Rumania, Dr. Moses Rosen, who is also the chairman of the Federation of Jewish Communities, denied yesterday a report in last Sunday's "Observer" that aliya from Rumania had been suspended.

Rabbi Rosen said the "Observer" report is untrue. There was no change whatsoever in the policy of the Rumanian Government regarding emigration to Israel. Those who want to go to Israel are at liberty to do so. I left Rumania only on Sunday afternoon, which means after the "Observer" story had been published, and I know of no change."

German couple send savings to aid wounded

A West German clergyman and his wife have donated DM5,000 out of their personal savings to help wounded Israel soldiers and their families.

The donation and a letter from Rev. Paul Achenbach and his wife, Caroline, of Bad Crozingen, arrived at the President's Residence re-cently. They said in their letter that they were sending the money to help alleviate the suffering caus-ed the Jewish People during the October war.

The President's office said Wednes-day that the Achenbachs are well known in Israel for their charitable works, including aid to Alyn, Akim, and other institutions.

The Lillehammer anomaly

SURROUNDED by tanks and armoured cars, Europe's major airports have become fortresses. Main oil refineries are ringed by army units. Lead-ing European personalities are guarded day and night.

At the same time two Arab ter-rorists on bail, awaiting trial in Rome for having plotted to shoot down an Israeli airliner with missiles, have disappeared, and an American girl, captured at London airport in the company of Arab plotters, was deported rather than put on trial.

This is part of the ludicrous reality of Europe's attempt to fight Arab terror.

For the past five years it has become almost a habit for many European nations to do their best not to apprehend Arab terrorists, but to deport them soon after they are captured. Britain released Leila Haled after Israeli security men seized her as she was trying to hi-jack an El Al plane, and West German police freed the Munich killers in a trade-off for a hi-jacked Lufthansa aircraft.

Together Britain, F r a n c e, Germany, S w i t z e r l a n d and Greece have freed almost 70 Arab terrorists. And now Eu-rope is trembling in fear. Mis-siles have reportedly disappear-ed from a Nato base, and others presumably have been smuggled onto the continent by Libyan diplomats.

The policy on terror is like European policy on oil — each country for itself. Just as France has sought to make unilateral oil deals with Arab producers in the hope that it can elude oil blackmail, so has it sought to buy immunity from Arab terror activities. Yet only last week, French police discovered a secret hideaway of explosives stored for use by the terrorists.

Even as the failure of Eu-rope's policy on Arab terrorism is clear — a policy grounded in releasing the guilty — six men and women are being tried in Oslo for their part in the Lillehammer Affair, which, by the evidence, was apparently an effort to stem the terrorist menace.

The anomaly of this trial — lying in the relentless applica-tion of the law against the op-ponents of terror — is too rea-dily apparent. It has also been recognized in Norway, where a leading newspaper commented that the accused are subject-ively not guilty.

If this anomaly would move the countries of Europe to im-plement their own laws and uti-lize their own law enforcement agencies against Arab terror instead of watching the law be applied against those who fight it, European airports would not have to be ringed with troops.

But no signs of such wisdom or the joint preventive effort that it would entail have ap-peared.

DIG IN YOUR HEELS

To the Editor of The Jerusalem Post

Sir, — Along with other Zionists, I have been devouring all news from your weekly and from American newspapers concerning military and diplomatic developments, as well as internal political matters in Israel. While washing one's political linen in public can be rather embarrassing, it is nevertheless one of the healthy signs of a democracy at work. Thus, the current discourse over failings and concurrent political backbiting fail to upset me.

What does disturb me, however, is the apparent embryonic emergence of some Israeli public opinion, signalled by a dispatch in "The New York Times" of November 26 entitled "Moderates in ruling Israeli party, spurred by the war, fight to unseat hard-line leaders." The end result would inevitably produce a weak bargaining posture at the upcoming peace negotiations and a total withdrawal to pre-1967 borders, accompanied no doubt by "ironclad" guarantees of Israel's future security by the U.S., the U.N., by that paragon of trustworthiness in international relations, the U.S.S.R., and of course by those very Arab nations which have sworn to destroy Israel and every Jew therein, for the better part of a century.

My aliya will not depend upon current internal political developments; but when I ascend onto Israeli soil next July, it will be with foreboding if, in the meantime, Israeli political leadership has placed any stock whatsoever in any empty guarantees and pious pressurings of Henry Kissinger and Richard Nixon. Whatever heavy pressure and threats are applied, they must be resisted to the very last. Israel will perish without absolutely defensible borders in depth.

Thus I plead, Israelis, for every Jew breathing today and yet unborn: Reject those "doves" among you, dig in deep your heels east and west of Suez, stand eyeball to eyeball with Brezhnev and Sadat, Nixon and Kissinger, and refuse to budge one inch until you have secured the borders and other prerequisites to the survival of our Jewish Nation. We know here the heavy price in blood and lives paid the last few weeks by you, and the gloom prevailing over the loss and maiming of 4,000 of the cream of your youth. But he assured that, from the world over, Jewish men and women will ever be arriving to replace and replant the eternal Jewish seed in the eternal Jewish Homeland.

STUART L. BRAUN
Westport, Conn., November 26.

SUPPORT FROM JAPAN

To the Editor of The Jerusalem Post

Sir, — Arabs blackmail Japan, exploiting oil as a political weapon. They even demand military assistance, which is forbidden by the Japanese Constitution. They also demand severance of diplomatic relations with Israel, which can never be done because of the just moral issue involved.

It is a fact that many people support the new pro-Arab Middle East policy of the government, claiming that there is no other way to secure oil. But it is also a fact that many people criticize this policy and believe that surrender to blackmail invites more blackmail. The Japanese are a proud people and the policy of our sovereign and independent country must be made in Tokyo and not in an Arab capital.

We support Israel, not because she is small, but because justice is on her side.

MASAYUKI TAKAHASHI,
Youth Committee,
Japan-Israel Friendship Association
Tokyo, December 17.

Sharif picks Israelis for bridge circuit

LONDON (UPI). — Egyptian movie star and bridge champion Omar Sharif is doing his bit to help bridge the differences between his country and Israel.

Sharif has chosen Israel's leading players Mori Stampf and Adrian Schwartz as teammates for this month's Cutty Sark international bridge tour of Britain, the organizers announced yesterday.

Special security measures will be taken in view of Sharif's "provocative choice of colleagues," a spokesman for the spnsors said.

English internationals Jeremy Flint and Boris Schapiro are also in the squad, which opens the tour in Glasgow on January. 28.

MAGAZINES NEEDED

To the Editor of The Jerusalem Post

Sir, — We are a group of English-speaking soldiers serving "somewhere" in the south.

As we lack reading material in English, we should be very grateful if some of your readers would send us magazines dealing with news, sports, cars, geography, photography — in short anything which would be of interest to young soldiers. (We have no objection to receiving "Playboy" or similar periodicals.) Our address is Doar Tsvai 1093.

Our thanks to all those who oblige.

The Desert Reading Society
Somewhere in the South

Lecturers bring college to front

Jerusalem Post Reporter

HAIFA. — The Haifa University has "adopted" an armoured corps division on the southern front as its "educational ward." For a week now, University lecturers have gone down to the front lines to deliver series of lectures in their respective fields, staying several days with each unit, sharing their tents and their rations.

The subjects are scientific, literary or artistic, and the soldiers have responded to the experiment with enthusiasm. On home leave, they've come to the campus to ask for "more of the same."

432

Mrs. Meir presents her Government to President Katzir.

Abu Rodeis secret was foolish

To the Editor of The Jerusalem Post

Sir, — After the fire at the Abu Rodeis oil wells had been raging for 10 days, and after the Israeli public had been told that the fire was not caused by sabotage or negligence, but by a technical mishap, the Army Spokesman finally thought it proper to inform us that an Israeli Hawk missile had hit a rig and set the wells aflame. But to say that he thought it proper is actually a euphemism, for he only confirmed — reluctantly! — the report of a foreign correspondent who had to sneak out of the country in order to file his story.

We are glad to be informed that an investigating committee has been set up, but our joy would be even greater if somebody would investigate and tell us who it is that seems to consider the Israeli public not mature enough to hear the truth. Does there really exist in this country a person or a group of persons who think that the same Israelis who willingly accept the heavy burden of a country at war, the same Israelis who were widely praised for their maturity shown in the recent elections, cannot bear the truth behind a technical mishap?

Does this person, or do these persons, whoever they are, not realize that this attitude is a personal insult to all of us and that more harm is done to national security than they hoped to prevent by their irresponsible silence? Security, and a sense of security, depends more than anything else on the extent to which the citizen has faith in the wisdom of his leaders' actions. This faith has already been badly damaged in the Yom Kippur War. To withhold the truth from the people now, after the war, is not only foolish, it is an offence against security, for it undermines the public's morale.

YOHANAN ELDAD
Jerusalem, January 13.

'PRESS SHARES BLAME FOR COMPLACENCY'

Editors urge easing of army censorship

TEL AVIV. — Israel newspaper editors on Friday urged a relaxation of military censorship and one of them urged its total abolition.

They were speaking at the second session of a Press Council discussion on the functions and failings of the press during the emergency.

Noah Moses, editor of "Yediot Aharonot," said the fact that an Israeli missile caused the fire at Abu Rodeis could have been published here earlier, without harming security, as demonstrated by its eventual publication after the story broke abroad.

Mr. Moses said his paper had been approached on the eve of the October War by the army spokesman's office and by a "prominent person" to play down the enemy concentration at Israel's borders in order to avoid panic. By agreeing to such requests, the press shared blame for creating the pre-war atmosphere of complacency.

Today, said Mr. Moses, papers were publishing reports on shortages of personal equipment in the army and were printing letters from soldiers, something which had been banned before the war. But even in the past, the press had reported military trials for theft or disciplinary breaches in the face of pressure against publication.

Moses proposed establishment of a committee to examine press failings during the war. He also urged that military correspondents be given free run of the army.

Gershom Schocken, editor of "Ha'aretz," urged abolition of censorship, pointing to the U.S. as a country in which the media enjoyed freedom despite the danger of nuclear war. Had security matters been treated as openly in Israel's press as economic or political affairs, public opinion might have been alerted in time to the dangers of increasing Arab strength and become more sceptical of certain Israeli victory.

Willingly or unwillingly, the press agreed to restrict publication of information pertaining to military affairs. One result was that no military commentator of stature had arisen in the Israeli press as they had done in other fields. Freedom to publish might expose internal weaknesses but it was the preferable alternative in a democracy. There was no reason, said Schocken, to agree to kill a story anticipating appointments in the army command when the Defence Minister did not regard with particular severity the interview given by Aluf Ariel Sharon to the "New York Times."

Eliahu Salpeter, of the "Ha'aretz" editorial board, said that in the absence of an effective parliamentary opposition, Israel's press was duty bound to be critical in security matters as a means of pressure on the administration to remedy failings. But at the same time, this function must be limited by an awareness of the danger of giving information to the enemy.

Haim Izak, of "Davar," said the army was not immune from legitimate criticism. But it had to be kept in mind that Israel, even in peacetime, lived in a state of siege. A credibility gap had been created at the beginning of the war: but a full account of what was happening might have affected morale. Israel's unique attitude towards its army grew not out of militarism but out of its security situation.

Dr. Baruch Ben-Yehuda, who represents the public on the Press Council, said the press and television had created a feeling of depression during the war instead of boosting morale. They had failed to give Israel's victory the prominence it deserved and instead set up a "wail over the security failure."

The press, said Dr. Ben-Yehuda, should emulate the Biblical prophets who chastised in times of peace and comforted in times of trouble.

Dr. Y. Rotenstreich presided at the meeting. A third session is to be held next Friday.   *(Itim)*

SOLDIER'S PROTEST FROM THE FRONT

To the Editor of The Jerusalem Post

Sir. — I think someone in some administration is sick and needs help: I am sitting facing the encircled Third Egyptian Army, who are firing upon us daily, wounding and sometimes killing our boys, and yet we are giving them food to keep up their energy. What's wrong?

JERRY AFTER
Somewhere on the front, Jan. 6.

'COULD BECOME WORLD FACTOR'
Israel has plenty of oil stocks

TEL AVIV. — Israel's oil stores are in good shape, and the country even has a chance of becoming a factor on the map of the world oil-producers. This was the opinion of Fuel Directorate director Shimon Gilboa, expressed during an interview on Israel Radio Friday night.

The amount of oil Israel had stored was respectable even on a world level, Mr. Gilboa said. The country had not been affected by the Arab oil boycott, and was prepared to see it would not be so affected in the future.

As to the search for oil in Israel, he said its current stepped up pace should show results in the next five years. "It may be a bit pretentious for us to call ourselves an oil state," he said, "but I have perfect faith that we will find oil and constitute a non-negligible factor in the oil world."

Another interviewee on the same programme, Oil Institute head Menahem Hen, was unhappy with the slow pace of oil exploration so far. There had been too much reliance on Sinai oil, which between the Six-Day War and 1969 had covered nearly all Israel's fuel needs. Those responsible had failed to look for oil in unconventional places.

During the programme it was reported that the Government was to invest IL137m. in looking for oil, mainly along the coast from Nahariya to El Arish. Prof. Aviahu Ginsberg of Tel Aviv University said 15 years of test drilling had taught geologists something about the country's geological structure, and he thought there was oil along the coasts.

Meanwhile, on the subject of alternatives to oil, Development Ministry director-general Yosef Vardi said experts were working on utilizing a number of Israeli mineral deposits formerly thought uneconomical.

In an Israel TV interview broadcast Friday, Mr. Vardi said that while nuclear energy was the cheapest alternative, geologists had also found indications of coal, at a depth of 400 metres. They were also looking at the Hula basin peat, oil shale near the Dead Sea, and the possibilities of using solar energy and the earth's heat.

But he cautioned against putting too much hope on these sources right now. It would be six year's before an alternative would be found.

'Undue delay' in release of oil well story

TEL AVIV. — The Foreign Press Association on Friday charged the army spokesman with "undue and unreasonable delay" in revealing the true cause of the fire at Abu Rodeis.

Although admitting that the spokesman was technically correct in calling the fire "a technical mishap," the chairman of the association, Dan Bloom, pointed out in a statement that the spokesman later confirmed that the actual cause was an Israeli Hawk missile which homed in on the oil derrick. This was only after the story had been reported outside Israel, however.

"Despite Israeli denials, the effect of the blackout on information led to speculation abroad that it had been a deliberate act by the Israelis against the possibility of a return of the wells through the Geneva peace talks, or the result of Egyptian military action," Mr. Bloom wrote.

"The withholding of information, and the persistent refusal of authorities to allow newsmen to go to the scene to report the story on a first-hand basis, only contributes to the credibility gap which exists in Israel to an increasing degree since the Yom Kippur war," he said.

'Sinai oil earns $400m. a year'

TEL AVIV. — Israel would lose $400m. a year in oil revenue if it gave up Sinai, according to Harvard University economist Thomas Stopper.

The economist and oil consultant, whose article on Israel's economic interest in Sinai appeared in Thursday's "Christian Science Monitor," was interviewed Friday by an Israel Radio correspondent in the U.S. He said that the Egyptians would earn an extra $600m. a year if they got Sinai back. This would include Suez Canal revenues and the $300m. a year Israel has been getting from the Bala'in field, part of the Abu Rodeis complex. There Israel has stepped up production from the pre-1967 90,000 barrels a day to a present 120,000 he said.

He added that Israel is among the countries benefiting from the oil price hike: where the Egyptians sold Sinai oil for $1.50 a barrel, Israel was getting $8. The Abu Rodeis fire was only a temporary hindrance.

For more than security reasons, Dr. Stopper concluded, Israel will not be in a hurry to give up Sinai. *(Itim)*

To the Editor of The Jerusalem Post

Sir, — The voter never had it so difficult to decide to which party to give his vote. In all the parties, especially the major ones, there were people to whom he objected, often passionately, even if he supported that party's general line. His only chance to give vent to his dislike or mistrust was to vote for his party's opposition — often with an aching heart. Like previous elections, this one has finally shown the necessity to choose the man (or woman) rather than the party ticket, where one never knows who one's representative will actually be.

The voter who got the worst deal is the one who chose the smaller parties, who often shock him by giving their vote to one of the "big two," thereby using his vote for what may be a diametrically opposed purpose.

I hope that the next elections will therefore be on a personal basis. In the meantime, we need a broad coalition of all parties which alone will be able to make the historical decisions awaiting us.

W. MACKY

Tel Aviv, January 4.

making the State of Israel disappear?

Yet the Palestinians refuse to make such a basic statement. *They will not disavow their intention to liquidate Israel.*

In the face of such intransigence, it seems to this writer that the Geneva Conference can not accomplish much. Any hard-headed realist who reads the signs must see that accommodation with the Arabs is quite unlikely at this point. If so, why does Israel attend a peace conference— in fact, welcome a peace conference?

The answer is the tremendous desire the Israelis have to reduce their anxiety. They still nourish the hope, no matter how small or farfetched, of the possibility of peace.

I have spoken to many Israelis who say: As far as all the evidence goes, the Arabs do not want peace. But even if there is but one chance in a hundred that we are wrong, we must take that chance. Maybe the Arabs are hoodwinking Kissinger, yet it's a calculated risk we must take. Better to give up a strong strategic position at the Canal, better to allow the Third Army to escape, better almost anything than simply to see nothing on the horizon but the inevitability of war after war. We who are engulfed by this constant round of wars can take it; but we must give our children any chance there may be—no matter how remote—to escape this fate. We do not want to pass on to them a legacy of war and death. Therefore, a cease-fire; therefore, a conference in Geneva.

Not only is Israel deeply mistrustful of Arab intentions, it also realizes that it stands diplomatically isolated at this point. When the crunch came, and war materials from American bases in West Germany were being shipped to Israel by way of Bremerhaven, the German Foreign Ministry called upon the American ambassador and sternly rebuked him. Germany's policy, he said, was one of strict neutrality, and his government was firmly resolved not to be drawn into the Middle East conflict.

On its face, this sounded quite reasonable, but the fact was that only the United States was willing to provide Israel with munitions. The Arabs, of course, were receiving all the arms they needed.

The same excuse of neutrality was offered by all of America's NATO partners, save Portugal, the only country which permitted the United States to use the military bases on its territory from which to ship arms to Israel. Greece refused. Italy refused. Spain refused. West Germany refused. Great Britain refused.

It was almost unthinkable that the members of NATO would snub the king pin of their group—

but the unthinkable happened. The short-term interest loomed so important that the overall long-term interest receded. Thirsting for oil to feed its industry, Europe brusquely pushed aside the protective hand that held off the Russian Bear.

In his book *Confrontation*[1], Walter Laqueur reports that after the fighting ended in the Yom Kippur War, a Pentagon official declared:

> *We feel there wasn't one country in Western Europe, that if pushed to the wall, wouldn't have let Israel go under.*

Undoubtedly, that official overlooked Holland; but by and large, the estimate was correct.

What Israel fears most is the specter standing at its back, the Soviet Union, who has supported Israel's enemies to the fullest. No matter how many humiliations and rebuffs the Russians have suffered at the hands of its clients, the Soviets have still come back to support Egypt and Syria.

The question of the Israeli future and what can be done about it still remains overwhelmingly baffling. I find no ready answers; certainly no pat answers.

I must emphasize that not even Kissinger has announced, in a public statement anywhere, that the Arabs have avowed that they are now willing to accept Israel's existence.

Or would be willing to accept Israel's existence if certain territories were returned to them. Or if the Palestinian refugees were paid compensation. Or if the Palestinians were permitted to establish, outside the borders of Israel, a state of their own. Or whatever.

Thus far, all ceasefires and disengagements have been engineered through a unilateral relinquishment by Israel of territory and of strategic positions. The Arabs have given nothing—not even kind words.

But this one-way process must inevitably have its limits. The Israeli public will stand for just so much. There is a point—and perhaps it has now been reached—beyond which the Arabs will not be able to pry concessions from Israel without yielding a quid pro quo. Realistically, this can be nothing less than an open avowal to accept Israel as one of the nations of the area.

I see no signs anywhere that the Arabs are about to make such an historic about-face. I see no signs anywhere that Kissinger is ready to insist that Cairo or Amman or Damascus make such a

1. Published by Bantam Books, Inc. 1974

Economy is recovering from the shock of war

ONE HUNDRED DAYS AFTER...

By MOSHE ATER

Jerusalem Post Economic Editor

A HUNDRED days after the outbreak of the Yom Kippur War, and almost three months after the cease-fire, it would be useful to review our economic situation. Unfortunately, the requisite data are scarce.

Some of the statistics available are outdated, some are no longer being published for security reasons. One is thus forced to draw conclusions, probably too sweeping, from far too few indications, and from hints which may be biased.

The picture thus obtained confirms one's personal impression that economic activity has recovered from the first shock of the war and is proceeding on a fairly high level—certainly higher than we had expected we could maintain (or afford). But it is not easy to find out how this has been achieved, and how ends are being met in the changed circumstances of neither-war-nor-peace.

Economic resilience seems most marked as far as employment is concerned. In spite of the massive call up, which keeps at last 20 per cent of the nation's active manpower under arms, the labour shortage is little more acute than it was before the war. Nor do we have the large pockets of jobless predicted as a result of dislocations caused by the war. The number of vacancies registered with labour exchanges in December was almost identical with that of a year before, and the figure for unfilled vacancies was only slightly lower. The number of persons looking for work increased by one-third from September to November, but most of it was seasonal and in December, the figure dropped almost to the 1972 level. The figure for unemployed remained very low. Difficulties in finding work were encountered mainly by clerical and service personnel—reflecting the decline of commercial activity and tourism. Many of these work-seekers were women, probably including many who were not major breadwinners.

Does this mean that some stabilization has been attained? The figures could be interpreted that way, implying that pre-war employment included much featherbedding, that the need for industrial re-adjustment and vocational shifts has been exaggerated, that most of the Arab labour has by now come back, and that the bulk of the labour shortage is in the building and catering industries, which are now operating at a reduced level. However, one may also argue that the adjustment process has not yet started in earnest, that more labour is going to be discharged shortly.

Business activity

Figures concerning commercial turnover — though not exactly reliable — also indicate the rapid recovery of business activity. A survey carried out by the Tel Aviv Chamber of Commerce found that sales of food and medicines were not at all affected by the war and its aftermath. Other branches reported a drop to 50-30 per cent of the September sales volume in October (and even less for furniture sales), but a steady improvement in the next two months.

In December, sales of motor vehicles and components were only 10-15 per cent lower than before the war, sales of electrical appliances more than half their September volume, and household goods were one-third down. Even furniture was back at 40 per cent of the pre-war sales. However, in this field too one must beware of rash conclusions. First, part of the December turnover probably reflected demand pent up during the previous two months of slack sales. Second, part of the sales of cars and consumer durables apparently were purchased in anticipation of expected price rises.

No doubt the government will do its best to revamp the economy by pump-priming, housing, investment and even private consumption. But if home demand is expanded while local supply is handicapped by a labour shortage and other bottlenecks, the balance must be covered by imports, more exactly by the foreign trade deficit (excess of imports over exports), which had been growing at an alarming rate even before the war. How then has our foreign trade developed since? Surprisingly, exports proceeds last October-November were only a little less than in 1972. However, exports of manufactures other than diamonds declined by almost 10 per cent, and provisional forecasts for the first half of 1974 envisage a drop by a full 30 per cent.

Diamond exports had already started to decline last August and are currently nose-diving, owing to the world recession which is having a particularly hard effect on the diamond trade.

Obviously, the crucial factor remains the inflow of unrequited foreign capital which is expected to soar, largely due to vastly bigger loans and donations from Jews abroad (quite apart from the U.S. Government's military aid). The ongoing recovery of Israel's economy is squarely based on this Jewish charity. Without it we would have already been in a precarious situation. Thanks to it, we can weather the current emergency period and adjust ourselves to new circumstances. But does the current recovery imply such adjustment?

pronouncement. Without such pronouncement, the Israelis are surely going to stop doling out their bargaining chips free of charge. Faced with an impasse, the Arabs are likely to once again start a war, or to threaten Israel to the point where she is forced, in self-protection, to make a pre-emptive strike.

As this book goes to press, on July 22, 1974, the New York Times carries a report by Anne Sinai, the editor of the Mid-East Information Series, a quarterly journal published by the American Academic Association for Peace in the Middle East. Ms. Sinai, who recently returned from Egypt where she investigated present conditions and the political tempo of the country, reports that the Egyptians today insist:

...that if their conditions for peace are not met in full, they will scrap all their development projects. They would, they say, rather be poor and proud, than rich and dishonored.

So much for the Egyptian trend towards peace.

Ms. Sinai goes on to disclose that there is a considerable quotient of cupidity in this posture. She continues:

It all seems to me to be based on the old idea of getting huge amounts of baksheesh—bribery—from the rich American brother.

Putting it in much more blunt language, the Egyptians have been coddling Kissinger in order to shake him loose from some American dollars, and not from any real desire to conclude peace with Israel.

I close this report with three quotations.

The great Hillel said, "If I am not for myself, who will be for me?"

The sages of the Talmud said, "All members of the house of Israel are responsible one for the other."

And in a very recent interview reported in *Newsweek,* Emanual Sivan, Chairman of the History Department at the Hebrew University in Jerusalem, a young man of 38, when asked what his mood was about Israel's situation, described his feeling as one of "optimistic desperation."

I leave it to the wisdom of the reader to fuse these three quotations which span the centuries. They contain within them the concerted folk wisdom of the Jewish people.

LETTER TO A FALLEN SON

Dear Gabi,

Today they brought us the booklet with the names of the fallen. I read them, name after name, all 2,522 of your comrades-in-arms, and suddenly I began to realize how much pain and sorrow, grief and despair it encompasses, all the tears shed for every one of you, the sleepless nights, the anguish and the inner struggle to accept the fact that none of us left behind will ever see our sons again.

Somehow it seems impossible to realize that you are no longer with us. Months have passed since you gave your young lives, but when I close my eyes I see you all marching by, as though at an Independence Day Parade, 2,522 of the flower of our youth, endless lines of a hand-picked elite, the human shield of the nation.

I did not know you all, only a few friends of yours, friends in spirit, in arms and in death: Hanoch, who lost an eye, yet refused to be evacuated and fought on till the bitter end; Eitan, who preferred death to desk duties; Efi, Nimrod and Ronnie, who led their men with so much brilliance, devotion and care; Oded, who rushed to the front and was killed instantly. And you, Gabi, who kept on fighting, though you had been wounded twice.

None of you wanted to be heroes, all you did was to obey orders. I have talked to soldiers who were led by you or your friends. What they told would fill countless pages, but in essence it was simply that you never feared, panicked or despaired. You gave your commands quietly and clearly in a manner that gave confidence and comfort to your men. Multiply by 2,522 these few stories of boys I had the privilege to know, and volumes of unsurpassed heroism, unselfishness, loyalty and self-sacrifice could be written. And in the end, you have a plain, white-jacketed booklet of names.

To remember the fallen is the life-line between two worlds: the world of the dead and the world of the living. For thousands of years the redemption of our great nation has demanded sacrifices. That is a price that must be paid. You young men have fallen and in doing so you commanded us to live — to carry on.

But how? Did you give your lives so that we should become a divided nation, whose leaders accuse each other, who sow mistrust and confusion? None of you died for a political party, all of you died silently, doing your job and obeying orders. Why can't we interpret your legacy — redeem the nation silently, industriously, faithfully and lovingly. The election campaigns are over, a government has been elected. Let us now bury our grievances, forget our individual ambitions and work together, to the best of our ability, for one great goal, to make Israel a homeland worth the sacrifices our sons have made. If we do this we shall have fulfilled our obligations. If we do this, we shall be cherishing their memory.

Gabi, Hanoch, Eitan and all you others rest in peace. We will try to make your dreams come true.

Lovingly,

Your (bereaved) father

EPILOGUE
Elie Wiesel

The essay which appears on the following pages was entitled "Against Despair," and was delivered as the first annual Louis A. Pincus Memorial Lecture under the auspices of the United Jewish Appeal at its 1974 National Conference, held on December 8, 1973.

Though this piece never appeared in the columns of The Jerusalem Post, its aptness as a fitting epilogue to the story recounted in these pages will become immediately apparent to every reader.

The author of this book wishes to express his deep thanks to Elie Wiesel for permission to reprint this moving essay.

IT HAPPENED IN 1961. Golda Meir, then Israel's Foreign Minister, came to the United States and went to see President John F. Kennedy with an urgent request. It's natural. What can a good Jewish grandmother ask from a good Catholic President? Weapons, of course—what else? Except that John Kennedy said no. He was in the early stages of his Administration and going through a period of utopia; he was convinced that he—and he alone—could bring peace to this tormented world. He believed in the necessity and the possibility of general disarmament, coexistence and détente—and here comes Golda straight from Jerusalem and what does she want? Weapons. How shocking…

He received her with his usual charm; he was known for his graciousness with ladies…But when she brought up the subject that was on her mind, he objected; why not talk about something else? Golda, being stubborn, said: "No, nothing else is *as* important." Kennedy insisted: "Mrs. Meir," he said, "you arrive from the Land of the Bible, let us talk about the Bible." "Later," said Golda. "Security first. And security means weapons." Thereupon Kennedy said: "I'll give you money." And Golda replied: "Money, you'll give to the UJA—we need weapons." Kennedy tried to head her into another direction; he said: "We'll give you political support abroad, diplomatic support in the United Nations." Her reply: "Thank you, we'll take it—but we need weapons." Finally, he went so far as to suggest a formal security pact with guarantees and iron-clad pledges that if attacked, Israel would be defended by the Sixth Fleet. But Golda kept on repeating: "Thank you, thank you for all your offers but what we need most, what we want most—is weapons."

Only then did Kennedy get angry: "Mrs. Meir, I don't understand you," he exclaimed. "Whenever I see you, you speak to me about weapons. Whenever I see your Jewish friends here, *they* speak to me about weapons. What is the matter with all of you? Why are you so obsessed with weapons—and nothing else?"

"I'll tell you why," Golda answered after a long silence. *"You see, Mr. President, I belong to an ancient people. Twice in our history our country has been destroyed, our capital demolished, our Temple reduced to ashes, our sovereignty robbed and our children dispersed to the four corners of the earth—yet somehow we have managed to remain alive. Do you know how? I will tell you. Because of the shopkeeper in Bialystok and the tailor in Kiev, the industrialist in New York and the diamond merchant in Amsterdam, the student in Paris and the visionary in Safed. Though they came from different backgrounds, different lands, speaking different tongues, they had one thing in common—a dream that one day our sovereignty would be restored, our children ingathered and our Temple rebuilt…Mr. President, our Temple has not been rebuilt yet, we have just begun. And should this beginning be erased, then the shopkeeper in Bialystok and the watchmaker in Paris, the tailor in Kiev and the rebel in Leningrad, the talmudist in Brooklyn and the visionary in Safed—all these Jews who have a dream in common—would no longer even be capable of dreaming."*

441

Well, President Kennedy had a poetic sense of history. He didn't say a word for a long moment. Then he pushed a certain button—which worked—and in came one of his assistants and, believe it or not, because of this story, Golda Meir received the first Hawk missiles for the Israeli Air Force…

What does this story prove? It proves that Jewish tales are useful—and important—and timeless; it proves that the Jewish dream cannot be shattered, must not be forgotten. And also that all Jews in Jewish history are related as are the events in it—they are all interdependent.

Columbus discovered America in the same year that Jews left Spain and went into exile. As you know, his aim was to reach India, where the Ten Lost Tribes were supposed to live in their own kingdom; that was why he hired some Hebrew-speaking crew members for the journey. Accidentally, he landed on the shores of this new world—but then, there are no accidents in Jewish history; nothing happens without purpose. Columbus had to discover a haven for our people's descendants who, many generations later, would be exiled from still other countries.

Dreyfus was an assimilated Jew, as was Theodore Herzl. Their "accidental" meeting brought about the Zionist adventure—and what an adventure it is…Here, the smallest anecdote has a dramatic significance of its own. For instance: from newspaper reports we learned that Captain Dreyfus' granddaughter came last year to settle in Israel—thus the story of this Jewish family came full circle. But—what if Herzl had not attended what was then the trial of the century?

Another anecdote: on his first official visit to the United States, the late Prime Minister Levi Eshkol—who was a great Jew, a great statesman too—was received at the White House by Lyndon Johnson with full military honors. It was a poignant scene to see Eshkol, representing one of the smallest nations on earth, being escorted by the leader of the mightiest nation under the sun, to review the honor-guard. When the band played the *Hatikvah,* something happened to the distinguished Jewish visitor; he let his emotion show; there were tears in his eyes. An hour or so later a friend asked him what had gone through his mind while listening to Israel's national anthem. "Strange," said Eshkol. "I was back in my little *shtetl* near Kiev; I saw myself as a young boy leaving *heder* and running, running from a mob of hooligans who were after me, and I thought: only a Jew like Eshkol, who had his roots both in Kiev and in Jerusalem, only he could serve as a bridge between Kiev and Jerusalem—between the *shtetl* of yesterday and the independent statehood of today—only he could think of a Jewish child running in fear while being honored at the White House."

For there is a link between the frightened Jewish child and the proud leader of Israel's sovereign nation. Were Israel to forget that child, it would not be Israel…what is one for the other? An answer? A question?

"Somewhere," said Rebbe Nahman of Bratzlav, "there lives a man who asks a question to which there is no answer; a generation later, in another place, there lives a man who asks another question to which there is no answer either—and he doesn't know, he cannot know, that *his* question is actually an answer to the first."

To us, however, questions remain questions. Our existence in the Diaspora is a mystery, as is the emergence of Israel. How did we survive—and why is our survival constantly threatened? To me, the essence of Jewish history is mystical and not rational. From the strictly rational viewpoint, we should have long ago yielded to the pressures and laws of the enemy and agreed to leave the stage gracefully, if not voluntarily—as other ancient civilizations have done. The mystery of our survival is matched only by our will to survive in a society embarrassed and annoyed by our presence—and, to a degree, understandably so.

Remember Dostoyevsky's Grand Inquisitor? He sends Jesus back and the reader condemns him for this. But read the scene again and your attitude will change: suddenly you will understand the Grand Inquisitor even though you cannot justify his move; he is disturbed by a Jesus who disrupts the existing order, calls many things into question and makes everybody feel guilty—better let Jesus return to heaven…

Alone, the individual Jew would have disappeared centuries ago—but a Jew is never alone; Judaism is a remedy against solitude. When Jacob remained alone—before his mysterious struggle with the unnamed angel—he was not alone, not really: Israel was with him—in him. And conversely: when Israel is alone, Jews everywhere will do their utmost to strengthen their bonds with Israel.

A Jew is forever surrounded, if not shielded, by his community—both visible and invisible. The enemy is forever aware of this. Since the Jew represents more than himself, his death means more than his own.

The Germans often conducted their infamous

"actions" on Jewish holidays. They organized massacres on *Tisha b'Av*—so as to make us experience the Destruction of the Temple in our own person—and on *Purim*—so as to avenge Haman and his sons—and on Passover—so as to make us regret the good times in Egypt. They aimed to turn the Jewish past against Jews, the Jewish tradition against the Jewish people. By killing thousands and thousands of Jews in Babi-Yar on *Yom Kippur,* they wished to destroy the spirit and the meaning of the eternal dimension of *Yom Kippur.* They, too, were capable of lending symbolic connotations to their acts.

Never before have Jews been so organically linked one to another. Shout here and you will be heard in Kiev. Shout in Kiev and you will be heard in Paris. When Jews are sad in Jerusalem, we are moved to tears everywhere. Thus, a Jew lives in more than one place, in more than one era, on more than one level. What is being Jewish if not being possessed of a historical consciousness which transcends that of the individual? If our tradition stresses the notion that each and every Jew stood at Sinai, that each and every Jew heard God proclaim His Law, it is to make us realize that we are older than we seem, that our memory does not begin with our own—and so, my young son is older than the oldest of my teachers.

This is part of what my contemporaries and I have learned from recent events. An assault on Jews anywhere means an attempt to humiliate Jews everywhere. The name of our secret is history and not geography. Therein lies our strength. The enemy knows it. His attempts at killing Jews are aimed at erasing Jewish history. We never give up, but neither does the enemy. Hence Jewish sadness is so specific and so peculiarly rich; it has a past which joy has not. Even now, our sadness is rooted in other times and earlier tragedies. Legend has it that Rabbi Yitzhak Lurie, founder of the Safed School of *Kabbala,* was able to relate his own suffering to the suffering of his ancestors in Egypt and in Babylon; when a Jew is in pain, he experiences more than his personal share. Our sadness now is due to the *Yom Kippur* War, but it began much before *Yom Kippur.*

Yes, that is the key word: sadness. That is what we all felt since the treacherous aggression against our people. That feeling dominated all the others. More than fear and anguish, more than bitterness and anger, we felt inundated with sadness. No hate, only sadness. From the very first moment, we were overcome by profound melancholy and could not shake it off.

We thought: "Well, here we go again…another war, the fourth since our nation was reborn. Would there ever be an end to this absurd bloodshed?" Once more young men would kill and be killed on both sides…Once more, we would inevitably, inexorably be compelled to choose between the role of victor and that of vanquished, between triumph and death, between military victory and survival. And yet we want neither. We want neither to humiliate the enemy nor to allow him to humiliate us; we want neither to kill nor to be killed.

All we want is to live and teach others the sanctity of life, all we want is to build peace and build in peace, and bear witness that man is not necessarily man's enemy, that every war is senseless, that the solution lies in compassion and that compassion is possible.

All we want is peace and yet—here we go again …Again there is war—and do we hate war. We know how ugly it can be—and is. The very first war, the one between Cain and Abel, taught us that he who kills, kills the brother in himself. That is why "Thou shall not kill" is one of the Ten Commandments. Is that why the world forces wars upon us? To prove to us that we are like everybody else? That we, too, can find glory in war? But, we do not. Jewish warriors are different— they are sad warriors. In 1967, in spite of their stunning victories, they did not rejoice. As they returned from battle, they even seemed angry— for having had to inflict suffering onto others. This time their sadness—and ours—was deeper: many, too many of our own lost their lives.

Remember? The uncertainty of the first days. The first reports. The first setbacks. The first pictures. One I shall never forget: a young soldier, a *Sefer-Torah* in his arms, led into captivity. The first names, the first faces. You closed your eyes and you saw faces, faces, so many faces. Friends and their children, friends and their friends. Who was still alive? Who was in what hospital with what wounds? Like Job, we sat in mourning and like Job we felt alone—abandoned by our allies and friends. Forsaken, betrayed.

So—how can one not be sad today? How can one be Jewish in this Gentile world of ours and not succumb to despair?

There are objective questions we must face, questions which engender their own sadness, such as: How was it all possible? Why was Israel not prepared? Why weren't we better equipped to handle the situation? Israel is going through a kind of catharsis. Its soul-searching is deep and thorough and reaches into all spheres of society. The war has affected everybody. People are not the same. The change is deeper than after the 1967

443

war. In June '67 we knew a unique moment of elevation and exaltation; we were confronted with Jerusalem, and through Jerusalem, with some mystical aspect of our destiny. Now, the confrontation was of a different nature and I hesitate to name it. It was a confrontation with our weakness…

What were the mistakes? Where lay our failures? Where did we go wrong—and why? I do not know, nor do I pretend to know. Yet since 1967 increasingly one had the feeling that things seemed too beautiful to last forever. You couldn't help but think of Napoleon's mother, who, thinking of her children sitting on prestigious thrones all over Europe, said sadly: *"Pourvu que cela dure,"* it cannot last, not forever. We should have had the same feeling about Israel: too victorious, too strong, too joyous. The world around us was too envious, too corrupt, too poisoned.

And then there was something else—more basic—which had to do with the most important event in our history: the Holocaust. If we won in '67, it was because the terms of reference were those of the Holocaust. In 1973 it was different: the terms of reference were those of '67. In other words, the Holocaust, which was a most powerful motivation then, was almost absent now. That Event was left far behind. We allowed it to be distorted, used and misused: politicians comparing Harlem to the Warsaw Ghetto and Vietnam to Auschwitz. In our own midst, some voices were heard contending that Jews paid too much attention to Holocaust themes. (Not so long ago, one could read an "analysis" in the Jewish Telegraphic Agency urging a more "realistic" approach to the Holocaust, claiming that, after all, Jews were not the only victims who died during that period and pointing out the fact that there was music even in Auschwitz.) Well, if such views are expressed in public without protest, that means that our entire community has grown dangerously insensitive to an event which naively some survivors had thought would continue to haunt all Jews forever, if only to save them from indifference and complacency.

Is that the reason for our despair today? Yes—and it is but one among many. And yet, and yet…

On the eve of *Simhat-Torah,* every rabbi in America was faced with the question: "What were the Jews to do during this particular holiday? Should they or should they not celebrate *Simhat-Torah?"* And the answer was unequivocally: "Yes—they should." It wasn't easy? Never mind. They could not rejoice? They felt unable to sing and dance? Never mind. Because there were so many reasons against celebrating, we had to celebrate.

I remember two episodes. One took place in a train carrying hundreds of Jews to their death. They were pressed together so that they could hardly move or breathe. Suddenly an old rabbi exclaimed: "It is *Simhat-Torah* today; have we forgotten what Jews are ordered to do on *Simhat-Torah?"* Somebody had managed to smuggle a small *Sefer-Torah* aboard the train; he handed it to the rabbi. And they began to sing, to dance vertically, and they went on singing and dancing and celebrating the Torah, all the while knowing that every step, every word was bringing them closer to their end.

The second episode took place inside the kingdom of night. In one of the barracks, several hundred Jews gathered to celebrate *Simhat-Torah.* In the shadow of shadows? Yes—even there. On the threshold of the death-chambers? Yes—even there. But there was no *Sefer-Torah.* So how could they organize the ritual *Hakafot,* the traditional procession with the sacred scrolls? As they were trying to solve the problem, an old man—old?… the word had no meaning there—an old man noticed a young boy—who was so old, so old—standing there looking on and dreaming. "Do you remember what you learned?" asked the old man. "Yes, I do," replied the young boy. "Really?" said the old man, "you really remember *Shma Yisrael?"* "I remember much more," said the young boy. *"Shma Yisrael* is enough," said the old man. And he lifted the boy from the ground and began dancing with him—as though *he* were the Torah. And all joined in, they all sang and danced and cried. They cried but they sang with fervor—never before had Jews celebrated *Simhat-Torah* with such fervor.

For in our tradition, the celebration of life is more important than the mourning over the dead. When a wedding procession meets a funeral in the street, the funeral must stop so as to allow the wedding procession to proceed…although surely you know what respect we show toward our dead… a wedding, symbol of life and renewal, symbol of promise too, has precedence.

Our tradition orders us to affirm life and proclaim hope—always. Any *Shabbat* interrupts all mourning. And what is *Shabbat* if not the embodiment of man's hope and his ability to strive for hope with joy?

In more general terms, Judaism teaches man to overcome despair. What is Jewish history if not an endless quarrel with God? Pascal put it somewhat differently: "The history of the Jewish people," he said, "is but a long love affair with God." As in every love affair there are quarrels and reconciliations, more quarrels and more reconciliations. Then how is one to explain that neither of the two sides gave up on the other in despair? God had every reason—he had to lose hope. He created man, and man sinned right away, if only by obeying his wife. He had children, who though alone in the entire world, were jealous of one another and ended in violence and murder. Still God did not give up. Adam had a third son who had children—mankind by then was so wicked that God decided to drown it in the floods. Still there was Noah. And Sodom. And Gomorra. Yet God does not despair. Later, he chooses to maintain His faith in His people even though our ancestors were not the easiest people to handle... Three days after the crossing of the Red Sea, they were already complaining. Shortly after the majestic spectacle at Sinai, they hurried to worship a golden calf... After witnessing more wonders and more miracles than any other generation they still kept on annoying God. Why did He not give up on them in despair?

Conversely, the same is true of our people. There were many periods in our past when we had every right in the world to turn to God and say "Enough...since You seem to approve of all these persecutions, all these massacres, have it your way...let your world be without Jews...either You are our partner in history or not. If You are, do Your share; if not, we consider ourselves free of past commitments. Since you choose to break the Covenant, so be it." And yet, and yet...

We went on believing, hoping, invoking His name. In the endless test with God, we proved to Him that we were more patient than He, more compassionate, too. In other words: we did not give up on Him either. For this is the meaning of being Jewish: never to give up—never to yield to despair.

Faced with despair, the Jew had three options. He could choose resignation, total resignation—and some of us did so one generation ago. Remember all those processions, all those nocturnal processions of men and women and children going silently to the mass graves...

Or we could seek refuge in self-delusion—and some individual Jews tried it in some places: assimilation was meant to be an option in some quarters. Or conversion. Yes, there were Jews who came to the realistic conclusion that since Jewishness was forever linked to suffering, they had to give it up to protect their children and even themselves.

But then there exists a third option—the most enriching and exciting of the three. To face the situation and do one's utmost to surmount it— as a Jew.

Our enemies are powerful? All right, we shall fight them nonetheless. They will our destruction? No matter—we shall resist them in our own Jewish way, which means that we shall not allow them to tell us when to be joyous and when to mourn, when to sing and when to be silent! I shall not allow them to determine my holidays and my days for remembrance. It is not up to them to tell me whether I should or should not celebrate Simhat-Torah! *These decisions belong to us—and we make them as free and sovereign Jews. That was why we had to celebrate* Simhat-Torah. *It wasn't easy to rejoice with a heavy heart? Never mind! In spite of the tears, in spite of the pain and the agony, we had to rejoice—and let the world know that Jews can sublimate the pain and transmute agony! And that Jews are able to draw from their despair new reasons for hope. We did so one generation ago when our reasons to despair were infinite; those who emerged from that ordeal were stronger than their brethren in free lands. They were the strongest Jews in history, and their strength, paradoxically, had its source in the Holocaust.*

That is the lesson Judaism teaches us: that one must turn every experience into a life force. One must not let the enemy impose his laws. Our strength is in our freedom. Ultimately *we* decide what to do—what to be.

The enemy wants us to be angry so as to let anger distort the image we have of ourselves? We will not let him. He wants us to open ourselves to hate and despair? We will not listen.

For, in conclusion, we must emphasize one more belief: true, we have many reasons to despair— but we also have many reasons not to despair.

True, many peoples and many leaders have abandoned us, betrayed us—but we have not betrayed our people, our people has not abandoned its children. The Jewish people emerged from this event strengthened and purified—and wiser.

Newspapers and speakers tell you that many myths were shattered in the *Yom Kippur* War? Maybe—but the "myth" of Jewish solidarity remained intact. As did the "myth" of the self-sacrifice of our youth.

Israeli youngsters have never been so heroic— and have never paid with so many lives. As a

445

people, we have never been so united —
so dedicated.

As Jews, we came out of this war with a heightened awareness of our duties — and with a more luminous and intense vision of what *Ahavat Yisrael,* love for our fellow Jews, really means.

Voltaire said: "When all hope is gone, death becomes a duty" — not so for Jews. When all hope is gone, Jews invent new hopes. Even when we are beyond despair we justify hope.

One day, Hasidim came to tell the great Rebbe Nahman of Bratzlav of new persecutions against Jews in the Ukraine. The Master listened and said nothing. Then they told him of pogroms in certain villages. Again, the Master listened and said nothing. Then they told of slaughtered families, of desecrated cemeteries, of children who were burned alive. The Master listened, listened and shook his head: "I know," he whispered, "I know what you want me to do — you want me to shout with pain, to howl with despair, I know, I know...but, I will not, you hear me, I will not." And, after a long silence, he began shouting louder and louder: *"Gewalt Yiden, zeit sich nit meyaesh!"* Jews, for heaven's sake, do not despair...*Gewalt Yiden,* Jews, do not despair.

In Ringelblum's Archives, I discovered that there was a Bratzlaver *"Shtibel"* in the Warsaw Ghetto. Above the entrance — an appeal which read like an outcry: "For heaven's sake, Jews, do not despair." Thousands of Jews were killed every day and yet the Hasidim of Rebbe Nahman were urged — indeed ordered — not to despair!

The same slogan is to be found today at the entrance to the Bratzlaver *"Shtibel"* in Jerusalem — and it has been repeated by scholars and soldiers alike. It may sound strange, but I have received scores of letters from embattled Israel — from a variety of friends, not all religious — yet everyone of them made mention of Rebbe Nahman's call against despair.

It is more needed now than at the time it was first uttered. Our people has lost many of its children. We are alone — terribly alone. And sad, terribly sad. We are entering difficult times. The era ahead of us will be critical. And yet, and yet...

We owe it to our past not to lose hope. Say what you may, despair is not the solution. Not for us. Quite the contrary: we must show our children that in spite of everything, we keep our faith — in ourselves and even in mankind, though mankind is not worthy of such faith. We must show our children and theirs that three thousand years of history cannot end with an act of despair on our part.

With our creativity, with our celebrations, we shall justify them, we shall purify them. Other peoples have more reasons to give up in despair. To despair now would be a blasphemy — a profanation.

Gewalt Yiden, do not permit the enemy to rob us of our joy and our hope: to give up would be his victory and he does not deserve it. Nor do we deserve defeat — we have never been worthier of victory than now. Were we right in celebrating Simhat-Torah? Yes, absolutely. And we must go on celebrating it. Not only on Simhat-Torah *but every day. That will be our way of proclaiming our faith in* Klal-Yisrael, *in* Ahavat-Yisrael *and therefore in* Netzach-Yisrael: *our faith has never been so needed nor so justified.*